Contents

Introduction to

Norfolk and Suffolk

Jutting out into the North Sea above London, the ancient counties of Norfolk and Suffolk form an incredibly diverse region. Like Britain's southwest corner, Norfolk and Suffolk feel like a place apart from the rest of the country: they're not on the way to anywhere, and, unusually in a densely populated country like England, they boast few truly large urban centres. The two regional capitals, Norwich and Ipswich, are thriving and enticing places, especially Norwich with its cathedral and old centre, but beyond here it is a region of small market towns and idyllic villages scattered across often curiously empty landscapes, with a skyline punctured by medieval church towers that seems hardly to have changed in centuries.

Norfolk and Suffolk are within easy reach of the capital and the Midlands, yet are far enough off the beaten track to retain a rural quality that's rare this far south in England. Both counties have become a little more discovered over the past two or three decades – parts of the north Norfolk coast are firm Chelsea tractor territory, and Southwold and Aldeburgh have always been genteel resorts – but the landscape remains either wild and uncultivated or given over to farmland, and there are few concessions to urban ways. Suffolk is the gentler of the two: smaller, more refined and less remote, although its coast – a mix of heath, marsh and dune – feels quite separate from the rest of the county. Norfolk is Suffolk's big brother, larger, rawer and more diverse than people imagine, with landscapes ranging from the sandy forests and heathlands of the Brecks (the driest region in Britain) to the wetlands of the Broads, and the dunes and long sandy beaches of the north and east coasts.

Where to go

Norwich, Norfolk's capital and home to a third of its population, has one of the country's finest cathedrals and a lovely old centre whose pubs, restaurants and shops could keep you entertained for days. Beyond here, **King's Lynn** and **Great Yarmouth** are old ports fallen on

ABOVE WINDMILL ON THE BROADS **RIGHT** ST PETER & ST PAUL, SWAFFHAM

THE ROUGH GUIDE TO

Norfolk & Suffolk

written and researched by

Martin Dunford and Phil Lee

roughguides.com

hard times mostly, but not without their charms, especially King's Lynn, whose perfectly preserved quayside harks back to its days as a member of the Hanseatic League; Great Yarmouth has great beaches and a range of kiss-me-quick attractions. East of Norwich, the glorious expanse of the **Broads** remains one of the county's prime attractions, great for boating and watersports but also the UK's primary wetland, nowadays protected in what is East Anglia's only National Park. It blends almost imperceptibly into the beautiful beaches and dunes of the **east coast**, most appealing around **Winterton**, **Horsey** and **Waxham**, although these days the **north coast**, between the old-time seaside resorts of **Cromer** and **Hunstanton**, draws the bulk of the crowds, a wild coastline whose charms coalesce around fine beaches like **Holkham Bay**, seaside hubs such as **Wells** and **Blakeney** and handsome Georgian towns like **Holt**. Central and western Norfolk is less well known, home to the mysterious expanse of field and dykes that is Norfolk's portion of the **Fens**, worth visiting not only for the unique watery landscape but also for back-of-beyond villages, birdwatching centres such as Welney, and of course the iconic cathedral of **Ely**, in Cambridgeshire. Central Norfolk revolves around the marvellous woody heaths of **Breckland**, which is punctuated by lovely villages such as **Castle Acre** and small towns like **Swaffham**, **Wymondham** and **Thetford**. To the south, Norfolk blends into Suffolk along the **Waveney Valley**, where **Diss**, **Bungay** and **Beccles** bridge the gap between the two counties.

Suffolk's greatest attractions are not in **Ipswich**, its capital, but it's a more enticing town than you might think, and a base for visiting **Constable Country**, a string of bucolic villages famously inhabited – and painted – by the English landscape painter. Inland, Suffolk's former glories are evoked in the old wool towns of **Lavenham** and **Bury St Edmunds**; to the north, the **Suffolk coast** up to the old fishing port of **Lowestoft** is home to some of the region's most alluring resorts in **Aldeburgh** and **Southwold**, and, north of Ipswich, one of its most attractive provincial centres in **Woodbridge**. The coast in between is unspoilt and in places wild, with the **Minsmere** RSPB reserve and some glorious stretches of marsh, heath and woodland that feel a world away from anywhere.

THE GLORY DAYS

It's not just the landscape that marks out Norfolk and Suffolk. This is one of England's most historic regions, and the cradle of its medieval prosperity, when it was the richest part of the British Isles, growing fat on the proceeds of the **weaving** industry, which nurtured wool towns like Lavenham and North Walsham, the ports of Ipswich and of course Norwich, and the now almost vanished communities of Dunwich and Worstead. It was the most densely populated part of England at this time, and you can feel the history everywhere, whether it's in the church towers that puncture the horizon in every direction – Norfolk has a greater concentration of **medieval churches** than anywhere on earth – or the otherwise ordinary town centres whose grand monuments and oversized churches hark back to more prosperous times. Most of the region's churches are kept unlocked, too, which makes it easy to base a trip around the best ones (see box, p.31).

NORFOLK AND SUFFOLK

THEY ARE FROM ROUND HERE: AN EAST ANGLIAN TOP TWENTY

As essentially backwater counties, it can be a challenge to name many famous East Anglians, but the region actually punches above its weight in the celebrity firmament.

Benjamin Britten Born in Lowestoft, long-time resident of Aldeburgh, and perhaps the greatest twentieth-century English composer.

Bill Bryson The best-selling travel writer and adoptive native of Norfolk lives near Wymondham and never misses an opportunity to speak up for the county.

Richard Curtis The director of *Four Weddings & A Funeral* (not to mention his equally famous wife, Emma Freud) is just one of two big-noise film directors living in Walberswick.

Brian Eno The record producer was born and still lives in Woodbridge when not hobnobbing with Davids Byrne and Bowie.

Stephen Fry The twitter-addicted national treasure was born in Reepham and is still a vocal resident of the county, as well as being a director of Norwich FC.

Paul Greengrass What on earth is it about Walberswick that attracts top-flight British film folk? We're not sure, but Greengrass (of *Bloody Sunday*, *Bourne Supremacy* and *Captain Phillips* fame) is just the latest luvvie to washup on the southern shores of the Blyth.

Amanda Holden It's perhaps no surprise that the *Britain's Got Talent* judge used to have a holiday home near Burnham Market. She still visits, and is a great advocate for Norfolk.

John Hurt The venerable actor lives near Cromer but is not a native of the county – he came here, he says, because it was not on the way to anywhere, which is one of the best reasons we can think of.

Bernard Matthews Famed for his "turkey Twizzlers", Matthews oversaw his Norfolk turkey empire from Great Witchingham Hall, northeast of Norwich, until his death in 2010.

Beth Orton A native of East Dereham, the singer-songwriter returned to Norfolk a few years ago and holed up in a house near Diss.

As far as we know, she's still there.

George Orwell So Suffolk-bred he named himself after its major river (he was born Eric Blair) and wrote several of his early books at the family home in Southwold.

Alan Partridge Steve Coogan's creation deliberately stereotypes the parochial nature of East Anglia. His local career peaked with his own show on Radio Norwich, and petered out somewhat on North Norfolk Digital.

John Peel The much-missed DJ lived in southern Suffolk for over thirty years, and since his death has given his name to Stowmarket's Creative Arts Centre.

Griff Rhys Jones The comedian, writer and all-round TV entertainer lives in Holbrook on the Shotley peninsula, from where he sails his classic wooden boat.

W.G. Sebald The Anglo-German writer and UEA academic adopted East Anglia as his own. He died in 2001 and is buried in the churchyard at Framingham Earl.

Ed Sheeran The stadium-playing troubadour was brought up in Framlingham, where his parents still live, and where he can still occasionally be spotted between world tours.

Delia Smith The TV chef (see p.51) is the majority shareholder of Norwich FC, but – whisper it! – she lives in Suffolk.

Christine Truman British Grand Slam tennis champions are few and far between but one of them – the 1959 French Open winner – lives and still plays tennis in Aldeburgh.

Twiggy The iconic 1960s model was spotted walking on the beach in her beloved home of Southwold by the marketing director of M&S, who snapped her up immediately!

Tim Westwood The Radio One DJ was perhaps the inspiration for TV's Ali G, but he comes from – oh dear – Lowestoft.

When to go

There is no bad **time to go** to Norfolk and Suffolk, but they're best when the weather is warm and dry and the crowds at their most comfortable – in May, June, early July and September. Late July and August can be busy, especially the Broads and coast, though many beaches are big enough to absorb the crowds. As both counties are drier than much of England, spring and autumn can be nice, with April and September the peak months for spotting migratory birds. Even in winter (often the best time to see seals and waterfowl) you'll find enough sunny days to make a trip worthwhile, plus there are loads of rainy-day activities just in case, and some seriously good places to hunker down for food and drink.

Author picks

We've spent a lot of time in Norfolk and Suffolk, and we're keen on all aspects of both counties, from the obvious heavyweight sights to their many hidden corners. What follows is a selection of some of the things that for us make Norfolk and Suffolk unique and fascinating places to visit.

Paddling your own canoe The Broads are glorious for all kinds of boating, but there's nothing quite like travelling by canoe through their remoter reaches (pp.66–67).

A swift half A multitude of breweries and brilliantly sited pubs mean that both counties are the perfect places to construct a trip not only around tasting the local brews but also feasting on locally sourced food – two things you can easily do at Woodforde's brewery (p.74) and its next-door pub, the *Fur and Feather* (p.74).

Among the ruins The counties' prominence in the Middle Ages means that you usually can't go far without encountering the remnants of a medieval priory or abbey, most often in an evocatively ruined state; for example at Castle Acre (p.198), Leiston (p.262), Baconsthorpe (p.142) and Binham (p.139).

Flippers and feathers Wildlife alone is a reason to visit both counties: otters have returned to the Broads and the region is home to more than a quarter of Britain's rarest species; you can spot seals on the north (p.139) and east (p.103) coasts, and lots of rarely seen birds at a range of reserves such as Minsmere (p.266), Titchwell (p.159), Strumpshaw Fen (p.115) and Cley Marshes (p.137).

Walking Arguably the best way to see Norfolk and Suffolk is on foot, and a number of long-distance footpaths make their way through both counties, including two wonderful coastal paths – the Norfolk Coast Path (p.125) and Suffolk Coast Path (p.243) – plus the Wherryman's Way (p.65), the Weavers' Way (p.65) and others.

> Our author recommendations don't end here. We've flagged up our favourite places – a perfectly sited hotel, an atmospheric café, a special restaurant – throughout the Guide, highlighted with the ★ symbol.

FROM TOP LOCAL OYSTERS AT ORFORD; BINHAM PRIORY; GREY HERON, MINSMERE; NORFOLK COAST PATH SIGN

22
things not to miss

It's not possible to see everything that Norfolk and Suffolk have to offer in one trip – and we don't suggest you try. What follows, in no particular order, is a selective taste of the region's highlights, from beautiful beaches and outstanding nature reserves to splendid stately homes and tasty local treats. All highlights have a page reference to take you straight into the Guide, where you can find out more. Coloured numbers refer to chapters in the Guide section.

1 MESSING ABOUT IN BOATS
Pages 66–67
Kick back under the endless sky on the Broads, with only the creak of the rigging and the swish of the water for company. Bliss.

2 BIRDWATCHING
Pages 330, 115, 159 & 163
Both Norfolk and Suffolk have some of the best RSPB reserves in the country – Minsmere, Strumpshaw Fen, Titchwell Marsh and Snettisham.

3 EAST RUSTON VICARAGE GARDEN
Page 93
North Norfolk's most glorious and inventive garden; visiting is like walking around a restless horticultural brain.

4 ORFORD NESS
Page 253
Orford itself feels like the end of the road, but take a boat on to Orford Ness to really experience the eerie wildness of the Suffolk coast.

9

5 ST HELEN'S, RANWORTH
The "Cathedral of the Broads" is a typical Norfolk church, with some beautiful original features. But the view over Broadland from its tower is a rare bonus.

6 LOCAL BREWS
East Anglia is home to a collection of excellent local breweries, some of which you can visit, and most of which sell their wares in local pubs and make a showing at summer beer festivals throughout both counties.

7 NORWICH CATHEDRAL
This is where the county's medieval glories reach their peak.

8 FRAMLINGHAM
The ultimate self-sufficient Suffolk town, but not just a nice place to live – it's got good places to stay and to eat, and a couple of great historical sights.

9 WINTERTON-ON-SEA
Winterton beach is lovely, but yomping across the vast area of dunes behind is even better.

10 SEAL-SPOTTING
A walk to Horsey beach or a boat trip or walk out to Blakeney Point are the two best ways to spot the Norfolk coast's colonies of grey seals – and, in winter, their pups.

10

16 HORSEY MERE AND WINDMILL
Page 103
A focus for adventures on land and water, with the Mere and its wonderful drainage mill looking out across to the coastal dunes.

17 IPSWICH WATERFRONT
Page 229
Dockland areas all over the country have been restored, but not many as successfully as this one.

18 CROMER CRABS
Page 128
Crab meat dressed and eaten from the half shell with a touch of lemon and pepper is a delicious Norfolk snack.

19 ALDEBURGH FESTIVAL
Page 260
Britten's local summer arts festival has been a huge success, and its venue, on the edge of Suffolk's marshes, is delightful.

20 BEWILDERWOOD
Page 82
An ecofriendly theme park that is rightly popular.

21 CONSTABLE COUNTRY
Page 284
This ravishing and unchanged landscape inspired the painter's best-known work.

22 HOLKHAM BAY
Page 149
The ultimate flat and sandy Norfolk beach, with the sea almost invisible at low tide.

Itineraries

These suggested itineraries cover the best of what Norfolk and Suffolk have to offer, whether it's medieval churches, outdoor activities, beaches or just enjoying the countryside. There's no need to follow them slavishly, but we hope they give you a taste of the richness and diversity of the region.

A WEEK IN NORFOLK

You could spend a month in Norfolk and still find something new. However, if you have just a week this selection of places to stay takes in the best of what the county has to offer.

❶ Norwich There's no better place to start a tour of Norfolk than its capital, which is one of the country's truly great cathedral cities. **See p.34**

❷ Swaffham You wouldn't stay here for the town itself, but it has a great hotel and is a good base for Breckland's northern reaches, Castle Acre and even parts of the Fens. **See p.188**

❸ Wells-next-the-Sea An enticing seaside town, with none of the airs and graces of other parts of the north coast, and the best base for Holkham beach. **See p.146**

❹ North Walsham The town is nothing special but it has a nice boutique hotel and is close to some of the best places on the east coast, including Norfolk's most enticing garden at East Ruston. **See p.91**

❺ Horning One of north Norfolk's most picturesque villages, and with a couple of good places to sleep and eat too – a great place from which to explore the northern Broads. **See p.80**

❻ Bungay Technically just over the river in Suffolk, but the best springboard for the sights of the beautiful Waveney Valley. **See p.216**

A WEEK IN SUFFOLK

It's a small county packed full of interest – if time is tight, this makes an enjoyable week.

❶ Bury St Edmunds There's no more appealing town in the country, and few better introductions to Suffolk. **See p.307**

❷ Constable Country The countryside and villages of the Stour Valley have a timeless beauty even if you don't give two hoots for the painter. **See p.284**

❸ Woodbridge and the Deben estuary The small-town charms of Woodbridge make it a great overnight stop, and it has some good places to stay too. Plus there's plenty to explore in the nearby area. **See p.243**

❹ Aldeburgh and Snape A cut above most seaside towns, with some excellent hotels and restaurants and as cool a vibe as you ever get in Suffolk, plus the attraction of annual festivals at nearby Snape Maltings. **See p.254**

❺ Southwold With its pier and sandy beach, and genteel high street with plenty of good places to eat, it's no surprise that a beach hut in Southwold can cost tens of thousands. Luckily you can stay at one of several comfortable hotels and B&Bs. **See p.268**

❻ Beccles One of the most handsome small towns in the region, and the gateway to the southern Broads too, with a picturesque riverside and boats to rent. **See p.219**

ABOVE WELLS-NEXT-THE-SEA HARBOUR; SOUTHWOLD BEACH HUTS

MEDIEVAL EAST ANGLIA

❶ **Wymondham Abbey** The ruins of the abbey and its church are a magnificent reminder of this tiny town's past significance – a very Norfolk phenomenon. **See p.201**

❷ **Castle Acre** This picturesque village is full of medieval treasures, from its ruined priory and magnificent church to its eponymous castle; a great place to stay the night. **See p.198**

❸ **Oxborough** The church has some of the finest pre-Reformation devotional carving in England, and the hall is magnificent. **See p.196**

❹ **Castle Rising** Norfolk's most imposing medieval castle, its ruins tower over the surrounding fields and marshes. **See p.164**

❺ **Binham Priory** Just outside Blakeney, these are some of the most substantial priory ruins in the county – quite a claim in Norfolk. **See p.139**

❻ **Framlingham** Suffolk's favourite inland town has two unmissable historic sights: its castle, and the amazing Howard funerary monuments inside the Church of St Michael. **See p.250**

THE GREAT OUTDOORS

❶ **Cley Marshes Nature Reserve** Norfolk's oldest reserve is one of the county's best places to watch migrating birds and rare waterfowl, including bitterns and marsh harriers. **See p.137**

❷ **Holme Dunes Nature Reserve** A wonderful area of marsh, reeds and sand dunes at the west end of the north coast. **See p.161**

❸ **The Peter Scott Walk** This evocative walk to the naturalist's lighthouse home near Sutton Bridge takes you along the marshy banks of the Wash. **See p.174**

❹ **The Canoe Man** Joining one of his nature or bushcraft trails is a real adventure, and a great way to see the Broads and its wildlife. **See p.67**

❺ **Thetford Forest** The forest isn't that old, but it offers great chances to hike, bike and race huskies along miles of well-defined trails. **See p.210**

❻ **Dunwich Heath** This National Trust reserve is a great place for a ramble, exploring a section of the Suffolk Coast Path or linking up with the lovely Minsmere RSPB reserve. **See p.265**

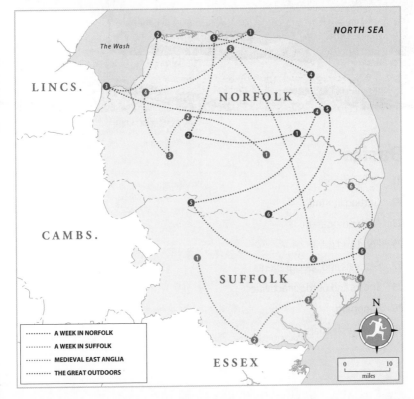

BOAT ON ALDEBURGH BEACH

Basics

Getting there

By road and rail, Norfolk and Suffolk are within easy striking distance of London and the Midlands, though neither county possesses a motorway, so journey times can be a little longer than you might expect. For international travellers, the obvious – and usually least expensive – way to reach either county is to fly into London and catch the train from there, but there are two regional airports – Norwich, in Norfolk, with a limited range of short-haul flights, and London Stansted, just fifteen miles or so southwest of Suffolk, with a wider range of flights, again largely short-haul. It's also easy to reach Norfolk and Suffolk by train from mainland Europe via London St Pancras station and there is a ferry route to Harwich, just south of Ipswich, from the Hook of Holland. Incidentally, the long-standing ferry service from Esbjerg, in Denmark, to Harwich is currently not in operation, though services may be revived (consult ⓦ directferries.co.uk for the latest information).

By car from around the UK

By car, the fastest route from London is the **A12** for Ipswich and most of Suffolk, and the **M11** then the **A11** for Norwich and most of Norfolk. Coming from the Midlands, the **A52/A17** will bring you to King's Lynn as will the much faster **A47**, whereas Suffolk is best reached from the Midlands via the **A1/A14**. The region's worst traffic jams are generally in Norwich, where the ring road can be a real pain, and during the summer season on the A149 between King's Lynn and Hunstanton.

By train

There are two main-line train services from **London** to Norfolk and Suffolk, one from London **King's Cross** to **Cambridge**, **Ely** and **King's Lynn**, the other from London **Liverpool Street** to **Colchester**, **Ipswich** and **Norwich**. Journey times are fairly short – King's Cross to King's Lynn takes about 1hr 30min, Liverpool Street to Norwich 1hr 50min. There are also two main **east–west train lines**, one from Ipswich to Bury St Edmunds, Newmarket, Ely and Cambridge, the other from Peterborough to Ely, Thetford and Norwich. There

are connecting trains to Peterborough from the likes of Leicester and Birmingham as well as a cross-country train that runs from Liverpool to Norwich via Manchester, Sheffield, Nottingham and Peterborough. Nottingham to Norwich takes about 2hr 30min; it's a somewhat epic 5hr from Liverpool. For information on routes, **timetables** and fares, contact National Rail Enquiries (ⓦ nationalrail.co.uk).

The key to getting the best **fares** is to be flexible with times, bearing in mind that most journeys will be cheaper – often much cheaper – in off-peak periods, characteristically Monday to Friday 10/10.30am to 3/3.30pm and all day Saturday and Sunday. As a sample fare, a standard return from London to Norwich can cost as little as £25 and as much as £60. If the ticket office at your departure station is closed and there is no ticket machine, you can buy your ticket on the train. Otherwise, **boarding without a ticket** will render you liable to paying the full fare plus a penalty fare. Note also that on Sundays, engineering work can add hours – literally – onto even the shortest journey.

From Europe, **Eurostar trains** (ⓦ eurostar.com) run roughly hourly to London St Pancras from Lille (1hr 20min), Paris (2hr 15min) and Brussels (2hr), with connections running into these three cities from all over Europe: Thalys (ⓦ thalys.com) provides some of the speediest international connections. To get from London St Pancras to Norfolk and Suffolk by train, you can either walk across to London King's Cross station (for King's Lynn) or take the underground to Liverpool Street station (for Ipswich and Norwich).

By bus

National Express (ⓦ nationalexpress.com), the UK's largest long-distance bus (or coach) operator, doesn't make much of a showing in Norfolk or Suffolk,

---

A BETTER KIND OF TRAVEL

At Rough Guides we are passionately committed to travel. We believe it helps us understand the world we live in and the people we share it with – and of course tourism is vital to many developing economies. But the scale of modern tourism has also damaged some places irreparably, and **climate change** is accelerated by most forms of transport, especially flying. All Rough Guides' flights are **carbon-offset**, and every year we donate money to a variety of environmental charities.

though it does run fast and frequent buses from **London Victoria** coach station to **Norwich** with fares from as little as £3. Neither does its main rival, **Megabus** (Ⓦmegabus.com), do much better, with only one route – London to **Norwich** (UEA). To plan a journey, contact **Traveline** (Ⓦtraveline.info), whose website carries comprehensive bus timetable details.

By plane

For travellers from **mainland Europe** and **Ireland**, the handiest airports for Norfolk and Suffolk are **London Stansted** (STN; Ⓦstanstedairport.com) and **Norwich** (NWI; Ⓦnorwichairport.co.uk). London Stansted, which is convenient for Norfolk and more especially Suffolk, has a particularly wide choice, and Norwich airport weighs in with over twenty European cities. **Norwich airport** is located about four miles north of the city centre along the A140. There is a patchy bus service (Mon–Sat only; every 30min–1hr; 25min) to the city centre from the airport's Park and Ride, but the taxi fare is only about £12. From **London Stansted**, there are regular long-distance buses to Thetford, Norwich and Ipswich as well as hourly trains to Cambridge and Ely for onward connections to Norfolk and Suffolk. **Long-haul destinations** mostly arrive at either London Gatwick or London Heathrow – and from London it's a short(ish) train journey to Norfolk and Suffolk (see below).

By ferry from mainland Europe

Drivers have a choice of **ferry** routes. The cheapest services are on the short, cross-Channel hops from the French ports of Calais and Dunkerque to Dover, but this leaves a longish drive to Suffolk and Norfolk via – or rather round – London. The most convenient port for both Norfolk and Suffolk is **Harwich**, in Essex, and there are regular ferries to Harwich from the Hook of Holland with Stena Line (Ⓦstenaline.co.uk). Fares vary enormously according to the date, time and length of stay. The sailing time from the Hook to Harwich is about 9hr.

Getting around

In both Norfolk and Suffolk, all the larger towns and villages are readily accessible by train or bus, but out in the sticks the smaller places can be a real hassle to reach if you don't have your own transport.

By train

The train network in Norfolk and Suffolk is reasonably dense with two south–north main lines originating in London, one linking **Cambridge**, **Ely** and **King's Lynn**, the other **Ipswich** and **Norwich** and points in between. There are also two main east–west lines, one connecting Norwich with **Thetford** and Ely, the other running from Ipswich to **Bury St Edmunds**, **Newmarket** and **Ely**. Among several branch lines, the most useful are those from Norwich to **Cromer** and **Sheringham**; **Marks Tey** to **Sudbury**; and Norwich to **Great Yarmouth**. The bulk of these services are operated by the Dutch-owned **Abellio Greater Anglia** (Ⓦabellio greateranglia.co.uk), though the London-to-King's Lynn route falls to **Thameslink & Great Northern** (Ⓦthameslinkrailway.com).

The essential first port of call for information on routes, timetables, fares and special offers is **National Rail Enquiries** (Ⓦnationalrail.co.uk), and it's always worth booking in advance. Abellio Greater Anglia also offers several sorts of Ranger and Rover tickets. The details are really rather complicated, but one of the more comprehensible is the **Anglia Plus One Day Pass**, which permits unlimited travel for just £18 per adult plus up to four children for just £2 each. The **Anglia Plus Three Days in Seven Pass** is in the same vein and costs £36 per adult. There's no need to book in advance for either of these passes – just turn up and go. There are also several sorts of nationwide railcard, which entitle the bearer to substantial discounts, though these have to be purchased beforehand. These include the **16–25 Railcard** for people aged between 16 and 25 (and full-time students of any age) and the **Senior Railcard** for those over 60.

By bus

A small army of local bus companies combines to serve most of the region's towns and villages most of the time, though as a general rule, the smaller the place the harder it is to reach. The main exception is the **Norfolk Coasthopper** (Ⓦcoasthopper.co.uk) which provides an exemplary service among the villages that lie dotted along the north Norfolk coast from Hunstanton to Cromer (see p.124); look into the useful Coasthopper Rover pass. To plan a journey in either Norfolk or Suffolk, contact **Traveline** (Ⓦtraveline.info).

TWENTY OF THE BEST PLACES TO STAY

NORFOLK

Bank House, King's Lynn. See p.174
Beechwood Hotel, North Walsham. See p.92
The Boathouse, Ormesby St Michael. See p.105
The Crown, Wells. See p.148
Gothic House, Norwich. See p.54
Gunton Arms, Thorpe Market. See p.92
Rose & Crown, Snettisham. See p.164
Ship Hotel, Brancaster. See p.158
Titchwell Manor Hotel, Titchwell. See p.159
White Horse, Brancaster Staithe. See p.157

SUFFOLK

Bildeston Crown, Bildeston. See p.301
The Crown, Westleton. See p.268
The Crown, Woodbridge. See p.246
Fritton Arms, Fritton. See p.113
Great House Hotel, Lavenham. See p.299
Ickworth Hotel, Horringer. See p.313
Old Cannon B&B, Bury St Edmunds. See p.311
Salthouse Harbour, Ipswich. See p.230
Swan Hotel, Lavenham. See p.299
Swan House, Beccles. See p.221

By car or motorbike

At risk of stating the obvious, the easiest way to explore Norfolk and Suffolk is by car. **Scenic routes** abound and although the coast attracts most of the attention, the region's inland villages can be delightful as can the rolling countryside. This is also one part of England where there are no motorways and instead you'll be mostly glued to the region's **"A" roads**, sometimes dual carriageway, but mostly not, which can add time to any journey but tend to give it more character. With the exception of Norwich, where hold-ups are common, traffic congestion is rarely a problem, though the main "A" roads north from London do get clogged on the weekend as does the A149 along the north Norfolk coast. Neither should you underestimate the **weather**: much to the chagrin of many locals, driving conditions can deteriorate quickly during rain, snow, ice, fog and high winds. BBC Radio Five Live (693 or 909 AM nationwide) and local stations feature regularly updated traffic bulletins, as does the Highways Agency website (Ⓦ highways.gov.uk).

Be aware that **speed limits** are not always marked, but you are expected to know (and obey) them: 20mph on residential streets; 30 or 40mph in built-up areas; 60mph on out-of-town single carriageway roads (often signed by a white circle with a black diagonal stripe); and 70mph on dual carriageways. Speed cameras are commonplace.

Vehicle rental

Car rental is usually cheaper arranged in advance through one of the multinational chains. Costs vary considerably, so it's well worth rooting around for a deal, but you can expect to pay around £30 per day,

£50 for a weekend or from £150 per week. You can sometimes find deals under £20 per day, though you'll need to book well in advance for the least expensive rates and be prepared for extra charges, primarily damage excess waiver (CDW). Few companies will rent to drivers with less than one year's experience and most will only rent to people between 21 and 75 years of age. Rental cars will be manual (stick shift) unless you specify otherwise.

Just Go (Ⓦ justgo.uk.com) can rent quality **motorhomes** sleeping four to six people, equipped with full bathrooms, kitchenette and bike racks, for £300–1000 per week, depending on the season.

Cycling

Precious few people would choose to get around East Anglia by **cycling** on the main "A" roads – there's simply too much traffic – but the region's quieter "B" roads and country lanes are much more appealing, especially as the National Cycle Network (see p.29) sustains many miles of cycling route in both counties. **Off-road** cyclists must stick to bridleways and byways designated for their use.

Accommodation

Accommodation in Norfolk and Suffolk covers everything from motorway lodges and budget guesthouses through to deluxe country retreats and chic boutique hotels. Atmospheric old buildings – former coaching inns in towns, converted mansions and manor houses in rural areas – offer oodles of

weekend, and an increasing number insist on a minimum two-night stay at the weekend too. Almost everywhere, standards are improving, a reflection of – and assisting – the area's burgeoning tourist industry.

This guide prioritizes independent hotels, but among the smaller chains, look out for **Flying Kiwi Inns** (Ⓦflyingkiwiinns.co.uk), a local mini-chain founded by the industrious New Zealander Chris Coubrough. They operate three first-rate hotels with restaurants: *The Ship Hotel*, in Brancaster (see p.158); *The Crown* in Wells (see p.148); and the *White Hart* in Hingham (see p.208).

historic atmosphere, but everywhere you should try to book ahead in the summer season, when vacant rooms can get thin on the ground. If you're stuck, the local tourist office (where there is one) will almost invariably lend a helping hand by booking a room on your behalf.

A loosely-applied nationwide **grading system** awards stars to hotels, guesthouses and B&Bs. There's no hard and fast correlation between rank and price, never mind aesthetic appeal, but the grading system does lay down minimum levels of standards and service.

Hotels

Hotels vary wildly in size, style, comfort and price. The starting price for a one-star establishment is around £60 per night for a double/twin room, breakfast usually included; two- and three-star hotels can easily cost £80–100 a night, while four- and five-star properties will be around £150–200 a night – considerably more in country-house hotels. Many city hotels offer cut-price **weekend rates** to fill the rooms whereas seaside and resort hotels almost always charge more on the

B&Bs and guesthouses

B&Bs and **guesthouses** are often a great option for travellers looking for character and a local experience: the best – with fresh, house-proud rooms, hearty home-cooked food and a wealth of local knowledge – can match or beat a hotel stay at any price. At its simplest, a B&B (bed-and-breakfast) is a private house with a couple of bedrooms set aside for paying guests. Larger establishments with more rooms, particularly in resorts, style themselves **guesthouses**, but they are pretty much the same thing. Don't assume that a B&B is no good if it is ungraded in official listings, as some places simply choose not to enter into a grading scheme: in countryside locations, for instance, some of the best accommodation can be found in **farmhouses** whose facilities may technically fall short of official standards. Many village **pubs** also offer B&B accommodation. Standards vary widely – some are great, others truly awful – but at best you'll be staying in a friendly spot with a sociable bar on hand, and you'll rarely pay more than £80 a room.

Single travellers should note that many B&Bs and guesthouses don't have single rooms, and sole occupancy of a double or twin room will normally be charged at seventy or eighty percent of the standard rate.

TEN GREAT CAMPING AND GLAMPING SITES

Beeston Regis Holiday Park, West Runton. See p.130

Clippesby Hall Thurne, Suffolk. See p.97

Deepdale Backpackers & Camping, Burnham Deepdale. See p.157.

High Sand Creek Campsite, Stiffkey. See p.142

Ivy Grange Farm, Halesworth. See p.275.

Orchard Campsite, Wickham Market. See p.250

Suffolk Yurt Holidays, Wickham Market. See p.245.

Wardley Hill Campsite, Bungay. See p.218.

Waveney River Centre, Burgh St Peter. See p.119.

West Lexham, West Lexham. See p.199.

Hostels

The **Youth Hostel Association** (YHA; ⓦyha.org .uk) has three hostels in Norfolk – one each at Wells, Hunstanton and Sheringham – and another in Suffolk, at Blaxhall, near Aldeburgh. All four offer bunk-bed accommodation in dormitories and smaller rooms of two, four or six beds. Each of them also has a reasonable range of facilities, including a kitchen, and the overnight rate for a dorm bed is around £24 per person, £60 or so for a double room. The YHA is affiliated to the global network of **Hostelling International** (ⓦhihostels .com). If you're already an HI member, you qualify for the YHA's standard rates. Otherwise, you must pay a small supplement, or you can join HI in person at any hostel or online for £20 a year (£10 for under-26s). Family membership deals are also available.

Camping

There are scores of **campsites** in Norfolk and Suffolk, ranging from rustic, family-run places to large sites with laundries, shops and sports facilities. Costs range from around £5 per adult at the simplest sites up to around £20 per tent (including two adults) in the most sought-after locations. Many campsites also offer accommodation in static **caravans**, which are mostly large and well equipped, and quite a few have a selection of chalet-style (wooden) huts. *The Rough Guide to Camping in Britain* has detailed reviews of the best campsites, including several in Norfolk and Suffolk, or you might check out ⓦcampingand caravanningclub.co.uk. **Camping rough** is frowned upon just about everywhere.

Self-catering accommodation

Self-catering is a big deal in the tourist industries of both Norfolk and Suffolk with literally hundreds of properties – usually **cottages** – rented out either all year or just during the season. Traditionally, the minimum rental period is a week, but there's more flexibility in the market than there used to be and weekend lets are now far from uncommon. Expect to pay around £300 a week for a small cottage in an out-of-the-way location, maybe three times that for a larger property in a popular spot.

SELF-CATERING RENTAL COMPANIES

Best of Suffolk ☎ 01728 553064, ⓦ bestofsuffolk.co.uk.
Exemplary and extremely efficient lettings agency offering a wide range of upmarket properties all over Suffolk with a particular concentration of places along the coast. Hard to beat.

Landmark Trust ☎ 01628 825925, ⓦ landmarktrust.org.uk. A preservation charity that owns a goodly number of historic properties in Norfolk and Suffolk, each of which has been creatively converted into holiday accommodation. One particular highlight is the restored Martello tower at Aldeburgh.

Living Architecture ⓦ living-architecture.co.uk.
Keen to popularize adventurous modern architecture, this embryonic organization has Grayson Perry's "A House for Essex" as its most famous listing – but racks up a handful of remarkable and rentable properties in Norfolk and Suffolk too.

National Trust ☎ 03443 351287, ⓦ nationaltrustholidays.org.uk.
The NT owns over forty cottages, barns, houses and farmhouses in Norfolk and Suffolk, mostly set in their own gardens or grounds and mostly of some historical interest or importance.

Norfolk Country Cottages ☎ 01263 715779, ⓦ norfolkcottages .co.uk. Well-established lettings agency with a substantial portfolio of properties, everything from large manor houses through to cosy flint cottages in every part of the county, but especially on the coast.

Norfolk Hideaways ☎ 01485 211022, ⓦ norfolkhideaways .co.uk. Efficient and proficient Norfolk-based company, specializing in Norfolk coastal cottages but with properties in the Broads too.

Rural Retreats ☎ 01386 897172, ⓦ ruralretreats.co.uk. Upmarket agency with over fifty properties in Norfolk and Suffolk, mostly sympathetically modernized old cottages.

Suffolk Secrets ☎ 01502 722717, ⓦ suffolk-secrets.co.uk. A choice selection of rentable Suffolk properties – from handsomely converted old cottages to bijou modern dwellings. A well-regarded agency.

Food and drink

Changing tastes have transformed Norfolk and Suffolk's food and drink over the last decade. Great importance is now placed on "ethical" eating – principally sourcing products locally and using organic ingredients. Good-quality, moderately priced restaurants can now be found almost everywhere and the majority are independently owned, with barely a chain in sight. The East Anglian pub has rung the changes too: the traditional village boozer is on the wane and although lots of rural pubs have closed, scores have reinvented themselves, sprucing up their decor and serving both real ales and excellent food.

In turn, this culinary transformation means that there are now enough (gastro-)pubs and restaurants demanding top-quality ingredients to support a battalion of local food suppliers.

LOCAL BEERS, CIDERS AND JUICES

Adnams ⓦ adnams.co.uk. The ultimate successful local brewer, rooted in the heart of its Suffolk community yet producing a wide range of excellent draft and bottled beers. They have a great county-wide chain of classy beer and wine shops too.

Aspall ⓦ aspall.co.uk. Based at Aspall Hall and run by the eighth generation of the Chevalier family, Aspall ciders are another fine example of a brilliant Suffolk product that has gone national. Great cider, apple juice and vinegar.

Beeston Brewery ⓦ beestonbrewery.com. Small brewer based in Beeston, near Dereham, that produces half a dozen ales, from the light, easy-drinking Afternoon Delight to the heavier and stronger stout, Old Stoatwobbler.

Calvors Brewery ⓦ calvorsbrewery.com. This Suffolk producer is one of the youngest East Anglia breweries, and concentrates on English lager and ales from its headquarters just north of Ipswich. You can find its beers in shops and pubs all over Suffolk, as well as the odd Norfolk location.

Cliff Quay Brewery ⓦ cliffquay.co.uk. This small brewer from Ipswich supplies outlets around the city and half a dozen places outside with its range of five regular ales and innumerable seasonal brews.

Earl Soham Brewery ⓦ earlsohambrewery .co.uk. One of the best-established Suffolk brewers, whose Victoria Bitter can be found in many a decent Suffolk pub.

Greene King ⓦ greeneking.co.uk. This well-known brewery has been going for 200 years and hardly needs an introduction if you've been into a pub anywhere in Britain over the past two decades. But its beers are reliably good, and it's still based in its original Bury St Edmunds home.

Humpty Dumpty Brewery ⓦ humptydumptybrewery.com. This Norfolk brewer is based in a large shed in Reedham, and produces a wide and delicious range of ales despite being a relatively small affair. Their shop (see p.114) sells their own products, alongside brews from Belgium and local ciders.

Iceni Brewery ⓦ icenibrewery.co.uk. This small brewery on the edge of Thetford Forest brews a huge range of beers considering its size. The best place to buy them is at their tiny shop in Ickburgh, but you can also find them at local farmers' markets.

James White ⓦ jameswhite.co.uk. This fantastic rural Suffolk business has a royal warrant for its apple and other juices. Its fresh-pressed russet juice is a joy.

Lacons ⓦ lacons.co.uk. Proof, if any were needed, of the resurgence of East Anglian brewing, Lacons has just returned to Great Yarmouth after a break of 45 years – long enough for a pint or two, that's for sure.

Mauldons ⓦ mauldons.co.uk. Over 200 years old, this is one of Suffolk's most established brewers, but it remains a microbrewer at heart, producing seven draft ales and five bottled beers at its home in Sudbury. You can sample its wares at its own local, the *Brewery Tap* (see p.292).

Panther Brewery ⓦ pantherbrewery.co.uk. This small Reepham-based brewer punches way above its weight around Norfolk, with a wide range of authentic craft beers that are showcased in the annual Reepham Beer Festival in August.

St Peter's Brewery ⓦ stpetersbrewery.co.uk. Based just outside Bungay, St Peter's was started about fifteen years ago not by a brewer but a brand consultant. They brew some great beers, which are available at the on-site shop (see p.219) and in decent pubs across Norfolk and Suffolk.

Tipples ⓦ tipplesbrewery.com. With a name like Jason Tipple, he really had to start his own brewery, and he now produces half a dozen or so bottled ales from his Salhouse HQ, not far from Wroxham, as well as plenty of seasonal specials and so-called experimental ales.

Wagtail Brewery ⓦ wagtailbrewery.com. This great Norfolk brewery's ales can be found all over the county and a little bit beyond, both on draft and in bottles.

Wolf Brewery ⓦ wolfbrewery.com. Based just outside Attleborough since 1995, this is one of the best-established Norfolk microbreweries, producing a platoon of draft ales and a whole slew of bottled varieties.

Woodforde's ⓦ woodfordes.co.uk. Based in the heart of the Broads, Woodforde's supplies pubs all over Norfolk and Suffolk, and most people swear by at least one of its five or so draft beers and bottled equivalents.

Free-range Suffolk pork and Cromer crabs (see box, p.128) are obvious and widespread examples, but other memorable specialities include Brancaster and Stiffkey oysters and mussels, and Norfolk samphire. In many pubs and restaurants, locally sourced food ties in with a well-considered "**modern British**" menu that features old favourites – steak and kidney pies – with more adventurous concoctions – crab in beetroot sauce, for example. One casualty of the change has been the **teashop** or **tearoom**: once there were dozens, now there is just a light scattering, their decline assured by the irresistible rise of the gastropub and, in the larger towns, the chain-outlet coffee shops such as *Costa* and *Caffè Nero*.

Festivals and special events

Festivals are something of a growth industry in the UK and East Anglia is no exception, with lots of towns and villages designing new special-interest shindigs each and every year – not surprising, really, when you consider the roaring success of Southwold's Latitude music festival, for example, which only started in 2006. These new concoctions are grafted onto more established festivals, ranging from the agricultural delights of the Royal Norfolk Show to the studied gentility of the Aldeburgh Festival. The calendar below picks out some of the best, but for detailed local listings contact the appropriate tourist office (see p.33).

JANUARY–APRIL

Shrove Tuesday The last day before Lent – in February or March depending on the year. Known as "Pancake Day", this is when the English get down to some serious pancake eating. In 2011, an ancient Pancake Day tradition was revived in Dereham with the ringing of church bells, and Felixstowe holds the record for the largest number of pancakes tossed in the shortest amount of time (349 tosses in 2 minutes). Also celebrated with a Mardi Gras parade in Great Yarmouth.

MAY

Broads Outdoors Festival Two weeks in early May; Ⓦ outdoorsfestival.co.uk. Guided walks, jazz boats, wildlife tours – a host of things to do on and off the water in the Broads.
Folk on the Pier Three days in early May; Ⓦ folkonthepier.co.uk.

OUR FAVOURITE NORFOLK AND SUFFOLK RESTAURANTS
Bildeston Crown, Bildeston. See p.301
Bure River Cottage, Horning. See p.82
The Crown, Woodbridge. See p.246
Great House, Lavenham. See p.299
Gunton Arms, Thorpe Market. See p.92
Lavender House, Brundall. See p.115
Market Bistro, King's Lynn. See p.176
Narborough Hall, Narborough. See p.195
Saracen's Head, Erpingham. See p.78
Strattons, Swaffham. See p.194
Tatlers, Norwich. See p.57
Titchwell Manor Hotel, Titchwell. See p.159

Held in Cromer, this ambitious music festival celebrates all things folksy with concerts, gigs and workshops. Acoustic folk, folk rock, blues and world music are all represented and performances feature an international cast of artists.
Norfolk & Norwich Festival Two weeks in May; Ⓦ nnfestival .org.uk. This is Norwich's premier arts festival with a particular emphasis on music, especially jazz, contemporary and classical, plus oodles of theatre and dance. Showcases performing artists from every corner of the globe.
Bury St Edmunds Festival Two weeks in late May; Ⓦ buryfestival .co.uk. Small-town cultural knees-up with jazz, theatre, film, classical music and street theatre.

JUNE

Suffolk Show Two days in early June; Ⓦ suffolkshow.co.uk. Folksy/ rural celebration of the best of Suffolk's agricultural trade, with a special emphasis on animals, local produce and skilled craftsmen. Held on the Suffolk Showground on the edge of Ipswich.
Three Rivers Race Horning; last Sat in May or first Sat in June; Ⓦ threeriversrace.org.uk. For some this is the major sailing event of the summer, a sort of Norfolk Broads Le Mans, lasting right through the night and with over a hundred yachts in contention.
Aldeburgh Festival Two and a half weeks in June; Ⓦ aldeburgh .co.uk. Suffolk jamboree of classical music with a worldwide reputation. Established by Benjamin Britten in 1948. Book early to avoid disappointment. Core performances are held at the Snape Maltings, just outside Aldeburgh. See p.260.
Royal Norfolk Show Two days in late June/early July; Ⓦ royalnorfolkshow.rnaa.org.uk. The largest agricultural show in England showcases all things farming – from crops to livestock and beyond. Hearty sports and hearty, locally produced food too. Held on the Norfolk Showground, on the western edge of Norwich.

JULY

Latitude Festival Four days in mid-July; Ⓦ latitudefestival .co.uk. Relatively new music festival that has quickly become one of

England's best, featuring several hundred performers with add-ons in the shape of comedy, theatre, dance, poetry and cabaret. Held in Henham Park just outside Southwold. Headline acts in recent years have included Suede, The Waterboys, The Cribs and Portishead. See p.274.

The Shakespeare Festival Four days in mid-July; ⓦ cathedral .org.uk. Top-ranking Shakespearean performances held in the cloisters of Norwich Cathedral – great setting.

Holt Festival Last week of July; ⓦ holtsummerfestival.org. Attracting a well-heeled crew, this week-long festival features all the performing arts, from dance, poetry, literature and street theatre through to comedy and contemporary music.

AUGUST

Cromer Carnival One week in mid-Aug; ⓦ cromercarnival.co.uk. Family fun and entertainment culminating in an impressive Carnival Parade and a whopping firework display.

SEPTEMBER

Heritage Open Days Three days in mid-Sept; ⓦ heritage opendays.org.uk. A once-a-year opportunity to peek inside dozens of buildings that don't normally open their doors to the public. Coordinated by English Heritage; the properties concerned are dotted all over the region.

High Tide Festival Ten days in mid-September; ⓦ hightide.org .uk. Enterprising festival showcasing newly written plays plus workshops, panel debates and films. Held in Aldeburgh, Suffolk.

Yare Navigation Race Brundall; one day in late September; ⓦ coldhamhallsailingclub.co.uk. The biggest Norfolk Broad cruiser event on the southern Broads, with around eighty yachts racing between Brundall and Breydon Water.

OCTOBER

Norwich Beer Festival Late Oct; ⓦ norwichcamra.org.uk. Six days of happy, hoppy stupefaction in St Andrew's Hall, Norwich. CAMRA buffs abound.

Halloween Oct 31. All Hallows' Eve. In the last decade, British kids have taken to the mock horror of Halloween like ducks to water, parading round in ghoulish disguises mainly copied from the USA. Expect to be tricked-or-treated.

NOVEMBER

Aldeburgh Poetry Festival Three days in early Nov; ⓦ thepoetry trust.org. The Poetry Trust is one of the UK's leading poetry organizations and it has steered this festival into becoming a big poetic deal, attracting a wide range of new and established poets.

Bonfire Night Nov 5. In 1605, Guy Fawkes tried to blow up Parliament in the Gunpowder Plot, but for better or worse he failed and was subsequently executed for his pains. The English have celebrated Fawkes's failure ever since with bonfires and fireworks in every corner of the land. Traditionally, an effigy of Fawkes was burnt on the bonfire, though nowadays it's as likely to be a heartily disliked celebrity. Celebrated with particular gusto in Norwich at both Earlham Park and the Norfolk Showground.

DECEMBER

New Year's Eve Dec 31. Much carousing in the region's town and cities; more genteel tipsiness in the country.

Sports and outdoor activities

The average East Anglian may love his or her spectator sports, but most of the action takes place in England's big cities, well away from Norfolk and Suffolk, with two main exceptions – one football, the other horse racing. For participants, Norfolk and Suffolk offer a battery of outdoor activities, with three of the most popular being walking, cycling and beachcombing – or just lying on the beach and going for a dip now and again. Sailing is popular too, both on the coast and on the Norfolk Broads (see box, pp.66–67), and birdwatching is a major pastime as well (see p.330).

Spectator sports

Football games between Ipswich and Norwich excite intense local rivalry, though Norwich (see p.59) were promoted to the Premier League in 2015, leaving Ipswich (see p.227) behind in the Championship and, as a result, regular league fixtures between them are no more – at least for the time being. The other spectator sport hereabouts is **horse racing**, principally in horse-mad Newmarket (see p.314), which is home to two – flat – **racecourses**. They hold several meetings a year between April and October, including the Guineas festival in late April/May, which takes in two of the five classics on the flat racing calendar, the 1000 Guineas and the 2000 Guineas. There is also flat racing in Great Yarmouth (see p.110) and National Hunt racing at Fakenham (see p.144).

Walking

Norfolk and Suffolk are neither rugged nor especially wild, but their easy, rolling landscapes, long coast, rich birdlife and wide skies have combined to make them a very popular **walking area**. Almost all of the region's many tourist offices have details of local rambles, most of which are easily accomplished in a day and are physically undemanding, especially as clearly signed footpaths abound. General details of local walks are given in this guide and the region also possesses one of England's busiest **National Trails** (Ⓦnational trail.co.uk), the **Peddars Way/Norfolk Coast Path**. This waymarked path and track separates into two clearly defined sections, the less-used portion being the 46-mile Peddars Way, which stretches north from Suffolk's Knettishall Heath Country Park, following the route of an old Roman road as far as Holme-next-the-Sea on the Norfolk coast. The second section is the 45-mile Norfolk Coast Path, which ambles east along the coast from Holme-next-the-Sea to Cromer. Only a minority of walkers undertake the whole caboodle with most opting for short(ish) hikes, especially along the Norfolk Coast Path where the **Norfolk Coasthopper** bus (Ⓦcoasthopper.co.uk) provides handy public transport, making round trips relatively easy and convenient.

Other long-distance routes include the sixty-mile **Stour Valley Path**, linking Dedham Vale with Sudbury and Newmarket; the fifty-mile **Suffolk Coast and Heaths Path**, which follows the coast from Felixstowe to Lowestoft; the 56-mile **Weavers' Way**, an inland route between Cromer and Great Yarmouth; the twenty-mile-long **Paston Way**, from North Walsham to Cromer; the 70-mile **Angles Way**, from just beyond Diss to Great Yarmouth; and the 35-mile **Wherryman's Way**, a riverine route connecting Norwich with Great Yarmouth. There are also paths that start outside but finish up in Norfolk or Suffolk, like the 50-mile **Fen Rivers Way**, which starts in Cambridge and runs right up the Ouse and its tributaries to King's Lynn. There's just one designated national park in the region – **The Broads** (Ⓦbroads-authority.gov .uk), which is the UK's most important wetland and is mostly in Norfolk but noses its way across the border into Suffolk.

It almost goes without saying that even for a fairly short hike you need to be properly equipped. The East Anglian climate is relatively benign, but the weather is very changeable and on the coast in particular the wind can be bitingly chill. As for maps, walkers almost invariably stick to **Ordnance Survey** maps (OS; Ⓦordnancesurvey.co.uk), either in the Explorer (1:25,000) or the Landranger series (1:50,000). These can be used in conjunction with the companionable **Wilfrid George maps**, simple sketch maps showing items of interest and potential walking routes. These are available at most major tourist offices – for example Lavenham and Cromer – and cost around £2; they don't cover all of Norfolk and Suffolk, but they do cover the most visited bits of both.

Cycling

The UK's **National Cycle Network** (Ⓦsustrans.org .uk) is made up of 10,000 miles of signed cycle routes, a third on traffic-free paths (including disused railways and canal towpaths), the rest mainly on country roads. In Norfolk and Suffolk, NCN cycle routes loop their way through both counties, dropping by all the major towns – Norwich, Ipswich, Bury St Edmunds, Thetford etc – and a battery of villages. **Sustrans** produces an excellent series of waterproof maps (1:100,000) to help you on your way. There's also the **Norfolk Coast Cycleway**, following quiet roads and lanes from King's Lynn to Great Yarmouth; detailed maps of the route, which is a regional route of the Sustrans Hull-to-Harwich route, are produced by the Norfolk Coast Partnership (Ⓦnorfolkcoastaonb .org.uk) and are also available at larger tourist offices. In addition, most local tourist offices stock a range of **cycling guides**, with maps and detailed route descriptions, and have details of local cycle-rental companies, though these are not as plentiful as you would perhaps imagine. Expect to pay around £10–15 per day, with discounts for longer periods; you may need to provide credit card details, or leave a passport as a deposit.

Beaches

The elongated coastline of Norfolk and Suffolk boasts long stretches of golden sand interspersed with mudflats and salt marsh, shingle and pebble. Everywhere, the sea disappears into the distance at low tide, possibly to the frustration of bathers, but to the delight of kids who can nose around the tide pools, observe the lugworms casting up their coils and watch (or catch) the crabs. Perhaps the eeriest

---

TOP TEN BEACHES
Cromer See p.125
Holkham Bay See p.149
Holme-next-the-Sea See p.160
Hunstanton See p.161
Overstrand See p.98
Sea Palling See p.100
Southwold See p.268
Walberswick See p.237.
Wells-next-the-Sea See p.147
Winterton-on-Sea See p.105

part of the coast is between Hunstanton and King's Lynn, where the Wash empties into the ocean creating a mass phalanx of treacle-mud that attracts birds by the thousand and birdwatchers by the score. A number of beaches are currently recipients of **Blue Flag** quality awards, including Hunstanton, Cromer, Southwold and Lowestoft.

Sailing and watersports

Most visitors to the Norfolk and Suffolk seaside are content with bucket and spade, deckchair and ice cream, but others are after more activity with sailing exercising an enduring appeal. Among the resorts of the north Norfolk coast, Blakeney is the apple of the sailor's eye, though here you will need your own boat; whereas, just along the coast at Brancaster Staithe, the Sailcraft Sea School (Ⓦnorthshoresport.co.uk) organizes training sessions and rents out boats. There's also surfing with The Glide Surf School in Cromer (Ⓦglidesurfschool.co.uk) and windsurfing at Hunstanton with Hunstanton Watersports (Ⓦhunstantonwatersports.com). Away from the coast, the Broads are extraordinarily popular with boaters too, and here boat rental is easy and straightforward (see box, pp.66–67), whether you're a keen sailor (there is no better place in the country for safe yet demanding **sailing**); a canoeist (the reedy wetlands of the Broads is ideal **canoeing** country); or you just want to do as most people do and pootle around in a **motor cruiser**.

Shopping

Homogenization may be the name of the game in most of the UK, but in Norfolk and Suffolk small, independent shops have survived – even flourished – in substantial numbers with Norwich leading the retail resistance.

Many of the region's towns and larger villages have, for example, a weekly **market**, where local produce is a particular highlight – this is, after all, a predominantly agricultural region – and Country Markets (Ⓦcountry-markets.co.uk) has detailed listings of what's on and where. There's also a veritable battery of specialist **food shops** in the prime tourist zones with the north Norfolk and Suffolk coasts in the forefront. It's here on the coast you'll find a goodly number of fishmongers with the good old Cromer crab clinging onto many a gastronomic headline. **Farm shops** are a feature of

---

> **LOCAL FOOD HEROES: GREAT PRODUCERS, DELIS AND FARM SHOPS**
>
> **Blythburgh Pork** Ⓦfreerangepork.co.uk
> **Cley Smokehouse**, Cley. See p.137
> **Drove Orchards**, near Holme-next-the-Sea. See p.160
> **Emmetts**, Peasenhall. See p.265
> **Farm to Fork & Fish**, Horstead. See p.73
> **Gurneys Fish Shop**, Burnham Market. See p.155
> **Jimmy's Farm**, Ipswich. See p.234
> **Lawson's**, Aldeburgh. See p.138
> **Norfolk Farmhouse Ice Cream** Ⓦdannsfarm.co.uk
> **Pinney's**, Orford. See p.254
> **Tavern Tasty Meats**. Ⓦtaverntasty.co.uk
> **Wiveton Hall**, near Cley. See p.138

---

the region too, as well as roadside stalls selling the freshest of fruit and veg – Norfolk strawberries can taste absolutely wonderful.

Furthermore, some of the more prosperous towns – like Holt, Burnham Market and Long Melford – have a good range of **independent retailers** selling books, antiques and designer clothes, but these tend to be on the pricey side except in Norwich, which excels in bargain-basement specialist shops selling everything from vintage clothes to ancient furniture.

Travel essentials

Costs and passes

By comparison with the rest of western Europe, England in general and Norfolk and Suffolk in particular are competitively priced, less so in comparison with North America, Australia and New Zealand. If you're camping or hostelling, using public transport, buying picnic lunches and eating in pubs and cafés your **minimum expenditure** will be around £35/US$54/€48 per person per day. Couples staying in B&Bs, eating at mid-range restaurants and visiting some attractions should anticipate roughly £70/US$110/€96 per person, while if you're renting a car, staying in hotels and eating well, budget for £120/US$185/€165 each – but double that figure if you choose to stay in stylish deluxe hotels or grand country houses.

Many of the region's **historic attractions** are owned and/or operated by either the **National**

NORFOLK AND SUFFOLK'S TWENTY BEST CHURCHES

The Abbey, Wymondham. See p.201
Binham Priory church, Binham. See p.139
Holy Trinity, Blythburgh. See p.273
Holy Trinity, Long Melford. See p.294
St Edmund, Southwold. See p.270
St Helen, Ranworth. See p.75
St Margaret, Cley-next-the-Sea. See p.136
St Margaret, King's Lynn. See p.171
St Mary, Bury St Edmunds. See p.309
St Mary, Houghton-on-the-Hill. See p.207

St Mary, Stoke-by-Nayland. See p.289
St Mary, Thornham Parva. See p.306
St Michael, Framlingham. See p.250
St Nicholas, Blakeney. See p.139
St Nicholas, Salthouse. See p.135
St Peter Mancroft, Norwich. See p.48
St John, Oxborough. See p.196
St Peter & St Paul, Lavenham. See p.299
St Peter & St Paul, Salle. See p.80
Walpole St Peter, Walpole St Peter. See p.177

Trust (W nationaltrust.org.uk) or **English Heritage** (W www.english-heritage.org.uk), whose properties are denoted throughout this book with "NT" or "EH". Most of the lesser, smaller sites are free, but all the more prestigious locations attract a hefty-ish admission charge of about £7 and up. If you plan to visit more than half a dozen places owned by either, it's worth considering an annual membership – you can join online or in person at any staffed attraction. There are several different sorts of membership, but a standard, adult, year-long pass currently costs £60 (NT) and £50 (EH). Non-UK residents can, on the other hand, buy short-term passes for both English Heritage (9 days, £30; 16 days, £35) and National Trust properties (7 days, £25; 14 days, £30) from Visit-Britain (W visitbritainshop.com). Family discounts are available on these passes, which can be purchased online.

A number of **stately homes** are still in private hands and these charge substantial entry fees – £12 for Holkham Hall, £14 for Houghton Hall – whereas the region's privately owned museums and art **galleries**, of which there are a small number, charge modest admission fees starting from as little as £2. Norfolk and Suffolk are short of publicly owned museums and art galleries, but admission to them starts at about £5. Churches are usually free, though Ely Cathedral charges (£8) and Norwich Cathedral requests a donation.

Throughout this book, admission prices quoted are the full adult rate, unless otherwise stated. Concessionary rates – generally half-price – for **senior citizens**, under-26s, and **children** (aged 5–17) apply almost everywhere, from tourist attractions to public transport; you'll need official ID as proof of age. Children under 5 are rarely charged. Full-time **students** are often entitled to discounts too via an ISIC (International Student Identity Card; W isic.org).

Health

Citizens of all EU and EEA countries are entitled to **free medical treatment** within the UK's National Health Service (NHS), on production of their **European Health Insurance Card** (EHIC). The same applies to those Commonwealth countries that have reciprocal healthcare arrangements with the UK – Australia and New Zealand, for example. Everyone else will be charged and should, therefore, take out their own medical insurance. However, EU/EEA citizens may also want to consider private health insurance, both to cover the cost of items not within the EU/EEA scheme (eg repatriation on medical grounds) and to enable them to seek treatment within the private sector. No inoculations are currently required for entry into Britain.

For medical advice 24 hours a day, call the **NHS** non-emergency number, ☎111. Otherwise, minor issues can be dealt with at the surgery of any local **doctor**, also known as a **GP** (General Practitioner), whereas medical emergencies are treated in hospital at 24hr "**A&E**" (accident and emergency) – or "**Casualty**" – sections; note that not all hospitals have A&E facilities. You can either make your own way to the nearest A&E or call an ambulance on ☎999.

LGBT travellers

England offers one of Europe's most diverse and accessible **LGBT** scenes, but most of the action is in the big cities, which tends to leave most of Norfolk and Suffolk high and dry (with the notable exception of Norwich). Countrywide listings and news can be found at PinkNews (W pinknews.co.uk) and *Gay Times* (W gaytimes.co.uk). For information and links, go to W gaybritain.co.uk and W gaytravel.co.uk. The age of consent is 16.

Maps

There's a bewildering variety of **road maps**, but the best – or at least the clearest – are those produced by **A-Z Maps** (ⓦaz.co.uk), whose excellent and competitively priced *A-Z Super Scale Britain* (1:100,000) includes inset maps of Norwich and Ipswich. The same company also publishes a wide range of detailed city street maps, including maps of Norwich and Ipswich (both at 1:16,000), and produces county maps for both Norfolk and Suffolk (1:17,000), each of which has literally dozens of village and town street maps. For hiking you'll need Ordnance Survey maps (see p.29).

Newspapers

There are lots of local newspapers in Norfolk and Suffolk, but the best coverage of regional news, scandal and gossip is provided by the **Eastern Daily Press**, which covers all of Norfolk as well as north Suffolk. The other regional daily is the **East Anglian Daily Times**, which covers Ipswich and the rest of Suffolk; and both papers publish a monthly magazine on Norfolk and Suffolk respectively, full of the usual glossy ads, lifestyle and property articles. The major local newspaper for Norwich and its surroundings is the **Norwich Evening News**, while the **Evening Star** does the same job for Ipswich and around.

Opening hours

Opening hours for most businesses, shops and offices are Monday to Saturday 9am to 5.30 or 6pm, with many shops, especially in the popular tourist areas, also open on Sundays (generally 10.30 or 11am until 4 or 5pm). Big supermarkets have longer hours (except on Sundays), sometimes round the clock. Some towns have an **early closing day** (usually Wednesday) when most shops close at 1pm, but this custom is on the wane. **Banks** are usually open Monday to Friday 9am to 4pm, and Saturday 9am to 12.30pm or so. You can usually get fuel any time of the day or night in larger towns and cities, but in rural areas keep an eye on that petrol gauge.

Phones

With the irresistible rise of the mobile phone (cell phone), public **payphones** are increasingly thin on the ground, especially in the countryside. Where they have survived, they take coins (minimum charge 40p) and some also accept credit cards. The English have taken to **mobile phones** like ducks to water, but outside of the towns in both Norfolk and Suffolk network coverage is frustratingly patchy. The UK mobile network is on the 900/1800 MHz band – the band common to the rest of Europe, Australia and New Zealand (but not North America). Phoning UK **directory enquiries** is inordinately expensive; instead look online at ⓦbt.com. Business and service numbers are searchable at ⓦyell.com.

Smoking

Smoking is banned in all enclosed public spaces, including restaurants, cafés, pubs and offices, and on all public transport. Hotel rooms that are designated specifically as smoking rooms are exempt – but the vast majority of hotels and B&Bs impose smoking bans throughout their premises anyway. All of this means that smokers have taken to the great outdoors, though quite a few pubs have created sheltered outside areas specifically for them – and some are even heated.

Time zones

The UK is on **Greenwich Mean Time** (GMT), five hours ahead of US Eastern Standard Time, eight

PUBLIC HOLIDAYS

New Year's Day January 1
Good Friday Variable March/April
Easter Monday Variable March/April
May Day Bank Holiday First Monday in May
Spring Bank Holiday Last Monday in May
Summer Bank Holiday Last Monday in August
Christmas Day December 25
Boxing Day December 26
(If Jan 1, Dec 25 or Dec 26 fall on a Sat or Sun, the next weekday becomes a public holiday)

hours ahead of US Pacific Standard Time, ten hours behind Australian Eastern Standard Time and twelve hours behind New Zealand. There are, however, variations during the changeover periods involved in **daylight saving**; the UK moves its clocks forward one hour on the last Sunday in March and one hour back on the last Sunday in October. During this summer period, the UK is on **British Summer Time** (BST).

Tourist information

The body promoting inbound tourism to the UK is **VisitBritain** (visitbritain.com), with offices worldwide and a comprehensive website. A network of regional tourist boards supplements the agency's work with **Visit East Anglia** (visiteastofengland.com) covering Norfolk and Suffolk. In turn, their work is supplemented by two county-wide organizations – **Visit Suffolk** (visitsuffolk.com) and **Visit Norfolk** (visitnorfolk.co.uk).

There are also tourist offices in all the larger towns – Ipswich, Norwich, Sudbury et al – and some villages and coastal resorts. Staff here will often be able to book local accommodation and sell guidebooks, maps and hiking leaflets. Details of all these local tourist offices are in this guide. There is a scattering of specialist information centres too, like those advising on the Broads National Park and those attached to all the larger nature reserves.

Travellers with disabilities

Generally speaking, Norfolk and Suffolk have reasonably good facilities for **travellers with disabilities**. All new public buildings – including museums, galleries and cinemas – must provide wheelchair access, train stations and airports are usually fully accessible, and many buses have easy-access boarding ramps. In the towns, kerbs and signalled crossings have usually been dropped, but in the villages this remains something of a rarity – indeed in many places there's no pavement at all. More positively, the number of accessible hotels and restaurants is growing, and reserved parking bays are commonplace. One useful point of reference is **Tourism for All** (tourismforall.org.uk), which has generic advice, listings and information.

Travelling with children

Facilities in Norfolk and Suffolk for **travelling with children** are up to par with the rest of the UK. Breastfeeding is allowed in all public places, including restaurants, cafés and public transport, and baby-changing rooms are available widely, including in malls and train stations. Under-5s aren't charged on public transport or at attractions and 5- to 16-year-olds usually get a fifty-percent discount. Children aren't allowed in certain licensed (that is, alcohol-serving) premises – though this doesn't apply to restaurants, and many pubs have family rooms or beer gardens where children are welcome. As for pastimes, children can spend hour after hour on the beach, building sandcastles, catching crabs and going for a paddle, but there is a scattering of specific attractions too – we've listed ten of the best (see box below). For more general advice, check out babygoes2.com.

TEN GREAT FAMILY ATTRACTIONS

Africa Alive, Lowestoft. See p.279
Bewilderwood, Horning. See p.82
Dinosaur Adventure, near Norwich. See p.53
Fritton Lake, near Great Yarmouth. See p.112
Gressenhall Farm & Workhouse, East Dereham. See p.200
Merrivale Model Village, Great Yarmouth. See p.109
Pleasure Beach, Great Yarmouth. See p.109
Pleasurewood Hills, Lowestoft. See p.278
Under the Pier Show, Southwold. See p.271
West Stow Country Park and Anglo-Saxon Village, West Stow. See p.314

Norwich

NORWICH CATHEDRAL

1

Norwich

Partly because it's tucked away in a corner of England far away from the nearest motorway, Norwich is often misunderstood. Neither has the city done well in popular culture – mention the city to the average Briton and you're likely to hear about Delia Smith, the revered but distinctly staid television chef and writer; Bernard Matthews, the turkey king who famously described his birds in a full flourish of the Norfolk dialect as "bootiful"; and Alan Partridge, the laughably inept presenter of Radio Norwich, as played by the comedian Steve Coogan. By such stereotypes images are made and reputations tarnished, but in fact Norwich is a go-ahead place with a sound and diverse economy, a flourishing cultural life, a major university, a lively restaurant and bar scene, and, for a small city, a surprisingly varied range of independent shops.

Nestling within a sweeping bend of the River Wensum, the narrow cobbled lanes – and irregular street plan – of Norwich's compact centre are a delight to explore on foot. The city's architectural pride and joy is the beautiful **cathedral**, while its imposing **castle** holds one of the region's most satisfying collections of fine art. Elsewhere, the **Market Place** – and its sprawling open-air market – lies at the very centre of the city and, nearby, is the distinctive **Norwich Lanes** with its cobbled streets and independent shops. The city's hallmark, however, is its medieval churches, thirty or so squat flint structures with sturdy towers and sinuous stone tracery. Many are no longer in regular use and are now in the care of the Norwich Historic Churches Trust (ⓦnorwich-churches.org), whose website describes each church in detail and gives opening times. For centuries, it was the Protestant Church that led the intellectual way here, but this role has now passed to the much-vaunted **University of East Anglia (UEA)**, whose sprawling campus holds the top-ranking Sainsbury Centre for the Visual Arts. And finally, as the capital of Norfolk, Norwich lies at the hub of the region's transport network, serving as a potential base for visiting the Broads and as a springboard for further Norfolk ramblings.

Brief history

Norwich boasts a long and distinguished **history**. It was one of the five largest cities in Norman England, serving a vast hinterland of **East Anglian** cloth producers, whose work was brought here by river and then exported to the Continent. The city's isolated position beyond the Fens meant that it enjoyed closer links with the Low Countries in Western Europe than with the rest of England – it was, after all, quicker to cross the North Sea than to go cross-country to London. The local textile industry, based on **worsted cloth** (named after the nearby village of Worstead), was further enhanced by an influx of Flemish and Huguenot weavers, who made up more than a third of the population in Tudor times. By 1700, Norwich was the second richest city in the country after London.

    With the onset of the Industrial Revolution, however, Norwich lost ground to the northern manufacturing towns – the city's famous mustard company, **Colman's**,

PLANTATION GARDEN

Highlights

❶ Norwich Cathedral Without doubt the city's most magnificent building, a stirringly beautiful medieval structure of imposing grace and elegance. **See p.39**

❷ Plantation Garden This delightful garden, hidden away in a wooded dell, is a charming surprise. **See p.49**

❸ Norwich Castle Museum and Gallery The castle may be something of an architectural disappointment, but not its superb collection of Norwich School paintings. **See p.49**

❹ The Sainsbury Centre for Visual Arts There's

money in those supermarkets and the Sainsbury family have turned a portion of their profits into this well-endowed collection. **See p.52**

❺ Gothic House Smashing B&B, arguably the city's best and certainly the most distinctive – all at a very reasonable price. **See p.54**

❻ Cinema City Watch the best of the cinematic crop at this excellent art-house cinema. **See p.58**

❼ Norwich Puppet Theatre Simply brilliant puppet theatre, whose performances cater for children and adults alike. **See p.58**

HIGHLIGHTS ARE MARKED ON THE MAP ON P.38

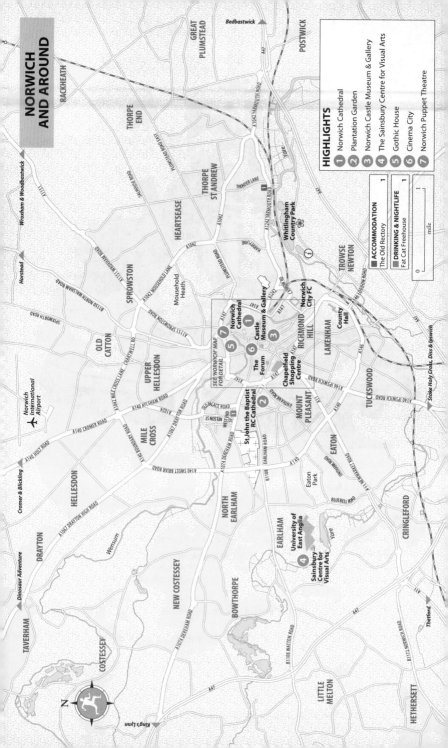

NORWICH AND AROUND

HIGHLIGHTS

1. Norwich Cathedral
2. Plantation Garden
3. Norwich Castle Museum & Gallery
4. The Sainsbury Centre for Visual Arts
5. Gothic House
6. Cinema City
7. Norwich Puppet Theatre

ACCOMMODATION
The Old Rectory 1

DRINKING & NIGHTLIFE
Fat Cat Freehouse 1

0 — mile

FESTIVALS

For a smallish city, Norwich punches well above its weight when it comes to **festivals**. Calendar highlights include:

The UEA Literary Festival Ⓦ uea.ac.uk /events. At the University of East Anglia, and attracting a heavy-duty bunch of writers and intellectuals, whose lectures and workshops spread over almost two months beginning in late February.

Norfolk & Norwich Festival Ⓦ nnfestival .org.uk. Held over two weeks in May, this is Norwich's premier arts festival, with an international cast of jazz, classical and world musicians and lots more.

The Shakespeare Festival Ⓦ cathedral .org.uk. Five days of Shakespearean performances held in the cloisters of the cathedral during July.

The Autumn Literary Festival Ⓦ uea.ac.uk /events. At the University of East Anglia. Similar to the UEA Literary Festival (see above) but beginning in late September.

Norwich Beer Festival Ⓦ norwichcamra .org.uk. Six days of hoppy satisfaction in The Halls in October.

remains one of its few industrial success stories (though it is now part of Unilever) – but there again this helped preserve much of the ancient street plan and many of the city's older buildings. Norwich's relative isolation has also meant that the **population** has never swelled to any great extent and today, with just 140,000 inhabitants, it remains an easy and enjoyable city to negotiate and explore.

Norwich Cathedral and around

The logical place to start an exploration of **Norwich** is the **cathedral**, a magnificent structure sitting proud in its own grounds – the leafy and expansive **Upper and Lower Close**. The Lower Close backs onto the **River Wensum**, a pleasant spot for a stroll, while the front of the cathedral pushes out towards **Tombland**, home to one of the city's more interesting medieval churches, **St George's**, which is itself but a hop, skip and a jump from one of the cutest corners of the city, **Elm Hill**.

Norwich Cathedral

The Close, NR1 4EH • Daily 7.30am–6pm • Free, but donation requested • ☎ 01603 218300, Ⓦ cathedral.org.uk

Of all the medieval buildings in Norwich, it's the **cathedral** that fires the imagination, a mighty, sandy-coloured structure finessed by its prickly octagonal spire, which rises to a height of 315ft, second only to Salisbury Cathedral in Wiltshire. From the front, the cathedral looks no more than imposing, but from the south, from the Lower Close (see p.44), the full intricacy of the design becomes apparent, the thick curves of the flying buttresses and the rounded sweep of the ambulatory chapels – unusual in an English cathedral – set against the straight symmetries of the main trunk. The cathedral is entered via the **Hostry**, a glassy, well-proportioned visitor centre located just to the right of the main doors. There are often modest displays of local art here, both secular and religious, plus a café whose attractive modern architecture is rather better than the food.

The nave

The interior of the cathedral is pleasantly light thanks to a creamy tint in the stone and the clear-glass windows of much of the **nave**, where the thick pillars are a powerful legacy of the Norman builders, who began work here in 1096 at the behest of a certain **Herbert de Losinga**, the city's first bishop. An interesting figure, Losinga had bought the bishopric of East Anglia from King William II just five years before. This itself was common practice, even if it was against church law, but Losinga's conscience still

1

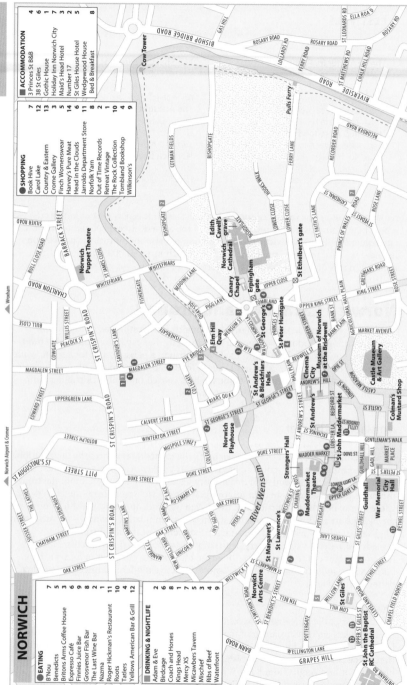

NORWICH

● **EATING**

B'Nou	7
Benedicts	5
Britons Arms Coffee House	3
Expresso Café	6
Finnies Juice Bar	9
Grosvenor Fish Bar	8
The Last Wine Bar	2
Nazma	1
Roger Hickman's Restaurant	11
Roots	10
Tatlers	4
Yellows American Bar & Grill	12

■ **DRINKING & NIGHTLIFE**

Adam & Eve	2
Birdcage	6
Coach and Horses	8
Kings Head	1
Mercy XS	7
Micawbers Tavern	5
Mischief	3
Ribs of Beef	4
Waterfront	9

● **SHOPPING**

Book Hive	7
Carol Lake	12
Country & Eastern	13
Crome Gallery	3
Finch Womenswear	14
Harvey's Pure Meat	5
Head in the Clouds	6
Jarrolds Department Store	11
Norfolk Yarn	8
Out of Time Records	2
The Rock Collection	1
Tombland Bookshop	10
Wilkinson's	9

■ **ACCOMMODATION**

3 Princes St B&B	4
38 St Giles	6
Gothic House	1
Holiday Inn Norwich City	7
Maid's Head Hotel	3
Number 17	2
St Giles House Hotel	5
Wedgewood House Bed & Breakfast	8

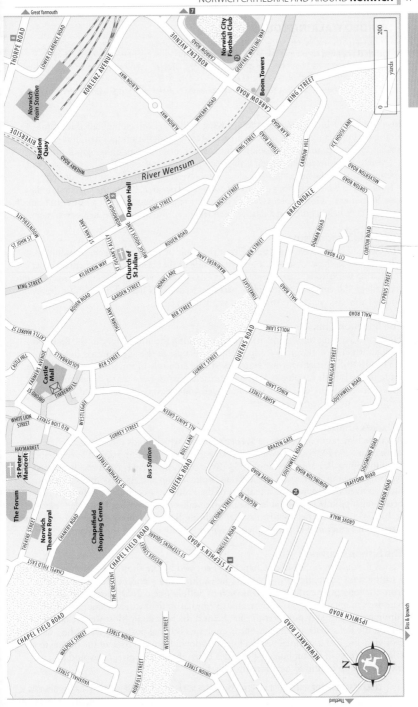

1

Great Yarmouth

THORPE ROAD

LOWER CLARENCE ROAD

KOBLENZ AVENUE

ALBION WAY

Norwich Train Station

RIVERSIDE

WHERRY ROAD

Station Quay

WHERRY ROAD

ALBION WAY

KOBLENZ AVENUE

Norwich City Football Club

CARROW ROAD

GEOFFREY WATLING WAY

Boom Towers

KING STREET

River Wensum

KING STREET

ALAN ROAD

STUART ROAD

ICE HOUSE LANE

MILVERTON ROAD

CORTON ROAD

Dragon Hall

HORNBOROUGH LANE

KING STREET

ARGYLE STREET

BRACONDALE

CARROW HILL

MONTERGATE

ST ANN LANE

ST JULIAN'S ALLEY

MUSIC HOUSE LANE

ROUEN ROAD

BER STREET

MARINERS LANE

DOMAN ROAD

CITY ROAD

CORTON ROAD

ST JOHN ST

KILDERKIN WAY

Church of St Julian

HORNS LANE

TIMBERGATE

HALL ROAD

CYPRUS STREET

KING STREET

ROUEN ROAD

GARDEN STREET

THORN LANE

BER STREET

QUEENS ROAD

HOLLS LANE

HALL ROAD

CATTLE MARKET ST

GOLDEN BALLS

BER STREET

SURREY STREET

KINGS LAND

TRAFALGAR STREET

CASTLE HILL

FARMERS AVENUE

Castle Mall

TIMBERHILL

ASHBY STREET

ALL SAINTS GREEN

SOUTHWELL ROAD

ORFORD ST

WESTLEGATE

WHITE LION STREET

RED LION STREET

SURREY STREET

BULL LANE

BRAZEN GATE

SOUTHWELL ROAD

HOWINGTON ROAD

SIGISMUND ROAD

TRAFFORD ROAD

ELLANOR ROAD

HAYMARKET

St Peter Mancroft

Bus Station

QUEENS ROAD

GROVE ROAD

GROVE WALK

The Forum

Norwich Theatre Royal

CHANTRY ROAD

ST STEPHENS STREET

Chapelfield Shopping Centre

VICTORIA STREET

REGINA RD

KINGSLEY ROAD

THEATRE STREET

CHAPEL FIELD ROAD

THE CRESCENT

WESSEX STREET

ST STEPHENS SQUARE

ST STEPHEN'S ROAD

IPSWICH ROAD

CHAPEL FIELD EAST

CHAPEL FIELD ROAD

WALPOLE STREET

UNION STREET

WESSEX STREET

NEWMARKET ROAD

VAUXHALL STREET

NORFOLK STREET

UNION STREET

Thetford

Diss & Ipswich

0   yards   200

N

> **GUIDED WALKING TOURS**
> Bookable at the tourist office (see p.54), the city's Blue Badge Guides run a programme of
> **guided walking tours** that take in all the leading sights, seasoned with anecdotes (April–Oct
> between three weekly and one per day; 1hr 30min; £4). The programme also includes themed
> walks – "In the footsteps of Nelson" and so forth – but these cost a pound or two more and last a
> little longer (May–Sept 5–6 weekly). For more ideas on Norwich walks, go to ⓦvisitnorwich.co.uk.

troubled him. Much to the irritation of King William, Losinga hightailed it off to
Rome to do penance to the pope, who accepted his resignation, granted him
absolution and promptly reappointed him as bishop – what an obliging pontiff.

The nave's architectural highlight is the **ceiling**, a finely crafted affair whose delicate and
geometrically precise fan vaulting is adorned by several dozen roof bosses recounting
– from east to west – the story of the Old and New Testaments from the Creation to the
Last Judgement. Without binoculars it's difficult to make these out, but a mirror in front of
the altar does help a little and a touch-screen terminal, also in the nave, helps even more.

The Gooding tombstone

The east end of the nave is separated from the choir by the **choir screen**, or pulpitum.
Close by, set in the wall on the south (right) side of the screen, is the cathedral's most
interesting **tombstone**, that of one Thomas Gooding, where a grimacing skeleton carries
a warning: "All you that do this place pass bye. Remember death for you must dye. As
you are now even so was I. And as I am so shall you be".

The Bauchon Chapel

From the Gooding tombstone, it's a few paces along the ambulatory to the **Bauchon
Chapel**, which is noteworthy for its memorial plaque to the MP Thomas Buxton
(1786–1845), a social reformer who played a leading role in the abolition of the slave
trade in the British Empire in 1807. Thereafter, Buxton went on to campaign against
slavery itself; his tireless efforts were rewarded when slavery was abolished across the
empire just over twenty years later.

St Luke's Chapel

After the Bauchon Chapel comes **St Luke's Chapel**, which holds the cathedral's finest
work of art, the *Despenser Reredos*, a superb painted panel commissioned to celebrate the
crushing of the Peasants' Revolt of 1381 (see p.324). It's a naive, emotionally charged
painting showing the Passion, Crucifixion, Resurrection and Ascension of Christ, but it
only survived the iconoclastic attentions of the Protestants during the Reformation by
becoming a plumber's worktable. The painting takes its name from Henry le Despenser
(c.1341–1406), otherwise known as the "Fighting Bishop", who spent much of his time
warring in France and England when he wasn't beating down on the peasantry.

The bishop's throne

Across the aisle from St Luke's Chapel, and encased by the choir, is the **bishop's throne**,
a sturdy stone structure dating back to the eighth century and possibly moved here
from the long-gone cathedral at Dunwich in Suffolk (see p.265). Norman bishops were
barons as much as religious leaders, and to emphasize their direct relationship with the
Almighty they usually put their thrones behind the high altar. Most were relocated
during the Reformation, but this one occupies its original position. The bishop of
Norwich also had a spiritual prop: a flue runs down from the back of the throne to a
reliquary recess in the ambulatory, the idea being that divine essences would be
transported up to him to help him do his job.

HUFF AND PUFF AT THE CATHEDRAL

The peaceful calm of Norwich Cathedral may be its most striking feature today, but over its long history there have been all sorts of ecclesiastical rows and arguments, with the reforming **Bishop Edward Stanley** (1779–1849) falling foul of his colleagues in the 1830s. Stanley changed the times of the morning service and the organist went on strike; he was relaxed about men wearing hats in church and the dean was enraged; the bedesman stopped praying for the departed until he got a pay rise; and Stanley's proposal to place a cross on the outside of the church was opposed by just about everyone. Fortunately, everyone united with him to condemn the new railway, which was offering day-trips to the Norfolk countryside: Stanley wrote to the directors of the train company complaining that the ride "Could only be paid for by the sacrifice of the family's Sunday dinner ... to say nothing of the temptation to drinking and to excess of even worse kinds ... [at such] dens of iniquity" – goodness knows what he would have said if the trippers had been going to Great Yarmouth instead.

The cloisters

Accessible from the south aisle of the nave are the cathedral's beautifully preserved **cloisters**. Built between 1297 and 1450, and the only two-storey cloisters left standing in England, they contain a remarkable set of sculpted bosses, similar to the ones in the main nave, but here they are close enough to be scrutinized without binoculars. The carving is fabulously intricate and the dominant theme is the Apocalypse, but look out also for the bosses depicting Green Men, originally pagan fertility symbols.

Norwich School and the Upper Close

In front of the cathedral's main doors stands the medieval **Canary Chapel** (no public access). This is the original building of **Norwich School**, whose blue-blazered pupils are often visible during termtime – the rambling school buildings are adjacent. A statue of the school's most famous pupil, **Horatio Nelson** (see p.156), faces the chapel, standing beside a cannon with telescope in hand – a suitably maritime pose. It does not quite stand up to close examination, though: poor old Nelson would appear to have lost his original nose and the new snout is too big by far. The statue is on the green of the cathedral's **Upper Close**, which is itself guarded by two ornate and imposing medieval gates: Erpingham and, a hundred yards or so to the south, **Ethelbert**. The **Erpingham gate** is the more interesting, dating from the 1420s and named after Thomas Erpingham, who had it built to celebrate his safe return from the Battle of Agincourt, where he commanded the archers – his kneeling figure with sword at his side is on the gable.

The Edith Cavell memorial

Beside the Erpingham gate is a memorial to **Edith Cavell**, a local woman whose heroic exploits were once famous across the British Empire. A nurse in occupied Brussels during World War I, Cavell was shot by the Germans in 1915 for helping Allied prisoners to escape, a propaganda disaster for the Kaiser exacerbated by Cavell's stoic bravery: the night before her execution, she famously declared "Standing as I do, in view of God and eternity, I realize that patriotism is not enough, I must have no hatred or bitterness towards anyone". Cavell was initially buried in Brussels, but after the war she was reinterred in Norwich – her grave is outside the cathedral ambulatory.

The Lower Close and a river walk

Just beyond the Upper Close, extending east towards the river, is the pedestrianized **Lower Close**, where attractive Georgian and Victorian houses flank a scattering of wispy silver birches. Straight on from the close, the main footpath continues east to the city's medieval watergate and the adjacent **Pull's Ferry**, a good-looking, seventeenth-century flint structure named after the last ferryman to work this stretch of the river. It's a picturesque spot and from here (during daylight hours) you can wander along the riverbank path either south to the train station or north to Bishopgate, then back to Tombland (see below). Beyond Bishopgate, the path continues north and then west along the river to Elm Hill (see below) and St George's Street. On the route north you pass **Cow Tower**, a 50ft-high, brick watchtower with arrow slits and gun ports where the bishop's retainers collected river tolls. This is one of the few surviving pieces of Norwich's fortified walls, which once stretched for over two miles, surrounding the city and incorporating thirty such circular towers and ten defensive gates. Up until the 1790s, the gates were closed at dusk and all day on Sundays.

Tombland

The cathedral's Erpingham and Ethelbert gates face out onto **Tombland**, a wide and busy thoroughfare whose name derives from the Saxon word for an open space. In medieval times, Tombland was the site of all sorts of markets – from cattle to religious trinkets – and it was here that the followers of Robert Kett camped out during the rebellion of 1549, much to the terror of the city's burghers (see p.325).

St George's

Tombland, NR3 1AF · Tues–Thurs 9am–2pm · Free

On the west side of Tombland stands **St George's**, an attractive, mostly fifteenth-century flint church with an impressive clock tower. Entry is via the south porch, whose carved bosses include one showing St George standing on a dragon, and although the interior is largely Victorian, the church holds a splendid Jacobean pulpit. Behind the organ there's also the **tomb** of a long-forgotten city father, the splendidly named Alderman Anguish, who kneels with his wife flanked by their offspring, five of whom carry skulls representing those children who predeceased him.

Elm Hill and St Peter Hungate

At the north end of Tombland, fork left into Wensum Street and cobbled **Elm Hill**, more a gentle slope than a hill, soon appears on the left. J.B. Priestley, in his *English Journey* of the 1930s, thought this part of Norwich to be overbearingly Dickensian, proclaiming it "difficult to believe that behind those bowed and twisted fronts there did not live an assortment of misers, mad spinsters, saintly clergymen, eccentric comic clerks, and lunatic sextons". Not for the first time, Priestley was being more than a little "poetical" – and the street's quirky half-timbered houses are in fact really rather appealing. While you're here, take a look at **Wright's Court**, down a passageway at no. 43, as this is one of the few remaining enclosed courtyards that were once a feature of the city. Elm Hill quickly opens out into a triangular square centred on a plane tree, planted on the spot where the eponymous elm tree once stood. It then veers left up to **St Peter Hungate** (March–Oct Sat 10am–4pm & Sun 2–4pm; free; ⓦ hungate.org.uk), a standard-issue, fifteenth-century flint church whose bare and bleak interior now holds a (very) modest display of stained glass retrieved from several local churches.

The Norwich Lanes

Perhaps the most enjoyable part of the city to wander is the **Norwich Lanes** (ⓦ norwichlanes.co.uk), a cobweb of narrow lanes and alleys that lie sandwiched between the Market Place and St Benedict's Street. It's here you'll find many of Norwich's best independent shops (see p.58), a gaggle of good bars and restaurants (see p.56 & p.57), a brace of old and diverting churches and the idiosyncratic **Strangers' Hall** with its assorted – and unassorted – bygones.

The Halls: St Andrew's and Blackfriars

St Andrews Hall Plain, NR3 1AU • Mon–Sat 9am–5pm • Free • ☎ 01603 628477, ⓦ thehallsnorwich.com

Just west of Tombland, on the northern edge of the Norwich Lanes, stand **The Halls**. These two adjoining buildings – **Blackfriars Hall** and, on the left, **St Andrew's Hall** – share the same entrance and were originally the chancel and nave, respectively, of a Dominican monastery church. Typical of a medieval friary church, the nave was used for the lay congregation, the smaller chancel by the friars alone. Imaginatively recycled, The Halls are now used for a variety of public events, including concerts, but the whole complex is looking a little frayed at the edges and a much needed revamp is promised. The Halls display a large collection of civic paintings, mostly indeterminate bishops and aldermen, but in Blackfriars is a splendid **portrait of Nelson** from three years before his death, shown in all his maritime pomp and completed by one of his friends, **William Beechey** (1753–1839), a talented artist who made a name for himself painting the most powerful men and women of the age.

St Andrew's church

St Andrews St, NR2 4AD • Late March to late Oct Thurs 2.30–5pm, Sun 11.30am–12.30pm • Free • ☎ 01603 498821, ⓦ standrewsnorwich.org

Opposite The Halls, up the slope and across the street, is **St Andrew's church**, a large and impressive structure equipped with a handsome square tower and massive windows, which render the nave light and airy. The highlights of the interior are the two alabaster tombs of the **Suckling Chapel**, one of Robert Suckling (d.1589), the other of John Suckling (d.1613), another member of the clan, who is depicted in his favourite suit of armour with his wife lying beside him kitted out in her fanciest Elizabethan dress.

Museum of Norwich at the Bridewell

Bridewell Alley, NR1 1AQ • Tues–Sat 10am–4.30pm • £5.20 • ☎ 01603 629127, ⓦ museumsnorfolk.org.uk

From St Andrew's church, it's a few yards to the **Museum of Norwich at the Bridewell**, whose warren of narrow rooms and corridors is jam-packed with information about the city. The ground floor tracks through the history of Norwich with due emphasis on its wool-based boom times, and there is a small section on the building's use as a prison too. Upstairs, there's a splendid old pharmacy, an intriguing section on the city's shoemaking industry and two larger sections illustrating life in Norwich 1900–1945 and 1945–1990. Almost everywhere you look there are fascinating bits and bobs, from vintage valentine cards to the contents of a neighbourhood grocery shop as of the 1970s. There's also a small feature on the benighted Peter the Wild Boy (1713–1785), found speechless and naked in the forests of Germany, brought to England and, after many ups and downs, temporarily imprisoned here in the Bridewell.

Strangers' Hall

Charing Cross, NR2 4AL • Mid-Feb to May & Oct–Dec Wed 10am–4pm & Sun 1–4.30pm; June–Sept Wed–Fri 10am–4pm, Sun 1–4.30pm • £4.50 • ☎ 01603 667229, ⓦ museumsnorfolk.org.uk

Strangers' Hall is the city's most unusual attraction. Dating back to the fourteenth century, it's a veritable rabbit warren of a place stuffed with all manner of bygones including ancient fireplaces, oodles of wood panelling, a Regency music room and a Georgian dining room. Allow an hour or so to explore its nooks and crannies, though the most impressive room – the **Great Hall**, with its church-like Gothic windows, old portrait paintings and rickety staircase – comes right at the beginning. The hall is named after the Protestant refugees who fled here from the Spanish Netherlands to avoid the tender mercies of the Inquisition in the 1560s; at the peak of the migration, these "Strangers" accounted for around a third of the local population.

St John Maddermarket

Maddermarket, NR2 1DS · Mon, Wed & Sun 10am–4pm, Thurs & Sat 11am–3pm · Free · ⓦ visitchurches.org.uk

Named after madder, the yellow flower the weavers used to make red vegetable dye, **St John Maddermarket**, a couple of minutes' walk south of Strangers' Hall, is one of thirty medieval churches standing within the boundaries of the old city walls. Most of these churches are redundant and rarely open to the public, but this is one of the more accessible, courtesy of a dedicated team of volunteers. Apart from the stone trimmings, the church is almost entirely composed of flint rubble, the traditional building material of east Norfolk, an area chronically short of decent stone. The exterior is a good example of the Perpendicular style, a subdivision of English Gothic, which flourished from the middle of the fourteenth to the early sixteenth century and is characterized by straight vertical lines – as you might expect from the name – and large windows framed by flowing, but plain, tracery. By comparison, the interior is something of a disappointment, its furnishings and fittings thoroughly remodelled at the start of the twentieth century, though there's compensation in a trio of finely carved Jacobean tombstones.

Outside, the arch under the church tower leads through to the Maddermarket Theatre, built in 1921 in the style of an Elizabethan playhouse (see p.58).

St Benedict's Street and around

One of Norwich's most pleasing thoroughfares is **St Benedict's Street**, lined with restaurants and shops and flanked by no fewer than three dilapidated and deconsecrated **medieval churches**. From east to west, these begin with **St Lawrence's** – named after a Roman Christian who was roasted alive for his faith – which was the scene of rioting in the 1860s when the rector allowed a group of Catholic monks to take part in church services. Next up is **St Margaret's**, with its handsome Decorated-style windows, and then there is **St Swithin's**, which has been turned into the Norwich Arts Centre (see p.58).

From St Benedict's, a sequence of narrow lanes leads to **Pottergate**, which looks like it hasn't changed much for many years, its pretty trail of old houses meandering out towards **Cow Hill**, which cuts up to Upper St Giles Street (see p.49).

The Market Place and around

The social hub of Norwich is the **Market Place**, an immediately attractive square, whose capacious open-air market is overlooked by **City Hall** and the glassy Forum leisure complex. The square is also bordered by the aesthetically pleasing **Royal Arcade** mini-mall and the city's finest church, **St Peter Mancroft**. Last but not least, the square is an obvious starting point for two of the city's more outlying attractions, the secretive greenery of the **Plantation Garden** and the clunking religiosity of the **Catholic Cathedral of St John the Baptist**, both of which are a little less than ten minutes' walk away to the west via St Giles Street.

Market Place

Market Place, NR2 1NH · Market Mon–Sat 8.30am–5.30pm · ☎ 01603 213537, ⓦ visitnorwich.co.uk

Norwich **Market Place** has long been the site of one of the country's largest open-air markets, with over 190 stalls selling everything from bargain-basement clothes to local mussels and whelks. Three very different but equally distinctive buildings oversee the market's stripy awnings, the oldest of them being the fifteenth-century **Guildhall**, a

1

capacious flint and stone structure begun in 1407. Opposite, commanding the heights of the Market Place, is **City Hall**, an austere brick pile with a landmark clock tower built in the 1930s in a Scandinavian style – it bears a striking resemblance to Oslo's city hall. Three large bronze doors provide some decorative intricacy here, as each is carved with six small reliefs depicting historical scenes and local industry, from the ravages brought on the city by the Black Death to the coming of the Danes, a girl at a silk loom to a man at a machine filling tins with mustard. In front of City Hall is a **war memorial**, designed by Edwin Lutyens in the 1930s, and beside it is **the Forum**, a large, flashy glass structure completed in 2001 and now home to the city's main library and the tourist office (see p.54).

St Peter Mancroft

Chantry Rd, Market Place, NR2 1QZ • Mon–Sat 10am–3.30pm (till 4pm in summer) • Free • ☎ 01603 610443, ⊕ stpetermancroft.org.uk

On the south side of the Market Place is Norwich's finest church, **St Peter Mancroft**, whose long and graceful nave leads to a mighty stone tower, an intricately carved affair surmounted by a spiky little spire. The church once delighted John Wesley, who declared "I scarcely ever remember to have seen a more beautiful parish church", a fair description of what remains an exquisite example of the Perpendicular with the slender columns of the nave reaching up towards the delicate groining of the roof. Completed in 1455, the open design of the nave was meant to express the mystery of the Christian faith with light filtering in through the stained-glass windows in a kaleidoscope of colours. Some of the original glass has survived, most notably in the east window, with its cartoon strip of biblical scenes, from the Virgin nursing the baby Jesus through to the Crucifixion and Resurrection.

Gentlemen's Walk and the Royal Arcade

Just below St Peter Mancroft stands the *Sir Garnet Wolseley* pub, sole survivor of the 44 alehouses that once crowded the Market Place – and stirred the local bourgeoisie into endless discussions about the drunken fecklessness of the working class. Just below the pub is **Gentlemen's Walk**, the city's main promenade, which runs along the bottom of the Market Place, and this in turn leads to the **Royal Arcade**, an Art Nouveau extravagance from 1899. The arcade has been beautifully restored to reveal the swirl of the tiling, ironwork and stained glass, though it's actually the eastern entrance, further from Gentlemen's Walk, which is the fanciest section. Inside the arcade, at no. 15, is **Colman's Mustard Shop**, which is often referred to as a museum – it isn't, unless you count a few display boards explaining the history of mustard in general and the Colman's company in particular.

NORWICH'S RENAISSANCE MAN: THOMAS BROWNE

St Peter Mancroft is the final resting place of **Thomas Browne** (1605–1682), a doctor, philosopher and naturalist who is little known today but was once a major figure, renowned for his *Religio Medici* ("The Religion of a Doctor"), a combined religious testament and intellectual dalliance with digressions into everything from alchemy to astrology. Predictably, the Catholics didn't like Browne's freewheeling ways and the pope put the book on his *Index Librorum Prohibitorum* ("List of Prohibited Books"). Browne's tomb is just in front of the church's high altar and is marked by a **memorial plaque** commissioned by his wife, who lies buried close by. This isn't without its ironies: Browne wanted to be cremated, railing against the potential indignities of burial – "to be knaved out of our graves, to have our skulls made drinking bowls and our bones turned into pipes, are tragically abominations escaped by burning burials". And so it proved: Browne's skull was extracted from his grave to be kept on display in a doctor's surgery for almost a century; it was only put back in his grave in 1922.

Upper St Giles Street

Heading west from the Market Place, **St Giles Street** cuts a mediocre path up to the rather more interesting **Upper St Giles Street**, whose dinky little shops and stores are something of a genteel enclave. Here also is the **church of St Giles** (no fixed opening times; ☏ 01603 623724), an especially handsome structure mostly dating from the fifteenth century. Built of flint, but with a fancy stone porch, the church has a wide and high nave topped off by a splendid hammer-beam roof, but the furnishings and fittings are largely Victorian.

The Catholic Cathedral of St John the Baptist

Unthank Rd, NR2 2PA • Daily 7.30am–7.30pm • Free • ☏ 01603 624615, ⓦ sjbcathedral.org.uk

Towering over the ring road at the top end of Upper St Giles Street is the **Catholic Cathedral of St John the Baptist**, a huge clunker of a building constructed at the end of the nineteenth century in an exuberant flourish of the neo-Gothic style. The fifteenth Duke of Norfolk footed the bill – appropriately, as the Norfolks have long been one of England's leading Catholic families – and the cathedral was built on the site of what had been the city prison. Aesthetically, it's a very cold building whose most appealing feature, apart perhaps from its sheer bulk, is its stained-glass windows. The architect, George Gilbert Scott (1811–1878), was famous for his Gothic Revival churches and workhouses, but he died while work was in progress here in Norwich and the cathedral was completed by his brother, John Oldrid Scott (1841–1913).

The Plantation Garden

4 Earlham Rd, NR2 3DB • Daily: April to mid-Oct 9am–6pm; mid-Oct to March 10am–4pm • £2 • ☏ 07504 545810, ⓦ plantationgarden.co.uk

Below the Catholic cathedral, the **Plantation Garden** is a simply delightful spot, where mature trees overhang a sweet little dell, complete with a fancy stone stairway that leads up to the cutest of thatched cabins (a glorified garden shed) with a pagoda-style water fountain as an added decorative bonus. The gardens date from the late nineteenth century when a local businessman, one Henry Trevor, turned the medieval chalk quarry immediately behind and below the Cathedral of St John the Baptist into an ornate garden. Sadly, within the space of a few years it had been forgotten and neglected. In the 1980s, however, the garden was rediscovered, cleared and turned into the version you see today.

Norwich Castle and around

Despite its commanding position in the heart of the city, **Norwich Castle** has had a chequered history, the repository of all things grim when it served as a prison. Today, however, it houses the city's most important art collection, featuring the work of the Norwich School (see box, p.50), and is also a good starting point for the enjoyable stroll southeast down to **Carrow Bridge**, spanning the River Wensum.

The Castle Museum and Art Gallery

Castle Meadow, NR1 3JU • July–Sept Mon–Sat 10am–5pm, Sun 1–5pm; Oct–June Mon–Sat 10am–4.30pm, Sun 1–4.30pm • £8.50; special exhibitions extra • Guided tours of castle dungeon & battlements £2.75 • ☏ 01603 495897, ⓦ museumsnorfolk.org.uk

Glued to the top of a grassy mound right in the centre of town – with a modern shopping mall drilled into its side – the stern walls of **Norwich Castle**, replete with their conspicuous blind arcading, date from the twelfth century. To begin with they were a reminder of Norman power and then, when the castle was turned into a prison, they served as a grim warning to potential law-breakers. Now thoroughly refurbished, the castle holds the **Castle Museum and Art Gallery**, spread over two floors surrounding a central rotunda.

The galleries

On the **lower level** there's a child-friendly gallery devoted to Boudicca and her Roman enemies (see box, p.321); a more substantial **Natural History** section, with a small army of stuffed animals, mostly from Norfolk; the Twinings Tea Pot gallery; and the much more diverting **Colman Art galleries** (see below). The **upper level** chips in with a second child-friendly gallery, this one devoted to the Anglo-Saxons and the Vikings, which comes with a reasonable range of archeological finds. Here also is a modest display on the Royal Norfolk Regiment; an Egyptian gallery, with half a dozen "mummies" thrown in for good measure; and a space for temporary exhibitions.

Stairs lead from the main body of the museum to the **castle keep**, though this is no more than a shell, its gloomy walls rising high and severe. Exhibited here is a bloated model dragon, known as Snap, which was paraded round town on the annual guilds' day procession – a folkloric hand-me-down from the dragon St George had so much trouble finishing off. To see more of the castle, sign up for one of the regular guided tours, which explore the battlements and dungeons.

The Colman Art galleries

The **Colman Art galleries** boast an outstanding selection of work by the **Norwich School**, whose leading figures were John Crome – aka "Old Crome" – and John Sell Cotman (see box below). Crome and Cotman have a beautifully lit gallery to themselves and their paintings are also exhibited in other galleries alongside other, arguably less talented, members of the School such as Alfred Priest and James Stark. Fine examples of the work of Crome include his elegiac *Norwich River: Afternoon* and the lonely-looking *A Road with Pollards*. Another gallery is devoted to English watercolours and yet another to paintings of East Anglia in the twentieth century, including several by **Alfred Munnings** (see p.288), one of England's most traditional painters whose speciality was horses – or rather sentimental visions of them as in *The Horse Fair* and *Sunny June*. Look out also for the canvases of a string of leading English painters, including **Thomas Gainsborough**'s (see p.290) glossy portrait of a local MP, *Sir Harbord*

THE NORWICH SCHOOL

Often neglected, frequently ignored, the **Norwich Society of Artists** – now usually referred to as the **Norwich School** – was founded in 1803 by two local, self-taught painters, **John Crome** (1768–1821) and **Robert Ladbrooke** (1770–1842). Both men were working class – Crome was the son of a weaver – which may partly account for their ambitious, even earnest, statement of purpose: "[the Society was to enquire] into the rise, progress and present state of painting, architecture and sculpture, with a view to point out the best methods … [of attaining] … greater perfection". A popular man, Crome soon attracted other like-minded artists to the Society, which organized its first exhibition in 1805 to great acclaim. Crome was the most talented member of the society by a long chalk, his vigorous, vital paintings of the Norfolk countryside greatly influenced by both the realism of Dutch seventeenth-century painters and that of his contemporary, Suffolk's John Constable: like Constable, for example, Crome painted identifiable species of trees rather than the generalized versions of his artistic predecessors.

After Crome's death, the prolific **John Sell Cotman** (1782–1842) became the society's leading light, holding the group together until it unravelled after he left Norwich for London in the early 1830s. Cotman churned out etchings, engravings and oil paintings, but it is for his **watercolours** that he is best remembered, each displaying a precise tone and line, the hallmarks of his technique. Cotman's early watercolours were restrained, sometimes austere, but later he began to mix rice-paste into his palette, which allowed him to work in a heavier, more flamboyant style.

The Norwich Society was always hard-pressed to find a patron – and all of the members struggled with money – but, curiously enough, it was the purchasing power of a local tycoon and art collector, the mustard baron **Jeremiah James Colman** (1830–98), that kept the Norwich School out of the artistic limelight. He snaffled up all their best work for his private collection, though in fairness he did bequeath many of his paintings to the city of Norwich in the 1880s.

THE ADVENTURES OF DELIA SMITH

Gastronomic guru **Delia Smith** (born 1941) has arguably done more to change the face of British cooking than anyone else. Raised in Surrey, Smith left school at 16 without a single O-Level to her name, trying her hand at hairdressing and working in a travel agency before getting a job as a washer-upper at *The Singing Chef*, a tiny restaurant in Paddington, London. It was here that she began to help with the cooking, beginning a meteoric rise that saw her appointed cookery writer for the *Daily Mirror's* magazine in 1969 – the same year as one of her cakes appeared on the cover of the Rolling Stones' album, *Let it Bleed*. In 1972 she became the cookery columnist for the *Evening Standard*, but it was her **TV appearances** that really made her name, beginning in the mid-1970s with *Family Fare* and as the resident cook on BBC East's regional programme *Look East*. Smith's easy, modest style and relaxed presentation made her trusted and liked by millions of Brits – so much so that by the 1990s, the mention of a particular ingredient in one of her recipes, either on TV or in one of her cookery books, could jump-start sales to an extraordinary extent – the so-called "**Delia effect**." In 2003, Smith announced her retirement from television, though she did do further stints in 2008 and 2010, before a second (apparently permanent) retirement in 2013. Worldwide sales of her cookbooks rack up to over 21 million.

Smith and her husband, Michael Wynn-Jones, live near Stowmarket in Suffolk (see p.302). They were already season-ticket holders at **Norwich City FC** when they were invited to invest in the club, which had fallen on hard times. They became majority shareholders in the club in 1996, a position they retain.

Harbord, and **William Hogarth's** (1697–1764) *Francis Matthews Schutz in his Bed*, with poor old Francis suffering from the most terrible of hangovers.

Church of St Julian and Dragon Hall

St Julian's Alley, NR1 3QD • Church: daily 7.30am–6pm • Free • ☏ 01603 622509, ⓦ norwich-churches.org

Southeast of the castle via King Street is the **Church of St Julian**, whose round stone tower attests to its Saxon origins. The interior is a modest affair, but the adjoining chapel is more interesting: formerly a monastic cell, it served as the retreat of St Julian, a Norwich woman who took to living here after experiencing visions of Christ in 1373. Her mystical *Revelations of Divine Love* – written after twenty years' meditation on her visitations – was the first widely distributed book written by a woman in the English language, and has been in print ever since.

Close by, at 115–123 King St, **Dragon Hall** is an extraordinarily long, half-timbered showroom built for the cloth merchant Robert Toppes in the fifteenth century. Bowed and bent by the passing centuries, the hall has a handsome façade, but as it's no longer open to the public, you can't pop in to examine the wonky beams of the roof.

Carrow Bridge and around

King Street runs down to **Carrow Bridge**, where you'll spy the ruins of two medieval boom towers, which once formed part of the city's defences – with the terraces of **Norwich City football ground** looming just behind (see p.59). From the boom towers, a **riverside walk** follows the Wensum round to the **train station**, a large and handsome structure of red brick and stucco that looks a little like a French chateau. Completed in 1886, it had a moment of cinematic fame when it featured in Joseph Losey's 1971 film *The Go-Between*.

The University of East Anglia (UEA)

UEA, NR4 7TJ • Main entrance: Earlham Rd (B1108) • Open access • ☏ 01603 456161, ⓦ uea.ac.uk • Bus #25 from either Castle Meadow or the train station

The **University of East Anglia (UEA)** occupies a sprawling, semirural campus on the western outskirts of the city. The university enrolled its first students in 1963, but from small and surprisingly humble beginnings, it soon administered a major cultural shock to what was then a sleepy Norwich. In the early 1970s, UEA students were conspicuous for their radicalism, uniting in their flares, Afghan coats, bangles, beads and beards to occupy the university buildings in a series of mass **sit-ins**. The reasons were complex, but although there was certainly a political edge (the Miners' Strike, Vietnam), it was just as much to do with personal freedoms: in 1969, for example, university cleaners still had to report students who had overnight "guests". Those radical days are long gone, but you can still get a sense of how adventurous a place it was once if you wander the elevated walkways to UEA's most distinctive buildings, **Norfolk Terrace and Suffolk Terrace**, halls of residence built in the shape of ziggurats to an inspired design by Denys Lasdun (1914–2001).

The Sainsbury Centre for Visual Arts

UEA, NR4 7TJ • Tues–Fri 10am–6pm, Sat & Sun 10am–5pm • Free except for temporary exhibitions & events • ☎ 01603 593199,
🌐 scva.ac.uk

For the casual visitor today, UEA's key attraction is the **Sainsbury Centre for Visual Arts**, which occupies a large, shed-like building designed by Norman Foster at the western end of the university campus. The centre is named after its original benefactor, the supermarket king Robert Sainsbury (1906–2000), who began collecting fine and applied art in the 1930s. He gifted three hundred pieces to the Centre in 1973, since when the collection has quadrupled in size.

Well lit and well presented, key pieces include a *Mother & Child* by **Henry Moore**, a bronze cast of **Edgar Degas'** famous *Little Dancer*, a *Torso in Metal* by Jacob Epstein, and several sketches by **Picasso**. There is also a platoon of paintings by **Francis Bacon** (1909–92), most memorably an *Imaginary Portrait of Pope Pius XII* and *Study of a Nude*. In 1955, Bacon also painted the portrait of his friend/ sponsor Robert Sainsbury, though it's hard not to think he approached this commission with his tongue firmly in his cheek – it looks as if someone has just poked Sainsbury in the eye.

From the ground floor, the permanent collection continues on two mezzanine levels, where there are several Henry Moore sketches and a cabinet of tiny Roman figurines, but pride of place here goes to a strangely unsettling *Bucket Man* sculpture by **John Davies** (b.1946). Other parts of the centre are devoted to an ambitious programme of temporary exhibitions and a reserve, holding paintings and sculptures that can be viewed, but are not on display as such.

Around Norwich

In every direction, Norwich's suburbs fade seamlessly into the open countryside, where a network of country lanes mazes across farmland to connect to a string of tiny villages. Within easy striking distance of the city centre, both **Mousehold Heath** and **Whitlingham Country Park** offer good walking, and a little further afield is a noteworthy theme park designed for kids – **Dinosaur Adventure**.

THE BOUDICCA WAY

The **Boudicca Way** (🌐 boudiccaway.co.uk) is a long-distance **footpath**, which runs the forty-odd miles south from Norwich to Diss (see p.212), starting and finishing at the two main-line train stations. For most of its course, it runs parallel with the **A140**, itself an old Roman road, passing through a string of pretty villages set amid quiet countryside.

Mousehold Heath

Spreading over a hilly parcel of land just to the northeast of the city centre,
Mousehold Heath once extended east almost as far as the Broads. The remaining
heath was bequeathed to the city council in 1880, but by then its character
had begun to change, with the open heathland rapidly disappearing beneath a
covering of scrub and woodland as locals stopped grazing their animals and
collecting their winter fuel here. Plans are afoot to extend the patches of
remaining heathland, but in the meantime most of the area is wooded, its dips
and dells explored on a network of **footpaths**, several of which begin beside
Gurney Road, which cuts right across the heath. The heath does support a varied
wildlife, but the particular highlight is the spring gathering of mating frogs
around **Vinegar Pond**.

Whitlingham Country Park

Whitlingham Lane, Trowse, NR14 8TR • Visitor centre (in the old flint barn) April–Dec daily 10am–2pm & 2.30–4pm • ☎ 01603 632307,
Ⓦ norfolk.gov.uk

Stretching out along the southern bank of the River Yare just to the east of the city
centre, **Whitlingham Country Park** is one of the city's most popular attractions, its
assorted woods, meadows and wetland crisscrossed by easy footpaths. It's also home to
an **Outdoor Education Centre** where the emphasis is on all things watery – from
canoeing and kayaking through to sailing and windsurfing – plus a handy **Broads
Authority** office (Ⓦ broads-authority.gov.uk), which also has a café and runs trips on its
solar-powered boat, *Ra*.

Dinosaur Adventure

Weston Park, Lenwade, NR9 5JW • Daily: late March to mid-July & early Sept to late Oct 9.30am–5pm; late July to early Sept 9.30am–
6pm; late Oct to late March 9.30am–4pm • £10.95, £11.95 in peak season; under-15s £11.95, £13.95; under-3s free •
☎ 01603 876310, Ⓦ dinosauradventure.co.uk

The **Dinosaur Adventure** theme park occupies a sprawling, partly wooded site about
twenty minutes' drive northwest of Norwich via the A1067. Apart from the petting
animals, there are lots of "prehistoric" adventures geared towards kids, whether it be a
walk along the Dinosaur Trail or a ball-clattering time at the Jurassic Putt Crazy Golf.
Don't expect too much in the way of subtlety.

ARRIVAL AND DEPARTURE   NORWICH

By plane Norwich Airport (Ⓦ norwichairport.co.uk)
is located about four miles north of the city centre
along the A140. There are buses from the Park &
Ride beside the airport to Norwich bus station
(Mon–Sat only; every 30min–1hr; 25min); a taxi fare
costs about £12.

By train Norwich train station is on the east bank of the
River Wensum, a 10min walk from the centre along Prince
of Wales Rd. For journey planning, by bus or train, consult
Ⓦ travelineeastanglia.org.uk.

Destinations Bury St Edmunds (hourly; 1hr, change at
Stowmarket); Cambridge (hourly; 1hr 20min); Cromer
(hourly; 45min); Ely (2 hourly; 1hr); Great Yarmouth (hourly;
35min); Ipswich (every 30min; 40min); King's Lynn (hourly;
1hr 30min, change at Ely); London Liverpool St (every
30min; 1hr 50min); London Stansted airport (hourly; 1hr
50min, change at Ely); Sheringham (hourly; 1hr);

Stowmarket (hourly; 30min); Thetford (2 hourly; 30min).
By bus Long-distance buses mostly terminate at the main
bus station in between Surrey Street and Queen's Road,
about 10min walk from the centre. Some services also stop
in the city centre on Castle Meadow.

Destinations Holt (Mon–Sat every 1–2hr; 1hr 20min);
King's Lynn (hourly; 1hr 50min); London Victoria (every
1–2hr; 3hr 30min).

By car Whichever way you approach Norwich you'll hit the
inner ring road, which gives access to every part of the city
centre – eventually. Traffic jams are commonplace and the
myriad lanes and alleys of central Norwich – never mind
the one-way system – make driving complicated, so once
you've parked up it's best to explore on foot. There are a
dozen or so city-centre car parks with one of the largest and
most convenient being next to the castle at the Castle Mall
shopping centre.

1

GETTING AROUND AND INFORMATION

By bus Norwich's more outlying attractions and hotels can often be reached by bus, but don't be amazed if this isn't possible: the city may have a brigade of competing bus companies, but services are patchy within the city. The hub of the local bus network is the series of bus stops on Castle Meadow. For journey planning, consult ⓦtravelineeastanglia.org.uk.

By boat City Boats (☎01603 701701, ⓦcityboat s.co.uk) operates cruises through Norwich along the River Wensum, starting near the train station and proceeding to Elm Hill Quay near the cathedral (Easter to late Sept Fri–Sun 1 or 2 daily; 1hr; £3, £6 return). The same company also offers longer cruises out from Norwich and into the Norfolk Broads; in all cases, advance reservations are recommended.

Tourist office In the glassy Forum building, overlooking the Market Place on Millennium Plain (April–Oct Mon–Sat 9.30am–5.30pm, Sun 10.30am–3.30pm; Nov–March Mon–Sat 9.30am–5.30pm; ☎01603 213999, ⓦvisitnorwich.co.uk).

ACCOMMODATION

Norwich has **accommodation** to suit every budget, but the city's most distinctive offering is its **B&Bs**, of which the city has a good selection. The two most appealing areas in which to stay are near the cathedral or north of the River Wensum in the vicinity of Colegate.

B&BS

3 Princes St B&B 3 Princes St, NR3 1AZ ☎01603 622699, ⓦ3princes-norwich.co.uk. In a great location, up a narrow lane yards from the cathedral, this B&B looks pretty dour from the outside – it occupies a plain red-brick Georgian terraced house that was once a rectory – but the four deluxe, en-suite rooms inside are attractively furnished in pastel shades, and three of them have views over Blackfriars Hall (see p.46). **£120**

38 St Giles 38 St Giles St, NR2 1LL ☎01603 662944, ⓦ38stgiles.co.uk. A cross between a B&B and a hotel, this deluxe establishment has five en-suite rooms of varying size and description, but they all have silk curtains, top-whack bedding and Bang & Olufsen TVs. Breakfasts feature home-made bread, freshly baked croissants, fresh fruit and cereals – with the option of a full English instead. It's in a handy location too, a few yards from the Market Place, on the first floor above other premises. **£130**

★**Gothic House** King's Head Yard, Magdalen St, NR3 1JE ☎01603 631879, ⓦgothic-house-norwich.com. This particularly charming B&B occupies a slender, three-storey Georgian house down a little courtyard off Magdalen Street. The interior has been meticulously renovated in a period style with plates, prints, curios and paintings liberally distributed throughout. The two boutique bedrooms are reached via the most delightful of spiral staircases, and although not en suite, this really is no inconvenience. Highly recommended – and the host is a gold mine of information, too. **£95**

Number 17 Colegate, NR3 1BN ☎01603 764486, ⓦnumber17norwich.co.uk. Behind its attractive wooden facade, this family-run guesthouse has eight en-suite guest rooms decorated in a cosy, albeit slightly frugal, style with solid oak flooring to boot; two of the rooms are larger family rooms. The home-cooked breakfasts can, if the sun is out, be taken in the courtyard. Good location, too, in one of the nicest parts of the centre. **£90**

Wedgewood House Bed & Breakfast 42 St Stephens Rd, NR1 3RE ☎01603 625730, ⓦwedgewoodhouse .co.uk. In a large Victorian house just off the inner ring road to the southwest of the city centre, this comfortable B&B has half a dozen well-maintained, en-suite rooms decorated in a neat and trim modern style. Has parking and offers home-cooked breakfasts and a warm welcome. **£75**

HOTELS

Holiday Inn Norwich City Carrow Rd, NR1 1HU ☎08714 234896, ⓦholidayinn.co.uk. Holiday Inns are, of course, fairly commonplace, but this one is especially good with large and extremely comfortable rooms with all mod cons, and a spacious public area on the ground floor. The decor is modern-minimalist throughout, and the buffet breakfast is top-ranking. However, what really distinguishes this hotel is its location – it adjoins Norwich City football ground and the best rooms have panoramic views of the football pitch. There's a small premium charge on match days, but if you're visiting when Norwich FC are at home to regional rivals Ipswich ("The Tractor Boys"), then you won't get a room for love nor money. **£90**

★**Maid's Head Hotel** 20 Tombland, NR3 1LB ☎01603 209955, ⓦmaidsheadhotel.co.uk. This engaging, family-owned hotel is delightfully idiosyncratic – a rabbit warren of a place with all sorts of architectural bits and pieces, from the mock-Tudor facade to the ancient, wood-panelled bar and the (sadly routine) modern extension. There are 84 guest rooms in total, which vary considerably in character; some are period but most are modern, large and comfortable. These have recently been upgraded to a high spec, with an ecofriendly heating system installed. What's more, the location, bang in the centre opposite the cathedral, can't be beaten. If you are a light sleeper, note

Black Eagle

7% abv

Imperial Stout

NORFOLK TENDER
TASTY ASPARAGUS

£2·50 PA
BUNCH

1

that you should avoid those rooms overlooking Wensum Street, especially at the weekend as local drunks wend their not-so-merry way home. **£110**

★**Old Rectory Hotel** 103 Yarmouth Rd, Thorpe St Andrew, NR7 0HF ☎01603 700772, ⊛oldrectory norwich.com. In a handsome, ivy-clad Georgian villa, this appealing hotel holds eight commodious, en-suite rooms. The five rooms in the main house are decorated in a modern and very relaxing rendition of country house style, while those in the Coach House annexe are more modern. The grounds are extensive and there's an outside pool, but in the winter guests gather round the open fire. Outstanding breakfasts, plus a smart dining room/restaurant where the food is first-rate with due emphasis given to local, seasonal

ingredients: try the roasted breast of woodpigeon salad. The hotel is located close to the River Yare on the A1242, a couple of miles east of Norwich train station. **£130**

St Giles House Hotel 41 St Giles St, NR2 1JR ☎01603 275180, ⊛stgileshousehotel.com. This deluxe hotel, Norwich's fanciest, occupies a handsome Edwardian building just a few yards from the Market Place. It was designed in a sort of grand French imperial style by George Skipper, for many years the city's leading architect and the man responsible for the Royal Arcade (see p.48). The exterior, with its columns and balustrade, is impressive – perhaps overly so – and inside, each of the twenty-odd rooms is distinctive, though most combine new, sometimes adventurous shades with retro flourishes. **£130**

EATING

Norwich has a scattering of top-ranking **restaurants**, but perhaps its most distinctive offering is the **cafés** that dot the **Norwich Lanes** (see p.45) between the Market Place and St Benedict's Street. Many have an eco/boho edge, the main problem being that they come and go with alarming speed: we have selected a couple which look like staying the course. The other problem is that many cafés and restaurants close on Sundays and Mondays.

CAFÉS

Britons Arms Coffee House 9 Elm Hill, NR3 1HN ☎01603 623367, ⊛britonsarms.co.uk. Home-made quiches, tarts, cakes and scones plus pies and salads in a quaint Elm Hill thatched house with a terraced garden. There's a roaring open fire in winter too – very cosy. Tues–Sat 9.30am–5pm.

Expresso Café 12 St George's St, NR3 1BA ☎01603 768881, ⊛expresso-online.co.uk. Pleasant and pleasantly decorated café that does a good line in coffee. The snacks and sandwiches are fairly average, but at least the place is an independent. Mon–Sat 7am–5pm & Sun 9am–4pm.

Finnies Juice Bar 19 Lower Goat Lane, NR2 1EL ☎07900 983909. Hole-in-the-wall café at the heart of the Norwich Lanes with a boho vibe, great juices and made-in-front-of-you "artisan" pizza at £2.50 a slice. Mon–Sat 9.30am–5pm.

★**Roots** 6 Pottergate, NR2 1DS ☎01603 920788, ⊛rootsnorwich.co.uk. This excellent, split-level café and bistro is a family-owned affair where they prepare all the food on site. Prides itself on sourcing its ingredients locally – and the results melt in the mouth, from scones and pastries through to chicken, duck and steak. In the evenings, when reservations are recommended, main courses start at £12. Tues–Fri 9.30am–10pm, Sat 10am–10pm & Sun 10am–4pm.

RESTAURANTS

Benedicts 9 St Benedict's St, NR2 4PE ☎01603 926080, ⊛restaurantbenedicts.com. Recently upgraded and revamped in tasteful modern style – all simple lines and bright whites – this appealing, family-owned restaurant

offers a well-considered modern British menu. Try, for example, the locally-caught sea bass or mullet with turnips, Jersey Royals and passion fruit. A two-course meal costs £30, less at lunchtimes. Tues–Sat noon–2.30pm & 6–10pm.

B'Nou 46 St Benedict's St, NR2 4AQ ☎01603 765440, ⊛b-nou.com. Cosy little restaurant decorated in pastel shades, where the tapas-style menu has an international flavour, though Mediterranean dishes are to the fore. Tapas from as little as £5. Tues–Sat 7pm–midnight.

★**Grosvenor Fish Bar** 28 Lower Goat Lane, NR2 1EL ☎01603 625855, ⊛fshshop.com. A fish and chip shop with bells: the funky decor is inventive, but this plays second fiddle to the delicious fish and chips, not to mention the veggie burgers, meat pies and more imaginative dishes – tuna with wasabi beans for one. Eat in or takeaway, which is slightly cheaper. Fish and chips from £5. Mon–Sat 11am–7.30pm.

★**The Last Wine Bar** 76 St George's St, NR3 1AB ☎01603 626626, ⊛lastwinebar.co.uk. Imaginatively converted old shoe factory, a couple of minutes' walk north of the River Wensum, offering a relaxed and very amenable wine bar in one section and an excellent restaurant in the other. The food is firmly modern British, with the likes of braised lamb shank with carrots and parsnips in a rosemary jus; mains around £17. Daily noon–4pm & 5–11.30pm; kitchen closes 10.30pm.

Nazma 15 Magdalen St, NR3 1LE ☎01603 618701, ⊛nazmabrasseries.co.uk. Many locals swear this is the city's best Indian restaurant – and they may well be right. The menu covers all the classics, each prepared from scratch with the freshest of ingredients, but it's particularly strong on Bangladeshi cuisine. The decor is smart, modern and very appealing too. Mains average around £11, slightly less for takeaway. Daily noon–2.30pm & 6pm–midnight.

Roger Hickman's Restaurant 79 Upper St Giles St, NR2 1AB ☎ 01603 633522, ⓦ rogerhickmansrestaurant .com. Impeccable service, attractive furnishings and fittings and a frequently inspirational menu are the hallmarks of this stylish restaurant, the choicest in town. The menu is every inch modern British and conscientious efforts are made to source ingredients locally – try, for example, the pan-fried John Dory with braised fennel, mussel and saffron casserole. Two-course set meal £36, less at lunchtimes. Tues–Sat noon–2.30pm & 7–10pm.

★**Tatlers** 21 Tombland, NR3 1RF ☎ 01603 766670, ⓦ tatlersrestaurant.co.uk. Enticing contemporary restaurant – all plain-wood floors and deep-red walls

– where they stick to local, seasonal ingredients when they can. The portions are a little *nouvelle*, but there's a good wine cellar to compensate. Try the wood pigeon. Mon–Sat noon–2pm & 6–9pm.

Yellows American Bar & Grill Norwich City Football Club, 33 Carrow Rd, NR1 1HS ☎ 01603 218209, ⓦ canarycatering.co.uk/yellows. Most British football fans are condemned to eat grotty fast-food with unimaginable ingredients, but not here – as befits a club partly owned by the country's favourite cook, Delia Smith (see box, p.51). The place is kitted out in a brisk, modern style, the service is fast, and they rustle up the best burger in town – no mistake. Kitchen: Tues–Thurs 11.30am–9pm, Fri & Sat 11.30am–10pm.

DRINKING AND NIGHTLIFE

Norwich heaves with **pubs**, and although many have been badly treated by the developers with ersatz themes and tacky copycat decor, a goodly number have bucked the trend. Some have maintained their traditional appearance, others have survived by offering a wide range of real ales, and yet others have ventured into the idiosyncratic-meets-surreal. As for **clubs**, Norwich cannot really compete with its big-city British rivals, but it does muster a handful of places where locals gather, all high-heels, short skirts and short-sleeved shirts, no matter what the weather.

PUBS

Adam & Eve 17 Bishopgate, NR3 1RZ ☎ 01603 667423. There's been a pub here for seven hundred years and this warren of a place is still a popular spot for the discerning drinker, with a changing range of real ales and an eclectic wine list supplied by Adnams. Mon–Sat 11am–11pm, Sun noon–10.30pm.

Birdcage 23 Pottergate, NR1 1BA ☎ 01603 633534 ⓦ thebirdcagenorwich.co.uk. Extraordinary pub with a classic Art Deco exterior and a self-proclaimed "Bohemian" interior, all recycled furniture, modern art and vintage postcards on the walls. It all works very well – a treat for the eyes – and the pub casts a wide net with light bites, board games, cocktails, cabaret and cupcakes. Mon–Wed & Sun noon–11pm, Thurs–Sat noon–midnight.

Coach and Horses 82 Thorpe Rd, NR1 1BA ☎ 01603 477077, ⓦ thecoachthorperoad.co.uk. Boisterous boozer attracting a youthful crew, not least because of the three big-screen TVs and the inexpensive bar food. It's also home to the small-time Chalk Hill Brewery, who make a first-class range of ales – knock your socks off with their Old Tackle brew (at 5.6 percent). Daily 11am–midnight.

Fat Cat Freehouse 49 West End St, NR2 4NA ☎ 01603 624364, ⓦ fatcatpub.co.uk. Award-winning pub with a friendly atmosphere and a fantastic range of well-kept, top-quality draft ales. Also sells a wide range of bottled beers, ciders and perries, and there's takeaway if you don't want to hang around. The pub is located to the northwest of the city centre off the Dereham Rd. Mon–Wed & Sun noon–11pm, Thurs–Sat noon–midnight.

★**Kings Head** 42 Magdalen St, NR3 1JE ☎ 01603 620468. The perfect drinkers' pub with precious little

in the way of distraction – there are certainly no one-armed bandits here. Content yourself instead with an outstanding selection of real ales supplemented by an equally impressive, international range of bottled beers with Belgium leading the alcoholic charge. In two smallish rooms, so you may need to be assertive to get served. Mon–Thurs & Sun noon–11pm, Fri & Sat noon–midnight.

★**Micawbers Tavern** 92 Pottergate, NR2 1DZ ☎ 01603 626627. Lodged in an old beamed building on one of the city's prettiest streets, this friendly and busy pub is a local par excellence, featuring an outstanding range of guest ales on draft. There's sports TV and home-cooked food, too. Mon & Tues 5–11pm, Wed & Thurs 3–11pm, Fri & Sat noon–11.30pm, Sun noon–10.30pm.

Mischief 8 Fye Bridge St, NR3 1HZ ☎ 01603 623810. The counterfoil to the *Ribs of Beef* just across the bridge, *Mischief* has dispensed with any claim to comfort with its plain furniture and bare wooden floors – this is youthful drinking territory, make no mistake, and students come here by the seminar load. Daily 11am–11pm.

Ribs of Beef 24 Wensum St, NR3 1HY ☎ 01603 619517, ⓦ ribsofbeef.co.uk. There's been a pub here for hundreds of years and the present incarnation is a lively, friendly kind of place that makes a play for the couple rather than the group – witness the comfy chairs and the thick carpet. Has a likeable riverside mini-terrace too. Daily 11am–11pm.

CLUBS AND VENUES

Mercy XS 82 Prince of Wales Rd, NR1 1NJ ☎ 01603 627666, ⓦ mercynightclub.com. Very large and very flashy nightclub with a thunderous sound system, acres

1

of neon lighting and massive, heaving dancefloors. Subtle it isn't – good fun it is. Fri & Sat 10pm till the wee hours.

Waterfront 139–141 King St, NR1 1QH ☎01603 632717, ⓦfacebook.com/waterfrontnorwich. This club and alternative music venue, which occupies what was once an old beer bottling plant, showcases some great bands, both big names and local talent, and offers club and DJ nights too. Run by the University of East Anglia's student union. Fri & Sat from 9pm, plus additional gigs.

ENTERTAINMENT

★**Cinema City** Suckling House, St Andrew's St, NR2 4AD ☎08719 025724, ⓦpicturehouses.com. Easily the best cinema in town, featuring the pick of new releases plus themed evenings and cult and classic films. Has three screens. Also has live feeds, from, for example, the New York Met, and regular late-night horror films, billed as "Friday Frighteners".

Maddermarket Theatre St John's Alley, off Pottergate, NR2 1DR ☎01603 620917, ⓦmaddermarket.co.uk. With a long and distinguished pedigree, this amateur theatre company offers an interesting range of modern theatre mixed up with the classics. The building is interesting too – it's in the style of an Elizabethan theatre.

Norwich Arts Centre 51 St Benedict's St, NR2 4PG ☎01603 660352, ⓦnorwichartscentre.co.uk. Adventurous venue with a varied programme of film, comedy, dance, theatre and music plus art exhibitions. Performances are held in St Swithin's, a recycled medieval church, and there's a café too.

Norwich Playhouse 42–58 St George's St, NR3 1AB ☎01603 598598, ⓦnorwichplayhouse.co.uk. Opened in the mid-1990s, this enterprising and popular venue offers a varied programme, featuring everything from dance, cabaret, stand-up comedy and celebrity chit-chats to rock and pop concerts, ballet and panto.

★**Norwich Puppet Theatre** Church of St James, Whitefriars, NR3 1TN ☎01603 629921, ⓦpuppettheatre.co.uk. This long-established puppet theatre company has an outstanding reputation for the quality of its puppets and the excellence of its performances, with recent shows including *Thumbelina* and *Pirates, Mermaids and Sea Beasts*. Some performances are aimed at young children – who are simply enraptured – while others are for adults, and there are regular workshops too. Children's tickets cost around £9, £15 or so for adults. The company is housed in a deconsecrated medieval church beside the Whitefriars roundabout.

Norwich Theatre Royal Theatre St, NR2 1RL ☎01603 630000, ⓦtheatreroyalnorwich.co.uk. This 1300-seat Art Deco theatre is the city's major performance venue. It casts its artistic net wide, but for the most part it's mainstream stuff with a large helping of classical music thrown in for good measure.

SHOPPING

For a smallish city, Norwich does extremely well for **independent shops**, which combine to sell everything from vintage clothing and vinyls to chichi fashion and fine art. Attempting to capitalize on this, the narrow lanes and alleys between the Market Place and St Benedict's St have been designated the **Norwich Lanes** (see p.45), though in fact this excludes what is arguably the city's most diverting shopping strip, **Magdalen Street**, which is neither neat nor pretty, but does hold a real hotchpotch of great little stores. Of course, Norwich has its fair share of multinational shopping chains and these are at their ritziest in the **Chapelfield Shopping Centre** (ⓦchapelfield.co.uk), beside the inner ring road.

Book Hive 53 London St, NR2 1HL ☎01603 219268, ⓦthebookhive.co.uk. Norwich's leading independent bookshop, which stocks a personally chosen selection of titles divided into five main categories: fiction, art and design, children's books, cookery and poetry. There's a café, a children's book room, easy chairs, and – best of all – knowledgeable, interested staff. They also host events here – book launches, signings, kids' workshops and so forth. Mon 10am–5.30pm, Tues–Sat 9.30am–5.30pm, Sun 11am–4pm.

Carol Lake 91 Upper St Giles St, NR2 1AB ☎07743 494985, ⓦcarollake.co.uk. Inventive and well-regarded designer who seems able to turn her hand to just about everything, from dresses, shirts and scarves to cushions, screens and upholstered furniture. Also acts as an interior-design consultant. She works on the premises, so there are no set opening hours – either ring the bell and take pot luck or call ahead to book an appointment.

Country & Eastern The Old Skating Rink, 34 Bethel St, NR2 1NR ☎01603 663890, ⓦcountryandeastern .co.uk. One of Norwich's most distinctive shops, this barn-like store, lodged in what was once the city's skating rink, offers all sorts of Asian goods, from Buddha statues and delicately carved Burmese wall-panels to rugs, Thai jewellery and Indian paintings. Apparently, the owners make regular trips to Asia to source the material and take pains to patronize independent artisans. Mon–Sat 9.30am–5pm.

Crome Gallery 34 Elm Hill, NR3 1HG ☎01603 622827, ⓦcromegallery.co.uk. One of the prettiest streets in

Norwich, Elm Hill has a fair smattering of fine art and antique shops, but this is perhaps the most diverting, selling vintage maps and sketches, plus a good selection of local land- and seascapes, both antique and modern. They offer a picture framing service, too, and mount temporary art exhibitions. Mon–Sat 10am–5pm.

Finch Womenswear 14 St Benedict's St, NR2 4AG ☎ 07446 023230, ⊕ finchnorwich.com. Inventive and contemporary independent women's clothing and accessory shop featuring up-and-coming designers as well as more established names and brands. Affordable prices too. Tues–Sat 11am–6pm.

Harvey's Pure Meat 63 Grove Rd, NR1 3RL ☎ 01603 621930, ⊕ puremeat.org.uk. There are several good butchers in Norwich, but this is the pick of the bunch. They take pride in sourcing their organic meat locally to the highest welfare standards, and with no chemicals or drugs. They do cured meats too – ham, bacon etc – but their particular speciality is game – in season, pheasant, partridge, grouse, hare, woodcock and snipe. Mon–Wed 8am–4pm, Thurs & Fri 8am–5pm, Sat 8am–4pm.

Head in the Clouds 13 Pottergate, NR2 1DS ☎ 01603 620479, ⊕ headintheclouds.info. Peering into the window of this "head shop", you could be forgiven for thinking you've been beamed back into the 1970s, a land of flared trousers and Afghan coats – and it's true, as the owner proudly proclaims, that nothing much has changed here for several decades. So, stock up on your incense sticks, badges, pipes and vintage hippy clothes, and get down to the groove, man; Peace and Love. Mon–Sat 9.30am–6pm, Sun 11am–5pm.

Jarrolds Department Store 1–11 London St, NR2 1JF ☎ 01603 660661, ⊕ jarrold.co.uk. A Saturday shopping trip to Jarrolds has been a popular outing for many a local for many a year. Perhaps surprisingly, Jarrolds has remained independent and its flagship premises, here on London St, covers all the retail bases from sports to travel, arts and crafts to PCs, wedding gifts to fashion. Mon, Wed & Fri 9am–5.30pm, Tues 9.30am–5.30pm, Thurs 9am–7pm, Sat 9am–6pm, Sun 10.30am–4.30pm.

Norfolk Yarn 11 Pottergate, NR2 1DS ☎ 01603 927034, ⊕ norwichlanes.co.uk. Family-run business that caters to every knitter around with a hard-to-beat range of wools in

every colour imaginable – and then some. Also offers practical advice and problem solving plus workshops. Mon–Sat 9.30am–5.30pm.

Out of Time Records 4 Magdalen St, NR3 1HU ☎ 01603 610139, ⊕ outoftimerecords.co.uk. Something of an institution, this long-established shop groans and heaves with vinyl and to a lesser extent CDs, a veritable Aladdin's cave of all things audio. It reflects the enthusiasms of its owner, Eric White, who first opened his doors way back in 1986. There's a lot of rock memorabilia on sale here, too, plus a mail order service. Mon–Sat 10am–4.30pm.

Retreat Vintage 26a Magdalen St, NR3 1HU ☎ 07599 044968. Norwich has a good line in secondhand and vintage clothes shops and this is one of the best, offering an idiosyncratic selection of women's dresses, coats, blouses, skirts, shoes, belts and handbags from the 1920s to the 1980s. There's a smaller men's section as well. Tues–Sat 10.30am–5.30pm.

The Rock Collection 16 Lower Goat Lane, NR2 1EL ☎ 01603 625055, ⊕ rockcollection.co.uk. Alternative street- and club-wear store specializing in niche collections from rockabilly to rave via punk and goth. Featured designers include Darkside, Cyberdog, and Famous Stars and Straps. They also play host to the occasional band signings. Mon–Sat 9.30am–5.30pm, Sun 10.30am–4.30pm.

Tombland Bookshop 8 Tombland, NR3 1HF ☎ 01603 490000, ⊕ tomblandbookshop.co.uk. In an attractive old building close to the cathedral, this secondhand and antiquarian bookshop is just ideal – its bookshelves are well-organized and arranged, the whole caboodle permeated by that lovely and distinctive smell of old books. As they themselves say, "from belly-dancing to Bauhaus, botany to bee-keeping, there will be a book for the keen collector or the serendipitous reader" – though a particular specialism is East Anglian history. Mon–Fri 9.30am–5pm, Sat 9.30am–4.30pm.

Wilkinson's 5 Lobster Lane, NR2 1DQ ☎ 01603 625121, ⊕ wilkinsonsofnorwich.com. There's something really refreshing about this independent tea and coffee merchant, who take great care to buy the best of the crop, then sell it here in these quaint old premises. Mon–Sat 9am–5.30pm.

DIRECTORY

Car rental There are several car rental firms at the airport as well as in the city centre. Options include Europcar at the airport (☎ 03713 843416) and Enterprise in the city centre (☎ 01603 216868).

Football Norwich City Football Club – The Canaries – play at their stadium on Carrow Rd, near the train station (☎ 08448 261902, ⊕ canaries.co.uk).

Library The main city library is in the Forum building just

behind the Market Place on Millennium Plain (Mon–Fri 9am–8pm, Sat 9am–5pm; ☎ 0344 800 8006).

Post office There's a central post office inside the Castle Mall Shopping Centre, on Castle Meadow (Mon–Sat 9am–5.30pm).

Taxis There are several taxi stands in the city centre with one of the busiest being in front of the Guildhall, on the Market Place. Alternatively, call Beeline Taxis on ☎ 01603 767676.

The Broads and northeast Norfolk

WINDMILL, WOMACK WATER

The Broads and northeast Norfolk

Generally known as the Broads, the pancake-flat region between Norwich and Norfolk's east coast and reaching down into northern Suffolk is a haunting wilderness of lake and river, reedbed and marsh, huge skies and distant horizons, cut only by windmills and the gaff-rigged sails of far-off yachts. Three rivers – the Yare, Waveney and Bure and their various tributaries, notably the Thurne and Ant in the north, and the Chet in the south – meander across these flatlands, converging on Breydon Water before flowing into the sea at the old port and seaside resort of Great Yarmouth.

In places these rivers swell into wide expanses of water called "broads", which were long thought to be natural lakes. In fact they're the result of several centuries of extensive peat cutting in an area where peat was a valuable source of energy and wood was scarce. The pits flooded when sea levels rose in the thirteenth and fourteenth centuries to create the Broads, and this is now the largest wetland area in the country (and one of the most important in Europe), a haven for bird- and wildlife. You can see grebes, herons and, if you're lucky, a kingfisher or two; you might also catch a glimpse of the rare swallowtail butterfly, which is unique to the area, and it's not unusual to spot an otter poking its whiskered snout out of the water.

It's a beautiful area, and has been popular as a tourist destination for the best part of a century. However, during the 1970s and 1980s the Broads' delicate ecological balance was under threat: the careless use of fertilizers poisoned the water, and phosphates and nitrates encouraged the spread of algae; the decline in reed cutting – previously in great demand for thatching – made the Broads partly unnavigable; and the enormous amount of pleasure-boat traffic began to erode the banks. National Park status was accorded to the area in 1988, and it is now tightly regulated by the **Broads Authority** (see p.29).

The Broads – or Norfolk Broads, as they are often known, although they include parts of northern Suffolk – break neatly down into the **Northern Broads** and **Southern Broads**, separated by the large and slightly daunting expanse of Breydon Water. The Northern Broads is the busier of the two, focused on big boating centres like **Wroxham** and popular villages like **Horning**, **Ludham**, **Stalham**, **Acle** and **Potter Heigham**, and boasting the largest two broads, Barton Broad and Hickling Broad. To get to the Southern Broads, you have to pass through Great Yarmouth, which puts a lot of people off, and as a result the Yare and Waveney rivers are for the most part free of the summertime congestion you get further north. **Reedham** and **Brundall** are the two

EAST RUSTON VICARAGE GARDEN

Highlights

❶ Horning This is the classic Broadland village – with a great location on a bend in the Bure, good restaurants and one of the region's best riverside pubs. **See p.80**

❷ Bewilderwood Tom Blofeld's magical Broads fantasyland for kids is very easy to reach, and great fun. **See p.82**

❸ Electric Eel, How Hill One of several wildlife trips you can take into the reedy heartland of the Broads, but maybe the best. **See p.86**

❹ East Ruston Vicarage Garden There are lots

of beautiful gardens in Norfolk, but if you only have time to visit one, make it this – a garden fantasy created from scratch over the last three decades. **See p.93**

❺ Horsey 's Seals Visit the windmill, sail on, or walk around Horsey Mere, and best of all take in the seal colonies of the nearby coast. **See p.103**

❻ Winterton-on-Sea The best beach settlement along this stretch of coast, with golden sands, wonderful dunes, a beach café and a nice village pub. **See p.105**

HIGHLIGHTS ARE MARKED ON THE MAP ON P.64

main boating centres on the Yare, and you can follow the river all the way into Norwich; **Loddon** and neighbouring **Chedgrave** are smaller, quieter options on the tributary of the Chet. You should also, though, consider heading way south to Oulton Broad, on the fringes of Lowestoft in Suffolk (covered in chapter 7), and to Beccles (covered in chapter 5), known as the "gateway to the Broads", which is a handsome small town on the River Waveney.

The small towns of **Aylsham** and **North Walsham** are pleasant centres on the northern fringes of the Broads, and both have a number of excellent accommodation choices. Finally there's the **east coast**, which has more to it than the seaside tack and low-level deprivation of **Great Yarmouth**, Norfolk's largest port and resort, and overall is a refreshingly unpretentious antidote to Norfolk's better-known north coast. The Broads landscape blends seamlessly into the coast around **Horsey** and **Waxham**, while small-scale resorts like **Winterton**, **Mundesley** and **Overstrand** boast great Blue Flag

THE BROADS AND
NORTHEAST NORFOLK

0   2
miles

NORTH SEA

HIGHLIGHTS

1 Horning
2 Bewilderwood
3 Electric Eel, How Hill
4 East Ruston Vicarage Garden
5 Horsey's seals
6 Winterton-on-Sea

FOOTPATHS AND CYCLE TRAILS

If you're not getting out on the water (see box, pp.66–67) you need to at least take some advantage of the region's network of **footpaths** and **cycle trails**. There are a number of bike rental points dotted around the region, and walkers might consider dipping into the 56-mile **Weavers' Way**, which winds through some of the best parts of the Broads on its way from Cromer to Great Yarmouth (see p.29), or the 35-mile **Wherryman's Way**, which skirts Breydon Water from Great Yarmouth, and then follows the Yare as far as Whitlingham Country Park on the edge of Norwich (see p.53). And of course there are any number of shorter options, including the Angles Way from Great Yarmouth to Thetford (p.29), the Paston Way (p.93) up on the northeast coast, along with several boardwalked paths through nature reserves and along the edges of the most scenic broads and rivers. There is also a plan to link the Bure, Ant and Thurne rivers with a brand-new foot- and cyclepath, the Three Rivers Way – ⓦthreeriversway.org.uk.

2

BIKE RENTAL

The Canoe Man Wroxham. See p.67
Broadland Cycle Hire Bewilderwood, Horning, NR12 8JW ☎07887 480331, ⓦnorfolkbroadscycling.co.uk
Clippesby Hall Hall Lane, Clippesby, NR29 3BL ☎01493 367800, ⓦclippesby.com
Riverside Tearooms The Green, Stokesby ☎01493 750470, ⓦstokesby.org.uk
Sea Palling Cycle Hire Waxham Barn, NR12 0EE ☎01692 598592, ⓦnorfolkbicyclehire.co.uk
Waveney River Centre Staithe Rd, Burgh St Peter, NR34 0BT ☎01502 677343, ⓦwaveneyrivercentre.co.uk

RIVERSIDE PATHS AND BOARDWALKS

Barton Broad See p.83
Carlton Marshes See p.278
Cockshoot Broad See p.74
Filby Broad See p.104
Hickling Broad See p.87
Horsey Mere See p.103
How Hill See p.86
Ranworth Broad See p.75
Rockland Broad See p.118
Salhouse Broad See p.73
Surlingham Broad See p.117

beaches and sumptuous dunes, although the ongoing problem of coastal erosion – at its worst around the village of **Happisburgh** – means that parts of this beautiful landscape are under threat.

INFORMATION

THE BROADS

Tourist information The National Park – otherwise known as the Broads Authority (ⓦbroads-authority.gov.uk) – has jurisdiction over much of the riverside and marshland and maintains a number of information centres throughout the region. At any of these, you can pick up a free copy of the annual *Broadcaster*, a useful guide to the Broads as a whole (and to which this writer is a contributor), as well as lots of other advice and practical information.

Wroxham and around

Straddling the River Bure at one of its few crossing points, the small town of **WROXHAM** styles itself as the "capital of the Broads", and with good reason – it's home to more boatyards than anywhere else in the national park and is dependent on the boating industry to survive; it also makes a good base for visiting some of the most picturesque Broadland villages in the surrounding Northern Broads area, notably Salhouse and Ranworth. It's not a very attractive place in truth, made up of two villages: **Wroxham** proper, on the south side of the river, and **Hoveton**, on the north. The latter is home to the bulk of the town centre and most facilities, including the main town moorings and pretty riverside park, and perhaps Wroxham's most famous attraction, **Roys** – "the largest village store in the world", whose department store, supermarket, garden centre, toy shop and various other dependencies make up most of the town's commercial activity.

2

MESSING ABOUT IN BOATS

The best way by far to appreciate the fragile beauty of the Broads is to get out on the water. Naturally, there are many ways to do that. **Motor cruisers** are the most popular option, but you can also rent a **sailing boat** or a **canoe**, or take any number of **guided boat trips**. The Broads are above all the perfect place for a spot of novice boating. You don't need any experience – at least if you opt for engine rather than sail, which is what most people do. Not surprisingly, it's crowded in peak season, but the area has a tardis-like ability to absorb visitors, and even in the height of summer it's possible to escape to somewhere that feels like the middle of nowhere, with only – if you're sailing – the creak of your sheets and the swish of the water for company. There are lots of options for renting boats by the day or even the hour if you don't want to commit to a full week or weekend. Better yet, get out in a canoe and explore the smaller waterways that aren't so easily navigable by larger craft.

BOAT TRIPS

Big Dog ferry, Beccles See p.219
Broads Tours, Wroxham See p.70
Electric Eel, How Hill See p.86
Fairhaven Water Garden See p.96
Fritton Lake Launch Trips See p.112
Gentleman Jim, Rollesby Broad See p.104
Liana, Hoveton See p.70
Museum of the Broads See p.89

Ra, Whitlingham Great Broad See opposite
Ranworth Broad trips See p.75
Ross's Rivertrips, Horsey Mere See p.103
Southern Comfort, Horning See p.80
Visitor Centre, Hickling Broad See p.87
Waveney Princess, Oulton Broad See p.278

BOAT RENTAL

Barnes Brinkcraft Riverside Rd, Wroxham, NR12 8UD ☎ 01603 782625, ⓦ barnesbrinkcraft.co.uk. Wroxham-based family firm offering motor cruisers, dayboats and even canoes.

Ferry Marina The Marina, Horning, NR12 8PS ☎ 01692 631111, ⓦ ferry-marina.co.uk. Cruisers by the week or day from this versatile and reliable outfit. They also rent holiday cottages, and have various other facilities – a pool, café and fish and chip shop among them.

Freedom Boating Holidays Kingfisher Boatyard, Bungalow Rd, Norwich, NR7 0SH ☎ 01603 858453, ⓦ freedomboatingholidays.co.uk. Motor cruiser, dayboat, overnight boat and canoe rental.

Herbert Woods Broads Haven, Potter Heigham, NR29 5JD ☎ 01692 670711, ⓦ herbertwoods.co.uk. Motor cruisers and dayboats from one of the pioneers of Broads tourism. Holiday cottages too.

Hoseasons ☎ 08448 471356, ⓦ hoseasons.co.uk. The largest selection of motor cruisers available for rent on the Broads, from bases in Wroxham, Stalham, Acle, Brundall and Beccles.

Hunter's Yard Horsefen Rd, Ludham, NR29 5DG ☎ 01692 678263, ⓦ huntersyard.co.uk. This yard has a wonderful collection of classic, gaff-rigged Broads yachts and half-decker sailing boats for rent by the day. It also offers skippered sails to give you a taster, and runs RYA and youth courses.

Martham Boats Cess Rd, Martham, NR29 4RF

☎ 01493 740249, ⓦ marthamboats.com. Specialists in both classic wooden Broads motor cruisers and sailing yachts; it also has half-deckers, cruisers and canoes for rent by the day.

Norfolk Broads Direct The Bridge, Wroxham, NR12 8RX ☎ 01603 782207, ⓦ norfolkbroadsdirect .co.uk. Cruisers by the week from this Northern Broads stalwart, which is one of the biggest and best boatyards in the National Park, with excellent service and one of its newest fleets. They also hire dayboats and run river trips with Broads Tours – see opposite.

Posh Boats Ferry Marina, Ferry Rd, Horning, NR12 8PS ☎ 01692 631111, ⓦ poshboats.co.uk. Boatyard that does what it says on the tin – motor cruisers that are a cut above the old tubs you see most of the time on the Broads. As such it's more expensive, but it might just be worth it.

Richardson's The Staithe, Stalham, NR12 9BX ⓦ richardsonsboatingholidays.co.uk. Long-standing family-run firm that runs the largest fleet on the Broads, renting motor cruisers by the week.

Sanderson Marine Riverside, Reedham, NR13 3TE ☎ 01493 700242, ⓦ sandersonmarine.co.uk. Firm with around a dozen motor cruisers for rent – perfect for exploring the Southern Broads.

Swancraft Riverside, Brundall, NR13 5PL ☎ 01603 712362, ⓦ swancraft.co.uk. Boat rental and boatbuilding business that has about fifteen motor cruisers of varying shapes and sizes.

Whispering Reeds Staithe Rd, Hickling, NR12 0YW

ⓦ whisperingreeds.net. Great, family-run boatyard and boatbuilder that does motor cruiser and dinghy rental by the day and the week.

DAYBOATS, CANOES AND PADDLEBOARDS

Bank Boats Staithe Cottage, Wayford Bridge, NR12 9LN ☎ 01692 582457, ⓦ bankboats.co.uk. Boat and canoe rental from a great family-run business, perfectly placed for exploring the upper reaches of the Ant and North Walsham & Dilham Canal, and Barton Broad.

Broads Tours The Bridge, Wroxham, NR12 8RX ☎ 01603 782207, ⓦ broadstours.co.uk. Dayboat hire and regular river trips on their big mock paddle steamer, *Queen of the Broads* (see p.70).

★**The Canoe Man** 10 Norwich Rd, Wroxham, NR12 8RX ☎ 01603 499177, ⓦ thecanoeman.com. The Canoe Man brings originality and adventure to the Broads, with a whole range of activities including straight canoe rental from a range of locations, guided canoe trails, bushcraft experiences and teepee canoe trips. They also have bikes for rent and offer all sorts of information and tips on exploring the area. A great place to start any discovery of Broadland.

CC Marine Wherry Boatyard, 35 Northgate, Beccles, NR34 9AU ☎ 01502 713703, ⓦ ccmarinebeccles .co.uk. Dayboat hire from a small, friendly yard right on the river.

Ferry Marina Ferry Rd, Horning, NR12 8PS ☎ 01692 631111, ⓦ ferry-marina.co.uk or ⓦ daycruisers .co.uk. Dayboat rental (see p.81).

Richardsons Fineway The Rhond, Hoveton, NR12 8UE ☎ 01603 782309, ⓦ finewayleisure.co.uk. Dayboat rental from the Wroxham base of the Broads' biggest hire fleet.

Freedom Boating Holidays Kingfisher Boatyard, Bungalow Rd, Norwich, NR7 0SH ☎ 01603 858453, ⓦ freedomboatingholidays.co.uk. Dayboats, canoes and boats for rent.

HE Hipperson Gillingham Dam, Beccles, NR34 0EB ☎ 01502 712166, ⓦ hippersons.co.uk. Dayboats and houseboats for rent by the river on the outskirts of Beccles.

JB Boats 106 Lower St, Horning, NR12 8PF ☎ 01692 631111, ⓦ jbboats.co.uk. Small boatyard close to the centre of Horning that often does the cheapest dayboats in the area.

Moonfleet Marine The Staithe, Stalham, NR12 9DA ☎ 01692 580288, ⓦ moonfleetmarine.co.uk.

Dayboats for hire from their yard right next door to the Museum of the Broads (see p.89).

Norfolk Paddle Company Pleasure Boat Inn, Hickling, NR12 0YW ☎ 07841 977802, ⓦ norfolk paddleco.co.uk. Paddleboards, canoes and kayaks for hire.

Phoenix Repps Staithe Boatyard, Potter Heigham, NR29 5JD ☎ 01692 670460, ⓦ phoenixfleet.com. Canoe and dayboat rental.

Rowan Craft Big Row, Geldeston, NR34 0LY ☎ 01508 518598, ⓦ rowancraft.com. Dayboat and canoe rental from an idyllic spot in the Geldeston boat basin.

Sutton Staithe Boatyard Sutton Staithe, NR12 9QS ☎ 01692 581653, ⓦ suttonstaitheboatyard .co.uk. Dayboat hire and canoes from a small boatyard tucked away on Sutton Staithe, handy for exploring the upper reaches of the Ant and Barton Broad.

Waveney River Centre Staithe Rd, Burgh St Peter, NR34 0BT ☎ 01502 677343, ⓦ waveneyrivercentre .co.uk or ⓦ daycruisers.co.uk. Dayboats and canoes from this fabulous spot on the Waveney River.

Waveney River Tours Bridge Rd, Oulton Broad, NR33 9JS ☎ 01502 574903, ⓦ waveneyrivertours .com. Boats for hire by the day. They're also the operators of the *Waveney Princess* (see p.278).

Whispering Reeds Staithe Rd, Hickling, NR12 0YW ☎ 01692 598314, ⓦ whisperingreeds.net. Dayboat and canoe rental, plus houseboat holidays.

SAILING FOR PEOPLE WITH DISABILITIES

Nancy Oldfield Trust Irstead Rd, Neatishead, NR12 8BJ ☎ 01692 630572, ⓦ nancyoldfield.org.uk.

Sailability Oulton Broad ☎ 01502 573556, ⓦ waveneysailability.co.uk.

BROADS AUTHORITY INFORMATION CENTRES

Whitlingham Broad Daily throughout the year 9am–5pm. See p.53.

Hoveton April–Oct daily 9am–5pm. See p.65.

How Hill April–Oct daily 9am–5pm. See p.86.

USEFUL GENERAL WEBSITES

ⓦ www.broads-authority.gov.uk

ⓦ enjoythebroads.com

ⓦ discoverthebroads.com

ⓦ norfolkbroads.com

St Mary

St Mary's Close, NR12 8NX · ⓦ wroxham.churchnorfolk.com

Tucked away on its own, south of the river, just off the main road into town, Wroxham's church of **St Mary** is – unusually for a Broadland church – often kept locked. In any case, its most distinctive feature is on the outside: a magnificent Norman doorway, stained blue, which the architectural historian Nikolaus Pevsner described as "barbaric and glorious", though it's hard to see if the porch doors are closed. At any rate, it's a peaceful spot – quite unlike anywhere else in Wroxham.

St John

Horning Rd, NR12 8NX · ⓦ hovetonstjohn.churchnorfolk.com

North of the river, Hoveton's church of **St John**, is in a much less peaceful position than St Mary's, but is more likely to be open. A small church, it has an ancient intimacy all of its own. Inside, you'll find a fifteenth-century beamed roof and some fifteenth-century stained glass details in the windows of the nave (though its red-brick tower is a Victorian addition). The most distinctive features, however, are the many memorials to the Blofeld family (see box opposite), on whose estate the church stands.

Wroxham Miniature Worlds

Horning Rd West, NR12 8QJ · £9.95, children £7.95 · ☎ 01603 781728, ⓦ wroxhamminiatureworlds.co.uk

Across the road from Hoveton and Wroxham mainline station, **Wroxham Miniature Worlds** modestly describes itself as the "largest indoor modelling attraction in the UK". Inside are some of the largest model railways you'll ever see on display, including

BURE VALLEY RAILWAY

Just across the road from Wroxham's main-line station on the edge of the village, the **Bure Valley Railway** (see p.76) runs from Wroxham up to Aylsham. You can also walk or cycle the **Bure Valley Path**, which shadows the rail line.

THE NAME'S BLOFELD, HENRY BLOFELD...

The **Blofelds** have been major players around these parts for many years, and among others have produced the genial cricket commentator Henry Blofeld, and his nephew Tom, who lives at nearby Hoveton House (no relation to Hoveton Hall) and is responsible for the Bewilderwood books and children's theme park (see p.82). Intriguingly, Tom Blofeld's grandfather John was something of a mystic and a practising Buddhist who lived in China for years. He was at school with Ian Fleming and is believed to have been the inspiration for the eponymous Bond villain.

2

wonderful, imaginative depictions of the UK, Europe and Japan. It's not just for model train enthusiasts, however, and also has a Scalextric track, a Lego city and all manner of vintage toys from years gone by. All in all a welcome addition to Wroxham and Hoveton's range of sights, plus it has a café and a shop for railway enthusiasts.

St Peter

St Peter's Lane, NR12 8RL • ⓦ hovetonstpeter.churchnorfolk.com

Hoveton's other church, **St Peter**, is just off the Stalham road on the Hoveton Hall estate, on the northern outskirts of the village. The unusual step-gabled building, built of red brick and with a thatched roof, is full of memorials to the Buxton family – the current incumbents of Hoveton Hall.

Hoveton Hall Gardens

Off the Stalham Rd, NR12 8RJ • Mid-April to mid-Sept daily 10.30am–5pm • Guided tours first Wed of the month, 11am; guided wildlife tours third Wed of the month, 11am • £7, children £3.50, family tickets £19 • ☎ 01603 782558, ⓦ hovetonhallgardens.co.uk

On the northern outskirts of Hoveton, just past St Peter's church a mile or so up the Stalham road, **Hoveton Hall Gardens** are a delightful and diverse fifteen acres in the

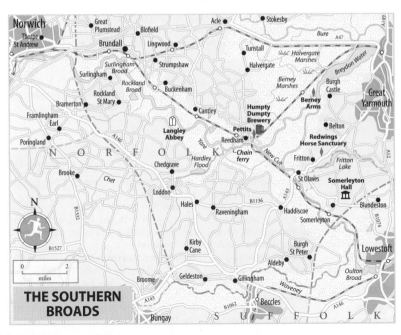

THE SOUTHERN BROADS

2

BOAT TRIPS FROM WROXHAM AND HOVETON

You can make river trips in both directions from Wroxham and Hoveton. The **Liana**, a small, Edwardian-style launch, plies the waters between Hoveton and Belaugh (June–Sept daily, hourly 11am–4pm; April, May & Oct weekends, bank hols, Easter week and half-term daily, hourly 11am–4pm; £7, children £6, family tickets £19.50; tickets and info from the Broads Information Centre in Hoveton). It leaves from the Hoveton riverbank just behind the Broads Information Centre (see below) and makes a pleasant, hour-long journey that takes in one of the most scenic stretches of the Bure. It only takes eight people, so you may need to book. A very different sort of trip, **Broads Tours**' mock paddle steamer, *Queen of the Broads*, runs several times a day from the Wroxham side of the river (close by the Norfolk Broads Direct moorings) and heads downriver to a choice of Wroxham Broad, Salhouse Broad and Horning Reach (March–June, Sept & Oct usually 2 trips daily at 11.30am & 2pm; July & Aug several trips daily 10.30am–4pm; 1hr trips to Wroxham Broad £7.50; 90min trips to Salhouse Broad £8; 2hr trips to Horning Reach £9.50; ☎01603 782207, ⊛broadstours.co.uk).

grounds of a Georgian house. They have fine spreads of daffodils in April and beautiful displays of azaleas and rhododendrons in May and June, while midsummer sees the old walled gardens turn into a riot of colour. There are some secluded water gardens, with tiny streams crossed by bridges, and lovely lakeside and woodland walks that take in a puzzle trail for kids, a makeshift bird hide and a recently restored, early nineteenth-century glasshouse. There's also a decent little café by the entrance, with plants for sale next door.

Wroxham Barns

Tunstead Rd, NR12 8QU • Daily 10am–5pm • Farm entry £6.25, under-2s free • ☎ 01603 783762, ⊛ wroxhambarns.co.uk

Just over a mile north of Hoveton, **Wroxham Barns** is a successful development that has plenty for children and adults alike – craft shops and galleries, a fine food store stocked with lots of local ciders and ales, and a garden centre. It's also home to a small "junior farm" with goats, sheep, cows, pigs and donkeys to pet and feed, a "championship" minigolf course, a funfair during summer and school holidays, and an excellent café and restaurant which serves great coffee and may be the area's best bet for lunch (see below).

Wroxham Broad

On the eastern edge of Wroxham is **Wroxham Broad**, reached by taking The Avenue, one of the largest of the broads and great for sailing, at its best during several annual **Wroxham Regattas**. These are organized by the Norfolk Broads Yacht Club – one of the area's most venerable sailing establishments – whose clubhouse sits on the far corner of the broad.

ARRIVAL AND INFORMATION   WROXHAM

By train Wroxham is 15min by train from Norwich: Hoveton and Wroxham station, on the Bittern line between Norwich and Sheringham, is on the edge of the village on the Coltishall road, on the far side of Roys car parks. Connections include Salhouse, Worstead, North Walsham, Cromer and Sheringham. You can also get to Coltishall, Buxton and Aylsham on the Bure Valley Railway (see p.76).

By bus Buses from Norwich stop on the main road,

outside Roys, as do buses on to Horning, Ludham and Great Yarmouth.

By boat There are free moorings on the southern (Wroxham) side of the river, and also on the Hoveton side, in the direction of Coltishall, where there's a nice riverside park.

Broads Information Centre Station Rd, Hoveton, NR12 8UR (April–Oct daily 9am–5pm; ☎ 01603 782281).

ACCOMMODATION

IN TOWN
Coach House 96 Norwich Rd, NR12 8RY ☎01603

784376, ⊛coachhousewroxham.com. Well-located, cosy B&B on the Wroxham side of the river, just 5min

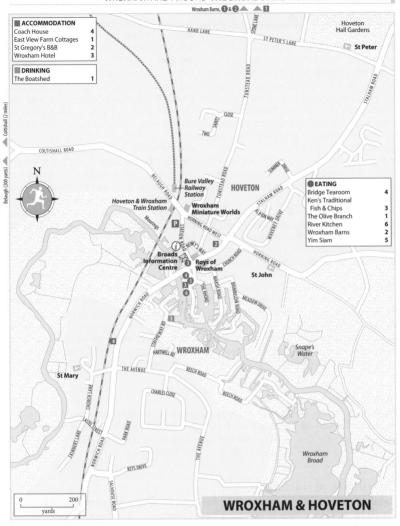

ACCOMMODATION

Coach House	4
East View Farm Cottages	1
St Gregory's B&B	2
Wroxham Hotel	3

DRINKING

The Boatshed	1

EATING

Bridge Tearoom	4
Ken's Traditional Fish & Chips	3
The Olive Branch	1
River Kitchen	6
Wroxham Barns	2
Yim Siam	5

WROXHAM & HOVETON

from the centre of the village, with three bedrooms – two doubles, one twin – and including a really good breakfast. **£85**

St Gregory's B&B 11 Stalham Rd, NR12 8DG ☎ 01603 784319, ⓦ stgregoryswroxham.co.uk. Local artist Chris Hutchins' place is a home from home in the heart of Hoveton with a double and a twin-bedded room, both en-suite, and excellent breakfasts. Both the house and the rooms are lovely, and Chris and Sue will make you very comfortable. Hard to fault, really. **£75**

Wroxham Hotel The Bridge, NR12 8AJ ☎ 01603 782061, ⓦ arlingtonhotelgroup.co.uk/wroxham. Nicer than it looks from the outside, with eighteen en-suite rooms, some

of which have balconies overlooking the river. **£100**

OUT OF TOWN

East View Farm Cottages Stone Lane, Ashmanhaugh, NR12 8YW ☎ 01603 782225, ⓦ eastviewfarm.co.uk. These two self-catering cottages are the ultimate in rural tranquillity, tucked away in a bucolic location just north of Hoveton, not far from Wroxham Barns. One cottage sleeps two, the other six, and it's as environmentally friendly a place as you could wish for, with energy-saving appliances in the cottages and its own wind turbine. There's even the added bonus of the fabulous miniature railway in the grounds. One week from **£650**

2

EATING AND DRINKING

IN TOWN

The Boatshed The Peninsula, Staitheway Rd, NR12 8TH ☎01603 781952, ⓦboatshedwroxham.co.uk. Hard to find among the riverside cottages but well worth searching out, this ramshackle joint has comfy chairs and pine tables and a vast range of real ales on tap, including many of the best local breweries alongside others from farther afield. Sit outside to best appreciate its riverside location. Live music too. Daily noon–11pm.

Bridge Tearoom The Bridge, NR12 8DA ☎01603 781817. Right by the bridge, this greasy-spoon café does a good line in big breakfasts and hot lunches. Mon–Sat 8.45am–4.45pm.

Ken's Traditional Fish and Chips Norwich Rd, NR12 8DA ☎01603 783739. Hungry sailors make a beeline for Ken's famous chippy – just a takeaway, and nothing special to look at, but renowned for the lightness of its batter and the tastiness of its chips. Expect to queue. Daily 11.30am–2.30pm & 4.30–7.45pm.

River Kitchen Riverside Rd, NR12 8UD ☎01603 926560, ⓦtheriverkitchen.co.uk. A welcome addition to the Wroxham eating scene, not least for its outside terrace right on the water. They do great breakfasts plus wonderful cakes and brownies; lunches consist of sandwiches and salads, a tart of the day, catch of the day, and excellent warm buns (£9.50), filled with pulled pork, fish cakes,

burgers, grilled halloumi and other good things. Daily 9.30am–4pm (from 8.30am on Sat).

Yim Siam 3 Riverside Centre, NR12 8AJ ☎01603 7811133, ⓦyimsiam.co.uk. Really good, authentic Thai food, in a place you wouldn't expect to find it, tucked away in a shopping precinct in the centre. Starters from £4.95, mains from £8.95. Well worth a visit, and they do takeaways too. Tues–Sun noon–3pm & 5.30–11pm.

OUT OF TOWN

The Olive Branch Market St, NR12 8AH ☎01603 737555, ⓦolivebranchnorfolk.com. In the centre of Tunstead, the next village north from Hoveton, this place describes itself as a "cycling café" and does great lunches for hungry cyclists and anyone else who happens to be passing. A nice vibe in a nice location, and the food is good too – "King of the Mountain" burger, anyone? Sandwiches, soups, salads, fish and quiches – and, yes, excellent burgers (from £9). Daily 9am–5pm.

Wroxham Barns Tunstead Rd, NR12 8QU ☎01603 777106, ⓦwroxhambarns.co.uk. One of the best places to eat in and around Wroxham, with an excellent restaurant where you could have just coffee and a cake, a sandwich or a full lunch from their list of specials – think Brancaster mussels, smoked haddock and bacon chowder, rare-breed sausage and mash or grilled fillet of sea bass – all made using local ingredients. Daily 10am–5pm.

Belaugh

Between Wroxham and Coltishall, the riverside village of **BELAUGH** lies at the end of a winding side-road off the main road. It's a peaceful spot with a handful of free moorings and the church of **St Peter** high above the river, in which what's left of a medieval rood screen shows ten of the eleven loyal disciples.

Coltishall and Horstead

Just three miles upriver from Wroxham, the sprawling village of **COLTISHALL** really represents the westernmost fringe of the Broads proper (the river is not navigable beyond this point by commercial craft). It's a pleasant place, once a centre for boatbuilding, its public **staithe** (with plenty of free moorings) fringed by green meadows and close to the *King's Head* (see below). Just past here, the thatched church of **St John the Baptist** has a light whitewashed interior, full of stained glass and grand memorials, beyond which is the heart of the village and a bridge over the river, which separates Coltishall from its sister village of **HORSTEAD**. Here you'll find both the excellent *Recruiting Sergeant* pub (see opposite) and a good local farm shop (see opposite).

ACCOMMODATION

COLTISHALL AND HORSTEAD

COLTISHALL

King's Head 26 Wroxham Rd, NR12 7EA ☎01603 737426, ⓦkingsheadcoltishall.co.uk. Four en-suite double rooms above the pub (see opposite), well located by the riverside green in Coltishall. Rooms are reasonable sizes

and fairly recently refurbished. Breakfast included. **£75**

Norfolk Mead Hotel Church Loke ☎01603 737531, ⓦnorfolkmead.co.uk. This comfortable Georgian hotel enjoys a fabulous location on the Bure, tucked away down a lane in Coltishall. It has eleven cool and contemporary rooms – very spacious and comfy, with large bathrooms, some of them overlooking the grassy water meadows that stretch down to the river and the hotel's private moorings. The public areas are very relaxing, as if you were lazing around in a (rich) friend's country house for the weekend, and there's a cosy bar and an excellent restaurant. **£125**

HORSTEAD
★**Recruiting Sergeant** Norwich Rd, NR12 7EE ☎01603 737077, ⓦrecruitingsergeant.co.uk. Five boutique rooms on two upstairs floors to stagger off to after eating in this great local gastropub (see below), all in a style that is as classic and contemporary as the food. **£80**

EATING

COLTISHALL
A Piece of Cake 18 High St, NR12 7DH ☎01603 736090, ⓦcoltishallcakes.co.uk. Two local mums set up this great little café a couple of years ago, and it was just what Coltishall needed, a community hub and place to enjoy a tea or coffee, superb home-made (including gluten-free) cakes and light lunches – jackets, sandwiches etc. Lovely cream teas, too. Mon–Sat 9am–4pm, Sun 9.30am–3.30pm.

King's Head 26 Wroxham Rd, NR12 7EA ☎01603 737426, ⓦkingsheadcoltishall.co.uk. The focus is on food in this friendly pub, right by the village staithe, and in fact it's one of two good places for dinner in Coltishall and Horstead with starters from £6.95 and mains from £16.95. The menu changes regularly, but expect Cromer crab tartlet or locally smoked eel followed by slow-cooked pork belly or pan-fried duck breast. It has rooms upstairs too (see opposite), and serves an excellent breakfast as well as

lunch and dinner every day. Kitchen daily 8am–10am, noon–2.30pm & 6–9pm.

HORSTEAD
★**Recruiting Sergeant** Norwich Rd, NR12 7EE ☎01603 737077, ⓦrecruitingsergeant.co.uk. This is one of the best places hereabouts for good gastropub food, with a great choice of daily specials for around £15 – hearty cooking that's deliberately simple and contemporary: skate wing, sea bass, smoked haddock with mash, calves' liver, or just steaks and burgers from the farm shop across the road (see below). The atmosphere is relaxed, with a roaring fire in winter and outside tables in summer, but the food and service is of restaurant standard – and worth the trip to Coltishall alone. Kitchen Mon–Fri noon–2pm & 6–9pm, Sat noon–2.30pm & 5.30–9.30pm, Sun noon–8.30pm; pub daily 11am–11pm.

SHOPPING

Farm to Fork & Fish Norwich Rd, Horstead, NR12 7EE ☎01603 266129, ⓦfarmtoforkandfish.co.uk. Great farm shop with deli, butcher's and fishmonger's counter,

and fantastically fresh local produce. Tues–Fri 8am–6pm, Sat 8am–4pm.

Salhouse and Salhouse Broad

NR13 6RX • Moorings £8 overnight, £4 during the day; canoes £10/hr, £22/3hr, £33/6hr • ☎01603 722775, ⓦsalhousebroad.org.uk

A couple of miles south of Wroxham, the village of **SALHOUSE** gathers around its **pub**, *The Salhouse Bell*, from where you can make the ten to fifteen minute walk to the signposted trail down to **Salhouse Broad**. This easy stroll finishes up at one of the prettiest of the smaller northern Broads – no more than a wider stretch in the Bure really, shielded from the main body of the river by spits of land covered by lines of trees. There are moorings on the bank, and riverside paths lead around the wooded hill just above and down to a small children's playground by the shore. There are **canoes** and kayaks for rent here, **camping** is available at a small, rustic campsite (see p.74), plus you can take the ferry across the river to the nature reserve at Hoveton Great Broad.

All Saints church

Bell Lane, NR13 6HD • Mon–Sat 9.30am–4.30pm • ⓦsalhouse.churchnorfolk.com

Like so many Norfolk churches, Salhouse's **All Saints** is a mile or so outside the village, on the Wroxham road, a thatched affair with a squat fifteenth-century tower that was never finished (hence its shape), although the main body of the church is at least two centuries older than this. Inside is a dark, cosy church with a number of curious features, including a wrought-iron hourglass on the pulpit, presumably to prevent the priest from droning on too long, and a rood screen topped – for once – by its "rood" or cross; behind it take a look at the sixteenth-century "sacring" bell, which used to be rung to celebrate Mass – one of very few left in the country.

2

Brick Kilns Norwich Rd, Little Plumstead, NR13 5JH ☎ 01603 723043, ⓦ thebrickkilns.co.uk. This distinctive pink-washed pub about a mile south of Salhouse has two very comfy double rooms and one twin upstairs. Also serves hearty pub grub downstairs, unusually including a full menu of vegan and vegetarian options as well as all the usual pub standards and a good array of fish. Most mains go for around £10–13. Kitchen daily

noon–2.15pm & 6–9pm; pub daily 11am–11pm. **£65**
Salhouse Broad Camping Corner, NR13 6RX ☎ 07795 145475, ⓦ salhousebroad.org.uk. A great rustic campsite with pitches for tents, as well as a "camping pod" (a simple wooden hut) that sleeps ten adults. Basic facilities but a great position right on Salhouse Broad. Steel firepits available and lots of firewood for sale. Pitches **£16** plus **£3** per person; camping pod **£20**

Hoveton Great Broad

April–mid-Sept 10am–5pm • Free

About a mile downriver from Wroxham, on the north bank of the Bure across the river from Salhouse Broad, **Hoveton Great Broad** is a protected area, and can only be accessed from the river, and visited on foot by following a laid-out nature trail. It's privately owned, and the trail is sadly only about half a mile long; but it is well marked, winding through the woodland and swamp around the broad, and it represents one of the best chances you'll get of seeing a swallowtail butterfly, not to mention dragonflies and various birds, such as marsh harriers, woodpeckers and kingfishers. There are plans afoot to dredge the broad and add a canoe trail, using lottery funding, so accessibility may increase in future years. For now, though, you can only reach Hoveton Great Broad with your own boat or by taking a **ferry** from Salhouse Broad (Thurs & Sun noon & 2pm; £3.50 return, children £1).

Woodbastwick

About ten minutes' walk beyond Salhouse Broad, around three miles southeast of Wroxham, **WOODBASTWICK** is one of the prettiest villages in the area. Its nucleus of thatched cottages nestle around a green, overlooked by the thatched church of **St Fabian and St Sebastian**, which has a nice churchyard and was refashioned inside in the nineteenth century by the prolific Gothic Revival architect George Gilbert Scott.

Woodforde's brewery

Woodbastwick, NR13 6SW • Mon–Fri 10am–4.30pm, Sat & Sun 11am–4.30pm • Tours £10, 90min • ☎ 01603 720353, ⓦ woodfordes.co.uk

For most people Woodbastwick's main draw is **Woodforde's brewery**, one of the best known and most successful of Norfolk's many independent brewers. The brewery is on the edge of the village, next to their *Fur and Feather* pub (see below); you can visit its **shop and visitor centre** and join one of their excellent tours (the only way to see inside the brewery itself), which take you through the brewing process and give you a tasting at the end. Wherry is their standard bitter, and very good it is too, kept on tap at pubs across East Anglia, but they also do a range of other beers. These include the stronger Nelson's Revenge, light and refreshing Sundew and fearsomely strong Headcracker.

Fur & Feather Slad Lane, NR13 6HQ ☎ 01603 720003, ⓦ thefurandfeatherinn.co.uk. A large, well-run family-friendly establishment owned by Woodforde's brewery next door that naturally serves Woodforde ales as well as cooking up some handsome pub grub, some of it using the

beer as an ingredient. Try the seafood medley or the excellent whole roasted pheasant. Kitchen Mon–Fri 11am–9pm, Sat 10am–9pm, Sun 10am–8pm; pub Mon 11am–9pm, Tues–Thurs 11am–9.30pm, Fri 11am–10pm, Sat 10am–11pm, Sun 10am–9pm.

Cockshoot Broad

It's a short walk from the centre of Woodbastwick through the Bure Marshes down to the south bank of the Bure River, where you could once cross the river to Horning by way of a foot ferry, but sadly no longer. You can still, though, follow the boardwalked path along the river for fifteen minutes or so to picturesque Cockshoot Dyke and on to the NWT-managed **Cockshoot Broad** – a wonderfully secret spot, viewable from a bird hide and known for its waterlily beds, home to schools of buzzing damsel- and dragonflies during high summer.

Ranworth

Situated on the southern side of Malthouse Broad (Ranworth Broad is next door, and is a nature reserve, not accessible to ordinary boats), the village of **RANWORTH**, around five miles southeast of Wroxham, has free moorings on its staithe, where there's also a car park, café and shop, an NWT information office, and, across the road, a decent pub, *The Maltsters* (see below).

St Helen

Ranworth, NR13 6HT • Mid-March to Oct Mon–Fri 10.30am–4.30pm, Sat & Sun 2–5pm; Nov to mid-March Sat & Sun 2–5pm • ⓦ broadsideparishes.org.uk

Ranworth is best known for its church of **St Helen**, the so-called "Cathedral of the Broads" for both its treasures and the marvellous views from the top of its 100ft bell tower, though it's a strenuous climb up steep and irregular steps, with a couple of ladders at the top to negotiate as well. Inside, the font, bang in front of the entrance, dates from the building's foundation in the eleventh century. The rest is mainly fifteenth-century, and its most impressive feature is the rood screen at the opposite end of the nave, painted with saints and with the rose of Ranworth on the back. Just in front is a similarly ancient lectern, decorated with the symbol of St John the Evangelist on one side and a fifteenth-century verse on the other, although it normally supports the so-called *Antiphony*, kept in a display case to the right of the entrance – a late fifteenth-century illuminated service book that is in fantastic condition.

Malthouse and Ranworth broads

Visitor centre April–Sept daily 10am–5pm; Oct same hours weekends and half-term only • ☎ 01603 270479

Small open boats make regular trips (10min; £1.50) from Ranworth staithe across **Malthouse Broad** and into adjoining **Ranworth Broad**, which is an NWT nature reserve, dropping you off at the informative **visitor centre** and viewing gallery built out into the water there. You can also reach Ranworth Broad and the visitor centre on foot – take the boarded path from the staithe or off the road that winds behind St Helen's church. The NWT run regular trips on Ranworth Broad (45min; £6) and also operate trips to Cockshoot Broad (see opposite) on Sundays during July and August (£14), though you must book these in advance.

EATING   RANWORTH

The Maltsters The Hill, NR13 6AB ☎01603 270900, ⓦ ranworthmaltsters.com. This village pub has been serving the sailors who pitch up here for years and has recently had a very welcome revamp, with a lick of paint and an upgraded menu that includes good burgers, salads and baguettes as well as more substantial fish and meat mains for £9.95–12.95. Outside seating available. Kitchen daily noon–3pm & 6–9pm; pub daily 10am–11pm.

Aylsham and around

The market town of **AYLSHAM** is not really part of the Broads, but it is the terminal for the Bure Valley Railway (see p.76) from Wroxham. It's a pleasant enough place, and like most Norfolk towns, life revolves around the **marketplace**, home to a twice-weekly market and overlooked by the *Black Boys Hotel*. There's not much to see apart from the considerable attraction of **Blickling Hall**, a couple of miles to the north, but the town is one of nine "**cittaslow**" communities in the UK (Ludlow in Shropshire was the first), an offshoot of Italy's Slow Food movement, designed to promote local food and food producers. Aylsham hosts a popular food festival at the beginning of October each year (ⓦslowfoodaylsham.org.uk).

St Michael and All Angels

Church Terrace, NR11 6BZ • ⓦ aylshamparishchurch.org.uk

On the far side of Aylsham's Market Place, the church of **St Michael and All Angels** was built in the early part of the fifteenth century under the English prince John of Gaunt (Aylsham was one of his dominions) on the proceeds of the town's linen trade. It sports a font carved with symbols of the Evangelists and the lower part of a rood screen painted with various saints (some of them defaced during the Reformation), both of which are contemporary with the building.

Bure Valley Railway

Aylsham Station, NR11 6BW • Aylsham–Wroxham £8 single, £12.50 return, family return £33 • ☎ 01263 733858, ⓦ bvrw.co.uk

Five minutes' walk south from the Market Place, Aylsham's station is home to the **Bure Valley Railway** – an old-fashioned mini (15-inch gauge) train line that runs from Aylsham down to Wroxham in the heart of the Broads, taking in Brampton, Buxton and Coltishall along the way. Engines are either steam- or diesel-powered, and the nine-mile trip to Wroxham takes 45 minutes. If you don't want to take the train you can walk or cycle the **Bure Valley Path**, which shadows the rail line – and the river – all the way.

ARRIVAL AND INFORMATION   AYLSHAM

By train You can reach Aylsham from the Broads proper by way of the quaint Bure Valley Railway (see above), which runs from Wroxham via Coltishall and other villages to a station 5min walk south of Aylsham town centre.

By bus Aylsham lies on the main bus line between Norwich and Sheringham (daily except Sun, every 30min; 40min).

Tourist office In the station (Jan–Easter & Oct–Dec daily except Wed & Sat 10am–2pm; Easter–Sept daily 10am–4.30pm; ☎ 01263 733903).

ACCOMMODATION AND EATING

IN TOWN

Black Boys Hotel Market Place, NR11 6EH ☎ 01263 732122, ⓦ blackboyshotel.co.uk. Aylsham's best pub has eight comfortable rooms upstairs, in one of which – the large Nelson suite overlooking the marketplace – the great man is said to have danced on one of the occasions he visited the town. Downstairs, the bar is cosy and the restaurant is pretty good too, as you would expect from the people who also own the nearby *Bucks Arms* (opposite) and the *Recruiting Sergeant* down the road in Coltishall (p.73). Starters cost around £6.95 and classic English mains (chargrilled pheasant, game pie, several fish options) £10.95–14.95. Mon–Sat noon–2pm & 6–9pm, Sun noon–9pm. **£65**

Old Pump House Holman Rd, NR11 6BY ☎ 01263 733789, ⓦ theoldpumphouse.com. Housed in a lovely double-fronted Georgian house with a secluded garden, this B&B has five very comfortable en-suite rooms and serves brilliant, locally sourced breakfasts. **£125**

Tinsmith's House 23 Oakfield Rd, NR11 6AL ☎ 01263 586187, ⓦ tinsmithshouse.com. This very stylish three-storey house was indeed originally the local tinsmith's and is now a highly desirable boutique B&B, with just two bright, spacious and modern rooms decorated with the owners' contemporary art. **£110**

OUT OF TOWN

Walpole Arms The Common, Itteringham, NR11 7AR ☎ 01263 587258, ⓦ thewalpolearms.co.uk. Just outside Aylsham, Itteringham's cosy old village pub has a focus on food, serving a light lunch menu during the day and a slightly heavier, more refined menu in the evening. The menu changes daily but is usually just half a dozen starters and mains, including burgers and steaks from the grill, a couple of fish dishes and a veggie option. Very good food and a nice environment in which to eat it; there are tables outside, too. Lunch mains £10–13, dinner mains £13–17, plus set lunch menus – £14 for two courses, £19.50 for three courses. Mon–Sat noon–2.30pm & 6.30–9.30pm, Sun noon–3pm.

Redwings Horse Sanctuary

Spa Lane, NR11 6UE • Mon & Fri–Sun 10am–4pm • Free • ☎ 0870 0400033, ⓦ redwings.org.uk

Just outside Aylsham is a branch of the **Redwings Horse Sanctuary**, which has its headquarters near Great Yarmouth (see p.113). The sanctuary is open all year to visitors, who can come by to see the various horses, ponies and donkeys they have rescued and taken in. There are regular tours and demonstrations, a café, shop and a play area for kids – though really the animals themselves should be enough to keep your little ones entertained.

2

Blickling Hall

Blickling, NR11 6NF • **Park** Daily dawn–dusk • Free • **House** Mid-Feb to mid-July & early Sept to Oct Wed–Sun 11am–5pm; mid-July to early Sept Mon & Wed–Sun 11am–5pm • £12.60, children £6.70, family £32.20 (includes gardens) • **Gardens** Jan to mid-Feb Thurs–Sun 11am–4pm; mid-Feb to Oct daily 10am–5.30pm; Nov & Dec Wed–Sun 11am–4pm • £8.10, children £4.50, family £23.60; NT • ☎ 01263 738030, ⓦ nationaltrust.org.uk

Built by Sir Henry Hobart in 1629 – just a couple of miles north of Aylsham, on the site of a mansion that once belonged to the Boleyn family – **Blickling Hall** is a mixed bag. It's a superb example of a Jacobean mansion from the outside, while its interior is furnished in the style of an Edwardian country house, dating from when it was the residence of the British ambassador to Washington, Lord Lothian (who bequeathed it to the National Trust in 1940). It's his portrait that oversees the dining room, laid out for dinner, but there are also examples of the Hobart family coat of arms, surmounted by the family bull – above the main entrance and on the ceiling of the Great Hall, for example. For the most part it's an "upstairs-downstairs" type of experience, with servants' quarters downstairs, where you can listen to recordings of staff who worked here in 1930 – the footman, cook, gardener; while upstairs there is a series of bedrooms, state-of-the-art 1930s bathrooms, and most impressively the **Long Room**, almost 130ft long and now a library with some ten thousand books, although it was built to suit a more modern purpose – for Sir Henry to keep fit when the weather was poor. There's also the so-called **Great Room**, home to a tapestry given to Sir Henry by Catherine the Great that was so large that the room had to be built around it. Two **Gainsborough portraits** – of the second earl and his wife – hang on either side of the fireplace.

The **grounds** of Blickling Hall incorporate formal gardens, extensive woodlands, a lake and the weird, pyramid-like mausoleum of the second earl. There's also a decent café and gift shop, a fabulous secondhand bookshop (where there's another café), a stamp shop and regular plant sales (all Jan to mid-Feb & Nov to mid-Dec Thurs–Sun 11am–4pm; mid-Feb to Oct daily 10.15am–5.30pm). The best **place to eat**, though, is the *Bucks Arms*, right outside the Hall; there are also rooms to stay in here, so you can wake up to a rather wonderful view of Blickling (see p.77).

St Andrew's, Blickling

Blickling, NR11 6NG • ⓦ blickling.churchnorfolk.com

Right by the enrance to Blickling Hall, **St Andrew's** is an many ways a typical medieval Norfolk church, with the obligatory font adorned by cheerful lions and some medieval brasses of the Boleyn family among others. It was, though, considerably renovated in the nineteenth century and has a magnificent marble tomb memorial to the eighth Lord Lothian in the nave, a bearded figure reclining on his bier with two spectacular Victorian angels tending to him.

ACCOMMODATION AND EATING   **BLICKLING**

Bucks Arms NR11 6NF ☎ 01263 732133, ⓦ bucksarms .co.uk. Right outside Blickling Hall, this welcoming gastropub has four comfortable and atmospheric rooms upstairs with four-posters and private bathrooms, two of which have wonderful views over the Hall. Downstairs retains something of the feel of a local pub: the food is high quality and local, with ciabatta sandwiches, sausage and mash and more adventurous choices like chicken and chorizo casserole, all £7.95–12.95. It does roasts on Sundays, "pie and a pint" nights on Mondays, and fish and chip suppers on Thursdays. Mon–Fri noon–2pm & 6.30–9pm, Sat noon–2.30pm & 6.30–9pm, Sun noon–2.30pm. **£100**

Wolterton Park

Wolterton Hall, Wolterton, near Erpingham, NR11 7LY

Built in the early 1700s for Horatio Walpole (brother of Britain's first prime minister), **Wolterton Park**, just outside the village of Erpingham about four miles north of Aylsham, has been empty for much of the last two centuries, and is a rather forlorn sight these days. The grounds are the real attraction, with miles of waymarked paths that lead around the lake and past the tower of the estate's ruined church, and eventually to another Walpole property, Mannington Hall, to which the Walpoles decamped in the nineteenth century. At time of writing the Hall had just been sold, and its future was unclear – watch this space.

ACCOMMODATION AND EATING   ERPINGHAM

★ **Saracen's Head** Wolterton, NR11 7LZ ☎01263 768909, ⓦsaracenshead-norfolk.co.uk. This Georgian inn is well situated for the north Norfolk coast, the Broads and the east coast, and has six nicely turned-out en-suite double bedrooms. The location – "in the middle of nowhere but centre of everywhere", say the owners Tim and Janie Elwes – feels very remote despite its convenience, and nothing is too much trouble. It has a great ground-floor restaurant, serving inventive, seasonal and above all local food – the menu even tells you how far the ingredients have travelled. Choose from pigeon and pork terrine or crispy duck salad to start, and wild sea trout or roast loin of Wolterton lamb to follow; there are usually a couple of veggie options, too. Or just have a drink in the bar or courtyard. Starters from £6.50, mains from £12. Tues–Sun noon–2.15pm & 6.30–8.30pm; Oct–June closed Tues lunchtimes. **£100**

Mannington Gardens

Mannington Hall, Itteringham, NR11 7BB • Gardens June–Aug Wed–Fri 11am–5pm, Sun noon–5pm; late May & Sept Sun noon–5pm • £6 • ⓦmanningtongardens.co.uk

Set around the moated fifteenth-century Mannington Hall, about five miles northwest of Aylsham, are lovely **Mannington Gardens**, complete with beautiful lawns and roses, fern gardens, woodland and wildflower meadows, a lake and miles of trails that link up with the Walpoles' sister estate, Wolterton Hall, about a mile away to the east (see above). There are lots of plants for sale, too.

Usually only the gounds are open to the public, but if you time it right then you may be able to visit **Mannington Hall** itself, which remains the home of Lord and Lady Walpole, the descendants of the first British prime minister. They run open days during the summer months, when Lord and Lady Walpole themselves show you around the house. Afterwards, take time out at the *Greedy Goose* tearooms (same opening hours as the hall), which serves sandwiches, cakes and cream teas with home-made jam to die for.

ACCOMMODATION   MANNINGTON HALL

Amber's Bell Tents Mannington Hall, NR11 7BB ⓦambersbelltents.co.uk. Eight bell tents in a large field just outside the main entrance to Mannington Hall, plus a beautiful shepherd's hut in a secluded enclosure in the grounds of the hall itself. The tents can comfortably sleep a family of four and have wood-burning stoves inside, plus barbecues and picnic tables outside; the shepherd's hut sleeps two and also has a wood-burner, plus a veranda and barbecue pit outside. There is a games room, a pizza oven and a sauna, toilet and shower facilities just outside the hall, and bikes for hire from the site. Tents **£115**, shepherd's hut **£99**

Alby Craft Centre

Cromer Rd, Erpingham, NR11 7QE • Tues–Sun & bank hols 10am–5pm • Free • Gardens April–Nov Tues–Sun & bank hol Mon 10am–4pm • £2.50 • ☎ 01263 768563, ⓦ albycrafts.co.uk

About five miles north of Aylsham, just outside Erpingham on the main road to Cromer, **Alby Crafts Centre** is a collection of cottages and farm buildings that have been converted into creative studios and galleries, home to a thriving complex of artists and craftspeople making and selling their products direct to the public, along with a gallery, tearoom and gift shop. It's worth a stop and a browse, particularly during summer when they open the gardens to the public – four acres of strikingly planted beds and borders set around several ponds and a small area of woodland.

St Agnes, Cawston

Cawston, NR10 4AG • Daily 9am–6pm or dusk • ⓦ st-agnes.org.uk

Around three miles west of Aylsham, the modest village of **CAWSTON** holds one of the county's most lauded churches, **St Agnes**, whose sturdy tower, built at the end of the fourteenth century on the profits of the wool trade, rises high above a dinky flint entry porch and a long line of gargoyles. The interior holds an especially fine hammerbeam roof, decorated with a solemn band of angels who are positioned as if they are on medieval diving boards. There's also a fifteenth-century carved pulpit and a medieval rood screen in unusually good condition with twenty panels of saints, including St Agnes herself – depicted with a lamb on the far left.

St Michael the Archangel, Booton

Booton, NR10 4NZ • Daily 9am–6pm or dusk • ⓦ visitchurches.org.uk

A couple of miles south of Cawston, or about seven miles southwest of Aylsham, a handful of houses make up **BOOTON**. In the nineteenth century local clergyman Whitwell Elwin made his mark here, writing copious letters to Charles Darwin about evolution – the post office even allocated him his own post box – and organizing the construction of an unusual-to-bizarre Gothic Revival church, **St Michael the Archangel** (also called St Michael's & All Angels), whose two slender towers rise high into the sky. It's now owned by the Churches Conservation Trust and is well worth a visit. It has all sorts of fancy details – the west doorway was modelled on that of Glastonbury Abbey, the figures of angels are all modelled on Elwin's female friends, and there's even a minaret. As Edwin Lutyens said at the time, "It's very naughty, but in the right spirit".

Reepham

West of Cawston, it's a short drive to **REEPHAM** (around five miles west of Aylsham), whose neat and trim marketplace is at its liveliest on Wednesday, its market day. The town holds a particularly attractive assortment of Georgian buildings and is home to an odd multiplex of churches where three parish boundaries meet. One of the churches – **All Saints** – burnt down in the eighteenth century and was left as a ruin, but the other two – **St Mary** and **St Michael** – were amalgamated in the 1930s. St Michael is more or less just a church hall with some modern stained glass in the chancel, but St Mary is a dinky medieval church with a simple Norman font from 1200, some beautifully carved back pews and a superb medieval tomb, thought to be that of one William de Kerdiston who died in 1361. There's another William de Kerdiston – probably his son, who died in 1391 – memorialized in a partially damaged brass in front of the altar; it's normally covered with a red carpet.

St Peter and St Paul, Salle

The Street, NR10 4SE • Daily 9am–5pm or dusk • ⓦ salle.churchnorfolk.com

Around five miles west of Aylsham, **SALLE** – pronounced Saul – is not much more than a village green with a terrace of cottages edging one of Norfolk's finest churches, **St Peter and St Paul**, a fifteenth-century extravagance paid for by the wool of the hundreds of sheep that used to graze nearby. Two angels wave censers above the west door and the medieval pulpit still has its original paint, although the church's finest feature is the chancel roof, supported by the wings of angels. Look out also for elaborate carving on some of the pews, and memorial brasses sunk into the floor of the nave, one of which remembers Geoffrey Boleyn, whose son purchased Blickling Hall (see p.77) and was the great-grandfather of Anne.

St Peter and St Paul, Heydon

The Street, NR11 6AD • Daily dawn–dusk • ⓦ heydon.churchnorfolk.com

Two miles north of Salle, and about five miles northwest of Aylsham, **HEYDON** is a lovely village situated quite literally at the end of the road, with nowhere to go beyond the main street and picturesque village green, backed by the imposing bulk of the church of **St Peter and St Paul** – the main reason for visiting apart from the intrinsic prettiness of the place. The owners of the estate, the Bulwers, still live next door in Heydon Hall (no public access), a large fifteenth-century mansion surrounded by a strollable **park**. The church possesses a large and imposing manorial pew, but its main items of interest are the medieval murals on the north wall: badly weathered, but you can still make out the three living and three dead figures, painted to remind the congregation of their mortality.

EATING   **HEYDON**

Earle Arms The Street, NR11 6AD ☎ 01263 587376. This traditional country pub, with its beamed ceilings, open fires and wood panelling, offers a good range of draft beers plus bar food and snacks. Mains from £10. Kitchen Tues–Sun noon–2pm & 6–8.30pm; pub Tues–Sat noon–3pm & 6–11pm, Sun noon–11pm.

Horning and around

Just three miles downriver from Wroxham, the village of **HORNING** hugs a right-angle bend in the river. It is an altogether different kettle of fish from its neighbour – equally focused on the water and the boat industry, with a long main street that leads down to boatyards and a large marina, but one of the prettiest villages on the Broads, with a buzzy vibe that attracts visitors year-round to its handful of pubs, restaurants and cafés.

The main focus is the shops and village green, and the adjacent staithe, next to which *The Swan* pub (see p.82) looks out over Horning Reach and the marshes opposite. Once you've wandered along by the river and around the village's two greens, you've more or less seen Horning, although the village extends for another mile or so east. You can wander along Horning's straggling main street, which follows the river past numerous dykes and riverfront holiday homes, to Ferry Marina, down a turning to the right, where there are more moorings where you can watch the boats coming and going while having a drink at the *Ferry Inn*. You can rent a boat here, or take the foot ferry across to the far bank, where a boarded path leads to Cockshoot Broad (see p.74).

> ### THE SOUTHERN COMFORT
>
> Just beyond *The Swan* pub, the **Southern Comfort** (Lower St, Horning, HR12 8AA; March–Nov sailings 3–4 times a day; £8, family tickets £24; ☎ 01692 630262 , ⓦ southern-comfort.co.uk) Mississippi-style riverboat sets sail several times a day in the season for Malthouse Broad and other points east. The ninety-minute round-trip is accompanied by relaxed and informative commentary and a comfily old-fashioned bar downstairs serving drinks and snacks.

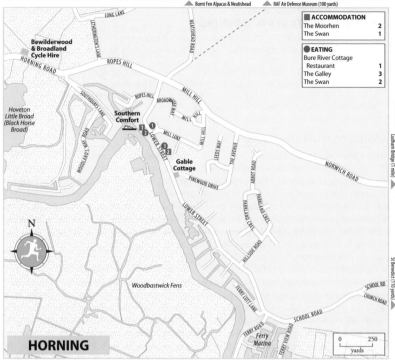

■ ACCOMMODATION	
The Moorhen	2
The Swan	1

● EATING	
Bure River Cottage Restaurant	1
The Galley	3
The Swan	2

HORNING

St Benedict

Church Rd, NR12 8PZ • ⓦ horning.churchnorfolk.com

About half a mile beyond the turn-off to Ferry Marina, a right turn by the village school leads to Horning's parish church of **St Benedict**, which enjoys a peaceful location by the river, and is worth popping into to see its fourteenth-century font, ancient priest's door and carved choir stalls, and a scale model of St Benet's Abbey (see p.84) just inside the entrance. Perhaps the most enjoyable thing, though, is the path that leads from the churchyard down to the church's own staithe – a marvellously tranquil spot among the reedbeds, where you can picnic and wave at the cruisers as they chug past.

ARRIVAL AND INFORMATION HORNING

By bus There are roughly hourly buses between Norwich and Stalham (40min), taking in Wroxham, Ludham and Potter Heigham on the way. They stop on the main road in Horning, just outside the village.

By boat There are free moorings outside *The Swan* and at the village staithe next door, and on the opposite side of the river (though you'll need to cadge a lift off someone if you want to get to the shops or the pub). There are also moorings at Ferry Marina, a 15min walk from the centre (the ones outside the *Ferry Inn* cost £10 overnight if you don't eat at the pub and the ones on the opposite bank are free); there are washing facilities, a

café, a fish and chip shop and even a swimming pool in the Helska complex in the marina. Finally there are a couple of moorings at Horning church staithe, half a mile further on – a wonderfully peaceful spot but with no facilities at all.

Cycle rental Broadland Cycle Hire, Bewilderwood, Horning Rd, NR12 8JW ☎07887 480331, ⓦnorfolk broadscycling.co.uk. Bikes from £16 a day, £60 a week; they also do rental by half-day or 2hr. They rent kids' bikes, tandems, baby seats, child trailers etc, and they have lots of maps and suggestions for local cycle routes.

2

HOLIDAY COTTAGES IN HORNING

There are tonnes of self-catering options around the village, many of them available through either **Horning Holiday Homes** (☎01692 630507, ⓦhorningholidayhomes.co.uk) or **Riverside Rentals** (☎01692 631177, ⓦriverside-rentals.co.uk). As for specific places, you could rent one of this guide's authors' beautiful holiday cottage, **Gable Cottage**, in the heart of the village (61 Lower St, NR12 8AA; ⓦnorfolkcottages.co.uk), which sleeps six. Or, if you crave a riverside location, you can't do better than the lovely **Ferry View** (Ferry View Rd, NR12 8PS; ⓦriverside-rentals.co.uk), which sleeps up to ten.

ACCOMMODATION AND EATING

★ **Bure River Cottage Restaurant** 27 Lower St, NR12 8AA ☎01692 631241, ⓦburerivercottagerestaurant.co.uk. Right opposite the pub in the centre of the village, this excellent fish restaurant run by a husband-and-wife team has a blackboard menu featuring changing specials like Brancaster mussels, pan-fried sea bream and fantastic locally smoked salmon. Not especially cheap – most starters go for £6–8, mains £13–18 – but one of the best places to eat for miles around. Tues–Sat 6–9.30pm.

★ **The Galley** 43 Lower St, NR12 8AA ☎01692 630088, ⓦthegalleyhorning.co.uk. It's hard to know what Horning residents would do without this fantastic deli and café, which specializes in high-quality produce (try the sausage rolls or home-made "Hornish" pasties) perfect for picnics and on-board lunches. The café serves coffee, sandwiches and light lunch dishes, and there's a dinky gift shop attached. Daily 10am–6pm.

★ **The Moorhen** 45 Lower St, NR12 8AA ☎01692 631444, ⓦthemoorhenhorning.co.uk. Horning is a great base for the Broads, and it has this really great B&B in the heart of the village, where Neil and Josie Grant offer a warm welcome, four very nicely furnished en-suite rooms and a fantastic breakfast. They also have a self-catering bunk-bedded cabin in the garden that sleeps five. Discounts for stays of three nights or more. £80

The Swan Inn 10 Lower St, NR12 8AA ☎01692 630316, ⓦvintageinn.co.uk/theswaninnhorning. This iconic Broads pub remains a cosy and welcoming place to this day, and does decent, reasonably priced food (starters £5–6, mains £10–15) – good burgers, steaks and decent-quality pub grub on the whole. Its outside terrace enjoys one of the best riverside views and it also has accommodation; the rooms are perfectly good, all en suite, and the best ones overlook the river. A good breakfast is included. Daily noon–9pm. £80

Bewilderwood

Horning Rd, NR12 8JW • Mid-March to Oct roughly daily 10am–5.30pm, but opening times are complex – check the website • Adults and children over 105cm £12, children 92–105cm £9, children under 92cm free • ☎01692 783900, ⓦbewilderwood.co.uk

Just outside Horning, off the main Wroxham road, **Bewilderwood** is one of the newest and biggest local attractions, a homespun theme park based on a series of books by local author Tom Blofeld. It's the reedy, watery world of the Broads brought to life, both a land of make-believe based on characters in the books and an oversized adventure playground, with rope bridges and ladders, treehouses and zip lines, all connected by boardwalks, forest paths and boats. It's pretty popular in summer, and might be worth avoiding on bank holiday weekends, but its mixture of spooky fantasy and adventure has something for kids of all ages, and there's a wittiness to the whole thing that's refreshing and fun. It has a policy of sustainability too, with everything made of wood, rope and other ecologically sound resources, though the undeniable wholesomeness of it all harks back to an age before such things seemed important.

RAF Air Defence Radar Museum

RRH Neatishead, NR12 8YB • April–Nov Tues & Thurs 10am–5pm; year-round second Sat of each month 10am–5pm • £8 • Guided tours every half-hour 10.30am–3pm; free • ☎01692 631485, ⓦradarmuseum.co.uk

Just north of Horning (a 10min walk from the village if you're on foot), RAF Neatishead shut down in 2004, but the buildings host the **RAF Air Defence Radar Museum**, a labyrinth of rooms and corridors that was a key centre of operations during World War II, and during the Cold War years too. There are rooms devoted to the Battle of Britain and a replica of the operations room at Neatishead in 1942, but the highlight is undoubtedly the Cold War operations room, which monitored most of the UK's airspace in the 1950s and 1960s and has been left pretty much as it was then, with banks of screens and a board on which operatives mastered the art of writing backwards. Next door a room remembers the glory days of nearby RAF Coltishall, which closed in 2006.

Burnt Fen Alpacas

Garden Cottage, Burnt Fen Rd, NR12 8LA • Visits by appointment only, £50 per group • ☎ 01692 630553, ⓦ burntfen.co.uk

A five-minute walk from Horning village, **Burnt Fen Alpacas** is a working alpaca farm that offers walks around their property including their own private broad with their herd of alpacas – great for kids who get to pet and feed these gentle creatures. Tours conclude with a coffee and a look in the owners' studio, where they make all sorts of things with alpaca wool – everything from woolly socks and hats to alpaca and silk scarves. They also run regular crafting courses working with alpaca wool in their own Mongolian yurt.

Barton Broad and Neatishead

The **River Ant** runs from the Bure in the south up to **Wayford Bridge** (see p.90) in the north, a meandering, roughly four-mile stretch that is one of the region's most picturesque. You could stop off at **How Hill** (see p.86) or **Irstead** staithes before reaching the wide expanse of **Barton Broad**, second largest of the Broads and recently dredged of the heavy silt and algae that was clogging it up as both a waterway and wildlife zone. Now fully restored to health, it's a beautiful spot: by boat you can follow the channel of Lime Kiln Dyke off to the left all the way down to the village of **NEATISHEAD**, where there is a shop and a good local pub – the *White Horse* (see below).

There are free moorings about 400yd from the village centre, left off the main road, and also half a mile or so further on at **Gay's Staithe**. Across the road from here is the car park for **Barton Boardwalk**, a ten-minute walk away across the fields, which is the best way of seeing the broad and its wildlife on foot, from various viewing platforms.

EATING   **NEATISHEAD**

White Horse Inn The Street, NR12 8AD ☎ 01692 630828, ⓦ thewhitehorseinnneatishead.com. This long-running local had a major revamp in 2014 and is now a fab gastropub with its own brewery. Unsurprisingly its range of beers is second to none, with lots of brews besides their own, and the food is varied and reliably good – everything from burgers (£8.95), steaks, sea bass and lamp rump to basics like fish and chips or sausage and mash, plus veggie risottos and burgers, all for £15 or less. Kitchen daily noon–9pm in summer.

Alderfen Broad

Daily dawn–dusk • Free • ⓦ norfolkwildlifetrust.org.uk

You can do a good and pretty easy circular walk from Neatishead down to the picturesque **Alderfen Broad**, an NWT-run nature reserve, about half a mile to the south. A path winds from a small jetty through the trees around its western edge, after which you can pick up the road that heads back north towards Neatishead – maybe an hour's walk in all.

Ludham and around

About three miles east of Horning, **LUDHAM** is a quiet Broadland village which clusters around a bend in the main road. It's home to a pub and tearooms, and has a good village shop, **Throwers** (☎ 01692 678248, ⓦ throwers.co.uk). It also has free moorings at **Womack Staithe**, five minutes' walk from the centre of the village, at the end of a long inlet of the Thurne River, and there are nice walks in the marshes roundabouts.

St Catherine

High St, NR29 5AB • Daily dawn–dusk • ⓦ ludham.churchnorfolk.com

The main thing to see in Ludham is the church of **St Catherine**, for once bang in the centre of the village. The late fifteenth-century building has a wooden beamed roof and a painted rood screen that is one of the finest in the county – beautifully preserved, with its ranks of saints on one side and Queen Elizabeth I's coat of arms on the other, added hastily on her accession to the throne in 1558. In the north aisle, the mangled old alms chest also dates from the mid-sixteenth century, while the font at the back of the church is late fifteenth century, carved with figures of the Evangelists and images of wild men and – unusually – wild women, clad in skins and carrying clubs.

ARRIVAL AND INFORMATION   LUDHAM

By bus Buses roughly hourly from Wroxham/Hoveton (15min), Horning and Potter Heigham stop in the centre of the village.

By boat Ludham's staithe, with free moorings, is a 5min walk from the village centre at the head of Womack Water, where there is also a shop and other facilities.

EATING

Al Fresco Tea Rooms Norwich Rd, NR29 5QA ☎ 01692 678384. Right in the centre of the village opposite the church, this is the place in Ludham for morning coffee, light lunches and afternoon tea and cakes. Good cream teas too. Tues–Fri 10am–4pm, Sat & Sun 11am–5pm.

The King's Arms High St, NR29 5QQ ☎ 01692 678386, ⓦ kingsarmsludham.co.uk. Right on the bend in the road, *The King's Arms* is both a good locals' pub and a reasonable venue for food, with a very large menu. Mon–Sat 11.30am–midnight, Sun noon–midnight.

Ludham Bridge

The main road from Horning to Ludham crosses the River Ant at **LUDHAM BRIDGE**, about a mile from Ludham proper, where there's a straggle of houses, a couple of shops and a gallery (see p.87), plus free moorings and a boatyard. You can follow a footpath north along the river for about a mile and a half and double back to *The Dog* **pub** on the main road (see p.86) – perhaps an hour's walk in all. *The Dog* also has a small **campsite** during the summer months.

St Benet's Abbey

St Benet's Rd, NR29 5NU • Daily 24hr • Guided tours May–Sept Wed 2pm, Sat & Sun 3pm • Free • ⓦ stbenetsabbey.org

A turning just past Ludham Bridge leads down to the ruins of **St Benet's Abbey**, which date back to the twelfth century, although they are dwarfed by the remains of the windmill a local farmer built behind the abbey gatehouse six centuries later. There are moorings here for boats, and this is probably the best way to get here – following in the footsteps of the Bishop of Norwich who still arrives here by water with much pomp and ceremony for an annual ecumenical service every August. The abbey feels isolated even today, but it was even more so before the surrounding marshes were drained,

---

EDWARD SEAGO

Ludham was the home of the artist **Edward Seago** (1910–74), not exactly a household name nowadays but an accomplished painter of oils and watercolours that depict the Broads and other parts of Norfolk. He was a favourite of the royal family's, in particular the Queen Mother, to whom he donated two paintings a year. He lived at the **Dutch House**, down Staithe Road on the left, and created a wonderful garden there that stretches down to Womack Water and is open to the public on selected days during June and July under the National Gardens Scheme or by appointment (☎ 01692 678225, ⓦ ngs.org.uk).

2

when it was, in effect, situated on an island. The abbey was originally a Saxon foundation that prospered throughout the Middle Ages, when it was the greatest landowner hereabouts, until the mid-sixteenth century and the Dissolution. It's still a sacred site but apart from the bishop's annual visit remains a fairly bleak spot, and you need a fair amount of imagination to re-create the thriving monastic life that once was based here.

ACCOMMODATION AND EATING   LUDHAM BRIDGE

The Dog Johnson St, NR29 5NY ☎ 01692 630321, ⓦ thedoginnludham. The closest pub to Ludham Bridge, and good enough, with a decent selection of ales and food plus regular live music. It also has a small adjacent campsite open all year round. Daily noon–3pm & 6–9pm. **£8**

Hall Farm Cottages Hall Farm, NR12 8NJ ☎ 01692 630385, ⓦ hallfarm.com. A beautiful grouping of holiday cottages in a peaceful location well off the main road near Ludham Bridge, and handy for both Horning and Ludham. Dog-friendly too. Half a dozen cottages in all, sleeping anything from two to seven people. One week from **£296**

How Hill

Norfolk Broads Study Centre, NR29 5PG • Gardens June–Oct daily 11am–4pm; rest of year weekends only • Free, but donations encouraged • ☎ 01692 67855, ⓦ howhilltrust.org.uk

Just outside Ludham, the Arts and Crafts-style mansion of **How Hill** was designed and built by architect Thomas Boardman in 1904 as his family home, and enjoys an enviable position perched on a hummock overlooking the River Ant and the adjoining woods and marshes. These days it's occupied by the How Hill Trust, which runs all sorts of residential courses pertaining to Broadland – on birds and wildlife, art, gardens and walks – and oversees the extensive grounds and gardens. There's a public staithe with lots of moorings and it's a nice place to stop off, especially if you're water-borne. You can visit Toad Hole Cottage (see below), and walk parts of How Hill's grounds on various loops, including the gardens for the displays of azaleas and rhododendrons, or just follow the river downstream for a short while.

Toad Hole Cottage

How Hill, NR29 5PG • April, May & Oct Mon–Fri 10.30am–1pm & 1.30–5pm, Sat & Sun 10.30am–5pm; June–Sept daily 9.30am–6pm • Free

The one building on the estate that's open to the public is **Toad Hole Cottage**, a marshman's cottage down near the river that was occupied until the early twentieth century, after which it was used as a playhouse by the Boardman children (it was the Boardman brood who named it). It was restored in the 1980s and now serves as a Broads National Park information centre, beautifully and authentically kept in the style of the marshfolk who would have occupied it in the eighteenth century, with a stocked larder and living room with wood-burning stove and various tools for reed cutting, eel catching and rabbit foraging. The two upstairs bedrooms have hot water bottles to combat the winter winds off the reedbeds, and the picture on the living room mantelpiece is of the last person to occupy the house, along with his wife and two children, until his death in 1910.

THE ELECTRIC EEL

How Hill's Toad Hole Cottage has a little shop and Broads Information Centre that sells tickets for trips on board the **Electric Eel** (April, May & Oct Sat & Sun hourly 11am–3pm; June–Sept daily hourly 10am–4pm; £7, family tickets £19.50; ☎ 01692 756096), which leaves from the staithe just beyond. These last just under an hour and are an absolute delight, taking you deep into the marshes on the far side of the Ant, a beautiful trip through narrow channels and dykes fringed by high reeds. You get out to walk (or sometimes wade) to nearby Reedham Water, where you can spot birds from a hide, and the guide provides binoculars and lots of background on the wildlife and unique vegetation you can see.

A BRUSH WITH THE BROADS

Ludham Bridge is home to local artist Linda Matthews' excellent **Broad Skies Gallery** (Tues–Sat 10am–5pm; ☎ 01692 630845, ⓦ broadskiesgallery.co.uk), which displays her own oil and watercolour scenes of Broadland, Norfolk and France, along with the work of other local artists. It's a lovely place, with a small café and lots of space to browse, and offers drawing and painting **courses** (ⓦ paintncanvasholidays.co.uk), often based at the Waveney River Centre (see p.119) or Clippesby Hall (see p.97), among other places. Linda also runs the brilliant **Brush with the Broads** festival of plein-air painting every September (ⓦ abrushwiththe broads.co.uk), the only event of its type in the UK.

2

ACCOMMODATION   **HOW HILL**

How Hill Windmill The Mill House, NR29 5PG ☎ 01692 678575, ⓦ norfolkholidaywindmill.co.uk. Its sails have gone, but this early nineteenth-century grain mill still makes an atmospheric place to stay, sleeping four in a large living area and two small upstairs bedrooms. One week from **£625**

Potter Heigham and around

It's a pity, but **POTTER HEIGHAM**, on the Thurne River, is one of the Broads' least attractive villages, split in two by the A149 and with a riverside area (the bit that most people see) dominated by the car parks and unalluring buildings of various boatyards. Prominent among these is Herbert Woods, who have been based in Potter since the youngish Woods took over the family boatbuilding business in 1929 and are still thriving today; their purpose-built Broads Haven headquarters can be seen for miles around. Otherwise there's not much to see apart from **Lathams** discount store, which sells pretty much anything you might want, and the village's famous medieval **bridge**, which dates from 1385 and is so low that it is almost impossible to get through without a pilot, or indeed at all at high tide.

St Nicholas

Church Rd, NR29 5LE • ⓦ norfolkchurches.co.uk

The only other structure of note in Potter Heigham is the church of **St Nicholas**, on the edge of the more attractive part of the village, across the A149, a ten-minute walk away from the riverside. It's a thatched building with a distinctive round, crenellated tower and a hammerbeam roof, below which is a series of fourteenth-century wall paintings, including a startlingly naturalistic series depicting the Seven Acts of Mercy. The churchyard is very peaceful, and there are some good circular walks you can do from here, down to the edges of Hickling Broad and back.

ARRIVAL AND DEPARTURE   **POTTER HEIGHAM**

By bus Potter Heigham is connected by roughly hourly buses with North Walsham (40min), Stalham (20min) and Great Yarmouth (40min) and less frequently with Ludham, Horning and Hoveton.

By boat There are free moorings on either side of the old bridge at Potter Heigham. If you have a craft wider than about 3m or higher than 2.3m you won't get under Potter Heigham's bridge at all. In any case, you should only try it at low tide, take it very slowly, and head for the central point.

Hickling Broad

Hickling Broad Nature Reserve, NR12 0BW • Daily 10am–5pm • Non-NWT members £4 • **Visitor centre** Easter–Sept & Oct half-term daily 10am–5pm; rest of Oct weekends only • **Boat trips** £6.50 for 1hr trips, £8.50 for 2hr • ☎ 01692 598276, ⓦ norfolkwildlifetrust.org.uk

Those boating folk who manage to negotiate the bridge at Potter Heigham finish up eventually on **Hickling Broad**, a mile or so to the north, the largest broad of all and

2

NOWT SO QUEER AS HICKLING BROAD FOLK

Hickling Broad has attracted a colourful cast of characters over the years. Wildlife photographer and ornithologist **Emma Turner** lived here during the early part of the twentieth century, part of the time on an island in the middle of the Broad – still known as "Turner's Island" – and the rest in a nearby houseboat of her own design. She became known for her 1911 picture of a bittern – the first evidence that they weren't extinct in Britain – and later published a book about the birds of the Broads. Wildlife artist **Roland Green** was another who was captivated by the Broad and its surroundings: he lived in a disused wind pump here until his death in 1972, and spent years painting the geese, ducks and kingfishers he observed on the water. Whiteslea Lodge, right on the water and the property of the Cadbury family for many years now, has a number of his paintings, commissioned by one Lord Desborough in the 1930s. You can get a good view of it from the tower among the trees on the opposite bank, which is accessible on the Weavers' Way long-distance path, which skirts the Broad, and also on the NWT's boat trips.

location of a Norfolk Wildlife Trust-managed nature reserve on its eastern edge. Hickling is the Broads at its very best, a large expanse of water fringed by reedbeds which is home to some of the area's best and rarest wildlife – if you're going to see a swallowtail butterfly or a bittern, the odds are it will be here. It's also sublimely peaceful, and getting out on its shallow waters and paddling among its reedy fringes, preferably in a canoe or a rowing boat, is a joy.

You can access the edge of the broad by way of Staithe Road from the edge of **Hickling village**; there are moorings and a car park here and you can follow the path along the dyke down to a picnic spot by the water, although most people come to this part of the broad for the sailing club next door or to visit the **Pleasure Boat Inn** (see below) on the left.

You can also access the Broad by following the path from the *Pleasure Boat Inn* car park half a mile or so to the **NWT visitor centre** and car park, where you can buy tickets to enter the nature reserve. There are marked tracks through the reserve which take in stretches of reedbed, woodland and of course the banks of the broad, where there are bird hides for spotting marsh harriers, cormorants, herons and the elusive bitterns. One- and two-hour **boat trips** run from a landing stage down on the broad and are fantastic, taking you all around the broad, getting off at various points along the way and visiting a 60ft-high treehouse that gives predictably great views. By car, the visitor centre and nature reserve are reachable by taking the long muddy track a mile or so down Stubb Road, which leads off from beside *The Greyhound* pub (see below) in the centre of the village.

ACCOMMODATION AND EATING   HICKLING

★**Dairy Barns** Lound Farm, Hickling Lane, NR12 0BE ☎01692 598243, ⓦdairybarns.co.uk. Just outside Hickling – a stone's throw from the sea at Sea Palling – is this standout Broadland B&B, a working farm with nine boutiquey rooms that are spacious and well equipped, with flatscreen TVs, posh toiletries and power showers. They also have two lovely self-contained cottages for rent. Breakfasts are great and served in a beautiful converted barn. Very friendly and superb value. **£75**

The Greyhound The Green, NR12 0YA ☎01692 598306, ⓦgreyhoundinn.com. Right in the centre of Hickling village, this is a proper village pub, with both a very warm welcome and excellent food – steaks, burgers, fish and chips and posher options (Gressingham

duck, stuffed chicken) for £10–12, as well as sandwiches and bar snacks. Kitchen daily noon–2.30pm & 5.30–9pm.

Pleasure Boat Inn Staithe Rd, NR12 0YW ☎01692 598870, ⓦthepleasureboat.com. Owned by the same people who run the *Nelson Head* in Horsey (see p.104), this long-running pub enjoys a great location right on Hickling Broad staithe (free moorings available). It serves decent pub food, from both a simple bar menu – fish and chips, burgers, ham, egg and chips, home-made pies, ploughman's, filled baguettes – for £8–10, and a more refined evening menu of sea bass, steaks, duck breasts etc, for around £12. Kitchen daily noon–2.30pm & 5.30–8pm.

Stalham and around

A couple of miles east of Wayford Bridge, the centre of **STALHAM** has seen better days, and locals peg its relative demise to the opening of Tesco here a few years ago – after years of being refused planning permission. Despite that, the farmers' market is still going strong, twice a month on Saturday mornings at Stalham town hall, there's a general market on Tuesdays in the centre, and the high street is still a fairly attractive stretch with all the amenities you could need. Like Potter, though, the town is split in two by the A149, with the staithe and boatyards a short walk away on the opposite side of the main road.

St Mary's

High St, NR12 9AU • ⓦ stalhambenefice.org.uk/stalham

Stalham's parish church of **St Mary** has had a stunted tower since its belfry collapsed in the sixteenth century; the bells were sold to the Dutch after this catastrophe, but the ship carrying them went down with all hands and it's said that the bells can still be heard tolling when a storm is forecast. Inside, the church has a lovely, very well preserved fifteenth-century font, carved with the Trinity on one side and the baptism of Christ on the other, and images of the apostles around the bowl.

The Museum of the Broads

The Staithe, NR12 9DA • **Museum** Easter–Oct daily 10.30am–5pm • £5, family tickets £13 • **Falcon boat trips** Tues–Thurs on the hour 11am–3pm • £4, families £12 • ☏ 01692 581681, ⓦ museumofthebroads.org.uk

There are a couple of boatyards, notably Richardsons, across the main road from the centre at Stalham Staithe, close to which the **Museum of the Broads** does a good if somewhat nostalgic job of summarizing the uniqueness of Broadland. You can climb into the cabin of a wherry, while other sheds have displays on the history of the Broads, its wildlife and its tourism, even on Roys of Wroxham (see p.65). There are plenty of historic craft on display, too, including an old commissioner's launch, various reedlighters, dinghies and other sailing vessels. From Tuesdays to Thursdays you can also take a trip on the museum's Victorian steam launch, the *Falcon*.

ARRIVAL AND DEPARTURE   STALHAM

By bus Buses stop on the main road and link Stalham roughly hourly to Cromer (1hr) and Great Yarmouth (1hr), North Walsham (20min), Wroxham (40min) and Norwich (1hr).

By boat There are free moorings at Stalham's town staithe, across the A149 by the Museum of the Broads.

ACCOMMODATION AND EATING

Hunsett Mill Chapel Field, NR12 9EL ☏ 01485 211022, ⓦ hunsettmill.co.uk. On the banks of the River Ant, just outside Stalham and a mile or so north of Barton Broad, this converted mill house – next to a listed nineteenth-century drainage mill – is the perfect Broads self-catering retreat, and the winner of various awards for the boldness of its design (it was also one of Kevin McCloud's favourites on *Grand Designs*). It sleeps up to nine people in its five bedrooms, and enjoys a wonderfully secluded waterside location. One week around £2500

The Mermaid's Slipper The Staithe, NR12 9BY ☏ 01692 580808, ⓦ the-mermaids-slipper.co.uk. Right by the water at Stalham Staithe, this is perhaps Stalham's

best place to eat, housed in a converted barn and serving a wide-ranging menu of fresh, well-cooked food – mostly meat dishes such as pork medallions, lamb shanks and steaks – with starters and desserts for £6.95 and mains for £16.95. The service is pretty good, too. Wed–Sat 6.30–9pm, Sun 12.30–3pm.

The Swan Inn 90 High St, NR12 9AU ☏ 01692 582829, ⓦ stalhamswan.co.uk. The heartbeat of Stalham is not Tesco's but *The Swan*, which has been well updated and serves coffee and pastries in the morning and decent pub food at lunchtime and evenings, including all the pub classics, burgers, pasta dishes and a good kids' menu. Main meals around £10 but plenty for less. Free wi-fi. Kitchen daily noon–9pm.

Sutton

Just south of Stalham, **SUTTON** is a sprawling village with its own staithe, again on the far side of the A149, where there are free moorings and sustenance and **accommodation** at the *Sutton Staithe Hotel* (see below), and **canoe rental** from **Sutton Staithe Boatyard** (£20 for 3hr, £30 for 6hr; ☎01692 581 653, ⓦsuttonstaitheboatyard.co.uk).

Sutton Pottery

Church Rd, NR12 9SG • Mon–Fri 9am–6pm • ☎01692 580595, ⓦsuttonpottery.com

The main thing to visit in the village is the **Sutton Pottery** where Malcolm Flatman throws – and sells – his own unique style of pots and invites you in to watch, buy and indeed learn to make your own, with regular three-hour lessons and residential courses.

2

ACCOMMODATION	SUTTON
Sutton Staithe Hotel Sutton Staithe, NR12 9QS ☎01692 583156, ⓦsuttonstaithehotel.co.uk. A good location right on the staithe and twelve decent if fairly	basic en-suite rooms. It also serves food and drink to the hungry boaters moored at the staithe and shows football on its big TV screen. **£65**

Holy Trinity Church, Ingham

Ingham, NR12 9AB • ⓦingham.churchnorfolk.com

About a mile east of Stalham, there's nothing much to the village of **INGHAM**, but its church of **Holy Trinity** is a beautiful, soaring Gothic building from the early fourteenth century, with a light interior and a number of carved effigy tombs contemporary with the building. One, unfortunately defaced and graffitied, is of **Roger du Bois** and his wife Margaret, who died in 1300 and 1315 respectively; in the choir is an effigy of another medieval aristocrat, **Sir Oliver de Ingham**, a more flamboyantly posed figure, again rather damaged, oddly nestling on a bed of pebbles, although there's a better example of this in Reepham (see p.79).

ACCOMMODATION AND EATING	INGHAM
The Star School Rd, Lessingham, NR12 0DN ☎01692 580510, ⓦthestarlessingham.co.uk. Just outside the village of Lessingham, a mile or so north of Ingham, this is a really friendly pub with a big fireplace in the bar and a more formal restaurant out the back. It specializes in good-quality pub grub – various steaks, gammon, Norfolk sausages with mustard mash – for £10–15; always lots of veggie options too. Dog-friendly. Tues–Sat noon–2.15pm & 6–8.30pm, Sun noon–2.30pm.	four en-suite rooms in the converted stable block. Nice rooms furnished in a crisp, modern style, a marvellously peaceful location and, as you might expect, an excellent breakfast served next door. The pub's menu changes regularly but is short and well considered, with around half a dozen starters and mains – think Cromer crab salad with King's Lynn brown shrimps, or pork belly crackling with apple boudin and pulled pork fritter followed by pan-roast sea bass with samphire. Prices are moderate to high – starters £7–9 and mains £15–
The Swan Sea Palling Rd, NR12 9AB ☎01692 581099, ⓦtheinghamswan.co.uk. This ancient coaching inn is now an upscale gastropub run by chef-patron Daniel Smith, with	25 – but they do good-value lunch and dinner menus and a lovely two- or three-course Sunday lunch. Tues–Sun 11.30am–3pm & 6–11pm. **£105**

Wayford Bridge

Following the River Ant north from Barton Broad takes you eventually to **Wayford Bridge**, the navigable northern limit, where you can rent a canoe from **Bank Boats** (£23 for 3hr, £35 for 3–6hr, £48 for 24hr; ☎01692 582457, ⓦbankboats.co.uk) if you want to go further north on the North Walsham & Dilham Canal (see p.93); only non-powered boats are allowed on the canal up to Honing and Smallburgh.

ACCOMMODATION	WAYFORD BRIDGE
Wayford Bridge Inn NR12 9LL ☎01692 583259, ⓦnorfolkbroadsinns.co.uk. This old standby has fifteen	nicely furnished if slightly bland en-suite rooms (mostly doubles, but also a couple of twins and a family room) amid

comfy public areas and a good restaurant. Despite being acquired a few years back by Marco Pierre White, it hasn't changed all that much, and who knows now if it ever will? Decent enough value though, and a good location. **£85**

North Walsham and around

The small market town of **NORTH WALSHAM** was at the centre of the Norfolk weaving trade in the Middle Ages, its light Walsham cloth bringing huge prosperity to the town in the fourteenth and fifteenth centuries. It's a pleasant if unexciting little place, life as ever revolving around the lead-topped **Market Cross** at the end of the High Street, built in 1602 after a fire gutted most of the town centre. The town has a couple of good places to stay and to eat, which is a bonus because there are a number of attractions in the countryside around – and of course it's only three miles or so from the coast at Mundesley (see p.98).

St Nicholas

Market Place, NR28 9BT • ⓦ saint-nicholas.org.uk

Just off the Market Place are the peaceful precincts of the church of **St Nicholas**, the largest parish church in Norfolk. It was built on the proceeds of the fourteenth-century wool trade, when its vast rood screen would have filled the width of the building, though now only the bottom painted panels of this survive. There's an elaborate Paston family memorial in the high altar – they once owned a lot of North Walsham, and much else besides in the area (see p.99) – and the interior is impressive for its sheer size, although sadly not much else survives and the once-grand tower is a ruin. However, when it was built it was second in height in the county only to Norwich Cathedral.

The Cat Pottery

1 Grammar School Rd, NR28 0DS • Mon–Fri 9.30am–5pm, Sat 11am–1pm • Free • ☎ 01692 402962

While you're wandering around the centre of North Walsham, look in on the **Cat Pottery**, an eccentric collection of railway paraphernalia and hand-crafted pottery cats (with the odd dog and rabbit thrown in), housed in a ramshackle collection of cottages and outbuildings.

Norfolk Motorcycle Museum

Station Yard, NR28 1JH • Daily 10am–4.30pm, closed Sun Oct–Easter • £4 • ☎ 01692 406266, ⓦ mc-museum.freeserve.co.uk

Across the main road and opposite North Walsham station, the **Norfolk Motorcycle Museum** is a curious and higgledy-piggledy collection of British bikes numbering over a hundred machines, the oldest of which date back to the 1920s. An affectionate memorial to a vanished industry, gathered together in a project of lunatic dedication by an enthusiastic founder, who may well be on hand to dispense bike wisdom.

Davenport's Magic Kingdom

108 Cromer Rd, NR28 0NB • Open Feb–Dec; see website for precise opening times • £11, children £8, family tickets £35 • ☎ 01692 405254, ⓦ davenportsmagickingdom.co.uk

Rather unprepossessingly housed in a giant warehouse on the outskirts of town, **Davenport's Magic Kingdom** is a relative newcomer among North Walsham's attractions – basically a collection of magic memorabilia from across the ages run by Roy Davenport, the great-grandson of a famous magician and purveyor of magic paraphernalia in late nineteenth-century London. Exhibits include re-creations of items used by Houdini, a "puzzle zone", a mock-up of the original shop and plenty more, and there are regular magic shows and a well-stocked, up-to-date magic shop for aspiring conjurors to browse.

ARRIVAL AND DEPARTURE
NORTH WALSHAM

By train North Walsham's station is a short walk from the town centre, just across the A149. It's on the Bittern Line, with roughly hourly connections to Norwich (30min) and Hoveton (12min) in one direction, and to Cromer (18min) and Sheringham (30min) in the other.

By bus North Walsham is a hub for a lot of local bus routes

– to Norwich (every 30min; 1hr), Aylsham (every 2hr; 25min), Cromer (hourly; 40min), Mundesley (hourly; 20min), Stalham (hourly; 20min) and Great Yarmouth (hourly; 1hr 20min), among others. Buses stop at the train station, outside Roys department store and at other locations around the town centre.

ACCOMMODATION AND EATING

IN TOWN

★**Beechwood Hotel** 20 Cromer Rd, NR28 0HD ☎01692 403231, ⌖ beechwood-hotel.co.uk. There's one very good reason to stay in North Walsham, and that's Don Birch and Lindsay Spalding's lovely boutique hotel, whose seventeen very comfortable rooms hark back to the days of Agatha Christie, who was a regular guest here when it was a private house. There's lots of Christie memorabilia, and just a hint of the country-house murder mystery about the place, but the easy affability of the hotel soon kicks this into touch. The annexe has four more contemporary rooms, there's a cosy bar and a lovely garden out the back, and the great restaurant serves a "ten-mile" dinner menu, using ingredients sourced no more than ten miles from the hotel. Service is first class, as is the food – the fixed-price menu is good value for three courses (£40). The menu changes regularly, but if you can, try the loin of Norfolk lamb on dauphinoise potatoes or fillet of beef with horseradish mash. They also do a good Sunday-lunch menu for £26. Mon–Sat 6.45–8.45pm, Sun noon–2.30pm & 6.45–8.45pm. **£100**

The Olive Tree 1 Bacton Rd, NR28 0RA ☎01692 404900, ⌖ theolivetreenorfolk.com. Incongruously located in a caravan and chalet park on the edge of town, this restaurant isn't the sort of place to benefit from passing traffic, but features slick presentation and an airy contemporary dining room, which opens onto a swimming pool. Also, of course, there's the food, which is very good, served from either a simple lunch menu – burgers, fish and chips, pasta (all around £11) – or a more varied dinner menu, featuring sea bass, salmon, rib-eye steaks and lots of pasta and risotto dishes (mains around £13.95–17.95). Lovely desserts, too, for around £5: try the chocolate taster (chocolate three ways, basically) or the Norfolk cheeseboard. Look out for the all-day summer Saturday barbecues outside on the patio. Tues 6–8.45pm, Wed–Sun 12.45–2.45pm & 6–8.45pm.

Scarborough Hill Hotel Old Yarmouth Rd, NR28 9NA ☎01692 402151, ⌖ arlingtonhotelgroup.co.uk /scarhill. A mile or so south of the town centre, this small country house-style hotel is an extremely peaceful place to stay, and although some of its rooms could do with a little TLC, they're large and well furnished, and the public areas have a pleasingly homely feel. It feels miles from anywhere, but North Walsham isn't far away, and the bar is comfortable and the restaurant reasonable. **£80**

OUT OF TOWN

The Green House B&B North Walsham Rd, Thorpe Market, NR11 8TH ☎01263 834701, ⌖ greenhouse norfolk.co.uk. This lovely old flint house right on picturesque Thorpe Market's village green has five very nicely furnished, spacious rooms, with large, recently refurbished bathrooms, a big and comfy downstairs sitting room with honesty bar and large adjacent breakfast room. The garden out the back has an almost Mediterranean feel and the decor is a pleasing mix of classic and contemporary, the walls decorated with the owner's collection of cartoons. **£80**

★**Gunton Arms** Cromer Rd, Thorpe Market, NR11 8TZ ☎01263 832010, ⌖ theguntonarms.co.uk. Owned by a London art dealer, and decorated with his edgy contemporary art collection, this estate pub has eight rooms upstairs, all en-suite, ranging from small well-priced doubles to grander "superior" rooms, most of which have views over the adjacent deer park – and occasionally of the herd that provides the ingredients for the steaks and sausages in the fab downstairs restaurant. The menu changes regularly and the cooking is excellent, portions hearty, and the vibe very convivial indeed. Good, English cooking at its best, and one of the standout places in the county. Starters £7.50–12.50, mains £13–23. Bar food noon–10pm; restaurant noon–3pm & 6–10pm. **£95**

Worstead

Like North Walsham, **WORSTEAD**, about three miles south, was at the heart of Norfolk's medieval wool and weaving trade and its name survives in the close-textured woollen cloth that originated here. These days it's no more than a small village, but its large church of **St Mary** epitomizes the wealth and strength of the wool trade, and still boasts a few remnants of its fourteenth-century heyday – a painted rood screen and a beautiful hammerbeam roof, although like North Walsham's church, its size is the most notable feature.

Before you move on, have a drink and maybe a bite to eat at **The White Lady**, virtually next door to the church, just off the main square, which also has rooms (see below). Another good reason to visit is **Worstead Festival** (ⓦworsteadfestival.org), a music and arts affair that takes over the entire village for a weekend in late July.

ACCOMMODATION AND EATING   **WORSTEAD**

The White Lady Front St, NR28 9RW ☎01692 535391, ⓦthewhitelady.co.uk. This village pub has five large and comfortably furnished double rooms upstairs, all with en-suite bathrooms (one with a bath). The rooms are nicely furnished and comfortable, and Worstead a good location, handy for both the Broads and the coast. The pub downstairs is a slightly spartan affair, but a friendly joint, with a good choice of real ales, especially local varieties (including Humpty Dumpty brews on tap), and pub grub – steaks, excellent burgers, "Hunter's Chicken", sandwiches and hot baguettes. Mon–Sat noon–2pm & 6–9pm, Sun noon–3pm. **£80**

Honing

About four miles southeast of North Walsham, across the other side of the A149 from Worstead, **HONING** is an attractive village whose church of **St Peter and Paul**, with its elegant high tower, occupies a lovely location on a hill just outside the village, and whose centre is mainly made up of the woods of **Honing Common**. The **North Walsham & Dilham Canal** runs right through its centre, a now disused waterway that was built to extend the navigability of the Ant as far as North Walsham in the early nineteenth century. It was never much of a success and is only properly navigable from Honing down to Smallburgh and Wayford Bridge, both about three miles south, where you can rent **canoes**, but its banks and bridges make the village an even more appealing spot.

East Ruston Vicarage Garden

East Ruston, NR12 9HN • Late March to late Oct Wed–Sun & bank hols 1–5.30pm • £8, children £1, tours £40 per person • ☎01692 650432, ⓦe-ruston-oldvicaragegardens.co.uk

The best thing to see in the area around North Walsham is **East Ruston Vicarage Garden**, created by Alan Gray and Graham Robeson in the early 1970s out of nothing. Gray and Robeson have worked miracles with the thirty-acre site, which isn't even well suited to gardening, and their fantasies and themes dominate throughout – a woodland area, overlooked by East Ruston's church, the dry, stony yet lush Arizona garden, several walled and sunken gardens, and the King's Walk, whose yew obelisks lead right up to the vicarage itself. It's everything a garden should be: escapist, calming and always surprising, and so cleverly planned that even its increasing popularity has not diminished its charms, with the crowds easily swallowed up by the garden's nooks and corners. It's easy to get lost but that's part of the joy of the place, and once you've emerged you can enjoy tea and cake at the café and maybe buy a plant or two before you leave. They run guided tours every month; check the website for details.

THE PASTON WAY AND PIGNEYS WOOD

The **Paston Way** footpath starts in North Walsham, from St Nicholas Church, and follows the Mundesley road out of town, east to the coast and then up to Cromer. It's a lovely path and its early stretches provide a good stroll into the countryside beyond North Walsham, following an old railway line to **Pigneys Wood** (ⓦpigneyswood.co.uk), home to a 450-year-old oak tree and a number of marked walking trails and picnic areas. Walking out to here and back is a two- to three-mile walk and should take no more than an hour and a half.

Butchers Arms Oak Lane, NR12 9JG ☎ 01692 650237. Decent, old-fashioned village local right on the green in East Ruston – a peaceful location even at the busiest times. They serve food, and it's a cosy, quirky place to come after visiting East Ruston Vicarage Garden (see p.93). Kitchen noon–2pm & 7–8.30pm.

Bacton Wood

Bacton, NR28 9UE • Daily dawn–dusk • ⓦ forestry.gov.uk/forestry/englandeastanglianoforestbactonwood

About two and a half miles northeast of North Walsham, **Bacton Wood** is an ancient piece of woodland now owned by the Forestry Commission, although many of its indigenous trees have been replaced with evergreens. There are parking spaces among the trees on the corner of Old Hall Road, and three colour-coded trails and cycleways help you to explore it fully.

All Saints Church, Edingthorpe

Church Lane, Edingthrope, NR28 9TJ • ⓦ edingthorpepcc.co.uk

Half a mile north of Bacton Wood, around four miles northeast of North Walsham, the hamlet of **EDINGTHORPE** has a unique village church, **All Saints**, occupying a very lonely spot – almost on a hill, in fact – just outside the village, with a thatched roof and a tapered round tower that is one of Norfolk's most elegant. Inside is a beautifully bare, whitewashed church full of traces of its age – a damaged but still richly decorated rood screen with paintings of saints and wonderfully delicate tracery and fragments of fourteenth-century wall paintings showing St Christopher and the Seven Acts of Mercy.

SS. Peter & Paul, Knapton

Pond Lane, NR28 0SB • ⓦ knapton.churchnorfolk.com

North of Edingthorpe, five miles northeast of North Walsham, the village of **KNAPTON** also has a church worth visiting, **SS. Peter & Paul**, which has a magnificent double hammerbeam roof decorated with angels (not unlike the one in Swaffham), dating from 1503, and which some claim was created from the remains of a shipwreck off nearby Mundesley. It's in perfect condition, and still decorated with 160 figures of angels, apostles and prophets – a stupendous achievement, not only for the completeness of its religious vision but also for the sheer practical skill involved.

St Botolph, Trunch

North Walsham Rd, NR28 0QE • ⓦ trunch.churchnorfolk.com

Three miles north of North Walsham, the small village of **TRUNCH** has a shop and a pub, but is really worth visiting for its church of **St Botolph**, a mainly fourteenth-century building with a wealth of carved features, notably the arms and undersides of the misericords in the choir, and the rather more primitive graffiti on the choir stalls, dating from Victorian times when this part of the church was used as a schoolroom. As usual the choir is separated from the rest of the church by a rood screen, and this one is very finely carved and painted with good depictions of various saints. There's also a fine hammerbeam roof, decorated with angels, though perhaps not quite as impressive as those in Knapton and Swaffham. The church's most distinctive feature is its font canopy, carved out of oak in 1500, and boasting a wealth of intricate detail – tendrils, fruit, leaves – though the bright paint that would once have covered it has long gone.

Acle and around

About ten miles east of Norwich on the A47, **ACLE** is the last major stop on the northern Broads before Great Yarmouth. It gives its name to the bridge over the Bure, about half a mile or so north of the town, where there are free moorings and a shop. The town itself (a large village, really) is nothing special, but it enjoys a lovely location, good not only for boating but also for exploring some of Broadland's most evocative – and flattest – countryside on foot.

2

St Edmund the King and Martyr

The Street, NR13 6QY • ⓦ acle.churchnorfolk.com

Acle's church of **St Edmund the King and Martyr**, in the centre of the town, has a crenellated Saxon round tower, believed to date back to the ninth century, and a thatched roof. Inside, its fifteenth-century font is still partially painted and carved with images of wild men with clubs and the Virgin and Christ, while at the other end of the nave there is a delicate, painted rood screen of a similar age. Look out too for the inscription on the north wall of the choir dating back to the plague of 1349, which describes "the black beast plague raging hour by hour".

ARRIVAL AND DEPARTURE   ACLE

By bus Acle is well connected by bus about every 30min with Lowestoft (1hr), Great Yarmouth (15min) and Norwich (35min).

By boat There are free moorings at Acle Bridge, where there is also a shop, and moorings on the opposite side of the river at the *Bridge Inn* pub (see below), who charge £4 (refundable if you eat at the pub).

ACCOMMODATION AND EATING

IN TOWN

Bridge Inn Old Rd, Acle Bridge, NR13 3AS ☎ 01493 750288, ⓦ norfolkbroadsinns.co.uk. Large pub right by Acle Bridge that has moorings, free wi-fi and a cosy bar and restaurant that does decent food from a large menu – better than you might expect given its size and location. Standards predominate – fish pie, steak-and-ale pie, lasagne, steaks, gammon, a range of burgers – and they have a good kids' menu and plenty to keep little ones entertained in the garden outside. Most main dishes cost between £9 and £12; the mooring fee is £4 and refundable from anything you buy in the pub. Kitchen daily noon–

9pm; pub Mon–Sat 11am–11pm, Sun 11am–10.30pm.

OUT OF TOWN

Old Vicarage Moulton St Mary, NR13 3NH ☎ 07500 578369, ⓦ oldvicaragecamping.co.uk. A great campsite on a working farm between Acle and Cantley, in a beautiful location surrounded by marshes and woodland. It's an old-fashioned sort of place, tents-only and with no marked pitches, that positively encourages campfires on its free-to-hire braziers (firewood is £5). Hot showers and composting toilets. There's a £2 supplement for pets. <u>£8</u> per person, children <u>£3</u>

Stokesby

Heading east down the Bure from Acle Bridge towards Great Yarmouth takes you through beautiful countryside of big skies and open, treeless fields; coasting down here on a traditional Broads yacht with the wind behind you on a summer's day is one of the finest experiences of the Broads. About a quarter of the way to Yarmouth, **STOKESBY**, on the north bank of the river, is a pretty riverside village with a perfectly located pub, the **Ferry Inn** (see p.96), and free moorings if you eat there.

ACCOMMODATION AND EATING   STOKESBY

Braid Barn Hall Farm, Runham Rd, NR29 3EP ☎ 01493 369849, ⓦ braidbarn.co.uk. Incorporating a large grade-two-listed barn conversion just outside Stokesby, this B&B has three lovely boutique-style guest rooms, beautifully furnished and equipped with comfy king-size beds and flatscreen TVs. A highly desirable place to stay, walking distance from the village (and its pub) and close to lots of good walks. The breakfast is excellent, too. <u>£85</u>

2

Ferry Inn Riverfront, The Green, NR29 3EX ☎01493 751096, ⍟ferryinn.net. A newly refurbished, dog-friendly pub that serves good-quality, well-presented food – crab cakes, steak-and-kidney puddings, burgers, fish and chips for £10–12. There's a slightly more adventurous dinner menu, most of it locally sourced, which you can also enjoy outside by the blissfully peaceful river. Overnight moorings cost £5, redeemable against an evening meal in the pub. Kitchen Mon–Thurs noon–2pm & 6–9pm, Fri noon–3pm & 6–9pm, Sat & Sun noon–9pm; pub Mon–Thurs noon–3pm & 6–11pm, Fri noon–3pm & 6pm–midnight, Sat noon–midnight, Sun noon–11pm.

Riverside Stores & Tearooms The Green, NR29 3EX ☎01493 750470. Breakfasts, lunches and cream teas at this iconic Broads stalwart that uses mainly local produce. Bike hire available too. Daily 7.30am–6.30pm.

Upton Broad and Marshes

Upton Broad and Marshes, NR13 6EQ · Daily dawn–dusk · ⍟ norfolkwildlifetrust.org.uk

Around three miles north of Acle, the spread-out village of **UPTON** lies to the south of **Upton Broad and Marshes** – managed by the NWT, and viewable on foot by means of a series of well-maintained footpaths. It's one of the best places in the UK to see dragonflies, and offers great walks. **Upton village** itself retains its own pub, **The White Horse** (see below), after a spirited fight by the villagers who clubbed together to make an offer for the doomed business; it has been community-owned since 2012, and has recently added a villages shop to its premises.

EATING   UPTON

The White Horse 17 Chapel Rd, NR13 6BT ☎01493 750696, ⍟whitehorseupton.com. Excellent community-owned pub that does good food, including roasts on Sundays, fish and chips on Fridays, and much more in the pub grub vein. Great food and value, with only the sirloin steak costing more than £10. They also regularly host live music on Saturday nights. Kitchen Mon–Sat noon–9pm, Sun noon–6pm; pub daily noon–midnight.

South Walsham

The small village of **SOUTH WALSHAM** – just west of Upton Fen, about three miles northwest of Acle – is home to a nice pub in the **Ship Inn** (see below). North of the village proper and on the far side of Fairhaven Water Gardens, **South Walsham Broad** is more easily reached on foot from nearby **Pilson Green**. You can park your car by the broad, where there are free moorings and a couple of boatyards, and follow the footpath along Fleet dyke all the way up to the River Bure. Then either come back the same way or continue along the river and link up with the path down to the village of Upton and Upton Fen – a great circular walk that delivers you back to Pilson Green in around two hours.

St Mary and St Lawrence

The Street, NR13 6DQ · ⍟ southwalsham.churchnorfolk.com

Across the road from the *Ship Inn* (see opposite), the church of **St Mary** is one of two churches on this site that share the same churchyard – the other, **St Lawrence**, has fallen into ruin and its nave is now a fragrant garden. St Mary itself is intact, and is a classic large Gothic Norfolk church, although its stained-glass windows are fine examples of early twentieth-century work.

Fairhaven Water Gardens

School Rd, NR13 6DZ · Daily: March–Nov 10am–5pm (May–Aug Wed till 9pm); Dec–Feb 10am–4pm · £6.20 · ☎01603 270449, ⍟ fairhavengarden.co.uk

Right on the edge of the village of South Walsham, **Fairhaven Water Gardens** provide an easy (and wheelchair-friendly) glimpse of the swampy woodland that makes up so much of the Broadland landscape and is so often inaccessible, with paths that lead through the grounds of the Fairhaven estate. Wooden bridges cross narrow waterways and lead you past a 950-year-old oak, candelabra primulas (in spring) and down to the estate's private section of South Walsham Broad, which you can tour by boat (£3.75; 20min); they also run boat trips to nearby St Benet's Abbey (see p.84) from here (£6.75; 50min). There's a good café and gift shop, and a very nice nursery selling all manner of plants – all accessible even if you're not visiting the garden. Dog-friendly, too.

EATING SOUTH WALSHAM

Ship Inn 18 The Street, NR13 6DQ ☎ 01603 270049, ⓦ theshipsouthwalsham.co.uk. Owned by Matthew and Nicola Colchester of *Recruiting Sergeant* fame (see p.73), this is a great village pub that serves excellent gastropub food from a relatively simple menu. There are half a dozen starters, including belly of pork or crayfish cocktail for £6–7.95, and around ten mains, most around the £12–15 mark – simple stuff like fish and chips or liver and bacon, along with more adventurous meals such as skate wing and pan-fried duck breast; there are always a couple of veggie options, too. Kitchen Mon–Thurs noon–2pm & 6–9pm, Fri & Sat noon–2pm & 6–9.30pm, Sun noon–9pm; pub Mon–Sat noon–11pm, Sun noon–10.30pm.

2

Repps-with-Bastwick and Thurne

About a mile south of Potter Heigham, the village of **REPPS-WITH-BASTWICK** lines the road. There's not a lot to do here, but it is home to a nice old church – St Peter's, which has an elegant flint round tower – and the **Wind Energy Museum** (see below). You can follow a stretch of the **Weavers' Way** from here to **THURNE**, which sits at the end of a small cutting on the east bank of the river. There are a number of moorings and you can stock up on basic provisions at the *Lion Inn* (see below), a family-run pub which also has a small shop in summer. Beyond here the Bure meets the Thurne River at Thurne Mouth, and you can keep following the Weavers' Way two miles south to Acle Bridge, along the Bure. There are also free moorings about ten minutes' walk from the village in this direction.

Wind Energy Museum

Staithe Rd, Repps-with-Bastwick, NR29 5JU • April–Sept Fri & Sun 10am–2pm • £3, children under 10 free • ☎ 07796 407864, ⓦ windenergymuseum.wordpress.com

Located by the river in Repps-with-Bastwick, the quirky **Wind Energy Museum** is dedicated to telling the story of wind power over the past two centuries through its collection of wind-powered machinery, originally brought together by local engineer Bob Morse and now owned by Debra Nicholson. It also incorporates nearby **Thurne Mill** (April–Sept first & fourth Sun of each month 2–4pm; free), a nineteenth-century drainage pump just outside the tiny village of Thurne.

ACCOMMODATION AND EATING REPPS-WITH-BASTWICK AND THURNE

IN TOWN

Lion Inn The Street, Thurne, NR29 3AP ☎ 01692 670796, ⓦ lion-inn-thurne.co.uk. Nice traditional pub that enjoys a great location right by the staithe in Thurne, where there are lots of moorings owned by the pub. It serves a well-cooked and wholesome menu – good steaks, burgers (including a lobster and crab burger) and a great mixed grill for £18.50, as well as other good-value pub grub mains (including veggie options) for around £10. Lots of tables outside and regular live music at weekends. Kitchen daily noon–2pm & 6–9pm.

OUT OF TOWN

★**Clippesby Hall** Hall Lane, Clippesby, NR29 3BL ☎ 01493 367800, ⓦ clippesby.com. About a mile east of Thurne, this site has secluded pitches for camping, hook-ups for caravans, holiday cottages and lodges, as well as its own pub, a very nice outdoor pool, bike rental and a children's playground – all in all a fantastic spot to explore this part of the Broads, and indeed one of the best campsites in Norfolk. Pitches including tent, car and two adults £36

The east coast

Norfolk's **east coast**, south of Cromer down to Great Yarmouth, is less renowned and as a result much less gentrified than its northern neighbour. But it's no less spectacular, and in some places more so, with long unbroken stretches of dunes, sandy beaches and seal colonies basking in the water just offshore – and its lack of refinement is refreshing if you're fed up with the Chelsea tractors and bijou shops of Burnham Market. Most of the east coast's villages and resorts are little known and feel off the beaten track, though its only large town, Great Yarmouth, is for the most part a sad shadow of its former self as a fishing port and seaside resort. The only drawback is the steady erosion of the sandy cliffs and dunes that is threatening the very existence of some of the villages, with **Happisburgh** the most extreme example of a community that is literally falling into the sea (see p.102).

2

Overstrand

You wouldn't know it now, but the village of **OVERSTRAND**, just south of Cromer, was a fashionable resort at the turn of the twentieth century and had a very grand hotel that crumbled into the sea in the 1940s (coastal erosion was a problem even then). It has a good sandy **beach**, and you should take some time to wander through the **Londs**, a tiny quarter of flint cottages and narrow lanes, next to which is the **Pleasaunce**, designed by a young Edwin Lutyens in the 1890s for the heirs to the Flowers brewing fortune and with extensive gardens by Gertrude Jekyll. Today it's in use as a Christian holiday centre. Nearby, on Cliff Road, there's another building by Lutyens, a small red-brick **Methodist church**, and the great man was also responsible for **Overstrand Hall** on the edge of the village.

ARRIVAL AND DEPARTURE   OVERSTRAND

By bus Connected by bus #5 (roughly hourly) with Cromer (10min), Mundesley (15min) and North Walsham (30min) roughly every hour.

ACCOMMODATION AND EATING

Clifftop Café 22 Cliff Rd, NR27 0PP ☎ 01263 579319, ⓦ clifftopcafenorfolk.co.uk. The excellent *Clifftop Café*, above the beach, serves huge breakfasts (full English £7.95), crab sandwiches (£4.85) and hot lunches and jackets (around £6). It also has great views over the sea and outside tables. Very popular, and rightly so. Easter–Oct daily 8am–5pm, rest of the year Wed–Sun 8am–4pm.

Sea Marge Hotel 16 High St, NR27 0AB ☎ 01263 579579, ⓦ seamargehotel.co.uk. A large mock-Tudor masterpiece that was built as a country retreat by a German banker who was deported shortly after its completion due to the outbreak of World War I. It was rescued from serious neglect in the mid-1990s and now has 26 comfy rooms, a restaurant some rather grand public areas and gardens that stretch down to the sea. **£125**

Shoal Cottage 22 Cliff Rd, NR27 0PP ☎ 01263 576996, ⓦ clifftopholidays.co.uk. Clifftop cottage, right next to its sister concern the *Clifftop Café* (see above), sleeps eight people in four comfy bedrooms, some of which have wonderful views out to sea. One week in high season around **£1000**

White Horse 34 High St, NR27 0AB ☎ 01263 579237, ⓦ whitehorseoverstrand.co.uk. In the centre of the village, a block back from the sea, this is a good village pub that does good pub food, ranging from sandwiches and other standards to more exotic options such as pavé of cod with lobster bisque, braised oxtail or tapas. It also has eight first-class rooms furnished in a contemporary style – all en-suite and including an excellent breakfast. Kitchen daily noon–2.30pm & 6–9pm. **£84**

Mundesley and around

About five miles down the coast from Overstrand, **MUNDESLEY** is a long-standing resort, and another east-coast town dealing with the problem of coastal erosion, with a large, virtually derelict hotel perched on the edge of the cliff to prove it. Despite that it's a cheerful place, with a long stretch of mainly sandy (Blue Flag) beach lined by colourful beach huts, which is a very popular spot during summer. There's a tiny **Maritime Museum** in the coastguard station overlooking the beach (Easter & May–Sept daily 11am–1pm & 2–4pm; 50p; ⓦ mundesleymaritimemuseum.co.uk), with bits and bobs relating to Mundesley and the sea, fishing wrecks and the old lifeboat station. Across the road, **Adventure Island** is an elaborate twelve-hole minigolf course (daily 10am–4pm; £3; ⓦ adventureislandgolf.co.uk).

By bus Hourly buses run between Cromer (25min), North Walsham (15min) and the village centre.

Tourist office The visitor centre (Easter–Oct Mon–Sat 10am–4pm, Sun 10am–3pm; ☎01263 721070) is in a wooden hut just past the main parade of shops in the inland part of the village.

ACCOMMODATION AND EATING

Beach Café Beach Rd, NR11 8BG ☎01263 720608. On – yes – the beach, this popular café does fried breakfasts, sandwiches, fish and chips and other hot lunches. Mid-May to mid-Sept daily 10am–5pm; April to mid-May Sat & Sun only.

Corner House Café 2–4 Cromer Rd, NR11 8BE ☎01263 720509. Sweet little café just off the seafront that serves tea, coffee and cakes, breakfasts till noon, and sandwiches, salads and jackets for lunch. Mon 9am–3pm, Tues–Sat 9.30am–4.30pm, Sun 10am–3pm.

Manor Hotel Beach Rd, NR11 8BG ☎01263 720309, ⓦ manorhotelmundesley.co.uk. Recently updated red-brick Victorian hotel whose rooms are well equipped if fairly characterless, although some have great views out to sea – and it's dog-friendly. The bar and restaurant serve a wide-ranging menu – taking in everything from stir fries, steaks, burgers and lamb chops to chilli con carne and lasagne – decently priced at £10–12 for a main course. Kitchen daily noon–2pm & 6–9.30pm; bar daily 10.30am–11pm. **£112.50**

Stow Windmill

Stow Hill, NR28 9TG • Daily 10am–dusk • £2, children 50p • ☎01263 720298, ⓦ stowmill.co.uk

Just outside Mundesley, **Stow Windmill** is an early nineteenth-century flour mill that shut down in the 1930s and has been beautifully restored by Roger and Andrea Hough, who live in the miller's cottage behind. You can climb up through the mill's various levels by way of a series of vertiginous ladders, taking in lots of photos of the mill through its life, along with displays explaining the purpose of each level. It's beautifully done, and the views back across to Mundesley and the sea are lovely.

Paston

A couple of miles inland from Mundesley, just beyond Stow Windmill, the village of **PASTON** is named after the Paston family who were immensely powerful during the Middle Ages, and is still home to a magnificent thatched **barn** that dates from 1581, which was deliberately upstaged by their rivals the Wodehouse family in Waxham (see p.102). It's managed by Natural England due to its important colony of Barbatelle bats, one of the few in the UK, that lives in its rafters. Paston's church of **St Margaret** has a number of tomb memorials to family members, one a marble edifice showing a reclining Lady Katherine Paston, who died in 1628, and a much plainer monument to her husband, who died four years later.

Happisburgh and around

Unfortunately **HAPPISBURGH** is best known for the fact that it is slowly sliding into the sea. It certainly feels a bit more off the beaten track than other nearby villages – and indeed it is, situated well off the main road and signalled by its red-and-white-striped lighthouse, a famous landmark hereabouts. Sadly, Happisburgh's once-beautiful sandy beach is now littered with the mangled iron and concrete of the village's flood defences, which have so far failed to stop the sea eroding the crumbling cliffs at a rate of around 30ft a year. There are one or two hardy souls still here, but their houses are so desperately close to the cliff edge it's hard to see how any of the few properties that are left will survive much longer (see box, p.102).

St Mary

Church St, NR12 0PN • ⓦ happisburgh.churchnorfolk.com

The main part of Happisburgh village clusters just inland next to the church of **St Mary**, which occupies a commanding position above the sea – and in fact its elegant battlemented tower was a beacon for shipping until the building of the lighthouse. It's unusually large inside, with three aisles and a lovely fifteenth-century octagonal font carved with symbols of the Evangelists – and, in a county not exactly short of appealing churchyards, St Mary's is one of Norfolk's most atmospheric, not least because of the perpetual soundtrack of waves pounding below.

Happisburgh Lighthouse

Lighthouse Lane, NR12 0QA • Late July to early Sept Sun 11am–4pm, plus selected bank hol Mondays April–Oct • £3 • ☎ 01692 650442, ⓦ happisburgh.org/lighthouse

The other thing to see in Happisburgh besides the church and beach – and very much the symbol of the village – is the **Lighthouse** on the other side of the village. The UK's only independently run lighthouse, it's still functional, and when it's open to the public you can climb right up to the lantern and enjoy the glorious 360-degree views.

ARRIVAL AND DEPARTURE   HAPPISBURGH

By bus Buses run to Happisburgh roughly every two hours from Stalham (25min), Sea Palling (15min) and points in between and run onto Mundesley (20min) and finally North Walsham (30min). There are also connections to Norwich (1hr 45min), via Wroxham, and to Great Yarmouth (1hr 30min).

ACCOMMODATION AND EATING

Hill House Inn NR12 0PW ☎01692 650004, ⓦ hillhouseinn.co.uk. Great pub at the centre of the village, which has three rooms in a coach house and a converted signal box, the latter with wonderful views over the sea. One of the rooms upstairs was occupied by Sir Arthur Conan Doyle when on holiday here, where he was inspired by the landlord's son to write his short story, *The Adventure of the Dancing Men*, in 1903 – a fact confirmed by a blue plaque on the front of the building. Downstairs they serve a good range of ales and home-cooked food – basic pub grub, but a cut above the usual, with good burgers, jackets and baguettes and a range of suet puddings (around £10), plus lovely traditional desserts – spotted dick, treacle sponge – for around £6. The pub also hosts the very popular summer-solstice beer festival every June, with live music and around seventy beers and two dozen ciders available to taste. Kitchen daily noon–2.30pm & 7–9.30pm. **£60**

Smallsticks Café Cart Gap Rd, NR12 0QL ☎01692 583368, ⓦ smallstickscafe.co.uk. This small café just outside Happisburgh at Cart Gap, converted from a barn and with a small and sheltered outside courtyard, does breakfast, lunches and excellent cream teas. April–Oct daily 9.30am–5pm; Nov–March Sat & Sun 9.30am–4pm.

Cart Gap

There's a better stretch of beach than Happisburgh's – with golden sands and no debris – at **CART GAP**, about a mile south of the village, next to **Eccles-on-Sea**. It's no more than a huddle of shacks around a small car park, to which they have moved the Happisburgh RNLI lifeboat, but there is a good café nearby (see above).

Sea Palling and Waxham

A couple of miles south of Eccles-on-Sea, the sandy beach at **SEA PALLING** is pretty good, and has Blue Flag status, protected by the artificial reefs of rocks that have been built just offshore as part of the coastal flood defences, and backed by concrete walls set into the dunes. It's not the classiest place along here, with a huddle of tacky shops and snack bars, and arguably the beach is more pristine further south, but it's nice enough if the sun is shining.

The beach is better at **WAXHAM**, a mile or so south, where a path cuts through the dunes from behind the village to emerge onto gorgeous golden sands that are relatively untouched by flood defence works, and are backed by a high, dense line of dunes. Walk a little way further south and you may be lucky enough to see some of the seal colony that lives nearby.

2

HOLDING BACK THE TIDE: THE FUTURE FOR NORFOLK'S EAST COAST

Happisburgh is only the most extreme example of a problem that afflicts a great deal of Norfolk's eastern shore – **coastal erosion**, which since 1992 has claimed around 500ft and also increased vulnerability to **flooding** of low-lying land. There have been a number of major floods in the area over the centuries – a massive one in 1622, another in 1938, which inundated the area around Horsey, and again in 1953, when over 300 people were killed.

Many of the settlements along the coast are protected in some way from the North Sea, either by flood defences (as at Happisburgh), concrete supports on the dunes, which provide a barrier between the sea and the land, or artificial offshore reefs (as at Sea Palling). However, a 2008 **Environment Agency plan** concluded that it was impossible to hold back the sea for more than another twenty to fifty years at most, and that at some point local people had no choice but to submit to the inevitable and let the sea flood the area between Happisburgh and Winterton, creating an estuary and consigning six villages, five churches, acres of valuable farmland and around a fifth of the Broads National Park to the sea. Centuries ago the land would have looked like this anyway, they argued, and there isn't the money to maintain sea defences indefinitely. Not surprisingly this has affected property prices – and morale – and has led to a storm of protests from residents. **Happisburgh** is already fast, and visibly, disappearing, but **Hickling**, **Waxham** and **Horsey** are just some of the places where homes will be lost underwater if the EA plan is adopted, and there is no compensation for anyone affected. Conservationists have also argued against the salination of part of the UK's most important freshwater wetland. Whatever happens, there is no doubt that climate change means the sea will be almost impossible to contain entirely, and it seems likely that the landscape around Hickling and along the nearby coast will look very different a century from now.

Across the North Sea, the Netherlands has done a very good job of protecting low-lying and reclaimed land from the sea. However, such efforts need both overwhelming political will and a great deal of money, and these are in much shorter supply in the UK, at least in the relatively off-the-beaten-track rural communities of east Norfolk.

Waxham Great Barn
Coast Rd, NR12 0EE • April–Oct daily 9.30am–5pm • Free • ☎ 01603 629048

Waxham itself is tiny, and centres on **Waxham Great Barn**, a huge sixteenth-century thatched barn, 180ft long, that has been recently restored in Norfolk reed. Built by the influential and wealthy Wodehouse family in the mid-sixteenth century, you can admire its construction during a free audio tour, marvelling at the hubris that induced Thomas Wodehouse to build this giant structure, ostensibly to upstage a rival's barn in nearby Paston (a structure which still stands, and is 24ft shorter; see p.99). There's also a small café selling sandwiches, cakes and light lunches, and a car park.

St John
Church Rd, NR12 0DZ • Daily 10am–4pm • ⓦ waxham.churchnorfolk.com

Thomas Wodehouse died in 1571, and you can see his tomb in the church of **St John**, which is in a state of some disrepair but is nonetheless a beautiful and very peaceful spot, before heading off for a swim and a picnic on the beach.

ARRIVAL AND INFORMATION   SEA PALLING AND WAXHAM

By bus Sea Palling is connected roughly every two hours to Happisburgh (40min), North Walsham (50min) and Stalham (20min).
Cycle rental Sea Palling Cycle Hire is based at Waxham

Barn (April–Oct daily 10am–6pm; ☎ 01692 598592, ⓦ seapallingcyclehire.co.uk). From £16 a day for an adult bike, £35 for tandems; kids' bikes and tag-along kids' (and even dogs') extensions available too.

Horsey and around

HORSEY feels like a very remote spot, more of a hamlet than a village really, with a huddle of houses looking out across the marshes to sea, which is no more than a mile away and home to a large colony of seals which you can usually spot basking on the shore or bobbing in the waves. As well as visiting **Horsey Windpump**, you can do a circular walk around part of **Horsey Mere** to the village and back, or strike out across the fields and then down to the sea to view the **seal colonies** there – detouring if you like to the **Nelson Head** pub on the edge of the village (see p.104). The **beach** is reachable in ten minutes by a footpath from the pub, and there's a small car park behind the dunes, at the end of a track off the main road, just north of the village.

All Saint's Church

The Street, NR29 4EF • Daily dawn–dusk • Ⓦ horsey.churchnorfolk.com

The village's church, **All Saints**, is tucked away on the other side of the main road, and has a thatched roof and round Saxon tower, topped with a later octagonal belfry. There's not much to it inside apart from a late-Gothic rood screen and attached staircase, but it has a tranquil feel that stays with you long after you have left, and its churchyard is another candidate for one of Norfolk's best.

Horsey Windpump

NR29 4EF • March Sat & Sun 10am–4.30pm; early April Mon & Thurs–Sun 10am–4.30pm; mid-April to late Oct daily 10am–4.30pm • £3; NT • ☎ 01493 393450, Ⓦ nationaltrust.org.uk

Stark and proud against the dead-flat landscape of the eastern fringes of the Broads (Horsey Mere is the furthest east you can go by boat), **Horsey Windpump**, the 1912 replacement of an earlier drainage mill, is what brings most people here. It's owned by the National Trust and you can climb to the top deck and look out over the Mere and fens, viewing various displays on the way – on the wildlife of the area, Arthur Ransome (who featured Horsey in a number of his stories) and the massive storm of 1938, which flooded most of the land around. Down below, there's a tearoom where you can sit and watch the activity on the boats moored along the cutting.

Horsey Mere

Horsey Mere reaches a watery hand west back into the Broads from Horsey Windpump, a beguiling expanse of water in which John Betjeman documented a magical swim in his poem, *East Anglian Bathe*. There's a good walk around part of the Mere, following the dyke inland and then around the northern banks before turning north along Waxham New Cut to emerge on the far side of the village at Horsey Corner, where you can follow a track back to the church. You can also see the Mere and its wildlife on one of Ross Warrell's hour-long **riverboat trips**, aboard the *Lady Ann* (May–Sept five daily 10am–4pm; £7.50; ☎ 01692 598135, Ⓦ rossrivertrips.co.uk), which leave from Horsey Staithe; they also run early-morning bird-spotting trips for the super-keen.

ARRIVAL AND DEPARTURE   HORSEY

By bus Horsey isn't very well connected by public transport; the nearest bus stops are in Sea Palling to the north, which has connections with Wroxham (around 3 daily; 40min), and Martham to the south, which has at least hourly services to Great Yarmouth (55min).

By boat There are free moorings at the Horsey Windpump and along the cut to Horsey Mere, as well as at West Somerton staithe, about a mile away.

HORSEY'S SEALS

You can access Horsey's beach via a path that leaves from the *Nelson Head* pub or from opposite the *Poppylands Café*, and very nice it is too – at any time of year. However, it is perhaps best known for its thriving colony of grey seals, most popular between November and January, when the seals come ashore to breed and their babies are born. The beach is roped off at this time to protect them, but you can in any case get a good view from up in the dunes; at other times of year, as at Waxham or Winterton, you are sure to get a glimpse of a seal or two, either in the water or basking on the beach. Get more info from Ⓦ friendsofhorseyseals.co.uk.

ACCOMMODATION AND EATING

Horsey Barns The Street, NR29 4AD ☎ 0844 800 2070, ⓦ nationaltrustholidays.org.uk. Three beautifully restored timbered barns, owned and run by the National Trust, and perfectly placed too, right in the heart of Horsey, with the *Nelson Head* and footpath to the beach nearby. They sleep between three and six. One week **£850**

Nelson Head The Street, NR12 8UR ☎ 01493 393378, ⓦ thenelsonhead.com. Cosy pub on the edge of the village, a fifteen-minute walk across the fields from the windpump, which does excellent food and has various bits of Nelson-related memorabilia decorating its walls. The pub is dog-friendly, making it perfect for a stroll across the marshes to the beach and dunes, and they host a beer and cider festival in early September. Mon–Thurs noon–2pm & 6–9pm, Fri & Sat noon–2.30pm & 6–9.30pm, Sun noon–2.30pm & 6–9pm.

Poppylands Café Palling Rd, NR29 4EQ ☎ 01493 393393, ⓦ poppylands.com. About 400yd out of Horsey village towards Waxham, this place does good breakfasts, sandwiches and jackets, gammon steaks, fish and chips and the like at lunchtime, and a full, slightly more refined menu in the evening, featuring steaks, salmon and chicken. It's also got a quirky gift and antique shop upstairs and just across the road a path leads down to the beach. Summer daily noon–3pm & 6–9pm; winter weekends only.

Martham and the coast to Great Yarmouth

The large village of **MARTHAM** sits on the far eastern edge of the Broads, and has in fact as much in common with the seas as with the inland waterways of the Broads. It's an attractive if sprawling village, its centre set around a green as picturesque as anywhere in the county, and home to a couple of pubs, shops and other facilities. Its church, **St Mary the Virgin**, is a massive structure, and dominates the flat landscape for miles around. If you're lucky you'll be able to climb the church tower, which is occasionally open during the summer and on special occasions; but if not, make do with its classic fifteenth-century interior and rough carved font showing the seven sacraments.

ARRIVAL AND DEPARTURE   MARTHAM

By bus There are services at least every hour between Martham and Great Yarmouth (55min); they stop on White St, near the village green. Buses run every half an hour to Winterton from Martham (10min).

By boat Martham village staithe is about a mile north of the village, right at the end of the road that finishes at the Thurne River, and has some free moorings; there are also moorings at West Somerton, on the other side of Martham Broad.

Martham staithe and Broad

A mile or so outside Martham proper, the **village staithe** is a delightfully peaceful spot: the river is quieter here, as you have to negotiate the bridge at Potter to reach this stretch, and that deters the average boater. The road ends at the waterside, and there's a hand-operated bridge that can get you across to the other side. There are boats for rent by the day at Martham Ferry Boatyard (ⓦ marthamferryboatyard.co.uk), and just before that there's a stretch of dyke with moorings. You can make a circular walk from here down the Thurne River to **Martham Broad** and back to the village. Back towards the centre of the village, Martham Boats (ⓦ marthamboats.com) rents cruisers, yachts and canoes by the hour, day or week.

The Trinity Broads

Just south of Martham, the so-called **Trinity Broads** – Ormesby, Rollesby and Filby broads (along with the smaller Ormesby Little and Lily broads) – form a necklace of

BOAT TRIPS ON THE TRINITY BROADS

Just beyond the village of Rollesby, the main A149 crosses between Ormesby and Rollesby broads, and it's here you'll find the **Waterside** complex, home to a café and restaurant (see opposite) and boat trips on *Gentleman Jim* (April–Oct daily 11am–4.15pm; £3.75, family tickets £9.95; ⓦ thewatersiderollesby.co.uk), which take around forty minutes to tour both Rollesby and Ormesby Little broads just beyond. You can also rent rowing boats from £9.95 an hour.

water that stretches from the edges of Hemsby in the north down to Fleggburgh in the south. They are connected to the River Bure by way of Muck Fleet dyke, but this is not navigable and they are effectively cut off from the main body of the Broads proper. No motor-powered craft are permitted on these Broads, but you can tour part by electric boat, and rowing boat and canoe rental is available, plus there's a sailing club on Rollesby Broad. But for the most part you'll find them quieter and more tranquil than the rest of the northern Broads. The pity is that so little can be accessed on foot.

★**The Boathouse** Ormesby St Michael, NR29 3LP ☎ 01493 730342, ⓦ theboathouseormesbybroad.co.uk. This old waterside pub was recently transformed by the folk from *The Waterside* (see opposite) into the stunning restaurant with rooms and wedding venue you see now. The six upstairs guest rooms are lovely, and several overlook the water, plus there are a number of two-bedroom self-catering lodges in the grounds. Downstairs there is a comfy bar area at the front (plus some outside seating by the water) and a more formal restaurant area at the back) and they serve salads, sandwiches and pubby dishes at lunchtime (mains £10–12) and a slightly more refined

menu in the evening, when mains average about £15. A perfect Broads places to stay and to eat. Tues–Sat noon–3pm & 6–9pm, Sun noon–6pm. Rooms __£95__, lodges __£168__
The Waterside Main Rd, Rollesby, NR29 5EF ☎ 01493 740531, ⓦ thewatersiderollesby.co.uk. Owned by the same folk as the excellent nearby *Boathouse*, the *Waterside* complex has a really good café-restaurant that serves excellent lunches and has a lovely decked outside terrace overlooking the Broad. Lunch options include sandwiches, jacket potatoes and light meals like ham, egg and chips. Really good, well-presented food – and excellent service too. Daily 10am–5pm.

Thrigby Wildlife Gardens
Filby Rd, Thrigby, NR29 3DR • Daily 10am–dusk • £13.90, children £9.90 • ⓦ thrigbyhall.co.uk

Around five miles south of Martham, **Thrigby Wildlife Gardens** is a rather sweet, homespun little zoo with a conservation agenda. It hasn't got a huge selection of animals, but those it does have are well and humanely housed, and can be viewed from a series of ingeniously constructed walkways, which take you past snow leopards, gibbons and macaques, and a variety of birds, including two white cockatoos – the only survivors of an illegally transported cargo of eight confiscated at Heathrow a few years back and rescued by the zoo. There's also a reptile house with crocs, alligators and snakes, a "willow pattern" garden – complete with little bridges and Chinese horoscopes – and a "natural" playground for children, plus of course the obligatory café and gift shop.

Winterton-on-Sea
Around three miles east of Martham, the small village of **WINTERTON-ON-SEA** is much the best seaside village hereabouts, with a marvellous sandy beach backed by some majestic dunes that stretch halfway to Horsey to the north and offer some strenuous windswept walks. What's more, Winterton is the first point that really feels separate from the depressing tack of Great Yarmouth to the south. It's a lovely spot, and it's not uncommon to see seals basking in the waves offshore – there's a family of thirty or forty a little way north – and the dunes are home to terns, natterjack toads and the odd adder. There's a (pay) car park and an excellent small café – the *Dunes Café* (see below).

Dunes Café Beach Rd, NR29 4AJ ☎ 01493 394931. At the top of the path down to the beach, this is the perfect beach café, serving good breakfasts and lunches as well as lovely cakes, sandwiches and ice creams. Daily 10am–4pm, plus evenings in summer.
Fisherman's Return The Lane, NR29 4BN ☎ 01493 393305, ⓦ fishermansreturn.com. If you want to stay – and there are worse ways of spending a day or two than soaking up the peace of Winterton and its surroundings

– try the village pub, which has three en-suite double rooms. It's right in the heart of the village, and is a great dog-friendly local that serves good food from a light menu of jackets, omelettes, sandwiches, and lots of pub classics like fish and chips, burgers, steaks and chilli. Veggie choices and a kids' menu too. Daily noon–2.30pm & 6–9pm. __£80__
Hermanus Holidays The Holway, NR29 4BP ☎ 01493 393216, ⓦ hermanusholidays.com. Overlooking the sea, this is a family-run establishment whose unique

round thatched chalets were inspired by a trip to South Africa's Hermanus Bay. There are twelve roundhouses for couples overlooking the dunes, and a number of larger roundhouses and various other bungalows and chalets. The simply furnished one-bedroom chalets ingeniously squeeze a kitchen/sitting room, bedroom and bathroom into a space the size of the average policemen's telephone box. There's an outdoor heated pool, and a bar and restaurant on site, but you're only two minutes' walk from the pub. **£55**

2 Great Yarmouth and around

Not even the greatest apologist for run-down British seaside towns would make much of a case for **GREAT YARMOUTH** – or at least not for spending any amount of time there. And yet it's a hard place to dislike, a once majestic port that supported a fishing fleet of over a thousand vessels, most of them fishing for herring on and around the prolific Smith's Knoll, 25 miles offshore. It was an industry that thrived from the Middle Ages, when this was one of the country's wealthiest cities. The herring fleet supported Yarmouth until the turn of the twentieth century, when it entered a steep period of decline, just as its days as a seaside resort began to gather momentum, spurred on by the mid-nineteenth-century arrival of the railway. These days it's a faded mixture of the two: a port that barely survives, a so-called heritage quarter that blends tattoo parlours, Polish supermarkets and Elizabethan mansions, and a kiss-me-quick resort that fronts a beautiful stretch of sandy beach. It's not everyone's cup of tea, but there is plenty to see, and as your expectations aren't sky high, you might just be pleasantly surprised.

The Heritage Quarter

Yarmouth's **Heritage Quarter** is a slightly desperate tourist-board epithet for the neighbourhood of fairly run-down social housing and the odd historic attraction sandwiched between the town quay and the seafront. But its few attractions are for the most part worth seeing and it does repay a wander.

Elizabethan House Museum

4 South Quay, NR30 2QH • April–Oct Mon–Fri & Sun 10am–4pm • £4.50, family tickets £12.60; NT • ☎ 01493 855746, ⓦ nationaltrust.org.uk

The edge of Great Yarmouth's Heritage Quarter is marked by the Dutch-looking nineteenth-century town hall, just beyond which the sixteenth-century **Elizabethan House Museum** does a good job of re-creating domestic life during Yarmouth's glory years, with period furnishings, a hoard of silver coins and a display on the Civil War (Cromwell is said to have spent time here). It's educational and fun, with clothes to dress up in and lots of other stuff for kids.

The Lydia Eva

South Quay, NR30 2QH • April–Oct daily 10am–4pm • Free • ⓦ lydiaeva.org.uk

Moored right by the town hall on South Quay, the **Lydia Eva** joined the Yarmouth fishing fleet in 1930, when the herring industry had already peaked, and lasted less than a decade before being retired to work for the Ministry of Defence. She returned here in 2004 and, as the only surviving herring drifter in town, has been restored and is open as a museum, along with her sister ship, the *Mincarlo* in Lowestoft (see p.277). Climb aboard to see the bridge, engine room, wheelhouse, crew's quarters, galley and hold, and plenty of illustrated displays and films that do a great job of describing the herring industry when it was at its height – as do the keen volunteers in attendance.

Nelson Museum

26 South Quay, NR30 2RG • Feb–Nov Mon–Fri 10am–4pm, Sat & Sun 1–4pm • £3.95 • ☎ 01493 850698, ⓦ nelson-museum.co.uk

About halfway along South Quay, the **Nelson Museum** is one of the best of the

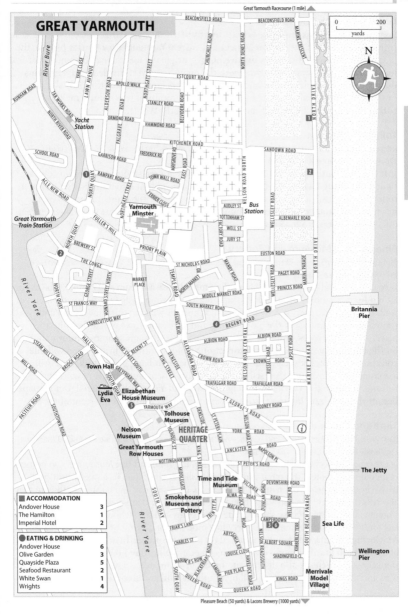

GREAT YARMOUTH

Heritage Quarter's museums, housed in a handsome Georgian mansion and telling the story of Norfolk's most famous son. It focuses on his naval career and love life, his leadership skills, and to some extent his appearance, and is an engaging and imaginative display for the most part, loaded with information and with a few touches that will appeal to kids.

Great Yarmouth Row Houses

South Quay, NR20 2RG · April–Sept Mon–Fri 11am–4pm · £4.50, family tickets £11.70; EH · ☎ 01493 857900, ⓦ www.english-heritage.org.uk

Immediately behind the Nelson Museum, the **Great Yarmouth Row Houses** provide the best extant example of these distinctive houses, originally merchants' residences that lined the narrow alleys running down to the quay. They were divided into tenements during the eighteenth century, and the port workers crowded into the "Rows" – the exhibition, spread across several of the big, empty rooms of two houses, mainly concentrates on the 1930s and the years of the World War II.

Tolhouse Museum

Tolhouse St, NR30 2SH · Late July to Aug Mon–Fri & Sun 10am–4pm, plus Easter hols & half-term weeks · £3.50, family tickets £9.80 · ☎ 01493 743930, ⓦ museums.norfolk.gov.uk

Just beyond South Quay, the **Tolhouse Museum** is housed in one of the town's oldest buildings, dating back to the twelfth century, a rugged flint structure that served for a time as Yarmouth's town hall and later became a prison. The museum focuses on the ne'er-do-wells and criminals of Yarmouth over the years, with some scary basement cells – again great fun for kids, with good, free audio guides.

Smokehouse Museum and Pottery

18–19 Trinity Place, NR30 3HA · May–Oct Mon–Fri 9.30am–5pm; Nov–April Mon–Fri 9.30am–3.30pm · £4.95, family tickets £14 · ☎ 01493 850585, ⓦ greatyarmouthpottery.com

Five minutes' walk from South Quay, the **Smokehouse Museum and Pottery**, housed in an old herring smokehouse built of ships' masts and timbers against the medieval town wall, is a fantastic place, run by Ernie Childs and his wife for thirty-odd years and showcasing the innards of the old building and a treasure-trove of nautical bits and pieces – rudders, ropes, ships-in-bottles, you name it. Ernie is a mine of information on the building and indeed on any aspect of Yarmouth life and history, and will talk you through both, between painting the sea scenes that hang on the walls and firing the commemorative pots they sell in the gift shop. There are a couple of constantly running films on the Yarmouth fishing industry and Yarmouth in general, but perhaps best of all is the building itself, infused with the smell of fish and the scent of the sea.

Time and Tide Museum

Blackfriars Rd, NR30 3BX · April–Oct daily 10am–4.30pm; Nov–March Mon–Fri 10am–4pm, Sat & Sun noon–4pm · £5.20, family tickets £14.50 · ☎ 01493 743930, ⓦ museums.norfolk.gov.uk

More or less opposite the Smokehouse Museum, the **Time and Tide Museum** is also housed in an old smokehouse, though it's an altogether slicker affair than its lesser-known rival, with a host of awards to its name. Deservedly so, for it's a great and engaging museum that also tells the story of the Yarmouth fishing industry and its demise, with exhibits on the smoking and curing process, showing the brine baths and smoke room, another giving a feel for life on board a drifter, and a very fine mock-up of a Yarmouth street in 1913, all convincingly documented and dramatized on the audio guide. There's the lingering smell of smoked fish in many rooms and upstairs you can walk around the rails of the old smokery itself; there are also displays on the rise of Yarmouth as a seaside resort, the world wars and the contemporary town. All in all a thoughtful and absorbing museum.

The seafront

Great Yarmouth's **seafront** stretches for about a mile north to south along Marine Parade, and is a fairly predictable mix of B&Bs, amusement arcades and cheap restaurants, anchored by the Britannia Pier to the north and the Wellington Pier to the south. It's not unpleasant, and compared to much of the Heritage Quarter feels positively vibrant; but the real attraction is the **beach** beyond, an unbroken strand of golden sand where you can ride donkeys, play crazy golf or just flop.

Sea Life

Marine Parade, NR30 3AH • Daily 10am–5pm • £15.60, two or more people £12.90 each • ☎ 01493 330631, ⓦ visitsealife.com

A worthy part of the nationwide family of aquariums, Yarmouth's **Sea Life** has an array of tanks of sharks, rays, penguins, sea horses and lots of fish. It's not a huge attraction, but it's very well done. The staff are helpful and enthusiastic and on hand to answer questions, deliver regular talks and run feeding times. Cheaper if you book online.

Merrivale Model Village

Marine Parade, NR30 3JG • End March to end Oct daily 10am–5.15pm, late July to Aug till 9pm • £7, children £6, family tickets £22 • ☎ 01493 842097, ⓦ merrivalemodelvillage.co.uk

Right on the seafront, just a few minutes' walk from Sea Life, the **Merrivale Model Village** is great, with paths that wind past all manner of creations – from churches hosting weddings to suburban streets witnessing robberies, villages to ruined abbeys. A railway winds through the various buildings, across bridges and through tunnels, past down-at-heel hotels and shopping parades, and when you've had enough you can enjoy a game of minigolf. What could be nicer?

Pleasure Beach

South Beach Parade, NR30 3EH • July to early Sept daily 11am–5pm, Aug till 9pm; also open selected days and times March–June, Sept & Oct; see website for details • Tokens £1 each, unlimited ride wristbands £17.50–19.95 • ☎ 01493 844585, ⓦ pleasure-beach.co.uk

If the beach and its associated attractions begin to pall, you can take in the rides at Yarmouth's **Pleasure Beach** at the southern end of Marine Parade, home to the UK's oldest wooden roller coaster and an excellent log flume ride – although much of the rest is pretty standard, er, funfair fare. If you're after a more sedate seafront experience, the **Pleasure Beach Gardens** just beyond should more than fit the bill.

ARRIVAL AND INFORMATION

GREAT YARMOUTH

By train Yarmouth's train station is on the edge of the town centre on Acle New Rd, not far from the mouth of Breydon Water on the far side of the Bure. Trains for Norwich (every 30–60min; 35min), via Acle (11min) and Brundall (20min).

By bus Buses stop at the Market Gates Rd bus station in the centre of town. There are buses to Norwich and Lowestoft (roughly every 20min; about 45min to both).

By boat The town's rather unprepossessing moorings are on the south side of the river, a 10min walk from the centre of town, at Great Yarmouth Yacht Station, Tar Works Rd ☎ 01493 842794. They cost £12 a night and have a range of facilities – water, electricity, toilets etc.

Tourist office On the seafront at 25 Marine Parade (Mon–Sat 9.30am–5pm, Sun 10am–5pm; ☎ 01493 84636, ⓦ great-yarmouth.co.uk).

ACCOMMODATION

Yarmouth doesn't have a great choice of accommodation, but look hard and you'll find something to suit, and the town does make a good base for visiting attractions in the surrounding area.

★**Andover House** 28–30 Camperdown, NR30 3JB ☎ 01493 8434490, ⓦ andoverhouse.co.uk. Just back from the seafront on the edge of the Heritage Quarter, this self-styled boutique hotel situated on one of Yarmouth's most elegant streets, is one of the best places to stay for miles around, with simply yet very stylishly furnished double rooms and a really good restaurant too (see below). **£85**

The Hamilton 23–24 North Drive, NR30 4EW ☎ 01493 844662, ⓦ hamilton-hotel.co.uk. There are

22 reasonably stylish rooms at this large guesthouse at the northern end of the seafront, most with flatscreen TVs. They include breakfast and are pretty good value, though doubles with sea views cost considerably more. **£55**

Imperial Hotel 13–15 North Drive, NR30 1EQ ☎ 01493 842000, ⓦ imperialhotel.co.uk. Spruce, recently refurbished, spacious rooms in what claims to be Yarmouth's best hotel. An excellent restaurant too, and the overall feel is of a proper, bustling hotel, rather than a guesthouse. **£100**

EATING

★**Andover House** 28–30 Camperdown, NR30 3JB ☎ 01493 8434490, ⓦ andoverhouse.co.uk. The

restaurant of this lovely boutique hotel is central Yarmouth's best, a self-consciously slick joint with a short menu that's

2

> **HAVING A FLUTTER**
>
> The flat racing (horse racing) season at Great Yarmouth's **racecourse** (☎01493 842527, ⓦgreatyarmouth-racecourse.co.uk) lasts roughly from mid-April until the end of October, during which time there are meetings every one to two weeks on average. The course is just north of the centre on Jellicoe Road – follow Marine Parade and its northerly extension, North Drive, for a little over a mile and you're there.

a mixture of well-presented classics – steaks, an excellent burger, pan-fried sea bass – and slightly more adventurous options such as slow-cooked spiced lamb or pan-roasted sea trout, and always a vegetarian option. Really good food, and moderately priced (starters around £7, mains £13–15) and a good wine list. Mon–Sat 6–9pm.

Olive Garden 42 Regent Rd, NR30 2AJ ☎01493 844641, ⓦolivegardenrestaurant.co.uk. Restaurant at the seafront end of Regent Rd that specializes in well-presented dishes with a Greek theme – beef *stifado*, lamb *kleftiko*, good steaks, fried halloumi, skewered scallops, and lots of meat and fish platters to share. Starters £4.50–6.95, mains from £10.95. On weekdays before 7pm you can get two courses and a glass of wine for £15.95. Mon 6–9pm, Tues–Thurs 6.30–9.30pm, Fri & Sat 6–10pm.

Quayside Plaza 9 South Quay, NR30 2QH ☎07500 740827, ⓦquaysideplaza.com. Good café serving breakfasts and lunches – salads, sandwiches and lots of other more substantial options from £6.95, including burgers, steaks, pan-fried sea bass and locally smoked fish

served with ratatouille and potatoes. It incorporates a store selling East Asian furniture and decorative objects. Mon–Wed & Sun 9am–4pm, Thurs–Sat 9am–10pm.

Seafood Restaurant 85 North Quay, NR30 1JF ☎01493 856009, ⓦtheseafood.co.uk. Long-running, popular family-run restaurant that serves the freshest fish you could imagine – plus great cheesecake for afters. Mon–Fri noon–1.45pm & 6.30–10.30pm, Sat 6.30–10.30pm.

White Swan 1 North Quay, NR30 1PU ☎01493 842027. One of Yarmouth's best pubs, and handily the closest one to the yacht station moorings on the river. A friendly place with a contemporary feel and decent food. Kitchen daily noon–2.30pm & 6–9pm.

Wrights 24 Regent Rd, NR30 2AF ☎01493 842658. Traditional restaurant on the main drag of Regent Road that's a good option for lunch, and a cut above most of the places along the seafront, from which it's only five minutes' walk. The menu includes burgers, steaks, omelettes, jackets and the odd Greek-influenced grill; most dishes £5–10. Daily 11am–7.30pm.

Around Great Yarmouth

There are many who would advise you to avoid staying over in Great Yarmouth, but the fact is there is plenty to see in the **surrounding area** if you do.

Caister-on-Sea

Just north of Yarmouth, there's not much to **CAISTER-ON-SEA**, which is a downbeat extension of its larger neighbour and home to the town's racecourse. However, its beach is nice enough, fringed with modest dunes and a beach café, and with the **Caister Lifeboat Station** (April–Oct Wed & Sun 10am–3pm; free; ⓦcaisterlifeboat.org.uk) just behind, famous for being one of only two non-RNLI stations in the UK (the other is at nearby Hemsby), and with a newly revamped visitor centre. There was a notorious lifeboat disaster here in 1901, when the lifeboat was launched for a rescue and then forced back onto the beach by heavy seas and overturned, killing nine of the twelve crew. During an inquest into the incident the survivors were asked why they set out, to which they got the memorable answer: "Caister men never turn back" (after which a nearby pub is named *Never Turn Back*).

The thirty turbines of **Scroby Sands Wind Farm** are clearly visible out at sea from the beach and provide power to around 40,000 homes, although they don't seem to put off the seals you can often see offshore. The town is also at pains to publicize its Roman connections, and the **Roman Fort**, back towards the main road, although it's a modest set of ruins. The town's other major sight, **Caister Castle** (mid-May to Sept daily except Sat 10am–4.30pm; £13; ⓦcaistercastle.co.uk), is more interesting, a set of elegantly crumbling ruins just outside the town, hiding a vintage car collection that ranges from the first-ever Ford Fiesta to a Lotus driven by Jim Clark in the 1960s.

Hemsby

To the north of Caister, **HEMSBY** is more of the same – seafront tack and caravan parks – but you may want to stop by if you're here during the **Hemsby Herring Festival** at the end of August: a grand term for what is basically the local lifeboat service cooking up herrings on the beach. They're rolled in oats and cooked in beef dripping, and after sampling one of these even Hemsby may begin to seem attractive.

Burgh Castle

Daily 24hr • Free; EH • ⓦ norfarchtrust.org.uk/burghcastle

2

BURGH CASTLE is both a suburb of Yarmouth and the site of Burgh Castle Roman fort, a remarkably intact example of an early fourth-century AD Roman fort, with gaspingly thick walls and the odd parapet to clamber about on. It's in much better shape than its cousin in Caister, with three of its four walls still standing, and its splendid location couldn't be more different: a beautiful, remote spot, overlooking the River Waveney, which spurs off the Yare just beyond Berney Arms and the marshes on the far side. They've built a visitors' car park nearby; you can park near the *Church Farm* pub and take in the round-towered church of **St Peter and St Paul** before moving on to the castle just beyond. After that you can walk down to the river and join the Angles Way footpath, taking it back alongside Breydon Water into Yarmouth, or – more appealingly – following it down past the Burgh Castle marina and *Fisherman's Inn* towards Fritton Lake (see p.112), Somerleyton (see p.112), or all the way to Oulton Broad (see p.278).

Breydon Water

RSPB reserve open year-round • ⓦ rspb.org.uk

The large expanse of **Breydon Water** forms the barrier between the northern and southern Broads, although it isn't in fact a broad at all, but a wide tidal estuary, where the rivers Yare, Bure and Waveney meet. It's over three miles long and about a mile across, and is very shallow – boats must stick closely to the marked channel or risk running aground. It is one of the Broads' bleakest spots, but is also an RSPB nature reserve. There is a bird hide on the north shore at the eastern end, which you can reach by following the Weavers' Way footpath from Great Yarmouth train station. You can follow this further along as far as the *Berney Arms* pub and the Berney Arms windmill beyond – a total distance of about five miles.

Berney Arms

Access to windmill on prebooked tours only • ☎ 01493 857900, ⓦ www.english-heritage.org.uk

At the far end of Breydon Water, on the northern bank of the River Yare, the nineteenth-century windmill at **BERNEY ARMS** is a landmark for miles around, and forms the focus of an odd settlement of mill, a pub and – across the fields – train station, and not much else. The mill is owned by English Heritage and is open to the public, while the pub is Norfolk's most remote inasmuch as it can only be reached on foot, or by river or train – and, as such perhaps, it is unclear whether it will remain open at present.

As for the **train station**, it's one of the country's most peculiar, and it's a miracle it exists at all: situated on the Wherry Line between Norwich and Yarmouth, it's a request stop that's not near anywhere; even the windmill and pub are about half a mile and a mile or so away respectively, along the Weavers' Way. The station opened in the mid-nineteenth century, on the insistence of Thomas Trench Berney, who owned the land that the railway company wanted to build their track on. He made it a condition that the station be built here "in perpetuity", and the company had no choice but to comply. After a while it became evident that no one got on or off at Berney Arms, and an agreement was hashed out; trains only stopped three times a week, Berney was paid compensation, and everyone was happy. Now trains stop at Berney Arms daily again

– infrequently, but there's plenty to do if you're stuck in between trains. Failing that, you can follow the riverside path all the way down to Reedham, seven miles away, which follows a part of the Wherryman's Way and takes about two and a half hours.

Somerleyton Hall and Gardens

Lowestoft, NR32 5QQ • April –Sept Tues, Thurs & Sun 11.30am–3.30pm; mid-July to Sept also Wed 11.30am–3.30pm • Hall and gardens £10.95, gardens only £6.45, children £5.95/4.45, family tickets £29/19 • ☎ 01502 734901, ⓦ somerleyton.co.uk

Situated on the southern fringes of Great Yarmouth, around four miles from the centre of town, the Somerleyton estate crosses the border between Norfolk and Suffolk, while the building itself, **Somerleyton Hall**, is a bit of a fake – a grand mock-Jacobean mansion rebuilt in the 1840s after an early seventeenth-century original for the railway entrepreneur Morton Peto, and since 1862 the home of the Crossley family. Fake or not, it's an impressive dwelling, and if you're lucky enough to coincide with its limited opening times, you can see the great ballroom, the parlour's oak carvings by Grinling Gibbons, the library and the family's collections of paintings and sculpture. Be sure to take in the gardens too, at their best in summer when the herbaceous borders and roses are in flower, but with lots more besides – lovely walled gardens, glasshouses designed by Crystal Palace architect Joseph Paxton, a super-long pergola and a fantastic, large maze – all harking back to the estate's Victorian heyday. Down by the river you can see the restored Herringfleet Windmill and enjoy lunch and a pint at the estate's pub, the *Duke's Head* (see below). There's also a very nice tearoom by the entrance that does great cakes, scones, sausage rolls and other goodies.

EATING   SOMERLEYTON

Duke's Head Slugs Lane, NR32 5QR ☎ 01502 730281, ⓦ dukesheadsomerleyton.co.uk. Right out by the Waveney at Somerleyton Hall, this is a great place to stop by for lunch or dinner if you're out that way (or even if you're not), with really good food served from short menus that focus on simple dishes well executed. Menus run the gamut from burgers, fish pie, fish and chips and pasta through to skate wing, bouillabaisse and excellent steaks, most for £10–14. Great home-made bar snacks, too. Mon–Sat noon–2.30pm & 6.30–9pm, Sun noon–8pm.

Fritton Lake

Church Lane, Fritton, NR31 9HA • April–Sept Sat, Sun & school hols 10am–5pm • £8.50, children £4.50 • ☎ 01493 488288, ⓦ somerleyton.co.uk

Part of the Somerleyton Hall estate, just across the border in Norfolk, **Fritton Lake**, off the main Beccles road, is basically a large adventure playground, with slides, zipwires and all the usual attractions, along with lots of other complementary attractions – rowing boats, canoes and launch trips on the lake, go-karts, cycle hire and pony rides, fishing, a short nine-hole golf course and other activities. You pay for parking, then per activity, but of course just sauntering around the lake on the marked-out nature trails is free.

St Edmund, Fritton

Church Lane, NR31 9EZ • ⓦ fritton.churchnorfolk.com

On the road to Fritton Lake, **FRITTON** village's round-towered parish church of **St Edmund** is a very ancient church, not far off a thousand years old, perhaps originally a wayside chapel that was enlarged in the fourteenth century. It's a small, simple

---

THE WALK FROM HALVERGATE TO BERNEY ARMS

The most satisfying way to get to Berney Arms isn't in fact by train, but by **walking** from the nearby village of **Halvergate** – about three miles in all, and an easy 45- to 60-minute hike across the marshes following a part of the **Weavers' Way** (see p.29). You can park your car on the farm track just east of the village, and then pick up the path which leads southeast past the disused Mutton's drainage mill – a glorious route on a bright, sunny day. The way is reasonably well marked – make sure you keep to it as at certain times of year the ground can be boggy – and crosses the rail line at **Berney Arms** station before hitting the river at the windmill.

church, but has a number of Saxon and Norman features, namely an unusually shaped apse, decorated with twelfth- and fourteenth-century fresco fragments depicting St Edmund's martyrdom, a giant fresco of St Christopher carrying Christ on his shoulders, in the nave, and a simple medieval rood screen separating the two.

ACCOMMODATION AND EATING   **FRITTON**

★**Fritton Arms** Church Lane, NR31 9HA ☎01493 484008, ⓦ frittonarms.co.uk. Right by Fritton Lake, this well-preserved Georgian house has nine large, light-filled rooms, as well as a two-bedroom suite that would suit a family or two friendly couples. There's access to the lakeside and formal gardens and all the walks around the Somerleyton estate, and a good bar-restaurant, making it quite a blissful place to stay all in all. The food is wonderful, with a short menu that uses ingredients from the estate – seasonal, and somewhat adventurous – on a daily-changing menu that makes the most of their wood-fired oven. A thoroughly foodie venue in an area where few such places exist, although the nice thing is it's also a good place just for a drink, with a pubby feel and a nice outside terrace looking down towards the lake. Mon–Sat noon–2.30pm & 6–9pm, Sun noon–5pm. **£130**

Redwings Horse Sanctuary

Caldecott Visitor Centre • April–Oct daily 10am–5pm • Free • ☎ 0870 0400033, ⓦ redwings.org.uk

Redwings is a nationwide concern and this is one of two bases in Norfolk – the other being near Aylsham (see p.75) – located opposite Fritton Lake between Great Yarmouth and Beccles, around four miles southwest of Great Yarmouth. Their mission is to rescue horses, ponies and donkeys who have suffered neglect or cruelty and they usually have around 110 to 115 horses, ponies, donkeys and mules here at any one time. Visitors can get up close to the animals, watch horse-care demonstrations and go on tractor rides, and there's a café and gift shop. The centre is also dog- and wheelchair-friendly.

St Olaves

A couple of miles northwest of Somerleyton (four miles southwest of Great Yarmouth), right by the crossing over the Waveney River, the small village of **ST OLAVES** is an odd mixture. Strictly practical down by the river, where boatyards and their sheds aren't an especially pretty sight, while also being an ancient village which grew up around its thirteenth-century **priory**, like the village named after an evangelical Norwegian king known for his friendly greeting, "Baptism or Death!" You can wander around what's left of the priory (not much), afterwards taking the weight off at the *Bell* by the river – which claims to be Broadland's oldest pub and serves predictable but good pub food. There are free moorings, too, if you're eating at the pub.

Reedham and around

Set on high ground above the fast-flowing River Yare, **REEDHAM** is probably the most attractive spot on the southern Broads, with a busy and appealing quayside and a handful of pubs and other attractions. It's famous for its swing railway bridge, and there's no way to cross the river here other than by the bridge or at Reedham's equally famous **chain ferry** a little way upstream; indeed there's no other crossing on the Yare between Norwich and Great Yarmouth.

Pettitts Animal Adventure Park

Church Rd, NR13 3UA • End March to end Oct daily 10am–5pm • £12.95, children £13.95, family tickets £49 • ☎ 01493 700094, ⓦ pettittsadventurepark.co.uk

Just strolling Reedham's quayside and watching the boats come and go is a pleasant enough way to while away an hour or two, but many people come here for **Pettitts Animal Adventure Park**, up above the quayside on the edge of the village, one of the most significant attractions hereabouts. It was formerly a small farm for kids, where you could pet goats and ponies, and to some extent it still is, with lots of other animals besides – pigs, rabbits, raccoons, some slightly sad owls, and many more, including a small reptile house. But the emphasis these days is on the rides: a mini railway loops around most of the site, and there are various fairground attractions, slides and a big adventure playground. Small children will like it well enough, but Disneyworld it ain't.

Humpy Dumpty Brewery

Church Rd, NR13 3TZ • Easter–Nov daily noon–5pm • 📞 01493 701818, 🌐 humptydumptybrewery.com

Immediately next door, the **Humpy Dumpty Brewery** is a little bit of compensation for the mums and dads who have trudged around Pettits, an excellent small brewery whose wide range of draft and bottled beers are on sale all over East Anglia and the Midlands. On quiet days you may be able to join a brewery tour but otherwise make do with its shop, which as well as selling Humpty Dumpty's beers also stocks ales from other Norfolk brewers, local ciders, a few Belgian beers and local produce.

St John the Baptist

Church Rd, NR13 3TZ • 🌐 reedham.churchnorfolk.com

Reedham's church of **St John the Baptist** is worth popping into to see its modern stained-glass windows – the church was gutted by fire in the 1980s and has been restored since with modern open-plan pews. There are also various memorials to the Berney family, best of which is the late sixteenth-century tomb showing Henry Berney, kneeling in prayer surrounded by members of his family.

ARRIVAL AND DEPARTURE   REEDHAM

By train Reedham's station is in the top part of the village, at the junction of Station Rd and Ferry Rd, and is on the main line between Norwich (22min) and Lowestoft (26min) with connections to Brundall (10min), Somerleyton (13min) and Oulton Broad (19min), among other places.

By bus A twice-daily bus connects Reedham station with Great Yarmouth (1hr), Acle (20min), Halvergate (20min) and points in between.

By boat There are free moorings on the Riverside quay in Reedham, very handy for all the village's facilities, and a lively spot in summer.

ACCOMMODATION AND EATING

Cupcakes Café 48 Riverside, NR13 3TE 📞 01493 700713, 🌐 cupcakes-reedham.co.uk. Right on the quay in Reedham, this is a small coffee shop, serving toasted sandwiches, jackets and the like. March–Oct Sat–Wed 10am–4pm.

Reedham Ferry Inn Ferry Rd, NR13 3HA 📞 01493 700429, 🌐 reedhamferry.co.uk. Right by the chain ferry and a bit of a Broads landmark, this pub is a cosy place for a drink and does decent pub food too. Mon–Fri noon–3pm & 6–9pm, Sat & Sun noon–9pm.

Reedham Ferry Touring Park NR13 3HA 📞 01493 700999, 🌐 reedhamferry.co.uk. Run by the same folk who run the ferry and the *Ferry Inn* (see p.96), this campsite is handy for Reedham and a good site in its own right, with the pub on its doorstep. Pitches £15

The Ship 19 Riverside, NR13 3TQ 📞 01493 700287. Festooned with flower baskets, and right by the railway bridge on the river, this has a good choice of pub grub (including a kids' menu and various daily specials), and a good riverfront garden with children's playground. Most mains – lamb shanks, chicken curry, steak pie – go for £8–10. Daily noon–2.30pm & 6.30–9.30pm.

Brundall and around

BRUNDALL is one of the major boating venues on the Southern Broads, and very easy to reach. Yet it's a disappointing kind of place, strung out along the river, with no real centre other than the area around the train station and the boatyards beyond, where the riverbank is lined with one holiday chalet after another – not one

> ### REEDHAM FERRY
> Reedham's **ferry** has operated on this spot since the early seventeenth century, and it still runs year-round (Mon–Fri 7.30am–10pm, Sat & Sun 8am–10pm; cars £4, day-return £7, motorbikes £2, foot passengers 50p; ⓦreedhamferry.co.uk), though at busy times be prepared for a wait – it only takes two cars at a time.

of the Broads' finest moments. You may come to pick up a boat, however, and for one other, unexpected reason: it's home to the region's premier restaurant, *Lavender House* (see below).

2

ARRIVAL AND DEPARTURE
BRUNDALL

By train There are two train stations in Brundall: the main one, down by the river, and Brundall Gardens, the next stop west. Both are on the main line between Norwich (15min) and Great Yarmouth (25min), on which trains run hourly.

By bus Buses stop on the main road in Brundall and connect roughly every half-hour with Norwich (20min), Acle (25min) and Great Yarmouth (45min), among other destinations.
By boat There are moorings at Brundall Bay Marina.

ACCOMMODATION AND EATING

IN TOWN
★ **Lavender House** 9 The Street, NR13 5AA ☎01603 712215, ⓦthelavenderhouse.co.uk. This lovely thatched restaurant in the centre of the village is reason enough to come to Brundall, the domain of celebrated chef Richard Hughes, serving an excellent-value three-course menu for £45, and a tasting menu for £59.95. The food is complex yet hearty, with lots of amuse-bouches and tasters between courses, and a very serious emphasis on Norfolk produce. Menus change every month but in general you can be sure to enjoy one of the county's finest culinary experiences – something you

can learn to re-create yourself at home by attending a course at Richard's in-house cookery school. Thurs–Sat 6.30–10pm, Sun noon–2.30pm.

OUT OF TOWN
The Station House Station Rd, Lingwood, NR13 4AZ ☎01603 715872, ⓦstationhouselingwood.co.uk. Between Brundall and Acle, Lingwood's Victorian former train station has been put to good use as a private house and bed and breakfast, with three double rooms. And trains still run on the line, so it's perfect if you're touring without a car. **£55**

Strumpshaw Fen
Strumpshaw Station • Daily: April–Sept 9.30am–5pm; Oct–March 10am–4pm • £3.50, children £1 • ☎01603 715191, ⓦrspb.org.uk
A mile or so down the road from Brundall, just across the railway line on the edge of Strumpshaw village (you park on one side and the fen is on the other), the RSPB reserve of **Strumpshaw Fen** is one of the best places to spot birds in Broadland, and is set up with well-maintained trails that take you through a variety of habitats – woodland, meadows and reedy fenland. There's a hide at the reception, and two others around the reserve, and although sometimes busy it can be glorious, the air rich with birdsong, and the reedbeds and water stretching far into the distance. It's worth taking the path through the woods and then along the river into the fenland area to get the full flavour of the place.

Strumpshaw Steam Museum
Old Hall, NR13 4HR • Mid-April to early Oct Sun 10.30am–3.30pm • £5, family tickets £12 • ☎01603 714535, ⓦstrumpshawsteammuseum.co.uk
Just beyond Strumpshaw village, a mile or so outside Brundall, the family-owned **Strumpshaw Steam Museum** was opened in the 1950s by Wesley Key and is now run by his grandson William. It displays steam and traction engines – one of the largest collections in the UK – and has a narrow-gauge railway and various countryside trails – not to mention the obligatory gift shop and café. They also host an annual and very well-attended steam rally every late-May bank holiday. Good, homespun fun.

Buckenham Marshes

Buckenham Station • Daily 24hr • Free • ☎ 01603 715191, ⊕ rspb.org.uk

A little further along the river from Strumpshaw Fen, a couple of miles downriver from Brundall, another RSPB reserve, **Buckenham Marshes**, stretches out to the river from Buckenham train station, where you can park and cross the line and then follow the path to the main hide, which is perfectly placed for the best of the marsh's bird- and wildlife. It's another beautiful spot, although it doesn't quite have the diversity of landscape of its neighbour. It's big on geese, and boasts the only regular winter flock of bean geese in England – you can see it between November and February – as well as lots of wigeon. Beyond the hide is the river, and you can follow this along through adjacent Cantley Marshes to Cantley (around a 40min walk), where you can pick up the train back to Buckenham.

Loddon, Chedgrave and around

The adjacent villages of **LODDON** and **CHEDGRAVE** together make up one of the southern Broads' most popular boating destinations – pleasant villages both, although of the two Loddon has most life. There are free moorings at Loddon staithe, and the main street leads up the hill from here to the centre of the village, where the flint parish church of **Holy Trinity** cuts an imposing presence off a large square (car park, really). The church interior is equally grand, the main feature a beautiful rood screen depicting a number of saints, including, oddly, a panel showing one St William of Norwich – a political addition, for St William was a posthumously canonized child who, it was claimed, was sacrificed by Jews in medieval Norwich and as such became a focus of anti-Semitic feeling at the time. In Chedgrave, **All Saint's** church is set on a mound above the river, tucked away behind a housing estate, and is unusual in that the roof of its tower is thatched. The building is Norman in origin, with an elaborately carved Norman arched doorway and stained glass from Rouen Cathedral.

The Chet and Hardley Flood

You can reach the **River Chet** by following a path from the main road – next to *Chedgrave House* B&B (see below) – that edges past the boatyards to pick up another path leading along the north bank of the river (you can also reach this from Chedgrave's church). The path leads in about twenty minutes to a thin strand between the river and the wide expanse of **Hardley Flood**, where there's a bird hide, and then continues on to Hardley Cross – basically the marker post between the district of Norwich and Great Yarmouth – and the Yare near Reedham, where it leads off left towards Hardley Marshes and beyond to Langley Dike, which you can follow up to Langley Abbey.

ARRIVAL AND DEPARTURE   LODDON AND CHEDGRAVE

By bus The fast #X2 buses between Norwich (25min) and Lowestoft (55min), via Beccles (15min), stop in Chedgrave (at the *White Horse* pub) and in Loddon – on High Bungay Rd, at the southern end of the High St – every half an hour.

By boat There are free moorings at Loddon staithe and a little further up the river at Chedgrave Common, within easy walking distance of the village.

ACCOMMODATION

Chedgrave House Norwich Rd, NR14 6HB ☎ 01508 521095, ⊕ chedgrave-house.co.uk. Just before the bridge at Loddon staithe, this is a homely B&B with three double bedrooms, and the price includes a very good breakfast. **£85**

Hall Green Farm Norton Rd, NR14 6DT ☎ 01508

522039, ⊕ hallgreenfarmbandb.co.uk. Just outside Loddon, this B&B has three very comfortable en-suite double rooms, each decorated with a different theme, in a converted dairy next door to the main house. Includes an excellent breakfast. **£65**

EATING

LODDON

Rosy Lee's Tearoom 37a Bridge St, NR14 6NA ☏01508 520204. Opposite Loddon staithe, and a bit of a local institution, *Rosy Lee's* is a great place for breakfast or lunch, with owner Caroline Dwen doing a good line in sandwiches, cakes, and light lunches using the fish fresh from her fishmonger's up the street. She sells work by local artists too. Mon–Sat 7.30am–5pm, Sun 8.30am–5pm.

★The Swan at Loddon 23 Church Close, NR14 6LX, ☏01508 528039, ⊚theloddonswan.co.uk. Another revamped Broadland pub, and one that has been done rather well, with a stripped-down yet still pub-like interior and distinctive, hearty British food. Slightly different menus for lunch and supper, but they overlap quite a lot – think wood pigeon and pea mousse or charred asparagus

and poached egg followed by flat-iron red poll beef or plaice with saffron potatoes. If you're overwhelmed by choice, go for one of the gourmet pizzas. Starters from £5, mains £10–15. Kitchen Mon–Sat noon–2.30pm & 6.30–9.30pm, Sun noon–4pm.

CHEDGRAVE

White Horse 5 Norwich Rd, NR14 6ND ☏01508 520250, ⊚whitehorsechedgrave.co.uk. Friendly local pub that's perhaps the town's best place for dinner, with a large menu of burgers, steaks, mussels, lasagne and lots of veggie options – mains around £10.95–13.95. Jackets, baguettes and various sharing platters available at lunchtime too for around £4–5. Daily noon–3pm & 6–9pm.

Surlingham and Church Marsh Nature Reserve

⊚ rspb.org.uk

North of Loddon, just a few hundred yards from the Yare, **SURLINGHAM** village is pretty enough, and well placed for great walking, but it's most often visited for the **pubs** on either side – the *Ferry House* and *Coldham Hall* (see below). You can do a relatively easy loop walk, just over a mile in all, starting at the *Ferry House*, following the river and continuing through **Church Marsh Nature Reserve** to Surlingham's small and immaculate church of **St Mary**, with its Norman door and hexagonal topped round tower. Just beyond here, on high ground overlooking the marshes, is the ruined Norman church of **St Saviour**, a gorgeous spot, where local naturalist (and conserver of nearby Wheatfen Broad) Ted Ellis chose to be buried – and who can blame him?

ACCOMMODATION AND EATING   SURLINGHAM AND CHURCH MARSH

IN TOWN

Coldham Hall NR14 7AN ☏01508 538366, ⊚coldhamhalltavern.co.uk. Recently revamped, *Coldham Hall* sits at the end of a long track through the marshes, a hard-to-reach riverside pub that looks over to Brundall across the water. It has gastropub pretensions, with a fairly adventurous menu and a restaurant feel. Not expensive (starters around £5.50, mains £10–15), with a menu that includes burgers and BLTs alongside fish cakes and Gressingham duck – all well executed, and they do tapas and filled baps too in case you're not that hungry. Moorings £10, but redeemable against food purchases. Kitchen Mon–Fri noon–2pm & 6–9pm, Sat noon–9pm, Sun noon–3pm; pub Mon–Fri noon–3pm & 6–11pm, Sat noon–11pm, Sun noon–6pm.

Ferry House 1 Ferry Rd, NR14 7AR ☏01508 538659, ⊚surlinghamferry.co.uk. Excellent riverside pub – cosy, dog friendly and family run, with free moorings and seating outside. It also serves a good menu of pub staples like jackets, baguettes and home-made soup, with mains from £7.95. Kitchen daily 11am–9pm; pub daily 11am–11pm.

OUT OF TOWN

Brasted's Manor Farm Barns, Framingham Pigot, NR14 7PZ ☏01508 491112, ⊚brasteds.co.uk. This award-winning restaurant, situated on the fringes of Broadland in the pretty village of Framingham Pigot, has six spacious boutique rooms that are perfectly in tune with the style and sophistication of the food they serve downstairs, furnished with antiques, king-sized beds (including a couple of four-posters), large bathrooms, posh toiletries and everything else you would expect from a B&B of this quality. The food is superb, as is the service, but prices are high (starters around £10–12, mains £25–30). It's a highly desirable and very successful wedding venue, too. Thurs–Sat 7–10pm, Fri also noon–2.30pm. **£270**

Water's Edge Woods End, Bramerton, NR14 7ED ☏01508 538005, ⊚watersedgewoodsend.co.uk. This old Broads pub was due a refurb, but it's been done up in a contemporary style that has left it feeling a bit characterless. A pity, because its riverside location is perfect; there are tables outside from which to enjoy it, and free moorings nearby. The food isn't bad, though, with a simple lunch menu of main courses for £10–12 and a

2

slightly more high-end and varied evening offering, with mains for £12–18. Kitchen Mon–Sat noon–3pm & 6–9pm, Sun noon–7pm; pub Mon–Fri 11am–3pm & 5pm–late, Sat & Sun 11am–late.

Rockland Broad

About five miles northwest of Loddon, **Rockland Broad** is one of the least-known Broads, but also one of the most beautiful – and characteristic – Broadland landscapes. The light and the views are glorious, and a well-laid path runs half a mile or so around one side, where you can spot all kinds of birdlife from the hide in its far corner, before continuing on along Fleet Dike. This links the broad with the main river, which you can follow all the way along to the *Beachamp Arms*, opposite Buckenham Marshes on the northern bank – about a half-hour walk following, in effect, the Wherryman's Way. There are free moorings at Rockland staithe, where the path starts, and a car park, and the recently reopened *New Inn* opposite.

Wheatfen Broad

The Ted Ellis Trust, Wheatfen Broad, The Cover, Surlingham, NR14 7AL • ☎ 01508 538036, ⊛ wheatfen.org

The area on the far (northern) side of Rockland Broad and Fleet Dike is **Wheatfen Broad**, home to a nature reserve initiated by the naturalist Ted Ellis, who made his home here while he was keeper of the natural history collection at Norwich Castle. He lived in the thatched cottage by the entrance to the reserve, and was one of the most vocal chroniclers and advocates of Broadland's beauty, and the need to preserve it for the future. Since his death in 1986, the marshes and watery channels of Wheatfen have been a nature reserve, with a series of paths down to the river – about an hour's walk there and back – that give you some appreciation of what Ted and his wife Phyllis (who lived here until her death in 2004) saw in this magical place.

St Margaret, Hales

Church Lane, NR14 6QL • ⊛ visitchurches.org.uk

The Norman church of **St Margaret** just outside the village of **HALES**, a mile or so southeast of Loddon, is typical of the churches in this part of Norfolk, but is perhaps the best. Abandoned in the 1970s due to its remote location and now owned by the Churches Conservation Trust, it's a gorgeous, truly out-there spot, and feels very old indeed, the exterior dominated by the finely carved sandstone shapes and tendrils of its Norman north door. Inside is small and bare, but there are traces of fourteenth-century wall paintings and a fifteenth-century font, carved with lions and roses and angels presenting shields.

Raveningham Hall and Gardens

Raveningham, NR14 6NS • April–Aug Thurs 11am–4pm, plus bank hol Sun & Mon 2–5pm • £5 • ☎ 01508 548152, ⊛ raveningham.com

About a mile or so east of Hales, and around three miles southeast of Loddon, nineteenth-century **Raveningham Hall** is the home of the Bacon family, who open their extensive **gardens** to the public on selected days during summer. The gardens were developed, more or less from scratch, by the mother of the current incumbent, Priscilla Bacon, who lived here for fifty years and created a series of very large herbaceous borders, as well as replanting and restoring the eighteenth-century walled garden, herb garden and rose garden. Since her death in 2000, the Victorian glasshouses have been refurbished and the gardens are dotted with a number of contemporary sculptures. You can look in on the estate's church of **St Andrew**, full of memorials to a long line of Bacons, and there's a spruce tearoom for a spot of tea and cake after your walk. All in all well worth a visit.

ALL ABOARD THE BETSIE JANE!

You can do short trips from Waveney River Centre to Oulton Broad on the beautifully restored 1930s day-cruiser, the **Betsie Jane** (late July to late Aug Wed & Sun 10am, noon, 2pm & 6pm; 90min; £10, children £8; ☏ 07789 401742, ⓦ betsiejane.co.uk). As well as the regular trips they do weekly Sunday breakfast runs (July & Aug Sun 9am; 90min; £20) plus dinner cruises and birdwatching trips on Breydon Water, and the *Betsie Jane* is available for private charters.

St Mary, Haddiscoe

Church Lane, NR14 6PB · ⓦ haddiscoe.churchnorfolk.com

There's no reason to stop in **HADDISCOE**, around five miles east of Loddon, other than to eat (see below) or to visit its church of **St Mary**, which occupies a commanding position on high ground on the edge of the village – a round-towered, originally Saxon building but with Norman features, notably the tower windows and the main doorway, which is fringed with decorative carving and is topped by a relief said to depict St Peter. Inside is pretty bare, but it's worth peeking in to see a fine and clear remnant of its original paintwork in the nave – a figure of St Christopher holding Christ.

Burgh St Peter

A few miles southeast of Haddiscoe, the village of **BURGH ST PETER** feels very out of the way, and it is, but just beyond the village is the excellent **Waveney River Centre** (see below). This hub of boat and tourist traffic is a complex of moorings (£10–14 a night), campsite and cabins, with lots of facilities including a heated indoor pool, a store and a nice pub with rooms – the *Waveney Inn* (see below). You can also take a foot ferry from here (£3 return) across the river to Carlton Marshes (see p.278), from where you can walk to Oulton Broad and Lowestoft (see p.276).

Just beyond there's the distinctive ziggurat-like tower of the flint and brick church of **St Mary the Virgin** (ⓦ achurchnearyou.com), a long, thin, thatched building whose odd tower was added in 1795 to serve as the local Boycott family mausoleum. The church is intriguing inside too, with a late fourteenth-century font decorated with rosettes and grotesque faces. Interestingly, it was a member of the Boycott family – Charles – who gave the word "boycott" to the English language in the late nineteenth century, when his brutal enforcement of rents and eviction of tenants led to him being ostracized – or "boycotted" – by the local community.

ACCOMMODATION AND EATING

Waveney Inn Staithe Rd, NR34 0BT ☏ 01502 677599, ⓦ waveneyinn.co.uk. Part of the Waveney River Centre complex (see below), the *Waveney Inn* has seven en-suite rooms – five doubles, one twin and a family room – some of which have views over the river and marshes. They are spacious and beautifully kitted out, with flatscreen TVs, big comfy beds and large bathrooms. Rates include use of the Centre's indoor pool and the fo0ot ferry across the river, plus an excellent breakfast in the downstairs pub/restaurant, which the rest of the time serves a high-quality menu including everything from baguettes and sharing platters to steaks, burgers and pasta. You can order anything in small, regular or large portions – a neat idea that makes you wonder why no one else does it – and

there's a nice terrace overlooking the marshes. Kitchen Mon–Sat 8–10am, noon–2.30pm (3pm on Sun) & 6–9pm; bar daily 8am–11pm. **£110**

★**Waveney River Centre** Staithe Rd, NR34 0BT ☏ 01502 677599, ⓦ waveneyrivercentre.co.uk. An oasis of activity in what feels like the middle of nowhere, the Waveney River Centre is many things rolled into one – a well-equipped campsite, right by the water, that also has pods for glamping and self-catering apartments. It also offers moorings to hire boats and rents dayboats, canoes and bikes at what must be one of the best locations from which to explore this part of the Broads National Park. There's also a nice indoor pool. Camping from **£11**; pods **£70**; apartments from **£1000** a week

The north Norfolk coast

CRAB POTS, WELLS-NEXT-THE-SEA

The north Norfolk coast

About forty miles from one end to the other, the north Norfolk coast is one of the UK's top tourist destinations – and no wonder. There's something for just about everyone here beneath the wide skies of Norfolk, from the kiss-me-quick resorts of Cromer and Hunstanton to the chichi, metropolitan delights of Burnham Market and a string of wildlife reserves, where the birdwatching is simply superb. Add to this a series of long sandy beaches, a platoon of excellent hotels and a brigade of first-class restaurants and it's easy to see why the region is quite so enduringly popular.

3

The north Norfolk coast begins (or ends) at **Cromer**, perhaps the most appealing of the larger resorts on account of its handsome setting, perched on the edge of blustery cliffs with its pier poking nervously out into the ocean. A few miles to the west is another well-established resort, **Sheringham**, though here the shoreline is buttressed by concrete sea defences, and then it's on to **Weybourne**, smaller and more subdued, but with another slab of sandy beach. Thereafter, and almost without interruption, the shoreline becomes a patchwork of marshes, creeks, sand dunes and shingle spits, which combine to offer a haven to millions of **birds**, both resident and migratory. The small villages backing onto these creeks and marshes were once important seaports, but the silting up of the coast did for them economically until tourism refloated the local economy in the 1960s. This is north Norfolk at its most beguiling, beginning with a quartet of lovely little places – **Salthouse**, which has a superb medieval church; **Cley**, where there is a major nature reserve as well as several excellent food stores; **Blakeney**, with its attractive harbour, enticing hotels and restaurants; and **Stiffkey**, with its huddle of old houses and riverine meadows.

Beyond Stiffkey is **Wells-next-the-Sea**, a relative giant with a population of 3000, though this swells to nearly 10,000 in the summer months. Wells is at its prettiest on the Buttlands, where Georgian mansions flank an open green, but although its "next-the-sea" tag may have been accurate once, the town now lies about a mile inland from its beach, a magnificent tract of sand bordered by pine-clad dunes. Pushing on from Wells, you soon reach **Holkham Hall**, an imposing eighteenth-century pile set in the middle of an enormous estate, part of which includes the wide, pristine sands of Holkham Bay. To the west of Holkham lies the studied gentility of the **Burnhams** – especially Burnham Market, a favourite with well-heeled Londoners, and Burnham Thorpe, the childhood home of Nelson. Beyond, the coast quietens down, its salt marshes and muddy creeks flanked by the tiniest of hamlets, each of which gives ready access to the coast. Among them, Brancaster Staithe, **Brancaster** and **Holme-next-the-Sea** are particularly appealing, while Titchwell holds an important nature reserve. Just to the west of Holme, at the humdrum resort of **Hunstanton**, the coast veers south to

Highlights

❶ Cromer pier Battered by the ocean and attacked by molluscs, Cromer pier has somehow managed to survive – walk out along it, high above the waves, and enjoy the views. **See p.126**

❷ Felbrigg Hall Neither grandiloquent nor pompous, this exquisite country house is Jacobean architecture at its finest. **See p.130**

❸ Priory Maze and Gardens These delightful themed gardens have a natural feel and the maze is large and suitably puzzling. **See p.132**

❹ Blakeney Point Nudging out into the ocean, this elongated spit is a wild and windy spot,

famous for its terns and seals. Enjoy the hike or take a boat trip. **See p.137 & P.139**

❺ Cley Smokehouse Local seafood smoked in Cley – hard to beat and decidedly delicious. **See p.137**

❻ Holkham Bay and beach Wide and inviting bay holding one of Norfolk's finest beaches – acres of golden sand set against hilly, pine-dusted dunes. **See p.149**

❼ Holme Dunes National Nature Reserve This gorgeous, pristine stretch of coastline with its long beach and sand dunes attracts birds by the thousand. **See p.161**

HIGHLIGHTS ARE MARKED ON THE MAP ON PP.124–125

run alongside the Wash, whose mudflats extend as far as King's Lynn (see p.168), with the quiet villages of **Snettisham** and **Castle Rising** as well as the too-popular-for-its-own-good royal estate of Sandringham nearby.

The other major attractions hereabouts are a short distance inland, principally Little Walsingham, an ancient village (one of **the Walsinghams**) that was the country's most important place of pilgrimage throughout the medieval period, and a charming stately home, the National Trust's Felbrigg Hall near Cromer. There's also the pretty little market town of **Holt**, the splendid grounds of Sheringham Park, and the workaday town of **Fakenham**.

GETTING AROUND
THE NORTH NORFOLK COAST

By train There's an hourly train service on the Bittern Line (ⓦ bitternline.com) from Norwich to Sheringham via a string of minor stations and Cromer.

By bus A battery of local buses traverse north Norfolk, but easily the most useful is the Norfolk Coasthopper bus (ⓣ 01553 776980, ⓦ coasthopper.co.uk), which runs along the coast between Cromer and King's Lynn via a whole gaggle of coastal towns and villages, including Blakeney, Sheringham, Wells and the Burnhams. Frequencies vary on

different stretches of the route, and there are more services in the summer than in the winter, but on the more popular stretches buses appear every 30min or hourly (less frequently on Sun). There are lots of different tickets and discounts, but perhaps the handiest is the Coasthopper Rover, which provides unlimited travel on the whole of the route for either one day (£9.30), three days (£18.50) or seven days (£33); they can be bought from the driver. For route planning by train and bus, go to ⓦ travelineeastanglia.org.uk.

THE NORTH NORFOLK COAST

LONG-DISTANCE FOOTPATHS

For walkers, the **Norfolk Coast Path**, which runs the 46 miles from Cromer to Hunstanton, is an especially fine way of exploring the north Norfolk coast's nooks and crannies as it edges through belts of sand dune, along muddy creeks and past salt- and freshwater marshes. As you might expect from the flatness of the terrain, it's all easy going with barely any inclines along its entire course. The path intersects with the 61-mile **Weavers' Way** (see p.29) at Cromer (see below) and with the 47-mile **Peddars Way**, which begins near Thetford, at Holme-next-the-Sea (see p.160). A National Trail guide (ⓦ nationaltrail.co.uk) covers the route in detail, otherwise you'll need the appropriate OS Explorer map.

Cromer and around

Dramatically poised on a high bluff, **CROMER** should be the most memorable of Norfolk's coastal resorts, but its fine aspect is undermined by a certain shabbiness in its narrow streets and alleys – an "atrophied charm" as Paul Theroux called it – though things are on the mend with new businesses arriving to add a touch of flair, while the town council keeps a string of mini-parks and **gardens** in immaculate condition. It's no more than the place deserves: Cromer has a long history, first as a prosperous medieval port and then as a fashionable watering hole after the advent of the railway in the 1880s. The Victorians

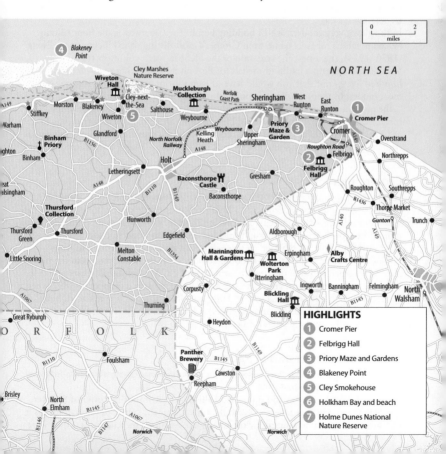

HIGHLIGHTS
1 Cromer Pier
2 Felbrigg Hall
3 Priory Maze and Gardens
4 Blakeney Point
5 Cley Smokehouse
6 Holkham Bay and beach
7 Holme Dunes National Nature Reserve

and then the Edwardians built a bevy of grand hotels along the seafront, but the gloss soon wore off and only the dishevelled *Hotel de Paris* has survived as a reminder of all the bustles and top hats, its imposing red-stone facade topped by a copper-green cupola. There are three things you must do here: take a walk on the **beach**; stroll out onto the **pier**; and, of course, grab a **crab**. Cromer crabs are famous right across England and several places sell them, cooked and stuffed every which way and reliably fresh (see box, p.128). There are enjoyable clifftop walks too, top of the pile being the thirty-minute stroll east along the sea cliffs from Cromer to the Overstrand lighthouse, plus a pair of stately homes within easy striking distance just inland – **Felbrigg Hall** and **Blickling Hall**.

The Gangway

Cromer doesn't have a natural harbour and from time immemorial local seamen have had to haul their boats in and out of the ocean up and over the shingle beach. Finally, in 1902, the town got round to building a ramp and this, **The Gangway**, survives today, its cobblestones lipped to provide leverage for the horses and mules that once lent a helping hoof moving goods up from the beach to the town.

The Henry Blogg Museum

The Rocket House, The Gangway, NR27 9ET • April–Sept Tues–Sun 10am–5pm; Oct–Nov, Feb & March Tues–Sun 10am–4pm • Free • ☎ 01263 511294, ⓦ rnli.org

In the glassy, very modern RNLI building beside The Gangway is the **Henry Blogg Museum**, which takes its name from Cromer's most distinguished lifeboatman. Blogg (1876–1954), the long-time coxswain of the lifeboat, was a volunteer for no fewer than 53 years, picking up a hatful of medals for his bravery and saving nigh-on nine hundred lives – not that you would have known it from meeting him. Blogg was the most modest of men, quiet to the point of retiring, and never boastful.

The museum's main exhibit is the lifeboat on which Blogg undertook most of his missions, but the vintage photos of old lifeboat crews are perhaps more interesting, hinting at a tightly knit world of thick jumpers, big sea boots, flat caps and alarmingly ponderous cork lifejackets. Curiously – and like most of his sea-mates – Blogg never learned to swim.

Cromer Pier

Cromer Pier (Pavilion Theatre), NR27 9HE • ☎ 01263 512495, ⓦ cromer-pier.com • Folk on the Pier festival ⓦ folkonthepier.co.uk

From the Henry Blogg Museum, it's a brief stroll over to the **pier**, whose gift shop, café and fast-food joints culminate in the **Pavilion Theatre**, whose light-entertainment treats pull in the crowds with everything from Michael Jackson impersonators to the rather more enticing "Folk on the Pier", a three-day festival of folk music held in May. Behind the theatre is the present **Lifeboat Station**. Over the years, repairs to the pier have cost a small fortune: the first cast-iron pier of 1822 lasted just 24 years before it was swept away in a storm and its wooden replacement came a cropper in 1897 when a coal boat accidentally smashed into it. Four years later, the pier was replaced, but storms and nautical collisions have been a regular handicap – in 1993, for instance, an oil rig bumped into the pier and almost sliced it into two.

Church of St Peter and St Paul

Church St, NR27 9HA • **Church** Sept– May daily 9am–4pm (June–Aug till 5pm) • Free • **Tower** Early May to late Oct Mon–Fri 10.30am–4.30pm, Sat 11am–3pm • £1.50 • ☎ 01263 514990

With its slender buttresses and pinnacled balustrade, the imposing tower of **St Peter and St Paul**, at 160ft the tallest in Norfolk, lords it over the centre of Cromer just as it was supposed to – a declaration by the town's late-medieval merchants that they were

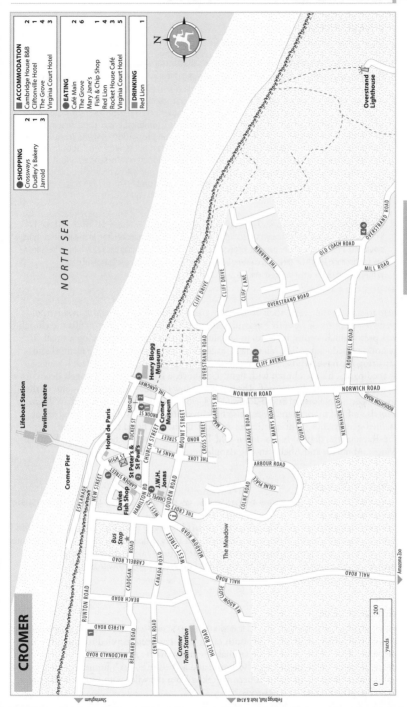

● SHOPPING	
Crossways	2
Dudley's Bakery	1
Jarrold	3

■ ACCOMMODATION	
Cambridge House B&B	2
Cliftonville Hotel	1
The Grove	4
Virginia Court Hotel	3

■ EATING	
Café Main	2
The Grove	6
Mary Jane's Fish & Chip Shop	1
Red Lion	4
Rocket House Café	3
Virginia Court Hotel	5

■ DRINKING	
Red Lion	1

CROMER

NORTH SEA

A HARD SHELL?

No one really knows why **Cromer crabs** are so delicious, but there's no shortage of theories: some say it's to do with the quality of the waters off Cromer, others put it down to the skill of the crab fishermen, but perhaps the most likely explanation is the relatively slow speed at which they grow. There are enough crabs to keep a fair-sized industry ticking over in several parts of the UK, but the Minimum Landing Size (MLS) stipulated by EU/UK regulators varies: Cromer crabs can be landed when they reach 4.5 inches (115mm), elsewhere it's 5.5 inches (140mm), a discrepancy that reflects the Cromer crab's slow rate of growth. This would seem to mean that the flesh of the Cromer crab is a good deal more tender than the faster-growing versions and has a higher proportion of white meat to dark. Currently, the Cromer crab fleet consists of around a dozen boats, who tend about two hundred baited crab pots, long-lined together and positioned on the seabed about three miles offshore. The genuine article is reddish-brown in colour with a distinctive pie-crust-shaped edge to its shell (or carapace). The **crabbing season** begins in March and ends in October and, although Cromer crabs are distributed far and wide, there are some key outlets in the town itself:

Davies Fish Shop 7 Garden St, NR27 9HN ☎01263 512727. Long-established fishmonger's specializing in boxed and dressed crab, not to mention kippers and smoked haddock. They have their own crabbing boat – so they really do know what they're doing.

J.W.H. Jonas 7 Chapel St, NR27 9HJ ☎01263 514121. Down an ancient lane, in an ancient courtyard, this cubbyhole of a shop has a daily catch of fresh-from-the-boats fish plus a good supply of crabs.

here to stay. In the event, their confidence was misplaced: the general movement of trade to the ports of western England marooned Cromer and by the 1780s the church was pretty much a ruin, its wardens keeping vermin at bay by employing a small platoon of hedgehogs. The Victorians saved the church, rebuilding the chancel and repairing the **nave**, whose huge Perpendicular windows, with their tinted, lozenge-shaped panes, fill the church with light. Up above, a handsome set of angels decorates a magnificent hammerbeam roof. The finest window of them all, at the east end of the south aisle, is by **Edward Burne-Jones** (1833–98), who worked closely with William Morris and did more than anyone else to rejuvenate what was then the dying art of stained-glass making. This particular window, in the full florid flourish of the Pre-Raphaelites, depicts half a dozen Old Testament figures – Enoch, Elijah, Samuel, Moses, Abraham and Abel – among dappled greenery.

Cromer Museum

Church St, NR27 9ES • March–Oct Mon–Fri 10am–4pm, Sat & Sun noon–4pm; Nov–Feb Mon–Sat 10am–4pm • £3.75 • ☎01263 513543, ⓦ museums.norfolk.gov.uk

Cromer Museum dips and delves into the town's history as a seaport, fishing village and Victorian seaside resort. The particular highlight is its collection of old sepias and, more unusually, an assortment of autochrome colour pictures taken of local scenes and people by the pioneering photographer **Olive Edis** from 1905 onwards. Edis had her studio just along the coast in Sheringham.

Amazona Zoo

Hall Lane, NR27 9JG • April–Dec daily 10am–5pm • £11.50, children (4–16yrs) £8.50, under-4s free • ☎01263 510 741, ⓦ amazonazoo.co.uk

An old patch of woodland to the south of Cromer has been recycled to house the **Amazona Zoo**, where most of the animals are native to the Amazon. There are around a dozen featured areas, including a hothouse and a "Feline Forest", home to puma, ocelot and jaguar. None of the animals here are taken from the wild, with most coming from breeding programmes in sister zoos.

ARRIVAL AND INFORMATION

By train Somewhat miraculously, Cromer has managed to retain its rail links with Norwich (hourly; 50min) and Sheringham (hourly; 10min); from the station, on Holt Road, it's a 5min walk northeast into the centre.

By bus Buses to Cromer mostly terminate at the east end of Cadogan Rd, on the western side of the town centre. Cromer is on the route of the Norfolk Coasthopper (see p.124) and also has a regular bus service to Holt (Mon–Sat every 30min; 30min).

CROMER

Tourist office The North Norfolk Information Centre is on the south side of the town centre on Louden Road (Sept to mid-May daily 10am–4pm; late May to Aug Mon–Sat 10am–5pm & Sun 10am–4pm; ☎01263 512497, ⓦ visitnorthnorfolk.com).

Guided walks The tourist office sells a good range of local walking maps and has the details of a varied programme of guided walks around both Cromer and its immediate surroundings.

ACCOMMODATION

Cambridge House B&B East Cliff, NR27 9HD ☎01263 512085, ⓦ cambridgecromer.co.uk. In a hard-to-beat location, with wide views out to sea, this B&B occupies a classic, Victorian terrace house on the clifftop in the centre of Cromer. There are six bedrooms, most en suite, and each has high ceilings and is modestly decorated in a modern style. Home-cooked breakfasts; £10 reduction for shared facilities. No cards. __£74__

Cliftonville Hotel 29 Runton Rd, NR27 9AS ☎01263 512543, ⓦ cliftonvillehotel.co.uk. Among the big old mansions that line up along Runton Rd just west of the town centre facing out to sea, this is the smartest, its grand Edwardian foyer equipped with an impressive double staircase and oodles of wood panelling. After the foyer, the rooms beyond can't help but seem a tad mundane, but they are large and they all have sea views. __£120__

The Grove 95 Overstrand Rd, NR27 0DJ ☎01263 512412, ⓦ thegrovecromer.co.uk. Tucked away in its own grounds on the Overstrand edge of Cromer, this is one of the town's nicest places to stay: a small 16-room hotel in an elegant Georgian house, with a glamping site made up

of bell tents and yurts (each sleeping four people) and six self-catering cottages, plus an excellent restaurant (see below). The hotel rooms are well-equipped without being flash and there's a lovely relaxed feel to the place, with enough to do to keep you from getting into the car for a few days: there's an indoor heated pool, a garden, a children's play area, and you can walk to the beach and into town through the woods. Double __£100__; yurt __£120__; cottage (four people, one week) __£800__

Virginia Court Hotel Cliff Ave, NR27 0AN ☎01263 512398, ⓦ virginiacourt.co.uk. This recently revamped, medium-sized hotel, arguably Cromer's best, has super-comfy beds, super-thick towels, super-warm duvets and super-fast wi-fi. The hotel dates back to Edwardian times, hence the capacious foyer with its wide, sweeping staircase, and the atmosphere is very much that of a traditional seaside hotel, friendly and relaxed. It's in a handy location too, on a quiet residential street a couple of minutes' walk from the immaculate greenery of North Lodge Park, and the owners are a gold mine of local information. The restaurant (see below) is excellent, as well. __£120__

EATING AND DRINKING

Café Main 50 Church St, NR27 9HH ☎01263 515070, ⓦ cafemaincromer.co.uk. This popular modern café serves the best coffee in town along with a good line in snacks and cakes. If the sun is out, you can join the scramble for a seat on the mini pavement terrace. Mon–Sat 8.30am–5pm, Sun 9.30am–4pm.

The Grove 95 Overstrand Rd, NR27 0DJ ☎01263 512412, ⓦ thegrovecromer.co.uk. The restaurant of elegant *Grove* hotel, with its modern British menu (mains from £17), has received rave reviews. Daily 6–9pm & Sun noon–2.30pm.

Mary Jane's Fish & Chip Shop 27 Garden St, NR27 9HN ☎01263 511208. Many Norfolk tourists are fastidious about their fish and chips with allegiances strongly argued and felt. This family-owned place is especially popular, not for the decor (which is very basic), but for lightness of the batter and the freshness of the fish. Eat-in or takeaway. Daily 11.30am–9pm.

Red Lion Brook St, NR27 9HD ☎01263 514964, ⓦ redlioncromer.co.uk. Right in the centre of old Cromer,

on the ridge facing out to sea, this lively pub has a grand old bar behind which are parked enough spirits to destroy even the hardiest of livers. A good supply of real ales and above-average pub grub too. Daily 11am–11pm.

Rocket House Café RNLI building, The Gangway, NR27 9ET ☎01263 519126, ⓦ rockethousecafe.co.uk. Offering sparkling views over the beach, pier and ocean from its giant windows – and outside from its blustery terrace – this café has the best location in town by a long chalk, though the food lacks subtlety – stick to the salads (which start at just £5) and the crab. Mon–Fri 9am–5pm, Sat 10am–5pm & 6–9pm, Sun 10am–5pm.

Virginia Court Hotel Cliff Ave, NR27 0AN ☎01263 512398, ⓦ virginiacourt.co.uk. The lovely *Virginia Court Hotel*'s (see above) restaurant is appropriately excellent, with due emphasis on local, seasonal ingredients – try, for example, the roast duck with an orange and redcurrant jus; mains average £14. Accommodation and dinner deals available. Daily 6.30–8.30pm.

3

SHOPPING

Crossways 1 Chapel St, NR27 9HJ ☎01263 513207. For better or worse, you don't see many shops like this any more, a good traditional tobacconist with every sort of cigarette and cigar you can think of, plus snuff, which is – apparently – enjoying something of a revival. Mon–Sat 9.30am–5pm.

Dudley's Bakery 21 Tucker St, NR27 9HA ☎01263 519777. The best baker's in town where a wide range of breads is supplemented by pies, cakes and quiches. Mon–Sat 7am–4pm.

Jarrold 33 Church St, NR27 9ES ☎01263 512190, ⓦjarrold.co.uk. A branch of the independent Jarrold's department store from Norwich (see p.59), this is easily the best stationers in town, with good sidelines in jigsaws and games, local maps and travel guides. Mon–Sat 9am–5.30pm.

East and West Runton

Cromer has a lovely sandy **beach**, but it can get a little crowded and if you're after a little more solitude, you may prefer **the Runtons**, just to the west of Cromer, before you reach Sheringham. First up along the main coastal road, the A149, is **EAST RUNTON**, where static caravans line up along the sea-bluff and a narrow lane, **Beach Road**, cuts down from the main road to a long strip of sandy beach. Neighbouring **WEST RUNTON** is a little bit larger, and here **Water Lane** cuts off the A149 to weave its way though the village before emerging beside crumbling sea cliffs with another slice of sandy beach extending east back towards Cromer. There's a smashing campsite here, too (see below).

ARRIVAL AND DEPARTURE   EAST AND WEST RUNTON

By bus Buses to East Runton, including the Norfolk Coasthopper (see p.124), pull in at the foot of Beach Road

(see above), while those to West Runton stop at the main road junction, where the A149 meets Station Road.

ACCOMMODATION

Beeston Regis Caravan & Camping Park Cromer Rd, West Runton, NR27 9QZ ☎01263 823614, ⓦbeestonregis.co.uk. First impressions of this site, which lies just to the east of Sheringham on the north side of the A149, may not be too favourable – there are a few too many static caravans for that – but campers share a lovely little patch perched immediately behind the sea cliffs; there's even a steep staircase leading down to a small sandy beach. The Norfolk Coasthopper (see p.124) stops close by. Camping pitch for two (including car and hook-up) **£24**

Felbrigg Hall

Felbrigg, NR11 8PR • **House** March–Oct Mon–Wed, Sat & Sun 11am–5pm • £9.85 (house and gardens); NT • **Gardens** March–Oct daily 11am–5pm; Nov to mid-Dec Thurs–Sun 11am–4pm • £4.65 • **Parkland** Daily dawn to dusk • Free • ☎01263 837444, ⓦnationaltrust.org.uk

Felbrigg Hall, situated just a couple of miles southwest of Cromer off the A148, is a charming Jacobean mansion. The main facade is particularly appealing, the soft hues of the ageing limestone and brick intercepted by three bay windows, which together sport a large, cleverly carved inscription – *Gloria Deo in Excelsis* – in celebration of the reviving fortunes of the family who owned the place, the Windhams. The interior is splendid too, with the studied informality of both the dining room and the drawing room enlivened by some magnificent seventeenth-century plasterwork ceilings and sundry objets d'art. Many of the paintings were purchased by William Windham II, who undertook his Grand Tour in the 1740s – hence the two paintings of the Battle of the Texel by Willem van de Velde the Elder, and the six oils and twenty-odd gouaches of Rome and southern Italy by Giovanni Battista Busiri.

The surrounding **parkland** divides into two, with woods to the north and open pasture to the south. Footpaths crisscross the park and a popular spot to head for is the medieval **Church of St Margaret's** in the southeastern corner, which contains a fine set of brasses and a fancy memorial to William Windham I and his wife by Grinling Gibbons (1648–1721), widely regarded as the finest woodcarver of his day. Nearer the house the extensive walled **garden** features flowering borders and an octagonal dove house, while the stables have been converted into particularly pleasant **tearooms**.

Sheringham and around

SHERINGHAM, a popular seaside town with a shingle beach, just four miles west of Cromer, has an amiable, easy-going air, its narrow High Street dotted with souvenir shops, cafés and chip shops. One of the town's more distinctive features is the smooth **pebbles** that face and decorate many of its houses, a flinting technique used frequently in this part of Norfolk. The downside is that the power of the waves, which makes the pebbles smooth, has also forced the local council to spend thousands rebuilding the sea defences, and the resultant mass of reinforced concrete makes for a less than pleasing **seafront** – despite the best efforts of **The Mo**, one of north Norfolk's more enjoyable museums. Sheringham's two main attractions are, however, elsewhere – in the hilly expanses of **Sheringham Park** to the southwest of town and in the volunteer-run **North Norfolk Railway**, whose trains shunt along the five miles of track from Sheringham to Holt (see p.142).

The Mo Museum

Lifeboat Plain, NR26 8BG • March–May & Oct Tues–Sat 10am–4.30pm, Sun noon–4pm; June–Sept Mon–Sat 10am–4.30pm, Sun noon–4pm • £3.70 • ⓣ 01263 824482, ⓦ sheringhammuseum.co.uk

Spread over two floors, **The Mo** – aka Sheringham Museum – focuses on the town's nautical past, its prime exhibits being a substantial collection of vintage fishing boats

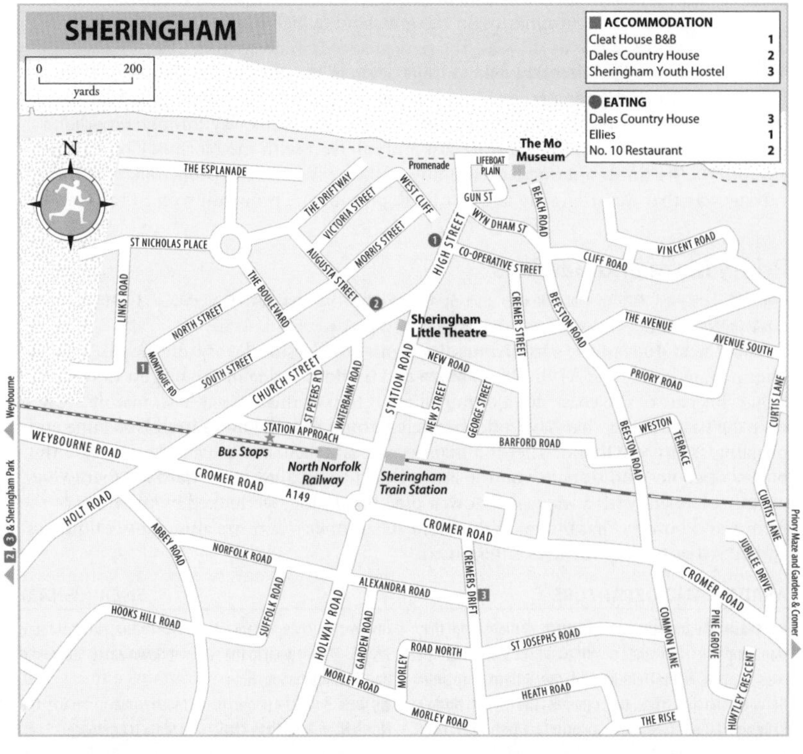

and lifeboats alongside archive film of dramatic sea rescues. There are also displays on old Sheringham, something on wind farms, and a viewing tower that rises high above its immediate surroundings. The museum puts on a lively programme of temporary exhibitions and events too, for example a feature on ganseys, the traditional woven jumper worn by local fishermen, and a "Spooky Pirate Treasure Trail" for kids.

Sheringham Park

Upper Sheringham, NR26 8TL · **Park** Daily dawn to dusk · **Visitor centre** Mid-March to Sept daily 10am–5pm; Oct Wed–Sun 10am–5pm; Nov to mid-March Sat & Sun 11am–4pm · Free, but parking £5; NT · ☎ 01263 820550, ⓦ nationaltrust.org.uk · Reached from Sheringham along the B1157, or from Cromer and Holt along the A148; buses run to the park from both Cromer and Sheringham train stations

Stretching over a large and distinctly hilly chunk of land just a couple of miles to the southwest of town, **Sheringham Park** was laid out to a design by Humphry Repton (1752–1818), one of England's most celebrated landscape gardeners. Repton professed himself very pleased with the result – Sheringham Park was "my most favourite work", he proclaimed, though the commission was not without its problems: following a carriage accident in 1811, Repton was confined to a wheelchair which severely limited the number of inspectorial visits he could make.

Over the decades, Repton's original design has been modified on several occasions, but the broad principles have survived, most memorably in the several **lookout points** that dot the wooded ridge running across the southern half of the park. Here also, among the Scots pine, sweet chestnut and oak, are two later additions, the magnificent, 50-acre **rhododendron garden**, seen at its best from late May to early June, and the **Gazebo** on top of Oak Wood Hill, where a steep modern stairway leads up to a viewing platform that offers sumptuous views over the coast. Further north, the park gets flatter and more agricultural, culminating in the grassland, which backs onto its honey-coloured **sea cliffs**, while in the west the park shades into heathland.

Three, clearly signed **circular walking trails** begin at the entrance: the shortest is the half-mile jaunt to the **Temple**, a modest ornamental folly on top of Temple Hill, and the longest is the five-mile **Ramblers' Route**, which threads its way through woodland and across open farmland to hit the coast and intersect with the Norfolk Coast Path (see p.29). The third, intermediate walking trail, the two-mile **Repton Trail**, uses the carriageway that was originally laid out by Repton before proceeding on to the Gazebo.

Priory Maze and Gardens

Cromer Rd, Sheringham, NR26 8SF · April–Oct daily 10am–5pm; Nov–Feb Wed–Sun 10am–4pm · £5.50, children £3 · ☎ 01263 822986, ⓦ priorymazegardens.co.uk · The Norfolk Coasthopper bus (see p.124) stops 450 yards from the Gardens

Situated next door to the battered medieval ruins of Beeston Priory, on the east side of Sheringham beside the A149, **Priory Maze and Gardens** is one of the biggest draws along this part of the coast. It's a beautiful collection of themed gardens, mainly created over the past decade, that have a deliberately natural feel; the **maze** itself is as large and puzzling as any you'll find. There's a plant centre attached, and a really nice café, with plenty of choice and seats out on the lawn. But the real draw is the **gardens** themselves, artfully planned, with a water meadow, a pine plantation overlooked by the ruins of the priory, and borders that bloom with colour in summer. There are also plenty of quizzes and activities to keep the kids entertained.

ARRIVAL AND DEPARTURE   SHERINGHAM

By train Sheringham has two train stations and they stand opposite each other, on either side of Station Rd. The main station is the terminus of the Bittern Line from Norwich (hourly; 1hr); the other is the North Norfolk Railway station (see box opposite), which has been restored to its appearance as of 1963. From either station, it's a 5–10min walk to the seafront down along Station Rd and its continuation, High St.

By bus Buses to Sheringham mostly pull in beside the North Norfolk Railway station, on Station Approach.

ACCOMMODATION

Cleat House B&B 7 Montague Rd, NR26 8LN ☎01263 822765, ⚑cleathouse.co.uk. This deluxe B&B, in a sympathetically modernized Edwardian house, a 5min walk from the seafront, offers three very comfortable, en-suite guest rooms, each of which is decorated in a modern rendition of period style. The breakfasts are excellent, there's a summer patio, and the overnight rate includes an afternoon cream tea when you arrive. April–Sept minimum two-night stay on weekends. **£110**

Dales Country House Lodge Hill, NR26 8TJ ☎01263 824555, ⚑dalescountryhouse.co.uk. In a superb location, just a couple of miles inland from Sheringham on the edge of Sheringham Park, this manor-house hotel occupies a rambling Edwardian mansion that was designed for a local bigwig – one Commodore Henry Douglas King, MP – in 1910 with the original Victorian rectory as its architectural base. With its tall and slender chimneys, half-timbering, ruddy-coloured stonework and turret, it's an impressive building and much of the interior is impressive too, beginning with the splendid wood-panelled foyer and dining room. Other parts of the house are not so endearing, reflecting its one-time use as a residential home, but the best of the 21 guest rooms are captivating, complete with mini-terraces, four-posters, oak furniture and open fireplaces. You can also access Sheringham Park direct from a gate in the hotel grounds. **£170**

Sheringham Youth Hostel 1 Cremer's Drift, NR26 8HX ☎0845 3719040, ⚑yha.org.uk. This well-equipped hostel occupies a large Victorian house on the south side of Sheringham, just beyond the A149 and a 5–10min walk from the town's train and bus stations. Among its facilities there is a cycle store, a self-catering kitchen, a laundry and a dining room, though there's only wi-fi (free) in the public rooms. There are one hundred beds in two- to six-berth bedrooms and family rooms are available, too. Dorm beds **£15**, doubles **£35**

EATING

Dales Country House Lodge Hill, NR26 8TJ ☎01263 824555, ⚑dalescountryhouse.co.uk. The *Dales* is a smashing hotel (see above) and it also possesess a very competent restaurant. The menu exhibits both flair and imagination: try, for instance, confit of wild rabbit for starters, followed by the roast rump of lamb served with parmentier potatoes, herbs, shallots, sautéed courgettes and mint jus; mains start at about £15. Daily noon–2pm & 6.30–9.30pm.

Ellies 14 High St, NR26 8JR. Kiosk and simple café selling Norfolk's own Ronaldo's ice cream in a mouthwatering battery of flavours, from chocolate and ginger to cinnamon, pineapple, coconut and lavender. Yum, yum. Daily 11am–5pm, later in season.

No. 10 Restaurant 10 Augusta St, NR26 8LA ☎01263 824400. Many visitors think this is the best restaurant in Sheringham – and it definitely has the prettiest premises, the windows of its Edwardian facade showing off a tasty batch of cakes and scones. The menu is well considered – the cod fillet with spring onion risotto and red pepper sauce (£15) is a good example – and they serve snacks too. Meals Wed–Sat noon–2pm & 6.30–9.30pm; teas, coffees and snacks Wed–Sat 10am–noon.

ENTERTAINMENT

Sheringham Little Theatre 2 Station Rd, NR26 8RE ☎01263 822347, ⚑sheringhamlittletheatre.com. This popular, 180-seat theatre offers a wide-ranging, all-year programme of music, art, comedy, film and theatre, but the highlights are the Christmas panto and the Summer Rep of classical and contemporary plays, anything from Wilde to Ayckbourn and running from July until September.

THE NORTH NORFOLK RAILWAY

Never a big player, the **Midland & Great Northern Joint Railway** (M&GN – familiarly known as the "Muddle and Get Nowhere") served much of Norfolk and Lincolnshire from its establishment in 1893 through to nationalization in the 1940s, though most of its routes were closed not long afterwards. One of the company's branch lines ran southwest from Sheringham to Holt, and this five miles of track was adopted by the volunteer enthusiasts of the **North Norfolk Railway** (NNR) in 1965, with the first vintage steam trains chugging down the "**Poppy Line**" two years later. The NNR is now a firm fixture of the Norfolk tourist scene, its steam and vintage diesel trains rumbling through the countryside with stations at Sheringham, yards from the ordinary train station (see opposite), Weybourne, Kelling Heath and Holt (see p.142).

The NNR (☎01263 820800, ⚑nnrailway.co.uk) operates services throughout the year (April & Oct on most days; May–Sept daily; Nov–March limited service). A return fare from Sheringham to Holt costs £12, singles £7.

Weybourne and around

Travelling west from Sheringham, the A149 meanders through a pretty rural landscape offering occasional glimpses of the sea and a shoreline protected by both a slab of marshland and a giant shingle barrier erected after the catastrophic flood of 1953. After about four miles you reach **WEYBOURNE**, whose huddle of houses falls either side of the main road. In the middle of the village, **Beach Lane**, a side road on the right, leaves the A149 to weave its way down to the shoreline, where a large shingle mound protects this part of the seashore and abuts a wide shingle **beach**. Likely as not, you'll spot a handful of anglers with their lines tugging in the surf – the beach shelves straight into the ocean, putting deep water close at hand. This is unusual for Norfolk and raiding Danes took full advantage in the ninth and tenth centuries, grounding their boats here at Weybourne before marching inland. Much later, in Elizabethan times, there was a real local panic when it was thought the Spaniards were heading for Weybourne, but they failed to show up, leaving the anchorage to a boisterous bunch of pirates, who made a living hereabouts until the late 1800s.

ARRIVAL AND DEPARTURE   **WEYBOURNE**

By train The NNR station (see box, p.133) is about one mile south of Weybourne's main street (the A149), along Station Rd and on Sandy Hill Lane, NR25 7HN.

By bus The Norfolk Coasthopper bus (see p.124) uses the bus shelters outside the *Ship Inn*, on the A149 in the centre of the village.

EATING

The Ship Inn The Street, NR25 7SZ ☎01263 588721, ⓦtheshipinnweybourne.com. This family-run pub, in a substantial, early twentieth-century building beside the A149, offers well-above-average bar food featuring a good range of local produce. An excellent selection of Norfolk ales too. Mains from £10. Kitchen Mon–Sat noon–2.30pm & 5.30–8.30pm, Sun noon–8pm; pub daily noon–11pm.

Kelling Heath

Holgate Hill, NR25 7HW • Open access • Free • ⓦnorfolkcoastaonb.org.uk

On the other side of the A149, just southwest of Weybourne, lies **Kelling Heath**, a protected parcel of heathland mostly covered by gorse, heather and bracken, though its northern slopes sustain a mixed woodland. The heath is crisscrossed with walking paths, which are most readily reached from the car park on Holgate Hill – take the Holt Road south from Weybourne and veer right.

The Muckleburgh Military Collection

Muckleburgh House, Weybourne Rd, NR25 7EH • April–Oct daily 10am–5pm • £10 • ☎01263 588210, ⓦmuckleburgh.co.uk

The vintage tank parked beside the A149 just to the west of Weybourne marks the entrance to the **Muckleburgh Military Collection**, whose assorted military hardware, much of which dates from World War II, is dotted around what was once an anti-aircraft training camp. Pride of military place goes to the **tanks**, including Soviet, German, US and British examples, and visitors are offered a cross-country ride in an American personnel carrier. If you stump up an extra £100, you can also have a bash at driving a tank for about forty minutes – and great fun it is too, in a very noisy kind of way.

Salthouse

With marshes to the north and heathland to the south, the tiny hamlet of **SALTHOUSE**, just a couple of miles west of Weybourne, may seem inconsequential today, but its flocks of sheep once provided a rich living for the lord of the manor. Indeed, such was the wealth of the local lord that the peasantry exacted retribution during Kett's Rebellion of 1549 (see p.325), when they polished off one of the family, William Heydon, who now lies buried in St Peter Mancroft in Norwich (see p.48). Today, the main evidence of the wealth and power of the Heydons is the **church of St Nicholas** (daily 10am–4pm), stuck on top of a grassy knoll at the insistence of Henry Heydon, its prominent position both a reminder to the faithful and a landmark for those at sea. Mostly dating from the sixteenth century, the church is an imposing structure, its aisle windows tall and slender, its tower squat and strong, but the interior is bare and bleak, even though the handsome timber ceiling does its best to cheer things up. The church also holds the **tomb** of Henry Stanforth, who died in 1751 at the age of 69, his qualities epitomizing all that was ideal in the Georgian gentleman: Stanforth was "an affectionate husband, an indulgent parent and a generous friend". It's also possible to reach the seashore at Salthouse along **Beach Lane**, which leaves the A149 at the east end of the village, but all you'll find at the end of the lane is a shingle hump and a shingle beach.

3

ARRIVAL AND DEPARTURE   SALTHOUSE

By bus The Norfolk Coasthopper (see p.124) pulls in beside The Green, a small triangular slab of grass beside the A149.

EATING

Cookies Crab Shack The Green, NR25 7AJ ☏01263 740352, ⓦsalthouse.org.uk. Overlooking the A149, *Cookies*, which comprises a tiny shop, a plastic gazebo and a glorified garden shed, has something of a cult following, not for the decor – which is simple in the extreme – but for the freshness and variety of the seafood. Crabs, prawns and smoked fish lead the maritime way, but there's lots more to choose from including samphire, a local delicacy harvested from the surrounding mudflats and salt marshes from late June to mid-September. Oct–March daily 10am–4pm; April–Sept daily 9am–6pm.

Salthouse Dun Cow Purdy St, NR25 7XA ☏01263 740467, ⓦsalthouseduncow.com. The only pub in Salthouse, the *Dun Cow* has been refurbished in gastropub style, its bare-brick walls and wooden beams left intact. The food is strong on local seafood and meat with mains starting at around £15. Kitchen daily 11am–9pm; pub daily 11am–11pm.

ADMIRAL SIR CLOUDESLEY SHOVELL LOSES HIS WAY

A big man with a big wig, **Sir Cloudesley Shovell** (1650–1707) was born in Cley and joined the Royal Navy as a cabin boy at the tender age of 14. Keen to earn promotion, Shovell taught himself navigation and his skilled seamanship then saw him scuttling up through the ranks in smart order. In 1676, Shovell hit the big time, becoming something of a national hero when he led two daring raids against the pirates of North Africa. Over the next twenty years, Shovell was involved in a series of naval battles until finally, in 1704, he was rewarded by his appointment as Rear Admiral of England. So far so good, but Shovell's career came to an untimely end just three years later: sailing from Gibraltar to Portsmouth, Shovell's fleet lost its bearings and struck the rocks off the **Scilly Isles** with the loss of four ships and two thousand men, one of the greatest disasters in British naval history.

Shovell avoided the ignominy of facing a board of enquiry by **dying** when the fleet ran aground, though there were some oddities about his death. Shovell's body was found seven miles from where his ship went down, so it seems likely he got away in a rowboat before this itself was wrecked – and the crew drowned – when they tried to come ashore at Porthellick Cove on St Mary's, or so it was assumed. On her deathbed some thirty years later, a certain **Mrs Thomas**, a Scilly islander, confessed that she had discovered the half-conscious Shovell on the seashore and had promptly smothered him for his large emerald ring. Mrs T then produced the ring and gave it to the attendant clergyman, who passed it back to the Shovell family. Meanwhile, after several comings and goings, the admiral's body ended up being buried in Westminster Abbey. There's a small display on Shovell in **Strangers' Hall** in Norwich (see p.46).

Cley-next-the-sea and around

Heading west from Salthouse on the A149, it's about half a mile to the Cley Marshes nature reserve (see opposite) and another three-quarters of a mile to the distinctive windmill at the start of **CLEY-NEXT-THE-SEA**, once a busy wool port but now little more than a row of flint cottages and Georgian mansions set beside a narrow, marshy inlet that (just) gives access to the sea: at high tide, the sea once swept over the marshes, but these were encased behind a new set of sea defences in the 1940s. In medieval times, the tides went much further, which explains why Cley's fine medieval **church** is located half a mile inland at the very southern edge of the current village, overlooking **The Green**, which was itself once the main harbour. Church apart, Cley's main draws are gastronomic with a pair of excellent shops (see opposite) on the main street, which doubles as the A149.

Church of St Margaret

Holt Rd, NR25 7UD • Daily 9.30am–4.30pm or dusk

Cley's architectural pride and joy is the church of **St Margaret**, whose most striking feature is its entrance **porch**, a two-storey, fifteenth-century extravaganza with the priest's chamber up above and a vaulted chamber down below, complete with a woman chasing a fox in the central boss. There's more unusual – and unusually secular – carving inside, where the arches of the **nave** frame a series of cameos, from a lion gnawing a bone to St George tackling a distinctly unfrightening dragon, and the bench ends are decorated with the most playful of monster-gargoyles. The nave and the now ruined transepts were completed in the Decorated style in the early fourteenth century and there were plans to rebuild the glum-looking tower and chancel, but these were abandoned when the Black Death reached Cley in 1349, killing over half the population: the village never really recovered.

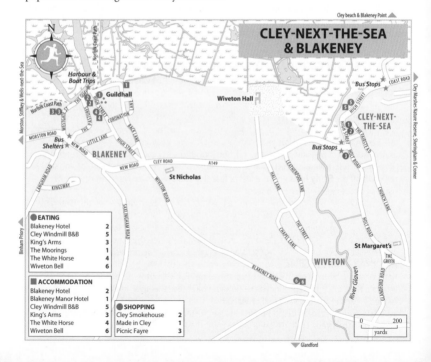

ARRIVAL AND DEPARTURE   CLEY-NEXT-THE-SEA

By bus The Norfolk Coasthopper bus (see p.124) stops outside Picnic Fayre on Cley's main street (the A149).

ACCOMMODATION AND EATING

★**Cley Windmill B&B** The Quay, NR25 7RP ☎01263 740209, ⓦcleywindmill.co.uk. This outstanding B&B occupies a converted windmill complete with sails and a balcony offering wonderful views over the surrounding marshes and seashore. The guest rooms, both in the windmill and the adjoining outhouses, are decorated in attractive period style and the best, like the Stone Room, have handsome beamed ceilings. At peak times, there is a minimum of a two- or three-night stay. The *Windmill*'s smart and very agreeable restaurant specializes in traditional, home-made English cooking and a three-course set meal costs £32.50 per person; advance reservations are required. Self-catering arrangements are possible as well. Dinner sittings at 7.30pm. **£180**

SHOPPING

★**Cley Smokehouse** High St, NR25 7RF ☎01263 740282, ⓦcleysmokehouse.com. This superb smokehouse sells a wide range of freshly smoked shellfish, fish and cured meats as well as home-made pâtés. Everything is smoked on site and their kippers are near impossible to beat. Mon–Fri 9am–5pm, Sat 8.30am–5pm, Sun 9.30am–4.30pm.
Made in Cley High St, NR25 7RF ☎01263 740134, ⓦmadeincley.co.uk. Of the several fine and applied art shops in Cley, this is the pick. They sell jewellery, prints and modern sculpture, but above all it's for their pottery they are praised, imaginative pieces for domestic use, from oven to tableware, and mostly made of hard-wearing stoneware clay. Next door to the Smoke House. Mon–Sat 10am–5pm, Sun 11am–4pm.
Picnic Fayre The Old Forge, High St, NR25 7AP ☎01263 740587, ⓦpicnic-fayre.co.uk. Squeezed into the old village forge, this long-established deli has been catering to urban – and urbane – tastes since it opened in 1984. Holiday-makers come from miles around to buy the freshly baked bread, dip into the antipasti, and make a selection from a wide range of cheeses, mustards, chutneys, jams and marmalades. Mon–Sat 9am–5pm, Sun 11am–4pm.

Cley Marshes Nature Reserve

A149, NR25 7SA • **Visitor centre** Daily: April to late Oct 10am–5pm; late Oct to March 10am–4pm • £5 • ☎01263 740008, ⓦnorfolkwildlifetrust.org.uk

Roughly midway between Cley and Salthouse along the A149 is **Cley Marshes Nature Reserve**, whose conspicuous, roadside **visitor centre** attracts birdwatchers like bees to a honeypot. Owned and operated by the Norfolk Wildlife Trust (NWT), the visitor centre has displays on local wildlife, sells books on the same, has OS maps, and issues **permits** for entering the reserve, whose salt- and freshwater marshes, reedbeds and coastal shingle ridge are accessed on several **footpaths** and overseen by half a dozen **hides**. You can avoid the £5 charge by walking round the edge of the reserve, but you'll miss out on the hides.

On foot to Blakeney Point

Lifeboat House, Blakeney Point National Trust information centre: April–Oct daily dawn to dusk • Free • No telephone, ⓦnationaltrust.org.uk

On the west side of the Cley Marshes Nature Reserve – and about 400 yards east of Cley village (see opposite) – is the mile-long byroad that leads to the shingle mounds of **Cley beach**. This is the starting point for the four-mile hike west out along the spit to **Blakeney Point**, a national nature reserve famed for its colonies of terns and seals. The **seal colony** is made up of several hundred common and grey seals, and the old **Lifeboat House**, at the end of the spit, is now a National Trust information centre. The shifting shingle can make walking difficult, so keep to the low-water mark, which also means that you won't accidentally trample any nests. The less strenuous alternative is to take one of the boat trips to the point from Blakeney or Morston (see box, p.139). The Norfolk Coast Path passes close to Cley beach too, and then continues along the northern edge of the Cley Marshes Nature Reserve (see above).

Wiveton Hall fruit farm, café and farm shop

Wiveton Hall, 1 Marsh Lane, NR25 7TE · **Café & shop** April to early Nov Mon–Fri 10am–4.30pm, Sat & Sun 9.30am–4.30pm · ☎ 01263 740515, ⓦ wivetonhall.co.uk

Wiveton Hall fruit farm, café and farm shop, just off the A149 midway between Cley and Blakeney, casts its gastronomic net as widely as possible. Visitors can pick their own fruit and veg in the fields, buy local produce at the farm shop, and pop into the café, a charming rustic-rural kind of place with a homely feel and offering excellent home-made snacks and meals: the café uses the farm's produce wherever and whenever possible. From the café, it's a few yards to **Wiveton Hall**, a sprawling country house, parts of which, including some of the Dutch-style gables, date back to the seventeenth century. One wing offers self-catering accommodation and there are holiday lets in several estate cottages, too – see the website for details.

Glandford

3

Glandford Shell Museum Church House, NR25 7JR · Easter–Oct Tues–Sat 10am–12.30pm & 2–4.30pm · £2 · ☎ 01263 740081, ⓦ shellmuseum.org.uk

From Cley, it's a mile or so south to **GLANDFORD**, a pretty little hamlet whose flint and red-brick cottages were built at the behest of a local landowner, Sir Alfred Jodrell (1847–1929), at the beginning of the twentieth century. Jodrell was well known for his charitable acts, but this does not seem to have extended to his political opponents: the story goes that when he asked one of his labourers how he was going to vote, the man rashly told him he was a "Radical", so Jodrell sacked him on the spot. It was the same Jodrell who built a small hall to display his substantial collection of seashells; this is now the **Glandford Shell Museum**, a cosy sort of place with seashells drawn from every corner of the globe. Mixed in among them are all sorts of curios, including a pair of albatross skulls, some intricate mother-of-pearl carvings and a rusty Cromwellian cannon ball.

ACCOMMODATION AND EATING   GLANDFORD

Wiveton Bell Blakeney Rd NR25 7TL ☎ 01263 740101, ⓦ wivetonbell.co.uk. On the road from Cley to Glandford, you will almost certainly spot the *Wiveton Bell*, which occupies an attractive, whitewashed building right next to the crossroads. The restaurant here has won all sorts of plaudits, not least for its lively menu – try, for example, the tomato, spinach and saffron risotto (£12.50). There are six deluxe bedrooms here too, each of which is both comfortable and luxurious – self-styled "French chic", and that sums it up nicely. Daily noon–2.15pm & 6–9pm, Sun till 8.30pm. **£120**

SHOPPING

CleySpy Glandford, NR25 7JP ☎ 01263 740088, ⓦ cleyspy.co.uk. There's everything for the birder here, from monoculars and binoculars to tripods and night-vision gear. Most of the stuff is new, but there are secondhand items too, and the staff are informed and helpful. Mon–Sat 10am–5pm, Sun 10am–4pm.

Blakeney and around

BLAKENEY, a mile or so to the west of Cley, is delightful. Once a bustling seaport exporting fish, corn and salt, Blakeney even provisioned two ships for the Crusades and accommodated an émigré colony of Dutch merchants, but that was long before its harbour silted. Nowadays it's a lovely little place of pebble-covered cottages sloping up from the creekiest of harbours. Crab sandwiches are sold from stalls at the quayside, family-run shops flank the winding high street, and footpaths stretch out along the sea wall to east and west, offering long, lingering views over the salt marshes with their deep and sticky mudbanks and abundant birdlife.

The Guildhall

Back Lane, NR25 7NR • Open access • Free; EH • ⓦ www.english-heritage.org.uk

At low tide, Blakeney harbour is no more than a muddy creek ideal for a bit of quayside crabbing and mud sliding. Yet here also is one reminder of the village's long history, the battered remains of the medieval **Guildhall**, though the locals were hardly overawed by its antiquity – right up until the 1950s, they grew rhubarb in its dark and gloomy, brick-vaulted undercroft.

The church of St Nicholas

Wiveton Rd, NR25 7NJ • Daily 9.30am–4.30pm or dusk

Blakeney's second noteworthy building is the **church of St Nicholas**, a large and sterling structure stuck on a grassy hillock beside the A149 at the south end of the village. Dating from the fifteenth century, the church's main tower and nave are made of flint rubble with stone trimmings, the traditional building materials of north Norfolk; but it's the second, smaller, minaret-like **tower** above the chancel that grabs most attention because no one is really sure why it's there: too slender to carry a bell, too angular to have been a stair turret, the usual explanation is that it served as a beacon to those out at sea, which seems strange when the main tower is much taller and more conspicuous. The church's **interior** is not exactly riveting, but it does hold a fine oak and chestnut hammerbeam roof and a mildly engaging set of twentieth-century stained-glass windows outlining the early history of Christianity in Britain. The late thirteenth-century chancel is the only survivor from the original Carmelite friary church.

3

Binham Priory

Binham, NR21 0DQ • **Grounds and ruins** Access at any reasonable time • **Church** Daily: April–Sept 9am–6pm; Oct–March 9am–4pm • Free; EH • ⓦ www.english-heritage.org.uk

The substantial remains of **Binham Priory** boast a handsome rural setting about four miles southwest of Blakeney, on the edge of the hamlet of **Binham**. The Benedictines established a priory here in the late eleventh century, but long before its suppression in 1540 it had gained a bad reputation, its priors renowned for their fecklessness. One of the worst was William de Somerton, a fourteenth-century figure who funded his dabblings in alchemy by selling the church silverware and then the vestments. Neither were the monks a picture of contentment – one became insane through excessive meditation, so the prior had him flogged and then kept in solitary confinement until his death. Today, the porridge-like ruins focus on the priory church, whose nave was turned into the parish church during the Reformation. Inside, the nave arcades are a beautiful illustration of the transition between the Norman and Early English styles with a triple bank of hooped windows shedding light on the austere interior. Among the fittings, look out for the delicately carved **font** and the poppy-head **bench ends**, worn smooth by the touch of generations of worshippers. Look out also for the remains of the former **rood screen** kept at the back of the church. The Protestants whitewashed

---

BOAT TRIPS TO BLAKENEY POINT

Blakeney harbour is linked to the sea by a narrow channel, which wriggles its way through the salt marshes, and is only navigable for a few hours on either side of high tide. Depending on these tides, there are **boat trips** from either Blakeney or Morston quay, a mile or two to the west, to either Blakeney Point (see p.137) – where passengers have a couple of hours at the point before being ferried back – or to the seal colony just off the point. The main operators advertise departure times on blackboards by Blakeney quayside or you can reserve in advance with **Beans Boats** (☎ 01263 740505, ⓦ beansboattrips.co.uk) or **Bishop's Boats** (☎ 01263 740753, ⓦ norfolksealtrips.co.uk). Both the seal trips and those to Blakeney Point cost £10.

the screen and then covered it with biblical texts, but the paint is wearing thin and the saints they were keen to conceal have started to peep out again.

ARRIVAL AND INFORMATION — BLAKENEY

By bus Buses to Blakeney, principally the Norfolk Coasthopper (see p.124), pull in at the Westgate bus shelter, a couple of minutes' walk from the harbour.

Blakeney Quayside Cottages ☎01263 741533, ⓦ blakeneycottages.co.uk. For longer stays in Blakeney, this efficient company rents out a handful of quaint cottages. Advance reservations are strongly recommended as the cottages go quick. Cottage per week in high season (half the price in winter) **£500**

ACCOMMODATION

Blakeney Hotel The Quay, NR25 7NE ☎01263 740797, ⓦ blakeney-hotel.co.uk. *The Blakeney* is one of the most appealing seaside hotels in Norfolk, occupying a handsome, rambling building with high-pitched gables and pebble-covered walls – all in a smashing location right down by the quayside. The hotel has a heated indoor swimming pool, a secluded garden, cosy lounges with exquisite sea views and an excellent restaurant (see below). The cheaper rooms can be poky and somewhat airless, so it's worth paying more – up to a maximum of £300 – for one with views out across the harbour and the marshes. Off-season special deals and discounts are legion. **£200**

Blakeney Manor Hotel The Quay, NR25 7ND ☎01263 740376, ⓦ blakeneymanor.co.uk. This medium-sized hotel occupies an old courtyard complex in a prime location, a few yards to the east of the harbour. The modern rooms are neat and trim, if somewhat routine, and there's an attractive garden. **£100**

King's Arms Westgate St, NR25 7NQ ☎01263 740341, ⓦ blakeneykingsarms.co.uk. Blakeney's best pub (see below) has seven en-suite guest rooms decorated in a straightforward modern style. The majority overlook the marshes and one has a kitchenette. **£80**

The White Horse 4 High St, NR25 7AL ☎01263 740574, ⓦ adnams.co.uk. Now part of the excellent Adnams group from Southwold, *The White Horse* has been thoroughly revamped and modernized. Its nine guest rooms are kitted out in smart modern style, each finished off in soft pastel shades. There's a good restaurant here, too (see below), and the hotel is only a minute or two from the quay. **£115**

EATING

Blakeney Hotel The Quay, NR25 7NE ☎01263 740797, ⓦ blakeney-hotel.co.uk. This excellent hotel (see above) offers delicious lunches and afternoon teas in the sea-facing lounges and the more formal restaurant, where, in the evenings, a three-course set meal costs £29. The restaurant menu is modern British – try, for example, the seared fillet of black bream with sautéed potatoes and confit shallots with chive sauce. Kitchen daily noon–4pm & 6.30–9pm.

King's Arms Westgate St, NR25 7NQ ☎01263 740341, ⓦ blakeneykingsarms.co.uk. The best pub in Blakeney by a long chalk, this traditional boozer, with its low, beamed ceilings and rabbit-warren rooms, offers top-ranking bar food, largely English but with an international bent: try, for example, the home-made steak and Adnams ale suet pudding with rich onion gravy (£13), or the warm butterbean, blue cheese and tarragon tartlets with roasted red pepper coulis (£12). Kitchen daily noon–2pm & 6–9pm.

★**The Moorings** High St, NR25 7NA ☎01263 740054. Informal little bistro, painted in bright and cheerful colours, where the menu is strikingly creative and is particularly strong on Norfolk fish and shellfish, though other local foods feature too, including meat, game and vegetables. A typical main course is sautéed lamb kidneys with pancetta and rosemary and white bean ragout (£17). Tues–Sat 10.30am–9.30pm.

The White Horse 4 High St, NR25 7AL ☎01263 740574, ⓦ adnams.co.uk. Recently overhauled, *The White Horse* bar-cum-restaurant offers a good-quality, locally sourced menu featuring English dishes, often with a twist. Try, for instance, the calf's liver with creamed potatoes, onion and pancetta (£13) or the fish and chips (also £13). Kitchen daily noon–9pm; bar daily 11am–11pm .

Morston

It's just over a mile west from Blakeney to minuscule **MORSTON**, where the main event is the **quay**, more accessible by boat than its neighbour and a departure point for boat trips to Blakeney Point and its seal colony (see box, p.139). The National Trust owns Morston Quay and operates an **information centre** here, and this has displays on local flora and fauna. There are no fixed opening hours, but the centre is usually open two hours either side of high tide in summer with restricted hours in winter. The quay is also crossed by the Norfolk Coast Path (see p.29).

ARRIVAL AND DEPARTURE

MORSTON

By bus In Morston, the Norfolk Coasthopper (see p.124) stops just off the main road (the A149) about 200 yards

from Morston Hall, and at the south end of the lane leading down to the quay.

ACCOMMODATION AND EATING

Morston Hall Hotel The Street (A149), NR25 7AA ☎01263 741041, ⓦmorstonhall.com. Deluxe hotel in an immaculately updated country house of traditional flint and brick that sits pretty beside the A149. The rooms are smart and really rather grand, with heavy drapes and lots of country house-style flourishes, and the gardens are kept in tip-top order. All this luxury doesn't come cheap,

especially as room prices include a set dinner menu at the hotel's much-vaunted restaurant, where they work hard to create the most enticing of menus: parmesan terrine with carrot ribbons and brown-bread tuile is a characteristic starter. Their set-menu dinner costs £66, Sunday lunches a more affordable £37. Lunch sitting Sun 12.30pm; dinner sitting daily 7.30pm. **£340**

Stiffkey

The main coastal road, the A149, is unkind to **STIFFKEY** (pronounced "Stewkey"), three miles west of Morston: trapped between high flint walls, the road narrows to a single file, bottling up the traffic and creating long queues in summer. What the locals think of all this congestion is not hard to imagine, especially as Stiffkey is, at least when the cars have gone, a pretty little place whose haphazard string of cottages lies dotted to either side of the meandering River Stiffkey. An ancient village – it appears in the Domesday Book – it was the Saxons who named the place "island with stumps of trees" after its watery location, and its long history is typical of villages hereabouts. Generations of agricultural labourers were pretty much at the beck and call of the local landowners, though here at least they could earn a little extra money by gathering cockles from the salt marshes to the north of the village; these "**Stewkey Blues**" are still a delicacy, their shells stained blue by the mud in which they live.

One further curiosity is **Camping Hill**, the wooded rise beside the A149 at the east end of the village: it's not named after "camping" as we know it, but rather Stiffkey's

---

SCANDAL AT THE VICARAGE

The villagers of Stiffkey had a real shock in the 1930s when the alleged activities of their local clergyman, **Harold Francis Davidson** (1875–1937), hit the national headlines. By all accounts, Davidson was a diligent man, regularly visiting his parishioners and undertaking all sorts of charitable acts. This made him extremely popular with the ordinary folk hereabouts, but the local landowners, fearing subversion, did not take to him at all, especially **Major Philip Hamond**, who conspired to bring about his downfall. He recruited a solicitor called **Henry Dashwood**, who looked for scandal in the charity work Davidson did in London, where the rector had taken a particular interest in the poorly paid young girls who worked at Lyons Tea Rooms. Davidson always insisted he was just trying to help the girls; Dashwood said it was much more than that – and the dispute went to a Church of England ecclesiastical court in 1932. The clinching evidence was two photos showing Davidson in close proximity to partly clad girls, though Davidson insisted they were forgeries. Whatever the truth, he was defrocked, though that was not quite the end of the story: Davidson went on to appear in public entertainments, trading on his fame. In one, he was placed in a barrel that was apparently being roasted in an oven while a figure dressed as the devil prodded him with a pitchfork; in others he entered a lion's cage where he proclaimed his innocence. In the event, it wasn't a good career choice as one of the lions mauled him and he died shortly afterwards, though this was more the result of medical incompetence than the efforts of the animal. Davidson was buried back in Stiffkey, where attending his **funeral** was, to all intents and purposes, an act of defiance: three thousand mourners turned up and his widow wore white. The scandal was revived in **The Prostitute's Padre**, performed at Norwich Playhouse in 1997, and in John Walsh's 2008 novel *Sunday at the Cross Bones*.

former community free-for-all in which two mini-mobs would try to get a ball from one "goal" to another amid black eyes, broken noses and sometimes much worse.

ARRIVAL AND DEPARTURE   STIFFKEY

By bus Buses, principally the Norfolk Coasthopper (see p.124), pull in on the main road (the A149) beside Stiffkey Stores.

ACCOMMODATION AND EATING

High Sand Creek Campsite Vale Farm, Greenway, NR23 1QP ☎ 01328 830235. Signed from the A149 on the west side of Stiffkey, this straightforward, low-key campsite is geared up for tents with its pitches spread over a hedge-sheltered hillside that looks out over the salt marshes. It's also a stone's throw from the Norfolk Coast Path. Open mid-March to mid-Oct. Tent pitches from **£12**

Stiffkey Red Lion 44 Wells Rd, NR23 1AJ ☎ 01328 830552, ⓦ stiffkey.com. Beside the main road, at the west end of the village, this charming pub has been sensitively modernized, keeping its original low-beamed ceilings, stone floors, cosy rooms and country benches. The food is first-rate, its staple of English cuisine usually varied by a couple of pasta dishes. The steak and Guinness pie with baby vegetables and new potatoes (£12) is especially tasty. Immediately behind the pub is a new hotel block, comprising ten modern, chalet-style guest rooms, each of which has either a small terrace and garden or, on the first floor, a private balcony. There are some welcome eco features too, like the sedum roof and the rainwater-flush toilets. Kitchen daily noon–2.30pm & 6–9pm; pub daily 11am–11pm. **£120**

SHOPPING

Stiffkey Stores The Old Coach House, Wells Rd, NR23 1QH ☎ 01328 830489, ⓦ stiffkeystores.com. There may be a lot of north London about this shop and café, but although the assorted knick-knacks are distinctly chichi, the cakes really are superb. Try, for example, the soft and moist, deliciously tangy almond cake. Also sells cards, gifts, kitchenware, bread and a battery of local farm produce. Daily 8am–5pm.

Holt and around

Neat and trim, spick-and-span **HOLT**, just five miles southeast of Blakeney, is the prettiest town in north Norfolk and has long attracted the praise of passing travellers: "Holt is most picturesquely situated, [rendering] it perfectly charming" wrote one, though that grumpy old radical William Cobbett (1763–1835) was less impressed, moaning that it was distinctly "old-fashioned". Most of Holt was burnt to a cinder in a great fire of 1708 and in its place rose the Georgian buildings that characterize the town today, lining up along the attractive **Market Place**. In recent years, Holt has also proved particularly adept at pulling in the tourist money and its streets now boast a string of independent shops and stores – a retail treat.

Baconsthorpe Castle

Baconsthorpe, NR25 6LE • Open access in daylight hours • Free; EH • ⓦ www.english-heritage.org.uk • Just over 3miles from Holt: take the signed country lane running southeast from the A148 on the edge of Holt, go through Baconsthorpe village and then watch for the signed (but easy to miss) turning on the left

Deep in the Norfolk countryside, the extensive ruins of **Baconsthorpe Castle** are a monument to the failed ambitions of the Heydon family, who ruled the local roost for several generations. It was here, in their salad days, that the Heydons built themselves a grand moated and fortified manor house, raising the inner gatehouse in the fifteenth century and adding the outer gatehouse not long afterwards. The inner gatehouse was strong enough to shelter the family in times of danger – and it needed to be, as these were troubled times and the Heydons were a quarrelsome lot. It all went wrong for the Heydons in the late sixteenth century, when one of the clan – Sir William – ended up in debt and thereafter much of the property fell into ruin, though the outer gatehouse was inhabited until 1920. Despite the years of neglect, much has survived, including a slice of the curtain wall and moat, plus the

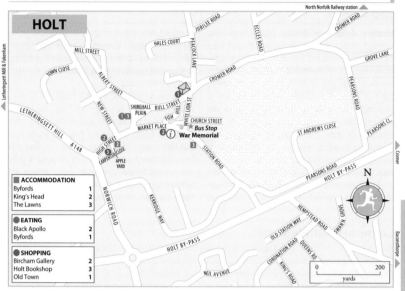

ACCOMMODATION
Byfords	1
King's Head	2
The Lawns	3

EATING
Black Apollo	2
Byfords	1

SHOPPING
Bircham Gallery	2
Holt Bookshop	3
Old Town	1

imposing flint walls of both gatehouses, each of which is punctuated by delicately carved stone doorways and window lintels.

ARRIVAL AND INFORMATION · HOLT

By train Holt is not on the regular train network, but it is on the North Norfolk Railway (see box, p.133), whose station is a mile or so east of town along the Cromer Road.

By bus Sanders Coaches (w sanderscoaches.com) links Holt with several other towns in Norfolk. Buses arrive and depart from the Market Place.
Destinations Cromer (Mon–Sat hourly; 45min); Fakenham (Mon–Sat every 2hr; 45min); Norwich (Mon–Sat every 1–2hr; 1hr 20min).

Tourist office In the centre of town at 3 Pound House, Market Place, NR25 6BW (Easter to mid-May, Sept & Oct Mon–Sat 10am–2pm; mid-May to Aug Mon–Sat 10am–5pm; ☎01263 713100, w visitnorthnorfolk.com).

ACCOMMODATION AND EATING

Black Apollo 24 High St, NR25 6BH ☎01263 712495. Cosy little café in the centre of Holt selling the best – and most varied range of – coffees in town. Tasty snacks too. Mon–Sat 8am–5pm, & Sun 10am–4pm.

Byfords 1 Shirehall Plain, NR25 6BG ☎01263 711400, w byfords.org.uk. Promoting itself as a "Higgledy-piggledy World of Pleasure" may be rather excessive, but *Byfords* attempts to hit all the bases, its substantial town-centre premises holding a deli (with home-made bread, cakes, pies and pre-cooked, frozen dinners), a café and a restaurant which dip into several cuisines – think "posh" pizza, paella and curry; mains around £13 – plus a self-styled "posh B&B" with sixteen guest rooms. Every effort has been made to keep the original character of the building, most of which dates back to the early 1900s – hence the exposed brick and flint work and oak flooring. Otherwise, it's all high spec, from Bang & Olufsen TVs, to power showers and underfloor heating.

Incidentally, visitors queue up for the breakfasts – try the kippers from Cley Smokehouse (see p.137). Kitchen daily 8am–9.30pm; drinks till 11pm. **£150**

King's Head 19 High St, NR25 6BN ☎01263 712543, w kingsheadholt.org.uk. Upstairs, above the *King's Head* pub, there are three, en-suite B&B rooms with a somewhat austere demeanour, only softened by the exposed beams and cheery paintwork. Great big beds too. Breakfast is served at *Byfords* (see above), the sister business. **£100**

The Lawns 26 Station Rd, NR25 6BS ☎01263 713390, w lawnshotelholt.co.uk. In a distinctive brick building, complete with an unusual turret tower, this family-owned hotel has eight guest rooms with fairly humdrum furnishings and fittings. The rooms are large and the hotel is a stone's throw from the centre of town, but the public areas are not especially enticing. More positively, the breakfasts are very good – especially the kippers. **£95**

3

SHOPPING

Bircham Gallery 14 Market Place, NR25 6BW ☎ 01263 713312, ⓦ birchamgallery.co.uk. Holt has a clutch of art galleries and although some of them verge on the tourist-twee, others are distinctly more upmarket and this is the pick of the artistic crop, its well-lit premises displaying regularly rotated displays of ceramics, prints, paintings, jewellery, sculpture and glassware. There's a good showing here for local contemporary artists and the gallery is perhaps at its strongest in its prints, many of which feature Norfolk land- and seascapes. Mon–Sat 9am–5pm.

Holt Bookshop 10 Appleyard, NR25 6AR ☎ 01263 715858, ⓦ holtbookshop.co.uk. Named in a poll as one of the UK's top independent bookshops, this bright and amenable store has more than 12,000 books on its shelves with special attention given to local interest titles, of which it has a comprehensive selection. Readings and cultural events too. Mon–Sat 9am–5pm, July–Dec till 5.30pm.

★**Old Town** 49 Bull St, NR25 6HP ☎ 01263 710001, ⓦ old-town.co.uk. Running the flag for British manufacturers, this excellent clothes shop has its own on-site workshop, where they turn out around fifty garments a week using British cottons, woollens and linens wherever possible. The clothes are made to order – as opposed to made to measure – with corduroy and moleskin being two of the most popular, fustian-type fabrics. Tues–Sat 10am–5pm.

Letheringsett Watermill

Riverside Rd, off the A148, NR25 7YD · **Mill operating hours** Usually Tues, Wed & Fri 11am–3pm · **Shop** Mon–Fri 9am–4pm & Sat 9am–1pm · Self-guided tours of the watermill during shop hours · £4 when the mill is working, £3 when it's not · ☎ 01263 713153, ⓦ letheringsettwatermill.co.uk · Buses from Holt Market Place (Mon–Sat 1–3 daily; 5min).

Letheringsett Watermill, a rare example of a fully working watermill, is located in the hamlet of **LETHERINGSETT**, which bunches up on the east bank of the River Glaven, just a mile west from Holt along the A148. There's been a watermill here since Norman times, maybe earlier, but the current brick building – an imposing and severe structure, four storeys high – dates from 1802. The mill still supplies many types of flour and bread to local businesses and there's a shop here, too. In Victorian times, Letheringsett was home to a renowned blacksmith, **Johnson Jex**, whose inventiveness endeared him to the local gentry – his speciality was making watches to his own design.

EATING

LETHERINGSETT

King's Head Holt Rd, NR25 7AR ☎ 01263 712691, ⓦ kingsheadnorfolk.co.uk. This well-run inn occupies a distinctive, two-storey brick building a few yards from the A148. The interior has been cleverly kitted out with all sorts of bygones, from old books to countrified furniture, but the open fires are original. The menu is strong on local, seasonal ingredients – they even have their own herd of cattle in an adjacent field – and features the likes of Norfolk duck cassoulet with mixed-leaf salad and vegetable crisps. Mon–Sat noon–2.30pm & 6.30–9pm, Sun noon–8pm.

Fakenham and around

It's hard to say quite why, but **FAKENHAM**, a medium-sized market town twelve miles southwest of Holt, seems to have missed the tourist money and although its **Market Place** is flanked and fringed by a pleasant assortment of old brick buildings, there's precious little sign of the bijou shops that are such a feature of Holt, its smaller neighbour. The town is at its busiest on horse-racing days – **Fakenham Racecourse** (☎ 01328 862388, ⓦ fakenhamracecourse.co.uk) lies just to the south of town – but otherwise it's a quiet sort of place. It is near several popular attractions, though, specifically **Pensthorpe Nature Reserve** to the east, the **Thursford Collection** to the northeast, and **Houghton Hall** to the west. There are a couple of good places to stay near Fakenham too – all of them lie to the west of town near the main road, the A148.

Museum of Gas and Local History

Hempton Rd, NR21 7LA • April, May & Oct Thurs 10.30am–1pm; June–Sept Thurs & Fri 10.30am–3.30pm • Free • ☎ 01553 762151,
Ⓦ fakenhamgasmuseum.com

Fakenham's main sight is the **Museum of Gas and Local History**, the only surviving town gasworks in the whole of England. It displays all the gear used for the manufacture of gas from coal – retorts, condensers, purifiers – in a technology that was rendered redundant when gas was discovered beneath the North Sea. There are also examples of vintage gas fires, lights, cookers and heaters. It's located a few minutes' walk south of the Market Place.

Pensthorpe Nature Reserve

Fakenham Rd, Fakenham, NR21 0LN • Daily: March–Dec 10am–5pm; Jan & Feb 10am–4pm • £11.25 • ☎ 01328 851465,
Ⓦ pensthorpe.com

Norfolk's most popular nature reserve, **Pensthorpe** occupies a large slab of land and lagoon about a mile from the centre of Fakenham. A network of footpaths negotiates most of the reserve, where waterfowl gather by the hundred and Norfolk's birdlife is supplemented by (clipped-wing) imports from round the world. One part of the reserve is dedicated to declining species – there is a red squirrel hutch and a corncrake breeding programme – and there are also several themed gardens. If you like things a little wilder, there are bird hides on the edge of Pensthorpe where you can observe waterfowl in a less constrained environment.

ARRIVAL AND DEPARTURE

FAKENHAM AND AROUND

By bus Fakenham is connected by bus to a hatful of Norfolk towns and villages, including Holt (Mon–Sat every 2hr; 40min) and Norwich (Mon–Sat hourly; Sun every 2hr; 1hr). One useful local service is to East Rudham, 7 miles to the west, where buses halt in front of the *Crown Inn* (Norfolk Green's bus #X8; every 1–2hr; 15min). In Fakenham, buses pull in on Oak St, just to the north of the Market Place.

ACCOMMODATION AND EATING

Congham Hall Grimston, PE32 1AH ☎ 01485 600250, Ⓦ conghamhallhotel.co.uk. In a rural setting just south of the A148 – and thirteen miles west of Fakenham – this deluxe hotel occupies a handsome Georgian mansion surrounded by well-tended gardens and with its own capacious herb garden. The rooms have been decorated in smart-to-lavish period style and there is a fully equipped spa. Off-peak, you can book bed and breakfast (from £120), but peak-period rates are inclusive of dinner. The hotel restaurant is smart and classy, featuring local produce and offering such delights as roasted Norfolk plaice with capers and spinach; mains average £18. Daily noon–2pm & 6.30–9pm. **£220**

Crown Inn The Green, East Rudham, PE31 8RD ☎ 01485 528530, Ⓦ crowninnnorfolk.co.uk. There's not much going on in the hamlet of East Rudham, but the *Crown* is a real treat of a hotel, occupying an intelligently renovated old country pub, its interior now decked out with suitably rustic furniture and fittings. The *Crown* has half a dozen comfortable bedrooms painted in creams, beiges and greys, and equipped with brass bedsteads. The restaurant, where the daily specials are chalked up on a blackboard above the open fireplace, offers such delights as tagliatelli with crayfish and walnuts, or sea bass with squash and chorizo risotto. Mains average a very reasonable £15. Mon–Sat noon–2.30pm & 6–9pm, Sun noon–8pm. **£100**

Manor Mews Tattersett, PE31 8RS ☎ 01485 528508, Ⓦ manormews.co.uk. This family-run, high-spec conversion of old farm buildings consists of nine spacious cottages for two guests or more and the former farmhouse, which sleeps 22. The owners have chosen to keep things simple and light with wood or stone floors, open fireplaces and the like, plus self-catering facilities. They have thought about energy conservation as well – most of the cottages have ground-source heat pumps. The *Mews* is in a rural setting, just off the A148 a mile or two from East Rudham, in the scattered hamlet of Tattersett. Advance reservations required. Two-person cottage for seven nights **£400**

The Thursford Collection

Thursford, NR21 0AS • April to late Sept Mon–Fri & Sun noon–5pm • £9.50 • ☎ 01328 878477, Ⓦ thursford.com • About four miles northeast of Fakenham via – and signed from – the A148.

One of Norfolk's most popular attractions, the **Thursford Collection** holds what the owners claim is the world's largest collection of steam engines and organs with pride of place going to the whopping Wurlitzer, played with pizzazz by the resident organist twice daily. There are also fairground rides, tourist shops, restaurants and a playground, plus regular screenings of silent films.

Houghton Hall

Houghton, PE31 6UE (signed from the A148) • **House** Early June to late Oct Wed, Thurs, Sun & Bank Holiday Mon 12.30–5pm, last admission 4.30pm • **Grounds and garden** Early June to late Oct Wed, Thurs, Sun Bank Holiday Mon 11.30am–5pm • £14 (house & grounds); £10 (grounds & garden) • Additional opening on Fri & Sat evenings – see website for dates • ☎ 01485 528569, ⓦ houghtonhall .com • About nine miles west of Fakenham via the A148

Built for England's first Prime Minister, Sir Robert Walpole (1676–1745), **Houghton Hall** is a grandiloquent, early eighteenth-century pile, whose assorted state rooms include the imperious **Stone Hall**, which comes complete with a bust of Sir Robert dressed up as a Roman and looking distinctly haughty – no one ever accused him of being modest. Perhaps the most appealing room, in a gaudy sort of way, is the **Saloon**, which was kitted out in all its luxury by **William Kent** (1685–1748), the hall's principal architect and designer. Kent was especially fond of classical Greek and Roman allegories – hence the painting of *Apollo Driving his Chariot of the Sun* in the ceiling's central octagon. After the house, you can wander the **grounds** and **garden**; Houghton also puts on a programme of temporary art exhibitions.

Wells-next-the-Sea and around

Despite its name, **WELLS-NEXT-THE-SEA**, some eight miles west of Blakeney, is situated a good mile or so from open water. In Tudor times, before the harbour silted up, this was one of the great ports of eastern England, a major player in the trade with the Netherlands. Those heady days are long gone and although it's now the only commercially viable port on the north Norfolk coast, this is hardly a major boast. More importantly, Wells is also one of the county's larger tourist resorts, and even though there are no specific sights among its narrow lanes, it does make a convenient base for exploring the surrounding coastline, especially Holkham Hall (see p.149) and Holkham Bay (see p.149); Wells is also the terminus of a toy-town tourist train, the **Wells & Walsingham Light Railway**.

The Buttlands and Staithe Street

Wells divides into three distinct areas, starting with the prettiest part of town, **The Buttlands**, where a broad rectangular green is lined with oak and beech trees and framed by an attractive medley of old, mostly Georgian houses and pretty little

---

THE WELLS & WALSINGHAM LIGHT RAILWAY

The **Wells & Walsingham Light Railway** (WWLR; A149, Wells, NR23 1QB; ☎ 01328 711630, ⓦ wellswalsinghamrailway.co.uk) is proud to be the longest **10¼-inch narrow-gauge steam railway** in the world, its two locomotives chugging their way the four miles south from Wells to Walsingham along what was originally a branch line of the Great Eastern Railway. The WWLR opened in 1982 largely thanks to the tireless endeavours of Roy Francis and it's now operated and maintained by a devoted team of volunteers. Wells station is southeast of town, just over a mile from the quayside beside the A149; the Norfolk Coasthopper bus (see p.124) stops nearby. Trains run from April to Oct (4–5 daily; 30min each way) with an occasional off-season service – see website for details. Adult return £9, child £7; one-way £7.50/£5.50.

WELLS-NEXT-THE-SEA

ACCOMMODATION	
The Crown Hotel	4
The Globe Inn	3
The Merchant's House	2
Pinewoods Holiday Park	1
Wells YHA	5

EATING	
The Crown Hotel	2
The Globe Inn	1

SHOPPING	
Saltmarsh Coast Gallery	1

3

cottages; the green takes its unusual name from the time it was used for archery practice (a butt being the earthen mound behind the target). North from here, across Station Road, lie the narrow lanes of the **town centre** with **Staithe Street**, the minuscule main drag, flanked by old-fashioned knick-knack stores, charity shops, ice-cream kiosks and cafés.

The harbour and beach

Staithe Street leads down to **The Quay**, a somewhat forlorn affair inhabited by a couple of amusement arcades and a big old warehouse or two, reminders of the town's previous role as a major port. Beginning here also is the mile-long byroad that scuttles north to the **beach**, a handsome sandy tract backed by pine-clad dunes. The beach road is shadowed by a high flood defence and the tiny, narrow-gauge **Wells Harbour Railway** (Easter to mid-Oct; trains every 20–30min from 10.30am; £3 return), which scoots down to the beach every twenty minutes or so.

Overlooking the start of the railway is a **monument** to the **lifeboatmen** who drowned in the worst disaster ever to befall the Wells lifeboat: in October 1880, in heavy seas amid a howling gale, the Wells lifeboat, *The Eliza Adams*, saved the crew of one ship before setting out again to save the men of another. Before the lifeboat could complete this mission, however, it was hit by a freak wave and, even worse, the boat could not right itself after it capsized as its mast had got stuck in a sandbank. Twelve of the crew were washed from the boat and eleven lost their lives, leaving ten widows and 28 children to mourn their passing.

ARRIVAL AND INFORMATION

By bus Buses, including the Norfolk Coasthopper (see p.124), stop on Station Rd, in between Staithe St and the Buttlands; some also travel down to The Quay.

Tourist office In 2017, Wells tourist office (☎ 01328

WELLS-NEXT-THE-SEA

710885, ⓦ visitnorthnorfolk.com) will move into the newly redeveloped Maltings complex (see below), by the harbourfront at the foot of Staithe St. In the meantime, it will be on the hoof, but keeping its present phone number.

ACCOMMODATION

★ **The Crown Hotel** The Buttlands, NR23 1EX ☎ 01328 710209, ⓦ crownhotelnorfolk.co.uk. Of the two hotels on the Buttlands, this one has the edge, beginning with the building itself, an especially attractive, three-storey former coaching inn with a handsome Georgian facade. Inside, the first batch of public rooms is cosy and quaint, all low ceilings and stone-flagged floors, and upstairs the dozen guest rooms are decorated in an imaginative and especially soothing style, though opinions are divided on the (very colourful) acrylic designs on the toilet seats. £155

The Globe Inn The Buttlands, NR23 1EU ☎ 01328 710206, ⓦ theglobeatwells.co.uk. Not perhaps as lively as *The Crown* just along the street (see above), *The Globe Inn* does have seven very well-appointed guest rooms, each of which is decorated in a light and self-assured, vaguely rural style, complete with oak flooring. Two-night booking policy on most weekends. £160

The Merchant's House 47 Freeman St, NR23 1BQ ☎ 01328 711877, ⓦ the-merchants-house.co.uk. Occupying one of the oldest houses in Wells, parts of which date back to the fifteenth century, this deluxe B&B has just two, en-suite guest rooms – one with a four-poster bed. It has a handy location, too, just a couple of minutes' walk from the quayside. The dining room, where breakfasts are served, holds a wide supply of information on local sights and walks. Minimum stay of two nights July & Aug. £90

Pinewoods Holiday Park Beach Rd, NR23 1DR ☎ 01328 710439, ⓦ pinewoods.co.uk. *Pinewoods* has been welcoming holiday-makers for over sixty years, its popularity based on its location, right behind a long line of pine-clad sand dunes that abut a gorgeous stretch of sandy beach. It's now a sprawling complex that holds touring and static caravans, beach huts and cosy wooden holiday lodges with kitchen-diners, but there is no camping. There's a comprehensive range of facilities to cater for the crowds, from toilet blocks to shops. *Pinewoods* is a 15min walk from The Quay in Wells or you can take the Wells Harbour Railway (see p.147). The tariff for all the various options available at *Pinewoods* is necessarily complicated, but in high season a three-bed lodge catering for up to six guests for seven nights is £1200, whereas a four-night stay in a static caravan costs from £450

Wells YHA Church Plain, NR23 1EQ ☎ 0845 3719544, ⓦ yha.org.uk. Located on the southern side of town, just off the A149, this medium-sized YHA hostel occupies an imaginatively recycled old church hall, which dates back to the early twentieth century. Especially popular with groups, the hostel offers self-catering facilities and 31 beds in two- to four-bunk bedrooms. Reception is 8am–10am & 5–10pm. Dorm beds £18, doubles £40

EATING

The Crown Hotel The Buttlands, NR23 1EX ☎ 01328 710209, ⓦ crownhotelnorfolk.co.uk. *The Crown* prides itself on its food. You can eat in several areas, each with a different atmosphere from the slightly formal to the very relaxed, though the menu is the same throughout. British dishes are to the fore here, but often with a gastronomic flourish or two – try, for example, the roast chicken with new potatoes and cherry tomatoes in a red wine jus. Prices are very competitive, with mains

averaging £16. Mon–Sat noon–2.30pm & 6.30–9pm, Sun noon–9pm.

The Globe Inn The Buttlands, NR23 1EU ☎ 01328 710206, ⓦ theglobeatwells.co.uk. Well-regarded restaurant featuring locally sourced fish, meat and vegetables. The menu is modern British at its core, but there are all sorts of adventurous exceptions – walnut and gorgonzola ravioli, for example. You can eat in the bar too. Mains hover around £15. Daily noon–2.30pm & 6–9pm.

ENTERTAINMENT

The Maltings Staithe St, NR23 1AU ☎ 01328 710193, ⓦ wellsmaltings.org.uk. The Maltings, the large and conspicuous red-brick building down by the harbourfront, is currently being redeveloped as a mixed entertainment

and leisure complex that will house a cinema, performing arts, a theatre and the tourist office (see above). Work is scheduled to be finished in 2017.

SHOPPING

Saltmarsh Coast Gallery 35a Staithe St, NR23 1AG ☎ 07833 296654, ⓦ saltmarshcoastgallery.co.uk.

Wells's main street may have more than its fair share of tourist tat, but this excellent gallery, which showcases the landscape photography of Jon Gibbs and Gareth Hacon, really is very good, its prime images being of Norfolk in general and the Norfolk coast in particular. Apart from the photos, there are also art cards, calendars, acrylics and framed prints – all at surprisingly affordable prices: a good-size, framed photo will cost you about £100. Sat & Sun 10am–5pm, but extended hours throughout the season; see website for details.

Holkham Hall

Holkham, NR23 1AB • **Hall** April–Oct Sun, Mon & Thurs noon–4pm • **Walled gardens** April–Oct daily 10am–5pm • £12 (Hall & gardens); £2.50 (gardens only) • **Parking** Hall & Park April–Oct; £2.50 • ☏ 01328 710227, ⓦ holkham.co.uk • The Norfolk Coasthopper stops yards from the *Victoria Inn* at the north entrance of the estate, about a mile from the Hall

Holkham Hall, about three miles west of Wells along the A149, is a grand and self-assured (or vainglorious) stately home designed by the celebrated eighteenth-century architect William Kent for the first earl of Leicester, whose descendants still own the place in the person of the eighth earl, **Thomas Edward Coke**, who inherited the estate in 2015. The severe sandy-coloured Palladian exterior belies the warmth and richness of the interior, which retains much of its original decoration, notably the much-admired **Marble Hall**, with its fluted columns, coffered ceiling and intricate reliefs. The rich colours of the **state rooms** are an appropriate backdrop for a wide selection of paintings, including canvases by Van Dyck, Rubens and Gainsborough, and, if opulence is your thing, you'll be delighted by the resplendent **North State Sitting Room**, which is adorned by four seventeenth-century Brussels tapestries depicting the sun's annual progress through the signs of the zodiac, though for some obscure reason or another, the summer months are missing. Outside, visitors can wander the extensive **walled gardens** and drop by the **courtyard**, which is, at time of writing, being redeveloped to accommodate a new café, restaurant, gift shop and a free exhibition on the estate's **farming heritage**. The latter will pay fulsome tribute to the Coke family's pioneering efforts to improve agricultural practices hereabouts in the late eighteenth and nineteenth centuries.

Holkham Park

Holkham, NR23 1AB • Daily: April–Oct 9am–5pm; Nov–March 9.30am–5pm • **Parking** Hall & Park April–Oct; £2.50; no vehicular access Nov–March • **Cycle rental** May–Sept most days, beside the car park; £15 per day; ☏ 01328 713111 • **Lake cruises** June–Sept Mon, Thurs & Sun 11.30am–4.30pm; 25min; £4 • **Boat rental** July & Aug daily 11am–5pm; rowing boats £10 for 30min, canoes £8 for 30min, kayaks £6 for 30min • The Norfolk Coasthopper stops yards from the *Victoria Inn* at the north entrance of the estate, at the south end of Lady Anne's Drive

Holkham Hall's surrounding **parkland** is laid out on sandy, saline land, much of it originally salt marsh. The focal point is an eighty-foot-high **obelisk**, atop a grassy knoll, from where you can view both the hall to the north and the triumphal arch to the south. In common with the rest of the north Norfolk coast, there's plenty of birdlife – Holkham's **lake** attracts Canada geese, herons and grebes – and several hundred deer graze the open pastures.

Holkham Bay

Open access • Free • **Parking** on Lady Anne's Drive; Daily: April–Sept 6am–9pm; Oct–March 6am–6pm; £2 for 1hr, £3 for 2hr, £5 for 4hr, £6.50 for over 4hr; the £6.50 fee also covers parking at the Hall; arrive before 10am in summer to be sure of a spot • The Norfolk Coasthopper stops yards from the *Victoria Inn*, at the south end of Lady Anne's Drive, a 10min walk from the bay

Much admired, **Holkham Bay** boasts one of the finest beaches on this stretch of coast, its golden sands stretching out into the ocean with pine-studded sand dunes behind. The bay is at its prettiest at high tide, when the sea breaks through the shoreline to create a shallow lagoon, which ripples and glistens in the summer sun. The nearest you can get by car and bike is **Lady Anne's Drive**, a half-mile byroad-cum-car-park accessed from the A149 opposite the *Victoria Inn* (see p.150).

3

The northern end of Lady Anne's Drive intersects with the **Norfolk Coast Path** (see p.29), which heads off in both directions around the edge of the bay (2.75miles to Wells, 3.5miles to Burnham Overy Staithe), or you can stay put and enjoy the **birdlife**: warblers, flycatchers and redstarts inhabit the drier coastal reaches, while waders paddle about the mud- and salt flats. In winter, thousands of geese drop by after their long flight from the Arctic and in spring and summer ground-nesting birds such as the lapwing and the avocet congregate here. There are two bird hides a short walk to the west of Lady Anne's Drive; more are planned.

ACCOMMODATION   **HOLKHAM BAY**

The Victoria Inn Park Rd, NR23 1RG ☎ 01328 711008, ⓦ holkham.co.uk. Part of the Holkham estate, *The Victoria* has a fine location in between Holkham Bay and Holkham Hall, though the streaming traffic of the A149 does rather take the gloss off things. The inn has twenty guest rooms – ten in the original building, the rest in the Ancient House annexe close by – and each has a modern, country-house demeanour with all mod cons. **£160**

3

The Walsinghams

For centuries, **LITTLE WALSINGHAM**, five miles south of Wells, rivalled Bury St Edmunds and Canterbury as the foremost pilgrimage site in England. It all began in 1061 when the lady of the manor, one Richeldis de Faverches, was prompted to build a replica of the **Santa Casa** (Mary's home in Nazareth) in this remote part of Norfolk – inspired, it is said, by visions of the Virgin Mary. Whatever the reason, it brought instant fame and fortune to Little Walsingham and every medieval king from Henry III onwards made at least one trip, walking the last mile barefoot. Both the Augustinians and the Franciscans established themselves here and all seemed set fair when Henry VIII followed in his predecessors' footsteps in 1511. Yet, pilgrim or not, it didn't stop Henry from destroying the shrine in the Dissolution of the 1530s, and at a stroke the village's principal trade came to a halt. **Pilgrimages** resumed in earnest after 1922, when the local vicar, a certain Alfred Hope Patten, organized an Anglo-Catholic pilgrimage, the prelude to the building of an **Anglican shrine** in the 1930s – much to the initial chagrin of the diocesan authorities. Nowadays, the village does good business out of its holy connections as well as from the **WWLR** steam railway, which links it with Wells (see p.146).

Common Place and the High Street

Pocket-sized Little Walsingham has an attractive and singularly old-fashioned centre, beginning with **Common Place**, the main square, whose half-timbered buildings surround a quaint octagonal structure built to protect the village pump in the sixteenth century. The **High Street** extends south from here, overlooked by antique brick and half-timbered houses, several of which are given over to religious bookstores. The northern end of the High Street is also overseen by the impressive, if badly weathered, fifteenth-century **abbey gatehouse** of the old priory – look up and you'll spy Christ peering out from a window – though the abbey grounds beyond can only be reached from Common Place. At the south end of the High Street is the **Friday Market Place**, a tiny crossroads edged by a pretty medley of very old houses. Beyond here, about 200 yards out on the Fakenham Road, is the tumble-down stonework of the old **Franciscan Friary** (no access).

The Anglican shrine

Common Place, NR22 6EE • Open daily • Free • ☎ 01328 820255, ⓦ walsinghamanglican.org.uk

Dotted around Little Walsingham are a number of shrines catering to a variety of denominations – there's even a Russian Orthodox Church – but the main event is the **Anglican shrine**, beside Holt Road, a few yards to the east of Common Place. Flanked

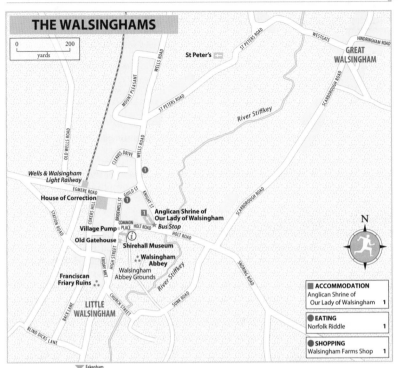

by attractive gardens as well as a visitor centre, where there's a small exhibition on the history of the cult, the shrine is a strange-looking building, rather like a cross between an English village hall and an Orthodox church. The interior holds a series of small chapels and a Holy Well with healing waters as well as the idiosyncratic Holy House – **Santa Casa** – which contains the much revered **statue** of Our Lady of Walsingham.

Shirehall Museum and Walsingham Abbey grounds

Common Place, NR22 6BP • **Shirehall Museum** April–Oct daily 11am–4pm • **Abbey grounds only** Nov–March Mon–Fri 9am–1pm & 2–5pm via the Walsingham Estate Office, 10 Common Place • £4, children £2.50 • Shirehall ☎ 01328 820510, Estate office ☎ 01328 820259; ⊛ walsinghamabbey.com

For most of the year, entry to the abbey grounds is via the mildly diverting **Shirehall Museum**, which has modest displays on the history of Little Walsingham, including a section on its role as a centre of pilgrimage. The Shirehall was also the seat of justice hereabouts as recalled by the original **Georgian Court Room** and an old holding cell. In the cell is a crude life-size model of **Rice Gavercoli** (see box, p.152), a local man who was transported to Australia in 1831 for breaking the machines that were threatening his livelihood as a day labourer.

Beyond the museum are the **abbey grounds**, whose lovely landscaped gardens stretch down to the River Stiffkey enclosing the **ruins of Walsingham Abbey**, primarily a large chunk of the east wall complete with its imposing Gothic window. Otherwise, the grounds are famous for their **bluebells**, which burst into flower in early February, signifying the start of spring and, in Christian terms, symbolizing the day, six weeks after his birth, when Joseph and Mary presented the infant Jesus at the Temple in Jerusalem as Jewish custom demanded.

> ## TOUGH JUSTICE
>
> Little Walsingham's **Shirehall** was where generations of Norfolk peasantry felt the full brunt of a legal system that gave short shrift to anyone who dared to attack the property of his or her social "superiors". In 1885, **Horace Pegg**, for example, set fire to a farmer's stack of wheat and barley and was given eighteen months in prison for his pains – but at least he didn't have to go far: Little Walsingham's **House of Correction** was just a few yards away off Bridewell Street (it's still there – but in a dreadful state of repair). However, Pegg and his fellow prisoners may well have preferred to serve their time elsewhere, for here in Walsingham the incarcerated experienced at first hand the shifting fashions in punishment. The worst time to be locked up was after 1836 when the authorities introduced the so-called **Pentonville System** of "Separation and Silence": the prisoners were kept in perpetual solitary confinement, and were compelled to wear masks when they took to the exercise yard. This system was founded on the pseudoscientific theory that defined crime as a contagious disease, but unfortunately for the theorists, the system drove so many prisoners crazy that it was abandoned a few years later.

Great Walsingham

If **GREAT WALSINGHAM** was ever "great", it certainly isn't today, comprising a handful of old flint houses scattered on either side of the River Stiffkey just half a mile or so (a 15min walk) north of Little Walsingham. The main reason to visit is the **church of St Peter**, a squat tumble of flint buildings sitting on a grassy knoll just to the west of the river and almost untouched since its construction in the early fourteenth century. The exterior is distinguished by the impressive gargoyles that adorn the tower and by some particularly fancy stone tracery round the windows; while inside pride of place goes to the forest of poppy-head bench ends carved with a menagerie of medieval life – from saints, flowers and mythical monsters to real-life creatures including a dog and a chameleon.

ARRIVAL AND INFORMATION   THE WALSINGHAMS

By train There are no regular train services to Little Walsingham, but the Wells & Walsingham Light Railway (see p.124) links it with Wells. The WWLR station is off Egmere Rd, from where it's a 5min walk south to Common Place: from the station, turn left along Egmere Rd and take the second major right, down Bridewell St.

By bus Norfolk Green's #29 bus service (☎ 01553 776980,

ⓦ norfolkgreen.co.uk) runs south from Wells (12min) to Fakenham (15min) via Little Walsingham, pausing outside the Anglican Shrine (Mon–Sat hourly, Sun every 1–2hr).

Tourist office At the Shirehall Museum, on Common Place, NR22 6BP (April–Oct daily 11am–4pm; ☎ 01328 820510, ⓦ visitnorthnorfolk.com). There is also a very good village website, ⓦ walsinghamvillage.org.

ACCOMMODATION AND EATING

Anglican Shrine of Our Lady of Walsingham Common Place, NR22 6EE ☎ 01328 820255, ⓦ walsinghamanglican.org.uk. Little Walsingham is light on hotel accommodation at least partly because the Anglican Shrine offers affordable lodgings in several locations in and around the village for pilgrims and non-pilgrims alike. The rooms are simply furnished – perhaps frugal would be a more accurate description – and are both en suite and with shared facilities; meals are also available. Note that during major pilgrimages, vacancies are rare. **£80**

Norfolk Riddle 2 Wells Rd, NR22 6DJ ☎ 01328 821903, ⓦ norfolkriddle.co.uk. A combined fish and chip shop and restaurant supplied – and owned – by the local farmers of the neighbouring Walsingham Farms Shop (see below). The restaurant lacks a certain cosiness, but there's no denying the tastiness of the food and by and large it's locally sourced – try, for example, the Farm Shop beef and ale pie (£11). East Anglian beers and ciders too. Wed–Sat (plus Aug Mon & Tues) 11.30am–2pm & 5–9pm, Sun 11.30am–2pm.

SHOPPING

Walsingham Farms Shop Guild St, NR22 6BU ☎ 01328 821877, ⓦ walsinghamfarmsshop.co.uk. Surprisingly large shop-cum-deli showcasing the produce of a raft of local farmers, especially meat, game

and veg. They have their own butcher's and also a kitchen, where they churn out pies and pâtés, soups, stews and puddings. Mon–Sat 9am–5.30pm, Sun 10am–4pm.

The Burnhams

Heading west from Wells on the A149, it's about five miles to **Burnham Overy Staithe**, a tiny hamlet whose easy ramble of old buildings nudges up against a creeky little harbour. This is the first of the **BURNHAMS**, the handful of villages that occupy this corner of Norfolk, the leading player being the postcard-pretty village of **Burnham Market**, where an attractive medley of Georgian and Victorian houses surrounds a dinky little green with an oh-so-cutesy stream flowing across the road whenever it rains. **Burnham Thorpe**, a mile or so to the southeast, is best known as the birthplace of **Horatio Nelson**, while further north **Burnham Deepdale** heralds a stretch of marshy coast that continues with neighbouring **Brancaster Staithe**, the main access point for the nature reserve on **Scolt Head Island**.

Burnham Market

3

BURNHAM MARKET attracts a well-heeled, metropolitan crew, in no small measure on account of *The Hoste* (see below), an old coaching inn beside the green that offers some of the best restaurant and bar food on the coast. There's quite enough money here to support several chichi shops and food stores (see opposite), but there's only one sight as such, the **church of St Mary**, whose stumpy tower is easy to spot just beyond the west end of the green. Every inch a country church, the interior of St Mary's is of some mild interest for its three-seater sedilia (for the priest, deacon and subdeacon) on the south side of the chancel and the intricacy of the stained glass of the east window, which was inserted in 1953.

ARRIVAL AND DEPARTURE   BURNHAM MARKET

By bus The Norfolk Coasthopper bus (see p.124) stops beside the green on the Market Place in Burnham Market. It also travels through Burnham Overy Staithe, Burnham Deepdale and Brancaster Staithe on the A149, but it does not pass through Burnham Thorpe, which has no bus services.

ACCOMMODATION AND EATING

The Hoste The Green, PE31 8HD ☎ 01328 738777, ⓦ thehoste.com. One of the most fashionable spots on the Norfolk coast, this former coaching inn at the heart of Burnham Market has been sympathetically modernized. The hotel's guest rooms are round the back and range from the small (verging on cramped) to the much more expansive (and expensive). The decor is a modern rendition of country-house style and can be a little over-corked, but there's no denying the buzz of the place. As for eating and drinking, there's an antique bar at the front, complete

WHAT'S IN A NAME – THE BURNHAMS

There are of course exceptions, but most villages in Norfolk have **Anglo-Saxon names**, with many ending in "-ham" or "-ton". These two endings were largely interchangeable, meaning settlement, though sometimes – as in the case of the Burnhams – "ham" referred to a central habitation with "tons" surrounding it. Thus, **Burnham Market** seems to have been the centre of a Saxon village with outlying settlements at **Norton** ("north") and **Sutton** ("south"), though the latter was swallowed up by Burnham Market long ago. However, just to complicate matters, the "Overy" in **Burnham Overy**, though Anglo-Saxon, refers to its location – "over the river" – and the "Thorpe" in **Burnham Thorpe** is thought to be of Scandinavian origin.

with wooden beams and stone-flagged floor, but this is merely a foretaste of the several dining areas beyond. Throughout, the menu is a well-balanced mixture of "land and sea", anything from wood pigeon with strawberries to cod in beer batter with peas and chips. Main courses average £20 in the evening, slightly less at lunchtimes. For accommodation, weekend rates are always higher, with two nights usually a minimum stay. Lunch daily noon–6pm; afternoon teas daily 3–5.30pm; dinner daily 6–9.15pm. £160

The Railway Inn Creake Rd, PE31 8EN ☎01328 738777, ⓦ thehoste.com. The rail line to Burnham Market was closed in the 1950s, but the old train station has been tastefully modernized and converted by the owners of *The Hoste* into a pretty little hotel, with one of the rooms in an old railway carriage. Keys from *The Hoste*, from where it is a ten-minute walk. £135

Vine House The Green, PE31 8HD ☎01328 738777, ⓦ thehoste.com. Boutique hotel in a handsome Georgian townhouse across the green from *The Hoste* – which is where you get the keys. Eight deluxe guest rooms with all mod cons. £180

SHOPPING

Brazen Head Bookshop Market Place, PE31 8HD ☎01328 730700, ⓦ brazenhead.org.uk. In antique premises, this top-notch bookshop is especially strong on children's classics and classic novels, with a good sideline in local stuff as well. Stocks both new and secondhand titles. Mon–Sat 9.30am–5pm.

Grooms Bakery Market Place, PE31 8HD ☎01328 738289. Top-notch bakery offering a wide range of Italian and French breads plus specialist health-food loaves: multigrain, low-salt and so on. Mon–Fri 8am–5pm, Sat 8am–4pm.

Gurneys Fish Shop Market Place, PE31 8HF ☎01328 738967, ⓦ gurneysfishshop.co.uk. Outstanding fishmonger's selling smoked and fresh fish and shellfish, including local lobsters and crabs. Has a quaint and old-fashioned appearance too – entirely appropriate in this most gentrified of villages. Mon–Sat 9am–5pm, plus June–Sept Sun 10am–1pm.

Heirloom Toys & Clothing Emma's Court, off Market Place, PE31 8HD ☎01328 738950, ⓦ heirloomtoysand clothing.co.uk. This bijou shop sells a first-rate range of stuff for kids. Toys and clothes are its primary pull, but there's a lot more too, including all sorts of games. Mon–Sat 10am–5pm.

Humble Pie Market Place, PE31 8HF ☎01328 738581, ⓦ humble-pie.com. Local produce is the big deal here in this excellent, well-established deli, which sells everything from pies and tarts, chutneys, cheeses, chorizo and marmalades through to cakes and biscuits, not to mention all sorts of olives and precooked deli dishes. Mon–Sat 9.30am–5pm.

Whitehouse Books Market Place, PE31 8HD ☎01328 730270, ⓦ whitehouse-books.co.uk. Enterprising, independent bookshop stocking a wide range of titles as well as cards, CDs and wrapping paper. Also puts on special events, and it sells OS maps. Mon–Sat 9.30am–1pm & 2–5pm.

Burnham Thorpe

Straggling **BURNHAM THORPE**, a couple of miles – or a 30min walk – from Burnham Market, was the birthplace of **Horatio Nelson** (see box, p.156), who was born in the village parsonage on September 29, 1758. The parsonage was demolished years ago, but the great man is still celebrated in the village's **All Saints Church**, where the lectern is made out of timbers taken from Nelson's last ship, the *Victory*, the chancel sports a Nelson bust, and the south aisle has a small exhibition on his life and times. The other place to head for is the village pub (see p.156), where Nelson held a farewell party for the locals in 1793.

3

SHOT TO BITS – THE UPS AND DOWNS OF BEING NELSON

Born in Burnham Thorpe, the sixth of eleven children, **Horatio Nelson** (1758–1805) joined the navy at the tender age of 12, and was soon sent to the West Indies, where he met and married **Frances Nisbet**, retiring to Burnham Thorpe in 1787. Back in action by 1793, his bravery cost him first the sight of his right eye, and shortly afterwards his right arm. His personal life was equally eventful – famously, his infatuation with **Emma Hamilton**, wife of the ambassador to Naples, caused the eventual break-up of his marriage. His finest hour was during the **Battle of Trafalgar** in 1805, when he led the British navy to victory against the combined French and Spanish fleets, a crucial engagement that set the scene for Britain's century-long domination of the high seas. The victory didn't do Nelson much good – he was shot in the chest during the battle and even the kisses of Hardy failed to revive him. Thereafter, Nelson was placed in a barrel of brandy and the pickled body shipped back to England, where he was laid in state at Greenwich and then buried at St Paul's. It was, however, Nelson's express wish that he should be buried here in Burnham Thorpe, but to no avail – he was too much of a national/imperial hero to ever allow that to happen. In all the naval hullabaloo, Nelson's far-from-positive attitude to the landowners of his home village was soon glossed over too: in 1797, he sent a batch of blankets back to Norfolk to keep the poor warm, railing that an average farm labourer received "Not quite two pence a day for each person; and to drink nothing but water, for beer our poor labourers never taste…"

EATING AND DRINKING	BURNHAM THORPE

Lord Nelson Walsingham Rd, PE31 8HN ☎ 01328 738241, ⓦ nelsonslocal.co.uk. They have kept modernity firmly at bay here at this ancient village pub, from the old wooden benches through to the serving hatch and tiled floor. There's a good range of real ales plus above-average bar food – try, for instance, the Norfolk chicken breast wrapped in ham with a green-herb filling (£14). Kitchen daily noon–2.30pm & 6–9pm; pub Mon–Sat noon–3pm & 6–10pm, Sun noon–10pm.

Creake Abbey

North Creake, NR21 9LF • Open access in daylight hours • Free; EH • ⓦ creakeabbey.co.uk • Signed from the B1355 just north of North Creake

Heading south from Burnham Thorpe, it's about a mile to **Creake Abbey**, whose shattered remains boast a captivating setting near the River Burn amid woods and fields – and just a few hundred yards from Abbey Farm's attractive courtyard complex (see below). A handsome set of Gothic arches support what remains of the abbey's flint walls, but in truth this was never an important foundation, though it did come to a dramatic end: in 1506, the seven remaining monks died of the plague and, in fright, the abbot took flight and no one ever opened it up again.

SHOPPING	NORTH CREAKE

Creake Abbey North Creake, NR21 9LF ☎ 07801 418907, ⓦ creakeabbey.co.uk. Here on Abbey Farm, near the ruins of Creake Abbey (see above), a set of old, stable-like agricultural buildings has been turned into a pleasant little tourist complex. There's a café and a deli, a hairdresser's, a clothing store and an interior design shop – and all very cosy it is too. Farmers' markets are also held here on the first Saturday of each month, except January (9.30am–1pm) and there are vintage fairs as well. Daily 10am–5pm, but check website for special events and extended openings.

Burnham Deepdale and Brancaster Staithe

Heading north from Burnham Market, you rejoin the main coastal road, the A149, just a mile or two from minuscule **BURNHAM DEEPDALE**, the home of the assorted holiday facilities of **Deepdale Farm** (see opposite). From here, it's a couple of hundred yards to the beginning of **BRANCASTER STAITHE**, where a strip of housing falls either side of the main road. First impressions of the village are not especially favourable, but it is home to the tempting *White Horse* (see below) and it also runs parallel and very close to the marshes of the seashore – and the **Norfolk Coast Path** (see p.29). There are several access points, the most easterly being at the back of the *White Horse* car park.

Brancaster Staithe Quay and Harbour

Heading west from the *White Horse* along the A149, you'll soon spy the *Jolly Sailors* pub (see below) on the left. Opposite, on the right, an easy-to-miss unmarked lane leads down to **Brancaster Staithe Quay**, where a tumble of old fishermen's shacks and sheds flank the tiniest of jetties. The quay is now owned and operated by the National Trust, who are upgrading its facilities to cater for up to twenty local fishermen. The next turning on the right – Harbour Way – leads to **Brancaster Staithe Harbour**, home to all sorts of sailing boats and the starting point for Branta Cruises out to Scolt Head (see p.158); here also is the National Trusts's **Brancaster Activity Centre** (see below).

3

ARRIVAL AND DEPARTURE   BURNHAM DEEPDALE AND BRANCASTER STAITHE

By bus The Norfolk Coasthopper bus (see p.124) sticks to the main road, the A149, as it runs through Burnham Deepdale and Brancaster Staithe. There are bus stops outside Deepdale Backpackers, the *White Horse*, and the *Jolly Sailors*.

INFORMATION AND ACTIVITIES

Brancaster Activity Centre Down by Brancaster Staithe Harbour, this residential centre (Dial House, Harbour Way, PE31 8BW; ☎01485 210719, ⓦ nationaltrust.org.uk), owned and operated by the National Trust, organizes a wide range of outdoor pursuits for groups and schools. They also have a few activities open to the general public – particularly two-hour-long "Muddy Harbour"walks for £5 per person. Call or drop by for further details.

Branta Cruises Organizes a variety of coastal boat trips including excursions to Scolt Head. Most of their tours last about two hours, but longer trips are possible. Two-hour tours cost £30 per person; advance reservations are essential (Brancaster Staithe, PE31 8BU; ☎01485 211132, ⓦ brantacruises.co.uk). The departure point is Brancaster Staithe Harbour (see above).

Deepdale Farm Information Centre This useful, privately-run information centre (Deepdale Farm, PE31 8DD; daily 10am–4pm; ☎01485 210256, ⓦ deepdale farm.co.uk) has details of local walks and boat trips, sells road and hiking maps, and has tide times and internet facilities. They also operate a campsite and a hostel here (see below).

ACCOMMODATION AND EATING

BURNHAM DEEPDALE

Deepdale Backpackers & Camping Deepdale Farm, PE31 8DD ☎01485 210256, ⓦ deepdalefarm.co.uk. Full marks for ingenuity go to this lively, youthful and very amiable set-up, where they operate a combined campsite, info centre (see above), café and ecofriendly backpackers' hostel in creatively renovated former stables beside the main coastal road. They have also diversified into tipis and yurts. Dorms (not available in high season) £15; doubles £45; two-person tipi £60; two-person yurt £80

BRANCASTER STAITHE

★**Jolly Sailors** Main Rd, PE31 8BJ ☎01485 210314, ⓦjollysailorsbrancaster.co.uk. Relaxed and easygoing pub, kitted out in traditional style, where they do a good line in pizzas from as little as £9. Also daily specials, including a local speciality, Brancaster mussels, cooked every which way and also from £9. Kitchen daily noon–9pm; pub Mon–Sat noon–11pm & Sun noon–10.30pm.

★**White Horse** Main Rd, PE31 8BY ☎01485 210262, ⓦ whitehorsebrancaster.co.uk. This combined hotel, pub and restaurant backs straight onto the marshes, lagoons and creeks of the coast – and, even better, the northern part of the Norfolk Coast Path runs along the bottom of the hotel car park. The hotel divides into two sections: there are seven en-suite rooms in the main building, one of which is a split-level room with a telescope thrown in for free, and eight more at the back with grass roofs. The decor is light and airy with a few nautical bits and pieces dotted around for good measure. As for the restaurant, Brancaster is famous for its mussels and oysters and this is as good a place as any to try them, though there are all sorts of other temptations from local duck to local beef, with main courses averaging around £16. Restaurant daily noon–2pm & 6.15–9pm; bar food daily 11am–9pm; drinks Mon–Sat 11am–11pm, Sun noon–11pm. £140

SHOPPING

★**Fish Shed** Main Rd, PE31 8BY ☎01485 210 532, ⓦfishshed.co.uk. On the main coastal road, a couple of hundred yards west of the *White Horse* (see p.157), the Fish Shed is just how it sounds – a shed with fish in. But what a range: there's cod and haddock, mullet and brill, tuna and trout, but the place specializes in Norfolk stuff, most memorably lobsters, cockles, crabs, mussels, oysters, whelks and samphire. Daily 10am–4pm, but restricted opening hours in winter.

Scolt Head Island National Nature Reserve

The narrow creeks and salt marshes that spread north from Brancaster Staithe are protected from the ocean by **Scolt Head Island**, a national nature reserve managed by Natural England (ⓦnaturalengland.org.uk). The island, which is gradually growing westward, has four main habitats – sand dune, shingle, salt marsh and intertidal mudflats – and these attract a wide range of birdlife, especially breeding terns and wintering wildfowl plus waders like the shelduck, wigeon, teal and curlew. Access is difficult, impossible on foot, but the Deepdale Farm information centre (see p.157) has the details of local **boat operators** who sally out to the island in the summer, or you could try Branta Cruises (see p.157).

Brancaster and around

From Brancaster Staithe (see p.156), it's about a mile and a half west along the main road to tiny **BRANCASTER** – the first of a string of attractive hamlets on this stretch of the coast – which straddles the A149 within easy walking distance of both the marshes and the Norfolk Coast Path (see p.29). Brancaster once bordered the open sea and it was here that the Romans built a fort – **Branodunum** – but this disappeared centuries ago, the only reminders of its location today being a number of street names – "Roman Way", for example. An uneventful sort of place today, Brancaster was the site of a major scandal in 1833, when the *Earl of Wemyss* ran aground here in a surging storm. Several of the passengers drowned as the result of the incompetence of the captain; several others, washed ashore half-dead, were most likely stripped of their possessions by the villagers – as recorded on the (badly weathered) tombstone of Susan Roche in **Brancaster church graveyard**. At the west end of the village, a turning leads the three-quarters of a mile north across the reedy marshes to **Brancaster beach** (£4 parking), where the sands are backed by a ridge of dunes; at low tide, the sand flats extend as far as the eye can see to either side of a narrow creek-cum-river.

ARRIVAL AND DEPARTURE   **BRANCASTER**

By bus The Norfolk Coasthopper bus (see p.124) travels along the A149, stopping opposite the *Ship Hotel*.

ACCOMMODATION AND EATING

★**Ship Hotel** Main Rd (A149), PE31 8AP ☎01485 210333, ⓦshiphotelnorfolk.co.uk. Long a Brancaster landmark, the *Ship* once welcomed customs officers in search of smugglers and shipwrecked mariners in need of care and attention. Nowadays, as one of the Flying Kiwi mini-chain, it offers nine extremely pleasant guest rooms and a family suite, each of which is decorated in a sort of New Age-meets-country-house style with lots of creams and greys, lovely big beds, Ottoman bedside tables, metal stars hanging like chandeliers, tartan stair carpets and tartan bedspreads. The establishment also offers simply delicious restaurant and bar food with oysters, mussels and crab to the fore. The bar is low-ceilinged, warm and friendly, the restaurant relaxed and kitted out with all sorts of incidental bygones. If the weather is good, you can eat out in the garden. A typical main course is seared sea bass fillets with crab mash, baby fennel and shallot dressing (£18). Kitchen Mon–Sat noon–2.30pm & 6–9pm, Sun noon–8pm; bar daily 11am–11pm. **£155**

Titchwell

From Brancaster, it's a little less than a mile to the next hamlet along, **TITCHWELL**, where a handful of flint-walled houses plus the enjoyable *Titchwell Manor Hotel* (see below) spread out along the A149. Before its harbour silted up, Titchwell sat right next to the sea, a tiny fishing village whose inhabitants helped themselves to whatever was washed ashore, much to the chagrin of the local landowners, who had wreckage rights – if, that is, they could enforce them. As early as 1317, one lord of the manor wrote to the courts accusing some of his tenants of stealing what was rightfully his. The locals were, however, far from lawless, often helping out those pilgrims who trudged through the village on the way to Little Walsingham (see p.150) – and the old **stone cross**, which stands on a grassy mound beside the A149, appears to have been a waymarker on the old pilgrims' route.

ARRIVAL AND DEPARTURE   TITCHWELL

By bus The Norfolk Coasthopper bus (see p.124) travels along the A149, stopping in Titchwell about halfway between the one and only village crossroads and the *Titchwell Manor Hotel* (see below).

3

ACCOMMODATION AND EATING

★**Titchwell Manor Hotel** Main Rd (A149), PE31 8BB ☎ 01485 210221, ⓦ titchwellmanor.com. Facing out towards the salt marshes that roll down towards the ocean, this is one of the most enjoyable hotels on the Norfolk coast, an intelligent and extremely creative remodelling of what was originally a fairly modest, albeit large, Victorian brick building. There are nine guest rooms in the main building with more in the contemporary-style courtyard complex round the back, some of which are dog-friendly. Everything is high spec, from the top-quality duvets to the bespoke furniture. The hotel also boasts an outstanding restaurant as well as a couple of (similarly excellent) bar-like eating areas. The decor is appealing throughout – bright, sunny and somehow rather nautical. The menu is very British with traditional dishes superbly prepared – anything from fish and chips with mushy peas (£14) through to lobster thermidor with new potatoes (£20) – and the service is fast and efficient. Daily noon–9.30pm. **£140**

Titchwell Marsh Nature Reserve

Titchwell, PE31 8BB • Daily dawn to dusk • Free, but £5 parking • **Shop & information centre** March–Oct daily 9.30am–5pm; Nov–Feb daily 9.30am–4pm • ☎ 01485 210779, ⓦ rspb.org.uk/titchwell • The reserve is clearly signed from the A149 on the west side of Titchwell

Today, the old sea approaches to Titchwell harbour have become the RSPB's **Titchwell Marsh Nature Reserve**, whose mix of marsh, reedbed, mudflat, lagoon and sandy beach attracts a wide variety of birds, including marsh harriers, bearded tits, avocets, gulls and terns. A series of footpaths explore this varied terrain, and there are several well-positioned bird hides (including a super-duper Parrinder hide) and a very helpful shop-cum-information-centre.

Thornham

In *The King's England: Norfolk*, published in 1940, good old Arthur Mee got rather carried away when he came to describing **THORNHAM** – the next village along from Titchwell, around three miles west of Brancaster – declaring it had "grown old beautifully by a creek of the North Sea, and trees have risen like friends to shield it from the winds". Elegies apart, Thornham had a brief industrial flurry when the lady of the manor, Edith Ames-Lyde, established an iron foundry here in 1887, but it didn't last long – the factory closed down in the 1920s – and today Thornham is a quiet little place whose brick and flint cottages stretch north from the A149 to the edge of the marshes. On the west side of the village, **Staithe Lane** leads the mile or so north from the A149 to the **harbour**, where a couple of rickety jetties oversee the narrowest of creeks set amid an expanse of salt marsh and mudflat. Walkers can pick up the **Norfolk Coast Path** (see box, p.29) either at the harbour or in Thornham village as the path returns to the coast here after its detour inland around Titchwell. From the harbour, it takes about thirty minutes to walk along the path to the visitor centre at **Holme Dunes National Nature Reserve** (see opposite), which stretches as far as Holme-next-the-Sea.

ARRIVAL AND DEPARTURE   THORNHAM

By bus The Norfolk Coasthopper bus (see p.124) stops at Thornham's main crossroads, at the junction of the High St (the A149) and Church St; the latter leads to the *Lifeboat Inn* on Ship Lane (see below).

ACCOMMODATION AND EATING

Lifeboat Inn Ship Lane, PE36 6LT ☎01485 512236, ⓦlifeboatinnthornham.com. In ancient premises facing the fields just to the north of the A149, this rambling hotel possesses a particularly striking main hall, which comes complete with a whopping open fire and an assortment of stuffed animal heads. There are thirteen guest rooms and the pick are decorated in a modern rendition of country-house style and have views out towards Thornham harbour. The hotel also serves good-quality, locally sourced food in both the bar and its restaurant with mains such as pork belly and fish pie costing around £15. Daily noon–2.30pm & 6–9.30pm. **£90**

Drove Orchards

Thornham Rd (A149), PE36 6LS • **Farm shop** Daily 9am–5pm; restricted hours in winter – call ahead • ☎01485 525652, ⓦdroveorchards.com • **Café** Daily 9am–5pm, plus Thurs–Sat 6–9pm; restricted hours in winter • ☎01485 525179

A few miles west of Brancaster – beside the main road, between Thornham and Holme-next-the-Sea – is **Drove Orchards**, an enterprising concern which started out as an apple orchard. It has now diversified, selling a whole range of home-grown and local meat, cheese, fish, vegetables and fruit at their **Drove Orchard Farm Shop** – or, depending on the season, you can pick your own. Encouraged by the success of the shop, the owners have invited in other businesses and these now include a café and a fish and chip shop, plus interior design and clothing stores.

Holme-next-the-Sea and around

HOLME-NEXT-THE-SEA, about two miles west of Thornham, is the quietest of villages, its gentle ramble of old flint cottages and farm buildings nudging up towards the **sand dunes** of the coast. It's here that the Norfolk Coast Path (see p.29) intersects with the Peddars Way (see p.210), which follows the route of an old Roman road for most of its course. It's likely, though, that the Romans simply enhanced what was there before; any doubts on the matter were surely quashed when, in 1998, gales uncovered a fascinating prehistoric site in the sands just off Holme, comprising a circle of timber posts surrounding a sort of inverted tree stump. Dated to around 2050 BC, "**Seahenge**", as it soon became known, attracted hundreds of visitors, but fears for its safety prompted its removal to the Lynn Museum in King's Lynn (see p.173) and there's nothing to see here today.

To get to the junction of the two long-distance trails, go to the north end of **Beach Road** on the western edge of Holme and walk for a few minutes to the signed intersection on the other side of the golf course. From the intersection, the Norfolk Coast Path heads northeast, crossing the sand dunes of Holme Dunes National Nature Reserve (see opposite) en route to Thornham (see p.159). On the way, you'll pass within a few yards of the reserve's visitor centre, which can also be reached by car (see opposite).

ARRIVAL AND DEPARTURE   HOLME-NEXT-THE-SEA

By bus The Norfolk Coasthopper bus (see p.124) stops at the junction of the main road (the A149) and Peddars Way; from here it's a 5min walk north along Peddars Way to the centre of the village.

Holme Dunes National Nature Reserve

Holme-next-the-Sea, PE36 6LQ • **Reserve** Daily 10am–5pm, or dusk if earlier • £5 for the reserve's footpaths and bird hides, but you can walk through the reserve on the Norfolk Coast Path for free • **Visitor centre** April–Oct daily 10am–5pm, Nov–March Sat & Sun 10am–dusk • ☎01485 525240, ⍟norfolkwildlifetrust.org.uk • 40min walk to the visitor centre from the nearest Norfolk Coasthopper bus stop on the A149 at Holme

Owned and managed by Norfolk Wildlife Trust, the **Holme Dunes National Nature Reserve** stretches along the coast at the point where the Wash meets the North Sea. The extensive sand and mudflats here have long protected the coast and allowed for the formation of a band of sand dunes, which have, in their turn, created areas of salt- and freshwater marsh, reedbeds, and Corsican pine woodland. This varied terrain attracts all sorts of **birds**, with waders such as the grey plover, knot, bar-tailed godwit and sanderling zipping across the mudflats and migrant wildfowl like wigeon, brent geese and teal arriving in autumn to graze the marshes. In spring and summer, the shingle ridges on the beach attract nesting birds; for example, ringed plover and oystercatchers, while lapwing, redshank, snipe and avocet breed on the marshes. The reserve's **visitor centre** can be reached on foot from Thornham via the Norfolk Coast Path (three miles) and by car from Holme-next-the-Sea: from the A149, turn down Beach Road just to the west of Holme-next-the-Sea and, near the end of the road, turn right down the signed gravel track.

Hunstanton and around

The north Norfolk coast pretty much ends (or begins) at **HUNSTANTON**, a bustling seaside resort positioned just where the coastline turns south to run alongside the wide and stumpy Wash. The now-defunct railway reached here in 1862 and thereafter Hunstanton grew by leaps and bounds, sprouting scores of good-looking Victorian houses that are still a feature of the town, though today you'll be just as struck by the sheer awfulness of the modern development that has scarred the centre. The main attraction remains the **beach**, a lovely sandy tract backed by the stripy, **gateau-like cliffs** for which Hunstanton is well known, comprising a layer of red sandstone set beneath a band of white chalk. Beach and cliffs stretch north to **Old Hunstanton**, the site of the original fishing village and the place where a large and grassy park-cum-car-park backs onto the sea cliffs offering panoramic ocean views.

ARRIVAL AND INFORMATION   HUNSTANTON

By bus Hunstanton bus station is on Westgate, a couple of minutes' walk from the seafront Promenade. The Norfolk Coasthopper (see p.124) links the resort with King's Lynn, Heacham and points along the Norfolk coast.
Tourist office Hunstanton tourist office is in the Town

Hall, The Green, just off Cliff Parade, PE36 6BQ, (Daily: April & May 9.30am–4pm; June to mid-Sept 9.30am–5pm; mid-Sept to March 9.30am–3pm; ☎01485 532610, ⍟visithunstanton.info).

ACCOMMODATION AND EATING

Neptune 85 Old Hunstanton Rd, Old Hunstanton, PE36 6HZ ☎01485 532122, ⍟theneptune.co.uk. Well away from Hunstanton's tourist tat, on the main coastal road as it cuts through Old Hunstanton, this smart and agreeable hotel occupies a tastefully modernized old coaching inn, its six modern guest rooms equipped with all mod cons and white "New England-style" furniture. It's better known for

its restaurant, however, where the modern British menu features such delights as pan-fried gurnard with smoked aubergine, red pepper, wild garlic purée and spinach. A two-course set meal costs £42. Reservations are well-nigh essential. Tues–Sun 7–9pm, plus Sun noon–1.30pm. Double room with three-course dinner **£245**, room only **£160**

SHOPPING

World of Fun 2 St Edmund's Terrace, PE31 6RH ☎01485 532016, ⍟jokes-online.co.uk. Laugh until you

cry – or just cry. This is supposedly the largest joke shop in the world, stocking everything from the innocent and the harmless to the dubious and positively strange (a pecker whistle, would you believe). It's been going strong since 1978 with such perennial favourites as wigs, whoopee cushions, sneeze powder and joke sweets. Hahaha. Daily: May–Sept 9am–7pm; Oct–April 9am–5.30pm.

Heacham

From Hunstanton, it's the briefest of drives south to **HEACHAM**, whose semi-suburban tangle of narrow streets lies just inland from the army of static caravans that line up along the Wash. In 1929, the town was unexpectedly propelled into newspaper headlines when Mercedes Gleitze swam ashore here, becoming the first woman to swim across the Wash – accidental because she was actually aiming for Hunstanton. Similarly accidental is Heacham's connection with **Pocahontas** (c.1595–1617), a Native American from what is now Virginia, who helped the early English colonists in their assorted travails. Her relationship with the settlers was not straightforward – at one time the English held her captive – but she did end up marrying one of them, **John Rolfe**, whose family home was here in Heacham, and this was where he brought his wife during her extended visit to England. Pocahontas was presented at court, though quite how well she was received – as an honorary guest or freakish curiosity – is a matter of debate and, in the event, she never managed to get back home from England, dying on the return journey shortly after the boat set sail.

Norfolk Lavender

Caley Mill, beside the A149, on the eastern edge of Heacham, PE31 7JE · **Norfolk Lavender** Daily 9am–5pm · Free · ☏ 01485 570384, ⓦ norfolk-lavender.co.uk · **Farmer Fred's Adventure Play Barn** Mon–Fri 9.30am–6pm, Sat & Sun 10am–6pm · 1–3 year-olds £5.50 (off-peak £3.95); 4 years-plus £6.50 (off-peak £4.95) · ☏ 01485 579526, ⓦ farmerfredsplaybarnnorfolk.co.uk

The main reason to visit Heachem today is **Norfolk Lavender**, a popular tourist attraction, where the big pull is the lavender gardens and the lavender plant sales, though there are also a couple of gift shops, a rare breed animal centre, a farm shop and a large, indoor play area for kids – **Farmer Fred's Adventure Play Barn** – with slides, climbing frames, a maze and so forth.

Sedgeford

From Hunstanton, it's about four miles southeast to **SEDGEFORD**, whose flint cottages and old agricultural buildings spread out along the main road. There's no strong reason to hang around here, but there is an excellent **B&B**, *Magazine Wood* (see below), a little less than a mile to the east of the village beside the Peddars Way long-distance footpath (see p.210). Sedgeford was also home to the redoubtable **Sir Holcombe Ingleby** (1854–1926), one-time mayor and Conservative MP for King's Lynn, who was tried – but found innocent – for bribing his way into office by scattering free rabbits among the voters. It was the same Ingleby who, in World War I, became convinced that west Norfolk was infested with German spies after the first of several **zeppelin** bombing raids had hit the county. No spies were ever found, but the raids did create a real panic among the locals, one of whom described the zeppelin in true agricultural style as being "the size of a bullock, but sounding like a bee".

ACCOMMODATION   SEDGEFORD

★**Magazine Wood** Peddars Way, PE36 5LW ☏ 01485 570422, ⓦ magazinewood.co.uk. This deluxe B&B, deep in the Norfolk countryside, is strong on luxury with each of the spacious guest rooms decorated in an attractive modern style with king-size beds, plasma-screen TVs and superb bathrooms. Every room has a private terrace with wide views and each has a separate entrance independent of the main house/family home. Breakfasts are outstanding too. Note that satnavs will take you to Magazine Cottage, a distinctive flint and stone building beside the main road, the B1454, just to the east of Sedgeford; *Magazine Wood* is a few yards to the north along a narrow country lane. **£115**

Great Bircham Windmill

Great Bircham, PE31 6SJ • April–Sept daily 10am–5pm • Windmill £4.95, otherwise free • ☎ 01485 578393, ⓦ birchamwindmill.co.uk •
Ten miles southeast of Hunstanton

Pressing on from Sedgeford, it's a little over three miles east to **Docking**, where you turn right along the B1153 to get to **GREAT BIRCHAM**, or more specifically **Great Bircham Windmill**, which stands in a field to the west of the village – just follow the signs. There were once dozens of windmills dotted over the Norfolk countryside and this is a rare survivor, a sturdy, grey-yellow brick structure with a white top and sails dating from the nineteenth century. The windmill is in full working order and you can clamber up inside for a good look around. Afterwards you can wander round the huddle of little outhouses, where there's a café, a bookshop, a milking parlour and a cheese shop; you can also buy bread made from flour ground here at the windmill's bakery.

Snettisham and around

3

The A149 bypasses **SNETTISHAM**, just over four miles south of Hunstanton, and this has saved the village's pocket-sized centre from excessive development, its pleasant collection of old stone houses fanning out from the old-fashioned stores and shops of the **Market Place**. The village's main draw is the *Rose and Crown Hotel* (see p.164), but it is also a stone's throw from **Sandringham** (see p.164) and home to the handsome **church of St Mary** (April–Sept daily 9.30am–5pm; free), whose mighty stone tower and stone nave, perched on a grassy knoll on the east side of the village, are most unusual in Norfolk, where almost all the churches are built of flint. Dating from the fourteenth century, St Mary's was meant to impress and the highlight of the interior is the splendid stained glass of the west window, though the finely crafted eagle lectern also deserves a second look. Snettisham is also famous for the **Snettisham Treasure**, the richest Iron Age hoard ever found in the UK, unearthed by a ploughman in 1948; the key finds are now displayed in the British Museum in London.

Snettisham Nature Reserve

Beach Rd, PE31 7RA • Open access • Free • ☎ 01485 542689, ⓦ rspb.org.uk • No public transport

From Snettisham, it's about three miles to the shores of the Wash – take Beach Road west from the A149 and keep going. As you near the coast, you'll pass the signed gravel byroad that leads south to the RSPB's **Snettisham Nature Reserve**, which stretches along the mudflats of the Wash and includes the long and slender lagoons immediately behind. Footpaths negotiate the reserve and there are four strategically placed bird hides, with most birdwatchers timing their visit to coincide with the hour before high tide when thousands of **wading birds** are pushed off their feeding grounds out in the Wash onto the banks and islands in front of the RSPB's hides. The higher the tide, the greater the concentration of waders – ring ahead for advice on local conditions. From mid-November to late January, the reserve is also a superb spot to see **pink-footed geese** flying overhead in formation from their roosting grounds out in the Wash to their feeding grounds inland at dawn, the other way round at dusk. It is, however, best to avoid the three or four days either side of the full moon as the geese are not as reliable as normal on these days.

Beyond the turning to the nature reserve, **Beach Road** pushes on towards the coast, coming to a halt at a large car park immediately behind the seashore with static caravans and seaside chalets stretching away to the south. From the car park, you can wander out onto the mudflats or stroll along the sea wall.

ARRIVAL AND DEPARTURE   SNETTISHAM

By bus Buses pull in on the Lynn Road at the centre of the village, a couple of minutes' walk from the *Rose & Crown*.

ACCOMMODATION AND EATING

★**Rose & Crown** Old Church Rd, PE31 7LX ☎01485 541382, ⓦroseandcrownsnettisham.co.uk. If you are looking for a prime example of how to update a traditional village pub, this must be it. The owners have kept all the good parts, from the low ceilings, wooden beams and log fires through to the cosy little rooms, but added a sunny and attractive conservatory and upgraded sixteen guest rooms with sleep-deep beds and bright and cheerful decor.

The food, which is served in all of the three dining areas, is excellent too – try, for example, the Norfolk venison sausages with braised puy lentils (£10.75). As if this wasn't enough, they also serve an excellent range of local ales on draft. Kitchen Mon–Sat 7.30–10am & noon–9pm (Fri & Sat till 9.30pm), Sun 8–9.30am & noon–9pm; pub Mon–Sat 11am–11pm, Sun 11am–10.30pm. **£110**

Sandringham House

Sandringham Estate, PE35 6EN • **House & museum** Early April to Sept daily 11am–5.30pm, last entry 4.45pm; early Oct daily 11am–4.30pm, last entry 3.45pm • **Gardens** Early April to Sept daily 10.30am–5.30pm, last entry 4.30pm; early Oct daily 10.30am–4.30pm, last entry 3.30pm • **Visitor centre & gift shop** Daily 9.30am–4.30pm • £13.50 (house, museum & gardens), £9 (museum & gardens) • ☎ 01485 545408, ⓦ sandringhamestate.co.uk • Bus #12 from King's Lynn bus station to Sandringham visitor centre (early April to early Oct daily every 1–2hr; 40min)

Famous as the Christmas hidey-hole of Queen Elizabeth II, **Sandringham House**, off the A149 about five miles south of Snettisham and six miles northeast of King's Lynn, was built in 1870 on land purchased by Queen Victoria for her son, the future Edward VII. The house is billed as a private home, but few families have a drawing room crammed with Russian silver and Chinese jade and neither do many homes hold a substantial collection of Asian arms and armour, this particular lot being brought back from East Asia and India in 1876. The **museum**, housed in the old coach and stable block, contains an exhibition of royal memorabilia from dolls to cars, but much more arresting are the beautifully maintained **gardens**, a mass of rhododendrons and azaleas in spring and early summer. The estate's sandy soil is also ideal for game birds, which was the attraction of the place for the terminally bored Edward, whose tradition of posh shooting parties is still followed by the royals of today. For lovers of royalty, the **gift shop** sells all manner of "royal" trinkets, including tea towels and mugs.

Wolferton

Queen Victoria rarely did things by half, so when she bought Sandringham, she also opened the royal family's own train station at **WOLFERTON**, a tiny but incredibly prim-and-proper estate village a couple of miles to the west of the main house – and now on the far side of the A149 from Sandringham. Neither was this all: there's no way the royals were going to loaf around on the station platform, so the queen had a set of elegant waiting rooms built as well and, although the station was closed in the 1960s and has subsequently become a private home, the old mock-Tudor train station, the station platform and the old railway crossing gates have survived.

Castle Rising

Minuscule **CASTLE RISING**, roughly midway between King's Lynn and Sandringham, is a prosperous kind of place, its comfortable suburban streets fanning out from the substantial remains of its medieval **castle**, which sits on top of a grassy mound at the centre of extensive earthworks. Part hunting lodge, part fortified palace, the castle's salad days were done and dusted by the early sixteenth century, when it fell into disrepair. Castle Rising itself then became notorious as a **rotten borough**, electing a Member of Parliament despite its scant population, until the Reform Act of 1832 put an end to some of the electoral corruption.

The castle

Lynn Rd, Castle Rising, PE31 6AH • Daily: April–Oct 10am–6pm or dusk if earlier; Nov–March 10am–4pm • £4; EH • ☎ 01553 631330, ⓦ www.english-heritage.org.uk

Towering over the surrounding flatlands, **Castle Rising castle** is a powerful, imposing structure, some of whose finer architectural details have survived, most notably its precise blind arcading and interior galleries gouged out of the original defensive walls. An important medieval stronghold, it was here that **Queen Isabella** (1295–1358) lived during the last decades of her eventful life. Born in France, the young Isabella was married off to King Edward II of England, an unhappy match if ever there was one – Edward was almost definitely bisexual and, more importantly, he destabilized the throne by showering his male favourites with money and honours. Isabella eventually tired of all these shenanigans, deposing Edward and probably having him murdered, though the legend that he was killed by having a red-hot poker stuck up his back passage is most likely untrue. Isabella ruled as regent with her lover, Mortimer, until her son, **Edward III**, deposed the two lovers in 1330. The new king was not, however, bent on revenge: he did have Mortimer executed, but he spared his mother, who moved to Castle Rising, where she received a generous allowance – quite enough for her to hire a veritable army of Norfolk minstrels, grooms and huntsmen. Courtiers as well as the king himself regularly visited Isabella, who lived here for the rest of her life, developing her many interests – in religion, astrology and geometry.

The Church of St Lawrence

Lynn Rd, Castle Rising, PE31 6AG • Daily 9am–4.30pm • Free

Below the castle, the **village** holds a quadrangle of immaculately kept, seventeenth-century **almshouses**, whose elderly inhabitants still go to church in orange-red cloaks and pointed black hats, the colours of the original benefactor, the Earl of Northampton. The church in question is **St Lawrence**, of medieval foundation, but much mucked about by the Victorians, who added the conspicuous tower with the saddle-shaped roof that now rises above the central crossing. The church's finest features are the Norman dog-tooth decoration round several of the doorways and windows plus the Norman font with its three strange-looking cats' faces.

ARRIVAL AND DEPARTURE	**CASTLE RISING**
By bus Norfolk Green's #12 bus (5 daily; 15min; ⓦ norfolkgreen.co.uk) links King's Lynn bus station with	Castle Rising; get off in the centre of the village at the *Black Horse* pub.

EATING	
Unique Tea Rooms 28 Lynn Rd, PE31 6AF ☎ 01553 631211. There's not much choice in Castle Rising, but this cosy tearoom, in what was formerly the village post office, hits the mark, serving up traditional English food, mostly	home-made and including deliciously fruity scones. Eat either inside or in the large garden at the front. Tues–Sat 8.30am–8pm, Mon & Sun 8.30am–4pm.

SHOPPING	
Unique Gifts & Interiors Lynn Rd, PE31 6AG ☎ 01553 631500. An old barn stuffed with assorted furnishings and fittings from this Norfolk-based homes and gardens chain. The adjacent Unique Bridal	& Hats holds an extensive collection of hats, fascinators and costume jewellery, and there's a substantial bridalwear section too. Mon–Sat 10am–5pm, Sun 10.30am–4.30pm.

King's Lynn and the Fens

WIGGENHALL ST PETER

King's Lynn and the Fens

Norfolk's third largest town, King's Lynn is an ancient port that prospered on the back of its easy access to seven English counties, and its position straddling the canalized mouth of the Great Ouse river a mile or so before it slides into the Wash. It's not the most obvious holiday destination, but it does have a cluster of handsome old riverside buildings, and its lively, open-air markets attract large crowds. Many visitors head north from King's Lynn to the north Norfolk Coast, but there is interest, too, to the east and south of the town, in the part of the country known as the Fens, the smallest section of which lies in Norfolk. To the west you can follow the Peter Scott Walk to his former home near Sutton Bridge, and explore the medieval churches of the tiny communities here; while to the south, Downham Market is a base for a number of enticing villages, plus waterland attractions like the Welney Wetland Centre and Wicken Fen, across the border in Cambridgeshire. Also in Cambridgeshire, make time for Ely, whose imposing cathedral – the so-called Ship of the Fens – is the Fens' major historical attraction.

King's Lynn

KING'S LYNN was once one of the major ports of England. A member of the powerful Hanseatic League during the late Middle Ages, the town's merchants grew rich importing fish from Scandinavia, timber from the Baltics and wine from France, while exporting wool, salt and corn. The good times came to an end when the focus of maritime trade moved to the Atlantic seaboard, but its port struggled on until it was reinvigorated in the 1970s by the burgeoning trade between the UK and its EU partners. Unfortunately much of the old centre was demolished during the 1950s and 1960s to make way for commercial development, and as a result most of Lynn – as it's known locally – is not especially enticing. But in its historic core, around the waterfront, between the Purfleet and Millfleet inlets and around the so-called Saturday Market and Tuesday Market places, the medieval streets are remarkably untouched and the quaysides retain something of the feel of a seventeenth-century trading port.

The Custom House

Purfleet Quay, PE30 1HP • April–Sept Mon–Sat 10am–4.30pm, Sun noon–4.30pm; Oct–March Mon–Sat 10.30am–3.30pm, Sun noon–3.30pm • £1 • ☎ 01553 763044

Right on Purfleet Quay, the splendid **Custom House** overlooks a short and stumpy harbour once packed with merchant ships. It was erected in 1683 in a style clearly influenced by the Dutch, with classical pilasters, petite dormer windows and a rooftop balustrade, but it's the dinky little cupola that catches the eye, and its all-round elegant

ELY CATHEDRAL

Highlights

❶ King's Lynn waterfront An amazingly overlooked slice of life from mercantile medieval England. **See p.171**

❷ The Peter Scott Walk The blustery, evocative, coastal trek to the naturalist's Fenland hideaway. **See p.174**

❸ The Wiggenhalls This group of villages hosts Fenland's – maybe even Norfolk's – densest concentration of medieval churches and their treasures. **See p.178**

❹ Welney Wetland Centre Perfect all year round for novices and lazy twitchers. **See p.182**

❺ Ely Cathedral Rising magisterially out of the Fens, this is one of England's largest and most magnificent medieval cathedrals. **See p.183**

HIGHLIGHTS ARE MARKED ON THE MAP ON P.170

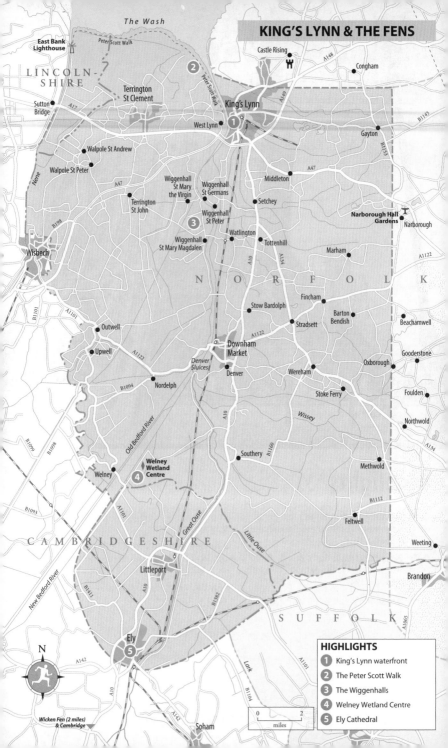

KING'S LYNN & THE FENS

The Wash

Peter Scott Walk

East Bank
Lighthouse

LINCOLN-
SHIRE

Castle Rising

Congham

A148

A149

Terrington
St Clement

Sutton
Bridge

A17

King's Lynn

Gayton

B1145

B1153

West Lynn

Walpole St Andrew

Walpole St Peter

Nene

A47

Middleton

A47

Setchey

Narborough Hall
Gardens

Narborough

Wiggenhall
St Mary
the Virgin

Wiggenhall
St Germans

Terrington
St John

Wiggenhall
St Peter

Wisbech

B1198

Watlington

Wiggenhall
St Mary Magdalen

Tottenhill

Marham

A1122

A10

A134

Marham

N O R F O L K

Fincham

B1101

A1101

Stow Bardolph

Stradsett

Barton
Bendish

Beachamwell

Outwell

A1122

Downham
Market

Wereham

Oxborough

Gooderstone

Upwell

A1122

Denver
Sluices

Denver

Stoke Ferry

Foulden

Nordelph

B1094

Wissey

Northwold

A134

A10

Old Bedford River

Southery

B1160

Methwold

B1098

B1099

Welney
Wetland
Centre

Welney

B1112

Feltwell

New Bedford River

B1093

Great Ouse

Little Ouse

Weeting

C A M B R I D G E S H I R E

Littleport

Brandon

A1065

S U F F O L K

A10

B1411

B1382

Ely

Lark

B1104

A1101

N

A142

Wicken Fen (2 miles)
& Cambridge

A143

Soham

0   2
miles

HIGHLIGHTS

1 King's Lynn waterfront
2 The Peter Scott Walk
3 The Wiggenhalls
4 Welney Wetland Centre
5 Ely Cathedral

proportions – Pevsner called it "one of the most perfect buildings ever built". The Custom House was in use until 1989, since when it has served as the tourist office (see p.174), and a couple of upstairs rooms have displays on the port and its heritage, including a number of matchstick models of the town's principal buildings. Out on the quayside giant boat-chains and a statue of King's Lynn native George Vancouver – best known for mapping the west coast of America in the late eighteenth century – with scroll in hand are further reminders of the town's maritime past.

The waterfront and around

The **waterfront** stretches west of the Custom House as far as **Millfleet Quay**, and is a beautifully preserved area, its Georgian and earlier frontages sliced through with evocative old alleys that lead back onto Queen Street and the centre of the old town. Most of the buildings along here are given over to non-maritime purposes these days, and not accessible to the public, but you can look in on the **Bank House Hotel** (see p.174), a beautiful Georgian building with a set of amazing cellars, and **Clifton House** (ⓦcliftonhouse.org.uk), which is occasionally open to the public and reckoned to be one of the most complete medieval merchant houses in England; it's owned by the former head of English Heritage Simon Thurley. The entrance – on Queen Street – is distinguished by its pair of twisted pillars and, if you're lucky enough to get inside, you can see tiled floors from the thirteenth century, a fourteenth-century vaulted undercroft and a magnificent brick Tudor tower.

Further down the quay, you can look in on **Marriott's Warehouse**, which is a café-restaurant these days (see p.176) but dates back to the 1580s and displays models of some of the town's medieval buildings, including one of the town in 1603, upstairs. Beyond here, the **Hanse House** (ⓦhansehouse.co.uk), built around 1475, is perhaps the country's most intact and authentic Hanseatic warehouse, consisting of a half-timbered upper floor that juts unevenly over the cobbles of St Margaret's Lane, a Georgian addition that fronts onto Saturday Market Place and a courtyard within that hosts weddings and houses a café and wine bar. Finally there's so-called **Hampton Court**, a little further on, a fourteenth-century merchant's building with a central cobbled courtyard, that has been converted to dinky flats.

Saturday Market Place

Behind the waterfront, the **Saturday Market Place** is one of the focal points of the old town, a thin triangle that is the older and smaller of the town's two marketplaces. It's home to Lynn's main parish church, St Margaret's (see below), and across the square is the city's prettiest building, the **Trinity Guildhall**, which has a wonderful, chequered flint-and-stone facade; this dates from 1421, and is repeated in the building's Elizabethan addition and the Victorian town hall immediately to the left. The Guildhall will soon be home to the "Stories of Lynn" exhibition, documenting the history of the town through various media and objects, not least the town's prized possession, the King John Cup, a bejewelled gold and silver goblet dating from 1325. Just opposite, across Queen Street, the peaceful courtyard of **Thoresby College** is accessible through its handsome medieval gateway from around 1510 – yet more evidence, if any were necessary, that history lurks around every corner in this part of King's Lynn.

St Margaret's

Saturday Market Place, PE30 5EB • ☎ 01553 772858, ⓦ stmargaretskingslynn.org.uk

The Saturday Market Place is dominated by the hybrid church of **St Margaret's**, a large and dignified building (one of the largest churches in the county) with an eighteenth-century organ and choir stalls covered with images of the Black Prince and Edward III.

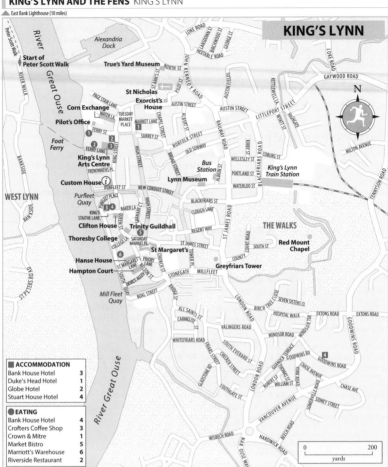

▲ East Bank Lighthouse (10 miles)

KING'S LYNN

N

Start of
Peter Scott Walk

True's Yard Museum

St Nicholas
Exorcist's
House

Corn Exchange

Pilot's Office

Foot
Ferry

King's Lynn
Arts Centre

Custom House

WEST LYNN

Purfleet
Quay

Clifton House

Thoresby College

Hanse House

Hampton Court

Mill Fleet
Quay

Trinity Guildhall

St Margaret's

Bus
Station

Lynn Museum

King's Lynn
Train Station

THE WALKS

Red Mount
Chapel

Greyfriars Tower

River Great Ouse

ACCOMMODATION

Bank House Hotel	3
Duke's Head Hotel	1
Globe Hotel	2
Stuart House Hotel	4

EATING

Bank House Hotel	4
Crofters Coffee Shop	3
Crown & Mitre	1
Market Bistro	5
Marriott's Warehouse	6
Riverside Restaurant	2

0   200
yards

The monarch is also remembered by the two medieval bronzes in the south aisle: the Walsoken brass, adorned with country scenes, recalling in particular the Peacock's Feast that was thrown for Edward when he visited the town in 1349, and the Braunche brass, named after a certain Robert Braunche, mayor of Lynn at the time and shown with his two wives.

King Street

Beyond the Custom House, **King Street** continues where Queen Street leaves off, and is the town's most elegant thoroughfare, lined with Georgian buildings and eulogized by none other than John Betjeman (a fan of Lynn, by all accounts) as one of the best walks in England. On the left, Ferry Lane leads down to the river and the departure point for the West Lynn ferry (see p.177). **St George's Guildhall** just beyond dates from 1410 and is one of the oldest surviving guildhalls in England. It was a theatre in Elizabethan times and is now part of the **King's Lynn Arts Centre** (see p.176). Behind, the *Riverside Restaurant* has a terrace overlooking the river (see p.176).

Tuesday Market Place and the Pilot's Office

The **Tuesday Market Place** is a handsome square by any standards, still surrounded by a good sprinkling of Georgian buildings and with the Rococo blue *Duke's Head Hotel*, dating from 1689, facing the plodding, Neoclassical **Corn Exchange** (now a theatre), on the far side. It's home to King's Lynn's main market on Fridays and, yes, Tuesdays.

Wander down to the riverfront, two minutes from the square, where the nineteenth-century **Pilot's Office**, with its octagonal brick tower, still does service as the King's Lynn Conservancy Board, looking after the port and harbour. A notice board outside displays the expected arrivals of ships from all over Europe to the docks just beyond.

Lynn Museum

Market St, PE30 1NL • Tues–Sat 10am–5pm • £3.95, families £11; free audio guide • ☎ 01553 775001, ⓦ museums.norfolk.gov.uk

Housed in the old Union Chapel by the bus station, bang in the centre of town, much of the refurbished **Lynn Museum** is given over to **Seahenge**, a circle of 556 oak timbers, preserved in peat, that were found to the north of here at Holme-next-the-Sea in 1998 (see p.160). The timber circle is reckoned to be around four thousand years old and was moved here amid much controversy in 2008. It's housed in an atmospheric gallery that showcases the timbers themselves, their original position and possible purpose, along with the giant upturned tree stump that stood in its centre – emphasizing what is thought to be its ritualistic purpose. The rest of the museum, in the wooden-beamed chapel, has displays on every aspect of life in Lynn and the region, including medieval times, World War II, the sea and the working lives of ordinary people, and there's a lot of good stuff for kids too.

True's Yard Fisherfolk Museum

North St, PE30 1QW • Tues–Sat 10am–4pm • £3, families £6 • ☎ 01553 770479, ⓦ truesyard.co.uk

The **True's Yard Fisherfolk Museum** is housed in some of the last remaining cottages in the heart of King's Lynn's North End district, once a hardcore fishing community, with the museum pretty much its only memorial. It's all very convincingly done, an affectionate commemoration of life in the old days, with lots of contemporary photos. The two cottages in the yards behind have been restored to how they were in the 1920s, when a family of seventeen lived there – as neat and prim as they must have been crowded, with more than a dozen layers of wallpaper uncovered and photos on the walls of the former occupants. An old smokehouse and smithy with more displays complete the picture. The museum also runs guided walks of the North End on Saturdays and Wednesdays in summer (£4), the price of which includes entry to the museum.

St Nicholas

St Ann St, PE30 1NH • Mon–Sat 11am–3pm • ⓦ stnicholaskingslynn.org.uk

The principal sight in this part of town is the nearby chapel of **St Nicholas**, an enormous structure that stood at the heart of the town's North End neighbourhood, and is now part of the Churches Conservation Trust. The spire was added by Gilbert Scott in the nineteenth century, but the large, cathedral-like church dates from the late fourteenth century and has recently received a massive restoration, with various interactive displays that help bring its history to life. It's pure medieval Gothic inside, with a fifteenth-century wooden roof punctuated by figures of angels holding musical instruments and lots of seventeenth- and eighteenth-century memorials to the merchants and seafarers who built King's Lynn, including one – a marble urn dedicated to Benjamin Keene – designed by Robert Adam and decorated with a harbourscape of Lisbon. The sixteenth-century benches in the corner of the west end are those of the consistory court, which met twice a year to adjudicate on moral matters, while the west doors are those of the original building

4

THE PETER SCOTT WALK

The **Peter Scott Walk** runs along the other side of the Ouse from the West Lynn ferry jetty to the **East Bank Lighthouse** – also known as Scott's lighthouse – on the River Nene (just across the county border in Lincolnshire), where the conservationist and artist lived from 1933 to 1939. Peter Scott was the only son of the Antarctic explorer **Captain Scott**, whose dying wish was that his son should be interested in natural history. Peter didn't let him down, founding among many other things the Wildfowl and Wetland Trust, one of whose nature reserves is at nearby Welney (see p.182), and promoting the conservation of Britain's wildlife throughout his life. Perhaps the best way to tackle the walk is to take a bus to Sutton Bridge and walk the three miles or so down the River Nene to pick up the path at Scott's lighthouse (you can also drive to the lighthouse, where there's a small car park). It's about eleven miles from here back to West Lynn, from where you can take the ferry across the river – or of course you can do the whole thing in reverse. The views over the Wash and the salt marshes and tidal flats are glorious, as are those inland over the Fenland that used to be under the sea, and you can spot redshanks, oyster catchers, curlews and much more along the way.

– painted green and red as they would have been in the fourteenth century. Outside, the gabled seventeenth-century building overlooking the churchyard is rather scarily known as the **Exorcist's House**; while **Pilot Street**, which winds around the back of the church, gives the best indication of how North End looked before the bulldozers moved in.

4 Greyfriars Tower and the Red Mount Chapel

Just outside the centre of Lynn, the brick and stone **Greyfriars Tower** is all that's left of a Franciscan friary that once stood here; it was restored in 2006 after an appearance on TV's *Restoration*. **The Walks**, across the road, is the city centre's main park, and features another historic building, the **Red Mount Chapel**, a former stop-off for medieval pilgrims on their way to Walsingham (see p.150), plus a café and a children's playground.

ARRIVAL AND INFORMATION   KING'S LYNN

By train King's Lynn's train station is a short walk east of the town centre across Railway Rd, the principal north–south thoroughfare that borders the centre's eastern edge, and down Waterloo St. It's at the end of the main line from London King's Cross (every hr; 1hr 40min), and is connected by hourly trains via Cambridge (45min), Ely (30min) and Downham Market (15min).

By bus The bus station is right in the centre, amid the main shopping area about 150m west of Railway Rd. There are buses west to Sutton Bridge (every 20min; 30min), roughly hourly buses to Wisbech that take in the Wiggenhalls (20min), and hourly buses to Downham Market (40min) and Denver (50min). There are also Coasthopper services to Hunstanton (every 30min; 35min) plus buses to Sandringham (every two

hours; 25min), Fakenham (every 30min; 40min) and Norwich (every 30min; 1hr 10min). There's also the #X1 from King's Lynn to Swaffham (40min), Dereham (1hr) and eventually Norwich (1hr 40min) roughly every 30min.

Tourist office By the river in the Custom House on Purfleet Quay (Mon–Sat 10am–5pm, Sun noon–5pm; ☎01553 763044, ⓦ visitwestnorfolk.com).

Walking tours One of the best ways to explore in Lynn's historical corners is to take one of the excellent walking tours that run regularly – choose from "Historic Lynn", "Maritime Trail" or the intriguingly titled "Darker Side of Lynn", among many others. All walks start at 2pm unless otherwise stated and last approximately 2hr; tickets cost £5 and are available from the tourist office (see above).

ACCOMMODATION

★ **Bank House Hotel** King's Staithe Square, PE30 1ED ☎01553 660492, ⓦ thebankhouse.co.uk. One of North Norfolk's best boutique hotels, and offering a chance to enjoy this fantastic Georgian merchant and banker's house, right on the quay in the heart of King's Lynn's historic district. There's a choice of eleven distinctive rooms, and a

great bar and restaurant (see p.176) that make it almost a destination in itself. Room rates vary according to size and levels of sumptuousness, but the cheapest so-called "cosy" doubles are excellent value and have lovely river views – as do several larger rooms. Owned by the Goodriches, who cut their teeth on the excellent *Rose & Crown* in Snettisham

THE FEN RIVERS WAY

The **Fen Rivers Way** runs for around fifty miles between King's Lynn and Cambridge, loosely following the route of the Great Ouse and then the Cam, via the Wiggenhalls, the Denver Sluices (see p.181) and Ely. Easy walking, and a great way to see the heart of the Fens, it links up with the Peter Scott Walk at King's Lynn by way of the West Lynn ferry.

(see p.164), the hotel is very friendly and also organizes guided walks around old King's Lynn with a local historian. Rates include a first-class breakfast. **£115**

Duke's Head Tuesday Market Place, PE30 1JS ☏0844 119484, ⓦ dukesheadhotel.com. This large historic hotel has had a bit of a makeover in recent years and while it's far from being King's Lynn's best place to stay, its rooms – in common with its public areas – are spacious and comfy and now have all the mod cons you would expect. **£110**

Globe Hotel Tuesday Market Place, PE30 1EZ ☏01553 668000, ⓦ jdwetherspoon.co.uk/home/pubs/globe -hotel. Nicely furnished, comfortable if fairly small rooms

in this busy Wetherspoon's hotel. Breakfast is served in the attached pub downstairs; it costs extra, but in typical Wetherspoon's style is cheap and quite cheerful. **£64**

Stuart House Hotel 35 Goodwins Rd, PE30 5QX ☏01553 772169, ⓦ stuarthousehotel.co.uk. Tucked away in a residential part of town, this small traditional hotel is just a 10min walk from the centre. It's a cosy old place with a busy bar downstairs that serves a good selection of real ales as well as hearty food. It has 24 well-furnished and thoroughly up-to-date rooms, although some can be a bit noisy if there's a function on downstairs. **£98**

EATING

★**Bank House Hotel** King's Staithe Square, PE30 1ED ☏01553 660492, ⓦ thebankhouse.co.uk. The warm, flickering lights of the *Bank House Hotel*'s (see p.174) bar and restaurant are wonderfully inviting from the relative darkness of King's Lynn's waterfront, and it's a very comforting feeling to be sitting in its elegant restaurant while the brown, sluggish Ouse lumbers by outside. The menu includes sandwiches for lunch and dinner, on top of a regularly changing all-day menu that features a great fish sharing platter, an excellent burger and more refined options like lamb rump, sea bream and mackerel. It's all topped off with delicious desserts and superb service, plus a lovely outside terrace. Starters go for around £6, mains £12–14, so it's very reasonably priced too. Daily: breakfast: 7.15–10am; lunch noon–6.30pm; afternoon tea 2.30–5.30pm; dinner 6.30–9pm (Fri & Sat till 9.30pm).

Crofters Coffee Shop 29 King St, PE30 1ET ☏01553 765565. Part of the Arts Centre complex, located in the undercroft of the St George's Guildhall, this serves as good a breakfast, light lunch or snack as you'll find in central King's Lynn, with a menu of sandwiches, jackets, salads and quiches. Mon–Sat 9.30am–4pm.

Crown & Mitre Ferry St, PE30 1LJ ☏01553 774669. A traditional cosy pub down by the water, with food – either on its riverside terrace or in its dining room with a roaring log fire. Basic pub grub – steaks, gammon, cottage pie – in generous portions, and a good selection of real ales. Daily noon–2pm & 6–9pm.

★**Market Bistro** 11 Saturday Market Place, PE30 5DQ ☏01553 771483, ⓦ marketbistro.co.uk. An unusually good local restaurant that serves excellent food in a stripped-down bistro environment. The food is hearty rather than refined, using locally sourced ingredients in an inventive and thoroughly up-to-date way – British tapas (Scotch eggs, ham hock terrine, etc), and mains like mussels, pollock with potato and leek terrine and blade of beef with oxtail. Great seasonal British food. Tues–Sat noon–2pm & 6–8.30pm, Sun noon–2pm.

Marriott's Warehouse South Quay, PE30 5DT ☏01553 818500, ⓦ marriottswarehouse.co.uk. Not only a great chance to see inside this historic building, but serving decent food and drink all day from 10am, too. The menu consists of hearty classics like fish and chips, omelettes, burgers and salads for £8.95–10.50; it doesn't change much throughout the day, but is beefed up in the evening with a few meat and fish dishes, such as sirloin steak for £16.95. Daily 10am–9pm.

Riverside Restaurant 27 King St, PE30 1ET ☏01553 773134. Housed in a handsomely converted, fifteenth-century warehouse overlooking the river at the back end of the King's Lynn Arts Centre, this is a decent venue with a good, varied menu featuring everything from lunchtime sandwiches, salads and burgers – which you can enjoy on their outside terrace – to slightly more refined dishes in the evening. Starters £5–6, mains £11–16. Mon–Sat noon–2pm & 6.30–9.30pm.

ENTERTAINMENT

King's Lynn Arts Centre 29 King St, PE30 1ET ☏01553 764864, ⓦ kingslynnarts.co.uk. Stages a wide range of performances and exhibitions both here and in several

other downtown venues, including the old Corn Exchange, on Tuesday Market Place.

WEST LYNN FERRY

Crossing the wide River Ouse in King's Lynn is made much easier, for pedestrians at least, by the mercifully still-running **West Lynn passenger ferry** which operates every day from the end of Ferry Lane, an alleyway off King St. It runs every 20min 6.45am–6.30pm (continuously 6.45–9am & 5–6.30pm) and costs £1 one-way, £1.50 return.

South and east of King's Lynn

The Fens is an amazing part of the country in many ways, but nowhere more so than the villages immediately to the **south and east** of King's Lynn where you'll find some of the finest medieval ecclesiastical architecture and art in Britain. The countryside is distinctive and oddly hypnotic: wide, endless fields of arable crops, split by drainage ditches and the slow-moving rivers of the Great and Little Ouse, the Nene and the Bedford – majestic thoroughfares that once carried convoys of commercial river traffic (hidden by dykes, you only become aware of them once you're upon them). With much of the land reclaimed from fen and marshland, there's naturally a Dutch feel to the landscape, as well as a captivating prettiness, especially around the **Wiggenhalls** and the villages to the south. The settlements to the north are more pedestrian sprawls of bungalows and workyards, scattered across the thunderous arterial roads of the A47 and A17, and interspersed between fields of crops – a hint of what is to come across the border in Lincolnshire (where, incidentally, you can pick up the Peter Scott Walk – see box, p.174).

Terrington St Clement

St Clement, Churchgate Way, PE34 4LZ • If closed, get the key from the house to the left of the church gate • Ⓦ tsc-church.org.uk

Four miles east of King's Lynn, **TERRINGTON ST CLEMENT** is the closest Fenland settlement with something worth seeing, a dull village on the whole but with an enormous parish church – **St Clement** – whose nave is the longest of any in the county (get the key from the house to the left of the church gate). In the north aisle is the massive wooden font cover, added in the sixteenth century, inside which there are paintings of the Four Evangelists added about a hundred years later; open the doors to peek in and look.

ARRIVAL AND DEPARTURE TERRINGTON ST CLEMENT

By bus There are roughly half-hourly buses (#505) from King's Lynn to Spalding in Lincolnshire which stop off at Terrington St Clement (20min) and Sutton Bridge just beyond, for the Peter Scott Walk (see box, p.174).

The Walpoles

In the far west of north Norfolk, just a stone's throw from the Lincolnshire border, the conjoined villages of **WALPOLE ST ANDREW** and **WALPOLE ST PETER** are nothing special in themselves, but the church of **St Peter** (Ⓦwalpolestpeterchurch.org) is known as the "Cathedral of the Fens" for its size, grandeur and fine proportions. There is a wealth of woodcarving inside – nothing incredible, but check out the animals and saints in the choir, which mostly date from the fifteenth century, and the faded saints on the chancel screen. Look too at the more low-key details at the western end: a sentry box used by ministers during rainy funerals, and a fine old table dating from the early seventeenth century. The Walpoles' sister church of **St Andrew** (Ⓦvisitchurches.org.uk) is a slightly more run-down version of St Peter, and is now owned by the Churches Conservation Trust – pick up the key from the house next door, 5 Kirk Rd. Inside it's strangely empty and rather damp, but a wonderful example of the period nonetheless.

ARRIVAL AND DEPARTURE THE WALPOLES

By bus The #63 runs from King's Lynn to Wisbech via the Walpoles (6 daily; 35min to Walpole St Peter's church).

THE FENS

One of the strangest of all English landscapes, the **Fens** cover a vast area of eastern England from just north of Cambridge right up to Boston in Lincolnshire. For centuries, they were an inhospitable wilderness of quaking bogs and marshland, punctuated by clay islands on which small communities eked out a livelihood cutting peat for fuel, using reeds for thatching and living on a diet of fish and wildfowl. Piecemeal land reclamation took place throughout the Middle Ages, but it wasn't until the seventeenth century that the systematic draining of the Fens was undertaken – amid fierce local opposition – by Dutch engineer **Cornelius Vermuyden**. This wholesale draining had unforeseen consequences: as it dried out, the peaty soil shrank to below the level of the rivers, causing frequent flooding, and the region's **windmills**, which had previously been vital in keeping the waters at bay, compounded the problem by causing further shrinkage. The engineers had to do some rapid backtracking, and the task of draining the Fens was only completed in the 1820s following the introduction of **steam-driven pumps**, leviathans which could control water levels with much greater precision. Drained, the Fens now comprise some of the most fertile agricultural land in Europe.

The Wiggenhalls

A short way to the south of King's Lynn, just off the main A10, the group of villages known as the **WIGGENHALLS** offer the most appealing glimpse of fens close to the town. Right on the river, the church of **St Germain** at **Wiggenhall St Germans** boasts a fine set of carved choir stalls and a perfect position by the Great Ouse. You can follow the riverside path from here two miles downstream to **Wiggenhall St Mary Magdalen**, or "Magdalen" as it's more often known, where the church of **St Mary Magdalen** was rebuilt in the fifteenth century by the same architect as the one at Walpole St Peter. It's a light, well-proportioned building with a beautiful wooden roof and ancient pews, though it's best known for the mid-fifteenth-century stained glass in the north aisle – mostly representations of saints and martyrs from the early Christian Church.

St Mary the Virgin

Church Rd, Wiggenhall, PE34 3EJ • If closed, get the key from Wiggenhall House, in front of the church • ⓦ visitchurches.org.uk

Of all the Wiggenhall churches, and despite not being right on the river, **St Mary the Virgin** enjoys the best position, outside the village surrounded by fields and with a resoundingly peaceful churchyard. Now part of the Churches Conservation Trust, it also holds quite a haul of treasure for such a remote site, not least a set of fifteenth-century pew carvings that are reckoned to be the finest examples of their kind in England. They're much larger than you usually find, often with two figures at each end and another – usually a saint – in a niche below, and are in a marvellous state of preservation, full of everyday details and observances. There's also an elaborate alabaster tomb in the aisle, with the life-sized effigies of local aristocrat Henry Kerville and his wife, who died in the early seventeenth century, together with beautifully realized and rather sad carvings of their children, who died before them, underneath. Check out, also, the beautifully coloured rood screen in the choir, with four saints on each side, which would alone be enough to draw you to the church.

EATING   **THE WIGGENHALLS**

Crown & Anchor 16 Lynn Rd, Wiggenhall St Germans, PE34 3EY ☎ 01553 617340. A homely and very friendly riverside pub that does a basic menu of pies, roasts and burgers for £8–10, and traditional desserts like jam roly-poly and spotted dick. Tues–Sat noon–2pm & 6–8.30pm, Sun noon–3.30pm.

Watlington

WATLINGTON is a pretty village centred around a large village green, and with a church – **St Peter and St Paul**, which has fine medieval bench-end carvings of the seven deadly sins – and a welcoming pub, *The Angel*, which does roasts on Sundays (see opposite).

OPIUM EATING IN THE NINETEENTH CENTURY

The Fens have always been poor, but a century ago, when the area was still prone to frequent inundations by water and all the problems associated with this, they were dirt poor, and unhealthy to boot, with those who lived here prone to debilitating "ague" and rheumatism brought on by the marshy environment. There wasn't much in the way of medical help, and many here turned to **opium** to enhance their miserable existence. As a result opium usage in the Fens was way above the national average in the nineteenth century and infiltrated all sectors of the population. It was given to children (thereby exacerbating an already high infant mortality rate), dropped into beer in the pub, and added to tea at home; and it wasn't unusual to see labourers asleep at their plough in the fields or bumping into the crowds on market day – indeed chemist's shops were often the busiest places when the rural poor came into town. As the Fens were drained, and the region in effect joined the rest of society, so opium usage declined, but there were still instances of it in the early part of the twentieth century.

EATING   WATLINGTON

The Angel 41 School Rd, PE33 0HA ☎01553 811326, ⓦtheangelpub.webs.com. Good local pub, right on the village green in Watlington, that does food all week – burgers, steaks, fish for £10–15 – and provides a very warm welcome. Kitchen Mon 6–9pm, Tues–Sat noon–2pm & 6–9pm, Sun noon–3pm; pub Mon 5–11pm, Tues–Thurs noon–2.30pm & 5–11pm, Fri–Sun all day.

Beers of Europe

Garage Lane, Setchey, PE33 0BE • Mon–Sat 9am–6pm, Sun 10am–4pm • ☎01553 812000, ⓦbeersofeurope.co.uk • Bus #37 (hourly) can drop you here on the way between King's Lynn and Downham Market

Situated just off the A10, in **SETCHEY**, about four miles south of King's Lynn, **Beers of Europe** is basically a large warehouse stacked full of beers you won't find elsewhere in Britain, and especially good on Belgian and German ales, together with the glasses to drink them from. There's an international selection of ciders, wines and weird spirits too, but as the name suggests beer is the thing here, and the selection of local and British ales is also strong.

ACCOMMODATION AND EATING   SETCHEY

Andel Lodge 48 Lynn Rd, Tottenhill, PE33 0RH ☎01553 810256, ⓦandellodge.co.uk. A good selection of double and twin rooms, all individually furnished, and a handy location on the main road midway between King's Lynn and Downham Market and just a mile or so from Setchey. The hotel has its own restaurant serving a good selection of steaks, duck, chicken and veggie options for around £12–15. Mon–Sat noon–2.30pm & 7–9pm, Sun noon–2.30pm. **£79.50**

Downham Market and around

Fifteen minutes by train south of King's Lynn, **DOWNHAM MARKET** is the gateway to the Norfolk Fens, and, although not much in itself, is a well-placed and pleasant base, within easy reach of some of the most alluring Fenland villages, and also some compelling natural attractions like the **Welney Wetland Reserve** and **Wicken Fen**. It's also within twenty minutes' drive or so of some of the best villages and attractions in the Brecks – **Oxburgh Hall**, **Gooderstone Water Gardens** and even **Thetford Forest** (see p.210).

The Market Place

Downham Market gathers around its **Market Place**, at the intersection of High Street and Bridge Street, marked by the town's iconic Victorian **clock tower**, a dinky cast-iron structure with a weather vane on top. There are weekly Friday and Saturday markets here.

4

ARRIVAL INFORMATION

DOWNHAM MARKET

By train The station is 5–10min west of the town centre – just follow Railway Rd then Bridge St to reach the Market Place. Regular connections to King's Lynn (15min), Ely (15min) and Cambridge (30min).

By bus Buses pull up just off Bridge St, and also at the nearby Tesco; there are hourly services to King's Lynn (40min) and to Denver village (10min).

Tourist office Next door to Tesco in the council offices on Priory Rd (Mon–Thurs 9am–5pm, Fri 9am–4.45pm; Easter to mid-Sept also Sat 9am–noon; ☎ 01553 616200).

ACCOMMODATION AND EATING

IN TOWN

Castle Hotel High St, PE38 9HF ☎ 01366 384311, ⓦ castle-hotel.com. Recently upgraded, the twelve en-suite rooms here vary quite a bit, with a mixture of doubles, twins and singles, but it's a friendly old place, and has a cosy bar and restaurant downstairs. Breakfast included. **£85**

Crown Hotel 12 Bridge St, PE38 9DH ☎ 01366 382322. Right in the heart of town, this creaky old coaching inn has a range of simply furnished but comfortable en-suite doubles upstairs and a busy bar downstairs serving food. Breakfast costs £7 extra. **£55**

★Dial House 12 Railway Rd, PE38 9EB ☎ 01366 385775, ⓦ dialhousebnb.co.uk. Between the station and the town centre, this is your chance to stay in a real gingerbread house. A small B&B beautifully kept inside and out, with three double rooms each named after the sisters who used to run a school for young gentlemen here. Look for the sundial on the side of the house. **£60**

The Railway Arms and Fenland Express Downham Market train station, PE38 9EN ☎ 01366 386636, ⓦ railway-arms.co.uk. Old-fashioned café and pub nestled into the train station, with a bar and two cosy rooms with comfy armchairs to sink into. Shelves of secondhand books too, all of which are for sale – just pop the money into the box. Good real ales and food, too. Café Mon–Thurs 5.30am–12.10pm & 3.30–5.10pm, Fri 5.30am–5.10pm, Sat 7.45am–12.10pm; bar Mon–Thurs 10am–12.10pm & 3.30–5.30pm, Fri 10am–10.30pm, Sat 10am–noon & 6–10.30am, Sun noon–2.30pm.

OUT OF TOWN

Timbers Lynn Rd, Fincham, PE33 9HE ☎ 01366 347747, ⓦ timberscountrylodge.co.uk. A few miles east of Downham Market, this complex of clapboard cabins arranged around a bar and restaurant building has 35 rooms in all, nicely furnished and with flatscreen TVs. Breakfast isn't included and costs £10, and the restaurant serves light bites at lunchtime and a fuller evening menu – fish and chips, burgers, steaks and the like. Mon–Thurs noon–9pm, Fri & Sat noon–9.30pm, Sun noon–8pm. **£60**

Holy Trinity, Stow Bardolph

Lynn Rd, PE34 3HT • ⓦ achurchnearyou.com/stow-bardolph-holy-trinity

A couple of miles north of Downham Market, just off the A10, **STOW BARDOLPH** is a pretty village that is home to the late twelfth-century **Holy Trinity** church, whose main feature is a chapel off the choir full of memorials to the local Hare family, who occupied nearby Stow Hall (the local pub, the *Hare Arms*, is named after them too). As well as simple memorials to the fifth and sixth baronets, who died in 1993 and 2000 respectively, there are more ornate memorial tablets to Hugo and Nicholas Hare, who died in 1597 and 1619 a large monument to Susanne Hare (sculpted in 1741) by the sculptor of Shakepeare's tomb in Westminster Abbey, and a reclining figure of Thomas Hare as a Roman general (1697). But most spooky is the wax effigy of Thomas Hare's daughter Sarah, who died in 1744 and had her likeness forever captured in wax – kept in a cupboard in the corner. Check out, too, the accomplished sixteenth-century carvings of hares (geddit?) at the far end of the choir stalls.

Church Farm Rare Breeds Centre, Stow Bardolph

Stow Bardolph, PE34 3HU • Mid-Feb to Oct daily 10am–5pm; Nov–Feb Thurs–Sun 10am–5pm • £7.50, children £6.80, family tickets £26.50 • ☎ 01366 382162, ⓦ churchfarmstowbardolph.co.uk

Almost next door to the church in Stow Bardolph, **Church Farm Rare Breeds Centre** is an unashamedly child-focused attraction, a small farm with sheep, goats and all sorts of pigs – and of course the cute lambs, kids and piglets that go with them. There are petting areas, tractor rides and a large children's play area (inside and out), and you can do walks on marked trails through adjacent Church Wood, although much of the focus is on the busy café and toyshop.

EATING AND DRINKING   STOW BOTOLPH

★**Hare Arms** Lynn Rd, PE34 3HT ☎ 01366 382229, ⓦ theharearms.co.uk. The village pub is also named after the family, and is a popular place. The food is a cut above average pub grub, with a large menu featuring good burgers, fish, sausages, steaks and veggie options – most of them for £10–12 and all locally sourced and beautifully cooked. They always have a few daily specials on too and there's a pleasant beer garden, full of peacocks. Kitchen Mon–Fri noon–2pm & 6–10pm, Sat & Sun noon–10pm; pub Mon–Fri 11am–2.30pm & 6–11pm, Sat & Sun noon–10.30pm.

St Mary, Barton Bendish

Boughton Long Rd, PE33 9DN • ⓦ visitchurches.org.uk

About seven miles east of Downham Market, **BARTON BENDISH** is more of a Breckland than a Fenland village, and has an interesting church – **St Mary's** – on its outskirts, which is now under the care of the Churches Conservation Trust and usually open during the day. Thatched, and without a tower, Pevsner called its west door "one of the best Norman doors in England", and its interior is one of Norfolk's finest too – wonderfully peaceful and with the traces of an ancient and mysterious painting of a woman on a cartwheel on the wall of the nave.

ACCOMMODATION AND EATING   BARTON BENDISH

★**Berney Arms** Church Rd, PE33 9GF ☎ 01366 347995, ⓦ theberneyarms.co.uk. This long-running place is now something of a gastropub with boutique rooms – three in the main building and four in the nearby stable block, plus a large suite in the old forge. Rooms are excellent value, and a good breakfast is included. There's a great, moderately priced menu, much of it sourced from the surrounding estate – think fish finger or beef and horseradish sandwiches, burgers, or maybe pan-seared scallops followed by venison or sea bream. They serve a set menu Mon–Fri & Sat lunch (two courses £12.50, three courses £15.50); otherwise starters are £5–6, mains £12–16. They also have a quirkily furnished garden front and back. Mon–Fri noon–2.30pm & 6–9pm, Fri & Sat noon–2.30pm & 6–9.30pm, Sun noon–8pm. **£65**

Denver Sluices

Sluice Rd, Denver, PE38 0EG • ⓦ environment-agency.gov.uk

In the village of **DENVER**, twenty minutes' walk from Denver Mill (see box, p.182) through an unspoilt Fenland landscape, **Denver Sluices** spread across the intersection

DENVER MILL

About a 25-minute walk from the centre of Downham Market, on the far side of the pretty village of Denver, **Denver Mill** is a nineteenth-century windmill that until relatively recently had been restored and was grinding its own flour, which was sold in its own shop, and operating as a tourist attraction and café with 50,000 visitors a year – proof that a sustainable business could be run from this historic structure. However, in 2011 one of the stocks on the windmill broke, scattering debris everywhere; the site was closed down and all trading ceased. Despite grants from other organizations to re-establish and develop what had been a thriving food and tourism business, the owners finally shut up shop in 2013, claiming the Norfolk Historic Buildings Trust had no interest in rescuing this historic building, and as such it has fallen into further disrepair, today presenting a rather sad spectacle – a great shame. Let's hope by the time we come to research the next edition of this guide something is once again up and running at Denver Mill.

of various channels of the Great Ouse and its drainage cuts. The first sluice was constructed here in 1651 by the great Dutch engineer Cornelis Vermuyden, and contributed greatly to the initial draining of the Fens, although it has been replaced and added to over the centuries. The complex is still a working one, and under the auspices of the Environment Agency, who host occasional drop-in events to explain how the sluices work and contribute to flood management in the area. Oddly, most of the water here is diverted way down south to Essex where they are more short of the stuff.

EATING AND DRINKING   DENVER

Jenyns Arms Sluice Bank Rd, PE38 0EQ ☎01366 383366, ⓦjenyns.co.uk. Right by the sluices outside Denver village, the *Jenyns Arms* has a perfect position by the river, and a garden from which to enjoy it. There's also basic pub grub, including fish and chips, burgers, steaks, and gammon, along with salads, jackets and sandwiches. Kitchen Mon–Thurs noon–2pm & 7–9pm, Fri & Sat noon–2pm & 6–9pm, Sun noon–9pm.

Welney Wetland Centre

Hundred Foot Bank, Welney, PE14 9TN • March–Oct daily 9.30am–5pm; Nov–Feb Mon–Wed 10am–5pm, Thurs–Sun 10am–8pm • £7.99, children £3.90, families £21.40 • ⓦ wwt.org.uk/wetland-centres/welney

Almost the perfect location for the novice or lazy twitcher, the **Welney Wetland Centre** occupies a complex of expensively assembled, cedar-clad and ecofriendly buildings astride the road and the marshland in between the New and Old Bedford rivers, about ten miles southwest of Downham Market (or ten miles northwest of Ely) and about a mile and a half outside the village of **WELNEY**. Twitchers aside, it can be a tremendously peaceful place, and is sensitively done, with total regard given to the birds' habitat. There're plenty of (accessible) observation points along a linear trail sandwiched between the river and fen, ranging from basic one-man hides to the large, centrally heated suite at the centre of the complex, where reference books are laid out for your edification and – if you've forgotten your binoculars – you can zero in on the best bits on CCTV (you can also rent binoculars for £5). In summer there's a trail where you are likely to see butterflies and dragonflies, and you might spot avocets and redshanks in spring and marsh harriers, curlews and sandpipers in autumn. By far the most popular time to be at Welney, though, is for the migration and feeding of winter Whooper and Bewick swans (which you can observe most evenings in floodlit comfort).

ACCOMMODATION AND EATING   WELNEY

Lamb & Flag Main St, PE14 9RB ☎01354 610242, ⓦlambandflagwelney.co.uk. Just over the border in Cambridgeshire, this is a large pub with a beer garden that does good food from a short menu of burgers, steaks and other staples – try the Fenman's steak pie – from around £10. Usually a blackboard of specials too. They also have a few B&B rooms upstairs. Kitchen Mon–Sat noon–2pm & 6.30–8.30pm, Sun noon–3.30pm; pub daily 11am–11pm. **£48**

Ely and around

Perched on a mound of clay above the Great Ouse river, about fifteen miles south of Downham Market, the attractive little town of **ELY** – literally "eel island" – was indeed an island until the draining of the Fens (see box, p.178). Before then the town was encircled by treacherous marshland, only traversable with the help of the local "fen-slodgers" who knew the firm tussock paths. In 1070, **Hereward the Wake** turned this inaccessibility to military advantage, holding out against the Normans and forcing William the Conqueror to undertake a prolonged siege. Centuries later, Victorian writer Charles Kingsley resurrected this obscure conflict in his novel *Hereward the Wake*, presenting the protagonist as the last of the English who "never really bent their necks to the Norman yoke" – a heady mix of nationalism and historical invention that went down a storm. "Norman yokes" don't have much resonance today and Ely's main magnet now is its magnificent Norman **cathedral**, visible for miles across the flat Fenland landscape. This makes Ely a worthwhile destination in its own right, but you may also want to take in nearby **Wicken Fen**, which is as close to a rare chunk of undrained and unmolested Fenland as you can get.

The High Street and Riverside

Ely is a pleasant small town, but apart from the cathedral it's hardly compelling. To the immediate north of the church, the **High Street** is a slender thoroughfare lined by cafés and old-fashioned shops. East of the dinky Market Place it becomes Waterside, leading down to **Riverside** – a relaxing stretch with a marina and footpath, a tearoom or two, an antique centre, a gallery and an entertainment complex in the splendidly restored **Old Maltings**.

4

Ely Cathedral

June–Sept daily 7am–6.30pm; Oct–May Mon–Sat 7am–6.30pm, Sun 7am–5.30pm • Mon–Sat £8 including ground-floor tour; Sun free, but no tour • There are also West Tower and Octagon tours (for an extra £6.50 each), best reserved in advance • ☎ 01353 660344, ⓦ elycathedral.org

Dating mainly from the late twelfth century, **Ely Cathedral** is one of the largest and most impressive churches in England, but outside at least it's also one of its least symmetrical, with one of its transepts having collapsed in a storm in 1701. The remaining transepts are an imposing sight, their dog-tooth windows, castellated towers and blind arcading possessing all the rough, brutal charm of the Normans. Inside, the nave is the fourth longest in the country at 538ft, its procession of plain late-Norman arches leading to the architectural feature that makes Ely so special, the **octagon**, built in 1322 to replace the collapsed central tower. Its construction, employing the largest oaks available to support some four hundred tonnes of glass and lead, remains one of the wonders of the medieval world, and the effect, as you look up into this Gothic dome, is simply breathtaking.

The first three bays of the **choir** were rebuilt at the same time as the octagon in the Decorated style – in contrast to the plainer Early English of the choir bays beyond. A commemorative plaque here marks the site of the shrine of **St Etheldreda**, founder of the abbey in 673, who, despite being twice married, is honoured liturgically as a virgin. The shrine once attracted pilgrims from far and wide, but it was destroyed in the Reformation. At the far east end of the cathedral, the thirteenth-century **presbytery** has two medieval **chantry chapels**, the more intricately carved of which is an elaborate Renaissance affair from 1488. The other marvel is the **Lady Chapel**, accessible via the north transept: it lost its sculpture and stained glass during the Reformation, but its fan vaulting remains, an exquisite example of the late English Gothic style.

The Stained Glass Museum and Cathedral Precincts

Museum Mon–Sat 10.30am–5pm, Sun noon–4.30pm • £4.50 • ☎ 01353 660347, ⓦ stainedglassmuseum.com

Close to the main entrance of the cathedral, the south triforium holds the **Stained Glass Museum**, exhibiting examples of this applied art from 1200 to the 1970s, including

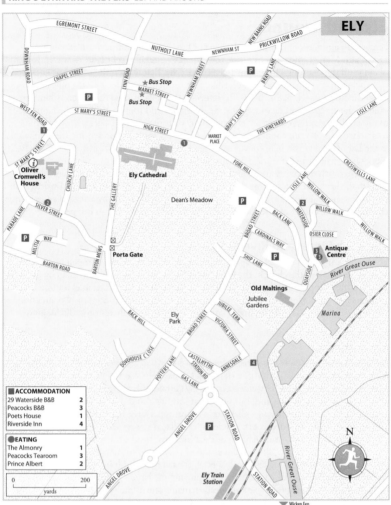

ELY

ACCOMMODATION
29 Waterside B&B	2
Peacocks B&B	3
Poets House	1
Riverside Inn	4

EATING
The Almonry	1
Peacocks Tearoom	3
Prince Albert	2

some especially fine work by William Morris and his circle. Outside, the **Precincts** of the cathedral boast a fine ensemble of medieval domestic architecture, an assortment of old stone, brick and half-timbered buildings that runs south from the Infirmary complex, abutting the presbytery, to the Prior's buildings near the Porta Gate. Many of the buildings are used by the King's boarding school – where the cathedral's choristers are trained – others by the clergy, but although you can't go into any of them, it's still a pleasant area to stroll; a free map and brochure are available from the cathedral itself.

Oliver Cromwell's House

29 St Mary's St, CB7 4HF • Daily: April–Oct 10am–5pm; Nov–March 11am–4pm • £4.90 • ☏ 01353 662062, ⓦ visitely.org.uk

Northwest from the cathedral is **Oliver Cromwell's House**, a timber-framed former vicarage, which holds a small exhibition on the Protector's ten-year sojourn in Ely, when he was employed as a tithe collector.

ARRIVAL AND INFORMATION

ELY

By train Ely lies on a major rail intersection, receiving direct trains from far and wide. From the train station, it's a 10min walk to the cathedral, straight up Station Rd and then Back Hill before veering right along The Gallery. Destinations Cambridge (every 15–20min; 15min); Downham Market (every 30min; 15min); King's Lynn (hourly; 30min); London King's Cross (hourly; 1hr 20min); Norwich (every 30min; 1hr).

By bus Buses stop on Market St immediately to the north of the cathedral.

Tourist office A couple of minutes' walk west of the cathedral in what was once Oliver Cromwell's House (see opposite) at 29 St Mary's St (Daily: April–Oct 10am–5pm; Nov–March 11am–4pm; ☎ 01353 662062, ⓦ visitely.org.uk).

ACCOMMODATION

29 Waterside B&B 29 Waterside, CB7 4AU ☎ 01353 614329, ⓦ visitely.org.uk. This cosy B&B near the river occupies a pair of little brick cottages dating back to the 1750s. Many original features have been preserved, including the beamed ceilings, and the remainder sympathetically modernized. If the sun is out, breakfast is taken in the garden. **£95**

Peacocks B&B 65 Waterside, CB7 4AU ☎ 01353 661100, ⓦ peacockstearoom.co.uk. *Peacocks Tearoom* (see below) has recently branched out into B&B accommodation, offering two cosy, well-presented, traditionally furnished suites down by the river. **£125**

Poets House 40 St Mary's St, CB7 4EY ☎ 01353 887777, ⓦ poetshouse.com. Apart from an apostrophe, this deluxe hotel lacks for nothing, its several guest rooms decked out in opulent, ersatz country-house style, with freestanding copper baths, big beds and rain showers. **£180**

Riverside Inn 8 Annesdale, CB7 4BN ☎ 01353 661677, ⓦ riversideinn-ely.co.uk. In a grand location overlooking the marina, this mid-range hotel, which occupies a substantial building dating back to the 1880s, has its guest rooms decorated in a pleasing version of country-house-meets-boutique style. Competitively priced. **£110**

EATING

The Almonry 36 High St, CB7 5JU ☎ 01353 666360, ⓦ elycathedral.org. Good café in a great location, with lovely views of the cathedral, albeit with a fairly pedestrian array of sandwiches and snacks. Daily 10am–5pm.

★ **Peacocks Tearoom** 65 Waterside, CB7 4AU ☎ 01353 661100, ⓦ peacockstearoom.co.uk. This riverside tearoom serves a delicious range of cream teas, salads, sandwiches, soups and lunches with the odd surprise: try the chocolate courgette cake. There's also an enormous

choice of teas from every corner of the globe. Wed–Sun 10.30am–5pm; June–Sept also Tues 10.30am–5pm.

Prince Albert 62 Silver St, CB7 4JF ☎ 01353 663494, ⓦ visitely.org.uk. Recently upgraded, this traditional neighbourhood pub has a first-rate selection of guest ales on tap, and a handy location– a short stroll from the cathedral. Pub grub and garden, too. Kitchen Mon–Fri noon–3pm & 5–9pm, Sat & Sun noon–8.30pm; pub daily noon–11.30pm, Sun noon–10.30pm.

4

Wicken Fen National Nature Reserve

Lode Lane, Wicken, CB7 5XP • **Nature Reserve** Daily 10am–5pm or dusk if earlier • **Cottage** April–July & Sept–Oct Sat & Sun 2–5pm; Aug Wed, Sat & Sun 11am–5pm • £6.45; NT • ☎ 01353 720274, ⓦ nationaltrust.org.uk • The NT's visitor centre organizes a variety of events and guided walks – call ahead or go online for details • **Dragonfly Centre** Late May to late Sept Sat & Sun 11am–4pm • ☎ 01353 720274, ⓦ british-dragonflies.org.uk

Wicken Fen National Nature Reserve, nine miles south of Ely, has the distinction of being Britain's first nature reserve – Darwin used to collect insects here. It is also one of the few remaining areas of undrained Fenland and as such is an important wetland habitat. It owes its survival to a group of Victorian entomologists who donated the land to the National Trust in 1899. The seven hundred acres are undrained but not uncultivated – sedge and reed cutting are still carried out to preserve the landscape as it is – and the reserve is easily explored by means of several clearly marked **footpaths**, the easiest of which is a three-quarter-of-a-mile romp along a boardwalk, passing one of the last surviving Fenland **wind pumps**. The reserve holds about ten **birdwatching hides** and there's also a visitor centre and an antique Fenland thatched cottage at the main entrance. As an added bonus, Wicken is also one of the best places in the UK to see dragonflies, reason enough for the British Dragonfly Society to establish a **Dragonfly Centre,** full of displays and with experts on hand to explain what you're looking at.

Central and south Norfolk

CYCLISTS IN THETFORD FOREST

5

Central and south Norfolk

A large and diverse area, central and southern Norfolk includes both some of the most scenic and some of the lesser-known parts of the region – namely the heaths and woodland of the Brecks of central Norfolk and the Waveney Valley along the county's southern border. These areas lie mostly in Norfolk, but the forests and heaths of Breckland dip a toe into Suffolk, and the Waveney River forms the delightful meandering border between the two counties, connecting some of their nicest small towns, Diss (in Norfolk), Bungay and Beccles (both actually in Suffolk). The land in between counts as one of Norfolk's most beautiful stretches of countryside.

At the heart of the region, Breckland is a notoriously dry area of forest and heathland that provides fine countryside for walking and a number of villages with pubs scattered across the countryside that are among the prettiest in East Anglia, not to mention a series of pleasant market towns to rest up in at the end of the day. **Swaffham** is the best placed of these, although nearby **Castle Acre** is also a good place to stay; **Wymondham**, **East Dereham** and **Watton**, to the southeast, are nice enough but not that great for accommodation. **Attleborough**, to the south, has its moments and is close to some decent countryside, as is **Thetford**, close to the border with Suffolk. Above all, try to make some time to visit **Thetford Forest**, whose pine woodland and heath is one of Norfolk's hidden secrets, full of well-marked trails that are ideal for walking, biking and even husky racing. To the west Breckland fades into the low-lying landscapes of the Fenland (see p.178), while to the east there is the valley of the Waveney River, where you can spend some time adjusting to the slower pace of life in the towns that straddle the border: **Diss** and **Bungay** both repay a visit – precisely for what it is hard to say, but like their close neighbour **Harleston** they have a small-town charm that is undeniably appealing. The same applies to **Beccles**, at the far end in the Waveney Valley, which is arguably the area's most handsome town and a perfect place from which to explore not only the immediate region but also the southern Broads, for which it is known as a "gateway".

Swaffham

It's hard to believe now, but like many Breckland towns, **SWAFFHAM** was once a large and relatively important place, the centre of an agricultural area that was as rich as anywhere in England during medieval times. Later it was a favourite haunt of Lady Hamilton and various Nelsons, and although those fashionable days are long gone, it's still a pleasant town. It's better known to some as (along with Wells and Downham Market) the filming location for the fictional market town of Market Shipborough in Stephen Fry's TV series, *Kingdom* (Fry himself lives nearby).

OXBURGH HALL

Highlights

❶ Strattons Hotel, Swaffham Eat, drink and sleep at one of the best small hotels in the county. **See p.193**

❷ Oxburgh Hall East Anglia is stuffed with glorious stately homes, but this fine moated manor is in the top three. **See p.196**

❸ Castle Acre Priory These represent some of Norfolk's most evocative abbey ruins, and are situated in one of its most picturesque small villages. **See p.198**

❹ Thetford Forest This isn't an ancient woodland by any means, but it is perhaps the jewel in Breckland's crown of heaths and forests. **See p.210**

❺ Locks Inn, Geldeston Great riverside pub in the middle of nowhere that has barely changed in years. Best reached by ferry for its real ales, hearty food and live music. **See p.221.**

HIGHLIGHTS ARE MARKED ON THE MAP ON PP.190–191

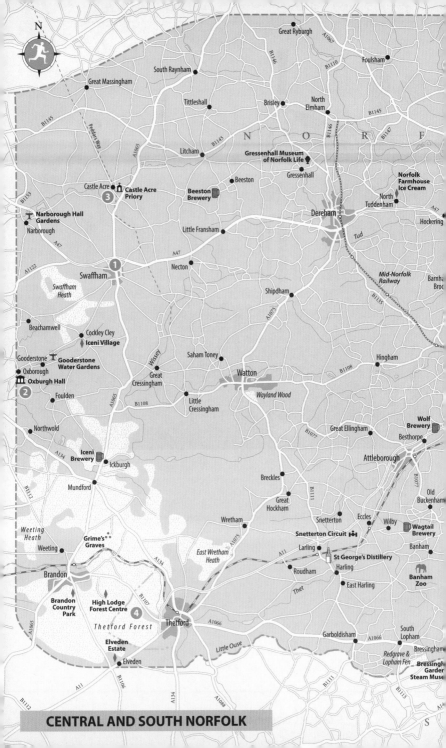

CENTRAL AND SOUTH NORFOLK

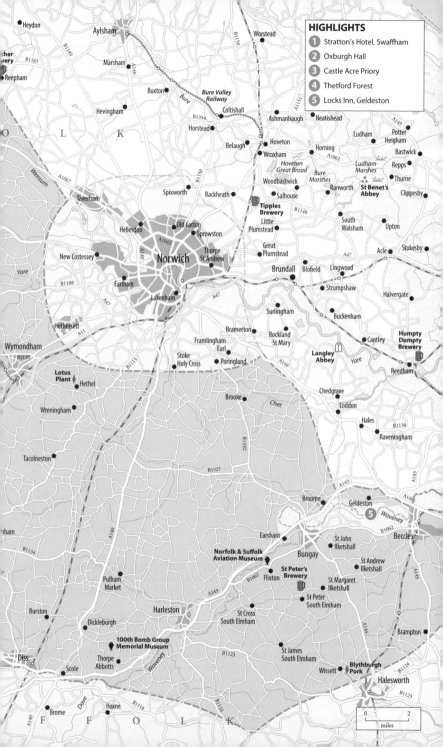

Heydon

Aylsham

Worstead

B1150

B1149

B1145

Marsham

A140

Buxton

Bure

Bure Valley Railway

Coltishall

B1354

Ashmanhaugh

Neatishead

A149

Reepham

Hevingham

Horstead

Belaugh

Hoveton

Wroxham

Horning

Ludham

Potter Heigham

Bastwick

N O R F O L K

Taverham

A1067

Wensum

Spixworth

Rackheath

Hoveton Great Broad

Bure Marshes

Woodbastwick

Salhouse

Ranworth

Ludham Marshes

St Benet's Abbey

Repps

Thurne

Clippesby

A1151

A1062

B1140

Upton

Old Catton

Sprowston

Tipples Brewery

Little Plumstead

South Walsham

Hellesdon

A140

Norwich

A1042

Thorpe St Andrew

Great Plumstead

Acle

Stokesby

New Costessey

Earlham

Lakenham

Brundall

Blofield

Lingwood

Strumpshaw

Halvergate

Yare

B1108

A47

A47

Hethersett

A11

Surlingham

Buckenham

Cantley

Humpty Dumpty Brewery

Wymondham

B1135

Bramerton

Rockland St Mary

Reedham

Framlingham Earl

Stoke Holy Cross

Poringland

Langley Abbey

Yare

A146

Lotus Plant

Hethel

Brooke

Chet

Chedgrave

Loddon

Wreningham

Hales

B1136

Raveningham

Tacolneston

B1527

B1332

A140

B1113

Broome

Geldeston

Waveney

A146

Beccles

B1062

Earsham

St John Ilketshall

Bungay

St Andrew Ilketshall

A144

A145

Norfolk & Suffolk Aviation Museum

Flixton

B1062

St Peter's Brewery

St Margaret Ilketshall

Pulham Market

Harleston

A143

St Cross South Elmham

St Peter South Elmham

Brampton

Burston

Dickleburgh

100th Bomb Group Memorial Museum

B1123

St James South Elmham

A144

A143

Diss

Scole

Thorpe Abbotts

Waveney

B1118

Hoxne

B1116

Wissett

Blythburgh Pork

Halesworth

B1124

B1123

Brome

Dove

S U F F O L K

B1134

0   2
miles

5

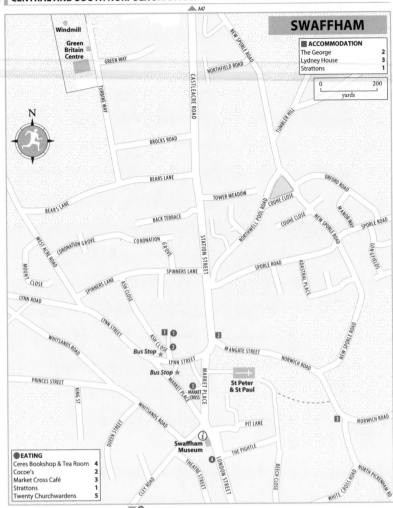

SWAFFHAM

■ **ACCOMMODATION**

The George	2
Lydney House	3
Strattons	1

0   200
yards

Windmill

Green Britain Centre

●**EATING**

Ceres Bookshop & Tea Room	4
Cocoe's	2
Market Cross Café	3
Strattons	1
Twenty Churchwardens	5

The Market Cross

Swaffham's central area focuses on the triangular **Market Cross**, appropriately graced by a statue of Ceres, Roman goddess of wheat and the harvest. There's a good market here on Saturday mornings, and not much goes on in Swaffham that can't be viewed from here.

St Peter and St Paul

Market Place, PE37 7AB • ⓦ swaffham.churchnorfolk.com

Just across the road from the Market Cross, Swaffham's church of **St Peter and St Paul** was built in the late fifteenth century. Its gorgeously preserved chestnut hammerbeam roof is the attention-grabber here, and there's a mirror in the nave to aid viewing of the 192 carved angels, all in immaculate condition, that decorate it. But there's much else to see besides: the church's good state of preservation may be down to the fact that Catherine Stewart, Oliver Cromwell's maternal grandmother, is buried here, and remembered by a memorial at the head of the south aisle. Other features include the 500-year-old wooden choir pews, which depict John Chapman, church warden in the fifteenth century, the so-called Pedlar of Swaffham (see box, p.194). Chapman funded the building of the unusually fancy tower and of the north aisle, where these pews used to rest, and he's depicted with his faithful dog, while his wife is shown opposite, with a rosary, behind the counter of a shop. Chapman and his wife also appear (in blue) in the tops of the windows in the north aisle – the only original stained glass. The church has a large and ancient churchyard that stretches way back beyond the building, where you might see the odd gambolling rabbit.

Swaffham Museum

4 London St, PE37 7DQ • Feb–Dec Mon–Fri 10am–4pm, Sat 10am–1pm • £3 • ☎ 01760 721230, ⓦ swaffhammuseum.co.uk

Housed in the town hall alongside the tourist office, **Swaffham Museum** has the usual jumble of locally gathered artefacts – including an impressive number of Saxon finds unearthed by an amateur local archeologist – but it also focuses on the bizarre personal collections of local people: baked-bean-tin wrappers, gadgets, toby jugs and cigarette cards. Upstairs is a model of the town in 1935, made by the cousin of Howard Carter, the Egyptologist who lived in Swaffham as a child. Carter has his own display, detailing his early life, along with his Tutankhamun discoveries, including a few Egyptian figurines and other objects – and Egyptian dressing-up clothes for kids.

Green Britain Centre

Turbine Way, PE37 7HT • July & Aug daily 10am–4pm; Sept–June Mon–Fri 10am–4pm • Free • Guided tours July & Aug daily on the hour 11am–3pm; Sept–June Mon–Fri at 11am, 1pm & 3pm • £6, children £4 • ☎ 01760 726100, ⓦ greenbritaincentre.co.uk

On the northern edge of town, ten minutes' walk from the Market Cross, Swaffham's **Green Britain Centre** showcases alternative energy and sustainability with displays, a café and a shop. You can see the "Green Bird" – a sort of giant sports car that's officially the fastest wind-powered vehicle on Earth, having clocked up to 126mph in 2009 – and the Nemesis, officially the UK's fastest electric car, with a top speed of 151mph. Outside there's an orchard with trees bearing all sorts of ancient apple varieties, an organic vegetable garden, a lovely tunnel of willows and an impressive rebuilding of the base of a typical Norfolk flint tower. There is also the giant blade of a Lincolnshire wind turbine, supposedly knocked off by a UFO in 2009 and a prequel to the working wind turbine that towers above the complex, the 300 steps of which you can climb if you coincide with a tour. If not, just standing at its base is still pretty awesome.

ARRIVAL AND INFORMATION

SWAFFHAM

By bus Buses stop in the centre, right by the Market Cross. The town is on the #X1 (every 30min) line between King's Lynn (30min), East Dereham (25min) and Norwich (1hr).

Tourist office Small office in the Swaffham Museum building, 4 London St (Tues–Sat 10am–4pm; ☎ 01760 724988).

ACCOMMODATION

The George Station St, PE37 7LJ ☎ 01760 721238, ⓦ goegrgehotelswaffham.co.uk. Don't be too put off by the "two-for-one" and "Sunday Carvery" signs outside, *The George* is nicer than you might think, with 28 comfortable if slightly characterless rooms. There's parking, a nice bar that serves food all day, and a restaurant serving lunch and dinner. The best rooms are in the old building, at the front. __£82__

Lydney House Norwich Rd, PE37 7QS ☎ 01760 723355, ⓦ lydney-house.demon.co.uk. Just across the meadow from the churchyard, on the edge of Swaffham

town centre, this mid-eighteenth-century Georgian house has eight bedrooms, most of them decently if a little uninspiringly furnished. The welcome is warm, and there's a downstairs bar. Includes breakfast. __£85__

★ **Strattons** Ash Close, PE37 7NH ☎ 01760 723845, ⓦ strattonshotel.com. Vanessa and Les Scott opened *Strattons* twenty years ago, and either they were remarkably ahead of the curve, or they have adapted it to be almost the epitome of a new breed of British boutique hotel, with an attractive historic building, a great restaurant

5

> ## THE PEDLAR OF SWAFFHAM
>
> A local legend tells the tale of the Pedlar of Swaffham, a poor man called **John Chapman**, who, having dreamt he went to London and made his fortune, decided to go to London to see what happened. Nothing much occurred, but he met a man who ridiculed him for following his dreams, telling him of a dream he had had that he'd found treasure under an old oak in a Norfolk town called Swaffham but wouldn't be so stupid as to go there to find it. Chapman of course went right back to Swaffham, found the oak, and dug up the treasure, making his fortune overnight and funding the rebuilding of the church and so many other civic projects that he's remembered throughout the town, most prominently on the town sign in the middle of the Market Cross.

(see below) and comfortable rooms, designed with flair and attention to detail, that make the most of their location. There are eight rooms in the main house, and half a dozen slick suites across the garden, including a couple with kitchens. Perhaps the best place to stay in Swaffham, and indeed in this part of Norfolk. **£155**

EATING

IN TOWN

Ceres Bookshop & Tea Room 20 London St, PE37 7DG ☎01760 722504, ⓦceresbookshopswaffham.co.uk. A few doors past the Swaffham Museum, the Ceres Bookshop is an excellent, large and well-stocked secondhand bookstore (though with a few new books too), with a tearoom at the back that does excellent home-made cakes. Tues–Sat 10am–4pm.

Cocoe's 4 Ash Close, PE37 7NH ☎01760 723845, ⓦstrattonshotel.com/cafedeli. Part of the *Strattons* hotel complex, this stylish café and deli does good coffee, great all-day breakfasts and light lunches and is licensed too. Hot dishes change each day and are written up on the blackboard – everything from fishcakes with fennel slaw to posh pies and salads. Free wi-fi. Mon 9am–3pm, Tues–Thurs 9am–5pm, Fri 9am–6pm, Sat 8am–6pm.

Market Cross Café Market Place, PE37 7AB ☎01760 336671. This homely café, with comfy seating upstairs and an outside terrace that overlooks most of what passes for life in central Swaffham, serves a quirkily individual lunch menu that ranges from quiches and lasagne to whitebait and Cajun spiced chicken. Great salads and filled ciabattas too, and home-made cakes. The food is fresh and good, portions generous and the service excellent, plus it's licensed. Mon–Wed 9.30am–3pm, Thurs 9.30am–6pm, Fri 9.30am–9pm, Sat 9am–9pm, Sun 10am–6pm.

★**Strattons** Ash Close, PE37 7NH ☎01760 723845, ⓦstrattonshotel.com. In the basement of *Strattons* hotel (see above) this popular, relaxed place, serving a modern British menu that is both traditional and inventive. It changes regularly, and there is a big emphasis on local suppliers – starters go for around £7, mains £14–18, and you can reckon on things like Binham Blue soufflé or wild rabbit *en croute* to start, followed by slow-cooked brisket or roasted cod fillet with mash and greens. Mon–Sat 6.30–9pm, Sun noon–2.30pm.

OUT OF TOWN

Twenty Churchwardens Cockley Cley, PE37 8AN ☎01760 721439. A cosy local between Swaffham and Gooderstone, dog-friendly and with book-lined walls, easy chairs, and a wood-burning stove in winter. The food is basic pub grub, but they do a good line in home-made pies; try the churchwarden's pie, filled with pork, herbs and a little chilli. Mon–Sat noon–2pm & 7–9pm, Sun noon–2pm.

Around Swaffham

Swaffham is perfectly placed for a number of outlying attractions – the woods of Swaffham Heath and Beachamwell Forest immediately to the southwest are crisscrossed by numbered paths and trails; **Gooderstone Water Gardens** are a beautiful, low-key attraction; and there's also the small village of **Oxborough** beyond, in the middle of glorious if unspectacular countryside – very rural, very pretty, and rather off the beaten track. The main thing to see here is **Oxburgh Hall**, but it's also worth visiting the **church of St John**, next door.

Narborough Hall Gardens

Narborough, PE32 1TE • May–Sept Wed & Sun 11am–4pm • £4 • ☎01760 338827, ⓦnarboroughhallgardens.com

About six miles northwest of Swaffham, at the centre of the village of **NARBOROUGH**, is the elegant country house of **Narborough Hall**, where Joanne Merrison has spent years reinvigorating not only the building but also the gardens. They are a fabulous sight in summer, especially the new borders established close to the house. It's a lovely destination both for garden-lovers and for children, with inventive trails and a treehouse overlooking a lake; there are paths along the tiny Nar River, which runs through the estate, and a walled fruit and vegetable garden that provides the ingredients for the Hall's excellent restaurant. Altogether it's a beautiful spot, laboured over with love, and the good news is you can sleep here too, in one of its spacious upstairs bedrooms.

ACCOMMODATION AND EATING   NARBOROUGH

★**Narborough Hall** PE32 1TE ☏01760 338827, ⓦ narboroughhallgardens.com. You can live it up for not much more than the price of a regular B&B at *Narborough Hall*, which has five handsome rooms upstairs and a self-catering cottage in the grounds – there are few better places to wake up than looking out on the gardens of this sumptuous house. The restaurant serves a regularly changing short menu based on ingredients from the Hall's beautiful kitchen garden and nearby farms – try the beef short ribs from the Sandringham Estate. Prices are reasonable for the location, with starters for £4.95–6.95 and mains £12.95–19.95. A real treat, whether you eat in the elegant main dining room or on the terrace, but you need to book. Wed–Sat 12.30–3pm & 5.30–10.30pm, Sun 11am–10pm. **£90**

Beachamwell

A short way southwest of Swaffham is the small village of **BEACHAMWELL**, whose unusual thatched church of **St Mary** anchors the large village green. It's around a thousand years old, Saxon in origin, with a round tower topped with a hexagonal turret that was added a couple of hundred years later. Inside is graffiti that dates back to the building of the church, scratched on a pillar at the back, including a depiction of a horned figure – the so-called Beachamwell devil.

ACCOMMODATION   BEACHAMWELL

The Great Danes The Green, Old Hall Lane, PE37 8BG ☏01366 328443, ⓦ thegreatdanes.co.uk. Right in the heart of the village, overlooking the green, is this inviting B&B-cum-hotel, with seven en-suite, simply but cosily furnished rooms with TVs. There's a small restaurant and bar downstairs, too, open every evening. **£80**

Gooderstone Water Gardens

The Street, Gooderstone, PE33 9BP • Daily 10am–5.30pm (or dusk, if earlier) • £6.50, children free • Tearoom May–Sept daily 10am–4.30pm • ☏01603 712913, ⓦ gooderstonewatergardens.co.uk

Around six miles to the southwest of Swaffham, **Gooderstone Water Gardens** are very much a family affair, and all the better for it – dug out on a whim by a local farmer thirty years ago, and lovingly restored by his daughter Coral Hoyos in 2002, who still

---

BRECKLAND: BRITAIN'S ATACAMA?

The Brecks – or **Breckland** – is one of Britain's most unusual lowland areas. Largely in Norfolk, it stretches roughly from Swaffham in the north, across to Brandon and Mildenhall (both in Suffolk) in the west and Watton in the east, and down to just past Thetford in the south. It's officially the driest place in Britain, with a more continental climate than the rest of the country, colder in winter and hotter in summer than the British average; incredibly, annual rainfall is on a par with Jerusalem. Its landscape, too, is distinctive, with sandy heaths and thick forests that are home to a variety of **wildlife** not readily found in other parts of the UK – woodlarks, stone curlews and nightjars are common here, as are various species of deer and muntjac. As such, the Brecks are a great place for **outdoor activities**: there are numerous footpaths for hiking, most spectacularly in Thetford Forest, and there's no better place in the country for biking, walking and horseriding. It's a great place to camp, too, although its main towns of Swaffham and Thetford provide excellent bases, as do a number of other villages in between.

5

oversees it (her brothers farm the adjoining land). It's a truly tranquil spot, its ponds and channels traversed by little bridges and fringed by majestic willows, offering splendid vistas at every turn; while its nooks and corners and perfectly placed benches absorb visitors with ease, and plentiful signs describe some of the more exotic species of plant. Follow the paths to the river and cross over for a nature trail through the reeds and woodland, or settle down in the bird hide to spot kingfishers on the lake – all before enjoying tea and Coral's home-made cakes in the tearoom. There are plant sales, too, by the entrance.

Oxburgh Hall

Oxborough, PE33 9PS • **House** Late Feb to mid-March & Oct Mon–Wed, Sat & Sun 11am–4pm; mid-March to late Sept Mon–Wed, Sat & Sun 11am–5pm; school hols & Aug also open Thurs & Fri 11am–5pm • **Garden** Same hours, plus Sat & Sun Nov–Feb • House & garden £8.90, garden only £4.90; NT • ☎ 01366 328258, ⓦ nationaltrust.org.uk/oxburghhall

Dominating the heart of the village of **OXBOROUGH**, the late fifteenth-century manor house of **Oxburgh Hall** is perhaps the major historical sight in this part of Norfolk. It was the family seat of the Bedingfield family from 1482, and is still officially their home (though it's administered these days by the National Trust) and is an impressive sight from the outside, still surrounded by its moat and at the centre of sumptuous grounds and gardens. Inside there are a wealth of period features: the Bedingfields were a devout Catholic family, and you can see a "priest hole" in which a priest would hide in the event of a raid during the Reformation, and a series of wall hangings stitched by Mary, Queen of Scots while in captivity. However, it's the building itself that is the real star, with a fortified gatehouse on one side, reached by a bridge, through which the courtyard is overlooked by tall brick towers; climb up onto the roof to appreciate it best, afterwards taking a stroll around the moat and gardens on a series of guided trails and woodland walks.

St John the Evangelist, Oxborough

Oxborough, PE33 9PS • ⓦ oxborough.churchnorfolk.com

Oxborough's fourteenth-century church of **St John the Evangelist** – in the centre of the village, next door to Oxburgh Hall – was an impressive construction until 1948, when its spire collapsed and destroyed most of the building, leaving only the choir intact. The church was never rebuilt; its churchyard and the open ruined nave make for a peaceful and bucolic spot, while the choir serves as the village chapel. But the church's real glory is the late fifteenth-century Bedingfield Chapel on the right, an unusual pre-Reformation treasure, with two magnificent carved terracotta tombs from the late fifteenth century that seem almost French in style, and point to the Catholic devoutness of the Bedingfield family. The main body of the choir has another pre-Reformation item – a brass lectern in the shape of an eagle, with slits in the beak to receive donations to the Church of Rome – so-called "Peter's Pence".

ACCOMMODATION AND EATING   **OXBOROUGH**

Bedingfeld Arms The Green, PE33 9PS ☎ 01366 38300, ⓦ bedingfeldarms.co.uk. This big, revitalized pub right in the centre of Oxborough, opposite Oxburgh Hall, is a lovely and very peaceful place to stay, with nine rooms divided between the main building and a separate coach house. The rooms in the pub are more classic in style, while those in the coach house are cheaper and a bit more contemporary, but all have flatscreen TVs and nice en-suite bathrooms. The pub serves excellent food (breakfasts are lovely, though cost extra) from a simple yet tasty menu using ingredients from the owners' family farm. There's a comfy bar in the middle and a dining room on either side, plus an outside terrace and garden, making it both a nice pub to drink in and a decent place to eat. Starters from £5.95, mains from £12.95. Kitchen daily noon–3pm & 6–9pm; pub Mon–Thurs & Sun 11am–12.30am, Fri & Sat 11am–1.30am. **£69**

CASTLE ACRE PRIORY (P.198) >

5 Castle Acre

One of west Norfolk's most immediately appealing large villages, **CASTLE ACRE** sits on a bluff above the Nar Valley about five miles north of Swaffham. Its centre is an improbably picturesque cluster of flint cottages set around a rectangular green, at the top of a steep hill, framed by the old bailey gate of the village's castle. It has a year-round population of less than a thousand, but punches far above its weight in terms of attractions, principally because the land here was gifted by William the Conqueror to one of his generals, Earl William de Warenne, who adopted it as his country seat and made it an important local powerbase for centuries to come. It's right on the Peddars Way long-distance footpath too, so gets its fair share of walkers stopping off at one of its places to stay.

St James

Priory Rd, PE32 2AE • ⓦ narvalleygroup.org.uk

Castle Acre's church of **St James**, at the far end of the village green, backs onto the ruins of the town's more famous priory, and is a large, three-aisled fifteenth-century Perpendicular-style church in classic Norfolk style. Inside is a soaring Gothic font cover and a beautiful painted rood screen in a good state of preservation featuring the Apostles – each shown with their symbolic emblem: St Thomas with a spear, St Batholomew with a knife, Andrew with a saltire – and a marvellous hexagonal pulpit decorated with the so-called "doctors" of the church, saints Augustine, Gregory, Jerome and Ambrose, dating from 1440.

Castle Acre Priory

Priory Rd, PE32 2XD • April–Sept daily 10am–6pm; Oct daily 10am–5pm; Nov–March Sat & Sun 10am–4pm • £6.20, children £3.70, family tickets £16.10; EH • ☎ 01760 755394, ⓦ www.english-heritage.org.uk

You can't move for ruined monasteries in Norfolk, but Castle Acre's **Priory** is one of the finest, the best-preserved Cluniac monastery in the country, with extant ruins spread across a fairly large and atmospheric site. Founded by the Earl of Warenne in 1077, at its height the priory was home to around 35 monks, though this was down to just ten by the time Henry VIII dissolved the monastery in 1537. Displays in the entrance building show how it would have originally looked and a good, free audio guide helps to bring the place alive as you stroll around.

The most impressive feature of the complex is the Norman west front off the priory church – the Cluniacs were known for their impressive buildings and elaborate ceremonies – but there are slices of Norman decoration throughout. You can access the quarters of the prior himself – a bedroom and an attached chapel – which are the most intact part of the Priory and overlook the cloister, and would have been very grand. Adjacent to the church is the cloister that lay at the heart of the complex, behind which are the remains of a stairway that led up to what was the monks' dormitory. At its far end this was attached to the Rere Dorter or latrine building, built above a diverted channel from the nearby River Nar – now picturesquely filled with reeds and wildflowers.

Castle Acre castle

Open 24hr • Free; EH • ⓦ www.english-heritage.org.uk

Castle Acre's **castle**, on the opposite side of the village centre to the priory, is the village's most ancient feature. Once again the work of the Warenne family, it fell into disrepair in the twelfth century, just as the priory rose to prominence, and there's not much of it left. But its position high up on a couple of mounds, looking over the very gently rolling countryside to the south, is superb both scenically and defensively, and it's a fun place to clamber about among the ruins. The keep is semi-intact, and there are walkways and wooden steps to help you on your way.

ARRIVAL AND DEPARTURE

By bus There are three buses a day from Swaffham Market Cross to Castle Acre – and it's just a 10min journey. Buses

CASTLE ACRE

stop outside Spar on Massingham Rd, 2min from the village green.

ACCOMMODATION AND EATING

Church Gate B&B Willow Cottage, Stocks Green, PE32 2AE ☎ 01760 755551, ⓦ churchgatecastleacre.co.uk. On the green, right by the churchyard, this traditional English tearoom has four comfy rooms, all en suite, not over-large but cosily furnished with TVs, and including breakfast. They also serve a simple menu of salads, sandwiches and baguettes (from £3.40), as well as hot dishes like jackets, omelettes, Welsh rarebit and poached eggs on toast (£4–5). Mon–Wed & Fri–Sun 10.30am–4.30pm. **£68**

Old Red Lion Bailey St, PE32 2AG ☎ 01760 755557, ⓦ oldredlion.org.uk. Castle Acre's budget alternative for three decades now, with a mix of dormitory accommodation and private rooms, some sharing a bathroom and some en suite. It's a great, friendly place, with an artsy vibe, a lovely courtyard garden and regular yoga classes. Rates include a self-service breakfast. Dorms **£22.50**, doubles **£50**

The Ostrich Stocks Green, PE32 2AE ☎ 01760 755398, ⓦ ostrichcastleacre.com. Right in the centre of Castle

Acre, this welcoming place does a good job as a hotel restaurant while still being a desirable village pub, with a wood-burning stove, a cosy main bar and five very well-finished en-suite double and twin rooms. It also serves thoughtful and beautifully cooked modern British food, with starters from £6.95 and mains from around £13.95 – think ham hock terrine or confit duck salad followed by rump of lamb, Cromer crab or beer-battered fish and chips. Or just have one of their gourmet sandwiches, salads or excellent deli boards. Always several daily specials on the blackboard, plus a kids' menu. Mon–Sat noon –3pm & 6–9pm, Sun noon–3pm. **£85**

West Lexham West Lexham Manor PE32 2QN ☎ 01760 755602, ⓦ westlexham.org. In the heart of a quiet village just a few minutes' drive from Castle Acre, the West Lexham estate is a supremely ecofriendly place to stay, with bell tents by a lake, treehouses in the woods and B&B and self-catering options too. Two-night minimum stay. Bell tents from **£90**, treehouses from **£150**

East Dereham and around

About fifteen miles west of Norwich, **EAST DEREHAM** – sometimes known simply as "Dereham" – is as close to the centre of Norfolk as you can get, a pleasant market town that is a good base for much of the county, although arguably this close to Norwich you may just as well be in the city. However, Dereham has an attractive small-town feel and is close to lots of worthwhile attractions – not least the excellent Gressenhall Farm and Workhouse to the north.

St Nicholas

Church St, NR19 1DN • ⓦ dereham.churchnorfolk.com

Just off Dereham's main drag, the town's parish church of **St Nicholas** was founded on the site of a shrine to a seventh-century Saxon saint, Withburga, whose body lay here until it was stolen in the tenth century and a spring erupted from her grave – you can see the well outside the west door, at the centre of a small overgrown grotto. The church itself is fifteenth century, with a separate sixteenth-century bell tower, and there are a number of items of interest inside: the highly polished eagle lectern, made in Liège in the late 1400s; the finely carved font of 1468, showing the seven sacraments – baptism up to unction; and a painted screen enclosing a chapel in the south transept which dates from 1488 and shows St Withburga herself, among other saints.

Opposite, in the north transept, there's a memorial to local poet **William Cowper**, who is buried in the church, and a stained-glass window from 1905 showing Cowper alongside quotes from his work and two pet hares that were given to him to alleviate (it's said) a bout of deep depression. Cowper wasn't the most pious of souls, and had a long-standing affair with one Mary Unwin, whose wish to be buried near her lover was frowned upon in local Dereham society; hence the ultra-plain black slab that marks her final resting-place in the north aisle.

5

Bishop Bonner's Cottage

Church St, NR19 1ED • May–Oct Tues & Thurs 2–4pm, Fri 10am–1.30pm, Sat 1–4pm • £2

Just outside the church of St Nicholas, a crooked old thatched flint cottage houses **Bishop Bonner's Cottage**, which has displays on Dereham's history and lots of photos and archeological bits and pieces. As for Bishop Bonner, this may indeed have been his home, and he had a fearsome reputation in the mid-sixteenth century, first as rector of Dereham and later as Bishop of London under "Bloody" Queen Mary, when he took it upon himself to rid the country of anti-Catholic "heretics". He spent the last ten years of his life in Marshals Prison, and was not, by all accounts, a nice man.

ARRIVAL AND DEPARTURE   EAST DEREHAM

By train Dereham no longer has a main-line station, but its old railway buildings on the edge of the town centre survive and house the northern terminus of the Mid-Norfolk Railway, which runs both steam trains and diesel locomotives down to Wymondham (see box, p.202).

By bus Buses stop in the centre of Dereham on the High St. Regular services to Norwich (every 30min; 35min), Swaffham (every 30min; 25min) and Kings' Lynn (every 30min; 1hr).

ACCOMMODATION AND EATING

IN TOWN

The Bull 25 High St, NR19 1DZ ☎01362 697771, ⓦgkpubs.co.uk/pubs-in-dereham/bull-pub. Decent town-centre pub with a well-priced and extensive pub menu that has plenty for £5–10. Plus the kitchen is open all day every day. Daily 11am–9pm.

The George Hotel Swaffham Rd, NR19 2AZ ☎01362 696801, ⓦthegeorgehoteldereham.co.uk. Right in the town centre, *The George* has five comfortable, spacious en-suite double and twin rooms. There's a restaurant downstairs that is perhaps the town centre's best place to eat, with a varied menu – everything from Thai green curry and lasagne to local pheasant, sausage and mash and racks of ribs. Most mains £10–12, and they do a two-course lunch for £11. You can eat in the bar if you prefer. Tues–Sun noon–3pm & 7–9.30pm. **£70**

Romany Rye Church St, NR19 1DL ☎01362 654160, ⓦjdwetherspoon.co.uk/home/hotels/the-romany-rye. Close by Dereham's parish church, this Wetherspoon's pub and hotel has 22 very nicely done double rooms, which are excellent value even though prices don't include breakfast. The downstairs pub follows the usual Wetherspoon's formula of well-priced drinks and food. **£64**

OUT OF TOWN

Greenbanks Hotel Swaffham Rd, Wendling, NR19 2NA ☎01362 687742, ⓦgreenbankshotel.co.uk. Small, privately owned hotel about five miles west of Dereham, just off the A47, that has eight recently refurbished guest rooms – three doubles, three twins, a suite and a family room – plus an indoor pool and a good restaurant that emphasizes fresh produce and veggie options. There's a slightly Mediterranean feel to the hotel's bright rooms and flower-filled courtyards, and the bonus of a beautiful fishing lake with a path all the way round. Note also that many rooms are kitted out for disabled access. **£120**

The Windmill 15–17 Mill St, Necton, PE37 8EN ☎01760 722057, ⓦthenectonwindmill.co.uk. A friendly village pub midway between Swaffham and Dereham, just off the A47, that does good pub food as well as more adventurous options, served in the bar or in a slightly posher restaurant. They do a set lunch menu – two courses for £12.50 – and in the evening à la carte starters and mains from £5.95 and £12.95 respectively. Kitchen Mon–Sat noon–2pm & 6.30–9pm (Mon from 7pm); Sun noon–4pm; pub Mon–Fri 11am–3pm & 6–11pm, Sat 11am–11pm, Sun noon–10.30pm.

Yaxham Mill Norwich Rd, Yaxham, NR19 1RP ☎01362 288185, ⓦyaxhammill.com. A few miles south of Dereham, this converted old mill has six en-suite double rooms, all comfortably furnished and very well priced, with rates that include an excellent breakfast in the attached restaurant. Tues–Sat 10am–11pm (kitchen till 9pm), Sun 10am–4pm. **£60**

Gressenhall Farm and Workhouse

Gressenhall, NR20 4DR • Early March to mid-Oct daily 10am–5pm, also Oct & Feb half-term weeks daily 10am–4pm • £10.50, children £7.50, family tickets £22–30 • ☎01362 869263, ⓦmuseums.norfolk.gov.uk

About two miles north of Dereham is the **Gressenhall Farm and Workhouse**, one of only three Victorian workhouses in the UK currently open to the public. Though essentially a museum of rural life in Victorian England, its best displays focus on its time as a workhouse. You can see the claustrophobic dungeon, where inmates were sent if they transgressed the strict rules, plus other rooms and artefacts, from here and other workhouses – like the wedge-shaped iron beds that allowed them to squeeze in more people; the laundry, with its original steam-powered machines and drying racks; and the men's exercise courtyard, complete with the inmates' graffiti. On the first floor, the workhouse's original clock ticks away, as it has done since the building opened in 1777, alongside display cases containing all manner of objects relating to rural Norfolk life – tools, toys, bottles and crockery. Perhaps the most interesting items are the photographs of Norfolk locations and people that you can browse through.

Outside you can visit the chapel and schoolroom, and mock-ups of village businesses – the post office, general store, blacksmith's and suchlike. There's also a a really good adventure playground, and a working farm run on traditional lines by volunteers, with rare breeds, a barn full of old farm implements and the chance to jump on Gressenhall's own tractor-pulled trailer. The farmhouse itself is kitted out as it would have been in Victorian times, and the walks you can do across the fields or down by the river are lovely.

North Elmham Chapel and St Mary, North Elmham

North Elmham, NR20 5JU • Free; EH • ⓦ www.english-heritage.org.uk

A short way north of Dereham, just off the main road in the village of **NORTH ELMHAM**, these ruins of the eleventh-century, Norman **North Elmham Chapel** make for a very atmospheric and peaceful spot. The church was in fact a replacement for an earlier Saxon foundation, which had served as the cathedral of the local diocese until this was moved to Thetford and later Norwich. Next door, the church of **St Mary** (ⓦelmhamchurchgroup norfolk.org.uk) is worth looking in on before you leave. The large Gothic structure contains a semi-intact rood screen, some medieval stained glass and a series of rustically carved medieval heads in the south porch – look for the one pulling a face.

Wymondham

Just nine miles southwest of Norwich, **WYMONDHAM** (pronounced "Wind'um") is a small town with plenty of character, once notorious for its connection with Robert Kett, a local landowner who led a peasants' revolt against enclosures of common land in Norwich in 1549, and was later executed along with his brother William. In 1615, Wymondham burned to the ground and had to be almost entirely rebuilt. Later it made its fortune as a weaving centre before declining in the nineteenth century. You'd be hard-pressed to find a good reason to stay in Wymondham with Norwich so near, but the abbey is certainly worth the journey, and there are a couple of good pubs – in town and nearby – in case you're on the hunt for lunch (see p.202).

The Market Cross

Wymondham's main street leads up to the market square and the early seventeenth-century **Market Cross**, raised up on stilts to protect documents and valuables from floods and other perils. Indeed, live rats used to be nailed onto its sides to deter vermin – until, that is, someone died after being bitten by one.

Wymondham Abbey

Church St, NR18 0PH • Mon–Sat 10am–5pm, Sun 1.45–4.45pm; guided tours Fri at 11.30am • Tours £4 • ☎ 01953 706062, ⓦ wymondhamabbey.co.uk

The main thing to see in Wymondham is the ruins of the town's Benedictine **Abbey**, at the other end of the high street from the Market Cross. Spread across green meadows, the site is dominated – as indeed is the town – by its twin-towered church, a twelfth-century construction whose nave is arguably the most beautiful in the county, with two

5

rows of Norman arches in soft grey Normandy stone supporting a wooden beamed roof decorated with over seventy carved angels. The neo-Gothic screen in the chancel is a memorial to the local casualties of World War I, while outside Robert Kett's brother, William, was strung up on the tower – a plaque marks the spot. From here there are some lovely riverside **walks** beyond the abbey, along the banks of the Tiffey River and across the bridge from the station.

Wymondham Heritage Museum

10 The Bridewell, NR18 0NS • March–Oct Mon–Sat 10am–4pm • £4 • ☎ 01953 600205, ⊛ wymondhamheritagemuseum.co.uk

Not far from the Market Cross, the **Wymondham Heritage Museum** has displays on its time as a House of Correction, with a basement dungeon and a remand cell upstairs, complete with recorded background and dialogue. There is also an exhibit on brush-making – for around two hundred years one of the town's major industries – and almost every other aspect of life in Wymondham that you could think of, including Robert Kett's Rebellion. Take a look at the lovely courtyard garden, too – originally the prison exercise yard.

ARRIVAL AND INFORMATION   WYMONDHAM

By train Wymondham's train station is just outside the centre across London Rd – about a 10min walk from Market Cross – and is quaint enough to have been used as the backdrop for Warmington-on-Sea's station in the 1970s series *Dad's Army*. It also has a good restaurant (see below). Wymondham is on the main line between Cambridge, Ely and Norwich and there are roughly hourly services to Attleborough (8min) and Thetford (25min). You can also reach East Dereham

on the Mid-Norfolk Railway, albeit from a different station on the other side of Wymondham (see box below).

By bus Buses stop right by the Market Cross, and there are services to Norwich (every 20min; 30min); Attleborough (every 20min; 20min) and Thetford (roughly hourly; 40min).

Tourist information In the Market Cross (April–Oct Mon, Wed & Fri 10.30am–2.30pm, Sat 10.30am–1.30pm; Nov–March Fri & Sat 10am–noon; ☎ 01953 604721).

ACCOMMODATION AND EATING

IN TOWN

Brief Encounter Wymondham Station Approach, NR18 0JZ ☎ 01953 606433. A spick-and-span café-restaurant that would look old-fashioned enough on its own, even without the ancient railway memorabilia decor. The menu is a short and deliberately simple roster of classics, from lasagne and steak and kidney pudding to liver and bacon and fish and chips – all for around £10 or less. Mon–Thurs 8.30am–4pm, Fri & Sat 8.30am–9pm, Sun 9.30am–4pm.

Green Dragon 6 Church St, NR18 0PH ☎ 01953 607907, ⊛ greendragonnorfolk.co.uk. Timbered old pub, tucked away off the end of Market St, near the abbey. Cosy and welcoming and something of a locals' joint, with a beer garden and serving basic pub classics alongside grander choices like rack of lamb and beef and chorizo lasagne – all served in hearty portions. Kitchen Mon–Thurs noon–3pm & 5.30–8.30pm, Fri & Sat noon–9pm,

Sun noon–8pm; pub Mon–Thurs noon–11pm, Fri & Sat noon–midnight, Sun noon–10.30pm.

OUT OF TOWN

Barnham Broom Hotel Honingham Rd, Barnham Broom, NR9 4DD ☎ 01603 759393, ⊛ barnham-broom .co.uk. About five miles north of Wymondham, this sprawling hotel fancies itself as one of the best places to stay around Norwich, and with some reason – it's got fifty-odd comfortable rooms, golf courses, a swimming pool and full fitness facilities. The restaurant is pretty good too. Decent value, especially as there are often deals on. **£95**

The Bird-in-Hand Norwich Rd, Wreningham, NR16 1BJ ☎ 01508 489438, ⊛ birdinhandwreningham.com. A couple of miles east of Wymondham, this country pub has eight new en-suite rooms in a purpose-built structure out back – very spacious, finished in a crisp, modern style,

---

THE MID-NORFOLK RAILWAY

Wymondham is the eastern terminus of the **Mid-Norfolk Railway**, which runs reconditioned steam and diesel trains to **East Dereham** (see p.199) from a station just beyond the abbey, taking in **Thuxton** (the main stop) and unmanned stations at **Yaxham** and **Kimberley Park**. The journey from Wymondham to Dereham takes 1 hour 40 minutes and there are 3–5 services a day during summer – go to ⊛ mnr.org.uk for timetables. Tickets cost £10–14 return for adults, £3 for children; family tickets £20–28.

LOTUS: NORMAL FOR NORFOLK?

Think of Norfolk and supercharged, state-of-the-art sports cars don't necessarily come to mind, yet the British sports car-maker **Lotus** has been associated with the county for almost half a century, when the company and its inspirational founder, **Colin Chapman**, took over part of the old RAF base at Hethel just east of Wymondham in 1966. They built a factory here, and used the disused runways as test tracks. Chapman was something of a Sixties legend, a flamboyant character and brilliant engineer who not only produced some of the design icons of the age (the Lotus Elan was driven by Emma Peel of *The Avengers*, and Roger Moore drove a submersible Lotus Elise in *The Spy Who Loved Me*, a decade or so later), but also built Lotus into the top British Formula 1 team of the age, winning half-a-dozen championships with state-of-the-art cars driven by great drivers like **Jim Clark**.

Clark died in an accident in 1968, and although fatalities weren't that unusual then, Lotus came under fire for designing cars that were considered too fast and too fragile. Later drivers included Jochen Rindt, Emmerson Fittipaldi and Mario Andretti, who won Lotus's last championship in 1978. However, the company declined in the 1980s – a process perhaps accelerated by Chapman's untimely death from a heart attack in 1982. The ensuing years saw changes of ownership, mounting debts, and finally a withdrawal from Formula 1 in the mid-1990s. Recent years have been kinder, with fresh injections of cash from the Far East and a reappearance on the Formula 1 scene. Lotus is also enjoying record sales for its successful road cars – the seminal boys' toy, the Elise, plus the Exige and the sleek Evora.

and with flatscreen smart TVs, plus they serve an excellent breakfast, though this is not included in the price. They also serve relatively upscale pub food in the cosy main bar or adjacent dining room – everything from burgers and steak-and-ale pie (£10–12) to good steaks and savoury bread-and-butter pudding. A good range of sandwiches and specials at lunchtime, too. They have a lot of seating outside and cook food on the barbecue out there during summer, plus they serve a special Sunday lunch menu. Kitchen Mon–Fri noon–2.30pm & 5.30–9.30pm, Sat &

Sun noon–9.30pm; pub daily noon–11pm. £80
The Pelican 136 Norwich Rd, Tacolneston, NR16 1AL ☎01508 489521, ⑩the-pelican-inn.co.uk. A few miles southeast of Wymondham is this welcoming, family-run place that serves a good choice of ales (some for sale in the ale shop, inside the pub) and great food in the pub and dining room – from hearty open sandwiches and fish and chips to beef bourgignon and confit of duck. Mains £9.95–15.95. There's a large garden and there are some rooms available, too. Daily noon–2pm & 6–9pm.

Lotus cars

Potash Lane, Hethel, NR14 8EZ • Factory Tours £39; Heritage Tours £69; track days from £169 • ☎01953 608547, ⑩lotusdrivingacademy.com

Just outside Wymondham, on the other side of the A11, is the headquarters of **Lotus cars**, which, despite many changes of ownership over the years, remains a Norfolk business at heart – and indeed one which has enjoyed something of a resurgence in recent years as the demand for its iconic, handmade sports cars has increased. You can view some of its products in the car park, or better still join one of the tours of the plant, which take in the full construction process from the chassis-build to the paint shop. True Lotus enthusiasts will want to add on a visit to the Lotus archive across the road on a so-called "Heritage Tour", where you can visit founder Colin Chapman's original Lotus workshops and see some of the team's Formula 1 cars. If money is no object, join one of their track days, when, as well as the plant tour, they offer expert tuition from one of the drivers out on the test track.

Attleborough and around

Halfway up the A11 between Thetford and Norwich, **ATTLEBOROUGH** has the feel of a village, its centre grouped around a small green – Queen's Square. There's not much to see here, but the town does have a good, contemporary hotel, and is the closest base for the Snetterton motor-racing circuit, just to the south, and one or two other nearby attractions.

5

St Mary

Church St, Attleborough, NR17 2AH • ☎ 01953 454977, ⓦ attleboroughchurch.org.uk

Right in the centre of Attleborough, the church of **St Mary** is a short, wide flint Gothic structure for the most part, although sections – like the tower – date back to Norman times; indeed, there was a church here as early as 856. The major feature, however, is the faded but still beautiful Gothic rood screen that fills the entire width of the building, decorated with images of saints and the coats of arms of the cathedral towns of England in the 1400s. Behind are the remains of a remarkably well-preserved fresco showing an Annunciation and various angels.

Peter Beales Roses

London Rd, NR17 1AY • **Gardens** Mon–Sat 9am–5pm, Sun 10am–4pm • Free • **Tours** April–Oct Mon–Fri ;1hr • £3.50 • ☎ 01953 454707, ⓦ classicroses.co.uk

This the home garden of the well-known specialist rose gardener, the late **Peter Beales**, who regularly won awards at the Chelsea Flower Show. It has three acres given over to variations on the rose, from large old-fashioned varieties to ramblers and small shrubs, set amid arches and pergolas. It's open all summer for private visits or guided tours, along with a garden centre and café that are open all year.

ARRIVAL AND INFORMATION   ATTLEBOROUGH

By train Attleborough's station is just off Station Rd, 200m south of the *Mulberry Tree*, and is on the main line between Cambridge (1hr 30min), Ely (50min) and Norwich (20min), with connections to Thetford (14min) and Wymondham (6min) every hour.

By bus Buses stop on Church St and there are services to Norwich every 30min (45min).

Tourist office Small office in the town hall on Queen's Square (Mon–Wed 9.30am–1.30pm, Thurs 9.30am–3pm, Fri 9.30am–12.30pm, Sat 9.30am–11.30am; ☎ 01953 456930).

ACCOMMODATION AND EATING

IN TOWN

Breckland Lodge London Rd NR17 1AY ☎ 01953 455202, ⓦ brecklandlodge.co.uk. This large bar-restaurant-hotel complex just outside of Attleborough on the A47 is owned by relatives of the people at the nearby St George's Distillery, and it has a similarly slick and contemporary approach. There are 32 neat rooms, nicely decorated and varying from smallish "standard" doubles to plusher and more spacious "premier" options, all with flatscreen TVs. Prices don't include breakfast, but food is served all day in the bar and restaurant, and although it's all a bit chainy in feel, the rooms are decent and the food honest, well-priced and served with a smile. **£65**

Mulberry Tree Station Rd, NR17 2AS ☎ 01953 452124, ⓦ the-mulberry-tree.co.uk. Right in the centre of town, not far from the train station, this boutique hotel is quite a find in humdrum Attleborough. Without question, it's the town's best place to stay, with six slickly decorated double rooms and a cool bar and restaurant that serves a mainly modern British menu with international touches. Think short ribs, salmon, steaks and swordfish (starters from £6.95, mains £11–16, sharing platters for £12), which you can enjoy in the restaurant proper, the bar or on the outside terrace. Mon–Sat noon–2pm & 6.30–9pm, Sun noon–3pm. **£85**

Pizzeria Bello Queen's Square, NR17 2AF ☎ 01953 459375, ⓦ pizzeriabello.co.uk. Next door to the town

hall in the centre of Attleborough, this is a decent Italian restaurant where you eat in a marquee out the back. They serve not just pizzas (from £7) but a good range of pasta dishes too (from £8). No license, so BYO wine and beer. Mon–Sat 9.30am–3pm, Sun 5–10pm.

Sherbourne House 8 Norwich Rd, NR17 2JX ☎ 01953 454363, ⓦ sherbourne-house.co.uk. Just outside the town centre, *Sherbourne House* is a lovely Georgian mansion with eight spacious rooms (seven doubles, one single). A very warm welcome – for pets too. It also has a small restaurant and bar. **£96.50**

OUT OF TOWN

The Angel Larling, NR16 2QU ☎ 01953 717963, ⓦ angel-larling.co.uk. Despite being right by the roaring A11, a few miles southwest of Attleborough, *The Angel* is a cosy, peaceful and very friendly place to stay, a long-established family business with five en-suite double rooms and a campsite in the adjacent meadow (April–Sept; £10 per pitch). One of the best places hereabouts, and deservedly CAMRA's Norfolk "pub of the year"' a few years ago, it also serves a big menu of home-cooked food – steaks, lamb chops, fish and chips – and specials from grilled cod to lamb korma. There's lighter stuff too, like burgers, omelettes and Welsh rarebit. It also hosts a popular August beer festival. Mon–Thurs & Sun noon–9.30pm, Fri & Sat noon–10pm. **£80**

Snetterton Circuit

Snetterton, NR16 2JU • Tickets £15–30; track days from £69 • ☎ 01953 887303, ⊛ snetterton.co.uk

Just off the A11 near Attleborough, the circuit at **Snetterton** was fashioned out of a series of USAF runways shortly after the war. It has just undergone a major revamp, redesigning its shape, with more corners and faster straights to become a virtually three-mile track. It hosts F3, the British Touring Car championship and the British Superbike championship, among other events, and tickets are reasonably easy to come by. In between major race meetings no one will stop you driving in and having a look around the paddock and pit lane. Better yet they run all sorts of "driving experiences" and "track days" on which you can take to the track yourself in your own car or bike, or in a single-seater or super car.

St George's Distillery

Harling Rd, Roudham, NR16 2QW • Daily 10am–5.30pm, tours on the hour 10am–4pm • £10 • ☎ 01953 717939, ⊛ englishwhisky.co.uk

Just off the A11, about five miles southwest of Attleborough, just outside the village of East Harling, St George's Distillery is one of very few specialist whisky producers in England and was the first to produce it in the country for a century. Set up by local farmer Andrew Nelstrop and his father in 2006, it released its first product in December 2009 (whisky has to be in the barrel for three years), and their products have so far been extremely well received. They hope to scale up to 120,000 bottles a year in time (by way of comparison, Glenfiddich makes over ten million) and the hour-long tour starts with a brief talk, before you're taken around the plant and the distilling process is explained in more detail. It's all very well done, and there's a tasting at the end in which their single malts more than hold their own – a fact demonstrated by the well-stocked shop, which is chock-full of high-end Scottish whiskies. They also run world whisky tours once a month, taking in the distillery tour but also tasting lots of whiskies from different parts of the world.

Old Buckenham

Just a couple of miles southeast of Attleborough, **OLD BUCKENHAM** is a small, pretty village, but its biggest claim to fame is that it's home to the largest village green in England. It can take a while to walk from one side to the other, but luckily there's a pub on each side to help you on your way – the traditional and very friendly *Ox & Plough* and the foodier, more upscale *Gamekeeper*. On the same side of the green as the *Ox & Plough*, **All Saints church** has a thatched roof, flint hexagonal tower and a font carved with cheeky faces under the bowl – although the church's real treasures are the choir stalls, whose ends are beautifully carved with the figures of Old Testament prophets.

EATING AND DRINKING   OLD BUCKENHAM

The Gamekeeper The Green, NR17 1RE ☎ 01953 860397, ⊛ thegamekeeperfreehouse.co.uk. The village's gastropub, with a cosy bar out front and a room given over to eating at the back, plus a beer garden. As you would expect, food is the focus here – and it's good, with options ranging from burgers, to meat and fish to veggie sharing platters and main courses from around £13.95. Kitchen Tues–Sat noon–2.15pm & 6–9pm, Sun noon–3pm; pub Tues–Sat noon–3pm & 6–11pm, Sun noon–5pm.

Ox & Plough The Green, NR17 1RN ☎ 01953 860004. A dog-friendly locals' joint, with tables outside and a very warm welcome. No food, though. Daily noon–11pm.

New Buckenham

Two miles east of Old Buckenham, the smaller village of **NEW BUCKENHAM** is not new at all, having been founded in the twelfth century. It focuses on a much more moderately sized village green distinguished by a shabby medieval loggia supported by wooden columns. On the edge of the village, towards Old Buckenham, a path leads off from a bend in the road to follow the overgrown bastions of a twelfth-century fortress – a popular spot for blackberry picking – while the church of **St Mary's**, just off the

5

village green, has a wooden roof supported by 22 stone corbels, carved with the likenesses of angels and bearded prophets.

EATING NEW BUCKENHAM

Inn on the Green Chapel St, NR16 2BB ☏01953 860172, ⍟innonthegreenfreehouse.com. This beautifully revitalized pub serves local ales and food in an interior that has been stripped down with care and attention to detail. Starters from £5.95, mains from £11.50, and the food – steaks, burgers, sea bass, pies – is deliciously simple contemporary pub grub. Kitchen Tues–Sat noon–2.15pm & 6–9pm, Sun 9.30am–2.15pm & 6.15–8pm; pub daily noon–3pm & 6–11pm (Sun till 10pm).

Banham

Roughly halfway between Attleborough and Diss, **BANHAM** centres on a rectangle of village green backed by its church of **St Mary the Virgin**, a typical Gothic Norfolk church that's home to a thirteenth-century wooden memorial effigy of local squire Sir Hugh Bardolph, painted to look like stone.

Banham Zoo

Kenninghall Rd, NR16 2HE • Daily: Jan–March 9.30am–4pm; April to mid-July 9.30am–5pm; mid-July to early Sept 9.30am–6pm; early Sept to late Oct 9.30am–5pm; late Oct to Dec 9.30am–4pm • Nov–Feb £11.75, children £8.10; April–Oct £18.10, children £12.65 • ☏01953 887771, ⍟banhamzoo.co.uk

Set in thirty acres of sumptuous grounds, **Banham Zoo** is a thriving small zoo and one of the most popular family attractions in south Norfolk, dating back to the late 1960s, when it opened as a monkey and ape sanctuary. Apes and monkeys are still some of the biggest attractions, but the zoo has expanded and hosts good collections of big cats (in particular snow leopards), giraffes (which you can get up close to by means of a unique walkway) and one of the best groupings of owls in the UK. Add in all the associated paraphernalia of train rides, kids' activities and regular feeding sessions with commentary, and it makes for a pretty good family day out.

Watton and around

WATTON lies at the centre of a region known as **Wayland**, situated on the far eastern edge of the Brecks. It's a small, fairly undistinguished market town (with a weekly general market and monthly farmers' market), whose small thirteenth-century parish church of **St Mary**, accessible on foot by way of a long avenue of truncated pines from near the Thetford crossroads, has an unusual round tower – although the inside is almost entirely Victorian. It does, however, retain a poor box from 1639, charmingly carved in the likeness of the vicar at the time. On the long, busy high street, check out the town's seventeenth-century **clock tower**, sandwiched between the terraces opposite the town sign which commemorates the sad tale of "Babes in the Wood".

ARRIVAL AND INFORMATION WATTON

By bus Buses stop on Watton's High St, outside *The Crown*, and run to Wymondham (every 30min; 30min), Norwich (every 30min; 1hr), Dereham (hourly; 30min) and Hingham (every 30min; 15min).
Tourist office At Dragonfly Gallery, Wayland House, High St (March–Dec Mon–Fri 10am–4pm, Sat 10am–1pm).

ACCOMMODATION AND EATING

IN TOWN
Willow House 2 High St, IP25 6AE ☏01953 881181, ⍟thewillowhouse.co.uk. Their moniker, "a little piece of countryside in the town", is hardly necessary, as it's at the end of Watton High St – not the most metropolitan location in the world. But it's a welcoming place, an ancient thatched building with simple and spacious refurbished double rooms in a separate building around the back. Rates include breakfast. It also has a bar and restaurant serving a simple bar menu of sandwiches and light dishes alongside

a short and uncomplicated menu of half a dozen starters and mains, plus a few steak and fish dishes. Starters around £6, main courses around £15. Mon–Sat noon–3pm & 7–9pm, Sun noon–3pm. **£80**

OUT OF TOWN
Broom Hall Richmond Rd, Saham Toney, IP25 7EX

☎ 01953 882125, ⓦ broomhallhotel.co.uk. Just to the north of Watton, this hotel is situated in a stately Victorian house at the centre of extensive gardens. It's fairly traditional, but the welcome is warm and the service helpful, and there's an in-house restaurant too. There are fifteen en-suite double rooms divided between the main house and a separate coach house. **£85**

Wayland Wood
ⓦ norfolkwildlifetrust.org.uk
Just a mile or so south of Watton, **Wayland Wood** is one of the largest forested areas in south Norfolk, and is said to have been the original inspiration for the fairy tale, "Babes in the Wood", in which a boy and his sister are left to die in a hostile forest. It's a less hostile place now, and managed by the Norfolk Wildlife Trust, with coppiced glades of oak and ash, interspersed with wildflowers – perfect for a walk that's easy on the feet and the eyes, with well-marked trails and bridleways leading through the trees.

East Wretham Heath
ⓦ norfolkwildlifetrust.org.uk
About seven miles south of Wayland Wood, towards Thetford, **East Wretham Heath** is another NWT property, a mixture of cratered heath and woodland of old Scots pine. Various paths wind around a couple of "meres" or shallow lakes – fed by springs and shallow in winter, deeper in summer, and home to various birdlife that complements the gangs of gambolling rabbits (dogs need to be kept on a lead).

St Mary's, Houghton-on-the-Hill
PE37 8FB • Daily 2–4pm
About half a mile off a small country road, roughly halfway between Watton and Swaffham at the end of a farm track, the church of **St Mary** enjoys a magnificent position topping the hill, far from any buildings and with views across the surrounding countryside. It was forgotten and partially derelict by the 1990s and was adopted by **Satanists**, run out of town by the local churchwarden, who in turn renovated the church and restored it to its former glory. Due to its history it's kept locked most of the time, but if you can time your visit with its limited opening times you will be rewarded with a series of medieval and earlier frescoes that include some of the best-preserved Saxon wall paintings in Europe. Even if you can't get here when it's open, come anyway – the churchyard and lovely location are ample compensation.

Hingham
A large village about six miles to the east of Watton, **HINGHAM** is a more immediately appealing destination than Watton, with a much larger parish church and two almost conjoined triangular greens either side, picturesquely fringed by Georgian houses and thatched cottages. The fourteenth-century church of **St Andrew** (Daily: April–Oct 9am–5pm; Nov–March–2pm) is a huge, cathedral-like structure with a high tower and a churchyard that spreads all the way around the church, although the large and majestic interior was revamped in the nineteenth century. There are some remnants of the original church in the choir – in particular a carved altar tomb – along with some elegant sixteenth-century stained glass. In the north aisle there's a bust of **Abraham Lincoln** of all people – his ancestor, Samuel Lincoln, was baptized in this church before emigrating to the New World in 1637.

5

The White Hart 3 Market Place, NR9 4AF ☎01953 850214, ⓦwhitehartnorfolk.co.uk. Part of chef Chris Coubourough's small Norfolk-based chain of restaurants and hotels, *The White Hart* occupies a distinctive and grand building and serves a good menu of well-executed British and continental dishes – as well as a more pubby menu – in a contemporary environment that sits well with the beams and fireplaces of this old coaching inn. Moderately priced, too: starters from £6.25, mains from £13.95, pub classics form £9.95. Daily noon–2.30pm & 6.30–9.30pm.

Thetford

The small town of **THETFORD** enjoys a relatively poor reputation across the rest of Norfolk, but it's a pleasant enough place, a small and long-established town close to the Suffolk–Norfolk border whose population was swelled by émigré Londoners during the latter part of the twentieth century. It's also one of the few towns in the county with a large immigrant population – mostly Portuguese who have arrived in the past two decades (around 30 percent of the town's 24,000 residents are of Portuguese descent). The centre has its share of charity outlets and boarded-up shopfronts, but there's a lively atmosphere, and its riverside location (the Little Ouse runs right through the centre) provides pleasant bankside walks.

It's also an ancient place, the home of Queen Boudicca during Roman times and later various Saxon royals; indeed, a hoard of Saxon treasure was discovered here and is on show at the British Museum. It was also the birthplace of US radical and reformer **Thomas Paine**, though its biggest claim to fame is its role in popular 1970s British TV comedy series *Dad's Army*, when it doubled as Warmington-on-Sea – a connection the town quite naturally makes the most of. All that said, the town's modest charms are soon exhausted,

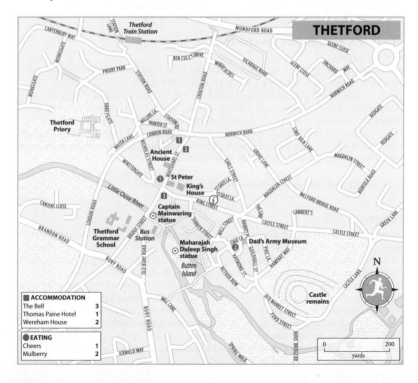

5

and there's no real reason to stay over apart from its handy location for visiting Thetford Forest and the southern reaches of the Brecks. You can follow the riverside path from the centre of Thetford to Brandon in the heart of **Thetford Forest**, a roughly two-hour journey.

King Street and around

The centre of Thetford is small and bisected by the Little Ouse River, quite pretty, despite a slightly frayed-around-the-edges appearance. The **bridge** over the river marks the centre of town; close by you'll notice a well-realized statue of **Captain Mainwaring** sitting pertly on a bench. From the bridge, pedestrianized **King Street** cuts through the centre, past the church of **St Peter**. Next door to the church, in front of the so-called **Kings House**, is a statue of the town's most famous son, **Thomas Paine**, who was educated at **Thetford Grammar** back across the river. Thetford's trio of interesting statues is completed by that of **Maharajah Duleep Singh**, the last Sikh ruler of the Punjab during the British Raj, who took over nearby Elveden Hall in the mid-nineteenth century (see p.211) and is ostentatiously commemorated with an elaborate statue on an island in the river, just beyond Captain Mainwaring.

The Ancient House

21–23 White Hart St, IP24 1AA · Tues–Sat 10am–5pm · £3.95 · ☎ 01842 752599

Around the corner from the church, the timbered **Ancient House** dates from 1490 and is home to the **Museum of Thetford Life**, which has displays on Thomas Paine and Duleep Singh. There's also the obligatory old kitchen and displays on who may have lived in the house, including one Betty Radcliffe, landlady at *The Bell* (see p.210), who lived here in the early nineteenth century and reportedly still haunts one of the rooms at the inn. However, the star attraction is the building itself – well preserved and properly ancient, with bare timbered walls and a distinctive, rickety old charm.

Thetford Priory

Water Lane, IP24 2AZ · Daily 10am–5pm · Free; EH · ☎ www.english-heritage.org.uk

Beyond the Ancient House, across the main road and accessible by subway (follow Minstergate from the bridge), **Thetford Priory** was one of the richest medieval monasteries in Norfolk, like Castle Acre (see p.198) a Cluniac foundation. Its extensive ruins, including a very well preserved fourteenth-century gatehouse (accessible through a private garden), are a peaceful and evocative spot for a stroll and a picnic lunch.

Dad's Army Museum

Cage Lane, IP24 2DS · April–Nov Sat 10am–3pm (till 4pm in Aug), July–Sept also Tues 10am–3pm · Free · ☎ dadsarmythetford.org.uk

On the far side of Market Place at the town's **Dad's Army Museum**, photographs from the series are displayed alongside all kinds of official memorabilia – and, for those who are really keen, there are monthly walking tours, led by a Captain Mainwaring lookalike, which take in all the key locations. Inevitably there's a shop, in which you can buy tea towels, mugs and even a replica of Pike's "stupid boy" scarf.

ARRIVAL AND INFORMATION   **THETFORD**

By train The station is 300m north of the centre, at the far end of Station Rd, which spears left off London Rd near the top of White Hart St. Thetford is on the main line from London, Cambridge and Ely to Norwich, with hourly trains to Norwich (40min), Attleborough (15min) and Wymondham (20min).

By bus The bus station is by the river. There are irregular services to Mundford (20min), Brandon (25min) and King's Lynn (1hr 10min), and one to Watton (every 2hr; 30min).
Tourist office Thetford's "Leaping Hare" information office is at 20 King St (Mon–Thurs 10am–3pm, Fri 10am–5pm, Sat 9am–3pm; ☎ 01842 751975).

5

THE PEDDARS WAY

The **Peddars Way** national footpath (Ⓦ nationaltrail.co.uk/PeddarsWay) runs through the heart of the Brecks, starting in Kettishall Heath just to the southeast of Thetford, and running north towards Swaffham before continuing on to meet the North Norfolk Coast Path at Holme-next-the-Sea (see p.160). It's a gentle route, much of it suitable for cyclists, and easiest to get a taste of from Castle Acre, just to the north of Swaffham, which it passes right through.

ACCOMMODATION

The Bell King St, IP24 2AZ ☎01842 754455, Ⓦ oldenglishinns.co.uk. This old, much expanded coaching inn by the river has 46 rooms of all shapes and sizes that are comfortable enough, if a little uninspiring. The best rooms are probably those that overlook the river in the modern wing, while those with the most character are in the old building, a couple of which – those facing onto King St – are said to be haunted, one by the ex-landlady of the hotel, who is commemorated in the Ancient House (see p.209). **£75**

Thomas Paine Hotel 33 White Hart St, IP24 1AA ☎01842 750372, Ⓦ thethomaspainehotel.co.uk. At the top of White Hart St, this place has eight large double rooms with en-suite bathrooms that have been fairly recently refurbished. There's also a decent bar and

downstairs brasserie, serving good steaks, fish and burgers as well as more Mediterranean meals and snacks. There's parking available, and the back end of the building, made up of three ancient cottages, has a reasonable claim to having been the birthplace of Thomas Paine – he's said to have watched proceedings on the nearby scaffold from his attic room. **£65**

Wereham House 24 White Hart St, IP24 1AD ☎01842 761956, Ⓦ werehamhouse.co.uk. Right in the heart of town, and run by a husband-and-wife team with years in the hotel business, this elegant old building at the top of White Hart St has eight en-suite rooms, not huge but comfortable enough. It's a friendly place, and the breakfasts are great – plus there's a bar and parking. **£80**

EATING

Cheers 3a White Hart St, IP24 1AA ☎01842 750170. The town's most central Portuguese restaurant, with a short, excellent-value menu specializing in superb steaks, fish and seafood. Try the steak on a stone – cooked at your table – or there's tuna, *bacalhau* and salmon, too, and a good Portuguese wine list. Mains £10–13. Tues–Fri 6–11pm, Sat & Sun noon–3pm & 6–10.30pm.

Mulberry 11 Raymond St, IP24 2EA ☎01842 824122. Thetford's classiest place to eat, serving modern British cuisine in a cosy setting, accompanied by a great wine list and excellent service. Think sirloin of Norfolk beef followed by treacle tart with clotted cream. Starters from £6.50, mains £17–22, and they also do a fixed-price menu midweek. Tues–Sat 6–10pm.

Thetford Forest

Straddling the Norfolk–Suffolk border, **Thetford Forest** is the largest stretch of low-lying forest in the UK. It's not an ancient woodland, only having been created after World War I to replace timber used during the war, and the pines here are not indigenous – indeed much of the native Breckland landscape was destroyed when the forest was created. Nonetheless it's a beautiful area, and the network of walking and cycling trails provides an outlet for all manner of hobbyists, including one of the largest contingents of husky-racing teams in the UK. The most central settlement for the forest is the small town of **Brandon** in Suffolk, but there's not much to it apart from its train station, either in terms of sights or facilities; you're probably best off staying at the excellent *Elveden Inn* or using Thetford or Mundford or even places further afield as a base.

High Lodge Forest Centre

Thetford Forest, B1107, IP27 0AF • Daily: March & Nov–Feb 9am–5pm; April, Sept & Oct 9am–6pm; May–Aug 9am–7pm • Parking £2.20 an hour/£11.50 a day • ☎01842 815434, Ⓦ forestry.gov.uk/highlodge

High Lodge Forest Centre is the best place to start if you're exploring Thetford Forest for the first time, with a good position well away from the main road, plenty of parking, a café and bike rental from **Bike Art** (daily: April–June, Sept & Oct 9am–5pm; July & Aug

9am–6pm; Nov–March 9am–4pm; ☎01842 810090, ⓦbikeartthetford.com). There are several loop walks from here, ranging from one to three miles, and cycle trails suitable for families and more serious mountain-bikers covering from six to ten miles. High Lodge is also home to the treetop rope-and-ladder outfit **Go Ape** (☎08456 439146, ⓦgoape.co.uk).

ARRIVAL AND DEPARTURE   THETFORD FOREST

By train Trains run hourly to Brandon station, just outside the centre of town across the river, from Cambridge (40min), and from Thetford (8min), Ely (17min), Attleborough (25min), Wymondham (30min) and of course Norwich (45min).

By bus Brandon and Mundford are connected by a couple of buses a day, but really the way to get around the forest is to walk or bike.

Brandon Country Park

B1106, Brandon, IP27 0SU • Daily: April–Oct 10am–5pm; Nov–March 10am–4pm • Free • ☎01842 810185, ⓦ brandonsuffolk.com /brandon-country-park.asp

Just outside Brandon, **Brandon Country Park** is another place to easily experience a little bit of Thetford Forest. It has a visitor centre with maps, books and information, plus a café, playground and walled garden. You can do a variety of marked walks, lasting from thirty minutes to three hours, and there's a well-marked four-mile mountain bike loop.

Elveden and the Elveden Estate

London Rd, Elveden, IP24 3TQ • Shops open Mon–Fri 9.30am–4.30pm, Sat 9.30am–5pm, Sun noon–5pm

On the edge of Thetford Forest, the village of **Elveden** is now a peaceful country village again since the re-routing of the nearby A11. It lies at the centre of the **Elveden Estate**, which was bought by the ex-ruler of the Punjab, Maharajah Duleep Singh, in 1849, on his exile from India. He rebuilt Eleveden Hall, and lived here until 1886, shortly after which the estate was bought by the earls of Iveagh, aka the Guinness family, who have owned it ever since and developed it into a considerable agricultural and commercial concern.

The hall itself is empty and not open to the public, but you can visit the parish church of **St Patrick and St Andrew**, which has the graves of the Iveagh dynasty in its churchyard, although most people just stop off to visit the estate's complex of **shops**, including a high-end food shop selling produce from the estate, various lifestyle and homeware shops, and a really good café-restaurant (see below). There is also a small waymarked loop through the forest opposite the car park that you can do to stretch your legs.

ACCOMMODATION AND EATING   ELVEDEN

The Courtyard London Rd, IP24 3TQ ☎01842 898068, ⓦelveden.com. A rather brilliant all-rounder, the Eleveden Estate restaurant serves great breakfasts until 11.15am and lovely lunches until 3.30pm. It's a bright, modern environment, the service is top-notch and the food delicious, whether you're sampling one of their excellent burgers or fishcakes or tucking into their Sunday roast lunches. Always lots of tempting specials too. Mon–Fri 9.30am–4pm, Sat 9.30am–5pm, Sun 10am–5pm.

Elveden Inn Brandon Rd, IP24 3TP ☎01842 890876, ⓦelvedeninn.com. Part of the well-run and beautifully updated Elveden Estate, the *Elveden Inn* is perhaps the most

perfect location for exploring this part of Thetford Forest and has four lovely boutique double and family rooms, crisply furnished in a contemporary style with flatscreen TVs and posh toiletries, plus it serves a tasty breakfast in the pub downstairs. The rest of the time it serves decent modern British food, much of it using ingredients from the Elveden Estate and offering some delicious takes on traditional British cookery – braised pigs' cheeks, leek and apple sausages – as well as classy spins on classic pub grub – fish and chips, burgers and suchlike. Starters from £5.95, mains from £11.95. Mon–Sat 7.30–9.30am & noon–9pm, Sun 7.30–10am & noon–8pm. **£105**

Weeting

Castle Open 24hr • Free; EH • ⓦ www.english-heritage.org.uk

Just across the river from Brandon, in Norfolk, the village of **WEETING** has a village

5

green boasting one of the longest thatched terraces you've ever seen – a full ten eyebrow windows long. On the edge of the village, **Weeting Castle** is not a castle at all but the remnants of a twelfth-century moated manor house, home of the de Plais family, who were tenants of Castle Acre's de Warennes (see p.198). It's an imposing ruin, but nothing more, although its location, surrounded by the peaceful fields and shaded by mature trees, is pretty much the perfect summer picnic spot. Next door, the round-towered village church of **St Mary** cuts an elegant figure, but it's usually locked.

Weeting Heath

Weeting, IP26 4NQ · April–July daily 7am–dusk; visitor centre April–July daily 9.30am–4.30pm · £4.25 · ⓦ norfolkwildlifetrust.org.uk

Weeting Heath, a mile outside the village, is an NWT reserve that occupies a pretty stretch of woodland housing several hides, from which you can spot the stone curlews that breed here in summer; you can also do a three-mile loop through the woods.

Grimes Graves

Lynford, IP26 5DE · April–Sept daily 10am–6pm; Oct Wed–Sun 10am–5pm · £3.80, children £2.20; EH · ⓦ www.english-heritage.org.uk

About three miles northwest of Thetford, at the end of a long track, the forest opens out to a vast and open grassy moonscape known as **Grimes Graves**, the earliest significant industrial site in Europe, dating from around 2000 BC. The craters are the result of Neolithic flint mines, one shaft of which you can descend 100ft down by ladder if you don a hard hat, from where galleries burrow deep into the ground in all directions. The mines were not identified as such until they were excavated in the 1870s, although they owe their collective moniker to the Anglo-Saxons, who named them after one of their gods, Grim.

Mundford

Approaching it from the main A134 from Thetford, the village of **MUNDFORD** doesn't look up to much at all, but it's a pretty village at its heart, with a main street of flint and thatched cottages and a small triangular green.

ACCOMMODATION AND EATING

Colveston Manor Mundford, IP26 5HU ☎01842 878218, ⓦ colveston-manor.co.uk. A farm-based B&B with four generously proportioned rooms (two doubles, one twin, one single) – all with their own bathrooms and a TV – furnished in traditional style, and with breakfast (included in price) using ingredients from the farm. It's a lovely, remote spot; you can wander the farm to your heart's content, and it couldn't be in a better position for the forest. If you're not coming by car, though, bear in mind that you are a good half-hour walk from the village. **£65**
The Crown Crown Rd, IP26 5HQ ☎01842 878233,

ⓦ the-crown-hotel.co.uk. This seventeenth-century village pub couldn't be in a more picturesque location, right in the heart of Mundford, and it has forty large rooms in the beamed main building and the converted barn next door, plus a large self-catering house for rent. Breakfasts are excellent, and you can eat lunch and dinner here too, from a slightly confusing array of menus. The food is filling rather than refined, but the bar menu standards are good and the T-bone steaks, sea bream and steak-and-mushroom pie they serve certainly hit the spot. There are always a few vegetarian options. All mains £7.95–13.95. Daily noon–3pm & 6.30–10pm. **£79.50**

Diss and around

Right on the southern border of Norfolk, at the western end of the Waveney Valley, is the appealing market town of **DISS**, unusually built around a lake (the Mere). It was much admired by John Betjeman, who gloried in its unremarkableness in his 1960s poem *A Mind's Journey to Diss*, which famously proclaimed to Harold Wilson's wife Mary how it would be "bliss, to go with you by train to Diss". These days Diss is still rather proud of its ordinariness, and it's nice to get a feel for the bliss that is Diss with a

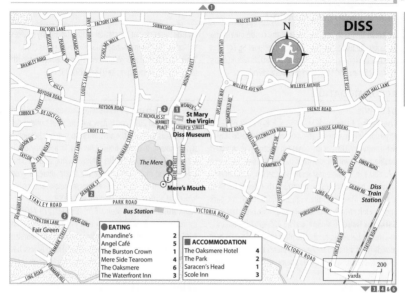

● EATING		■ ACCOMMODATION	
Amandine's	2	The Oaksmere Hotel	4
Angel Café	5	The Park	2
The Burston Crown	1	Saracen's Head	1
Mere Side Tearoom	4	Scole Inn	3
The Oaksmere	6		
The Waterfront Inn	3		

stroll around town, and to use it as a base for the various attractions nearby, including the excellent **Bressingham Steam Museum and Gardens** and Redgrave and Lopham Fen.

The Market Place

Diss's central **Market Place** forms a triangle at the top of the main street, Mere Street, and is home to a busy weekly market on Fridays. Housed in a wooden hut on the Market Place, **Diss Museum** (mid-March to Oct Wed & Thurs 2–4pm, Fri & Sat 10am–4pm; May–Aug also Sun & bank hols 2.30–4.30pm; free) has displays on the town, the Mere, and John Skelton, sometime poet laureate and rector of the church of **St Mary the Virgin**, at the top end of the square. The church is a very dignified building from the outside, although most of its originally fifteenth-century interior was refurbished in the nineteenth century.

The Mere

Mere Street leads, as you would expect, to the **Mere**, a picturesque spot surrounded by willows and with a spouting fountain at its centre. It's a natural lake, deeper than you might think (it reaches 65ft in places), and carpeted by thick mud so noxious that in times gone by eels were said to throw themselves out to die on the banks rather than live there. Happily the eels are long gone, and you can safely sit on the benches at the so-called **Mere's Mouth** and feed the ducks, or take a stroll through the park on the far side, where there's also a children's playground.

Fair Green

Beyond the Mere-side park, Denmark Street leads down to the main road through town, across which is **Fair Green** – arguably the prettiest part of Diss, with houses set around a large village green. The Waveney River is just beyond, and a path alongside leads a mile or so to **Roydon Fen**, a small nature reserve maintained by the Suffolk Wildlife Trust (ⓦsuffolkwildlifetrust.org).

ARRIVAL AND INFORMATION

DISS

By train Diss station, 500m east of the centre off Victoria Rd, is on the main line from London Liverpool St. Services also run to Norwich (every 30min; 20min), Ipswich (every 30min; 25min) and Stowmarket (hourly; 12min).

By bus Buses stop at the station on Park Rd. Hourly services to Harleston (20min), Bungay (45min) and Beccles (1hr).
Tourist office In a kiosk on Mere St, by the Mere's Mouth (Mon–Sat 9.30am–4pm; ☎ 01379 650523).

ACCOMMODATION

IN TOWN

The Park 29 Denmark St, IP22 4LE ☎ 01379 642244, ⓦ parkhotel-diss.co.uk. The most obvious place to stay in the centre of Diss, with nineteen recently refurbished double rooms with good-sized bathrooms and flatscreen TVs, and a reasonable restaurant too, serving food all day. They also have a self-catering cottage that sleeps six. Walk around the Mere from the High St and through the park and turn left onto Denmark St. Rates include breakfast. **£80**

Saracen's Head 75 Mount St, IP22 4QQ ☎ 01379 652853, ⓦ saracensheaddiss.co.uk. The plain en-suite doubles here provide good value for money, and there's the added benefit of an excellent breakfast in their downstairs restaurant. **£50**

OUT OF TOWN

The Oaksmere Hotel Rectory Rd, Brome, IP23 8AJ ☎ 01379 873940, ⓦ theoaksmere.com. This formerly rather run down country-house hotel was rescued by a local businessman in 2014 and is now without doubt one of the nicest places to stay in the area, with ten spacious boutique-style rooms in the main house plus four in a nearby coach house – all with flatscreen TVs, iPhone docking stations, posh toiletries and more. The grounds are lovely, there's a good restaurant with lots of outside seating (see below) and the bar is buzzy at all times of day. Excellent value. **£99**

Scole Inn Ipswich Rd, Scole, IP21 4DR ☎ 01379 740481, ⓦ scoleinn.co.uk. A mile or so east of Diss, on the main A1066 in the small village of Scole, this is an old Georgian coaching inn with 22 good-sized rooms. The business has been through multiple changes of ownership in recent years and it shows a bit, in the uneven service and – literally – of the building itself, which is creaking with age. The rooms are fine though nothing special, but downstairs there is a cosy old pub and restaurant serving decent pub grub. **£65**

EATING

IN TOWN

Amandine's St Nicholas St, IP22 4LB ☎ 01379 640449, ⓦ amandines.co.uk. Tucked away on an old renovated courtyard complex at the top of town, *Amandine's* does great vegetarian and vegan food at lunchtimes from a menu that changes every day – lots of soups, baked savouries and cakes and pastries. There's a nice outside terrace on which to enjoy it all, too. Tues–Sat 10am–3pm.

Angel Café 1 Fair Green, IP24 4BQ ☎ 01379 640758. A hippy-dippy local favourite, which does good cooked breakfasts and lunches, with home-made soups and quiches and lots of veggie options. Tues–Sun 8am–4pm.

Mere Side Tearoom Diss Publishing Bookshop, 40 Mere St, IP22 4AH ☎ 01379 642047, ⓦ disspublishing .co.uk. Next door to the tourist office, this café (which is part of a great independent bookshop) backs onto the Mere and serves coffee, sandwiches, soup and hot lunches. Mon–Sat 10am–4pm; shop Mon–Sat 9am–5.15pm.

The Waterfront Inn 43 Mere St, IP22 4AG ☎ 01379 652695. A very popular high-street boozer that does pub grub all day from £6.49 – burgers, salads and the usual standards – and has a terrace overlooking the Mere. Daily 11am–9pm.

OUT OF TOWN

The Burston Crown Mill Rd, Burston, IP22 5TW ☎ 01379 741257, ⓦ burstoncrown.com. Classic village pub that's both a cosy boozer and a food destination, with a menu – cooked up by Steve Kembery, ex-chef to U2 and Bruce Springsteen – that's a notch above your average pub. The all-day bar menu includes sandwiches, excellent home-made burgers, steak-and-kidney pie and the like (£9.50–14), and more refined dishes are served in the separate restaurant lunchtime and evenings – think rib-eye steak or sea bass fillet (£12–15). Kitchen Tues–Sat noon–2pm & 6.30–9pm, Sun noon–4pm; pub Mon–Sat noon–11pm, Sun noon–9pm.

The Oaksmere Rectory Rd, Brome, IP23 8AJ ☎ 01379 873940, ⓦ theoaksmere.com. Slick and popular, this is one of the best places to eat near Diss, serving a bright, adventurous menu that focuses on local produce. Starters from £7.50, mains from £15.95. They also serve a prix-fixe menu at lunchtimes and Tues–Thurs evenings – £19.50 for two courses, £24.50 for three. Part of the lovely *Oaksmere Hotel* (see above). Tues–Sat noon–2.30pm & 6.30–9.30pm, Sun noon–3pm.

Bressingham Gardens and Steam Museum

Bressingham, IP22 2AA • Late March to Oct daily 10.30am–5pm (July & Aug till 5.30pm) • Entry including train rides (Wed–Sun only) £13.99, children £9.99; entry only £8.99/£5.59 • ☎ 01379 686900, ⓦ bressingham.co.uk

This is two attractions in one, both of them the vision of Alan Bloom, who bought

Bressingham Hall in 1946 and indulged his two passions – collecting old steam engines and gardening. The result is a large complex encompassing the enormous **garden centre** next door, the **gardens** of Bressingham Hall and a **museum** of steam engines. Bloom's legacy has been continued by his sons, one of whom still lives in the grounds.

The **museum** is housed in several engine sheds, some of which have some very fancy engines indeed, including the former royal coaches of both the current Queen and Edward VII. You can peer in to see the sumptuous period fixtures and fittings. Another shed houses traction engines, a gleaming Post Office train and the collection of the **Dad's Army Appreciation Society**; its homage to the series, most of which was filmed in the area, is a rival to Thetford's better-known but much less accessible museum (see p.209). There are mock-ups of Jones the Butchers and Captain Mainwaring's bank and numerous photos of the Norfolk locations used, not to mention a portrait of actor Bill Pertwee by former England wicketkeeper Jack Russell – plus you can sit and watch key episodes which are repeated on a continuous loop. You can tour the gardens and the adjacent nursery on regularly running mini steam and diesel trains, and there's a carousel and other rides. As for the **gardens** themselves, they are a magnificent sight, best enjoyed during spring or summer. They consist of Alan Bloom's original "Dell" garden in front of the house, and his son Adrian's Foggy Bottom garden behind – a perfect counterpoint to the steam trains, though in their way no less man-made.

Redgrave and Lopham Fen

Low Common Rd, South Lopham, IP22 2HX • ☎ 01379 687618, ⓦ suffolkwildlifetrust.org

A few miles west of Diss, the Suffolk Wildlife Trust reserve of **Redgrave and Lopham Fen**, is the largest "valley fen" in England, and the source of not one but two of East Anglia's most significant rivers – the **Waveney**, which flows east from here to disgorge into the North Sea at Great Yarmouth, and the **Little Ouse**, which flows north to the Wash. It's a beautiful, relatively little known spot, a mixture of open marsh and woodland that was restored just over a decade ago and was for many years the only UK home to the rare fen raft spider (even now this is only found in two other places in the country). You can explore it on foot by taking one of five marked trails, ranging in length from the short Lopham Loop (500m), which provides a brief taster of the environment, to the Waveney Trail (6.5km), which takes in pretty much everything; the 2km-long Spider Trail is probably the best choice for a short walk.

100th Bomb Group Memorial Museum

Thorpe Abbotts, IP21 4PH • March, April & Oct Sat & Sun 10am–5pm; May–Sept Wed, Sat & Sun 10am–5pm • Free • ☎ 01379 740708, ⓦ 100bgmus.org.uk

A few miles to the east of Diss, just outside the village of Thorpe Abbotts, the airfield buildings of the **100th Bomb Group Memorial Museum** commemorate the US airmen of the 100th Bomb Group – "the bloody hundredth", as they were known, due to their heavy losses – who fought alongside the RAF during the last two years of World War II, flying B17 bomber missions between here and mainland Europe. The buildings and shelters that remain hold displays of uniforms, photos and personal effects and include a small chapel, with memorials to all those who died (the life expectancy of a bomber was just eleven missions); one holds the gun turret of a "Flying Fortress" and the blackboard showing the status of aircraft on June 6, 1944. You can also climb up to the control tower, still with its Bakelite telephones and control panel, and the balcony above, where you can contemplate the vast size of the original airfield, which covered no less than six hundred acres and encompassed three runways.

5

THE SAINTS

To the southwest of Bungay, and northeast of Halesworth, the flattish farmland of **The Saints** feels somehow off the map, a bleakish, windswept region that is crisscrossed by footpaths and byways. It's named for the numerous small villages in the area that take their name from a saint – either with the prefix "Ilketshall" or the suffix "South Elmham" – and although none are especially worth stopping at, the area has a unique feel, and of course there is always a medieval church to go with each saint. It's a good area to cycle through, and you can do a sixteen-mile loop from Bungay that takes in the villages of **Ilketshall St Andrew** and **St Lawrence**, before crossing the main Halesworth road – the A144 – to visit the Elmham villages and finish up at **St Peter's Brewery**, just between **St Peter South Elmham** and **Ilketshall St Margaret**. It's worth taking a picnic and making a day of it if you can, maybe stopping off at the eleventh-century ruins of **South Elmham Minster**, which hide among the trees in the grounds of South Elmham Hall farm.

Harleston

There are a number of Norfolk (and Suffolk) towns that seem to survive in a self-contained bubble, doing very nicely despite the encroachment of out-of-town shopping and the lure of bigger urban centres. Swaffham is one, Framlingham and Halesworth are others, and **HARLESTON**, about eight miles down the Waveney from Bungay, is yet another, with an attractive and relatively thriving main street that ends at the inevitable marketplace, and not all that much to see or appreciate apart from the enjoyable small-town vibe. There are lots of timbered houses, and you can stroll the town centre in twenty minutes, before enjoying a well-earned pint.

ARRIVAL AND DEPARTURE   HARLESTON

By bus Hourly to Bungay (20min) and Beccles (30min), and in the opposite direction to Diss (20min).

ACCOMMODATION AND EATING

Chameleon House 3 Redenhall Rd, IP20 9EN ☎ 01379 852030, ⊛ chameleonhouse.co.uk. An ancient building with a Georgian front that houses a restaurant – serving mainly Italian food – and three spacious, very comfortably furnished contemporary B&B rooms upstairs. They also have a galleried self-catering apartment behind that is suitable for a small family, and a lovely secluded garden. **£90**

JD Young 2–4 Market Place, IP20 9AD ☎ 01379 852822, ⊛ jdyoung.co.uk. This contemporary coaching inn offers eleven en-suite rooms – recently refurbished and with Freeview TV – and a popular bar and restaurant downstairs that's very much the hub of the town centre, with an attractive book-lined dining room and serving a good choice of food all day: sandwiches and burgers, beef-and-ale pie and fish and chips on the bar menu (£8.95–12.95), plus a more adventurous, refined restaurant menu with starters from £5.95, mains £10.95–19.95. Mon–Thurs 7am–10pm, Fri & Sat 8am–10pm, Sun 8am–9pm. **£95**

Bungay and around

"Welcome to Bungay, a fine old town", proclaim the signs, and it's hard to disagree that **BUNGAY**, just south of the border in Suffolk, would be a nice place to live. But there's not all that much to bring you here, beyond a possible change in lifestyle. Clasped in a

BUNGAY'S BLACK DOG

St Mary's is best known for the legend of the **black dog of Bungay** – in a terrible storm of 1577 a black dog ("black shuck") appeared and attacked the congregation, before descending on Blythburgh church (see p.273), leaving many dead and the locals terrified. Many speculated that the dog was an incarnation of the evil local landowner Hugh Bigod, who had terrorized the town three hundred years earlier; others felt it was an appearance by Satan himself. Whatever the truth, the black dog lives on – not least in Bungay's coat of arms.

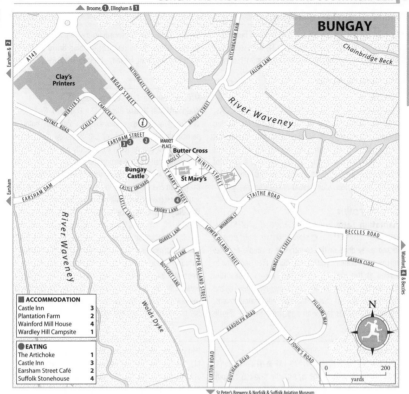

▲ Broome, ❶, Ellingham & ❶

BUNGAY

5

Chainbridge Beck

Earsham & ❷

A143

Clay's Printers

BROAD STREET

NETHERGATE STREET

DITCHINGHAM DAM

FALCON LANE

River Waveney

WEBSTER ST

CHAUCER ST

OUTNEY ROAD

SCALES ST

ⓘ

EARSHAM STREET ❷

❸❸

BRIDGE STREET

MARKET PLACE

CROSS ST

Butter Cross

TRINITY STREET

Bungay Castle

ST MARY'S STREET

St Mary's ❹

EARSHAM DAM

CASTLE ORCHARD

STAITHE ROAD

CASTLE LANE

PRIORY LANE

WHARTON ST

BECCLES ROAD

River Waveney

QUAVES LANE

LOWER OLLAND STREET

WINGFIELD STREET

GARDEN CLOSE

Earsham

ROSE LANE

BOSCOTT LANE

UPPER OLLAND STREET

Wainford ❶ & Beccles

PILGRIMS WAY

Wolds Dyke

BARDOLPH ROAD

ST JOHN'S ROAD

N

FLIXTON ROAD

SOUTHEND ROAD

■ ACCOMMODATION	
Castle Inn	3
Plantation Farm	2
Wainford Mill House	4
Wardley Hill Campsite	1

● EATING	
The Artichoke	1
Castle Inn	3
Earsham Street Café	2
Suffolk Stonehouse	4

0   200
yards

▼ St Peter's Brewery & Norfolk & Suffolk Aviation Museum

meander of the Waveney River, it's an odd mix of the well-to-do and shabby (Earsham Street is its most upscale stretch), but otherwise it's a smallish market town with a handful of low-key attractions and a couple of good gastropubs. A great place, in short, to just loaf about, before heading off to explore the countryside around.

St Mary's

St Mary's St, NR35 1AX • Ⓦ visitchurches.org.uk

The centre of Bungay isn't very big, and focuses on the Butter Cross and Market Place intersection, and the bulky fifteenth-century **St Mary's** church. Formerly part of a priory, the remains of which – the nun's choir – you can see outside. Badly damaged by a seventeenth-century fire, it's now owned and run by the Churches Conservation Trust.

Bungay Castle

NR35 2AF • Free • Ⓦ bungay-suffolk.co.uk/activities/castle.asp

Across the road from the church, Bungay's **castle** was built by Hugh Bigod in 1165, and, after it was destroyed by Henry II, rebuilt a hundred years later by his descendant Roger. The Bigods were a powerful Norman family hereabouts, and Hugh in particular was a vicious tyrant who by all accounts wasn't much admired by the local populace, eventually dying in Syria after embarking on the Crusades. There's certainly not much left of his edifice now, just the gateway and the evocative grassed-over ruins of the keep, accessible through *Jester's Café*, just off the Market Place.

By bus Bungay doesn't have a train station; buses stop opposite the Butter Cross or on Trinity St, with services to Beccles (hourly; 15–30min), Diss (hourly; 45min), Harleston (hourly; 20min) and Halesworth (every 30min; 30min).

Tourist office In the centre of town on Broad St (Mon–Thurs 9am–4.30pm, Fri 9am–4pm; ☎ 01986 892716).

ACCOMMODATION

IN TOWN

Castle Inn 35 Earsham St, NR35 1AF ☎ 01986 892283, ⓦ thecastleinn.net. By far the best accommodation option in the centre of Bungay, with four simple yet comfortable en-suite rooms overseen by rat-race escapees Mark and Tanya Hougham Martin, who are a fount of knowledge of everything to do in and around Bungay, and also run the fab downstairs restaurant (see below). **£95**

OUT OF TOWN

Plantation Farm Private Rd, Earsham, NR35 2AW ☎ 01986 805033, ⓦ plantationfarmhouse.co.uk. Tucked away deep in the countryside a couple of miles northwest of Bungay, you'll think you've died and gone to heaven at this idyllic country B&B. There's a beautiful garden and a wildflower-filled meadow, overlooked by the balcony of one of two beautifully decorated rooms. Fabulous breakfasts too, with eggs from owners Cherrie McCarron and Paul Cray's own hens. **£100**

Wainford Mill House Pirnhow St, Wainford, NR35 2RU ☎ 07855324055, ⓦ wainford.co.uk. Backing onto a particularly alluring stretch of the Waveney, this former watermill just outside town has recently been transformed into magical self-catering accommodation, with six bedrooms and a lovely kitchen and sitting room. There's a pizza oven in the garden and you can just row yourself into Bungay when you fancy some shopping. Minimum stay three nights. **£375**

Wardley Hill Campsite Wardley Hill Rd, Kirby Cane, NR35 2PQ ☎ 07733 306543, ⓦ wardleyhillcampsite .co.uk. Lovely campsite a few miles outside of Bungay that has a mixture of regular pitches and "too posh to pitch" alternatives including a couple of bell tents, a shepherd's hut and even a tree tent. A bucolic, peaceful place to camp or glamp, and very ecofriendly too, with partially solar-powered showers and compostable toilets. Camping (per person) **£6**, children **£2**, bell tents from **£60**, tree tent **£40**, shepherd's hut from **£75**

EATING

IN TOWN

Castle Inn 35 Earsham St, NR35 1AF ☎ 01986 892283, ⓦ thecastleinn.net. Bright, beautifully restored old pub that focuses squarely on food, and does so with some style. There are classic pub options and sandwiches at lunch, plus a good-value two-course menu for £16.50. The "Innkeeper's Lunch" (£11.50) is another popular choice while evening menus (mains around £15) feature everything from burgers to ribs, fish and some more adventurous dishes. Delicious, locally sourced food, very friendly and welcoming service, and a wine list that includes a white from nearby Fressingfield. You can also stay over (see above). Hours vary by season, so check online beforehand. Daily noon–8.30pm.

Earsham Street Café 11 Earsham St, NR35 1AE ☎ 01986 893103, ⓦ earshamstreetcafe.co.uk. One of the pioneers of the gentrification of Bungay's poshest street, the *Earsham Street Café* is still going strong, serving coffee, tea and cakes plus platters, sandwiches and hot lunches (£6–8). They also host regular themed dinner nights and have a courtyard garden out the back. Daily 10am–4.30pm.

Suffolk Stonehouse 18 St Mary's St, NR35 1AX ☎ 01986 894553, ⓦ suffolkstonehouse.co.uk. Bungay needs more places to eat, and this, the latest venture of the great people at the *Castle Inn* (see above), could yet herald the resurgence of St Mary's St, with fabulous pizzas and stone-baked pasta dishes (£7.50–11). Stripped down inside and very appealing, it's just what Bungay's food doctor ordered. Tues, Thurs & Sun 3–9pm, Fri & Sat 3–10pm.

OUT OF TOWN

The Artichoke 162 Yarmouth Rd, Broom, NR35 2NZ ☎ 01986 893325, ⓦ theartichokeatbroome.co.uk. Homely pub in an otherwise nondescript village just outside Bungay that serves a uniquely large selection of local real ales but also has a focus on food – pub food, really, but a cut above other places, and not expensive. Lunchtime mains go for £8–10, and there are plenty of veggie options, alongside home-made pies, sausage and mash, and a decent ploughman's. The evening menu is strong on meat and fish dishes – fish and chips, salmon, liver and bacon, lamb cutlets (£10–16) – but again has several veggie options. Kitchen Tues–Sat noon–2.30pm & 6.30–9pm, Sun noon–4pm; pub Tues–Sun noon–11pm.

Norfolk & Suffolk Aviation Museum

The Street, Flixton, NR35 1NZ • April–Oct Sun–Thurs 10am–5pm; Nov–March Tues, Wed & Sun 10am–4pm • Free • ☎ 01986 896644, ⓦ aviationmuseum.net.

Five minutes outside Bungay by car, the **Norfolk & Suffolk Aviation Museum** is an unexpected sight in the middle of the Suffolk countryside – two fields crammed full of mainly military aircraft, with a couple of hangars behind housing yet more planes and lots of aeronautical and military paraphernalia – models, uniforms, ejector seats – along with a couple of overflowing exhibition rooms devoted to both world wars. Among the aircraft on show is an English Electric Lightning, a Harrier jump jet and a wingless Spitfire, as well as the nose of a Vulcan bomber – an aircraft nerd's paradise basically, but with enough to interest the non-enthusiast, too. And if you've had enough of planes you can follow the **Adair Walk** from behind the museum, through a bucolic stretch of wet woodland down to a particularly idyllic bend in the Waveney River.

St Peter's Brewery

St Peter's Hall, South Elmham, NR35 1NQ • Tours Sat & Sun 11am, 12.30pm & 2pm • £7.50 • Shop Mon–Fri 9am–5pm, Sat & Sun 11am–4pm (Jan–Easter closed on Sun) • ☎ 01986 782322, ⓦ stpetersbrewery.co.uk

Bang in the centre of the Saints (see box, p.216), four miles south of Bungay, the buildings of **St Peter's Brewery** were an abandoned farm until the mid-1990s, when John Murphy – the founder of the multinational brand consultancy Interbrand – developed the brewery here. Murphy has done a great job in producing an award-winning selection of mainly bottled ales, around a dozen varieties in all. The real key, though, as he has acknowledged, was in bringing his marketing background to the fore and putting his products in distinctive and well-designed oval-shaped bottles that helped distinguish them from other small brewers who have sprung up in the last twenty years, particularly in East Anglia. You can take a tour of the plant, taste some beer and, of course, buy more of it in the shop. Across the courtyard, **St Peter's Hall** also houses a bar and restaurant.

Beccles and around

BECCLES is perhaps the most handsome town along the Waveney Valley, and the furthest south navigable mooring point for craft on the Broads. Like close neighbour Bungay it's actually in Suffolk (Norfolk begins across the river), and it has the same kind of self-contained, low-key prosperity as its neighbour, with an alluring Georgian centre that's home to the sort of small-scale sights that make visiting East Anglian market towns such a pleasure. It also has a few very good places to stay and eat.

St Michael the Archangel

The Walk, NR34 9AJ • ⓦ becclesparish.org.uk

The centre of Beccles sits high above the river, lofty heights only enhanced by the squat sixteenth-century stand-alone tower of the fifteenth-century church of **St Michael the Archangel**, which was built to the east of the church so as to avoid being too near the cliff. The interior was damaged in a fire not long after its completion, and doesn't hold all that much of interest, although Nelson's mum and dad (who was curate of the church) were married here in 1749 – they had Horatio (see box, p.156) nine years later.

BIG DOG FERRY

The **Big Dog ferry** (late March to late Oct daily 11am–7pm; one-way £6, return £10; children £3.50, £6; family tickets £15, £25; ☎ 07532 072761, ⓦ bigdogferry.co.uk) plies the route between Beccles Lido and Geldeston, a lovely forty-minute journey whether you choose to get out at the other end or not – though the delights of the *Locks Inn* (see p.221) should be more than enough to tempt you. It's not far into the pretty village of Geldeston, where there is another pub and Rowan Craft (see p.67), from whom you can hire a canoe or dayboat to take you back to Beccles.

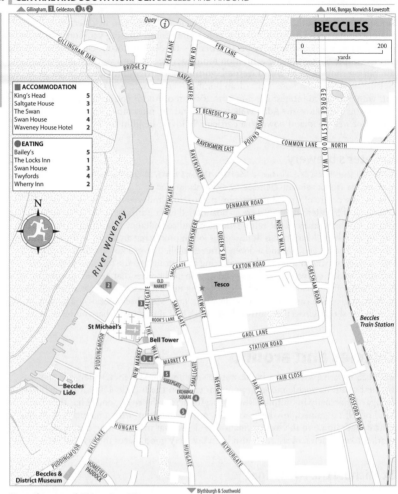

Beccles and District Museum

Leman House, Ballygate, NR34 9ND • April–Oct Tues–Sun 1.45–4.30pm • Free • ☎ 01502 715722, ⊛ becclesmuseum.org.uk

A short walk out of the immediate centre is the **Beccles and District Museum**, housed in an eighteenth-century schoolhouse with a garden overlooking the boatyards down below. It has the usual civic museum material – agricultural items, prints, photographs – but it's all quite well done, and there's a good model of the town as it looked in the nineteenth century, and usually a temporary exhibition or two on a local theme.

ARRIVAL AND INFORMATION   BECCLES

By train Beccles station is a 5min walk from the town centre, on Station Rd at George Westwood Way. Trains run hourly to Ipswich (1hr 10min), Woodbridge (50min), Saxmundham (30min), Oulton Broad (10min) and Lowestoft (15min).

By bus Buses stop at the train station and outside Tesco, and the town is well connected to Norwich and Lowestoft by the #X2 (every 30min), which runs via Loddon.

By boat The town staithe (and free moorings) are a 10min walk from the centre, at the end of Northgate. Dayboat rental is possible from CC Marine or HE Hipperson (see box, p.67). Ferries run upriver to Geldeston (see p.219).

Tourist office At Beccles town staithe, north of the centre (daily 9am–5pm; ☎ 01502 713303); there are toilets and all the usual facilities of a Broadland quayside.

ACCOMMODATION

IN TOWN

King's Head 6 New Market, NR34 9HA ☎01502 718730, ⓦjdwetherspoon.co.uk/home/pubs/the-kings -head-hotel. Wetherspoons took over this failing town centre hotel a couple of years ago and it's now quite a hub of activity, with the usual cheap food and ale and ten clean and tidy rooms upstairs, with refurbished bathrooms and all the facilities you'd expect – and great prices, though they don't include breakfast. **£39**

Saltgate House 5 Saltgate, NR34 9AN ☎01502 710889, ⓦsaltgatehouse.com. Situated in a large and elegant Georgian house in the heart of town, this family-run B&B has four well-furnished double and twin rooms, refurbished in the last year or so, with new bathrooms and comfy beds. The largest rooms are at the front but the quietest are at the back, overlooking a pretty courtyard garden. There's a bright breakfast room and comfy sitting room, both of which have a communal vibe. **£95**

★Swan House By the Tower, NR34 9HE ☎01502 713474, ⓦswan-house.com. *Swan House* is a Beccles institution, and it has an excellent location bang in the centre of town. The five boutique rooms make the most of the beams and creaky floors but also have smart TVs with Netflix, iPhone docking stations and funky, well-appointed bathrooms. Music in the restaurant (see below) is provided by the owner's carefully chosen playlists and each week he picks a movie theme, with a different film each day showing on a loop in reception. **£130**

Waveney House Hotel Puddingmoor, NR34 9PL ☎01502 712270, ⓦwaveneyhousehotel.co.uk. At heart a historic building, whose creaky sloping floors date back to the sixteenth century, and with a great location by the river. There are twelve guest rooms, which, although on the bland side, are pleasant enough. The restaurant downstairs is deliberately informal, good for just a drink or a full meal – both best enjoyed on the riverside terrace. **£100**

OUT OF TOWN

The Swan Loddon Rd, Gillingham, NR34 0LD ☎01502 470047, ⓦgillinghamswan.co.uk. Just outside Beccles, over the Norfolk border, *The Swan* has fourteen simply furnished but recently and tastefully updated rooms in an annexe behind the main building. A pub grub menu is served and there's a nice sun-trap terrace on which to enjoy a drink. Breakfast costs an extra £5. **£65**

EATING

IN TOWN

Baileys 2 Hungate, NR34 9TL ☎01502 710609, ⓦupstairsatbaileys.co.uk. A great food shop and deli with a Spanish flavour, which does set lunches for £13.50 as well as serving a delicious dinner menu on Friday and Saturday in the restaurant upstairs, with mains like monkfish, cod and pork belly confit for around £20. It's a wine merchant, too, specializing in Spanish wine. Mon– Thurs 9am–5pm, Fri & Sat 9am–11pm.

★Swan House By the Tower, NR34 9HE ☎01502 713474, ⓦswan-house.com. A contemporary hotel (see above) restaurant with stripped tables and squashy sofas in a bright double-aspect room, very much at the heart of the Beccles scene. The excellent menu changes regularly, but always has a balance of meat, fish and veggie dishes; starters are £6–7 and mains £15–18. They have a great beer list too, and they serve breakfast until 9.30am, morning coffee, and afternoon tea between the lunch and dinner services. Daily noon– 2.30pm & 6.45–9.30pm.

Twyfords Exchange Square, NR34 9HL ☎01502 710614, ⓦtwyfordscafe.co.uk. This café occupies a former gentlemen's outfitters right in the heart of Beccles, and does great coffee and cakes, salads and lots of sandwiches, including items like pulled pork and beef and Stilton melt. A place to drop into at any time of day, and with a garden out the back that's perfect in summer. Free wi-fi, too. Mon–Sat 8.30am–5pm.

OUT OF TOWN

★The Locks Inn Locks Lane, Geldeston, IP19 8AP ☎01508 518414, ⓦgeldestonlocks.co.uk. Across the border in Norfolk, about a mile outside the nearby village of Geldeston down a long dirt track, is a Broads pub par excellence, right on the river and not even on the national grid. It's remote enough to host regular, loud live music at weekends, while the rest of the time it specializes in folk nights, curry nights and a thousand other inventive offerings. You can even take a ferry there from Beccles (see box, p.219). Shorter hours in winter, so check ahead. Kitchen Mon–Fri noon–2.30pm & 6–9pm, Sat & Sun noon–9pm; pub Mon–Fri noon till late, Sat & Sun 11am–late.

Wherry Inn 7 The Street, Geldeston, NR34 0LB ☎01508 518371, ⓦwherryinn.co.uk. In the heart of the pretty village of Geldeston, this is a comfy village pub that serves simple but well-cooked and well-presented pub food – nothing fancy, but good steaks, burgers and fish and chips, plus excellent pies. Kitchen Mon & Wed–Fri noon– 2pm & 6–8pm (Fri till 9pm), Sat noon–9pm, Sun noon– 8pm; pub Mon, Wed & Thurs noon–3pm & 5.30–11pm, Fri & Sat noon–11pm, Sun noon–10pm.

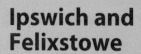

Ipswich and Felixstowe

CHRISTCHURCH MANSION, IPSWICH

Ipswich and Felixstowe

Situated at the head of the Orwell estuary, Ipswich is the largest town in Suffolk by some way, twice the size of its nearest rival, Lowestoft, although most people would struggle if you were to ask them to name a reason to visit. Certainly it's not seen as an alluring destination in its own right – at least not in the way, say, Norwich might be. It's not even technically a city, and has a reputation for seediness that most ports are saddled with, though one without any attendant glamour. However, the town is both more appealing and more historic than you might think, with any number of reasons to make a trip, not least the waterfront development, which on a good day is as nice a place to shoot the harbourside breeze as any in England.

Thirteen miles southeast, at the end of the Orwell estuary, **Felixstowe** is the port that stole Ipswich's thunder, and the most southerly town on the Suffolk coast. It too is not the county's most appealing corner but it is certainly its most economically productive, a powerhouse of a port that handles much of southern England's container traffic – hence the parade of trucks thundering continuously up and down the A14. Even Felixstowe has its good bits, though, and generally it's a decent resort with a long sandy beach and the tiny satellite village of Felixstowe Ferry to tempt you to stay a little bit longer.

Ipswich

IPSWICH is one of the oldest towns in the country, the Saxon stronghold of Raedwald, seventh-century ruler of East Anglia, whose burial site was at Sutton Hoo (see p.246). The town became a rich trading port in the Middle Ages, exporting the fruits of the Suffolk textile industry to the rest of Europe. It was home to one of the most popular medieval shrines, and to one of its most controversial figures, Cardinal Wolsey (see box, p.230), who made the town his power base. Later, Thomas Gainsborough lived and worked in Ipswich, and Tolly Cobbold established their brewing dynasty here.

The port declined at the start of the twentieth century and the town has a rather tawdry reputation today: its **centre** is made up of the usual pedestrianized precincts and chain stores and there's been some poor postwar redevelopment. However, the city is more handsome than you might expect, with pockets that are as vital and dynamic as any provincial British town, not least the redeveloped waterfront, where the impression is of a confident, resurgent city. There are some good museums, including **Christchurch Mansion**, with its collection of Gainsboroughs and Constables, and there's plenty to see nearby – along the scenic Shotley peninsula and in so-called **Constable Country**, a series of pretty villages and countryside where John Constable lived and worked.

Cornhill and around

If Ipswich has a focal point then it's **Cornhill**, a central square at the end of the town's main Tavern Street, flanked by a bevy of imposing Victorian edifices – the Italianate

Come on you Tractor Boys! p.227
Thomas Wolsey p.230

On the river p.231
Foodie Ipswich p.234

A CONTENTED RESIDENT OF JIMMY'S FARM

Highlights

❶ Christchurch Mansion Ipswich's most handsome building, and with an art collection that features work by local boys Gainsborough and Constable. **See p.227**

❷ The Waterfront One of the most successful dockside developments you'll find – don't come to Ipswich without seeking it out. **See p.229**

❸ Jimmy's Farm "As seen on TV", and a perfect attraction for kids, also featuring a great farm shop and restaurant. **See p.234**

❹ Landguard Fort This historic fort is by far the best venue from which to appreciate Felixstowe's unique port and harbour. **See p.236**

❺ Felixstowe Ferry Felixstowe – indeed Suffolk – at its best, and you could be a million miles away from the docks, with fresh fish stalls, a couple of places to eat and the ferry across the river to Bawdsey. **See p.237**

HIGHLIGHTS ARE MARKED ON THE MAP ON P.226

Town Hall (Tues–Sat 10am–5pm), now a venue for exhibitions of contemporary and local arts and crafts, the old Neoclassical post office next door, and on the other side of the square the pseudo-Jacobean Lloyds Building. Cut through from here to the end of the town's other main drag, Buttermarket, and the **Giles Statue**. This remembers the *Daily Express* cartoonist, Carl Giles (1916–1995), with a representation of "Grandma" from the popular strip that ran in the newspaper from 1945 until the early 1990s. The cartoon followed the daily fortunes of an ordinary family, of which Grandma was perhaps the most memorable member, although, as Giles himself claimed, her conversation amounted only to "ailments, horse racing and little else". With her dog at her feet, Giles' Grandma looks up to the building opposite where the cartoonist had his studio, while in the opposite direction the *Swan* pub on King Street is apparently where he often used to wind up after work (see p.234).

The Ancient House

On the corner of Buttermarket and St Stephen's Lane, Ipswich's most renowned building is the **Ancient House**, whose stuccoed exterior was decorated around 1670 in an extravagant style that makes it one of the finest examples of Restoration artistry in the country. There are plasterwork reliefs of pelicans and nymphs as well as representations of the four continents (that were known at the time) – Europe symbolized by a Gothic church, America a tobacco pipe, Asia an Oriental dome and Africa by a man astride a crocodile. The house is now a branch of the Lakeland homewares chain, and as such you're free to take a peek inside to view more of the decor, including yet more fancy stuccowork.

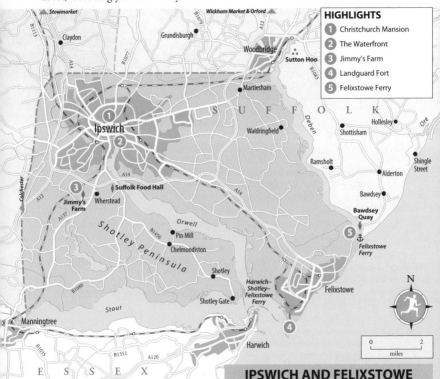

HIGHLIGHTS

1. Christchurch Mansion
2. The Waterfront
3. Jimmy's Farm
4. Landguard Fort
5. Felixstowe Ferry

IPSWICH AND FELIXSTOWE

St Mary-le-Tower

Tower St, IP1 3BE • Mon–Fri 9am–5pm, Sat 9am–noon • ☎ 01473 289001, ⓦ stmaryletower.org.uk

Ipswich is not a city, so doesn't have a cathedral, and the nearest it gets is the church of **St Mary-le-Tower**, whose spire is a familiar landmark wherever you are in the town centre. Although it's not even close to being on a par with Norwich's cathedral, and has been hugely updated over the years, it's an important symbol of the town, and there are some aspects of it that locals can be proud of – not least the magnificent nineteenth-century organ, the replacement of an original from 1680, on which regular recitals are given. The font is a typical example from the fifteenth century, decorated with images of lions and human heads, and the churchwardens' pews at the back of the church have finely carved ends showing dragons and devout monks while; in the north aisle you can see stained glass window memorials to the local Cobbold brewing dynasty. Look also for the nearby painted memorial to William Smart MP, which shows Ipswich as it would have looked when he died in 1599.

6

Ipswich Museum

High St, IP1 3QH • Tues–Sat 10am–5pm • Free • ☎ 01473 433550, ⓦ www.cimuseums.org.uk

On the edge of the town centre, the **Ipswich Museum** is an old-fashioned museum of the very best kind, with a wonderful main gallery full of traditional glass display cases full of stuffed birds and animals from the Victorian era and a very charming life-sized mock-up of a woolly mammoth. Upstairs are more birds and a gallery that concentrates on the history of Ipswich to the present day. There's also a good archeological section, with locally found Roman jewellery, tableaux of life in the fields and in a Roman villa, and a good array of Egyptian artefacts, well exhibited with children in mind. The ethnographic section, too, has costumes, weapons, and day-to-day items from the developing world, and a series of galleries focus on life in the town during World War II – again, really well thought out and great for kids.

St Mary-at-the-Elms

68 Black Horse Lane, IP1 2EF • ☎ 01473 216484, ⓦ stmaryattheelms.org.uk

Ipswich's quaintest town-centre church, **St Mary-at-the-Elms** is distinguished by its redbrick Tudor tower, although this was damaged by a fire in 2010. Dating back to the thirteenth century, the church is linked to the shrine of **Our Lady of Grace** which once stood nearby and was second only to Walsingham in stature until it was suppressed by Henry VIII in the 1530s. Today the church houses a copy of the wooden statue of the Virgin that used to reside in the shrine and somehow ended up in Nettuno, Italy.

Christchurch Mansion and Wolsey Art Gallery

Soane St, IP4 2BE • Tues–Sun 10am–5pm • Free • ☎ 01473 433554, ⓦ www.cimuseums.org.uk

A few minutes' walk north of the town centre, the 33-acre expanse of Christchurch Park is worth a stroll in itself, but it's also home to **Christchurch Mansion**, a handsome if much-restored Tudor building, attached to the **Wolsey Art Gallery** behind. It was built in the sixteenth century on the grounds of a priory seized for

---

COME ON YOU TRACTOR BOYS!

Ipswich Town FC are struggling to get back to their glory days under Bobby Robson in the 1960s and 1970s but still enjoy solid support locally, and of course loathe their East Anglian rivals Norwich City. They play at Portman Road, a 30,000-capacity stadium on the western edge of the town centre, five minutes' walk from Cornhill and the train station, and ten minutes from the Waterfront. For information and tickets, see ⓦ itfc.co.uk.

6

IPSWICH

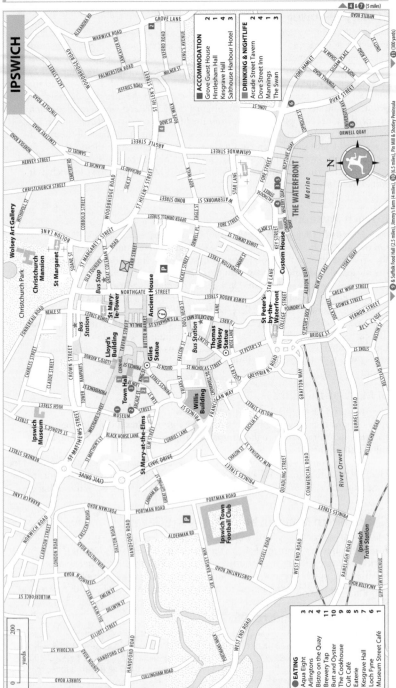

ACCOMMODATION
Grove Guest House	2
Hintlesham Hall	1
Kesgrave Hall	4
Salthouse Harbour Hotel	3

DRINKING & NIGHTLIFE
Arcade Street Tavern	4
Dove Street Inn	2
Mannings	1
The Swan	3

EATING
Aqua Eight	3
Arlingtons	2
Bistro on the Quay	4
Brewery Tap	11
Butt and Oyster	10
The Cookhouse	9
Cult Café	8
Eaterie	5
Kesgrave Hall	7
Loch Fyne	6
Museum Street Café	1

the crown by Cardinal Wolsey (see p.230) and later occupied in its eighteenth- and nineteenth-century heyday by the wealthy Fonnereau family, who added the various wings and extensions. There's quite a lot to see, starting in the impressive arcaded Great Hall in the Jacobean core, and finishing up in the Victorian wing, with its downstairs kitchen and servants' quarters – all sensitively and effectively filled with period furniture, vintage toys, paintings and other displays. There are paintings throughout, including one – *Hot Cockles* – by the Dutchman Adriaen van Ostade in the library, lots of portraits of the Fonnereau family, and various Tudor and Stuart portraits and landscapes by nineteenth- and twentieth-century Suffolk artists, including work by Thomas Gainsborough and Alfred Munnings and local scenes by Cor Visser, a Dutch painter who spent much of his life in Ipswich. Perhaps most unusual, though, are the early seventeenth-century *Hawstead Panels*, which occupy a room to themselves and were based apparently on an elegy by John Donne; they were painted on the death of one of the daughters of the family, and each depicts a different thought or prayer.

The attached **Wolsey Art Gallery** displays a collection of mostly Gainsborough and Constable paintings – the largest outside London and a homage to the area's most renowned painters. You'll find early landscapes and portraits of local eighteenth-century dignitaries by Gainsborough – notably one of local MP William Wollaston – and landscapes and family portraits by Constable, including the beautiful soft landscape of *The Mill Stream, Flatford* and a wonderfully verdant painting of his father's vegetable garden.

The Waterfront

Ipswich's wet dock or **Waterfront** dates from the nineteenth century, when its mills and warehouses were the focal point of the town's Victorian docks (the largest in Europe when they opened in 1845). Like inner-city port areas across the country, it fell into disrepair some time ago and is now in the process of being transformed into one of the city's most exciting new neighbourhoods, with a busy marina and a barrage of cool bars, restaurants and hotels; it's also been the home campus of the University of Suffolk since 2008. The area is something of a work-in-progress, but already its quayside main drag has been pretty successful in creating an almost Mediterranean ambience – squint across the masts of the marina on a summer's evening and you could almost believe you were in St Tropez. The cafés and restaurants along the water's edge certainly make a good fist of apeing life on the Riviera, none more so than the slick *Salthouse Harbour Hotel* (see p.230), while the stolid Neoclassical **Customs House** provides a reminder of yesteryear, complete with a grand portico and a wide double stairway.

St Peter's by-the-Waterfront

College St, IP1 1XF • Mon–Fri 10am–3.30pm • ☎ 01473 225269, ⊕ stpetersbythewaterfront.com

Just outside the Waterfront development, across the main road, is the church of **St Peter's-by-the-Waterfront** and the so-called **Wolsey Gate** next door. There has been a church here since the eleventh century and the current building dates from the 1500s when Cardinal Wolsey made it his own private chapel. It's deconsecrated now, but you may want to drop by to see the so-called *Ipswich Charter Hangings*, commissioned in 2000 to commemorate the granting of the town's first charter in 1200 AD and now permanently on display in the church. Designed by local ecclesiastical artist Isabel Clover, they show the history of the town in a series of eight bold and colourful tapestries, starting with the arrival of the Vikings and finishing up in the present day. They are full of recognizable local sights and attractions, from the Custom House to Portman Road – although the main motif is the river.

6

THOMAS WOLSEY

Perhaps the most famous and certainly the most influential prelate of the Tudor period, **Thomas Wolsey** was born in Ipswich in 1473, the son of a butcher, and it was here that he developed a power and influence that resonates to this day – in street names, memorials, ruins and a number of buildings around the town centre. His childhood home reputedly stood on St Nicholas Street, close by which a statue of Wolsey was unveiled in 2011. More prosaically there is a pub named after him just down the street, beyond which is the church of St Peter's-by-the-Waterfront, which was his place of worship. Outside the church there still stands a brick arch that is the only remnant of a college he founded. A close confidante of **King Henry VIII**, he became Archbishop of York in 1514 and **Lord Chancellor** a year later. He was unable to use his considerable influence on the pope to achieve the annulment of Henry's marriage to Anne Boleyn, though, and for that he was eventually stripped of office; he died shortly after in 1530.

Ipswich Transport Museum

Cobham Rd, IP3 9JD • April–Nov Sun 11am–4pm, plus additional weekdays 1–4pm during Easter, May, summer and bank hols • £5.50, children £3.50, family tickets £16 • ☎ 01472 715666, ⊚ ipswichtransportmuseum.co.uk

About a mile down Felixstowe Road from central Ipswich, the **Ipswich Transport Museum** isn't a must-see, but its vintage trams, buses and fire engines – the self-proclaimed largest collection of transport vehicles in the country derived from just one town – may provide respite from the weather, or indeed satisfy your family's public transport buff. There is a pristine tram from 1904, a 1923 trolleybus – which you can board – and even a Sinclair C5 electric car from 1985, one of the biggest transport flops in history. Nerdy grown-ups and nostalgia addicts will also enjoy the collections of milk floats, lawnmowers, bikes and prams, along with lots and lots of classic signs.

ARRIVAL AND DEPARTURE   IPSWICH

By train The station is on the south bank of the river, about a 15min walk from Cornhill along Princes St, and is very well connected to the rest of East Anglia.

Destinations Beccles (hourly; 1hr 10min); Bury St Edmunds (hourly; 35min); Cambridge (hourly; 1hr 20min); Diss (every 30min; 25min); Felixstowe (hourly; 25min); London Liverpool St (every 30min; 1hr 20min); Lowestoft (every 30min; 1hr 30min); Newmarket (hourly; 1hr); Norwich (every 30min; 40min); Oulton Broad (hourly; 1hr 25min); Saxmundham (hourly; 35min); Stowmarket (every 30min; 15min); Woodbridge (hourly; 15min).

By bus Buses arrive at and leave from various places around the town centre, mainly the Tower Ramparts bus station (Crown St) and the Old Cattle Market bus station (Turret Ln, a southerly extension of St Stephen's Ln). There are regular buses to Felixstowe from the Old Cattle Market station (every 15min; 40min) and Framlingham from the corner of Northgate St and Great Colman St (every 30min; 45min).

By car There are several well-placed car parks in the town centre, including one just off Tacket St at Cox Lane, just south of Tavern Lane, another right by the landmark glass Willis Building on St Nicholas St, and a third at the junction of Alf Ramsey Way and Portman Rd, right by the football ground.

INFORMATION AND TOURS

Tourist office Opposite Buttermarket shopping centre in St Stephen's Church (St Stephen's Lane, IP1 1DP; Mon–Sat 9am–5pm; ☎ 01473 258070, ⊚ visit-suffolk.org.uk).

Walking tours There are excellent themed guided walks around the city centre, starting at the tourist office (usually Tues & Thurs at 2.15pm; 90min; £4).

ACCOMMODATION

IN TOWN

Grove Guest House 14 Grove Lane, IP4 1NR ☎ 01473 221014, ⊚ groveguesthouseipswich.co.uk. Fairly centrally located B&B with five comfortable rooms, two of which are en suite and each furnished differently in a contemporary style. They serve an in-room continental breakfast. Follow St Helen's Lane to the end and make a right, or walk up from Fore St across Alexandra Park – both about ten minutes' walk. £61

★**Salthouse Harbour Hotel** Neptune Quay, IP4 1AX ☎ 01473 226789, ⊚ salthouseharbour.co.uk. Down on the resurgent Waterfront, housed in part in an imaginatively converted old warehouse, this is the city's best choice by some way, with seventy large, modern and funkily decorated rooms, many of which look out over Ipswich's yacht harbour. It's undeniably nice, and not necessarily what you thought Ipswich would be like, especially if you are enjoying the view from your bath while listening to music through the room's iPod dock. It also has an excellent restaurant, *Eaterie* (see p.232). **£120**

OUT OF TOWN

Hintlesham Hall Hintlesham, IP8 3NS ☎ 01473 652334, ⓦ hintleshamhall.co.uk. This country-house hotel a few miles west of Ipswich was owned for years by the proto-celebrity chef Robert Carrier and is still a very comfortable place to stay, with 32 large and very well-appointed rooms and suites divided between the main house and a converted stable block. Prices are good considering the location and facilities, which include a croquet lawn, tennis courts and subsidized green fees at the adjacent golf course. They also

have a rather grand restaurant, where the à la carte prices fit the surroundings, but the table d'hôte fixed-price menus, served during the week, are excellent value. **£85**

★**Kesgrave Hall** Hall Rd, Kesgrave, IP5 2PU ☎ 01473 333741, ⓦ milsomhotels.com/kesgravehall. On the furthest eastern edge of Ipswich, an ex-private school, and also once owned by the Tolly Cobbold brewing dynasty, this is a boutique hotel with a contemporary feel. Part of the small, mainly Essex-based Milsoms group, it has 23 rooms, around half of which are in the main house while the rest are in the former headmaster's quarters and various outbuildings. The rooms are sumptuous but not old-fashioned, kitted out with sound systems, flatscreen TVs and posh bathroom products, and the bar/lounge and restaurant (see p.232) are relaxed rather than stuffy. **£110**

EATING

IN TOWN

Aqua Eight 8 Lion St, IP1 1DQ ☎ 01473 218994, ⓦ aquaeight.com. This cool pan-Asian restaurant right in the heart of town serves lovely meze and finger food to share and has a small garden out the back in which to enjoy it. It also serves regular main courses for £10–15 – things like katsu chicken, teriyaki sea bass and wasabi steak, as well as the spectacular Alaskan black cod with miso sauce (£21.50). There are good-value lunch specials at £12.50 for two courses. Tues–Thurs noon–2.15pm & 6–9.30pm, Fri & Sat noon–2.15pm & 6–11pm, Sun 5.30–9.30pm.

Arlingtons 13 Museum St, IP1 1HE ☎ 01473 230293, ⓦ arlingtonsbrasserie.com. Big, airy restaurant, formerly home to the Ipswich Museum (see p.227), divided into an upstairs brasserie and downstairs café. Upstairs, mains go for £10.95–16.95, and are mainly tried-and-tested French favourites – beef bourguignon, cassoulet and steak frites – along with English standbys like fish pie and fish and chips, plus the inevitable burgers. The downstairs café does great coffee, bagels and croissants, as well as a delicious breakfast and a simple lunch menu of gourmet sandwiches (£7.95), big salads and jackets for around £7. Brasserie Mon noon–2pm, Tues noon–2pm & 5–8.15pm, Wed–Sat noon–2pm & 5–9pm; café Mon 8am–6pm, Tues–Thurs 8am–11pm, Fri & Sat 8am–1am, Sun 9am–5pm.

Bistro on the Quay Wherry Quay, IP4 1AS ☎ 01473 286677, ⓦ bistroonthequay.co.uk. This restaurant epitomizes the revitalization of the Waterfront, with its clean modern interior and big windows looking out onto the water. The food, too, is a contemporary take on some deliberately simple classics, with things like lemon sole, monkfish fillets, lamb shank and dauphinoise potatoes predominating. Mains go for £14.50–16.95 but there are good-value menus on offer too – £15.95 for three courses – and they do a short menu of light lunch specials for just £8–10. Mon–Sat noon–2pm & 6.30–9.30pm, Sun noon–2.30pm.

★**Brewery Tap** Cliff Rd, Cliff Quay, IP3 0AT ☎ 01473 225501, ⓦ thebrewerytap.org. Just beyond the more contemporary developments of the Waterfront, the *Brewery Tap* is almost the perfect boozer – a dockside pub, plumb by the entrance to what's left of the town's port, with a warm welcome, lots of space and great food. The lovely light lunch menu has mains for £6–9, and the more refined dinner options include main courses – from curried monkfish skewers or citrus-marinated guinea fowl breast to fish and chips, pork belly and the like – for around £13–16. They also serve fab bar snacks, including more varieties of pickled egg than you will have ever seen, and stock a great selection of beers, including Suffolk Calvors lager and their own Cliff Quay brews. A real haven in a pretty unappealing part of town, though only a 10min walk from the more obvious bars and restaurants of the Waterfront district. Kitchen Mon

ON THE RIVER

Orwell River Cruises (☎ 07773 369970, ⓦ orwellrivercruises.com) run trips aboard the *Orwell Lady* from their berth on the eastern side of the Waterfront. One trip goes to Pin Mill (see p.234), which leaves at 10am and 2.30pm and lasts 2hr 30min; another – 1hr longer – leaves at 2pm and goes further downriver to Harwich. Other options include cream tea cruises and themed evening cruises. The Harwich trips run 3–4 days a week during summer, and cost £19 per person (family tickets £59.50); Pin Mill cruises cost £15 per person (family tickets £48). There's also the *Victor* **sailing barge** (☎ 01473, ⓦ sbvictor.co.uk), also moored on the Waterfront, which runs supper, high tea and Sunday lunch cruises at various times during the week for £35–50 per person.

6–9.30pm, Tues–Sat noon–2.30pm & 6–9.30pm, Sun 10.30am–8pm; pub Mon 6–11pm, Tues–Fri noon–3pm & 6–11pm, Sat noon–11pm, Sun 10.30am–10.30pm.

Cult Café James Hehir Building, University Ave, IP3 0FS ☎ 01473 338166, ⓦ cultcafe.co.uk. It looks like a student joint and in a way it is, but it's run by the guys from the *Brewery Tap* (see p.231) and is one of the funkier places to eat on the Waterfront, serving good coffee, great breakfasts, and a fabulous lunch menu, consisting of all sorts of different snack-type dishes: burgers, Canadian poutine (chips, cheese curds 'n' gravy – hard to explain but delicious), Middle Eastern flatbreads and various sharing dishes. Most things cost under a tenner. Regular live music, too. Mon–Thurs 8am–11pm, Fri 8am–2am, Sat 9am–2am, Sun 9am–10.30pm.

★**Eaterie** Salthouse Harbour Hotel, Neptune Quay, IP4 1AX ☎ 01473 226789, ⓦ salthouseharbour.co.uk /eaterie. This restaurant lives up to the hotel's (see p.230) high standards, with curvy banquettes and a low-lit, New York warehouse feel that they pull off rather well. The food is hearty, but always served with a flourish and a keen eye for detail – the menu changes monthly, but there's always a good balance of fish and meat dishes; steak always features, cooked in summer on their "green egg" barbecue. Starters go for £7.50 or so, mains from £14, and there's a wide selection of wines (bottles start at £19). Not bad prices for the coolest location east of, er, Bury St Edmunds. Daily noon–5.30pm & 6–10pm.

Loch Fyne 1 Duke St, IP3 0AE ☎ 01473 269810, ⓦ lochfyne.com. A chain, but a good one, and in a handy location just off the Waterfront. The menu features the usual well-prepared selection of fish and seafood. Moderately priced, too, with most starters at around £5–7 and mains £13–17. Mon–Fri noon–10pm, Sat 9am–10pm, Sun 9am–9pm.

Museum Street Café Westgate House, Museum St, IP1 1HQ ☎ 01473 232393. A great little veggie café right in the heart of town, serving a regularly changing menu of really tasty vegetarian dishes, from pumpkin soup and butternut squash lasagne to sweet potato tortillas. Great value, and justifiably busy at lunchtime, it will be a hit even with your carnivore friends. Tues–Fri 9.15am–4.30pm, Sat 11am–4.30pm.

OUT OF TOWN

The Cookhouse Wherstead, IP9 2AB ☎ 01473 786616, ⓦ suffolkfoodhall.co.uk/restaurant. The excellent Suffolk Food Hall (see box, p.234) is home to a café and full-service restaurant, which is open daily for breakfast, lunch and afternoon teas (plus dinner on Fri & Sat) and has lovely views over the Orwell River. Mon–Thurs 8am–3pm, Fri & Sat 8am–9pm, Sun 8.30am–4.30pm.

Kesgrave Hall Hall Rd, Kesgrave, IP5 2PU ☎ 01473 333741, ⓦ milsomhotels.com/kesgravehall. Despite the relative grandeur of the surroundings, the restaurant of the *Kesgrave Hall* hotel (see p.231) is busy and relaxed at the same time, with stripped pine tables and an open kitchen. There are always daily specials or you can order à la carte from a menu that is deliberately informal, with dishes like guinea fowl Kiev, pan-fried sea bream, fish and chips and gourmet burgers. You can choose between "ample" (starter-size) and "generous" (main-course-size) portions in some cases. Prices are keen, with "ample" portions starting at £6.50 and "generous" ones at £14.50; most regular main courses go for £14–15 and wine starts at just £17.50 a bottle. Daily noon–9.30pm.

★**Maybush Inn** Cliff Rd, Waldringfield, IP12 4QL ☎ 01473 736215, ⓦ debeninns.co.uk/maybush. Owned by the same folk who have the *Butt & Oyster* in Pin Mill (see p.234) and a number of other scenic local pubs, this is a gloriously situated riverside boozer, right on the Deben roughly halfway between the A12 and Felixstowe Ferry. It does food all day – steaks and burgers, fish and chips, pasta and chilli, prawns and seafood – which you can enjoy from its large terrace overlooking the masts and grassy banks of the tranquil river. Reckon on anything from £10.95 to £13.95 for a main dish, more for steaks, but there are plenty of nibbles for less. Kitchen daily 9am–9.30pm; pub Mon–Sat 9am–11pm, Sun 9am–10.30pm.

DRINKING AND NIGHTLIFE

Arcade Street Tavern 1 Arcade St, IP1 1EX ☎ 01473 805454, ⓦ arcadetavern.co.uk. Great bar right in the centre of town that focuses on craft beers and has a frankly impressive list of bottled beers as well as lots of real ales and lagers on tap. It's not just a haunt of the cable-knit jumper brigade, though, and has a crisp, nicely furnished interior, an outside terrace and a small courtyard garden at the back. No food, apart from bar snacks, unless you are lucky enough to coincide with one of their "Streetfood Fridays", when local vendors are invited in to sell their frequently delicious wares to hungry punters. Tues 10am–3.30pm, Wed & Thurs 10.30am–11pm, Fri 10.30am–midnight, Sat 10.30am–1am.

★**Dove Street Inn** 76 St Helens St, IP4 2LA ☎ 01473 211270, ⓦ dovestreetinn.co.uk. Just outside the city centre, this is one of Ipswich's best locals, deceptively large inside, with a back room and courtyard and a cosy bar in the front. Lots of real ales (they host regular beer festivals), and an unusually wide choice of bottled beers too. They also serve a hearty menu of home-made chilli, curries, beef and ale pie and more for £5–6, and a great selection of bar snacks too. Mon–Sat noon–midnight (last entry 10.45), Sun noon–11pm (last entry 10.30pm).

Mannings 8 Cornhill, IP1 1DD ☎01473 254170, ⓦmanningsph.co.uk. A well-established city-centre pub from whose accommodating yet unpretentious sixteenth-century interior you can watch the comings and goings on the square. Some outside seating, too, and a garden at the back. If you're hungry, feast on their doorstep sandwiches or bowls of chips with various toppings. Mon–Wed 11am–8pm, Thurs–Sat 11am–11pm, Sun noon–5pm.

The Swan King St, IP1 1EG ☎01473 252485. Long-running pub which is one of the better city-centre pubs for a drink, but is also one of the best night-time places for music, with regular live bands – big with students. Mon–Wed noon–11pm, Thurs noon–midnight, Fri & Sat noon–1am, Sun 4–10.30pm.

Jimmy's Farm

Pannington Hall Lane, IP9 2AR • Daily 9.30am–5pm • £4.50, children £3.50, family tickets £15 • ☎08444 938088, ⓦjimmysfarm.com

Just outside Ipswich, **Jimmy's Farm** is the domain of TV farmer Jimmy Doherty, and featured in the Channel 4 series of the same name before Jimmy made *Friday Night Feast* with his mate Jamie Oliver. The farm focuses on rare breeds and has a great farm shop (see box below), and although you're not likely to see its celebrity owner or his wife Michaela, they're both still pretty active around the place, in which pigs, turkeys, chickens and goats abound, alongside "ferret world", a guinea pig village and a lovely hothouse full of butterflies. There are also well-marked walks through the surrounding woodland and a good restaurant, fashioned out of a wonderful beamed old barn and partly supplied by the farm, including Michaela's nearby vegetable patch – a well-tended spread if ever there was one.

The Shotley peninsula and Pin Mill

The **Shotley peninsula** extends to the southeast of Ipswich, an unusual and occasionally scenic mix of farmland, semi-suburban industry and housing and big riverside views. It culminates in the village of **Shotley Gate**, where you can look across to Harwich and the container port of Felixstowe (see opposite) on the far side of what is an enormous natural harbour. There's a footpath you can follow all the way along the Stour, and a foot ferry that goes to Harwich and Felixstowe (see p.237). Halfway along the Shotley peninsula, below the small village of Chelmondiston, tight against the muddy banks of the River Orwell, the tiny village of **Pin Mill** hogs a marshy inlet, its huddle of old houses edging a busy boatyard, whose vintage boats creak and groan with the tides. Once the haunt of smugglers, Pin Mill is a peaceful, very nautical place today, and you can stroll along the riverbank or hoof it up to Pin Mill, where a network of footpaths crisscross the hilly woodland that runs roughly parallel to the river.

EATING

Butt and Oyster The Quay, Pin Mill, IP9 1JW ☎01473 780764, ⓦdebeninns.co.uk/buttandoyster. This quarry-tiled seventeenth-century pub has a great location down the estuary from central Ipswich, and is well worth the short drive out of the town. It serves food all day – decent pub grub mainly, and great sharing platters. Some people of a certain age might recognize it from the TV series, *Lovejoy*, in which it starred as the *Three Ducks*. Kitchen Mon–Fri 10am–9.30pm, Sat & Sun 9am–9.30pm; pub Mon–Fri 10am–11pm, Sat 9am–11pm, Sun 9am–10.30pm.

FOODIE IPSWICH

Cornhill, right in the centre of Ipswich, hosts a regular, mainly food, market (all day Tues, Thurs, Fri & Sat), but the city's real foodie delights are outside the centre. Jimmy's Farm Shop (daily 9.30am–5pm; see above) is one of the best farm shops you'll find, selling all manner of meat and poultry, sausages and bacon from the farm's rare-breed pigs, and fruit and veg. The Suffolk Food Hall, in the shadow of the Orwell bridge in Wherstead (IP9 2AB ☎01473 786610, ⓦsuffolkfoodhall.co.uk.; Mon–Sat 9am–6pm, Sun 10.30am–4pm), is a fabulous one-stop shop for local produce, with a butcher's, deli, wet fish shop, bakery and much more. They host lots of foodie events, run cookery classes and are home to a restaurant, *The Cookhouse* (see p.232).

Felixstowe

Like Ipswich, **FELIXSTOWE** perhaps gets worse press than it deserves. It's the UK's largest container port, and one of the biggest in Europe, the target destination of the giant trucks and lorries that travel in convoys down the A14. But it's also a well-developed seaside resort, and while it's not the most glamorous place on the Suffolk Coast, it's not the worst either, with a pier and seafront promenade backed by rather lavish subtropical gardens that edge a long sand and shingle beach, and a pleasant town centre on the cliff above. There's not that much to see once you've strolled the prom and gone to the end of the pier or taken a dip in the sea, but you certainly wouldn't be aware of its port activities if you just stayed in this part of town, apart from the distant cranes on the skyline. Bear in mind, too, the waterside village of **Felixstowe Ferry**, where you can take a foot ferry across the Deben river-mouth to Bawdsey on the far side.

6

The seafront and town centre

Felixstowe's **seafront** is a classic English affair, with well-tended gardens and a promenade lined by mainly Edwardian hotels and B&Bs along Sea Road and Undercliff Road West. There's a run-down **pier** and a hideous leisure centre, but none of the seaside tack you'll

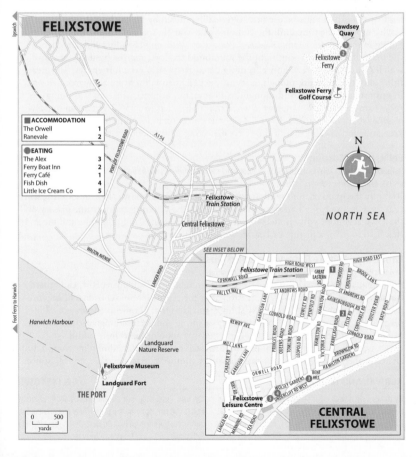

find in, say, Yarmouth, and there's even a hut selling fresh fish near the pier. Close by *The Alex* (see opposite), Bent Hill winds up to the **town centre** – similarly ordinary, focused on a partly pedestrianized shop-lined main street (Hamilton Road), and giving way to a quiet suburban network of Edwardian streets that spreads out on both sides.

The port

Bus #77 from the Orwell Hotel

Most of Felixstowe's sights – such as they are – are in the area around the **port**, an area that has its own unique appeal (ⓦdiscoverlandguard.org.uk). You can watch the ships passing from a viewpoint right by the docks, in the shadow of giant dockside cranes, joining the locals to gaze out across the channel to Essex while sipping tea in the excellent *Viewpoint Café*, run by the guys from *The Alex* (see opposite). You can also take the foot ferry to Harwich or Shotley Gate from here (see opposite), visit the port's old fort and tramp through the duney grasses of the nearby nature reserve.

Landguard Fort

Viewpoint Rd, IP11 3TW • April–Oct daily 10am–5pm, June–Sept till 6pm • £4, includes free audio tour; EH • ☎07749 695523, ⓦlandguard.com

The pentagon-shaped **Landguard Fort** guards the estuaries of the Orwell and Stour, and dates mainly from the early eighteenth century, although there were fortifications at least two hundred years before that. Originally ordered by Henry VIII, it was on active service most of the time until the end of World War II. You can wander around at will, taking in the barrack rooms, soldiers' washrooms, the long corridors and chambers of the magazine stores that run right the way round the fort, and the bastions up above, which give a good idea of how effective a defensive position the fort enjoys. The great thing about Landguard, though, is its untouched quality: there are a few mannequins in uniform and a small exhibition on its history, but otherwise its empty, echoing rooms are kept much as they were when the soldiers left in 1956, right down to a few original sticks of furniture. Even the eighteenth-century clock on the wall of the outer keep still works – almost as if they were expecting to resume operations here one day.

Felixstowe Museum

Viewpoint Rd, IP11 7JG • June–Sept Wed & Sun 1–5.30pm, also Thurs in Aug; Oct–May Sun & bank hols 1–5.30pm • £2 • ☎01394 674355, ⓦfelixstowemuseum.org

Right by the main channel, **Felixstowe Museum** is an enthusiastically-run local museum that focuses on nearby Landguard Fort and both the seafaring and wartime history of the town and port, with model aircraft and ships, paintings and other bits and pieces that help to paint a picture of Felixstowe past and present.

Landguard Nature Reserve and Bird Observatory

Viewpoint Rd, IP11 3TW • Open 24hr • ☎01394 673782, ⓦlbo.org.uk

Stretching along the coast in both directions from behind Landguard Fort, **Landguard Nature Reserve** makes for a pleasant stroll after the claustrophobic corridors of the fort itself, a stretch of grassy, hummocky shingle and sand that's home to an array of edible plants – sea kale, sea rocket – plus a variety of spring and autumn migratory birds, and in summer ringed plovers, which you can view (by appointment) from a bird observatory. It's an odd location, part nature reserve, part military dumping ground, but an atmospheric and unique spot that shows yet another side to multifaceted Felixstowe.

ARRIVAL AND DEPARTURE   **FELIXSTOWE**

By train Felixstowe's train station is at the top end of Hamilton Rd, and is accessible on foot through Great Eastern Square. It's the end of the line, so the only connections are with Ipswich (hourly; 25min).

By bus Buses stop outside the train station, at Great Eastern Square, opposite the *Orwell Hotel* on Hamilton Rd, and just to the north on High Rd West. Destinations include Felixstowe Docks and Felixstowe Ferry (both every 30min;

both 15 min), Ipswich (every 15min; 40min) and Woodbridge (every 2hr; 35min).

By boat Perhaps the nicest way to arrive in Felixstowe is by foot ferry. You can catch it in Bawdsey, just across the river from Felixstowe Ferry (every 30min: April & Oct 10am–5pm; May–Sept 10am–6pm; £1.80 one-way, £2.50 return; with bikes £3.50/£5; ☎07709 411511), or from Shotley Gate/Harwich across the river from Felixstowe Docks (May–Aug daily roughly every 2hr; 9am–5.15pm; Easter & Sept weekends only; Harwich–Felixstowe £6 one-way, £8 return; with bike £8/£10; ☎07919 911440, ☞harwichharbourferry.com).

INFORMATION AND TOURS

Tours The same people who run the foot and cycle ferries across Felixstowe harbour also run harbour cruises between Felixstowe and Harwich, ranging from a 10min trip around the harbour (£4) to a 35min trip to Harwich and back (£6). You must book in advance. More info on ☎07919 911440, ☞harwichharbourferry.com.

6

ACCOMMODATION

Orwell Hotel Hamilton Rd, IP11 7DX ☎01394 285511, ☞theorwellhotel.co.uk. At the top end of the high street, this resolutely traditional hotel, housed in a grand red-brick building 5–10min walk from the seafront, has sixty nice en-suite double rooms. With palatial and beautifully maintained public areas, a wood-panelled bar and a restaurant, the hotel is perfectly in tune with the Edwardian ambience of this part of Felixstowe. **£75**

EATING

The Alex 123 Undercliff Rd West, IP11 2AF ☎01394 282958, ☞alexcafebar.co.uk. Popular seafront place serving excellent food all day in its downstairs café and posher, more substantial meals in its upstairs brasserie – oysters, steaks, burgers and lots of fish and seafood. The café does all-day breakfasts, club sandwiches, fish and chips and burgers for around £9. Upstairs, starters are around £6, mains £12.95–16.95, plus they do a set lunch during the week (two courses £13, three courses £17). There's always a crowd, and it's the buzziest place in Felixstowe by some way, with a sea-facing outside terrace. Brasserie daily noon–9.30pm, Fri & Sat till 10pm; café daily 9.30am–11pm.

Fish Dish 69–71 Undercliff Rd, IP11 2AD ☎01394 670202, ☞myfishdish.co.uk. They call themselves a modern fish and chip restaurant, and that's exactly what they are – not only serving immaculate fish and chips with all the trimmings but lots of other less traditional fish dishes too, including charcoal-grilled sea bass and sea bream, fish pie, salt and pepper squid and plenty of veggie and meaty stuff too, much of it also cooked over charcoal. Good prices as well – fish and chips from £7.50, other mains around £13. Mon–Thurs & Sun 11.30am–7.45pm, Fri & Sat 11.30am–8.45pm.

Little Ice Cream Co 59–61 Undercliff Rd West, IP11 2AD ☎01394 670500, ☞littleicecream.co.uk. On the seafront opposite the leisure centre this coffee shop (with another branch in Colchester) does home-made ice cream in loads of flavours plus cakes, waffles and light lunches – sandwiches, quesadillas, tuna melts and BLTs, all for a fiver or so. Mon–Fri 10am–5.30pm, Sat 10am–8pm.

Felixstowe Ferry

Bus #76 from Great Eastern Square, Felixstowe to Western Ave, then a 10min walk

On the opposite side of central Felixstowe to the port, about a mile north of Felixstowe proper, the town's most appealing enclave is the tiny village of **Felixstowe Ferry**, marked by a couple of Martello towers, a huddle of houses, beach huts and boatyards as well as a wet fish shop (**Springtide Fish**), café and pub. You can take the **foot ferry** from here across to Bawdsey (see above), where the *Boatyard Café* does tea and snacks at lunchtime.

EATING

★**Ferry Boat Inn** IP11 9RZ ☎01394 284203, ☞ferryboatinn.org.uk. This fifteenth-century inn sits picturesquely on the village green facing the sea wall. It's a cosy pub, with a low-beamed interior and lots of different nooks and corners, fine for a drink but also very popular for food, with a large menu featuring fish and chips for around £12.75, pies and steaks, chicken curry and – when in season – mussels; baguettes and a good ploughman's complete the picture. Tables outside and on the green beyond. Kitchen Mon–Sat noon–2pm & 6.30–9pm, Sun noon–2pm & 6–8.30pm; pub Mon–Fri 11am–3pm & 5.30–11pm, Sat 11am–11pm, Sun noon–10.30pm.

Ferry Café IP11 9RZ ☎01394 276305. This immaculately painted and very popular shack by the ferry quay in Felixstowe Ferry has a slightly retro, US-diner feel and does good fish and chips (cheaper than the pub), along with breakfasts, burgers and sandwiches. Sandwiches from £5, burgers and fish from £8. Daily 9am–5pm.

The Suffolk coast

THE SCALLOP, ALDEBURGH BEACH

The Suffolk coast

The Suffolk coast feels a little detached from the rest of the county: the road and rail lines from Ipswich to Lowestoft funnel traffic a few miles inland for most of the way, along the busy A12, while patches of marsh, heath and woodland make the separation still more complete. It's a wilder region than you might expect, but it's also home to established resorts like Aldeburgh and Southwold, whose worldly charms are an appealing contrast to the more remote delights of Orford Ness and Dunwich, and the nature reserves at Dunwich Heath and Minsmere. There are other, cultural highlights too – the earthen mounds of Sutton Hoo, the medieval delights of Blythburgh and Framlingham and the Cold War spookiness of Rendlesham Forest. But the entire coast and its hinterland repays a visit: it's one of Britain's most diverse and untouched regions.

The coast really starts with **Felixstowe** (see p.235), although you can go no further than this without taking the first of the Suffolk coast's many foot ferries across the Deben River (see p.254). Across the river, **Bawdsey** is famous as the home of the last war's radar efforts, and is just a few miles from the unashamedly parochial town of **Woodbridge** – which is close to the Anglo-Saxon burial mounds of **Sutton Hoo** and the wilds of **Rendlesham Forest**. Further north, there's the relative isolation of tiny **Orford** and the nature reserves you can reach from its harbour, and beyond here the upmarket resort of **Aldeburgh**, famed for its links with Benjamin Britten and the **Aldeburgh Festival** – East Anglia's most compelling cultural gathering, which takes place every June at nearby **Snape Maltings**.

North of Aldeburgh, **Thorpeness** is an odd, purpose-built Edwardian resort village, while nearby **Leiston**, just inland, adds a dose of grit to the coast's predominantly genteel pleasures, a small town that flourished during the nineteenth-century Industrial Revolution and now supports the power station at nearby **Sizewell**, where two nuclear facilities are oddly plonked among the dunes and woods of Sizewell beach. Nearby **Saxmundham** is a pleasant small town and major rail hub, while **Framlingham**, a few miles west of the A12 artery, is the region's most alluring market town, with a fantastic castle and a pleasantly prosperous centre with a handful of enticing places to eat. Back on the coastal strip, between Sizewell and Southwold, lies perhaps the most appealing stretch of Suffolk's coast, a wildish area of heath, marsh and woodland around the RSPB reserve at **Minsmere** and the

Highlights

❶ **Sutton Hoo, Woodbridge** One of the country's most evocative and best Anglo-Saxon sites, well preserved and explained by the National Trust. **See p.246**

❷ **Framlingham** A few miles inland from the coast, this market town represents the essence of provincial Suffolk, and has a couple of great attractions to boot. **See p.250**

❸ **Fish huts, Aldeburgh** There's nothing quite like choosing and buying fish from the seafront at Aldeburgh then going home and cooking it up for tea. **See p.254**

❹ **Minsmere** This RSPB reserve gets busy, but somehow soaks up people into its glorious mixture of reedbeds, woodland and heath. **See p.266**

❺ **Holy Trinity, Blythburgh** This landmark building is one of Suffolk's finest churches, with wonderfully preserved medieval features. **See p.273**

❻ **Oulton Broad** Lowestoft's watery heart, and a perfect introduction to the glories of the Broads further north. **See p.278**

HIGHLIGHTS ARE MARKED ON THE MAP ON P.242

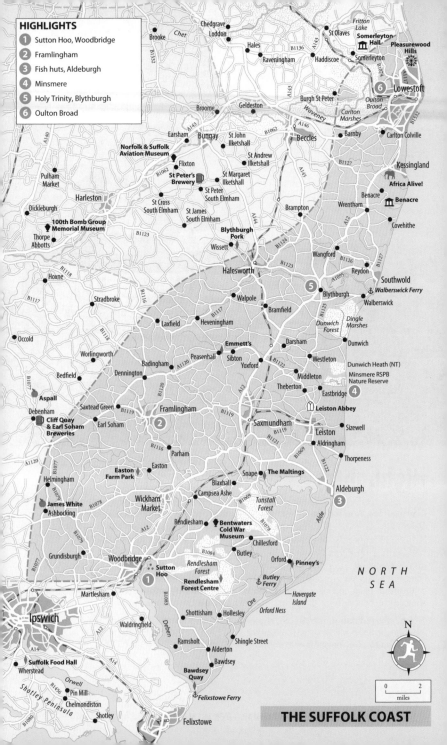

THE SUFFOLK COAST

WALKING THE COAST: TWO LONG-DISTANCE FOOTPATHS

The most obvious footpath through the Suffolk coastal region is the 50-mile-long **Suffolk Coast Path**, which must be the only footpath in Britain that starts with a ferry crossing, beginning as it does in Felixstowe Ferry and resuming on the other side in Bawdsey. It then heads up Orford, inland to Snape – it also, despite the name, doesn't always follow the coast – and then back out to Aldeburgh, from where it pretty much sticks to the coastline as far as Lowestoft. The other long-distance path is the delightful **Sandlings Walk**, a 55-mile-long path that begins in Southwold, where it connects with the Suffolk Coast Path, and heads south on a more inland route, through forest and heathland mainly, passing through Dunwich Heath, Snape, Rendlesham Forest and ending up in Ipswich.

National Trust-owned **Dunwich Heath** – great walking country at any time of year. **Dunwich** itself was the Felixstowe of the Middle Ages, but got swallowed up by the sea long ago and now lies mostly beneath the waves. But it's a lovely spot, and is only an hour or so's walk along the coast from the pretty village of **Walberswick**, popular for its beach, its yearly crabbing festival and the foot ferry to the outskirts of **Southwold**. This is Suffolk's largest and most popular resort, with the most all-round metropolitan vibe of the entire coast, full of Londoners dreaming of relocating, and some decent hotels and restaurants.

Just inland, at the head of the deep Blyth estuary, **Blythburgh**'s church, with its enormous tower, is a landmark for miles around, and the most impressive medieval monument along the coast. Further inland still, **Halesworth** is, like Framlingham, the epitome of the self-sufficient Suffolk market town, while further up the coast grim reality takes over in **Lowestoft**, where the fishing industry limps on manfully alongside the town's ailing resort business, neither with a great deal of conviction. However, even Lowestoft is not entirely without interest, with a number of attractions both in and around the town, and up towards the Norfolk border. It's also the jumping-off point for **Oulton Broad** and the Broads in general (see p.278).

Woodbridge and around

If you came to England for the first time and only went to **WOODBRIDGE**, you would go away with a skewed but not entirely false sense of modern Britain. The town claims to be the best place to live in the country (though it has a few rivals for that in Suffolk alone); it was voted among the top foodie destinations in the UK by *Country Living* magazine a few years back; and it generally wins praise and plaudits for the easy-going, locally focused pace of life. Naturally, the folk of Woodbridge want to keep all this to themselves, and in truth it's perhaps a better place to live than to visit, with a small and low-key selection of things to see. But its small centre is unspoilt and walkable, with an array of independent shops and cafés, good pubs and a couple of excellent places to stay, and an enticing riverside area down by the much-photographed Tide Mill. It's also within easy reach of **Sutton Hoo**, the most important Anglo-Saxon archeological site in the country.

Market Hill and around

The centre of Woodbridge focuses on the main shopping street of the **Thoroughfare** and, at the top of Church Street, **Market Hill**, a small square gathered around the Dutch-looking **Shire Hall**, built by Thomas Seckford in 1575. He was a confidante and courtier of Elizabeth I, and he lived for a while in the Tudor building next door to St Mary's church – now home to Abbey School – before moving out of town to sumptuous Seckford Hall (now a hotel – see p.245).

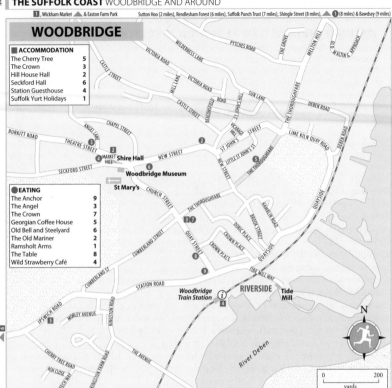

Wickham Market, & Easton Farm Park   Sutton Hoo (2 miles), Rendlesham Forest (6 miles), Suffolk Punch Trust (7 miles), Shingle Street (8 miles), (8 miles) & Bawdsey (9 miles)

WOODBRIDGE

ACCOMMODATION
The Cherry Tree	5
The Crown	3
Hill House Hall	2
Seckford Hall	4
Station Guesthouse	6
Suffolk Yurt Holidays	1

EATING
The Anchor	9
The Angel	3
The Crown	7
Georgian Coffee House	5
Old Bell and Steelyard	6
The Old Mariner	2
Ramsholt Arms	1
The Table	8
Wild Strawberry Café	4

Woodbridge Museum

5a Market Hill, IP12 4AU • Easter to late Oct Thurs–Sun 10am–4pm, daily during school hols • £1 • ☎ 01394 380502

Opposite the Shire Hall, **Woodbridge Museum** is just a couple of rooms really, with Anglo-Saxon finds from nearby excavations at Butley and a case of displays on Sutton Hoo, with replicas of the finds and a model of the ship, plus exhibits relating to Thomas Seckford (see opposite). There are also sections on the war years, and the second half of the twentieth century, when Woodbridge became, in the words of the museum, "the perfect place to live".

St Mary's

11 Market Hill, IP12 4LU • ⓦ stmaryswoodbridge.org

At the top of Church Street, just off Market Hill, Woodbridge's parish church of **St Mary** is a flint Gothic building from the mid-fifteenth century. Inside it has an octagonal font decorated with reliefs depicting the seven sacraments and the Crucifixion, which sits in the corner along with the painted wooden panels from the church's original rood screen, now preserved behind glass.

Riverside

Woodbridge is situated on a river, the Deben – in days gone by its main industry was shipbuilding – but you could spend a day here and not know it. The **Riverside** lies apart from the centre, on the far side of the railway tracks. It's no less picturesque for

BIKE HIRE ON THE COAST

What better way can there be to tour the Suffolk Coast than by bike? The great thing about **Suffolk Cycle Hire** (☎01394 461166, ⓦsuffolkcyclehire.co.uk) is that, although you can rent their bikes directly from their base in Rendlesham, they also deliver to lots of locations up and down the Suffolk coast, from Woodbridge to Southwold. They do all sort of bikes, including touring bikes and hybrids, as well as child seats and other accessories, and provide handy route maps of the region. You do need to book in advance, however – prices start at £15 a day for a regular adult bike, plus delivery.

that, and serves as a marina for Woodbridge's yachties, but has managed to avoid being overly spruced up. The exception is the beautifully refurbished white bulk of the late eighteenth-century clapboard **Tide Mill** (Easter–Sept daily 11am–5pm; £4, families £9), which once again has a fully functioning water wheel and houses a small museum, with a mixture of exhibits and a short film about the mill. They also have a glassed-in booth with window seats for watching the birds on the river.

7

ARRIVAL AND DEPARTURE

WOODBRIDGE

By train Woodbridge is on the main Ipswich–Lowestoft line, and its train station is down in the riverside part of the centre.
Destinations (trains hourly): Ipswich (18min); Lowestoft (1hr 10min); Oulton Broad (1hr 30min); Saxmundham (20min); Wickham Market (10min).
By bus Buses stop outside the railway station among other places. There are several, services to Ipswich, and the #62

bus runs to Wickham Market (8 daily; 10min), Framlingham (8 daily; 25min) and Saxmundham (4 daily; 45min). Other destinations include Aldeburgh (#63; roughly hourly; 1hr), Leiston (#64; roughly hourly; 40min), Orford (#71; 3 daily; 40min), Sutton Hoo (#73a; 1 daily; 10min & #71; 3 daily; 15min) and Rendlesham (#65; 7 daily; 20min).

ACCOMMODATION

IN TOWN

The Cherry Tree 73 Cumberland St, IP12 4AG ☎01394 384627, ⓦthecherrytreepub.co.uk. Friendly, family-run pub on the edge of the centre, serving well-cooked pub food lunchtime and evenings and with three very nicely furnished rooms fashioned out of a clapboard barn in the back garden, one of which is large enough for a family. Flat-screen TVs and parking, a 5min walk from Market Hill. **£110**
★**The Crown** Thoroughfare, corner of Quay St, IP12 1AD ☎01394 384242, ⓦthecrownatwoodbridge .co.uk. This updated pub, hotel and restaurant has ten double bedrooms, each individually designed with fresh and simple colours and a deliberately coastal, almost New England feel. There's a great restaurant and comfy bar downstairs, too, which serves a very good breakfast. **£120**
★**Hill House Hall** 30 Market Hill, IP12 4LU ☎01394 383890, ⓦhillhousehall.com. Right on the main square, this hotel has the town's best and certainly most central location, and is certainly its most historic, a thirteenth-century building that was upgraded in Tudor times. There are two double rooms, both with very comfy beds, and the beams and rickety floors are lovingly watched over by owner Sarenka Knight, who will tell you all about the building. Oddly, the *Sunday Times* reckoned it one of the 100 best places to stay in the world in 2011. **£85**
Station Guesthouse Station Rd, IP12 4AU ☎01394 384831, ⓦwoodbridgestationguesthouse.co.uk. Four

simple but very comfortable B&B rooms above the excellent *Whistle Stop Café* at Woodbridge train station, and the nice thing is you get a view of the river as well as the trains. **£75**

OUT OF TOWN

Seckford Hall Great Bealings, Woodbridge, IP13 6NU ☎01394 385678, ⓦseckford.co.uk. Just outside town across the A12, Seckford Hall was the home of Thomas Seckford, a high-ranking official at the court of Elizabeth I and a local philanthropist, and his marvellously preserved sixteenth-century seat was converted some time ago to a country-house hotel that does a good job of retaining the building's age and atmosphere while providing a decent degree of comfort. There's a lovely wood-panelled sitting room and beautiful gardens, and the guest rooms are very comfortable, most of them with recently refurbished bathrooms. There are some larger and more contemporary rooms and suites in the courtyard buildings opposite the entrance, where there's also a pool in the beautifully converted beamed barn. **£150**
★**Suffolk Yurt Holidays** Ufford Rd, Bredfield, IP13 6AR, ☎07907 964890, ⓦsuffolkyurtholidays.co.uk. In a very tranquil setting a few miles north of Woodbridge, these five spacious, beautifully furnished and well-equipped yurts provide as comfortable and peaceful a place to stay as you'll find anywhere in Suffolk. Minimum two-night stay. **£105**

EATING

IN TOWN

The Anchor 19 Quay St, IP12 1BX ☏01394 382649, ⓦtheanchorwoodbridge.co.uk. A great local pub just across the street from Woodbridge's quayside and station, whose various rooms make it not only a good place for a drink but a nice place to eat too, with a simple menu of pub grub staples that are a cut above the norm – burgers, bangers and mash, duck breast, cod fillet – all for £10–12 a dish; there are usually a few specials too. Always busy and very friendly. Kitchen Mon–Wed noon–2.30pm & 6–9pm, Thurs–Sat noon–2.30pm & 6–9.30pm, Sun noon–2.30pm & 6–9pm; pub Mon–Sat noon–11.30pm, Sun noon–10.30pm.

The Angel 2 Theatre St, IP12 4NE ☏01394 382660, ⓦtheangelwoodbridge.co.uk. Convivial pub with an area of comfy sofas and another, more traditional section, where you can enjoy its simple menu of sandwiches and bar snacks, fish and chips, sausage and mash, steaks and a few veggie dishes – easy stuff, but all locally sourced and beautifully cooked, good value for £10 a main dish. They usually have an interesting special or two as well – try the mussels and chips if they're on. They also stock a vast collection of spirits, including one of the world's largest collections of different gins. Kitchen Mon–Sat noon–2.30pm & 6–9pm, Sun noon–2.30pm; pub Mon–Thurs noon–3pm & 5–11pm, Fri noon–3pm & 5pm–midnight, Sat noon–midnight, Sun noon–10.30pm.

★**The Crown** Thoroughfare, corner of Quay St, IP12 1AD ☏01394 384242, ⓦthecrownatwoodbridge.co.uk. A really good, well-established hotel restaurant with great modern British food and a passionate attachment to English traditions and local suppliers, with fish and seafood from Lowestoft and local marsh-grazing lamb and beef. Considering the quality, it's not that expensive either, with starters from £7.50 and mains for £12.50–18. Rightly listed as one of the country's top fifty gastropubs in the *Independent* a few years back. Kitchen daily noon–3pm & 6–10pm; brunch served Sat & Sun 10am–noon.

Georgian Coffee House 47a Thoroughfare, IP12 1AH ☏01394 387292, ⓦgeorgiancoffeehouse.co.uk. Small café in the heart of town that's nothing special but makes for a handy place for jackets, sandwiches and light lunches – the latter around £7. Mon–Sat 9am–5pm.

Old Bell and Steelyard 103 New St, IP12 1DZ ☏01394 382933, ⓦyeoldebellandsteelyard.co.uk. Great old timbered pub in a crooked building dating from 1549, with good beer, a garden and a games room with bar billiards and more. A good, simple menu, too, with pub grub staples from £9.95. Ask about the daily specials. Kitchen Mon–Sat noon–2pm & 7–9pm, Sun noon–2pm; Mon–Fri 11.30am–3pm & 5–11.30pm, Sat 11.30am–12.30am, Sun noon–11pm.

The Old Mariner 26 New St, IP12 1DX ☏01394 382679, ⓦtheoldmariner.co.uk. Cosy old pub that serves food lunch and evening and usually has a wide choice of ales to enjoy in an interior of old quarry-tiled floor and ochre, nicotine-stained walls covered with rugby and nautical memorabilia. Food too – a basic pub grub menu and a tapas menu. Kitchen Tues–Sat noon–2pm & 6–9pm, Sun noon–2.30pm; pub Mon–Sat 11am–11pm, Sun noon–10.30pm.

The Table 3 Quay St, IP12 1BX, ☏01394 382428, ⓦthetablewoodbridge.co.uk. This brasserie-style restaurant is a good place for breakfast, lunch or dinner, with coffee and pastries in the morning, light lunches (minute steaks, salads) and a dinner menu of three or four starters and mains in the evening – pork and duck hash or potted crayfish followed by ribeye steak or lamb curry. Seating inside and out in the pleasant courtyard. Mon 10.30am–3pm, Tues–Sat 10.30am–3pm & 6–9pm, Sun noon–3pm.

Wild Strawberry Café 19a Market Hill, IP12 4LX ☏01394 388881, ⓦwildstrawberrycafe.co.uk. Good coffee, breakfasts and lunches are served in this bright modern café right on Woodbridge's main square. Mon–Fri 8am–5pm, Sat 9am–4pm; breakfast 8am–noon, lunch noon–2.30pm.

OUT OF TOWN

★**Ramsholt Arms** Dock Rd, Ramsholt, IP13 3AB ☏01394 411229, ⓦtheramsholtarms.com. About five miles south of Woodbridge, this riverside pub at Ramsholt (see box, p.248) sits right on the Deben estuary, with big picture windows overlooking the water, a homely, dog-friendly place with a large terrace and decent food – sandwiches and sharing platters, lots of fish dishes for £10–13, a children's menu and usually a few specials too. Hours vary by season (check website). Kitchen Mon noon–2.30pm, Tues–Sat noon–2.30pm & 6–9pm; pub Mon–Wed noon–5pm, Thurs & Fri noon–10pm, Sat 11am–11pm, Sun 11am–8pm.

Sutton Hoo

Tranmer House, IP12 3DJ • Jan to mid-March & Nov–Dec Sat & Sun 11am–4pm; mid-March to Oct daily 10.30am–5pm • £7.90, families £19.50, guided walks £2.50; NT • ☏01394 389700, ⓦnationaltrust.org.uk/sutton-hoo

About three miles outside Woodbridge, off the Orford road on the far side of the River Deben, **Sutton Hoo** – "hoo" means promontory or headland in ancient local dialect – is perhaps the most important Anglo-Saxon archeological site in the country. Now owned by the National Trust, it was discovered by local landowner Edith Pretty and amateur archeologist Basil Brown in 1939, who excavated a number of burial mounds in the remote countryside here, unearthing the forty-oar burial ship of an Anglo-Saxon warrior king, packed with his most valuable possessions, from a splendid iron and tinted-bronze helmet through to his intricately worked gold and jewelled ornaments. It's now believed to be the tomb of Raedwald, king of East Anglia, who died in 624.

The focus is the **exhibition hall**, where a very well mounted series of displays includes a mock-up of how they think the king may have been laid in his ship, although sadly there's not much in the way of treasure, as most of this is kept in the British Museum (including the famous helmet you see on all the Sutton Hoo posters). A short film tells the story of the finds and the Anglo-Saxons in general, and there are details of what was found in the other mounds, including another young warrior buried with his weapons and his horse next to him – his sword, belt buckles, even a comb, are on display. Next door to the exhibition hall, a **visitor centre** houses a ticket office, shop and café.

The **site** itself, just a short walk from the visitor centre, is very atmospheric, and there are a couple of viewing platforms, one right by the mound where they discovered the ship (which would have been hauled up from the river, several hundred feet below), and a couple of marked loop walks right around the entire site.

Suffolk Punch Trust

Hollesley, IP12 3JR • Late March to Oct Mon & Wed–Sun 10.30am–4pm (late May to mid-Sept till 5pm) • £9 • ☎ 01394 411327, Ⓦ suffolkpunchtrust.org

Just outside the village of Hollesley, about eight miles from Woodbridge, the **Suffolk Punch Trust** is a charity devoted to the breeding and preservation of the Suffolk Punch horse – a sturdy working breed that was used widely in agriculture for two centuries until farms became mechanized, and which has been bred at the stud farm here for over two hundred years. You can view the horses in a series of fields, paddocks and stables, along with rare breed pigs and other farm animals, farming equipment and a museum that harks back to the golden age of these magnificent creatures. There's a café, and all sorts of activities for kids – tractor rides, a petting area and more, making it well worth the stop.

Bawdsey

To the south of Sutton Hoo, about ten miles from Woodbridge, the village of **BAWDSEY** sits almost at the end of the main road, and as such feels like the back of beyond – a mood only enhanced by the shady churchyard of its church, **St Mary the Virgin**. Inside are memorials to the local Quilter family, who lived in nearby Bawdsey Manor, and the Cavells who occupied Bawdsey Hall, including a short spiel on Edith Cavell (see p.44). Look also at the Bawdsey altar frontal, embroidered with figures of God, Jesus and various saints in thirteenth-century Flanders (though the bolder stitching is Victorian).

Bawdsey Manor

Bawdsey, IP12 3AZ • **Transmitter block** Occasional Sat, Sun & Mon April–Sept 12.30–4.30pm • £4, children free • ☎ 07821 162879, Ⓦ bawdseyradar.org.uk

Just outside the village, **Bawdsey Manor** looks older than it is, a Victorian Gothic mansion built in the 1870s by William Quilter as a lavish holiday home, and which in 1936 became the secret Ministry of Defence research establishment that developed radar under Robert Watson Watt – an invention without which, arguably, the Allies would have lost World War II. It occupies a fantastic location, hugging a gorgeous stretch of the coast and overlooking the Deben estuary. Unfortunately it's now used for conferences and functions and is pretty much off-limits to the public – although you can see the main house and extensive gardens on the occasional guided tour. The concrete bunker of the original **transmitter block**, which played a crucial role in the Battle of Britain, is open sporadically though.

> **A WALK ALONG THE DEBEN ESTUARY**
>
> About five miles south of Woodbridge, **Ramsholt** is not so much a village as a handful of houses above a great riverside pub. You can do a shortish **walk** (45min–1hr) from the **Ramsholt Arms** (see p.246) following the estuary inland from the pub and then up into the woods after about a mile. Bear right in the woods, keeping the sandy quarry to your left, before joining a farm track to the round-towered church of **All Saints**. Take a right here, back towards the river, and then edge the fields before turning right again, following the signs through the woods and a few houses to join up with the main road above the *Ramsholt Arms*.

Bawdsey Quay

A mile or so from the village of Bawdsey, **Bawdsey Quay** is no more than a strip of houses, a small visitor centre and the grounds of Bawdsey Manor looking across the mouth of the Deben River to old Felixstowe. You can take the foot ferry to the other side, though you may need to hail the boatman from the quay; there is car parking on the quay and in the woods behind, and food at the **Boathouse Café** (March, April & Nov Fri–Sun 11am–5pm; May–Oct Mon & Thurs–Sun 11am–5pm; ⓦboathousecafe.co.uk).

Rendlesham Forest

Rendlesham Forest Centre, IP12 3NF · Daily dawn–dusk · Car park £3.50 all day · ⓦ forestry.gov.uk/rendlesham

Immediately east of Woodbridge, **Rendlesham Forest** is a Forestry Commission-owned stretch of coniferous woodland and heath – a beautiful area that's great walking, cycling and indeed camping country. The forest hit the national headlines in 1980 when were a series of UFO sightings here that have since passed into the folklore of conspiracy theories, partly because it is near Bentwaters USAF base and RAF Woodbridge.

The **Rendlesham Forest Centre** has parking and a small information centre with leaflets detailing a "UFO Trail", bike rental and forest camping nearby, and is a convergence point for bike trails and footpaths (there are three detailed circular routes you can do from here) – although the forest has any number of other car parks and clearings where you can park up and hike off into the woods.

ACCOMMODATION   RENDLESHAM FOREST

Forest Camping Butley, IP12 3NF ☎ 01394 450707, ⓦ forestcamping.co.uk. Lovely, dog-friendly campsite with good facilities, yet surrounded by the forest. Two people, car and a tent **£19**

Bentwaters Cold War Museum

Building 134, Bentwaters Park, Rendlesham, IP12 2TW · End April to early Oct first & third Sun of each month 10am–4pm · £5 · ☎ 07588 877020, ⓦ bcwm.org.uk

Housed in the former control tower, bang in the middle of the airfield that formerly served both the USAF and RAF Woodbridge, the **Bentwaters Cold War Museum** only serves to enhance the atmosphere of military secrecy that hangs over this part of Suffolk. Here you'll find operations rooms, mostly fitted with original equipment, that not only functioned during World War II and the Cold War but also as recently as 1986, when the US bombed Colonel Gaddaffi's complex in Libya, and during the first Gulf War.

Shingle Street

About eight miles southeast of Woodbridge, across the marshes on the far side of the village of Hollesley, **SHINGLE STREET** is a very desolate place. Its name is a misnomer as it's probably the only settlement in Suffolk without streets of any kind – just a long line of bungalows and cottages facing directly onto the beach and the North Sea. Until a

---

LIGHTS IN THE NIGHT: THE RENDLESHAM FOREST AFFAIR

No one outside of Suffolk would have heard of Rendlesham Forest if it wasn't for the events of December 1980, when on an evening before Christmas a number of air-force personnel witnessed strange lights in the trees and a "craft" or "object" with triangular landing gear. Since dubbed "**Britain's Roswell**", it was at first thought that an aircraft had crashed in the trees. The police were called but apparently could not find no evidence of anything much, claiming that the lights must have been those from nearby Orford Ness lighthouse. The site was revisited on Boxing Day and then again two days later, when scorch marks were discovered on the trees, higher levels of radiation recorded and more lights seen, but again nothing was done – and nothing was reported or revealed about the sightings until a couple of years later, when a memo by a local base commander, Colonel Charles Halt (the so-called "Halt Memo") was made public. It referred to the sightings in quite a lot of detail, mentioning how long the lights remained in the air (several hours) and the depressions that were found where the craft was said to have landed. Halt clearly felt that something unusual had been going on, and couldn't explain what it was.

To this day the incident has not been officially investigated, and this has of course allowed the conspiracy theories to flourish; but it's worth noting that as recently as 2010 Colonel Halt, now retired, defended his memo, claiming the sightings had been deliberately covered up by the MOD, USAF and the local police. There are many who believe that it was the cover-up of some sort of secret military exercise rather than UFOs, and it hasn't helped that the MOD recently admitted that a number of files relating to the incident had "disappeared". What really happened in Rendlesham will probably never be known, but there's no doubt that it's fun to speculate, and many do – see ⓦianridpath.com/ufo/rendlesham.htm or ⓦuk-ufo.org/condign/rendsec.htm, if only to see just how long a story like this can run (and run, and run…). You could also take one of the UFO trails that run through the woods from the Forest Centre (see opposite).

7

---

series of top secret documents were declassified in 1992, well before their official 2021 expiry date, all sorts of rumours circulated about Shingle Street, most luridly that around three thousand German soldiers, part of an attempted invasion force, were killed in a firefight here. Most of this has proved to be wartime propaganda, and what actually happened during World War II was not that remarkable, though a little scandalous: Shingle Street was forcibly evacuated in 1940 in anticipation of a German invasion, and three years later was a venue for the testing of new, experimental bombs. After the war it was deemed uninhabitable because of the number of mines that had been laid on its beach, and it wasn't until the late 1940s that these were cleared and people began to drift back. It has never regained the prosperity it once had, and is now mainly made up of holiday homes. You may find its eerie isolation compelling and even addictive, but without a holiday home of your own there's not much to keep you here, and you may be glad to head back inland to relative civilization.

Wickham Market

Not much more than a large village really, **WICKHAM MARKET** lies just off the A12, a few miles to the north of Woodbridge. It has a pretty main square that's home to most of the town's commercial activity, and its spiritual activity too, in the shape of the nearby church of **All Saints**, with its spired hexagonal tower. There's little else to Wickham Market, but there are some good places to stay nearby and just outside is the family attraction of **Easton Farm Park**.

Easton Farm Park

Easton, IP13 0EQ • Mid-March to Sept daily 10.30am–6pm, half-term daily 10.30am–4pm, Christmas hols daily 11am–3pm • **Farmers' markets** Fourth Sat of the month • £8.75, children £7.75, family tickets £31 • ☏ 01728 746475, ⓦ eastonfarmpark.co.uk

Just a few miles outside Woodbridge on the far side of the A12, this kid-friendly farm is a popular day out for families, with goats, sheep and rare breed cattle, Suffolk Punch horses, train and cart rides. It's a full-on affair for the most part, with lots of activities for kids of all ages, but it does also have attractive trails through the meadows by the river.

ARRIVAL AND DEPARTURE WICKHAM MARKET

By train Wickham Market's station is on the Ipswich–Lowestoft line and is situated three miles outside the town in the village of Campsea Ashe.
Destinations There are hourly trains to Ipswich (18min); Lowestoft (1hr 10min); Oulton Broad (1hr 30min); Saxmundham (20min); Woodbridge (10min).

By bus There are bus connections with Ipswich (lots of alternatives), Woodbridge (8 daily; 10min), Framlingham (8 daily; 15min), Saxmundham (#62; 4 daily; 35min), Aldeburgh (#63; roughly hourly; 45min), Leiston (#64; roughly hourly; 30min).

ACCOMMODATION

Orchard Campsite 28 Spring Lane, IP13 0SJ ☎ 01728 746170, ⓦ orchardcampsite.co.uk. Just outside Wickham Market, this was judged "campsite of the year" by *Camping Magazine* a few years ago, and quite right too – it's a great, family-oriented place, set among meadows and woodland which stretch down to the river. It allows campfires, and will even sell you the wood to start your own. It also has a gypsy caravan for rent, which sleeps four, and there's free wi-fi that works across much of the site. Pitches from **£20**, gypsy caravan **£190**

Framlingham and around

FRAMLINGHAM, or "Fram", as it's known to locals, is small-town Suffolk *par excellence*, grouped around a triangular market square and with an enticing, parochial feel typical of this part of the county. For once, this is matched by a couple of heavyweight attractions at the top of its main street – the castle and parish church.

Framlingham Castle

Church St, IP13 9BP • April–Sept daily 10am–6pm; Nov–March Sat & Sun 10am–4pm • £7.20, children £4.30, family tickets £18.70; free audiotours; EH • ☎ 01728 724819, ⓦ www.english-heritage.org.uk

The crenellations of **Framlingham Castle** cut a classic shape at the top of Church Street. The castle dates from the twelfth century, and was built by the Bigod dynasty (see p.216 & p.323), later becoming the seat of the dukes of Norfolk. It's little more than a shell inside, but the curtain wall, with its thirteen towers, has survived almost intact, a splendid example of medieval military architecture, many of them topped by elegant Tudor brick chimney stacks. Unfortunately nothing remains of the castle's Great Hall, where Mary Tudor was proclaimed Queen of England in 1553; Mary was responsible for freeing the Duke of Norfolk, Thomas Howard, from the Tower (see opposite). You can get good views of the castle from the outside by following the footpaths that lead around the moat and down to and around the lake or "mere" below, where you can see across the valley to Framlingham College.

St Michael's

Fore St, IP13 9BJ • ⓦ stmichaelschurch.onesuffolk.net

The large thirteenth-century church of **St Michael** is extraordinary, not because of the building, although this is impressive enough, but for the sepulchral monuments of the **Howard family**, perhaps the finest array of monumental sixteenth-century sculpture in the country, and also a brilliant snapshot of court life and relationships during the time of the Tudors.

The church has other highlights before you get to the tombs: the fourteenth-century font in the north aisle, a seventeenth-century organ (one of only two still in use in the UK), and the roof, whose carved fan vaulting fitted around the nave windows is ingenious, and contemporary with the church. But it's the **tombs** that steal the show, at the far eastern end of the church, in a chancel that was enlarged to accommodate them in the 1400s. To the right of the high altar, the tomb of Thomas Howard, Duke of Norfolk, is surrounded by the twelve Apostles, and the niches they stand in support the praying effigies of Thomas and his wife Anne, the daughter of Edward IV. Thomas Howard lived dangerously: he was a rival to Thomas Cromwell, and indirectly sent the latter to the gallows, shortly after which Henry VIII wedded his niece Katherine. Later he had the chancel enlarged to accommodate the family tombs, and he was lucky to survive to see its completion, for in 1546 he was charged with treason and would have been executed but for the death of Henry and an eleventh-hour pardon. Not so lucky was his brother Henry Howard, in the coloured alabaster tomb on the far left (lying next to his wife Frances), executed by Henry for the same offence; hence the coronet which rests by his side, not on his head. To the left of the altar is the tomb of Henry Fitzroy, the only illegitimate son of Henry VIII the king ever acknowledged, who married Thomas Howard's daughter, Mary, in 1533.

ARRIVAL AND DEPARTURE
FRAMLINGHAM

By bus Buses stop on Bridge St/Market Place in the centre of Framlingham and there are regular connections to Saxmundham (20min) in one direction and Woodbridge (30min) in the other.

ACCOMMODATION

The Crown Market Hill, IP13 9AN ☎01728 723521, ⓦframlinghamcrown.co.uk. Right in the centre of town, this sixteenth-century coaching inn, all flagstones, oak beams and creaky floors, has fourteen rooms. They are decently furnished and nice enough, and there's a cosy bar and restaurant downstairs and a pleasant courtyard in which to while away summer evenings. **£100**

★**The Round House** 30 Station Rd, IP13 9ED ☎01728 723779, ⓦtheroundhousesuffolk.co.uk. This conversion of an eighteenth-century windmill is without question Fram's nicest place to stay, a cool and elegant B&B just a couple of minutes' walk from the centre of town – and handily close to the *Station Hotel* (see below). There are three rooms, the nicest of which is probably the Garden Room, in the Victorian Gothic extension, below which is a guests' comfy sitting room. There's an honesty bar full of booze and non-booze items and they leave a flask of milk outside your room so you can have a proper cuppa – a thoughtful touch appreciated by all those who hate hotel room UHT. **£95**

EATING AND DRINKING

Common Room Café 22 Bridge St, IP13 9AH, ☎01728 768238, ⓦthecommonroomfram.com. Great, very friendly café run by an ex-chef from the Laxfield *King's Head* (see p.276) and serving proper home-cooking in the form of big breakfasts (£6.95), wholesome lunches and restorative sandwiches (£5.95). Mon–Fri 8am–5pm, Sat 9am–5pm, Sun 9am–4pm.

Dancing Goat Café 33 Market Hill, IP13 9BA ☎01728 621434, ⓦthedancinggoatframlingham.wordpress .com. Popular joint where locals sip good coffee and munch delicious cakes, sandwiches and panini in the cosy interior or outside on the main square. Good food and very friendly service. Mon–Sat 8.45am–5pm.

Lemon Tree 3 Church St, IP13 9BE ☎01728 621232, ⓦlemontreefram.com. Long-running café-restaurant that serves a contemporary menu focused on locally sourced ingredients. Lovely breakfasts, and starters for £5–6, main courses (cheeseburgers, fish platters) for £10.50–11.50, plus sandwiches and jackets for £7.95–8.95. Mon–Wed 9am–3pm, Thurs–Sat 9am–3pm & 6.30–9pm.

★**Station Hotel** Station Rd, IP13 9EE ☎01728 723455, ⓦthestationframlingham.com. Not much from the outside, but this old pub is a real haven on the inside, with a stripped-down interior that caters for local drinkers and foodies alike. Menus change daily and are written up on the blackboards, with simpler stuff at lunch – kedgeree, burgers, liver & bacon – and slightly more refined food in the evening, such as pork belly, venison, pan-fried squid and Dover sole. Really good food and service, with the atmosphere of a home cook's front room. The small garden out the back has a pizza oven that they fire up on summer evenings, plus they serve a proper roast on Sunday. Kitchen Mon–Sat noon–2pm & 6–9pm, Sun noon– 2.30 & 7–9pm.

St Mary's, Dennington

A couple of miles north of Framlingham, **DENNINGTON** is a tiny place but is home to an intriguing church in **St Mary's**, whose medieval benches and pews sport a fantastical series of carvings showing wild and folkloric figures and beasts. In particular there is a rare representation of a sciapod, a mythical creature that avoided sunlight by shading itself with its one, large foot – according to legend, sciapods would die if they smelled contaminated air, so they carried sniffable fresh fruit around with them everywhere. Elsewhere, and equally unusual, is a rare pyx canopy over the altar (pyx was the vessel in which the Holy Sacrament was kept), one of only two such surviving canopies in Europe.

Orford and around

Some eight miles north of Woodbridge, in one of the most secluded parts of Suffolk, the tiny, eminently appealing village of **ORFORD** was, like many of the Suffolk coastal towns, a working port in the Middle Ages. Like Woodbridge, its focus now is slightly inland, its centre a generously proportioned rectangle of houses between the castle and church, while half a mile away the harbour looks out to its most famous feature, the National Trust-owned nature reserve of **Orford Ness** – the largest shingle spit in Europe – which you can reach by boat.

Orford Castle

Orford, IP12 2ND • April–Sept daily 10am–6pm; Oct daily 10am–5pm; Nov–March Sat & Sun 10am–4pm • £6.50; EH • ☎ 01394 450472, www.english-heritage.org.uk

Orford's most impressive historic building is its twelfth-century **castle**, which lies just off the main square, built on high ground by Henry II, and under siege within months of its completion from his rebellious sons during the revolt of 1173–74. Most of the castle disappeared centuries ago, and it's only the lofty keep that remains, although its impressive stature hints at the scale of the original fortifications. There are lots of levels to investigate, and you can see what's left of the chapel, various latrines, a kitchen and well, and a bakery on the roof, where you can also savour the wide views over Orford Ness from the battlements. The upper hall also holds a pocket-sized town museum, which puts some flesh on local bones, as well as describing the various uses the castle has been put to over the years and hosting displays of local archeological finds.

St Bartholomew

Church St, IP12 2LW

Besides its castle, Orford's other medieval edifice is **St Bartholomew's**, on the other side of the main square, a large church where Benjamin Britten premiered his most successful children's work, *Noye's Fludde*, as part of the 1958 Aldeburgh Festival (see box, p.260). St Bart's is mainly fourteenth century but has been much messed about with since, and the original church here was a Norman construction – the arched remains of which you can see outside the church's east end, and on the left side of the choir inside. There's also a lovely font decorated with a depiction of the Holy Trinity on one side and a beautiful pieta on the other.

WALKS AROUND ORFORD

One of the best of the many walks around Orford is the five-mile hike **north** from Orford Quay along the river wall that guards the west bank of the River Alde, returning via Ferry Road, a narrow country lane that enters the village by the *King's Head* pub. Alternatively, you can head off in the opposite direction from Orford Quay, **south** along the north bank of the Ore, turning inland after about a mile and following the path across country to the top end of the village from where you can either turn right into the village (about three miles in all), or continue on and do a loop around the fields, also returning back into Orford by way of Ferry Road (about six miles).

Orford Ness National Nature Reserve

April–June & Oct Sat 10am–2pm; July–Sept Tues–Sat 10am–2pm; last ferry back 5pm • £9, NT members £4; families £22.50, NT members £10 • ☎ 01394 450900

Lying tight against the coast, and linked to the mainland at Aldeburgh to the north, **Orford Ness National Nature Reserve** is a six-mile-long shingle spit that has all but blocked Orford from the sea since Tudor times – and which, technically speaking, you could follow all the way to Aldeburgh. The spit's assorted mudflats and marshes nourish sea lavender beds, which act as prime feeding and roosting areas for wildfowl and waders. The National Trust runs boat trips across to the Ness from Orford Quay, and a five-mile hiking trail threads its way along the spit. En route, the trail passes a string of abandoned military buildings: some of the pioneer research on radar was carried out here, but the radar station was closed at the beginning of World War II for fear of German bombing – although the military stayed on here until the 1980s.

Havergate Island

7

Boats first Sat of each month at 10am, returning at 3pm; 20min • £19, RSPB members £12 • ⓦ rspb.org.uk

The second of the two places you can visit by boat from Orford harbour is the RSPB reserve at **Havergate Island**, best in spring and summer when you can see its colonies of avocets, wheatears and terns, and pintails and wigeons in autumn and winter, as well as hares, rabbits and other creatures. There's just one trail on the island, which runs for around a mile and a half to several bird hides, but no other facilities. If you can't coincide with a trip, you can always content yourself with a one-hour ride around the island on the passenger boat, *Regardless*, which runs regularly from the harbour during the summer (£10 per person; ☎01394 459984, ⓦorfordrivertrips.co.uk).

ARRIVAL AND DEPARTURE   ORFORD AND AROUND

By bus Buses pull up on the central square and connect 4–5 times daily with Melton, Sutton Hoo and Woodbridge. There is also one bus a day to Ipswich.

ACCOMMODATION

★ **Crown & Castle** Market Square, IP12 2LJ ☎01394 450205, ⓦcrownandcastlehotel.co.uk. There's no better place to stay overnight and enjoy Orford's gentle, unhurried air than at this excellent, revamped pub, whose modest-looking exterior doesn't quite do justice to the 21 stylishly simple guest rooms within and in the outbuildings behind. It has a good restaurant too, and standards generally are top-notch – as you would expect from former TV hotel inspector Ruth Watson's place. They offer a lot of good-value, dinner-included breaks if you plan to stay more than one night. **£135**

Jolly Sailor Quay St, IP12 2NU ☎01394 450243, ⓦjollysailororford.co.uk. The village's best place for a drink, but serving excellent food and with rooms as well – three doubles and one twin, well fitted out with en-suite bathrooms. **£115**

EATING

IN TOWN
Butley Orford Oysterage Market Square, IP12 2LH ☎01394 450277, ⓦbutleyorfordoysterage.co.uk. An institution for many years in Orford and indeed for miles around. Great fish and seafood, much of it caught, farmed and smoked locally by the family themselves (they have their own oysterage, as well as two fishing boats), which you can enjoy in a simple café-restaurant environment. No trip to Orford is complete without eating here. Daily noon–2.15pm, Wed–Sat also 6.30–9pm.

★ **Crown & Castle** Market Square, IP12 2LJ ☎01394 450205, ⓦcrownandcastlehotel.co.uk. An outstanding

---

BUTLEY–ORFORD FERRY

One of the Suffolk coast's four **foot ferries** runs during the summer from near Butley to just south of Orford – useful if you're following the Coast Path. It operates at regular intervals every weekend between Easter and the end of September, 11am–4pm, and weekends-only during April and October – £2 single, £3.50 for cyclists. Call ☎07913 672499 for more details.

BRIDGING THE GAPS: SUFFOLK'S COASTAL FOOT FERRIES

The Suffolk coast is full of annoying rivers and estuaries that cut deep into the coastline which can sometimes make travelling in a straight line difficult if you're walking the Suffolk Coast Path. To compensate for this there are four **foot ferries** that bridge the watery gaps at various points along the coast:

Harwich–Shotley–Felixstowe See p.236.   **Butley–Orford** See p.253.
Felixstowe Ferry–Bawdsey Quay See p.248.   **Walberswick–Southwold** See p.271.

7

restaurant, where the emphasis is on local ingredients and the food takes in both British and Italian classics (better than it sounds), with lots of good fish, seafood and locally farmed meat dishes – Orford skate, oysters and steak-and-kidney pie alongside calves' liver *veneziana* and Venetian braised octopus. Good lunchtime specials for around £10, sharing plates for £18 and evening main courses in the £17.50–19.50 range – all delicious. Daily 12.15–2pm & 6.45–9pm.

Jolly Sailor Quay St, IP12 2NU ☎01394 450243, ⓦ jollysailororford.co.uk. Really cosy, dog-friendly pub just back from the harbour, which is great for a drink, with a wood-fired stove in winter. Does excellent food, too – sandwiches, fish platters, steaks and burgers. Most things go for £10–12. There's also a kids' menu, and lots of good desserts. Daily 11am–3pm & 6–9pm.

★**Pump Street Bakery** 1 Pump St, IP12 2LZ ☎01394 459829, ⓦ pumpstreetbakery.com. The bread and pastries at this renowned local bakery are wonderful, as are the lunches and weekend brunch dishes, which you can

enjoy at their big communal table or a handful of seats outside. Very good coffee too – a pity it's not open every day. Wed–Sat 9am–4pm, Sun 10am–4pm.

Riverside Tearooms Orford Quay, IP12 2NU ☎01394 459797, ⓦ riversidetearoom.co.uk. Run by the folk who operate the *Regardless* passenger boat (see box, p.253), this is housed in one of the huts on Orford's quayside, and does good basic breakfasts and lunches, with outside seating on the terrace decking. Jan & Feb Sat & Sun 10am–4pm; April–Oct daily 9.30am–5pm; March & Nov Wed–Sun 10am–4pm.

OUT OF TOWN

The Froize Chillesford, IP12 3PU ☎01394 450282, ⓦ froize.co.uk. A couple of miles outside Orford, *The Froize* is known for well-prepared, seasonal modern British food that's all locally sourced – good on meat dishes especially, using local lamb, beef and venison, with lunch specials for a flat £16 a dish, plus dinner starters for £6.75 and mains for £17.50. Tues–Sun noon–2pm, Fri & Sat also 6.30–8.30pm.

SHOPPING

Pinney's The Old Warehouse, Quay St, IP12 2NU ☎01394 459183, ⓦ pinneysoforford.co.uk. The family who run the excellent *Butley Orford Oysterage* (see p.253)

also have a shop, a slick operation which sells fresh and smoked fish and seafood. Mon–Fri 10am–4.30pm, Sat 9am–4.30pm, Sun 10am–4pm.

Aldeburgh and around

Well-heeled **ALDEBURGH**, a small seaside town of only three thousand people situated just north of the meandering Alde River, is one of Suffolk's most popular coastal towns, and has a buzzy, prosperous vibe that draws visitors from far and wide. It's also known for its annual arts festival, the brainchild of composer Benjamin Britten, who lived here for many years, and nowadays the town has a small fishing fleet selling its daily catch from wooden shacks along the pebbled shore. But in essence it's a seaside resort, and an increasingly gentrified one at that, with a high street featuring a handful of national chains alongside an array of bijou local businesses. There are good hotels and B&Bs, and some of Suffolk's best places to eat – Aldeburgh pretty much has it all if you're looking for somewhere to stay for a while on the East Anglian coast.

The High Street and around

Aldeburgh's centre is clearly defined by its wide **High Street** which runs parallel to the seafront and the narrow side streets that run off at right angles, but this was not always the case: the sea swallowed much of what was once an extensive medieval town long ago. Nowadays the side streets run down to the pedestrianized seafront and the large stony **beach** beyond, the top end of which is lined with **huts** selling fresh fish.

Aldeburgh Lifeboat Station

Crag Path, IP15 5BP • Daily 10.30am–4.30pm • Free • ⓦ aldeburghlifeboat.org.uk

The pristine Aldeburgh lifeboat is poised and ready to launch in the **lifeboat station** on the beach, and you can peek inside for a look – the boat is surrounded by photos and memorabilia, including details of all recent rescue operations – and afterwards pop into the RNLI shop, whose cards, stationery and gifts make good Aldeburgh souvenirs.

St Peter and St Paul

Church Close, IP15 1DY • ⓦ aldeburghparishchurch.org.uk

The fourteenth-century flint church of **St Peter and St Paul** sits on a hill just off one end of the High Street, a large and very-well-looked-after church – as you would expect in a place like Aldeburgh. Inside there's a small display on Britten, close by the Britten Memorial Window, whose three stained-glass panels were designed by artist John Piper (who collaborated with Britten on set design) and depict the composer's three operatic parables for church performance – *Curlew River* in the middle, *Burning Fiery Furnace* on the right and *The Prodigal Son* on the left. Appropriately, there's also a memorial nearby to the eighteenth-century poet George Crabbe, who also lived in the town and inspired Britten's opera *Peter Grimes*. But most Britten devotees make their way to his and Pears' simple slate headstones at the far end of the large churchyard, where they are buried – just in front, as it happens, of their close friend the conductor and composer Imogen Holst, the only child of Gustav, who lived in Aldeburgh for much of her life until she died in 1984.

Aldeburgh Museum

Moot Hall, IP15 5LE • April, May, Sept & Oct daily 2.30–5pm; June–Aug daily noon–5pm • £2 • ☎ 01728 454666, ⓦ aldeburghmuseumonline.co.uk

A creaky timbered edifice, with a sundial on its side, sixteenth-century **Moot Hall**,

ALDEBURGH

Thorpeness
The Scallop

St Peter & St Paul Church
Fish Huts
Aldeburgh Museum (Moot Hall)
Boating Pond
Aldeburgh Cinema & Gallery
Bus Stop
Crag House
Lifeboat Station

Aldeburgh Bay

Aldeburgh

Westrow Reach

SLAUGHDEN QUAY

ACCOMMODATION	
The Brudenell	4
Martello Tower	5
Ocean House B&B	3
Wentworth Hotel	1
White Lion	2

EATING	
Aldeburgh Fish & Chip Shop	7
The Brudenell	8
Cragg Sisters	3
DPs	1
Golden Galleon	4
The Lighthouse	2
Munchies	5
Regatta	6

DRINKING	
White Hart	1

SHOPPING	
Aldeburgh Bookshop	1
Ives	4
Lawson's	2
Shingle & Sherbert	3

7

7

BENJAMIN BRITTEN

Born in Lowestoft in 1913, **Benjamin Britten** was closely associated with Suffolk for most of his life. He started composing music as a boy, and attended the Royal College of Music in 1930, where he wrote his first major work, a *Sinfonietta* for chamber ensemble. By the close of the 1930s he was an established composer of some renown, and had met his lifelong partner, the tenor **Peter Pears**, with whom he enjoyed both a loving and creative relationship for the rest of his life. Pears and Britten fled Britain for the US in 1939, as conscientious objectors, and stayed there until 1942, when they returned to Aldeburgh. They lived in Crag House, at 4 Crabbe St, on the seafront next to the boating pond, until 1957, when they supposedly grew tired of fans peering through the windows, and moved to the grander Red House (see opposite), about a mile out of town on the road to Leiston. The work of the nineteenth-century Suffolk poet George Crabbe formed the basis of the libretto of Britten's best-known opera, *Peter Grimes*, which premiered in London in 1945 (with Peter Pears in the main role) to great acclaim. It was followed a year later by Britten's *Young Person's Guide to the Orchestra*, igniting a burst of creative energy that led to a flood of operas and choral music – *Billy Budd, The Turn of the Screw* (his masterpiece for children), *Noye's Fludde*, a *Midsummer Night's Dream* and finally his last opera *Death in Venice*. He died in 1976, aged just 63, after undergoing heart surgery. Peter Pears outlived him by over a decade and continued to live in Aldeburgh until his death in 1986. He was buried next to Britten in the local churchyard, but their best memorial must really be the **Aldeburgh Festival**, which they founded in 1948 and which is bigger and stronger today than it has ever been (see box, p.260).

Aldeburgh's oldest building, began its days in the centre of town, but with the erosion that has swallowed half of the town centre over the centuries, it now finds itself almost on the beach. Inside, beneath its venerable beams, it houses the **Aldeburgh Museum**, whose displays take in all aspects of the town's history, including its prosperous years as a port, the lifeboats, its growth as a holiday resort and the war years.

The boating pond and Snooks

Next door to the Moot Hall is the **boating pond**, donated to the town by Elizabeth Garrett Anderson and a focus for families during summer who gather here to eat ice cream and watch the boats. Beside the pond is a statue of **Snooks** – the much-loved dog of a local doctor that is something of a symbol for the town, especially since the original statue was stolen in 2003. The current *Snooks* is a replacement, funded by locals chipping in after much public outcry.

The Scallop

A memorial to Benjamin Britten, on the northern end of Aldeburgh's beach, Maggi Hambling's 13ft-high steel **Scallop** sculpture has caused quite a rumpus in Aldeburgh since it was first unveiled in 2003, dividing opinion in the town between those who loathe it and would like it to be moved and those who feel it's a fitting tribute to Aldeburgh's most famous son, sited in the midst of the landscape that inspired him most. Hambling herself described the sculpture as a conversation with the sea, and it is pierced through with the words of the George Crabbe poem – *The Borough*, a grisly portrait of the lives of the fishermen of Aldeburgh – that inspired Britten to compose the opera *Peter Grimes*. It's designed, apparently, to induce a contemplative state, which it arguably has some chance of doing in this location – although it's more often used to shelter from the wind on Aldeburgh's blustery beach, and sadly of late has become a target for anti-*Scallop* graffiti.

The Red House

Golf Lane, IP15 5PZ · **Gallery, library, studio & garden** June–Sept Tues–Fri 2–5pm · **House tours** June–Sept Tues–Thurs & Sat 2.15pm & 3.15pm; 45min · Free; parking £5; free shuttlebus every 30min from Moot Hall June–Sept 2.05–4.05pm · ☎ 01728 451700, ⚑ brittenpears.org

There are reminders of Benjamin Britten and Peter Pears all over Aldeburgh, but the one that resonates most is the house in which they spent the last three decades of their lives together, **The Red House**, now home to the Britten-Pears Foundation. Britten and Pears moved here in 1957, when their home in the centre of town became too public and they agreed to swap homes with their good friend Mary Potter. Britten and Pears were extraordinarily happy here, and the house has been preserved more or less as it was when Britten died in 1976, although Pears lived on here until his own death in 1986. You can join a tour of the house proper at specific times (see above), and it holds various manuscripts and a revolving selection of correspondence with the greats of the music world; but above all it is interesting for the revealing minutiae of the composer's life and the circle of creative friends that gathered here.

The various outbuildings are just as fascinating. A gallery houses a permanent exhibition on Britten, with all manner of personal and artistic effects, from suitcases still with their luggage tags, passports, postcards to friends, even the invoice from the removal firm that moved their furniture here in 1957. There are also costumes from the first performance of *Noye's Fludde* in Orford church (see p.252), manuscripts and correspondence and set models from *Peter Grimes* – all enhanced by an excellent audio guide that climaxes with the closing bars of a performance of *War Requiem* conducted by Britten at the Albert Hall. Behind here is the library, a gloriously calm space, filled with Britten and Pears' collection of books, furniture, paintings and rugs – and one of the composer's two Steinway grand pianos. Across the courtyard Britten's studio occupies the top floor of another converted outbuilding, and is kept exactly as it looks in a 1958 photo on the wall, with Britten's other Steinway and his desk overlooking the garden – which you can also visit – where he composed *War Requiem* and other works between the late 1950s and early 1970s.

ARRIVAL AND DEPARTURE
ALDEBURGH

By bus Buses pull in along the High St and at Fort Green, near to Slaughden Quay, and there are hourly connections to Leiston (12min), Snape (20min) and the nearest train station at Saxmundham (30min). The same service also runs on to Wickham Market (1hr), Woodbridge (1hr 10min) and Ipswich (1hr 45min).

By car You can park along the seafront by the Moot Hall, on the High St, or there's a pay-and-display car park at the far end of the High St close to Slaughden Quay.

ACCOMMODATION

Aldeburgh is solid second-home territory, so the number of hotels and B&Bs is relatively low, and a lot of places are only available as self-catering, and rentable by the week. During the festival (see box, p.260) you'll need to reserve well in advance.

The Brudenell The Parade, IP15 5BU ☎ 01728 452071, ⚑ brudenellhotel.co.uk. This seafront hotel has been refurbished and updated relatively recently and is part of the same local hotel family as the *White Lion* at the other end of town and the *Thorpeness Hotel & Golf Club*. It's very comfy, with a yachty feel that sits very well with the Aldeburgh vibe. There's a cosy sitting room downstairs in which you can sip tea and look out over the sea, and the rooms are thoughtfully if not imaginatively furnished. Service is excellent, and there's a good ground-floor restaurant with outside terrace. **£175**

Martello Tower Slaughden Rd, IP15 5NA ☎ 01628 825925, ⚑ landmarktrust.org.uk. This heavily fortified Martello tower, right on the edge of the ocean about half a mile south of the centre of Aldeburgh along Slaughden Quay, provides the town's most distinctive accommodation, with two bedrooms, a roof terrace and parking. Four nights minimum stay from **£536**

Ocean House B&B 25 Crag Path, IP15 5BS ☎ 01728 452094, ⚑ oceanhousealdeburgh.co.uk. In a prime location, this immaculately maintained Victorian dwelling right on the seafront in the centre of town has just two guest rooms. One is a first-floor double the other a top-floor suite with double, bedroom and sitting room attached; both have great sea views and are en-suite. Great breakfasts, with home-made bread, and they also have a self-contained self-catering wing sleeping five. **£100**

7

Wentworth Hotel Wentworth Rd, IP15 5BD ☎01728 452312, ⓦwentworth-aldeburgh.com. With its series of Edwardian half-timber gables, this is a lovely seafront hotel, old-fashioned but briskly efficient, with elegant public areas and 35 lovely rooms, the best of which overlook the boats and fish huts on the beach. The welcome is professional rather than warm, but all in all the *Wentworth* nails the traditional British seaside hotel experience perfectly. **£175**

White Lion Market Cross Place, IP15 5BJ ☎01728 452720, ⓦwhitelion.co.uk. Relatively recently upgraded, and now making much better use of its perfect position on the seafront right by the Moot Hall, with a reception area that flows through into the hotel's popular restaurant and bar. It's basically the slightly less upscale sister of *The Brudenell* at the other end of the seafront, and the cheaper and somewhat less refined rival to the *Wentworth*, a few doors down. **£175**

EATING

Aldeburgh Fish & Chip Shop 226 High St, IP15 5DJ ☎01728 452250, ⓦaldeburghfishandchips.co.uk. Aldeburgh's two almost world-renowned fish and chip shops are owned by the same people, and they do mostly justify their huge reputations. This one, at the southern end of the High St, just does takeaways and you can expect to queue most evenings. Tues & Wed 11.45am–2pm, Thurs & Sat 11.45am–2pm & 5–8pm, Fri 11.45am–2pm & 5–9pm, Sun noon–2pm.

The Brudenell The Parade, IP15 5BU ☎01728 452071, ⓦbrudenellhotel.co.uk. The restaurant of the hotel (see p.257) has good sea views and a deliberately short menu (half a dozen starters and mains) that focuses on fish and seafood dishes with simple ingredients. Starters go for around £6.95, mains £12.95–18.95. Mon–Fri noon–2.30pm & 6.30–9pm, Sat & Sun noon–3pm & 6–9.30pm.

Cragg Sisters 110 High St, IP15 5AB ☎07813 552181, ⓦcraggsisters.co.uk. Busy serving tea in the same location since the days of Britten and Pears, and doing as good a job as ever. Mon–Fri & Sun 11am–4.30pm, Sat 11am–5pm.

DPs 106–108 High St, IP15 5AB ☎07854 920332. Short for *David's Place*, this is a handy local bar right on the high street that also does really good home-made Thai food, which they cook in the courtyard out the back. Most main courses around £10. Very convivial. Daily noon–midnight.

Golden Galleon 137 High St, IP15 3AR ☎01728 454685, ⓦaldeburghfishandchips.co.uk. If you want to sit down for your fish and chips, or to swap queues, try

Aldeburgh Fish & Chip Shop's sister establishment, the *Golden Galleon*, which also has another restaurant upstairs, the *Upper Deck* (check website for hours). Mon–Wed & Fri noon–2pm & 5–8pm, Thurs noon–2pm, Sat noon–2.30pm & 4.30–8pm, Sun noon–7pm.

★**The Lighthouse** 77 High St, IP15 5AU ☎01728 453377, ⓦlighthouserestaurant.co.uk. Perhaps Aldeburgh's best restaurant, this locals' favourite on two floors is a relaxed and informal place that serves breakfast, lunch and dinner seven days a week. The menu favours locally sourced ingredients and good, simple home-cooked food, with everything from excellent fish and chips, liver and bacon and burgers to pan-fried scallops and venison tagine with couscous. Mains go for £10.95–15.95. Always busy. Daily from 10am for coffee, lunch noon–2pm, dinner 6.30pm–late.

Munchies 163 High St, IP15 1AN ☎01728 454566, ⓦaldeburghmunchies.co.uk. This long-established joint – and distant relative of the excellent *Lighthouse* restaurant (see above) – remains one of the best places in town for coffee and a pastry or a gourmet sandwich. Daily 8am–4.30pm.

Regatta 171 High St, IP15 1AN ☎01728 452011, ⓦregattaaldeburgh.com. One of Aldeburgh's longest-established restaurants, and still a reliable choice, with a range of daily specials on a blackboard – including salmon smoked in their own smokehouse – and a creative menu with a British base that is especially strong on seafood. Light lunch dishes and sandwiches £6–9.50; otherwise mains average about £14. Daily noon–2pm & 6–10pm.

DRINKING

White Hart 222 High St, IP15 5AJ ☎01728 453205. Good locals' joint, a very friendly small pub with one big main room in which everyone mucks in together. Another side of Aldeburgh. Daily 11am–3pm & 6pm–midnight.

ALDEBURGH CINEMA AND GALLERY

Wouldn't you just know it, but opposite its fantastic local bookshop Aldeburgh has its own **gallery and cinema** complex, a dinky, toy-town affair at 152 High St (☎01728 452996, ⓦaldeburghcinema.co.uk) that has been screening films since 1919. It's a fairly small space, and one which was only saved from demolition in the 1960s when Benjamin Britten and other concerned locals clubbed together to save it – a very Aldeburgh sort of fate – and it's to the town's credit that it's still going. Plus, of course, the Gallery hosts regular exhibitions by local artists.

SHOPPING

★**Aldeburgh Bookshop** 42 High St, IP15 5AB ☎01728 452389, ⓦaldeburghbookshop.co.uk. Great independent bookshop that would grace the high street of a much larger town, let alone one the size of Aldeburgh. Good on local titles, biography and new fiction, and a layout that encourages you to pick up and browse. Quite a good children's section too. Mon, Tues & Thurs–Sat 9.30am–6pm, Wed 9.30am–5.30pm, Sun 10.30am–5.30pm.

Ives 160 High St, IP15 5AQ ☎01728 452264, ⓦivesices .co.uk. *The* place to go for an ice cream on the High St, but be prepared to queue in summer. April–Oct Mon–Fri 11am–5pm, Sat & Sun 11am–5.30pm; Nov–March Sat & Sun 10am–4pm.

Lawsons 138 High St, IP15 5AQ ☎01728 454052, ⓦlawsonsdelicatessen.co.uk. This sleek and refined deli continues to win awards for being one of the best of its kind in Suffolk, and it's pretty good, selling a thoughtful selection of deli goodies, although being in Aldeburgh it doesn't stand out as much from the crowd as it would in most places. Not cheap. Mon–Sat 9am–5pm, Sun 10am–2pm.

Shingle & Sherbert 158 High St, IP15 5AQ ☎01728 454308. Part of the craze for old-style sweets that's sweeping Britain, this is Aldeburgh's very own old-fashioned sweet shop. Mon–Sat 10am–5pm.

Snape Maltings

7

Bridge Rd, Snape, IP17 1SR • April–Oct daily 10am–5.30pm; Nov–March 10am–5pm • ☎01728 688303, ⓦsnapemaltings.co.uk

Just off the main road between Aldeburgh and the A12, **SNAPE** is more or less a straggle of houses with a good pub – the *Golden Key* – just off the main drag. However, the village is best known for the complex of former malthouses known as **Snape Maltings**, the main site of the Aldeburgh Music Festival and home to one of the finest concert venues in the country and much more besides; indeed the Maltings has grown into quite a commercial behemoth in recent years, with various craft shops and galleries, a food hall, a couple of cafés and a pub, the *Plough & Sail*. It's a pleasant place, and you could easily spend a couple of hours strolling around, afterwards maybe taking a walk along the river through the reedbeds to nearby Iken and its church (see below) – about two miles in all, and an easy, partly boardwalked route. The Maltings also hosts a farmers' market on the first Saturday of each month, and an annual food festival in September – ⓦaldeburghfoodanddrink.co.uk.

ARRIVAL AND DEPARTURE   SNAPE

By bus There are hourly connections between Snape and Aldeburgh (20min). Buses stop outside the *Crown* pub and the Maltings and generally travel on to Woodbridge.

ACCOMMODATION

OUT OF TOWN

Blaxhall YHA Hostel Heath Walk, Blaxhall, IP12 2EA ☎0845 3719305, ⓦyha.org.uk/hostel/blaxhall. Housed in the old village school at Blaxhall, a small village a couple of miles beyond Snape Maltings, this YHA hostel has 41 beds in two- to six-bed rooms, a self-catering kitchen, a café and a laundry. They also have a small camping area. Dorms <u>£15</u>; doubles <u>£35</u>

The Ship Inn School Rd, Blaxhall, IP12 2DY ☎ 01728 688316, ⓦblaxhallshipinn.co.uk. Cosy village pub that serves up good food and regular live music – mainly folk – and has eight neat, tidy and well-equipped en-suite rooms in a couple of clapboard outbuildings. Good breakfasts, too. <u>£75</u>

St Botolph's, Iken

Church Lane, IP12 2ES

A small, partially thatched church at the end of the road in the tiny hamlet of **IKEN**, sat

---

ALL ABOARD THE ENCHANTRESS

The irresistibly named **Enchantress** (3 times a day; 45min; £8.50, children £5; ☎01502 574903, ⓦwaveneyrivertours.com) makes the short journey from Grain Quay at Snape Maltings down the Alde River to Iken village and back.

ALDEBURGH: FESTIVAL TOWN

When Benjamin Britten launched the **Aldeburgh Festival** in 1948, in part as a showpiece for his own works and those of his contemporaries, he didn't know what he had started: Aldeburgh and its hinterland has since turned into a major festival venue in its own right, and Britten's festival in particular has grown exponentially. By the mid-1960s, it had outgrown the parish churches in which it began, and moved into a collection of disused malthouses, five miles west of Aldeburgh on the River Alde, just south of the small village of Snape (see p.259). The festival now takes place every June and lasts two and a half weeks. Core performances are still held at the Maltings, but a string of other local venues are pressed into service as well. Throughout the rest of the year, the Maltings hosts a wide-ranging programme of musical and theatrical events, including a three-day Britten Festival in October. For more information, contact Aldeburgh Music (☎01728 687110, ⓦaldeburgh.co.uk), which has box offices at Snape Maltings and on Aldeburgh High Street alongside the tourist office. Tickets for the Aldeburgh Festival itself usually go on sale to the public towards the end of March, and sell out fast for the big-name recitals.

But it's not just Britten's festival that brings visitors to Aldeburgh these days: the **Aldeburgh Food and Drink Festival** (ⓦaldeburghfoodanddrink.co.uk) takes place during the last weekend in September at the Maltings and at a variety of venues across east Suffolk, from Orford to Woodbridge and as far afield as Framlingham. There's also the **Aldeburgh Carnival** (ⓦaldeburghcarnival.com) which has been held across the third weekend in August for over half a century, and gives this normally relatively buttoned-up town the chance to let its hair down, with a parade, firework display and Chinese lantern procession.

on a headland on the wide Alde estuary, **St Botolph's** feels like a very special place – and indeed it is, founded by the eponymous saint in the seventh century, and later a Saxon, then a Norman, foundation. Its rough-hewn walls enclose a nave that contains a piece of a carved stone cross from the original Saxon church, most probably from the ninth century; while among more recent items the church has a beautifully carved medieval font, decorated with the symbols of the four evangelists.

Thorpeness

A couple of miles north of Aldeburgh, a bracing thirty-minute walk along the beach, **THORPENESS** is a slightly peculiar place, with a toy-town quaintness reminiscent of the 1960s TV show *The Prisoner*. Formerly a tiny fishing village, it was bought up in its entirety in 1910 by (ironically) a Scottish lawyer named Stuart Ogilvie, who was determined to re-create a retreat that was English to the core, turning it into his private holiday village, with a country club and golf course and an estate of mock-Jacobean and Edwardian holiday homes, some of which fringe Thorpeness's most distinctive and central feature, the Meare. The **Meare** was created as a boating lake with the help of Ogilvie's friend J.M. Barrie, who mocked up several Peter Pan-type locations on the islands in the middle. You can still tour the deliberately shallow lake by rowing boat, canoe or sailing dinghy (April–Oct daily 10am–5pm; £8 for 30min; ☎01728 832523). There's a shop and a café nearby, the **Meare Shop & Tearoom** (see opposite), with some tables overlooking the water. As for the rest of the village, a series of tracks lead through its centre to the sea, among which nestles a local pub, *The Dolphin* (see opposite), while the *Thorpeness Hotel & Golf Club* continues to this day.

ACCOMMODATION

The Dolphin Peace Place, IP16 4NA ☎01728 454994, ⓦthorpenessdolphin.com. Three very well turned out, dog-friendly rooms above Thorpeness's village pub – which incidentally serves very good food, including an excellent breakfast (see opposite). **£95**

The Dune House Aldeburgh Rd, IP16 4NR ⓦliving-architecture.co.uk. Situated right on the beach between Aldeburgh and Thorpeness, *Dune House* is the brainchild of the writer Alain de Botton and a firm called Living Architecture, whose aim is to introduce ordinary folk to the delights of modern architecture in amazing settings. Designed by a renowned firm of Norwegian architects, it

WALKS AROUND ALDEBURGH

Several **footpaths** radiate out from Aldeburgh, with the most obvious trail leading two miles north along the beach to Thorpeness, where you can pick up the **Suffolk Coast Path** towards Sizewell, a lovely passage along the cliffs through heathy landscapes almost as far as Sizewell, turning inland just by Sizewell Hall and cutting across the woodland and heath of the so-called **Aldringham Walks** back to Aldeburgh – an easy five miles (2–3hr walk) in all. You can also pick up the coastal path in the opposite direction – also known as the **Sailor's Path** – off the main road out of town beyond the golf course, which leads across country to Snape and through the reeds to the Maltings (about three miles). You can also pick up this path by taking a footpath across the marshes around halfway down the road to Thorpeness, crossing the old railway track after about 500m and continuing on to The Red House. Another option is to turn right when you hit the old railway and follow this for a mile or so towards Thorpeness, then branch off into the woods before turning right into North Warren, where after a short while a boardwalked path leads to a viewpoint for watching the wildfowl over the reeds. Continue on, either back around to Aldeburgh in a circle or to pick up the Aldringham Walks paths to the north.

7

makes the most of its big-skied beach location: all glass on the ground floor and with views in all directions, it almost invites the beach inside the house. A great place to stay, and the prices, while not within reach of everyone, are relatively modest considering the location and size – its five bedrooms sleep up to nine people. Four-night minimum stay. Around **£2000**
House in the Clouds Uplands Rd, IP16 4NQ ☎ 020

7724 3615, ⊛ houseintheclouds.co.uk. Thorpeness's best established unusual self-catering option, situated in the most prominent of Stuart Ogilvie's creations, is a five-storey pitched-roof clapboard tower bang in the centre of the village. You can't take your eyes off the views from its top-floor galleried games rooms, and the four double/twin bedrooms are suitably baronial to make the high prices seem like pretty good value. **£800** a night; one week around **£3000**

EATING

The Dolphin Peace Place, IP16 4NA ☎ 01728 454994, ⊛ thorpenessdolphin.com. Thorpeness's local is no ordinary boozer, as you might expect, but a stripped-down modern pub serving excellent and inventive food for around £12–14 a main course – excellent grilled fish and steaks along with some fairly fancy dishes and frankly magnificent chips. It's the home of the village store, too. Kitchen daily noon–2.30pm & 6–9pm; pub Mon–Fri 11am–3pm & 6–11pm, Sat 11am–11pm, Sun 11am–10.30pm (closed Mon Nov–March).
Meare Shop & Tea Room The Meare, IP16 4NW ☎ 01728 452196. Right by the Meare in the centre of Thorpeness, this hut-based shop and café does sandwiches, home-made quiche and ice creams and sells newspapers and basic provisions; plus it has a few tables by the water. Daily, hours vary.

Leiston and around

It's just inland from the Edwardian fantasy village of Thorpeness, but the gritty, grounded town of **LEISTON** couldn't be more different – indeed, aside from the tourist industry Leiston has been the area's main source of employment for years, first with the innovative Garrett works during the nineteenth and early twentieth centuries, and since the 1960s with the nuclear power station at the village of Sizewell – on what is, in effect, Leiston's beach. Leiston is also the home of Summerhill School, founded on the edge of town by A.S. Neill in the 1920s, a democratic institution in line with Neill's philosophy "to make the school fit the child instead of making the child fit the school", still going strong today.

The Long Shop Museum

Main St, IP16 4ES • June–Sept Mon–Sat 10am–5pm, Sun 11am–3pm; April, May & Oct Tues–Sat 10am–5pm, Sun 11am–3pm • £6 • ☎ 01728 832189, ⊛ longshopmuseum.co.uk

Right in the centre of Leiston, the **Long Shop Museum** was originally the site of the

Leiston Works. Founded by Richard Garrett in 1778, the Works produced agricultural tools and went on to become a pioneer of steam-driven machinery and equipment, employing over two thousand staff and exporting its products all over the world. The Garretts were quite a dynasty: Richard Garrett's granddaughter, Elizabeth Garrett Anderson, was a nineteenth-century feminist and the first woman to qualify as a doctor in the UK, while her younger sister, Millicent Fawcett, was an early campaigner for women's suffrage and founder of the feminist organization now named after her.

As for the museum, there is a steam engine – the *Sirapite* – in a separate shed, and threshing machines and old fire engines in another, and lots of fine details – not least the job vacancy cards from 1887, looking for "sober and hardworking boilermakers and engine erectors to travel to all parts of the British Empire, Austro-Hungarian Empire and Russia". But the heart of the displays are in the **Long Shop** itself, a giant vaulted engine shed, with traction engines, steam tractors and various other bits of machinery, including the dry-cleaning machines the Garretts manufactured towards the end of their days here. The gallery upstairs takes you through the finer points of the steam process, as well as later sources of energy, including the building of Sizewell A in 1966, then B in the 1990s, which replaced the Garretts as the lifeblood of the town.

ARRIVAL AND DEPARTURE   **LEISTON**

By bus There are roughly hourly connections to Aldeburgh (12min), Saxmundham (12min), Woodbridge (#64; 40min)   and Ipswich (1hr 50min).

Leiston Abbey

Abbey Rd, IP16 4TD • Always open • Free; EH • ⓦ www.english-heritage.org.uk

About half a mile outside Leiston are the ruins of **Leiston Abbey**, built in the fifteenth century as a replacement for a thirteenth-century abbey in Minsmere, and constructed from some of the stones from the previous complex. It met its fate a century or so later when it was dissolved under Henry VIII, but the ruins are reasonably substantial, and you can still make out the refectory, with its large Gothic window, the cloister space next door and the abbey church. It's all part of a large complex incorporating a music school and a wedding and conference operation housed in the nearby thatched medieval barns, and, just beyond, the rebuilt guesthouse from the original abbey.

Sizewell

A couple of miles out of Leiston, right on the sea, the village of **SIZEWELL** amounts to no more than a handful of houses, but its name has a notoriety that belies its modest size, home as it is to two of southern Britain's largest nuclear power stations, both of which dominate the coastal landscape for miles around. The southernmost and older of the two, the Magnox **Sizewell A** reactor, has been decommissioned, but its sister reactor to the north, **Sizewell B**, with its distinctive white golfball dome, is Britain's only functioning PWR reactor, and one of the most modern in the UK, completed in 1995. A third reactor, **Sizewell C**, is planned, and work is due to start in 2018. There is a visitor centre at Sizewell (Mon–Sat 9am–4pm; ☎01728 653974, ⓦsizewellbtours @edf-energy.com), and you can do a tour of the plant, but they need to be booked at least a month in advance; tours last around three hours. If you're not that organized – or interested – you can get up closer than you might expect on the beach.

ACCOMMODATION AND EATING   **SIZEWELL**

Beach View Holiday Park Sizewell Common, IP16 4TU ☎01728 830724, ⓦbeachviewholidaypark.co.uk. Though dominated by statics and caravans, this has a nice field for tents too, well positioned above the beach and across the road from Sizewell Hall and the Aldringham Walks (though of course also virtually in the shadow of the power station). It has good facilities, a bar and café and games room, too. Pitches **£30**

Sizewell Tea Sizewell Gap, IP16 4UH ☎ 01728 831108. Right by the beach and in the shadow of the power station, this is a great little café that does breakfasts till noon and lunches till 4pm (£6–8) – cosy inside and with tables outside during summer. Daily 9am–5pm.

Theberton

There's not much to the village of **THEBERTON**, a couple of miles north of Leiston, but its church of **St Peter** is a very elegant building, with a long main body, a lovely thatched roof, and a handsome crenellated hexagonal tower. Just inside the porch is a large fragment of a German zeppelin which was shot down in a nearby field in June 1917, killing all sixteen aircrew, who are remembered (but no longer buried – they were reinterred in a national cemetery for German war-dead in Staffordshire) by a plaque in the graveyard on the other side of the road. Otherwise the church is an ancient building, originally Norman, and half-timbered inside; it has a few remaining features from that time, including a lovely, carved arched doorway inside the vestry, along with a fifteenth-century font carved with angels and wild men with clubs – so-called woodwoses – and a pulpit from the same period.

Saxmundham and around

Just off the A12, about six miles inland from Aldeburgh, **SAXMUNDHAM** retains a pleasant small-town vibe, helped no doubt by the presence of its main-line station, which provides a lifeline for the towns and villages around, but hindered somewhat by the recent dumping of a giant Waitrose right in the middle of town. It's more upmarket than Leiston, but doesn't have the cachet – or indeed the cash – of, say, Framlingham. However, there are worse places to end up; there are a couple of things to help you pass the time, and it makes a good base for some of the area's most desirable villages and countryside.

St John

Church St, IP17 1EP
Right opposite Waitrose's car park, the church of **St John** is a flint-built edifice of the thirteenth century, though with parts dating back much earlier. It boasts a lovely wooden hammerbeam roof and a well-preserved font carved with images of the club-wielding "old man of Suffolk" known as a woodwose.

Saxmundham Museum

49 High St, IP17 1AJ · April–Sept & last week of Oct Mon–Sat 10am–1pm · Free · ☎ 01728 663583
Situated on the High Street right by the railway bridge, **Saxmundham Museum** is the most obvious local attraction, with several rooms containing an old-fashioned station booking office, and a number of good displays on the town and its history, including plenty of local anecdotes.

ARRIVAL AND DEPARTURE   SAXMUNDHAM

By train Saxmundham's train station is right in the centre of town just off the main street – follow Station Approach from Market St – and is connected every hour with Ipswich to the south (40min) and Lowestoft via Halesworth (15min) to the north (50min).
By bus Buses stop on the High St and there are hourly buses between Ipswich (every 2hr; 1hr 30min), Woodbridge (every 2hr; 1hr) and Aldeburgh (every 2hr; 15min).

ACCOMMODATION AND EATING

IN TOWN
★ **The Bell at Sax** 31 High St, IP17 1AF ☎ 01728 602331,
ⓦ thebellatsax.co.uk. Reinvented as a "restaurant with rooms", this old coaching inn is more or less the only show in

town in Saxmundham, with ten large double rooms that are spacious, comfortable and decent value; the flagstones and offbeat decoration of the lobby create a timeless yet contemporary vibe, and the bar is one of the nicest places to drink in town. The restaurant serves a straightforward and very well priced menu (starters around £5, main courses £10.95–15.95) covering everything from fish and chips and a very good burger to *moules frites*, pan-seared scallops, sticky Asian pork belly and a tasty fish platter. With really good cooking and service in a relaxed environment, it's a nice place to eat; their two-course lunch specials (£10) are a bargain, plus they serve a great Sunday brunch. Tues–Sat noon–2.30pm & 6–9.30pm, Sun 11am–3pm. **£80**

Bistro at the Deli 26a High St, IP17 1AJ ☎01728 605607, ⓦthebistroatsax.co.uk. Deli and café in one, offering coffee and tea, home-made cakes, sandwiches and light lunches from about £7.50. On Friday evening they also serve a full restaurant menu, with pizzas and proper mains for around £10. Mon–Thurs 8.30am–4.30pm, Fri 8.30am–3.30pm & 6–10.30pm, Sat 8.30am–1pm.

OUT OF TOWN

Alde Garden Low Rd, Sweffling, IP17 2BB ☎01728 664178, ⓦaldegarden.co.uk. Set in the grounds of the *Sweffling White Horse* pub, this is a fantastic small campsite that's perfect for people who don't really like camping, with a couple of yurts, a teepee, a gypsy caravan, and even a wooden house on stilts, known as "The Hideout". There are pitches available too in case you have your own tent, and a small cottage which you can rent by the week (about £550 in summer). Yurts, teepees and caravans minimum two-night stays from **£125**; hideout **£75**; pitches from **£14**

Yoxford

Straddling the A12 just north of Saxmundham, the large and very sought after village of **YOXFORD** was an important stopover in times gone by, occupying a key point not only on the London–Yarmouth road but on the road to Dunwich too, when the seaside town was one of the most important ports in the land. There's evidence in the form of a nineteenth-century road **sign**, pointing the way to Framlingham, Yarmouth and London, in the centre of the village. Right by the sign, the spired church of **St Peter** is the site of many memorials to the Blois family, who occupied the adjacent **Cockfield Hall**, the grounds of which back onto the village. Lady Jane Grey's younger sister Catherine was held here for the last two weeks of her life in 1568. She died, aged 27, after spending most of her adult life in captivity (like her sister, she was regarded by Elizabeth I as having a potentially legitimate claim on the throne). You can gain access to at least a little bit of the grounds by taking the path by the gatehouse opposite the church.

EATING YOXFORD

Main's 26 High St, IP17 3EU ☎01728 668882, ⓦmainsrestaurant.co.uk. Spick-and-span modern restaurant serving an imaginative – and short – menu of modern British food using local ingredients that changes every day – think pigeon breast, black pudding and chestnuts followed by sea bream with rosemary and chilli, roast pheasant or roast loin of pork. Fairly reasonably priced, with starters from £7 and mains around £15, and they serve brunch on Saturday mornings. Thurs & Fri from 7pm, Sat 9.30am–noon & 7pm till late.

SHOPPING

Yoxford Antiques Centre Askers Hill, IP17 3JW ☎01728 668844, ⓦyoxfordantiques.com. Just outside Yoxford on the way to Peasenhall is this great collection of furniture, books, garden benches and knick-knacks – eminently browsable and very decently priced. They also have a small café and a garden with a beautiful spreading willow and sculptures and benches dotted around. Mon & Wed–Sat 10am–5pm, Sun 10am–4pm.

Peasenhall

Travelling up the A1120 from the A12 and Yoxford, you soon reach **PEASENHALL**, six miles from Saxmundham. which has fair claim to being the prettiest village in a region of exceptionally pretty villages, its main street lined by alluring cottages and the sunken stream of the River Yox, crisscrossed by occasional footbridges. It no longer has a village pub, which is a pity, but it more than makes up for this with its village store and tearoom, **Emmetts**, on the main street (see opposite), another good tearoom, **Weavers**, at the other end of the village on the green (see opposite), and an excellent local butcher opposite, **J.R. Creasey**. All in all not a bad place to find yourself, especially if you're hungry and/or self-catering.

EATING

★**Emmett's** The Street, IP17 2HJ ☎ 01728 660250, ⓦ emmettsham.co.uk. Great village store which cures its own bacon and stocks all manner of deli goodies and fruit and veg, including Spanish products like chorizo and Serrano ham. It also has a small tearoom next door, in which you can sample many of its wares. Mon–Fri 8.30am–5.30pm, Sat 8.30am–5pm.

Weavers The Knoll, IP17 2JE ☎ 01728 660548. Peasenhall's main tearoom occupies a classic village-green location and serves breakfasts, coffee, sandwiches, cream teas and hot lunches. Well worth the stop in this village of foodie delights. Mon, Tues & Thurs–Sat 8am–5pm, Sun 10am–5pm.

Dunwich and around

Tiny **DUNWICH**, just over twelve miles up the coast from Aldeburgh, is probably the strangest and certainly the eeriest place on the Suffolk coast. The one-time seat of the kings of East Anglia, a bishopric and formerly a large port, Dunwich peaked in the twelfth century, since when it's been downhill: over the last millennium, something like a mile of land has been lost to the sea, a process that continues at the rate of about a yard a year. As a result, the whole of the medieval city now lies under water, including all twelve churches, the last of which toppled over the cliffs in 1919.

7

Dunwich Greyfriars

Dunwich, IP17 3DR • ⓦ dunwichgreyfriars.org.uk

The only things that survive from medieval Dunwich are the fragments of the **Greyfriars monastery**, which originally lay to the west of the city and now dangles near the sea's edge. You can access them from the Westleton road out of town, and although there's not much to see, it's an evocative sight, and one that brings home not only how grand a place Dunwich once was, but also just how close to obliteration the village has been for centuries.

Dunwich museum

St James St, IP17 3DT • March Sat & Sun 2–4.30pm; April–Sept daily 11.30am–4.30pm; Oct daily noon–4pm • £1 donation

Dunwich's dinky **museum**, located just down from *The Ship* pub (see p.266), and recognizable by the giant anchor outside, gives a potted history of the town, with displays on local wildlife and the erosion of the coast, a model of Dunwich as it was in the Middle Ages, and an interesting section on the many locals who decided to emigrate to Canada, including Lucy Woolner Macneill, the grandmother of Canadian author Lucy Maud Montgomery, who wrote one of the most popular children's books of all time, *Anne of Green Gables* – and famously returned to her Dunwich roots for her honeymoon.

Dunwich Heath

March to mid-July & mid-Sept to Dec Wed–Sun 10am–4pm; mid-July to mid-Sept daily 10am–5pm • Free, parking £4.80; NT • ☎ 01728 648501, ⓦ nationaltrust.org.uk

From Dunwich car park, it's possible to walk south along the seashore and then cut inland up and over the dunes to National Trust-owned **Dunwich Heath**, where heather and gorse spread over a slab of upland. You can also drive here – the turning is clearly signed on the more southerly of the two byroads to Dunwich. At the end of this turning, on the heath immediately behind and above the coast – the views are fantastic – the old **coastguard cottages** accommodate a shop and tearoom, and are available for self-catering (see p.266).

Minsmere RSPB Nature Reserve

Reserve Daily 9am–9pm or dusk • **Visitor centre** Daily 9am–5pm, Nov–Jan till 4pm • £8, children £4 • ☎ 01728 648281, ⓦ rspb.org.uk

A narrow lane off the main road into Dunwich branches off to the **Minsmere RSPB Nature Reserve**, a varied terrain of marsh, woods and heathland, and in the autumn a gathering place for wading birds and waterfowl, which arrive here by the hundred. It's best known for marsh harriers and avocets – the latter familiar from the RSPB's logo – and the reserve is also home to a small population of notoriously shy bitterns. It's a glorious place, and very well managed, with well-marked trails and hides, a huge car park and visitor centre, and a shop selling everything you could think of to do with birdwatching. There's a decent café too, serving hot food at lunchtime and snacks, tea and coffee all day.

Dunwich Forest

St Helena, IP17 3ED • Open all year • ⓦ forestry.gov.uk/dunwich

Just outside Dunwich, **Dunwich Forest** is co-managed by the Forestry Commission and the Suffolk Wildlife Trust and is home to loads of bike and walking trails, and you can link up with the trails to Dingle Marshes, which stretch towards Walberswick. It's a lovely spot, which is being gradually returned to its traditional state, with the coniferous trees that currently predominate being harvested and replaced by native deciduous woodland and pasture, much of which is grazed by a small herd of recently introduced Dartmoor ponies.

ARRIVAL AND DEPARTURE
DUNWICH

By bus There are a couple of buses every morning to Dunwich from Leiston, Darsham train station, Yoxford, Westleton and Theberton.

By car A sprawling, seashore car park gives easy access to both the village and this stretch of the coast.

ACCOMMODATION AND EATING

IN TOWN

Coastguard Cottages IP17 3DJ ☎ 0870 4584422, ⓦ nationaltrustcottages.co.uk. Three of the cottages at the Dunwich Heath National Trust centre have been converted into very comfortable apartments – one two-bedroom, two one-bedroom – and are available for rent. Two-night minimum stay. From **£397**

Flora Tea Rooms Beach Rd, IP17 3EN ☎ 01728 648433. Right by the beach in Dunwich, this is a Suffolk coast institution, basically a large hut serving big plates of excellent fish and chips, pies, burgers and salads to an assortment of birdwatchers, hikers and anglers. Outside seating too. Daily 11am–5pm.

The Ship IP17 3DT ☎ 01728 648219, ⓦ shipatdunwich .co.uk. Owned by the same people as *The Crown* at Westleton, some of the refurbished sixteen rooms here are on the smallish side but who cares? With its low wooden beams and wood-burning stove, this is a cosy, traditional pub and the food is great, made with locally sourced ingredients and including excellent fish and chips, fried in their secret-recipe batter (£12.50). Plus it's only in the dead of night that the peace and spookiness of the village really strikes home. Daily noon–3pm & 6–9pm. **£112.50**

OUT OF TOWN

★**Eel's Foot Inn** Eastbridge ☎ 01728 830154, ⓦ theeelsfootinn.co.uk. Just a few miles inland from Dunwich in the tiny village of Eastbridge, this old smugglers' haunt is a popular base for twitchers and walkers, with not only good pub food and drink but also six very nicely finished and extremely spacious en-suite double rooms in a building behind the pub. They serve a fairly basic pub grub menu, but it's a great base for walks, plus its large beer garden – complete with petanque court and kids' play area – was recently reckoned to be one of the UK's best by a national newspaper. Daily noon–2.30pm & 6.30–9pm. **£99**

A MINSMERE CIRCLE

Using the *Eel's Foot Inn* (see above) as your base, you can do a **walk** right around Minsmere reserve, taking in all of the forest, heath, marsh and coastal habitats without actually entering the reserve itself – five miles in all, and a good way of working up an appetite for a meal at the pub. You can do pretty much the same walk starting from the NT tearoom and visitor centre at Dunwich Heath.

MIDDLETON'S ALTERNATIVE TO BOXING DAY TELLY

A pretty village grouped around a green off the main road just south of Westleton, and with a pub, *The Bell*, **Middleton** is known for its **cutty wren festival**, an old English ritual that takes place every year on St Stephen's Day, more prosaically known as Boxing Day (December 26). It's an ancient event, dating back to times when people thought the wren to be the "king of all birds". Historically a wren was caught and killed and paraded around the village; nowadays it's a carved wooden effigy, but the ceremony still takes place, having been revived about twenty years ago. It begins after dark, when the participants blacken their faces with soot and dance around the village with the bird on a stick, finishing up at the village pub, where there's more dancing and the wren is ceremonially buried. What you might make of it is anybody's guess, but if you're in the area on Boxing Day, why not stop by and have a look?

Westleton

On the seaward side of the A12, a turning off the main road towards the sea leads a few miles to **WESTLETON**, a pretty village a couple of miles from Dunwich built around a large green and the thatched fourteenth-century church of **St Peter's**, though very unusually for Norfolk and Suffolk, it lacks a tower, as it was destroyed by a World War II bomb. Though there's not much to see in the church, the churchyard is a pleasant spot.

ACCOMMODATION AND EATING

★**The Crown** The Street, IP17 3AD ☎ 01728 648777, ⓦ westletoncrown.co.uk. This pub-restaurant became famous for fifteen minutes when the Duke and Duchess of Cambridge breezed by for a friend's wedding a few years back, and their 34 en-suite bedrooms, either in the main building or dotted about the various converted barns, are all beautifully finished, and are confidently classified as "good", "better", and "best" (presumably the royals went for "best"). They're all nice in any case, with even the cheapest rooms fairly recently refurbished with well-fitted bathrooms. The pub itself (open all day) has been well updated, with a stripped-down bar and a light-filled dining room, and serves an upscale but deliberately hearty British menu. Starters go for £5.50–8.50, while the mains (£12.25–17.50) take in confit duck, Blythburgh pork and usually a couple of fish dishes. They also serve a lunch menu of sandwiches, light dishes and specials for £7.50–10. Daily noon–2.30pm & 6.30–9.30pm. **£125**

Southwold and around

Perched on the cliffs just to the north of the River Blyth, **SOUTHWOLD** is a small town of around 1500 people that competes with Aldeburgh for the London tourist and second-homer trade. It was Suffolk's busiest fishing port in the sixteenth century, but in time lost most of its fishing industry to Lowestoft, just up the coast, and today, although a small fleet still brings in herring, sprats and cod, the town is primarily a seaside resort, a genteel and eminently appealing little place with fine old buildings, a long sandy **beach**, open heathland, a dinky harbour and even a little industry in the shape of the Adnams brewery. It's a gentility that wasn't to the liking of George Orwell, who lived for a time at 36 High St (a plaque marks the spot) with his parents. He heartily disliked the town's airs and graces, and soon fled to live more cheaply and "have less temptation from the world, the flesh and the devil".

Market Place and the Greens

The centre of Southwold is its triangular, pocket-sized **Market Place**, framed by attractive, mostly Georgian buildings, which sits at one end of the town's busy **High Street**. One of the great things about Southwold is that its centre is dotted with green spaces, left as firebreaks after the town was gutted by fire in 1659. The two most central are **East Green**, where you'll find the Adnams Brewery, and **South Green**, the largest, which looks out to sea and down across the fields towards the harbour. **North Green** is a smaller open space at the top of the High Street. But Southwold is a pretty green place all round, with common land stretching out west from the centre of town behind the High Street.

Adnams brewery

Sole Bay Brewery, IP18 6JW • Tours usually 2–3 daily during summer, plus separate weekly distillery tours • Brewery tours £12, distillery tours £10; tours last 1hr plus a 30min tasting and include a bottle of beer to take home; book online or at the Adnams shop on the corner of Pinkneys Lane and Queen St • ☎ 01502 727225, ⓦ brewerytours .adnams.co.uk

North from Market Place, **East Green** is the site of the **Adnams brewery**, its various buildings filling the air with vaguely malty fumes throughout much of the day. Adnams has been here for well over a century and not surprisingly remains an important local employer. But what's admirable about Adnams is the way it has turned a successful local business into a nationwide (and even international) one, investing in the latest brewing methods and cannily extending into the catering trade, with a number of wholly owned pubs and hotels and a great local chain of wine merchant and kitchen stores, Cellar & Kitchen (see p.273). They have also started distilling their own gin and vodka. You can take a tour of the brewery, viewing the state-of-the-art brewing process and finishing up with a tutored tasting and a trip to their store to taste wine.

SHOPPING

Adnams Cellar & Kitchen	1
Black Olive Deli	2
Southwold Books	3

ACCOMMODATION

The Blyth	3
The Brewer's House	4
The Crown	6
Home@21	2
Northcliffe	
Sutherland House	5
The Swan	7

EATING

The Blyth	2
Boardwalk	1
The Crown	5
Lord Nelson	7
Sole Bay Inn	3
Sutherland House	4
The Swan	6

7

The Lighthouse

Stradbroke Rd, IP18 6LU • Late March to Oct Wed, Sat & Sun 2–4pm, plus bank hol weekends and most of Aug daily 11am–1pm & 2–4pm • £4, children £3, family tickets £12 • ☎ 01502 724729, ⓦ trinityhouse.co.uk

On the opposite side of East Green to the Adnams brewery is Southwold's famous white **Lighthouse**, built in 1887 and open to the public on guided tours, which take you right the way up to the lantern, around 100ft high. Tours last twenty minutes and are not for those nervous about heights or confined spaces.

7

> **BOUTIQUE BEACH HUTS**
>
> Southwold's sandyish **beach** is backed by rows of candy-coloured huts which face out towards the ocean. There are some – nearest to the pier – for rent, for £20–25 a day, £100–140 a week (☎07842 528164, ⓦbeachhutsouthwold.co.uk), or you can bite the bullet and buy your own for around £75,000.

St Edmund's

Bartholomew Green, IP18 6AH • Daily 9am–4pm, July & Aug till 6pm

Just off East Green, right in the centre of Southwold, the large church of **St Edmund** is a light and very handsome mid-fifteenth-century church whose solid symmetries are balanced by a long sequence of elegantly carved windows. Inside there are lots of neo-Victorian additions and renovations, but some original features too, not least the stout wooden doors and a rood screen that goes the full width of the building, painted with images of angels on the left, apostles in the centre and Old Testament prophets on the right. Cromwell's troops hacked off their faces in the mid-seventeenth century – a similar fate befell the original font at the other end of the church. Beyond the rood screen, the choir stalls carry finely fashioned human and animal heads as well as grotesques, not least a depiction of a man in the throes of toothache. Look out also for "Southwold Jack", a brightly painted, medieval effigy of a man in armour nailed to the wall beside the font; he was once part of a clock, nodding belligerently as he struck the hours.

Southwold Museum

9–11 Victoria St, IP18 6HZ • Easter–Oct daily 2–4pm, Aug also 10.30am–noon • Free • ☎01502 726097, ⓦ southwoldmuseum.org

Just across the road from the town's parish church, **Southwold Museum** covers an awful lot in a relatively small space, from the rise and fall of the local fishing industry to the town's latter-day gentrification – all very well displayed following a recent renovation.

The Sailors' Reading Room

East Cliff, IP18 6EL • Daily 9am–5pm; Oct–March till 3.30pm • Free

From the Lighthouse, follow the seafront path right to the curious **Sailors' Reading Room**, built in 1864 in memory of a local Captain Rayley, one of Nelson's officers at the Battle of Trafalgar who had died the previous year. It's a peaceful haven, open to anyone, which serves as – yes – a reading room, designed to keep sailors occupied and out of the pub, and where only the ticking of the clock can disturb your browsing of the morning papers, boating magazines and Lloyds ship registers that are left on the tables. There's also a make-do Southwold **maritime museum**, with models of old ships, an array of painted figureheads from ships long since sunk and photos of the various local salts who helped to fund and build the place. The late W.G. Sebald, in his book *The Rings of Saturn*, regarded it as his favourite haunt in Southwold, "better than anywhere in the long winter months for looking out on the stormy sea as it crashes on the promenade".

Southwold Pier

Mon–Fri 9am–6pm, Sat 8.30am–7pm, Sun 8.30am–6pm; Under the Pier Show Mon–Fri & Sun 10am–6pm, Sat 10am–7pm • ⓦ southwoldpier.co.uk

Southwold Pier is the latest incarnation of a structure that dates back to 1899. Built as a landing stage for passenger ferries, it has had a troubled history – repeatedly damaged by storms, hit by a sea-mine and then partly chopped up by the army as a protection against German invasion in World War II. Recently revamped and renovated, and nowadays owned by the folk from the *Salthouse Harbour* (see p.230) and *Angel* hotels (see p.311), it's delightfully retro, with deliberately low-key attractions and almost classy gift shops in rows of humdrum white huts. Be sure to take in the ingenious **Waterclock**, made to promote the recycling of water in 1984 and still going; and don't on any account miss the **Under the Pier Show**, full of Tim Hunkin's off-the-wall handmade games, the most popular of which is unsurprisingly "Whack-a-banker", although you might also like to try "Rent-a'-Dog", "Gene-Forecaster" and "Brainwash". Afterwards relax at the *Boardwalk* restaurant (see p.272).

The Harbour

Just below the Market Place, **South Green** is the largest and prettiest of Southwold's greens, and you need to cross this to reach both Ferry Road and the ferry footpath that lead down to the **harbour**, at the mouth of the River Blyth – a ten-minute walk. It's an idyllic spot, where fishing smacks rest against old wooden jetties and nets are spread out along the banks to dry. A foot **ferry** (late April to late May & late Sept to late Oct Sat & Sun 10am–12.30pm & 2–5pm; late March to mid-April & late May to Sept daily 10am–12.30pm & 2–5pm; £1; ☎01502 724729), shuffles across the river to Walberswick from here (see p.273) and there are a couple of places for food and drink, notably the *Sole Bay Fish Co and Smokehouse*, where you can buy fresh fish and also eat it in the attached restaurant, and the *Harbour Inn* further up the river. You can do boat and seal-spotting trips on the *Coastal Voyager* from here too (see p.272), while in the opposite direction take in the current RNLI lifeboat station and the **Alfred Corry Lifeboat Museum** (Easter–Oct Mon–Fri 10.30am–12.30pm & 2.30–4.30pm, Sat & Sun 10.45am–4.30pm; free; ☎01502 723200, ⊛alfredcorry.co .uk), which houses a wooden rowing and sailing lifeboat from 1892 along with lots of accompanying background. Across the dunes from here the beach is glorious, and you can either follow it all the way back into Southwold proper or go back along the river to the *Harbour Inn* and then take the path that leads back into town across **Southwold Common**.

ARRIVAL AND INFORMATION   SOUTHWOLD

By bus Buses pull in on the High St, yards from the tourist office, and there are hourly buses to Halesworth (30min), where there's also a train station, to Lowestoft (40min) and Great Yarmouth (1hr30min), and to Beccles (25min).

By car There are two central car parks in the town, both free – one just off the common, close to the *Red Lion* pub,

the other at the opposite end of the High St just off York Rd, on the way to the water tower. There's also a large pay-and-display car park just north of the pier.

Tourist office Just off the Market Place at 7a Child's Yard (April–Oct daily 10am–5pm; Nov–March Mon–Sat 10am–3pm; ☎01502 724729, ⊛visit -sunrisecoast.co.uk).

ACCOMMODATION

The Blyth Station Rd ☎01502 722632, ⊛blythhotel .com. On the edge of the town centre, but just a 5min walk from the High St, the thirteen rooms here are cosily decorated in country style; and there's a good bar and restaurant downstairs. Dog-friendly too. **£115**

The Brewer's House 56 Victoria St, Southwold, IP18 6JQ ☎01502 722186, ⊛adnams.co.uk. The double-fronted Victorian former home of the Adnams head brewer is centrally placed and very comfortable, and has been beautifully refurbished by the brewery. It sleeps 6–8. One week **£1740**

The Crown 90 High St, IP18 6DP ☎01502 722186,

⊛adnams.co.uk. The less upmarket – and cheaper – of Adnams' two hotels in Southwold, with fourteen rooms above a bar-restaurant. Most of the rooms are large and have been recently refurbished, decorated in a contemporary style. **£165**

Home@21 21 North Parade, IP18 6LT ☎01502 722573, ⊛homeat21.co.uk. Near the pier, this seafront guesthouse occupies a well-maintained Victorian terrace house, whose rooms have been sympathetically updated and opened out. Four rooms, all en suite, and two of which are sea-facing. **£95**

Northcliffe 20 North Parade, IP18 6LT ☎01502 724074, ⓦnorthcliffe-southwold.co.uk. Of several guesthouses that line up along the seafront promenade, this is one of the nicest, with six very comfortable en-suite guest rooms all decorated differently. **£85**

Sutherland House 56 High St, IP18 6DN ☎01502 724544, ⓦsutherlandhouse.co.uk. The three rooms above this smart restaurant are all very comfy, but the pick is the room James II slept in when he was the grand old Duke of York, although the more expensive top-floor suite, with its adjoining sitting room, is perfect if you're staying a while or you're a family. **£145**

The Swan Market Place, IP18 6EG ☎01502 722186, ⓦadnams.co.uk. Delightful hotel which a rather splendid Georgian building right at the heart of Southwold. Some of the guest rooms are in the main building, which is a real period piece, its nooks and crannies holding all manner of Georgian details; others occupy the more modern, blander garden annexe at the back – the "Lighthouse Rooms" – and are a bit cheaper. **£185**

EATING

The Blyth Station Rd, IP18 6AY ☎01502 722632, ⓦblythhotel.com. The restaurant here has a more contemporary feel than the upstairs rooms, and serves a fairly simple menu encompassing starters at around £6.50 and mains for £13–17, along with a separate bar menu next door – fish and chips, sausage and mash, etc – although you can mix and match the two. Mon–Fri 6.30–9pm, Sat & Sun noon–8pm.

Boardwalk Southwold Pier, IP18 6BN ☎01502 722105. The pier's restaurant has always been a great spot to eat, and the food here is now better than ever, with a larger menu that includes everything from great fish and chips to burgers, steaks and sausage and mash. There are always a few surprising specials too. Most mains around £12.95. Daily 10am–8pm; lunch 11.30am–4pm, dinner 5–9.30pm.

The Crown 90 High St, IP18 6DP ☎01502 722186, ⓦadnams.co.uk. Deluxe bar food featuring local, seasonal ingredients, all washed down with Adnams ales. Mains here average £16–20 and you can eat in wood-panelled bar or restaurant at the front. Mon–Fri noon–2.30pm & 6–9pm, Sat & Sun noon–2.30pm & 6.30–9.30pm.

Lord Nelson East St, IP18 6EJ ☎01502 722 ☎079, ⓦthelordnelsonsouthwold.co.uk. A lively neighbourhood pub of low-beamed ceilings just back from the seafront. There's an emphasis on food, with a really good, locally inspired menu featuring crab, lots of good fish and seafood and Blythburgh pork sausages. Kitchen daily noon–2pm & 7–9pm; pub Mon–Sat 10.30am–11pm, Sun noon–10.30pm.

Sole Bay Inn 7 East Green, IP128 6JN ☎01502 723736, ⓦsolebayinn.co.uk. This couldn't help but be an Adnams pub, based as it is right opposite the brewery, and it's a convivial, one-bar place, with a stripped-back interior, that's popular with locals as well as tourists and serves decent pub food, with most mains – chicken curry, minute steak, fishcakes, lamb chops – £9–12. Kitchen daily noon–9pm; pub Mon–Sat 11am–11pm, Sun 11.30am–10.30pm.

Sutherland House 56 High St, IP18 6DN ☎01502 724544, ⓦsutherlandhouse.co.uk. Classy, modern British restaurant that's housed in one of Southwold's oldest buildings, home to the admiralty in days gone by. There's a strong local emphasis to the menu, and whether you're eating lunch or dinner here you can reckon on feasting on local sea bass and other fish, Blythburgh pork, Cromer crab and great steaks. Lunch mains go for £12–14, dinner main courses for £18–23. Tues–Sat noon–2.30pm & 6.30–8.30pm.

The Swan Market Place, IP18 6EG ☎01502 722186, ⓦadnams.co.uk. Southwold's best hotel offers its most upscale, if old-fashioned, dining experience, with great food served in an elegant dining room overlooking the Market Place, which always feels like a treat. It's moderately priced too, considering the environment and quality, and service is excellent. The food is fairly old-school, with a fixed-price menu costing £35 for three courses – pretty good value because the food is beautifully executed. Start with ballotine of quail or ham hock roulade followed by saddle of lamb or rib of beef; or you can order from the less-high-end bar menu, where they have a smaller and simpler selection of dishes for £10–12 a main course. Mon–Sat noon–2pm & 7–9pm, Sun 12.30–2.30pm.

OUT ON THE WATER

Coastal Voyager (☎07887 525082, ⓦcoastalvoyager.co.uk) operates a variety of sea and river trips from their base in Southwold Harbour. Their most popular trip is the 30min "Sea Blast", on their 400hp powerboat (£26, children £13, families £65), but if you want something gentler they also run a 3hr 30min cruise up the Blyth River (£25, children £12.50, families £66) and 3hr seal-spotting trips to Scroby Sands (£40, children £20, families £100). You can also opt to drive the powerboat yourself if you have £260 to spare.

THE SOUTHWOLD CIRCULAR

You can do a three-mile circular **walk** all the way around Southwold, by following the path to the harbour and then right up the Blyth River and across the marshes, and then back across the main road down to the coast just north of the pier. You can also follow the river all the way up to Blythburgh church (see below), about four miles in all, either then coming back the same way or having the *Coastal Voyager* pick you up or drop you off (see box, p.272).

SHOPPING

Adnams Cellar & Kitchen 4 Drayman Square, Victoria St, IP18 6GB ☎01502 725612, ⓦadnams .co.uk. Large store around the corner from the brewery that's typical of this great local chain, with a fantastic choice of wine and of course Adnams beer, kitchenware and a really good café out the back. Mon–Sat 9am–6pm Sun 10am–4pm.

Black Olive Deli 80a–80b High St, IP18 6DP ☎01502 722312, ⓦtheblackolivedelicatessen.co.uk. Great deli

right on the High St that has all the usual deli favourites, including a particularly good selection of fish and seafood products, home-made pies and, of course, olives. Mon–Sat 9am–5pm, Sun 10am–4pm.

Southwold Books 69 High St, IP18 6DS ☎01502 722283. It's actually a branch of Waterstone's, but you wouldn't know it, and at least Southwold has got its own bookshop back again after the previous one closed down. Mon–Sat 9am–5.30pm, Sun 10am–5pm.

7

Walberswick

Just across the River Blyth from Southwold lies the pretty little village of **WALBERSWICK**, another once-prosperous port now fallen (or risen) into well-heeled tranquillity. For many years it was the home of the English Impressionist painter Philip Wilson Steer (1860–1942), and, warming to the same theme, it's now a seaside escape with an arty, sometime celebrity undertow. There's not much to see as such, though you can stroll south along the coast to Dunwich (see p.265) and its annual crabbing festival is a popular event, indeed too popular in recent years – it has been cancelled because of the sheer numbers attending.

ACCOMMODATION AND EATING

★**The Anchor** The Street, IP18 6UA ☎01502 722122 ⓦanchoratwalberswick.com. This place strives to be a village local, a gastropub and a cool place to stay and succeeds pretty well at all three, offering a choice between the old-fashioned cosiness of its three doubles and one single in the main building and the more contemporary comforts of its six cedar-clad garden chalets outside, half of which are dog-friendly. It also has a convivial bar that always boasts a great choice of draught beers, and lunch and dinner menus that focus on Norfolk and Suffolk fish and seafood, local game and even local flour with which they make their home-made bread. A great place both to stay and to eat – never

better than when serving its excellent Saturday brunch, or one of its summer Sunday lunchtime barbecues. Kitchen Mon–Fri noon–3pm & 6–9pm, Sat & Sun noon–10pm. **£110**

The Bell Ferry Rd, IP18 6TN ☎01502 723109, ⓦthebellwalberswick.wordpress.com. Under new management, this local pub has six snug double rooms that are all individually designed and very comfy. A couple of rooms are big enough for a family and rates include breakfast. The downstairs pub is a rabbit warren of a place, with all sorts of ancient nooks and crannies, and a separate dining room. Kitchen daily noon–2.30pm & 6–9pm; pub daily 11am–11pm. **£90**

Blythburgh

The small village of **BLYTHBURGH** lies at the end of the Blyth estuary, which reaches inland from Southwold's harbour. Its church of **Holy Trinity** is known as the "cathedral of the marshes", and with good reason – its tower can be seen long before you reach the village, and it's an enormous church even by East Anglian standards. Inside it's a high, open structure, with a prominent, shining, beamed ceiling decorated with carved angels, as well as other details to seek out, such as the so-called "poppyhead" carving at the end of the pews, each one depicting one of the seven deadly sins, and the Jack o' Bell in the choir, who originally rang his bell every hour but now only does so to signal the arrival of the priest. Look also at the north door at the back of the church, scorched black in 1577 by the devil or "Black Shuck" – the ghostly black dog thought to roam East Anglia in the Middle Ages, who appeared the same night in Bungay (see p.216) – and, if you can manage the stairs, the restored priest's room above the porch, which is a haven of contemplation.

Covehithe

Just under five miles north of Southwold, **COVEHITHE** is technically at the end of the road, although the "end" keeps changing as coastal erosion causes the nearby cliffs to fall into the sea. That's not the reason the church of **St Andrew** is mostly a ruin; the once enormous church was deemed unviable in the seventeenth century and they let it fall apart while building the thatched edifice you see today, only keeping the church's massive tower. There's nothing much to see inside, apart from a beamed ceiling and medieval font, but the location, and especially the ruins, are uniquely atmospheric.

A sign warns against proceeding any further due to the instability of the cliffs beyond, but you can instead reach the nearby beach by taking a path off the main road – just back a little from the church, into the **Benacre Nature Reserve** – for ten minutes or so to where Covehithe Broad's reedy waters give way to bracken-topped cliffs and a sandy beach beyond. It's a lovely, untouched spot where you can spy marsh harriers, bearded reedlings and others.

You can also do a circular walk in the other direction taking in **Benacre Broad** to the north and then coming full circle back down the coast – about five miles in all, and pretty easy. Walk back up the road inland from St Andrew's church and take a path off to the right after about half a mile, alongside a section of wood. This leads across country and after about a mile and a half links up with the Suffolk Coast Path, which leads right back down to the coast, where it heads south, skirting the edge of Benacre Broad and finally finishing up at Covehithe.

Halesworth and around

The archetypal small Suffolk town of **HALESWORTH** is a self-sufficient sort of place rooted in the local farming community but one that has done a good job of updating itself, with a slightly artsy edge these days. Its pedestrianized main street – the **Thoroughfare** – is a bustling mix of low-key local businesses that leads to the *Angel Hotel* (see opposite) and small **Market Place** opposite, from which a path leads through to the precincts of the parish church of **St Mary**. Once you've seen these you've pretty much seen Halesworth, although there are pleasant walks to be done by the **river** and in the meadows just south of the centre known as **Millennium Green**.

LATITUDE FESTIVAL

Local lad George Orwell may have hated Southwold, but he might well have approved of the town's music festival, **Latitude**, which began in 2006 and now spreads over four days in the middle of July with happy campers grubbing down in Henham Park about five miles west of town, just across the A12. It bills itself as a festival with a literary and dramatic bent, and is deliberately a lot more family-friendly than the multitude of other British summer music fests.

Tickets generally go for around £200 including camping for the full long weekend; more from ⓦ latitudefestival.com.

St Mary the Virgin

1 Steeple End, IP19 8LL • ⓦ blythvalleychurches.org.uk

At the centre of Halesworth, the stout flint church of **St Mary the Virgin**, surrounded by a pleasant triangle of timbered and Georgian houses, was built on much earlier foundations, as evidenced by the so-called "Dane Stone" in the choir, a Saxon carving sunk into the wall on the right and showing arms reaching out to clasp branches and leaves. At the back of the church, the medieval font, with its carvings of woodwoses, is a more conventional feature.

Halesworth & District Museum

Halesworth Station, IP19 8BZ • Tues–Sat 10am–12.30pm, Wed also 2–4pm • Free • ⓣ 01986 873030, ⓦ halesworthmuseum.org.uk

Halesworth Museum, just out of the centre in the train station, has displays on local industry and local characters, including the re-creation of a local tailor's workshop and the collections of Haleworth botanist Sir William Hooker, who was the first director of Kew Gardens. It also has a model of the station's famous "moveable platforms", installed in 1880 to accommodate longer trains.

7

ARRIVAL AND INFORMATION   HALESWORTH

By train Halesworth is on the main Ipswich–Lowestoft line and its train station is just outside the town centre off London Rd – hourly trains to Lowestoft (30min) and Ipswich (55min).

By bus Buses stop at the train station and also opposite the town centre car park, and there are connections at least

every hour to Southwold (30min), and hourly to Saxmundham (30min), Aldeburgh (1hr) and Leiston (50min).

Tourist office You can get tourist information from the reception of the *Angel Hotel* on the Thoroughfare.

ACCOMMODATION

IN TOWN

Angel Hotel Thoroughfare, IP19 8AH ⓣ 01986 873365, ⓦ angel-halesworth.co.uk. At the far end of the Thoroughfare, the *Angel* is a bit of a hub, holding as it does the town's tourist office, a bar that's popular for both morning coffee and evening drinks, and a well-patronized restaurant. It's also a really cosy old coaching inn, with seven decently furnished en-suite doubles upstairs. **£75**

★ **Ivy Grange Farm** Butt's Rd, IP19 8RN ⓣ 07802 456807, ⓦ ivygrangefarm.co.uk. One of the best places to stay in Suffolk, *Ivy Grange Farm* is the delightful glamping site of two London escapees (Nick and Kim Hoare), who have five beautifully appointed and very cosy

yurts with wood-burners, BBQs and campfire pits to enjoy. The setting couldn't be better – very rural, with lots of birds and wildlife on your doorstep, but right on great cycling and walking routes. And Nick and Kim are great hosts. Minimum two-night stay. From **£90**

OUT OF TOWN

Rendham Hall Rendham, IP17 2AW ⓣ 01728 663440, ⓦ rendhamhall.co.uk. This homely B&B, based on a working dairy farm just outside Halesworth, has just two rooms – a family room and a double, both en suite. Very friendly, and in a beautiful location that's great for kids. **£75**

EATING

Angel Hotel Thoroughfare, IP19 8AH ⓣ 01986 873365, ⓦ angel-halesworth.co.uk. The *Angel Hotel* has both a busy bar serving a full menu lunchtimes and evenings and also the long-standing *Cleone's* restaurant, with pizzas from £5.50 and pasta and other mains from £9.95 on a short and pretty authentic Italian menu. Daily noon–2pm & 6.30–9pm.

Singtong Neeyom 37 Thoroughfare, IP19 8LE ⓣ 01986 873737, ⓦ singtongthairestaurant.co.uk. Virtually opposite the church, and housed in the old town police station, this is the place to go if you're tired of modern British food made with locally sourced ingredients.

Most mains cost around £9.95. Good Thai cooking, and a welcoming environment to enjoy it in. Tues–Sat 5.30–9.30pm.

Tilly's 10 Market Place, IP19 8BA ⓣ 01986 835899, ⓦ tillysofhalesworth.co.uk. Late of Southwold and now re-established in Halesworth, this deliberately retro-1920s café-restaurant has an all-day menu serving breakfast, lots of good light-lunch options – smoked fish chowder, Welsh rarebit, bubble & squeak (all around £7) – and a simple weekend evening menu where you can start with a prawn cocktail and follow with pan-roasted chicken or sea bass. It's all traditional food that suits the venerable building and determinedly old-fashioned atmosphere. Evening main courses go for around £12, starters around £5, and they also serve morning coffee and cream teas, and, unusually, a gluten-free menu too. Mon–Thurs & Sun 9am–5pm, Fri & Sat 9am–10pm.

Bramfield

The village of **BRAMFIELD**, a couple of miles south of Halesworth, is home to the *Queen's Head* pub and the church of **St Andrew**, a well-kept thatched church with a round tower, though one which is unusually separate from the main body of the church. Inside it has one of the best-preserved rood screens in Suffolk, with rich and clear paintings showing various saints. Look, too, at the seventeenth-century memorial for a certain Arthur Coke in the choir, a beautifully carved piece of work, which shows his wife lying by him with her baby daughter at her side (she died, apparently, in childbirth).

Laxfield

About six miles southwest of Halesworth, the pretty village of **LAXFIELD** feels quite remote, situated as it is in the no-man's-land between Halesworth and Framlingham. Its centre is marked by the timbered **Guildhall**, built in 1515 on the site of an earlier building, and home to a small museum (Easter & May–Sept Sat & Sun 2–5pm; free), with various exhibits relating to rural life in the area. Directly opposite, **All Saints** church is a fourteenth-century building that's unusual for its exceptionally wide timber roof, which covers an equally broad single aisle. It also has an impressive large font from the early sixteenth century, with carvings of the seven sacraments (although it could be in better repair), some early sixteenth-century pews carved with various creatures, and a giant fifteenth-century chest that used to hold church records.

EATING AND DRINKING

★**King's Head** Gorams Mill Lane, IP13 8DW ☎01986 798395, ⊛laxfieldkingshead.co.uk. Below the church, across the stream that runs through the village, this was proclaimed "Adnams Pub Of The Year" a few years ago, and is unusual in that it has no bar – just a room full of barrels that staff disappear into to get your order while you make yourself comfy in one of the pub's wood-panelled little rooms. There is also good food, served in a separate dining room – sandwiches, steaks, pan-fried sea bass, sausage and mash, etc. Very friendly, and especially cosy on a winter's night. Kitchen daily noon–3pm & 7–9pm; pub daily noon–late.

Lowestoft and around

Suffolk's second-largest town, **LOWESTOFT** is known for two things: fish and the seaside, two industries which to say the least are in decline – a fact that's unfortunately evident pretty much everywhere you look. The heart of the town, close by the **harbour**, is a down-at-heel mix of chain and Poundstretcher stores, while the harbour itself is a workaday fishing port that is a shadow of its former self. The southern end of the town's centre is its most alluring stretch, focusing on the **beach**, which is undeniably fine, a long strip of golden sand kept in immaculate condition and lined by a typically English seaside blend of Victorian terraces, pristinely planted gardens and beach huts. There's a small **pier**, and the East Point Pavilion close to the harbour houses the tourist office, but to be honest there's not a great deal to be gained in hanging around here unless you're going to the beach. There are things to see in Lowestoft, but the town's best attractions lie beyond the centre, either on the northern and southern edges of the centre by the sea, or amid the bypasses and roundabouts that encircle the town – specifically Oulton Broad, which provides the town's most alluring destination by some way.

The Mincarlo

Royal Plain, NR33 0AQ • May–Oct Mon–Thurs, Sat & Sun 10.30am–4pm • Free • ☎ 01502 565234, ⓦ lydiaeva.org.uk

Moored by the South Pier next to the lifeboat station, the **Mincarlo**, the last sidewinder trawler to be built in Lowestoft, offers a glimpse of life on board Lowestoft's fishing fleet at its height, fitted out much as it was when it was built in 1961.

Maritime Museum

Sparrow's Nest, Whapload Rd, NR32 1XG • May–Sept daily 10am–5pm • £2 • ☎ 01502 561963, ⓦ lowestoftmaritimemuseum.org.uk

Lowestoft's **Maritime Museum** is north of the town centre, just below the town's lighthouse, facing the beach (you can follow the seaside path all the way form the centre of town). It's a good local museum, crammed with artefacts pertaining to fishing, shipbuilding and World War II among other things. There are models of sailing and steam drifters, mock-ups of the cabin of a drifter and the bridge of a trawler, and lots of background on the fishing industry here in general, much of whose story is told in some constantly running short films – though the most tangible relics from the town's fishing past are the beach navigation buoys and rows of wooden racks across the road outside, once used for drying nets.

East Anglia Transport Museum

Chapel Rd, Carlton, Colville, NR33 8BL • July & Aug Tues, Thurs & Sat 2–5pm, Sun 11am–5pm; June & Sept Thurs & Sat 2–5pm, Sun 11am–5pm; April & May Thurs 2–5pm & Sun 11am–5pm • £7, children £5 • ☎ 01502 518549, ⓦ eatm.org .uk • Buses every 15min from the train station to Beccles Rd, from where it's a 5–10min walk

The **East Anglia Transport Museum** is not the Suffolk coast's most vital attraction. But this open-air museum of old trams, trains and buses does a great job of showing the development of mass transport over the past century or so. You can ride on trains, buses and trams and afterwards stop for a cup of tea at the museum's café.

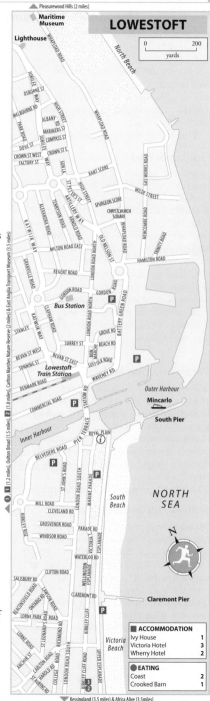

7

The Carlton Marshes Nature Reserve

Open 24hr; office Mon–Fri 9am–5pm • Car parking available

On Lowestoft's western edges, close to Oulton Broad, **Carlton Marshes** gives a hint of the Broadland landscape that lies just beyond, a wide-skied expanse of marshy grazing land, reeds and water. It's crisscrossed by paths and you can either do a loop back to the car park or continue on to Oulton Broad in about twenty minutes. Various birds are often spotted here – marsh harriers, kestrels, golden plovers, reed and sedge warblers and others, along with a number of different kinds of dragonfly.

Oulton Broad

Lowestoft's most compelling attraction, **Oulton Broad**, where the town takes on a riverside rather than seaside feel, is effectively the southern gateway to the Broads National Park. There's a gathering of shops and restaurants around the eastern end at **Mutford Lock**, where you can hire a dayboat or take a cruise around the Broad (1hr; £4.50) or up the river (1hr 30min; £8) on the *Waveney Princess*. The Broad itself is fringed by the grass and trees of Nicholas Everitt Park, where the **Lowestoft Museum** (April–Oct daily 1–4pm; free) is hosted by the crenellated flint Broad House and has displays of eighteenth-century Lowestoft porcelain, others pertaining to Lowestoft local luminaries including Benjamin Britten, and of course the fishing industry, and mock-ups of old living rooms, shops and suchlike. Or you can just sit and nurse a coffee at the **Quays Café** and watch dayboaters and yachtsmen try to make land at the nearby free moorings. It's busy here during summer, and summer evenings can be great fun, especially when the Broad hosts motorboat racing every Thursday evening.

Pleasurewood Hills

Leisure Way, Corton, NR32 5DZ • April, May & Sept Sat & Sun 10am–5pm; June Wed, Sat & Sun daily 10am–5pm; July daily 10am–5pm; late July to early Sept daily 10am–6pm; also Easter hols and half-term daily 10am–5pm • Ticket prices cheaper if bought online: £16.50–20, children £14.50–17 • ☎ 01502 586000, ⬤ pleasurewoodhills.com

Just to the north of the centre of Lowestoft, **Pleasurewood Hills** is rightly one of the town's main attractions. It's not quite Disneyworld, but it makes a decent stab at providing some genuinely terrifying rides – a state-of-the art loop-the-loop roller coaster, a couple of waterslides, a scary ghost ride – along with gentler attractions aimed at younger children, such as boat rides, a smaller roller coaster and much more. It's a nice place, well run, and makes for a decent family day out.

ARRIVAL AND INFORMATION   LOWESTOFT

By train Lowestoft's train station is right in the centre of town by the harbour; there are also stations on the other side of the town centre at Oulton Broad North and Oulton Broad South, and all three stations are connected roughly hourly with Ipswich (1hr 30min) and stations on the way – Darsham, Saxmundham and Woodbridge among them. Lowestoft is also connected by rail with Norwich roughly every hour (55min), taking in stops at Haddiscoe, Reedham, Acle and Brundall.

By bus The bus station is also centrally placed, a short walk north of the main train station on Gordon Rd, just behind the Britten Centre. The most useful bus is the #X1, which leaves every half an hour or so for Great Yarmouth

(30min), travelling from there right across Norfolk via Acle, Norwich, Dereham, Swaffham and King's Lynn as far as Peterborough (4hr 30min away). There are also buses, every half-hour, to Norwich via Beccles (35min) and Loddon (1hr), and also half-hourly services to Yarmouth, Hemsby and Caister beyond.

By car The most central car parks are those on Denmark Rd by the train station and across the river from here by the East Point Pavilion – both pay-and-display. However, there are often spaces free along Kirkley Cliff Rd.

Tourist office In the East Point Pavilion right on the seafront near the station and harbour (Mon–Sat 10am–5pm, Sun 10am–3pm; ☎ 01502 533600).

ACCOMMODATION

Ivy House Ivy Lane, Oulton Broad, NR33 8HY ☏01502 501353, ⓦivyhousecountryhotel.co.uk. *The Ivy House* has always been an undeniably nice place to stay, but it's better than ever after a recent makeover, with twenty very comfortable rooms in a series of barn conversions and other buildings that back onto the marshes and Oulton Broad. The gardens are lovely and there's a new bright and contemporary bar with outside seating, along with a long-established, excellent restaurant. **£140**

Victoria Hotel Kirkley Cliff, NR33 0BZ ☏01502 574433, ⓦthehotelvictoria.co.uk. An elegant old building, reasonably well refurbished, with lovely views over South Beach and 24 good-sized rooms, many of which have views of the sea. The rooms are slightly bland, but it's one of the better places to stay in Lowestoft, and enjoys a good location a 10min walk from the train station and main pier. **£95**

Wherry Hotel Bridge Rd, Oulton Broad, NR32 3LN ☏01502 516845, ⓦwherryhotel.com. Enjoying a perfect position facing Oulton Broad, the *Wherry* is a nice old-fashioned hotel with spacious, recently refurbished rooms with large bathrooms. It's not fancy, but the rooms are decent and have all you need, especially the ones with views over the water; and the bar and restaurant are convivial places of an evening. **£80**

EATING

Coast Kirkley Cliff, NR33 0BZ ☏01502 574433, ⓦthehotelvictoria.co.uk. The restaurant of the *Victoria Hotel* (see above) has perfect views over the beach from its sea-facing dining room, and locally themed seasonal menus that change every three months or so (£17 for two courses, £20 for three), as well as a bar menu with fish and chips, sausage and mash, steaks and the like (£10–12) in case you fancy something simpler. The food isn't bad and it's one of the town's most pleasant places to eat. Mon–Fri noon–2.30pm & 6.30–9pm, Sat & Sun noon–9pm.

Crooked Barn Ivy Lane, Oulton Broad, NR33 8HY ☏01502 501353, ⓦivyhousecountryhotel.co.uk. The restaurant of the *Ivy House* hotel (see above) offers Lowestoft's best chance of a slap-up gourmet experience, with an admirably restrained choice of five or so starters and mains for £5.95 and £16.95 respectively. It's a fairly safe menu – fillet of beef, lemon sole, calf's liver plus a veggie option – but the room itself is a lovely, eighteenth-century beamed affair, full of character. Mon–Sat noon–2pm & 7–9.30pm, Sun 12.30–7.45pm.

Kessingland

About four miles south of Lowestoft, the village of **KESSINGLAND** was home to the swashbuckling adventure writer H. Rider Haggard, who had a clifftop house here in the late nineteenth century. You can see why he chose it: it's a dramatic, almost forsaken location, its large foreshore of pebbles and marram grass giving way to a lovely strip of sandy beach. The parish church, **St Edmund**, is worth a peek for its massive tower and nautical stained-glass windows, and WG Sebald popped in on his *Rings of Saturn* trip, but otherwise there's not much reason to visit apart from as part of the windy walk north to Lowestoft (p.276) or south to Covehithe and Benacre (p.274) – or to visit its major attraction, Africa Alive (see below).

Africa Alive

White's Lane, Kessingland, NR33 7TF • Daily: late March to mid-July 9.30am–5pm; mid-July to early Sept 9.30am–6pm; early Sept to late Oct 9.30am–5pm; late Oct to late March 9.30am–4pm • April–Oct £18.95, children £12.95; Nov–March £12.95/£8.95 • ☏01502 740291, ⓦafrica-alive.co.uk

A slice of tropical savannah transplanted to Suffolk, the **Africa Alive** zoo unsurprisingly focuses on Africa and does it pretty well, a compact place with giraffes, rhino, zebras, ostriches and others roaming its central "Plains of Africa" enclosure, and other sections containing lions and cheetahs, lemurs and meerkats, monkeys and critically endangered creatures like the Somali wild ass. There are lots of activities during the day, and you can get up close to the lemurs, "meet the meerkats" and more – plus there are kids' play areas and minigolf, and the site as a whole is well kept and has numerous picturesque corners. Run by folk from Banham Zoo (see p.206), it's a decent day out, and one of Lowestoft's relative highlights, for families at least.

Inland Suffolk

FLATFORD MILL

Inland Suffolk

Stretching forty-odd miles north from the Essex border, inland Suffolk is deeply rural, its myriad hamlets and villages linked by an intricate network of country lanes. At first glance, the landscape changes very little, but change it does, from the valley meadowlands in the south through rolling farmland and on up to the plateau claylands of what is sometimes called High Suffolk. The River Stour weaves its way through the southern reaches of the region, creating the verdant vistas much admired by the painter John Constable – hence the tourist moniker "Constable Country" now attached to Dedham Vale. The National Trust's Flatford Mill celebrates the life and times of the painter, but otherwise it's the prettiness of the villages that remains the main draw hereabouts with Stoke-by-Nayland and Dedham leading the picture-postcard charge. The River Stour also runs through Sudbury, a pleasant little town that boasts an excellent museum devoted to the work of another highly regarded English artist, Thomas Gainsborough, and from here it's a short hop to another small town, Long Melford, home to a pair of stately homes and a particularly splendid church.

8

Sudbury, **Long Melford** and the other villages and towns dotted along the River Stour and its tributaries were once busy little places at the heart of East Anglia's medieval weaving trade. By the 1490s, the region produced more cloth than any other part of the country, but in Tudor times production moved on and, although most of the smaller places continued spinning cloth for the next three hundred years or so, their importance slowly dwindled. Bypassed by the Industrial Revolution, the southern reaches of inland Suffolk had, by the late nineteenth century, become a remote rural backwater, an impoverished area whose decline had one unforeseen consequence: with few exceptions, its settlements were never prosperous enough to modernize, and the architectural legacy of medieval and Tudor times survived. The two best-preserved villages are **Lavenham** and minuscule **Kersey**, both of which hold a battery of ancient, rickety half-timbered buildings, many painted in the bright yellows and pinks popular hereabouts – though they both heave with sightseers on summer weekends; whereas Clare and Cavendish, in the **Upper Stour River Valley**, are smaller and quieter.

Moving north, **Bury St Edmunds** can boast not just the ruins of its once-prestigious abbey, but also some fine Georgian architecture on its grid-iron streets; **Stowmarket** is home to the Museum of East Anglian Life; and nearby **Newmarket** is different again, a one-industry, monoculture town devoted to the racehorse with 16,000 people and 3000 horses. Both Bury St Edmunds and Newmarket are on the A14, which slices across inland Suffolk, and the scattering of hamlets to the north of this main

LAVENHAM

Highlights

❶ Flatford Mill Take a peek at the land- and riverscapes that inspired one of England's greatest painters, John Constable. **See p.284**

❷ Sudbury The home town of one of England's finest portraitists, Thomas Gainsborough, whose rich talents are celebrated in the Gainsborough House gallery. **See p.290**

❸ Holy Trinity, Long Melford In a county that seems to drizzle superb medieval churches, Holy Trinity is one of the most beautiful, if not the most beautiful of all. **See p.294**

❹ Lavenham With a small army of antique, half-timbered buildings, this lovely town is the cream of the scenic crop. **See p.297**

❺ Kersey Probably the prettiest village in Suffolk – there's hardly an architectural hair out of place. **See p.300**

❻ Bury St Edmunds Atmospheric old town, whose star turn is the crumbly ruins of its once-mighty abbey. **See p.307**

HIGHLIGHTS ARE MARKED ON THE MAP ON PP.286–287

HALF A DOZEN GREAT PLACES TO STAY

Black Lion Hotel Long Melford. See p.295
Great House Hotel Lavenham. See p.299
Swan Hotel Lavenham. See p.299

Old Cannon B&B Bury St Edmunds. See p.311
The Bildeston Crown Bildeston. See p.301
Ickworth Hotel Ickworth House. See p.313

---

thoroughfare are the quietest of places, the two particular highlights being **Eye**, complete with its battered castle and splendid church, and **Hoxne**, where one of the most popular saints of medieval England, King Edmund, met a grisly end.

GETTING AROUND   INLAND SUFFOLK

By train Inland Suffolk's principal train line links Ipswich with Stowmarket, Needham Market, Bury St Edmunds and Newmarket; you can also get to Sudbury, which is on a branch line off the London Liverpool Street–Colchester main line (change at Marks Tey).

By bus Bus services between the villages are patchy – and almost nonexistent in the evenings and on Sundays – so you'll find it difficult to get away from the towns. The situation isn't helped by the multitude of bus companies, though Chambers (⊛ chambersbus.co.uk), one of the largest, does operate an especially useful service linking Colchester, Bury St Edmunds, Lavenham, Long Melford and Sudbury (Mon–Sat hourly). For bus timetable information, go to ⊛ suffolkonboard.com or ⊛ travelineeastanglia.org.uk.

On foot For walkers, footpaths crisscross the area, with some of the most enjoyable being in the vicinity of Lavenham and Long Melford. All the local tourist offices sell easy-to-use walking leaflets. The main long-distance route is the Stour Valley Path, which runs for sixty miles, linking Dedham Vale with Sudbury and ultimately Newmarket.

Dedham Vale – Constable Country

Forming the border between Essex and Suffolk for much of its length, the **River Stour** weaves and wends its way through a handsome, quintessentially English landscape of farms and woodland with the thick grassy banks of the river keeping the Stour in check and at bay. Following the river inland from its estuary, the first major port of call is Sudbury (see p.290), but on the way it negotiates **Dedham Vale**, undoubtedly the prettiest part of the river valley and famous as **Constable Country**, for this was the home of John Constable (see box opposite), one of England's greatest artists, and the subject of his most famous works. Inevitably, there's a Constable shrine – the much-visited complex of old buildings down by the river at **Flatford Mill** – and among the area's assorted hamlets, two are extremely pretty: **Dedham**, just over the border in Essex, and **Stoke-by-Nayland**.

GETTING AROUND   DEDHAM VALE

By bus Exploring Dedham Vale by public transport is problematic – distances are small, but buses between the villages are generally infrequent. The best you'll do is the reasonably frequent bus from Colchester to Dedham (Mon–Sat every 1–2hr; 40min) or from Colchester to Stoke-by-Nayland and Nayland (Mon–Sat every 1–2hr; 25min/20min). For timetable, go to ⊛ suffolkonboard.com.

On foot Footpaths crisscross the area, with some of the most enjoyable being in the vicinity of Dedham village. All the Suffolk tourist offices sell easy-to-use walking leaflets.

Flatford Mill

"I associate my careless boyhood to all that lies on the banks of the Stour", wrote John Constable, who was born in East Bergholt, nine miles northeast of Colchester in 1776. The house in which he was born has long since disappeared, so it has been left to the hamlet of **FLATFORD MILL**, down by the river a mile or so to the south, to take up the painter's cause. The mill here was owned by his father and this was where Constable painted his most celebrated canvas, *The Hay Wain* (now in London's National Gallery), which created a sensation when it was exhibited in Paris in 1824: Constable rendered his scenery with a realistic directness that infuriated many of his contemporaries, but typically he justified this approach in unpretentious terms, observing that, after all "No two days are alike, nor even two hours; neither were there ever two leaves of a tree alike since the creation of the world".

Bridge Cottage and around

Flatford Mill, East Bergholt, CO7 6UL • Jan & Feb Sat & Sun 10.30am–3.30pm; March Wed–Sun 10.30am–5pm; April & Oct daily 10.30am–5pm; May–Sept daily 10.30am–5.30pm; Nov & Dec Wed–Sun 10.30am–3.30pm • Free, except for parking; NT • ☎ 01206 298260, ⓦ nationaltrust.org.uk

The **mill** itself – not the one he painted, but a Victorian replacement – is not open to the public and neither is neighbouring Willy Lott's Cottage, which does actually feature in *The Hay Wain*, but the National Trust has colonized several local buildings, principally **Bridge Cottage**, which was familiar to Constable and is now packed with Constabilia. None of the artist's paintings are displayed here, but there's a pleasant riverside tearoom to take in the view. Many visitors are keen to see the **sites** associated with Constable's paintings and, although there is something a tad futile about this – so much has changed – the National Trust does organize **guided walks** to these locations; the nearest are the remains of the dry dock next to Bridge Cottage and the *Hay Wain* view itself. Rather more rewarding, however, is the easy, two-mile stroll over to Dedham village – cross the bridge beside Bridge Cottage, veer right and keep going along the riverbank. Alternatively, you can rent a rowing boat from beside this same bridge and potter along peacefully to your heart's content.

8

THE EPITOME OF SINCERITY: JOHN CONSTABLE

The son of a well-heeled miller and corn merchant, **John Constable** (1776–1837) was born in **East Bergholt**, a village just to the north of Flatford Mill. His father wanted him to continue the family business, but in 1799 the young Constable persuaded his father to release him from his obligations, citing the successful sketching trips he had been making out into the Suffolk countryside. Constable then went on to train at the Royal Academy in London and it was here that he first encountered an international cast of great painters, from Rubens to Gainsborough. For several years thereafter, the artist spent the winter in London, returning to paint in and around East Bergholt during the summer, though from 1811 onwards he also made regular visits to, and painted many pictures of Salisbury, a city that was very much to his liking.

It's impossible to unpick the many and varied influences Constable absorbed at the Royal Academy, but with remarkable fortitude he broke with the Romantic, Italianate landscape tradition that was then in vogue, opting instead for finely detailed and observed landscapes reminiscent of the Dutch Realists of the seventeenth century. Perhaps even more remarkably, he introduced a startling freshness of light and colour to his paintings, capturing sunlight in blobs of yellow and white, storms with rapid and broken brushwork. Constable's inspiration was quite simply his delight in his rural surroundings – as he summed it up himself, "The sound of water escaping from mill dams, willows, old rotten planks, slimy posts and brickwork, I love such things".

Initially at least, matters both financial and matrimonial were difficult for Constable: his paintings were poorly received and the family of his proposed bride, Maria Bicknell, was dead set against the match. In 1816, however, his father died, which both secured his finances and enabled the marriage to take place. The next few years were the best of times for Constable. His paintings became increasingly popular and Maria, very much the love of his life, produced a fair brood of children. In 1828, the high times ended abruptly with the death of Maria, a shock from which he never really recovered, always being "prey to melancholy and anxious thoughts". He lies buried alongside his wife in Hampstead.

Constable is often considered as the most English of painters and it comes as a surprise to realize his immediate influence was actually far greater in France, where he inspired both the Barbizon School and the French Impressionists.

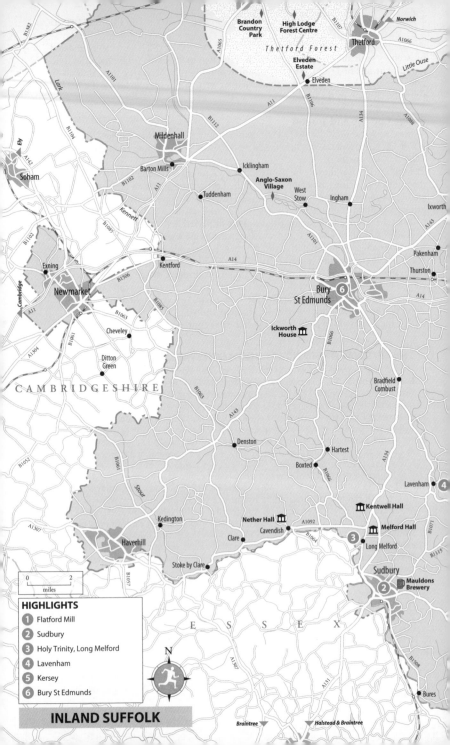

HIGHLIGHTS

1. Flatford Mill
2. Sudbury
3. Holy Trinity, Long Melford
4. Lavenham
5. Kersey
6. Bury St Edmunds

INLAND SUFFOLK

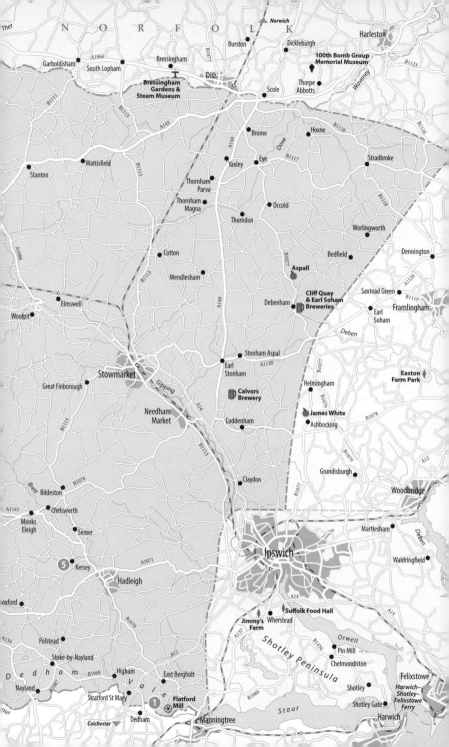

ARRIVAL AND DEPARTURE
FLATFORD MILL

By train The nearest station is Manningtree, on the Colchester to Norwich line, from where it's a couple of miles' gambol northwest to Flatford Mill.

By car Drivers will find Flatford Mill well signed from the B1070, which links the A12 and the A137. The Mill is located at the end of a country lane, which is itself a dead end.

ACCOMMODATION

The Granary B&B Flatford Mill, CO7 6UL ☎01206 298111, ⓦgranaryflatford.co.uk. In the annexe of an old granary, once owned by Constable's father, this appealing B&B has a real cottage feel with its beamed ceilings and antique furniture. The two ground-floor en-suite rooms open onto a garden bordering the River Stour. **£62**

Dedham

Constable went to school in **DEDHAM**, just upriver from Flatford Mill and one of the region's prettiest villages, its wide and lazy main street graced by a handsome medley of old timber-framed houses and Georgian villas. The main sight as such is **Dedham Parish Church of St Mary** (daily 9am to dusk; ⓦdedham-parishchurch.org.uk), a large and well-proportioned structure with a sweeping, sixteenth-century nave adorned with some attractive Victorian stained glass in the style of the Pre-Raphaelites. Constable painted the church on several occasions and today it holds one of the artist's rare religious paintings, *The Ascension*; frankly it's a good job Constable concentrated on landscapes – his figure of Christ floating in the sky manages to be both trite and unconvincing. Dedham is also popular with day-trippers, who arrive here by the coach-load throughout the summer, and one of the results has been the creation of the **Dedham Art and Craft Centre** (daily 10am–5pm; free; ☎01206 322666, ⓦdedhamart andcraftcentre.co.uk), housed in a converted church just along the main street from St Mary's. The centre holds over thirty stores, selling everything from clothes and furniture to photography, ceramics, jewellery and garden gubbins.

The Munnings Art Museum

Castle House, Castle Hill, CO7 6AZ • April–Oct Wed–Sun 2–5pm, plus bank hols 2–5pm • £6.50 • ☎01206 322127, ⓦsiralfredmunnings.co.uk

In front of the Art and Craft Centre, Dedham's main street swings right for the mile-long journey to the **Munnings Art Museum**, in Castle House, an expansive country villa set in its own grounds. Barely remembered today, Sir Alfred Munnings (1875–1959) was a major figure and president of the Royal Academy in the 1940s. He earned his artistic spurs as a poster artist for Caley's Chocolates of Norwich, but made a name for himself as an official war artist attached to the Canadian cavalry in 1918. It was then that he discovered his penchant for painting horses – with and without their riders – a skill that brought him scores of aristocratic commissions, though today his paintings of rural East Anglia rest more easily on the eye. It was Modernism that did for Munnings: as president of the Royal Academy, he savaged almost every form of modern art there was, creating enemies by the score and ensuring he was soon ridiculed as old-fashioned and out of touch. The museum displays a comprehensive range of Munnings' paintings and posters and although few would say they were inspiring, seeing them is a pleasant way to fill a (rainy) afternoon. A clearly signed **footpath** leads from the village cross beside the church to the museum – allow about fifteen minutes.

ARRIVAL AND DEPARTURE
DEDHAM

By bus Buses to Dedham stop in the centre of the village. There is a reasonably good service to Colchester (Mon–Sat every 1–2hr; 40min).

By car Reaching Dedham by car is easy enough, but note that it's a circuitous drive of around 5km from here to Flatford Mill (see p.284) via the A12.

ACCOMMODATION AND EATING

The Sun Inn High St, CO7 6DF ☎01206 323351, ⓦthesuninndedham.com. Among Dedham's several pubs, the pick is *The Sun*, an ancient place which has been sympathetically modernized. The menu is strong on local

DASTARDLY DEEDS IN POLSTEAD

There's no strong reason to visit the hamlet of **Polstead**, a couple of miles north of Stoke-by-Nayland, but the village was on everyone's lips in the 1820s on account of the **Red Barn Murder**, which shocked and titillated the whole of England. At first glance, it was a simple tale: a young mole-catcher's daughter by the name of **Maria Marten** had arranged to meet her lover **William Corder** at the Red Barn, a local landmark, from where they were to elope to Ipswich. Unluckily for Marten, Corder killed her instead and although he subsequently sent letters to her family purporting to come from Maria, the game was up when the authorities found her body buried in the barn – no one could say Corder was a master of subterfuge. Corder was quickly tracked down in London – where he had married someone else, a certain Mary Moore – brought back to Suffolk, and then tried and hanged in front of a huge crowd in Bury St Edmunds in 1828.

In itself the murder might have passed without too much attention, but during and after the trial, all sorts of details emerged which were bizarre and riveting in equal measure: to start with, Maria had already had two children, one with William's older brother, Thomas, and one with William himself – and, for that matter, there were persistent rumours that William and Maria had murdered their own child the year before. Neither was their elopement a secret: William had suggested to Maria that they meet at the Red Barn in the presence of Maria's stepmother, Ann Marten, who was probably having an affair with William herself. To add to this heady mix of infanticide and sexual shenanigans, there was also the gore: despite lengthy and detailed proceedings, the exact cause of Maria's death could not be ascertained – she was either shot, strangled or stabbed, or a combination of all three, but no one was sure. William Corder's guilt was, however, not in doubt, and his sentence exemplary: "…That you be hanged by the Neck until you are Dead; and that your body shall afterwards be dissected and anatomized". Cambridge University students did the honours, concluding – in the mumbo-jumble style of the phrenologists of the period – that Corder's skull showed strong signs of "secretiveness and destructiveness". Bits and pieces of Corder ended up at Moyse's Hall Museum in Bury St Edmunds (see p.311), as did a book giving an account of the murder bound in the poor bugger's tanned skin.

The Red Barn itself suffered for its notoriety too: literally thousands of sightseers visited Polstead, stripping the barn down for souvenirs and even turning its plank walls into toothpicks; the remains burnt down in 1842.

ingredients and offers a tasty range of both Italian and British dishes, all washed down by real ales; main courses average around £13. *The Sun* also has five en-suite rooms decorated in a creative blend of country inn and boutique hotel, from four-poster beds through to billowy, caramel-cream curtains. Kitchen Mon–Sat noon–2.30pm & 6.30–9.30pm, Sun noon–4pm & 6.30–9pm; pub daily 11am–11pm. **£135**

Stoke-by-Nayland and Nayland

North from Dedham, the B1029 dips beneath the A12 on its way to **Higham**, where you pick up the road to **STOKE-BY-NAYLAND**, four miles further west. This is the most picturesque of villages, where a knot of half-timbered and pastel-painted cottages cuddle up to one of Constable's favourite subjects, **St Mary's Church** (daily 9am–5pm), with its pretty brick and stone-trimmed tower. The doors of the church's south porch are covered by the beautifully carved if badly weathered figures of a medieval **Jesse Tree** (purporting to show the ancestors of Christ) and, although the interior is sombre and severe, it does boast a beautifully carved medieval font and a pair of splendid, seventeenth-century alabaster tombs, one each in the south and north chancel chapels. The village also has a pair of appealing pub-restaurants (see p.290).

Travelling southwest from Stoke-by-Nayland, it's two miles back to the River Stour at **NAYLAND**, a workaday little place whose most distinctive feature is the **church of St James** (daily 9am–5pm), whose square tower and copper-green spire poke high into the sky. Inside, behind the high altar, Constable's *Christ Blessing the Bread and Wine* is one of only three attempts he made at a religious theme – and, dating from 1809, it was completed long before he found his artistic rhythm.

ACCOMMODATION AND EATING

The Angel Inn Polstead St, CO6 4SA ☎01206 263245, ⓦangelinnsuffolk.co.uk. This agreeable country pub, with its bare-brick walls and rustic beams, offers a good-quality British menu – steak-and-ale pie, fish and chips – with mains averaging £13. *The Angel* also has half a dozen comfortable en-suite guest rooms, each of which is pleasantly kitted out in a sort of country house style with lots of creams. Kitchen Mon–Sat noon–2.30pm & 6–9.30pm, Sun noon–4pm & 6–9pm; pub daily 11am–11pm. **£110**

The Crown Polstead St, CO6 4SE ☎01206 262001, ⓦcrowninn.net. *The Crown* may fancy itself just a little too much, but there's no disputing the quality of the food or the inventiveness of the menu, with such delights as venison chop with horseradish and mustard butter, watercress and chips; mains start at £14. The decor is appealing too, with the open-plan restaurant decorated in a sort of low-key, country house style – flowery wallpaper and so forth. The same decorative approach has been followed in the eleven bedrooms, which are all kept in tip-top condition. Kitchen Mon–Sat noon–2.30pm & 6–9.30pm, Sun noon–9pm; pub Mon–Sat 10am–11pm, Sun noon–10pm. **£95**

Sudbury

With a population of around thirteen thousand, **SUDBURY** has doubled in size in the last forty years, to become by far the most important town in this part of the Stour Valley. A handful of timber-framed houses recalls wool-trade prosperity, but its salad days were underwritten by another local industry, silk weaving, which survives on a small scale even now. Sudbury's most famous export, however, is **Thomas Gainsborough**, the leading English portraitist of the eighteenth century, whose statue, with brush and palette, stands on the traffic-choked triangle of **Market Hill**, the town's predominantly Victorian marketplace. A superb collection of the artist's work is on display a few yards away in the house where he was born – Gainsborough's House. Sudbury also saw service as a major staging post on the journey north to Norwich and it was here that a young reporter by the name of **Charles Dickens** came to observe the general election of 1836, a process whose assorted corruptions he described in *The Pickwick Papers*, with Sudbury rebranded to obvious effect as the fictional *Eatanswill*.

Gainsborough's House

46 Gainsborough St, CO10 2EU • Mon–Sat 10am–5pm, Sun 11am–5pm • £6.50 • ☎01787 372958, ⓦgainsborough.org

Kept in excellent order, **Gainsborough's House** possesses an outstanding collection of the artist's work distributed over a couple of main floors. The house also offers a lively programme of **temporary exhibitions**, has a café and a garden, and organizes lessons and demonstrations in its Print Workshop, lodged in what was originally the coach house. As for the man himself, **Thomas Gainsborough** (1727–88), the son of a Sudbury cloth merchant, left his home town when he was just 13, moving to London where he was apprenticed to an engraver. Nevertheless, it seems he was soon moonlighting and the earliest of his surviving portrait paintings – his *Boy and Girl*, a remarkably self-assured work dated to 1744 – is displayed here in two pieces as someone, somewhere, chopped up the original.

In 1752, Gainsborough moved on to Ipswich, where he quickly established himself as a portrait painter to the Suffolk gentry with one of his specialities being wonderful "conversation pieces", so-called because the sitters engage in polite chitchat or genteel activity with a landscape as the backdrop. Stints in Bath and London followed and it was during these years that Gainsborough developed a fluid, flatteringly easy style that was ideal for his well-heeled subjects, who posed in becoming postures painted in soft, evanescent colours. Examples of Gainsborough's **later work** on display include the *Portrait of Harriet, Viscountess Tracy* (1763) and the particularly striking *Portrait of Abel Moysey, MP* (1771). In his last years, the artist also dabbled with romantic paintings of country scenes – as in *A Wooded Landscape with Cattle by a Pool* – a playful variation of the serious landscape painting he loved to do best; the rest, he often said, just earned

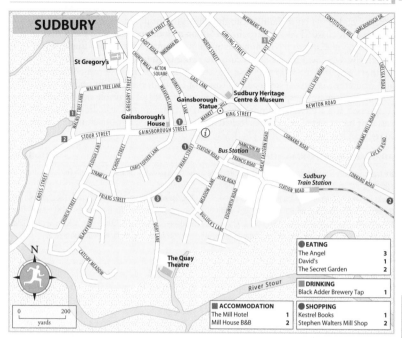

him a living. Gainsborough never bothered with assistants, with one exception, his nephew **Gainsborough Dupont** (1754–97), who has a room devoted to his work on the top floor.

Sudbury Heritage Centre and Museum

Gaol Lane, off Market Hill • Mon–Fri 10am–4pm • Free • ⓦ sudburysuffolk.co.uk/heritagecentre

Adjoining the Town Hall, the **Sudbury Heritage Centre and Museum** may be small and a tad short on exhibits, but its explicatory panels are well written and together they present a clear and concise history of the town. There are particularly good sections on the silk-weaving factories that kept the town going in the nineteenth century and the arrival of the **USAF in World War II**. The Americans began to arrive in numbers in 1943, congregating at a hastily prepared airstrip beside the tiny hamlet of Chilton Street, a few miles west of town. By the following year, there were no less than three thousand stationed in the vicinity of Sudbury, much to the delight of many local women, who found them much more attractive than the local men – they were generally bigger, better paid and with better teeth. Predictably, Suffolk men were less enamoured, coining various wry-to-bitter jokes about their predicament.

St Gregory's church

Gregory St, CO10 1BA • Daily 8.30am–5.30pm • Free • ☎ 01787 371445, ⓦ stgregoryschurch.org.uk

There are three medieval churches in Sudbury, but the only one of any real interest is the church of **St Gregory**, a large flint, rubble and stone-trimmed structure whose heavily buttressed tower pokes high into the sky on the west side of the town centre. Highlights of the interior include the painted ceiling of the chancel, the Victorian stained-glass windows, and more particularly the cover of the font, an extraordinarily ornate wooden structure dating from the fifteenth century. In an alcove, there's also a display on Richard II and his henchman **Simon of Sudbury**, one-time papal nuncio and Archbishop of Canterbury. Simon was appointed Lord Chancellor of England in 1380 and this was to cost him his life during the Peasants' Revolt, which convulsed much of southern England the following year. Taxation was the immediate cause of the rebellion and when the insurgents stormed the Tower of London, they caught and beheaded Simon, holding him responsible for the poll tax of 1381. The revolt was brutally suppressed and afterwards Simon's body went to Canterbury Cathedral, but his **skull** was sent here to St Gregory's: it's locked away in the vestry, but the church custodian is more than happy to show it to you if you ask.

ARRIVAL AND INFORMATION   SUDBURY

By train Sudbury train station is a 5–10min walk from the centre via Station Rd. There are hourly services to and from Marks Tey (in Essex) on the London to Colchester line.

By bus The bus station is on Hamilton Rd, just south of Market Hill. The main local bus company is Chambers (☎01787 375360, ⬡chambersbus.co.uk), who – among a batch of services – link Sudbury with Colchester and Bury St Edmunds.

Tourist office In the library, which is in the grand old Corn Exchange, metres from Market Hill (Mon–Thurs 9.30am–4.30pm, Fri 9.30am–4pm & Sat 10am–3.30pm; ☎01787 881320, ⬡sudburytowncouncil.co.uk).

ACCOMMODATION

The Mill Hotel Walnut Tree Lane, CO10 1BD ☎01787 375544, ⬡themillhotelsudbury.co.uk. Near the river on the west side of town, this distinctive hotel occupies an intelligently recycled Victorian mill, whose four floors rise high above their surroundings. The hotel has its original flagstone floors and water wheel, now enclosed within a glass case, but of its 62 rooms, those in the main building are more appealing than those in the adjoining annexe – specify if you book. **£90**

Mill House B&B Cross St, CO10 2DS ☎01787 882966, ⬡millhousesudbury.co.uk. This old house and cottage, whose exterior walls are painted terracotta, has a couple of comfortable, en-suite guest rooms, but its prime appeal is its conservatory and garden, which stretch down towards the River Stour. Central location and home-made breakfasts. **£65**

EATING AND DRINKING

Perhaps surprisingly, Sudbury's café and restaurant scene is distinctly pedestrian with only a handful of places worth a second look. Enjoyable or at least distinctive pubs are similarly thin on the ground, though there are a couple of notable exceptions.

The Angel 43 Friars St, CO10 2AG ☎01787 882228, ⬡theangelsudbury.co.uk. This traditional boozer has been rebooted in slick modern style, but the food gets mixed reviews. Probably a better bet for lunch than dinner with the likes of oven-roasted chicken with sautéed potatoes costing £13. Kitchen Mon–Sat noon–2pm & 5.30–9.30pm, Sun noon–3pm; pub Mon–Thurs noon–2pm & 5.30–11pm, Fri & Sat noon–11pm, Sun noon–3pm.

Black Adder Brewery Tap 21 East St, CO10 2TP ☎01787 370876, ⬡blackaddertap.co.uk. Not much in the way of decorative finesse here, but who cares when the big deal is the beer – a rotating selection of eight real ales on draught, but always including something from Mauldons, a local brewer producing, among several offerings, the sterling Black Adder stout. There's a courtyard patio out at the back, pub grub and occasional jazz gigs too. Mon–Thurs 11am–11pm, Fri & Sat 11am–midnight, Sun noon–10.30pm.

David's 51 Gainsborough St, CO10 2ET ☎01787 373919, ⬡davidsdelicatessen.co.uk. Neat and trim café-deli, where they turn out a tasty range of salads and light meals featuring local ingredients. Try, perhaps, the scrambled eggs and pancetta on toast. Mon–Sat 9am–5pm.

The Secret Garden 21 Friars St, CO10 2AA ☎01787 372030, ⬡tsg.uk.net. Independent tearoom with bells on, where the menu has French flourishes and they do their best to source locally. For lunch, you might try their ham, spinach and cheddar cheese salad for just under £10. Cosy, antique premises too. Mon–Sat 9am–5pm, plus Fri & Sat 7–10pm.

ENTERTAINMENT

Quay Theatre Quay Lane, CO10 2AN ☎01787 374745, ⬡quaytheatre.org.uk. Sudbury's main performance venue covers all the bases, from country to comedy, soul to skiffle. There's classical music too, plus jazz – Jacqui Dankworth has appeared here – and a good film programme organized by the town's Cinema Club.

SHOPPING

Kestrel Books 10 Friars St, CO10 2AA ☎01787 372735. Enterprising, independent bookshop, which stocks both new and secondhand titles. Also does sidelines in cards and jigsaws, road maps and local hiking maps. Mon–Sat 9am–4pm (Wed till 5.30pm).

Stephen Walters Mill Shop Cornard Rd, CO10 2XB ☎01787 372266, ⓦstephenwalters.co.uk. This factory shop – the mill (not open to the public) is next door – sells handbags and cushions as well as roll upon roll of fabric. The company moved here from London in 1894 and it was in Sudbury that they established a flourishing silk-weaving business, producing such items as parasols and black mourning crepe. They now focus on high-quality furnishing fabrics, with silk to the fore, as well as men's and women's clothing. The shop is located a 5–10min walk from the town centre. Tues 10am–3pm, Wed–Fri 10am–4.30pm, Sat 10am–2.30pm.

Long Melford

From Sudbury, it's just three miles to **LONG MELFORD**, which dates back to the Iron Age, though its heyday was as a cloth town in the fifteenth century. The village may share the same industrial history as its neighbours but it looks very different, its northern approach dominated by a long and conspicuous triangular **green**, which is itself flanked by **Melford Hall and Park**, one of Suffolk's most popular country houses. Beyond the green, the village is not much more than one long street, variously the High Street, Hall Street and Southgate, and this is flanked by a pleasing mix of architectural styles, from Georgian villas to Victorian red brick. The main street is also overlooked by the splendid **Church of the Holy Trinity** and lined by a good selection of shops, pub-restaurants and hotels. There's also a second country house on the northern edge of the village, **Kentwell Hall** – altogether quite enough to pull in tourists by the coachload.

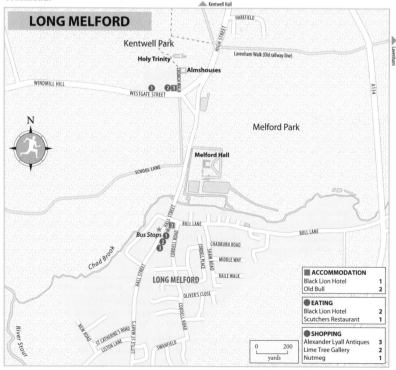

Melford Hall

Hall St, CO10 9AA • April Sat & Sun 1–5pm; May–Oct Wed–Sun 1–5pm • House and garden £7.20; garden only £3.60; NT • ☏ 01787 376 395, �🌐 nationaltrust.org.uk

The pepper-pot turrets and slender chimneys of **Melford Hall** were built at the behest of William Cordell, a prominent Elizabethan lawyer and Speaker of the House of Commons in the 1550s. The house goes round three sides of a courtyard, with its entrance set away from the village to face the garden. The general shape of the house may be Elizabethan, but much of the detail is not – cue the Georgian sash windows – and neither is the **interior**, which was badly damaged by fire in the 1940s. Highlights here include the splendid main staircase, the long gallery on the second floor and the Rococo fireplace in the drawing room, though most visitors are more interested by the **Beatrix Potter Room**, which features a selection of the author's watercolours and drawings. Potter (1866–1943), who was related to the Hyde Parkers, the long-time owners of Melford Hall, slept in the **Victorian Bedroom** when she stayed here, as she often did, bringing with her a travelling menagerie of toy animals.

Church of the Holy Trinity

High St, CO10 9DN • Daily April–Oct 10am–6pm; Nov–March 10am–4pm • Free • �🌐 longmelfordchurch.com

One of the finest churches in the whole of Suffolk, **Holy Trinity** occupies a gentle ridge on the northern edge of Long Melford, opposite Melford Park. Mostly dating from the 1490s, the church's long and lovely nave, with its elegant high pointed windows, marches up to a squat, square tower, which is topped by a set of elongated pinnacles. Inside, the first eight windows of the north aisle hold some especially beautiful, late-medieval **stained glass**, including – in the second frame from the left in the most westerly window – the figure of Elizabeth Talbot, said to be the inspiration for the original illustration of the Duchess in Lewis Carroll's *Alice in Wonderland*. At the east end of the north aisle is the **Clopton Chantry Chapel**, named after the former owners of Kentwell Hall (see below) and distinguished by a rare example of a **Lily Crucifix window** depicting Christ crucified on the leaves of a lily – most were destroyed during the Reformation. In the adjacent **Sanctuary** are the assorted tombs of another powerful family, the Cordells, with one of the clan, Sir William, lying there in his armour beneath a fancy set of columns and coffered arches.

Kentwell Hall

High St, CO10 9BA • Opening times vary – check website • £11.90 , garden & farm £8.90 • ☏ 01787 310207, �🌐 kentwell.co.uk

Approached along an avenue of lime trees just to the north of the village, moated **Kentwell Hall** has an impressive red-brick facade whose long line of gables is topped off by a pair of dinky, copper-green cupolas. A fire in the 1820s took care of most of the original interior and the house was pretty much a ruin when the present owners moved in during the 1970s, since when they have reinvented it as a major tourist attraction, creating, for example, a two-dimensional, brick-paved maze; a camera obscura fabricated from an old gazebo; and a rare breeds farm. They have also restored the old ice house and created a wildflower meadow. These specific attractions are supplemented by a lively programme of shows and special events, from medieval banquets to sheep-shearing.

ARRIVAL AND DEPARTURE   LONG MELFORD

By bus Buses pull in along the main street. One especially useful service is Chambers bus #753 (Mon–Sat hourly; �🌐 chambersbus.co.uk) running to and from Bury St Edmunds (50min), Colchester (1hr 15min), Sudbury (20min) and Lavenham (20min). There is also Beestons bus #236 (Mon–Fri every 2 hr; �🌐 beestons.co.uk) linking Long Melford with Clare (20min) and Cavendish (15min).

On foot Perhaps the happiest way to reach Long Melford is on foot from Lavenham (see p.297), four miles to the northeast. For the most part, the footpath follows the old railway line, which was closed down in 1961. In Long Melford, the main path emerges on the north side of the village opposite the entrance drive to Kentwell Hall.

ACCOMMODATION AND EATING

★**Black Lion Hotel** The Green, CO10 9DN ☎01787 312356, ⓦblacklionhotel.net. Quite simply the best place to eat and sleep in Long Melford, this small hotel occupies a good-looking Georgian building a few yards from the Church of the Holy Trinity. The interior is kitted out in country house style and each of the ten bedrooms has luxurious, heavy drapes and iron bedsteads. Guests can eat in the restaurant, which is smart and fairly formal, or in the bar – less formally and more economically. They are strong on local food – partridge pâté and Suffolk pork for example – and the menu offers some interesting variations on traditional English dishes as well as more straightforward favourites like shepherd's pie (for £14). Daily: lunch noon–2pm, afternoon tea 2–5pm & dinner 7–11pm. **£125**

Old Bull Hall St, CO10 9JG ☎01787 378494, ⓦoldenglishinns.co.uk. One of a largish chain, Old English Inns, this medium-sized hotel occupies a handsome half-timbered building that was originally built for a wealthy cloth merchant in the fifteenth century. Many of the original features have survived, from the squeaky wooden floors and open fireplaces through to the heavy oak beams in the foyer, but the 25 guest rooms are suitably modern, furnished in a pleasant and unfussy style. **£90**

Scutchers Restaurant Westgate St, CO10 9DP ☎01787 310200, ⓦscutchers.com. Smart and intimate, bistro-style restaurant offering a short but finely judged menu that features the likes of plaice fillet on a crab mash with a lemon butter sauce. Save space for a dessert – if it's on, their vanilla panna cotta with a compote of cherries is particularly delicious. Mains start at £19. The restaurant is a few yards west of the *Black Lion Hotel*. Thurs–Sat noon–2.30pm & 7–10pm.

SHOPPING

Alexander Lyall Antiques Belmont House, Hall St, CO10 9JF ☎01787 375434, ⓦlyallantiques.com. Upmarket, antique furniture shop whose forte is top-quality Georgian and Victorian mahogany, rosewood and walnut pieces, for example dwarf and revolving bookcases, pedestal desks, dining tables, corner cupboards, chest of drawers and chairs. Also do promising sidelines in mirrors, cameos and ceramics. Mon–Sat 10am–5.30pm.

Lime Tree Gallery Lime Tree House, Hall St, CO10 9JF ☎01787 319046, ⓦlimetreegallery.com. Of the several fine and applied art shops in Long Melford, this is arguably the pick, specializing in contemporary paintings and glassware. They are particularly keen on Scottish artists and they also organize several exhibitions every year. Mon–Sat 10am–5pm.

Nutmeg 8 Hall St, CO10 9JF ☎01787 311842, ⓦnutmeglongmelford.co.uk. Chic women's fashion shop, which specializes in smart, casual wear from an eclectic mix of designers – Lauren Vidal, Sahara, Great Plains and Chen. Particularly good for separates, but there's also a good selection of dresses and accessories. Mon–Sat 9.30am–5pm.

The Upper Stour River Valley

Heading west from Long Melford, the **A1092** stays close to the River Stour as it cuts a meandering route through meadows and farmland, acting as the county boundary between Suffolk and Essex at the same time. En route, the road slips through several little villages, among which **Cavendish** and **Clare** are the most appealing. The other village of some interest hereabouts is **Hartest**, which lies six miles north of Long Melford along narrow country lanes.

Cavendish

CAVENDISH is a tiny place, but it does have a whopping **green**, a sloping slab of grass framed by an attractive mix of old houses from Georgian villas to terracotta-painted cottages. The village looks prosperous, and it most certainly is, and it also has one real claim to fame as the final resting place of **Leonard Cheshire** (1917–1992) and his wife **Sue Ryder** (1924–2000), the joint founders of a highly regarded charity that cares for people with terminal and/or incurable illnesses both in the UK and abroad. The couple's good deeds are recalled by the pocket-sized **Sue Ryder Shop** (Mon–Sat 9am–5pm; ☎01787 282591), which overlooks the green. Nearby is **St Mary the Virgin's Church** (daily 9.30am–5pm or dusk), a handsome medieval structure where pride of place goes to an exquisite Flemish alabaster of the Crucifixion dating to the sixteenth century and now positioned on the north wall of the nave. St Mary's may look the picture of peace and tranquillity, but there were bloody goings-on here during the Peasants' Revolt of 1381. The local bigwig, a certain John Cavendish, was chased through the village by the rebels and managed to get to the church doors, where he grabbed the knocker and claimed sanctuary – but to no avail as the peasants chopped him up anyway: the **knocker** is still there, worn thin by thousands of hands over hundreds of years.

ARRIVAL AND DEPARTURE   CAVENDISH

By bus Beestons bus #236 (Mon–Fri every 2 hr; ⓦ beestons.co.uk) links Cavendish with Clare (10min), Long Melford (15min) and Sudbury (25min).

ACCOMMODATION AND EATING

The George The Green, CO10 8BA ☎ 01787 280248, ⓦ thecavendishgeorge.co.uk. Smart and very amenable country pub-cum-restaurant, where the lively menu often surprises – try, for example, the whole roasted quail, butternut squash, olive and hazelnuts (£15). *The George* occupies a very old building, many of whose features have been preserved and conserved. It also has five en-suite guest rooms decorated in soothing colours and with lots of period flourishes. Kitchen Mon–Sat noon–2pm & 6–9.30pm, Sun noon–3pm; pub daily noon–11pm. **£85**

Clare

Small and pretty, the tiny town of **CLARE** was fast out of the municipal blocks: as early as the eleventh century, it had a sizeable number of merchant-landowners and by the thirteenth it was a major cloth-producing town, churning out heavy-duty broadcloth by the cartload for export far and wide. Like the rest of Suffolk, it hit the economic buffers in the sixteenth century with the decline of the wool trade, but the townsfolk diversified and **Daniel Defoe**, for one, remarked on the number of turkeys in Clare, though he did not like the place at all: it was in his *Tour Thro' the Whole Island of Great Britain*, written in the 1720s, that he called it "a poor town and dirty". It is certainly neither today.

Clare Castle Country Park

Malting Lane, CO10 8NW• Daily dawn to dusk • Free • ☎ 07470 279363, ⓦ clarecastlecountrypark.co.uk

To protect his real estate in the 1070s, the local lord of Clare built a wooden motte-and-bailey castle down near the River Stour and the keep was, in its turn, replaced by a stone structure a couple of centuries later. Perched high on an earthen mound, the battered ruins of this **castle** are now incorporated within **Clare Castle Country Park**, which also holds the remains of another era – the railway age, with the old station, the station house and the shed of the former goods yard nestling among the greenery. There's also an unsigned footpath leading west along the river from the Country Park to **Clare Priory**, a modern pink-stone structure inhabited by Augustinian monks and built on the site of the medieval monastery, which was suppressed during the Reformation.

Ancient House Museum

26 High St, CO10 8NY • April–Sept Thurs, Fri & Sun 2–5pm, Sat 11.30am–5pm • £1 • ☎ 01787 277572, ⓦ clare-ancient-house-museum.co.uk

From Clare Castle Country Park, it's a short walk to the High Street, which runs north to the **Ancient House Museum** and its series of mildly diverting displays on the history of the town. Temporary exhibitions focus on all things Clare, though frankly the exterior of the building is the main pull on account of its fancy plasterwork (or pargeting).

Church of St Peter and St Paul

High St, CO10 8NY • Daily 9.30am–5pm or dusk • Free

The Ancient House faces out towards Clare's finest building, the **Church of St Peter and St Paul**, whose exterior, with its turrets, mighty windows and castellated tower, looks both dignified and serene. The interior is similarly imposing and a menagerie of medieval faces peer down from the upper reaches of the nave. Also in the nave is a large and really rather dramatic Stuart **gallery-pew** that looks like an opera box – the lords of Clare may have been equal before God with their fellow worshippers, but not that equal.

ARRIVAL AND DEPARTURE   CLARE

By bus Beestons bus #236 (Mon–Fri every 2hr; ⓦ beestons.co.uk) links Clare with Cavendish (10min), Long Melford (25min) and Sudbury (30min).

EATING

Number One Delicatessen & Café 1 High St, CO10 8NY ☎ 01787 278932, ⓦ numberonedeli.co.uk. This café and delicatessen, in the old village post office, serves a tasty line in sandwiches and light lunches. Prides itself on selling home-made food produced from locally sourced ingredients. Mon–Sat 9am–5pm.

Hartest

Distinguished by its lovely old houses, the hamlet of **HARTEST**, deep in the Suffolk countryside, frames an expansive green, where the war memorial stands proud and solitary. Hartest is located in what is sometimes called "High Suffolk", an area of rolling agricultural land very different from the flatter heaths, forests and fens to the north and east, though the village was once surrounded by thick woodland as recalled by its coat of arms, which features a stag standing tall against a boulder – the so-called Hartest stone, a legendary limestone hunk of rock that was supposedly immovable. A narrow country lane leads southeast from the village to **Giffords Hall Vineyard** (Shimpling Road, IP29 4EX; ☎ 01284 830799, ⓦ giffordshall.co.uk), which was planted about twenty years ago and now produces some of the region's best-regarded wines. They organize regular open days and tastings throughout the season – call ahead or check their website for details.

8

EATING

The Crown The Green, IP29 4DH ☎ 01284 830250, ⓦ thecrownhartest.co.uk. Hartest may be small, but its pub has survived – unlike those in many a Suffolk village. It's a good one, too, a sprawling affair situated just off the green and selling a range of tasty ales from its own microbrewery. Also offers above-average pub grub and has a well-kept garden. Kitchen Mon–Fri noon–2.30pm & 6–9.30pm, Sat noon–9.30pm, Sun noon–8.30pm; pub Mon–Thurs noon–11pm, Fri & Sat noon–midnight, Sun noon–10.30pm.

Lavenham

LAVENHAM, some seven miles northeast of Sudbury, was once a centre of the region's wool trade and is now one of the most visited villages in Suffolk, thanks to its unrivalled ensemble of perfectly preserved half-timbered houses. In outward appearance at least, the whole place has changed little since the demise of the wool industry, owing in part to a zealous local preservation society, which has carefully maintained the village's antique appearance by banning from view such modern frivolities as advertising hoardings. Such a setting has attracted the occasional film producer – though not perhaps as many as you would have thought: Stanley Kubrick used the Guildhall (see p.298) for several scenes of *Barry Lyndon*; parts of *Harry Potter and the Deathly Hallows* were filmed here in 2010; and, much more bizarrely, John Lennon and Yoko Ono made a short film in Lavenham in 1969, peering out from big black capes as a hot air balloon was launched from the Market Place in *Apotheosis 2*. Lavenham's musical connections don't end there: *Twinkle, Twinkle Little Star* was written by Jane Taylor, the daughter of the Reverend Isaac Taylor in the early 1800s, shortly after the poor old reverend had been driven out of the village by locals angry at his French revolutionary sympathies.

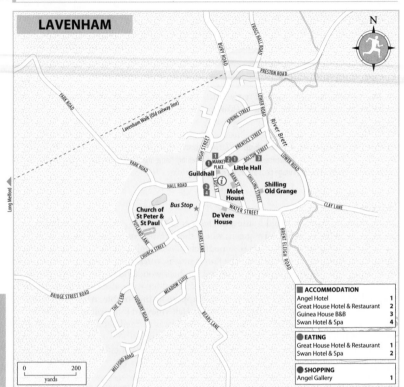

Guildhall

Market Place, CO10 9QZ · March–Oct daily 11am–5pm; Nov & Dec Thurs–Sun 11am–4pm; mid-Jan to Feb Sat & Sun 11am–4pm · £5.85;
NT · ☎ 01787 247646, ⓦ nationaltrust.org.uk

Lavenham is at its most beguiling in the triangular **Market Place**, an airy spot flanked
by pastel-painted, medieval dwellings whose beams have been bent into all sorts of
wonky angles by the passing of the years. It's here you'll find the village's most
celebrated building, the lime-washed, timber-framed **Guildhall of Corpus Christi**, erected
in the sixteenth century as the headquarters of one of Lavenham's four guilds. In the
much-altered interior (used successively as a prison and workhouse), there are modest
exhibitions on timber-framed buildings, medieval guilds, village life and the wool
industry, though most visitors soon end up in the walled garden or the teashop.

Little Hall

Market Place, CO10 9QZ · April–Oct Mon 10am–1pm, Tues–Thurs, Sat & Sun 1–5pm; last admission 1hr before closing · £3.10 · ☎ 01787
247019, ⓦ littlehall.org.uk

From the Guildhall, it's a few yards across the Market Place to another handsome
timber-framed building, **Little Hall**. Dating from the 1390s, but expanded and modified
in Tudor times, the Hall had become something of a ruin by the 1920s when the
Gayer-Anderson brothers rode to the rescue, repairing and reviving the place and
installing the objets d'art that are on display today. Back outside, the **view** down Prentice
Street from beside the *Angel Hotel* (see opposite) is one of Lavenham's most exquisite – a
line of creaky timber-framed dwellings dipping into the deep green countryside beyond.

Church of St Peter and St Paul

Church St, CO10 9SA • Daily: April–Sept 8.30am–6pm; Oct–March 8.30am–4pm • Free

Be sure to spare some time for the Perpendicular Gothic Church of **St Peter and St Paul**, which, with its gargoyle water spouts and carved boars above the entrance, is sited a short walk southwest of the centre on Church Street. Local merchants endowed the church with a nave of majestic proportions and a mighty flint tower, at 141ft the highest for miles around, partly to celebrate the Tudor victory at the Battle of Bosworth in 1485, but mainly to show just how wealthy they had become. Inside, the nave is suitably wide and mighty and the nave aisles hold two splendid chantry chapels, whose screens are simply exquisite, their delicate and intricate carving a wonderful illustration of sixteenth-century craftsmanship. In the floor, look out also for the tiny and really rather mournful **brass** of a baby in swaddling clothes, who died at just ten days old sometime in the seventeenth century.

ARRIVAL AND INFORMATION

LAVENHAM

By bus Buses to Lavenham pull in at the corner of Water and Church streets, a 5min walk from the Market Place. Chambers bus #753 (Mon–Sat hourly; ⌨ chambersbus .co.uk) links Lavenham with Sudbury (40min), Long Melford (20min), Bury St Edmunds (25min) and Colchester (1hr 35min).

Tourist office Just south of the Market Place on Lady St (mid-March to Oct daily 10am–4.45pm; Nov to mid-Dec daily 11am–3pm; Jan to mid-March Sat & Sun 11am–3pm; ☎ 01787 248207, ⌨ heartofsuffolk.co.uk). They sell a detailed, street-by-street village guide and can help with accommodation – there's plenty of choice but rooms still get mighty tight in the high season. They can also advise on – and sell maps of – local walking routes, with the most obvious stroll being the four-mile jaunt southwest to Long Melford (see p.293), mostly along the old railway line.

ACCOMMODATION AND EATING

Angel Hotel Market Place, CO10 9QZ ☎ 01787 247388, ⌨ theangellavenham.co.uk. A member of a small chain, the *Angel* has just eight, spick-and-span guest rooms, whose modest and modern fittings are enlivened by period flourishes – exposed beams, old open fires and so forth. Has a popular bar-restaurant too. **£90**

★**Great House Hotel & Restaurant** Market Place, CO10 9QZ ☎ 01787 247431, ⌨ greathouse.co.uk. Charming, family-run hotel bang in the centre of the village. There are five guest rooms here and each is decorated in a thoughtful and extremely tasteful manner, amalgamating the original features of this very old house with the new. Comfortable beds and a great breakfast round it all off. The hotel restaurant is similarly excellent, specializing in classic

French cuisine, with a three-course set lunch costing £25, dinner £35; you can also opt for à la carte. With such delights as belly of Suffolk pork confit and duck in cider, they have garnered rave reviews – so book ahead. Wed–Sun noon–2.30pm & Tues–Sat 7–9.30pm. **£120**

Guinea House B&B 16 Bolton St, CO10 9RG ☎ 01787 249046, ⌨ guineahouse.co.uk. In a dinky little house a short walk from the Market Place, this well-established B&B has two low-beamed, folksy-meets-cosy, en-suite guest rooms. No credit cards. **£75**

★**The Swan Hotel & Spa** High St, CO10 9QA ☎ 01787 247477, ⌨ theswanatlavenham.co.uk. One of a small chain, this outstanding hotel is a veritable rabbit warren, its various nooks and crannies dating back several hundred

8

NO CHANGE HERE: A WALKING TOUR OF OLD LAVENHAM

Lavenham is jammed to the gunnels with historic buildings, several of which are of particular interest, reflecting both the village's role as a centre of the wool trade during the reign of Henry VIII and a second spurt of industrial activity in Victorian times, when local factories turned out coconut matting and horsehair fabric. An especially fine example of a Tudor clothier's dwelling, **Molet House**, stands just off the Market Place on Barn Street, its splendid doorway set beneath a triple overhang of black and white timbers. Nearby **Shilling Street** boasts the finest assortment of Tudor facades in Lavenham, though the most conspicuous building – **Shilling Old Grange** – is a bit of a fraud, as its lower floor was "'invented" in the 1920s. Shilling Street connects with Water Street, the site of a former horsehair factory and the distinctly bendy **De Vere House**, whose odd angles and thick mullion windows look decidedly Dickensian. Just along the street is *The Swan Hotel* (see above), which incorporates the old Wool Hall, reopened after a thorough refit in 1965 by, bizarrely enough, the then Miss World, Dorset's own Ann Sydney.

years. There's a traditional lounge to snooze in – especially lovely in winter when the fire is stacked high with logs – plus a courtyard garden, an authentic Elizabethan Wool Hall, and a wood-panelled bar with mementoes of the American servicemen who hunkered down here in World War II; it's likely that the band leader Glenn Miller popped in for a pint or two. The guest rooms are very comfortable, and most have lots of original features – low wooden beams and so forth. *The Swan's* restaurant and brasserie are also first-rate, attracting by and large an older clientele, drawn here by the imaginative British-based cuisine with the likes of roasted wood pigeon and puy lentils. Mains start at around £18. Restaurant daily noon–2pm & 7–9pm; brasserie daily noon–2.30pm & 6–9.30pm. **£180**

SHOPPING

Angel Gallery 17 Market Lane, Market Place, CO10 9QZ ☏ 01787 248417, ⓦ angelgallerylavenham.com. Lavenham has more than its fair share of antique and souvenir shops – though, as befits such a prosperous place, there's precious little in the way of tourist tat. What's more, several artists have moved here in the last few years and you may be able to catch sight of their work here at the Angel Gallery, whose assorted paintings, sketches, ceramics and sculptures are displayed in a fifteenth-century wool merchant's house. Mon–Sat 10am–5pm.

Kersey, Hadleigh and around

Among the assorted towns and villages within easy striking distance of Lavenham, the prettiest is **Kersey**, where an improbably picturesque main street of timber-framed houses seems to have dodged just about every historical bullet since the seventeenth century. Neighbouring **Hadleigh** is larger and more mundane, though it does have one or two interesting old buildings, while straggling **Bildeston** is home to one of the county's most enjoyable country hotels.

Kersey

Minuscule **KERSEY**, nine miles southeast of Lavenham off the A1141, is one of the most photographed villages in Suffolk. Another old wool town, it now comprises little more than one exquisite street of rickety old houses, which dips in the middle to cross a ford that's inhabited by a family of fearless ducks. Kersey's more populous past is recalled by the large parish **church of St Mary** (daily 9am–4.30pm or dusk; free), visible for miles around, perched on high ground above the village. The tower is classic Suffolk – square, heavy and strong – but the south **porch** is unusually grand and indeed it may not have been built for the villagers at all, but for pilgrims visiting the miracle-making shrine of Our Lady of Kersey, which was chopped up during the Reformation. The interior is a bit of a disappointment, though six painted panels from the old rood screen dado have somehow managed to survive, including a picture of St Edmund holding an arrow to represent his martyrdom (see box, p.310).

ACCOMMODATION AND EATING   KERSEY

Bell Inn The Street, IP7 6DY ☏ 01473 823229, ⓦ kerseybell.co.uk. In ancient beamed premises dating from the fourteenth century (if not before), this village pub offers a tasty line in draft beers – there are usually three to choose from. Filling bar food and snacks are available too. Kitchen Mon noon–2.30pm, Tues–Sun noon–2.30pm & 6–8.30pm; pub Mon–Sat 11am–11pm, Sun noon–10.30pm.

Primrose Cottage Church Hill, IP7 6EF ☏ 07809 673375, ⓦ primrosecottagekersey.com. It's not big and it's certainly not cheap, but *Primrose Cottage*, which dates from the seventeenth century, does help to fill the accommodation gap in Kersey. The cottage has been sympathetically restored to a high standard; a particular highlight is the cosy lounge with its open fireplace. One en-suite bedroom, sleeps two. Minimum stay three nights. **£350**

Hadleigh

From Kersey, it's two and a half miles southeast to the market town of **HADLEIGH**, whose long and really rather workaday **High Street** runs parallel to, and just to the east of the

---

DOWN ON THE FARM

Really getting into the swing of the tourist market, 140-acre **Hollow Trees Farm** (Semer, IP7 6HX; core hours: Mon–Sat 9am–4.30pm, Sun 9.30am–4pm; ☏ 01449 741247, ⓦ hollowtrees .co.uk) offers "a farm experience that will delight all of your senses, from the noise of our busy farmyard to the smell of fresh baked bread". The shop sells their own vegetables and meat, there are a couple of clearly marked **farm trails**, and visitors can feed the animals in the livestock barn. Hollow Trees is located just north of Hadleigh in the hamlet of **Semer**.

River Brett. Locals from the surrounding villages pop in here to do their shopping, but for the passing visitor there are only a couple of buildings worth a second look, clustered close together, just west of the High Street and best reached via the elegant Georgian terrace that comprises **Queen Street**. Here, near the west end of Queen Street, stands **St Mary's church** (daily: May–Sept 9am–5.30pm; Oct–April 9am–3.30pm; ☏ 01473 824987, ⓦ stmaryshadleigh.co.uk), which mostly dates from the fifteenth century, being a good-looking replacement for several earlier versions. Legend asserts that Guthrum, the Danish chieftain and arch-rival of Alfred the Great, was buried underneath the south aisle in 889, but his remains have never been definitively identified. Opposite the church, across the graveyard, is the half-timbered **Guildhall**, every bit as immaculate as Lavenham's (see p.298), with the earliest sections dating to the 1430s. Behind the church is the ornate brickwork of the **Deanery Tower**, a fifteenth-century gatehouse whose palace was never completed. In the garret room at the top of the tower, the Oxford Movement, which opposed liberal tendencies within the Anglican Church and sought to promote Anglo-Catholicism, was founded in 1833 by local rector Hugh Rose.

ARRIVAL AND DEPARTURE
HADLEIGH

By bus Hadleigh is reasonably easy to reach by bus with Beestons (ⓦ beestons.co.uk) providing a particularly useful service (#91 Mon–Sat hourly) to and from Sudbury (30min) and Ipswich (1hr). Buses pull into the bus station on Magdalen Rd, immediately to the east of the High St.

EATING

Crabtree's Café Bar 66 High St, IP7 5EF ☏ 01473 828166, ⓦ crabtreescafebar.co.uk. Easily the liveliest place in Hadleigh, *Crabtree's* serves up tasty and traditional breakfasts and lunches – try, for example, their prawn cocktail open sandwich with salad (£6.50). Has a pleasant garden terrace and serves excellent coffee, too. Mon–Sat 8am–5pm (kitchen closes 3pm), Sun 10am–3pm.

Bildeston

From Hadleigh, it's about four miles northwest to the hamlet of **BILDESTON**, whose long and narrow High Street strings along the shallow valley of the River Brett. The original village actually started out on higher ground a few hundred yards to the west, but the villagers opted for a more sheltered location in the thirteenth century; though the church was never moved, which is why the **church of St Mary Magdalene** occupies a solitary location among fields a five- to ten-minute walk from the High Street along Church Road. It's a substantial affair, complete with an elaborate entrance porch, but the tower is new – the old one collapsed in 1975. Bildeston also possesses an outstanding hotel (see below).

ARRIVAL AND DEPARTURE
BILDESTON

By bus There aren't many buses to and from Bildeston, but there is a reasonably frequent service linking the village to Ipswich (Mon–Sat 3 daily; 50min).

ACCOMMODATION AND EATING

★**Bildeston Crown** High St, IP7 7EB ☏ 01449 740510, ⓦ thebildestoncrown.com. Village hotels don't come much better than this lovely place, which occupies an immaculately maintained, mustard-painted, half-timbered building

– plus adjoining annexe – at the heart of Bildeston. The hotel has around a dozen rooms, where top-of-the-range facilities – wide-screen TVs, a/c, luxuriant bathrobes, etc – are complemented by well-chosen modern and antique furnishings. The *Crown's* restaurant is similarly outstanding, its attractive modern decor respecting and including all sorts of period flourishes. The menu is modern British with added vim and gusto, featuring the likes of pigeon and duck liver Wellington with artichokes, greens and peppercorn sauce; mains average £17. They also have special tasting menus, a real feast that lasts a good couple of hours with game a particular speciality. Daily noon–2.30pm & 7–9.30pm. **£125**

Stowmarket and around

Northeast of Bildeston lies the market town of **STOWMARKET**, which, with a population of around 15,000 is a relative giant hereabouts, though it has been badly mauled by the developers, a fate that has also befallen its near neighbour, **Needham Market**. Just outside Stowmarket is the hamlet of **Great Finborough** and it's here that the **DJ John Peel** holed up for several decades – and lies buried in the churchyard.

Museum of East Anglian Life

Iliffe Way, IP14 1DL · Late March to early Nov Tues–Sat 10am–4.30pm, Sun 11am–4.30pm · £8.25 · ☎ 01449 612229, ⓦ eastanglianlife.org.uk

The main attraction in Stowmarket is the **Museum of East Anglian Life**, comprising a series of relocated old buildings moved here to a large site that features nearly two miles of woodland and riverside nature trails. Salvaged buildings include an old blacksmith's forge, a watermill, a grocer's, a Victorian schoolroom, a barn, an engineering workshop, a wind-pump and a carpentry workshop. There's also a "Tin Tabernacle", the simplest of structures where the Norfolk village of Great Moulton's Nonconformist residents once gathered to hear the word of God. The museum also owns a substantial collection of antique objects, photographs and books illustrating life and work in East Anglia in the nineteenth and early twentieth centuries, and organizes special exhibitions and events – anything from beer festivals to arts and crafts.

ARRIVAL AND DEPARTURE   STOWMARKET

By train Stowmarket train station is on Prentice Road, just across the river from (and to the east of) the town centre. Destinations Bury St Edmunds (2 hourly; 20min); Ipswich (2 hourly; 15min); Needham Market (hourly; 5min); Norwich (hourly; 30min).

By bus There's no bus station as such, but two main bus stops – one on Bury St (for Ipswich and points south and east), the other on Ipswich St (for Bury St Edmunds and points west); both are in the town centre.

Cotton Mechanical Music Museum

Blacksmith's Rd, Cotton, IP14 4QN · June–Sept Sun 2–5.30pm · £5 · ☎ 01379 783350, ⓦ mechanicalmusicmuseum.co.uk

The hamlet of **COTTON**, about five miles north of Stowmarket on the B1113, holds one real surprise, a **Mechanical Music Museum**, where a miscellany of fairground organs, barrel organs and suchlike are topped off by a mighty Wurlitzer cinema organ, all crowded into shed-like premises. It may all be a bit eccentric, but it's certainly good fun – as are the anecdotal guided tours.

Needham Market

No one could accuse **NEEDHAM MARKET**, five miles southeast of Stowmarket, of being excessively picturesque, but its long and workaday main street is home to the diverting **church of St John the Baptist** (daily 9.30am–4pm or dusk; free), which possesses one of the county's finest hammerbeam roofs – not that you'd guess it from the outside, as the church looks a bit of a mess: there's no tower and no churchyard and the original

FROM TOP ICKWORTH (P.313); BURY ST EDMUNDS (P.307) >

JOHN PEEL AND GREAT FINBOROUGH

Born near Liverpool, but a long-time resident of Suffolk, Robert Parker Ravenscroft (1939–2004) – better known as **John Peel** – was a key figure in the evolution of popular musical taste from the late 1960s until his death from a heart attack while on a working holiday in Peru. His main platform was as a DJ on BBC Radio 1, a station he broadcast on for several decades. His honest, sometimes confessional, warmly laconic style made him immensely popular among both his general listeners and professional musicians, many of whom he counted as friends. Many more were eternally grateful to him (or in some cases ungratefully not) for launching their careers – and Peel developed a peerless reputation for playing the obscure and the new. He was, for example, one of the first DJs to play reggae, psychedelic rock and punk, and he always championed the unusual, from Captain Beefheart to his favourite band of all, The Undertones. No wonder young hopefuls bombarded him with demo tapes and discs.

In the 1970s, Peel and Sheila, his wife, moved to a cottage – "Peel Acres" – in **Great Finborough** just west of Stowmarket. In his later years, Peel broadcast many of his shows from a studio in this house, which also had room enough for live performances. In 2003, Peel was persuaded to write his autobiography, but in the event he died before he could finish it, and the book was left to his wife to finish off, with **Margrave of the Marshes** finally published in 2005. Typically, Peel had often spoken wryly of his death: "I've always imagined I'd die by driving into the back of a truck while trying to read the name on a cassette and people would say, 'He would have wanted to go that way'. Well, I want them to know that I wouldn't."

Over a thousand people attended his funeral in Bury St Edmunds and, in accordance with his wishes, he was buried at St Andrew's church in Great Finborough, his tombstone engraved with a line from his favourite song, *Teenage Kicks* by The Undertones: "Teenage dreams, so hard to beat".

8

exterior has been clumsily amended. There is, however, no disputing the architectural virtuosity of the roof, its delicately carved horizontal timbers decorated by a veritable herd of angels, exquisite creatures whose wings are open and closed alternately.

ARRIVAL AND DEPARTURE   NEEDHAM MARKET

By train Needham Market train station is on Station Yard, a couple of minutes' walk from the High St – turn right for the 5min stroll to the church of St John the Baptist. Destinations Bury St Edmunds (Mon–Sat hourly, Sun every 2hr; 30min); Ipswich (Mon–Sat hourly, Sun every 2hr; 15min); Stowmarket (Mon–Sat hourly, Sun every 2hr; 5min).

By bus Most buses pull in opposite or next to *The Swan*, at the junction of the High Street and Station Yard.

SHOPPING

Alder Carr Farm Creeting St Mary's Rd, Needham Market, IP6 8LX ☎01449 720820, ⓦaldercarrfarm.co.uk. The flood plain of the River Gipping, the slender parcel of land between Needham Market High St and the A14, has been pretty much left for agricultural use – and it's here among the orchards that the enterprising owners of Alder Carr Farm have established a farm shop and deli, both stuffed to the rafters with local produce. There's pick your own in season too, as well as a nature trail, farmers' markets, craft shops and a play area. Shop Mon–Sat 9am–5pm, Sun 10am–4pm.

Debenham

The moisture-retaining clay soils around **DEBENHAM**, ten miles east of Stowmarket, produce some of the largest yields of barley and wheat in the UK, so it's no surprise that the village has an agricultural air – especially when today's giant-sized tractors, combines and harvesters rumble along the elongated High Street. Framing the High Street is a fetching mix of brick cottages, pastel timber-framed houses and Georgian villas, though the grandest building, a Neoclassical stone pile built for the Ancient Order of Foresters, is currently empty and up for sale. The village gets its name from the River Deben, which flows beside and beneath the main street. Incidentally, neither river nor town was responsible for the name of the Debenhams department store chain, though **William Debenham** (1794–1863), the founder of the store, was a Suffolk man, born just outside Lavenham.

By bus The most convenient bus stop is on Gracechurch St at the corner of Henniker Road; from here, it's under 400m to the High St. The most frequent service is to Ipswich (every 1–2hr; 40min).

EATING

Deben Rose 6 High St, IP14 6QJ ☎ 01728 860190. This pleasant little place is a flower shop with bells on – the bells being an unassuming café, where the Illy coffee is reliably good and the snacks and cakes are home-made. The bonus is that you can eat and drink amid the scent of the flowers. Mon–Sat 9am–5pm.

Helmingham Hall

Helmingham, IP14 6EF • Gardens May to late Sept Tues– Thurs & Sun noon–5pm • £7 • ☎ 01473 890799, ⓦ helmingham.com

From Debenham, it's five miles south to **Helmingham Hall**, a moated mansion sitting pretty in a substantial estate. The hall has long been the home of the Tollemache family, a brewing dynasty who threw in their lot with the Cobbolds of Ipswich to create the (now defunct) Tolly Cobbold business. You can't visit the house, but the estate and its gardens are open during the summer months and are vast – a fabulous mixture of borders, orchards and artfully planned walks and vistas. They also run cookery courses in the hall's kitchens (see website for details).

Eye and around

It may be within easy striking distance of Diss (see p.212), just over the border in Norfolk, but the pocket-sized town of **EYE**, around eleven miles northeast of Stowmarket, can't help but feel remote, a rural fastness that was once surrounded by water and marshland; hence its Saxon name, literally "island". Eye has the tiniest of main squares and it's here you'll find a conspicuous stone memorial to **Viscount Sir Edward Clarence Kerrison** (1821–86), long-time Conservative MP for Eye and paternalist of the first rank, commonly described as a "great friend of the agricultural labourer". He also burnished his local credentials by having Eye connected to the rail network, but this particular branch line was closed in 1931. Eye is also near the sprawling **Thornham Estate**, with its assorted tourist facilities and waymarked paths, and a delightful little church in the scattered little hamlet of **Thornham Parva**.

Church of St Peter and St Paul

Church St, Eye, IP23 7BD • Daily 9.30am–5pm or dusk, except during services • Free • ☎ 01379 871986, ⓦ eyeparishchurch.org

Eye is at its prettiest on **Church Street**, whose handsome medley of old cottages ambles down from the main square to both the **Guildhall**, an attractive timber-framed structure dating back to the fifteenth century, and the adjacent **church of St Peter and St Paul**, whose beautiful tower soars high above its surroundings, its contrasting panels, alternately stone and flint flushwork, an exercise in the Perpendicular. Inside, the most interesting feature is the fifteenth-century **rood screen**, whose dado sports a series of remarkably well preserved, albeit naive, almost doll-like – saints, including St Ursula, who shelters her acolyte-virgins, and St Barbara with a miniature representation of the tower in which she was, according to legend, imprisoned by her father.

Eye Castle

Castle Hill, off Castle St, Eye, IP23 7BD • Easter to Oct daily 9am–6pm or dusk; Oct– Easter Sat & Sun 9am–6pm or dusk • Free

From the church, it's easy to spot the prominent bramble-covered mound on which are perched the battered remains of **Eye Castle**, reached by clambering up a long wooden stairway in the castle grounds on Castle Hill, just off Castle Street – which itself

8

intersects with Church Street. The original motte-and-bailey fortress was erected in the eleventh century, but later fell into disrepair. A windmill was built here in the sixteenth century and a mansion was added in the reign of Queen Victoria, but the remains of both have vanished, leaving the crumbly stone walls of today. The ruins may be scant, but the wide views over the surrounding countryside are compensation.

ARRIVAL AND DEPARTURE

EYE

By bus Most buses to Eye pull in beside (or opposite) the Town Hall, on Lambeth St, from where it's a few yards to the minuscule main square and Church St. Among a limited range of services, there are buses to Ipswich (Mon–Sat every 1–2hr; 1hr), Diss (Mon–Sat every 1–2hr; 30min) and Hoxne (Mon–Fri 3 daily; 10min).

ACCOMMODATION AND EATING

Camomile Cottage Brome Ave, IP23 7HW ☎01379 873528, ⓦ camomilecottage.co.uk. Charming, timber-framed farmhouse, dating back to the sixteenth century, that has been creatively modernized to accommodate a handful of luxurious, en-suite bedrooms with all sorts of period details. To get there, head north from Eye along the B1077; Brome Avenue is a turning on the right. **£100**

Queen's Head 7 Cross St, IP23 7AB ☎01379 870153, ⓦ queensheadeye.co.uk. Refreshingly traditional, small-town pub with three bars, open fires and an excellent range of draft ales. Friendly place with first-rate bar food – try the fish and chips for £10.50. Kitchen daily 8.30–10.30am & noon–2pm, plus Mon–Sat 6–8pm; pub Mon–Sat 11am–11pm, Sun 11am–9pm.

Thornham Estate

Thornham Magna, IP23 8HH • Daily: April–Oct 9am–6pm; Nov–March 9am–4pm • Free • Parking Mon–Fri £2, Sat & Sun £3 • ☎01379 788345, ⓦ thornhamwalks.org

From Eye, it's a mile or two southwest to the **Thornham Estate**, where the **Thornham Walks** comprise over twelve miles of waymarked footpaths leading through woods, parkland and water meadows. There's also a walled garden, two cafés and a programme of special events with kids very much in mind, from bat evenings to den building. Maps of the estate are available at the entrance.

St Mary's church, Thornham Parva

Thornham Parva, IP23 8ES • Daily 9.30am–4pm or dusk • Free

On the northeast edge of the Thornham Estate, the scattering of houses that make up **THORNHAM PARVA** includes **St Mary's church**, a solitary affair, long bereft of its surrounding houses, whose ancient rubble walls are topped off by a splendid thatched roof. The simple, aisle-less interior bears witness to all sorts of historical tinkering – for a start there are both Saxon and Norman windows – and the faded wall paintings tell the tale of St Edmund (see box, p.310); but pride of place goes to the painted, fourteenth-century **retable** in which eight saints flank the Crucifixion. Saved from Thetford Priory during the Reformation, it's a beautiful work of art with a soft, sinuous quality: St Catherine, for example, holds the Catherine wheel on which she was martyred, her face gripped with a look of determined piety. Look out also for the engraved window on the south side of the nave, the work of the poet and artist **Laurence Whistler** (1912–2000) in tribute to his friend, the improbably named Lady Osla Henniker-Major.

Hoxne

The pretty little village of **HOXNE** (pronounced "Hoxon"), about four miles northeast of Eye, has one major claim to fame for it was here in 869 AD that the Anglo-Saxon ruler of East Anglia, **King Edmund**, came a cropper. A victim of excessive polishing, legend asserts that, after a defeat in battle, Edmund was hiding from his enemies, the Danes, beneath Hoxne's Goldbrook bridge when a local couple, who were on their way to church to get married, spotted the reflection of his glistening spurs in the river. They informed the Danes, who promptly captured him, tied him to a tree and shot him full of arrows – but not before Edmund laid a hex on the bridge, cursing any bride and groom who would ever use it in the future. Well into the nineteenth century, betrothed locals went to considerable trouble to avoid the bridge. Nonetheless, unpleasant curse or not, Edmund still ended up the most popular **saint** in East Anglia after various miracles were attributed to his body (see box, p.310).

The Goldbrook bridge and around

Today, a plaque on the **Goldbrook bridge**, at the south end of the village, remembers Edmund's betrayal and capture, and a clearly signed **Heritage Walk** begins here too, covering all the historical sites in the village and its immediate surroundings, including the spot where St Edmund's first chapel was erected and the place where he is supposed to have died. Maps of the walk are available at the car park on the bridge's far side.

There's also a small display on Edmund in the **church of St Peter and Paul** (daily 9am–4pm or dusk; free), at the top of the village beside the B1118. This display is supplemented by old photos of the village and information on the Hoxne hoard, a large collection of Roman coins found here in 1992 and subsequently transferred to the British Museum.

ARRIVAL AND DEPARTURE   HOXNE

By bus Buses pull in just north of the Goldbrook bridge on Low Street, though services are few and far between (especially Sun & evenings). The best of a poor job is the service to Eye (Mon–Fri 3 daily; 10min).

EATING

Swan Inn Low St, IP21 5AS. In 2015, this ancient inn, which occupies a good-looking half-timbered building a stone's throw from the Goldbrook bridge, closed down. At time of writing, there were moves to reopen it, possibly as a community-owned business.

Bury St Edmunds and around

One of Suffolk's most appealing towns, **BURY ST EDMUNDS**, ten miles north of Lavenham, started out as a Benedictine monastery, founded to accommodate the remains of **Edmund**, the last Saxon king of East Anglia. Edmund had been buried in Hoxne, where the Danes had murdered him, but later on he was dug up and reinterred in Bury, where his shrine became a major place of pilgrimage (see box, p.310). Almost two centuries later, England was briefly ruled by the kings of Denmark and the shrewdest of them, **King Canute** (or Knut), made a gesture of reconciliation to his Saxon subjects by granting the monastery a generous endowment and building the monks a brand-new church. It was a popular move and the abbey prospered, so much so that before its dissolution in 1539, it had become the richest religious house in the country, attracting hundreds of pilgrims eager to seek divine assistance via the mouldering bones of a now beatified Edmund.

Most of the **abbey** disappeared long ago, and nowadays Bury is better known for its graceful Georgian streets, lovely public gardens and clutch of enjoyable bars and restaurants. The town also acts as a supply centre for the surrounding villages, so it has a good range of shops, and is home to the **Greene King brewery** – though Bury's good looks are a tad spoilt by the hulking sugar-beet plant just outside the town centre.

Bury St Edmunds sits snug with rolling farmland stretching out towards every point of the compass except the northwest, where the A1101 is flanked by wooded heathland. Dotted over this rural terrain are several attractions, the pick of which is **Ickworth House**, the ancestral home of one of the aristocracy's oddest families, the Herveys, and you could also squeeze in detours to **Pakenham Mill**, the **Wyken Estate** and the re-created Anglo-Saxon Village at **West Stow**.

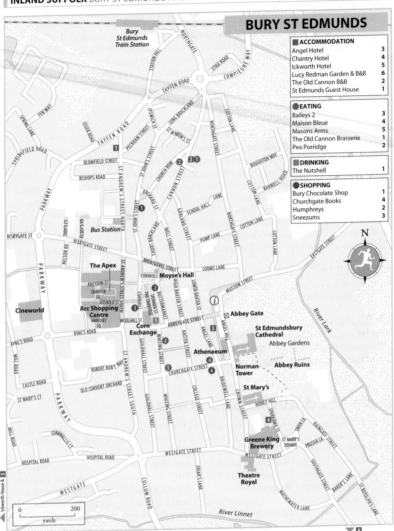

BURY ST EDMUNDS

■ **ACCOMMODATION**
Angel Hotel	3
Chantry Hotel	4
Ickworth Hotel	5
Lucy Redman Garden & B&B	6
The Old Cannon B&B	2
St Edmunds Guest House	1

● **EATING**
Baileys 2	3
Maison Bleue	4
Masons Arms	5
The Old Cannon Brasserie	1
Pea Porridge	2

■ **DRINKING**
The Nutshell	1

● **SHOPPING**
Bury Chocolate Shop	1
Churchgate Books	4
Humphreys	2
Sneezums	3

Angel Hill

Bury **town centre** has preserved much of its Norman street plan, a gridiron in which **Churchgate** was originally aligned with, and sloped up from – the abbey's high altar. It was the first planned town of Norman Britain and, for that matter, the first example of urban planning in England since the departure of the Romans. At the heart of the town is **Angel Hill**, a broad, spacious square partly framed by Georgian buildings, the most distinguished being the ivy-covered **Angel Hotel**, which features in Dickens' *Pickwick Papers*. Dickens also gave readings of his work in the **Athenaeum**, the Georgian assembly rooms at the far end of the square.

A twelfth-century **wall** runs along the east side of Angel Hill, with the bulky **Abbey Gate** forming the entrance to the Abbey Gardens and ruins beyond. An imposing structure dating from the middle of the fourteenth century, the gate's strong lines are emphasized by its castellated parapet and surly gargoyles – for, make no mistake, the gate was designed to overawe the locals. In 1327, the townsfolk had attacked the monastery, angered by its excessive power and wealth, and afterwards the abbot had this new gate built both to show exactly who was in control and to make sure it would never happen again.

Abbey Gardens and ruins

Abbey Gardens, off Angel Hill, IP33 1XL • Mon–Sat 7.30am–dusk, Sun 9am–dusk • Free

Ensconced within the immaculate greenery of the **Abbey Gardens**, the abbey **ruins** are themselves like nothing so much as petrified porridge, a rambling assortment of incidental remains with little to remind you of the grandiose Norman complex that once dominated the town. Thousands of medieval pilgrims once sought solace at St Edmund's altar and the cult was of such significance that the barons of England gathered here to swear that they would make King John sign their petition – the Magna Carta of 1215. A **plaque** marks the spot where they met beside what was once the high altar of the old abbey church, whose crumbly remains are on the far (right) side of the Abbey Gardens behind the cathedral.

St Edmundsbury Cathedral

Angel Hill, IP33 1LS • Daily 8.30am–6pm • Free, but £3 donation requested • ☎ 01284 748720, ⊕ stedscathedral.co.uk

On Angel Hill, the Anglican **St Edmundsbury Cathedral** is a hangar-like affair, whose most attractive features are its Gothic lantern tower and its beautiful painted roof. The tower was completed in 2005 as part of the Millennium Project, a long-term plan to improve the church, which has also involved the installation of a vaulted ceiling under the tower and the reconstruction of the cloisters. St Edmundsbury was only granted cathedral status in 1914, though it was a close call: many clergy would have preferred to see the neighbouring (and more interesting) church of **St Mary's** (see below) upgraded, but that church holds the tomb of Mary Tudor, the sister of Henry VIII and one-time Queen of France – and that was quite enough to put the church authorities off. Next door to the cathedral stands the twelfth-century **Norman Tower** (no access), a solitary structure whose rounded arches, blind arcading and dragon gargoyles once served as the main gatehouse into the abbey.

St Mary's church

Honey Hill, IP33 1RT • Mon–Sat 10am–4pm, 3pm in winter • Free • ☎ 01284 754680, ⊕ wearechurch.net

St Mary's church, just along the street from the cathedral, is a handsome structure that dates from the twelfth century, though most of what you see today is the result of an extensive revamp carried out in the 1430s. The revamp was not without its mishaps: the congregation was mumbling away one dark and stormy evening when the tower collapsed, narrowly missing the worshippers below, but covering them in dust and grime. St Mary's boasts an especially wide and well-lit nave, whose tall and slender pillars rise up towards a simply magnificent **hammerbeam roof**, where a full set of angels presides over the proceedings below, their wings unfurled as if ready for take-off. The central arch also catches the eye, not so much for its height but because of the richly coloured stained-glass window depicting the martyrdom of the saint-king Edmund. The window is cut in the shape of the original pilgrim's badge and was the work of **Thomas Willement** (1786–1871), a once famous stained-glass artist and dedicated medievalist.

Beside the high altar, two badly weathered table tombs commemorate local bigwigs – the delicately carved, tasselled cushions beneath the wife of Robert Drury are particularly delightful – and nearby, behind the altar at the far end of the church, is the simple **tomb of Mary Tudor** (1496–1533), the favourite sister of Henry VIII, after whom he named his leading warship, the *Mary Rose*; Mary was originally buried in the abbey,

---

EDMUND: SAXON SAINT AND HERO

Before the pagan Danes killed him in Hoxne (see p.306), **Edmund**, the last Saxon king of East Anglia (c.840–869) allegedly refused to save his life by abjuring his Christian faith and, in the way of would-be saints, his death was accompanied by miracles: the Danes threw his head into a wood, where the Anglo-Saxons discovered it guarded by a wolf, and when head and body were reunited, they miraculously re-attached themselves. Edmund was canonized early in the tenth century, the speed of his elevation no doubt influenced by the stirring account of his death provided by the **Anglo-Saxon Chronicle**, which recorded the history of the Anglo-Saxons at considerable length: "The heathens then became brutally angry because of Edmund's beliefs… They shot then with missiles, as if to amuse themselves, until he was all covered with their missiles as with bristles of a hedgehog, just as [Saint] Sebastian was. Then Hinguar, [the Danish chieftain], saw that the noble king did not desire to renounce Christ, and with resolute faith always called to him; Hinguar then commanded to behead the king and the heathens thus did. While this was happening, Edmund called to Christ still. Then the heathens dragged the holy man to slaughter, and with a stroke struck the head from him. His soul set forth, blessed, to Christ."

---

but her remains were moved here after the Reformation. Mary Tudor may have been Henry's favourite sister, but it didn't save her from being shipped off to France to be married to the ailing King of France, Louis XII, who, at 52, was 34 years her senior. Louis did not last long, so Mary's time as Queen of France was limited to just a few months and afterwards she hotfooted it back to England to marry the Duke of Suffolk.

8

Greene King brewery

Westgate St, IP33 1QT• Guided tours 1 daily Mon, Tues & Sun, 2 daily Wed–Fri, 4 daily Sat; 1hr 30min–2hr • Advance booking recommended • £12 • ☎ 01284 714297, ⓦ greeneking.co.uk

From St Mary's church, it's a couple of minutes' walk south along Crown Street to the **Greene King brewery**, where the visitor centre sells tickets for guided tours of the museum and the adjacent brewery. The tour is finished off by a pit stop at the Brewery Tap, where you can wet your whistle on the full range of their products; **Old Speckled Hen** is perhaps their most celebrated brew.

Theatre Royal

6 Westgate St, IP33 1QR • Tours See website for times; 1hr • £6.50, NT members free • ☎ 01284 769505, ⓦ theatreroyal.org

Across the street from the brewery stands the **Theatre Royal**, an attractive building of 1819 which is owned by Greene King, but leased to the National Trust, who in their turn have rented it out to a theatre company (see p.312). Sympathetically restored to its Regency appearance, the interior is the most intimate of auditoria and comes complete with a painted frieze and a painted ceiling plus a sweeping circle of dinky little boxes.

Corn Exchange

Bury's main commercial area lies just to the west of Angel Hill up along **Abbeygate**. There's been some intrusive modern planning here, but sterling Victorian buildings flank both the L-shaped **Cornhill** and the **Buttermarket** – the two short main streets – as well as the narrower streets in between. The dominant edifice is the **Corn Exchange**, whose portico is all Neoclassical extravagance with a whopping set of stone columns and a carved tympanum up above. Perhaps the Victorian merchants who footed the bill decided it was too showy after all, for they had a biblical quote inscribed up above the columns in an apparent flash of modesty: "The Earth is the Lord's and the Fulness Thereof".

Moyse's Hall

Cornhill, IP33 1DX • Mon–Sat 10am–5pm, Sun noon–4pm • £4 • ☎ 01284 757160, ⓦ moyseshall.org

Across the Cornhill from Smiths Row is **Moyse's Hall**, a modest museum lodged in an early medieval building, whose twin gables give the exterior the appearance of a church. It's likely that the abbot owned the hall, but it's possible it was built for a wealthy member of the small Jewish community that lived in Bury in the twelfth century. Frankly, the interior is hardly riveting, but there are several mildly interesting sections, one on the Suffolk Regiment, which was amalgamated with the Norfolk Regiment in 1959, and another in the "Death Gallery", which includes examples of the poor old cats that were habitually interred inside the walls of houses to ward off the evil eye. In the same room is a motley collection of instruments of torture plus one or two mementoes of William Corder, the **Red Barn Murderer** (see p.289), principally his death mask, his desiccated scalp and, most gruesome of the lot, a book bound with his skin.

The Apex

1 Charter Square St, IP33 3FD • Mon–Sat 10am–5pm, Sun 10am–4pm • Free • ☎ 01284 758000, ⓦ theapex.co.uk

Attached to the Arc Shopping Centre, **The Apex** is Bury's glitzy new performance venue (see p.312), its construction part of a sustained effort to enliven the town. The first floor here holds the **Apex Gallery**, a contemporary art gallery, whose temporary exhibitions have been very well received; most of the works on display are for sale.

ARRIVAL AND INFORMATION

BURY ST EDMUNDS AND AROUND

By train Bury St Edmunds' train station is on the northern edge of the centre, a 10min walk from Angel Hill via Northgate St.
Destinations Cambridge (hourly; 45min); Ely (every 2hr; 30min); Ipswich (hourly; 40min); Newmarket (hourly; 20min); Stowmarket (hourly; 20min).
By bus The town bus station is on St Andrews St North, from where it's a couple of minutes' walk south to the

Cornhill. Principal destinations include Long Melford (Mon–Sat hourly; 1hr) and Thetford (Mon–Sat hourly; 20–40min).
By car The A14 skirts the eastern edge of Bury St Edmunds; on-street parking is rarely a problem.
Tourist office In the town centre at the glossy new Apex performance centre (1 Charter Square, IP33 3FD; Mon–Sat 10am–5pm; ☎01284 764667, ⓦvisit-burystedmunds.co.uk).

ACCOMMODATION

Bury St Edmunds is especially popular with day-trippers, but there's still enough overnight trade to support a reasonable range of hotels and B&Bs either in or very close to the centre. If you're on a tight budget, stick to the B&Bs; if you're after luxury make a beeline for the out-of-town *Ickworth Hotel* (see p.313).

IN TOWN

Angel Hotel 3 Angel Hill, IP33 1LT ☎01284 714000, ⓦtheangel.co.uk. Long-established former coaching inn whose public areas have been remodelled in contemporary style. Beyond are over seventy bedrooms, some with a country house feel, others with a more modern one. Great location, a few yards from the Abbey Gardens. **£130**
Chantry Hotel 8 Sparhawk St, IP33 1RY ☎01284 767427, ⓦchantryhotel.com. There are seventeen guest rooms here in this privately owned hotel and they occupy the Georgian house at the front and the annexe behind. The decor is retro with big wooden beds and even the odd four-poster, though the bathrooms are routinely modern. A handy, central location too, but note that Sparhawk St can get very busy with speeding traffic. **£115**

★**The Old Cannon B&B** 86 Cannon St, IP33 1JR ☎01284 768769, ⓦoldcannonbrewery.co.uk. Arguably Bury's most distinctive B&B, there are a handful of neat modern guest-rooms here, all en suite, in an intelligently recycled brewhouse, itself attached to a microbrewery, restaurant and bar (see p.312). Over in the bar, the brews are strong – so you might be glad your bed is near at hand. Cannon St is on the north side of town, a 5min walk from the centre: to get there, take Northgate St from Angel Hill and watch for the (hard) turning on the left. **£130**
St Edmunds Guest House 35 St Andrews St North, IP33 1SZ ☎01284 700144, ⓦstedmundsguesthouse .net. Browns and creams with oak furniture are the order of the day in this pleasant B&B, which has nine en-suite guest rooms. Occupies a straightforward, three-storey brick house on the west side of the centre, a 5–10min walk from Angel Hill. Full English breakfast included. **£70**

OUT OF TOWN
Lucy Redman Garden & B&B 6 The Village, Rushbrooke, IP30 0ER ☎ 01284 386250, ⌨ lucyredman.co.uk. Tucked away in the village of Rushbrooke, about six miles southeast of Bury, this charming B&B occupies an immaculately maintained thatched cottage with gorgeous gardens. They have two en-suite guest rooms – one decorated in Moroccan style, the other Indian. Tasty breakfasts, too. **£100**

EATING

Baileys 2 5 Whiting St, IP33 1NX ☎ 01284 706198, ⌨ baileys2.co.uk. This cosy, modern place just off Abbeygate is the best teashop in town – no argument. The food is fresh, the service fast and the menu extensive, but you need look no further than the toasties (£5–6), which are lip-smackingly good. Mon–Sat 9am–4pm.

★**Maison Bleue** 30 Churchgate St, IP33 1RG ☎ 01284 760623, ⌨ maisonbleue.co.uk. Slick and sleek seafood restaurant noted for its outstanding (French-influenced) menu, covering everything from crab and cod through to sardines and skate. Main courses average £22. Tues–Sat noon–2pm & 7–9.30pm.

Masons Arms 14 Whiting St, IP33 1NX ☎ 01284 753955, ⌨ masonspub.co.uk. This pub-cum-restaurant, with its traditional interior, occupies a very old building, though the weatherboarding that covers the outside is entirely Victorian. The food is above-standard pub grub, featuring the likes of chilli con carne and roast beef. Mains around £13. Mon–Sat noon–11.30pm, Sun noon–11pm; kitchen open daily noon–9pm.

The Old Cannon Brasserie 86 Cannon St, IP33 1JR ☎ 01284 768769, ⌨ oldcannonbrewery.co.uk. This enjoyable and very relaxing place hits all the right notes: with a B&B (see p.311) in the adjoining brewhouse, the large and softly lit restaurant-bar offers an excellent range of daily specials with due prominence given to local ingredients – Norfolk mussels, Suffolk pork, Lowestoft cod. Main courses are competitively priced at around £14. The restaurant-bar also holds two brewing vats, evidence of the on-premises microbrewery, whose products include the award-winning dark ale Gunner's Daughter. Outstanding service, too. Kitchen Mon–Sat noon–9pm, Sun noon–3pm; bar Mon–Sat noon–11.30pm, Sun noon–10.30pm.

★**Pea Porridge** 28 Cannon St, IP33 1JR ☎ 01284 700200, ⌨ peaporridge.co.uk. In a small, terraced house just across the street from *The Old Cannon* (see above), this small and intimate restaurant has a homely feel and an inventive, thoughtful menu with mains averaging £17. One delicious choice is pigeon with beetroot and fondant potato in an artichoke jus. Tues–Sat 6.30–9pm, Thurs–Sat noon–1.45pm & 6.30–9pm.

DRINKING

★**The Nutshell** The Traverse, IP33 1BJ ☎ 01284 764867, ⌨ thenutshellpub.co.uk. At the top of Abbeygate, *The Nutshell* claims to be Britain's smallest pub and it certainly is small – only sixteen feet by seven, big enough for twelve customers or maybe fifteen, provided they can raise a pint without raising their elbows, though on one splendid occasion in the 1980s no fewer than 102 drinkers managed to squeeze inside on a charity gig. Successive landlords have warmed to the theme of size and the antique interior, with its wood panelling, benches and gnarled bar, has at one time or another held the world's smallest dartboard and snooker table. The desiccated body of a cat hanging from the ceiling is not the origin of the phrase "Not enough room to swing a cat", but the result of a traditional custom in which builders walled in cats behind the fireplace to ward off the evil eye; the cat was found during renovations. The pub provides some sterling beers, including Greene King's full-bodied Abbot Ale and Old Speckled Hen. Daily 11am–11pm.

ENTERTAINMENT

The Apex 1 Charter Square St, IP33 3FD ☎ 01284 758000, ⌨ theapex.co.uk. Casting its musical net far and wide, this is Bury's principal – and really rather flashy – performance venue for pretty much everything from heavy metal to Leo Sayer.

Cineworld Park Way, IP33 3BA ☎ 0871 2002000, ⌨ cineworld.co.uk. Bury's main cinema has eight screens, big enough to cater to both mainstream and arthouse tastes, and is handily located to the rear of the Arc Shopping Centre beside the inner ring road.

Theatre Royal Westgate St, IP33 1QR ☎ 01284 769505, ⌨ theatreroyal.org. Bury's principal performing arts venue offers a year-round programme of cultural events, from Shakespeare to pantomime.

SHOPPING

Bury St Edmunds possesses a reasonably good range of small, independent shops, though they are under increasing pressure from the glitzy new **Arc Shopping Centre** that has sprung up on the site of the old Cattle Market, just off St Andrews St. The town also has a busy and popular open-air provisions **market** held every Wednesday and Saturday on and around the Cornhill and the Buttermarket.

Bury Chocolate Shop 77a St John's St, IP33 1SQ ☎01284 724555, ⓦburychocolateshop.co.uk. In dinky, antique premises on one of the town's most pleasant shopping streets, this independent shop specializes in first-rate Belgian chocolates, all attractively displayed. Also has sidelines in all things sweet, from pastilles to children's novelties – chocolate-filled pencils, dinosaurs and so forth. Tues–Sat 10am–5pm.

Churchgate Books 22a Hatter St, IP33 1NE ☎01284 704604, ⓦchurchgatebooks.co.uk. In the old part of town, this enterprising, independent bookshop carries a wide selection of new, remaindered, secondhand and antiquarian books. They are particularly strong on local stuff – East Anglian history and so forth – and they even make a range of hand-crafted blank books in their own bindery. Mon–Sat 9.30am–5pm, and often Sun afternoons during summer.

Humphreys 16 Buttermarket, IP33 1PD ☎01284 763300, ⓦhumphreysbutchers.com. Traditional family butcher's shop that takes great pride in sourcing its beef locally from only the best-kept and best-raised herds. Also does a tasty line in game, including pheasants, grouse and wood pigeon, depending on the season. Mon–Sat 7am–5pm.

Sneezums 10 Cornhill, IP33 1BH ☎01284 752634, ⓦsneezums.co.uk. Not, as you might expect from the name, a supplier of snuff, but rather an independent shop selling an excellent range of watches, cameras, binoculars and telescopes, with a tasteful sideline in jewellery. Mon–Sat 9am–5.15pm.

Ickworth House

Horringer, IP29 5QE • **House** March to late July, Sept & Oct Mon, Tues & Thurs–Sun 11am–4pm; late July to Aug daily 11am–4pm; Nov & Dec Sat & Sun 11am–4pm • **Park** Daily 8am–8pm or dusk • **Gardens** Daily 9am–5.30pm • House, park & gardens £12.60; park & gardens only £6.25; park only, free; NT • ☎01284 735270, ⓦnationaltrust.org.uk

Surrounded by acres of parkland, **Ickworth House** is distinguished by its huge stone **rotunda**, commissioned by **Frederick Hervey**, the Bishop of Derry and Earl of Bristol in the 1790s. The Earl-Bishop loved all things Italian, hence the design of the rotunda, but when he died in 1803, his new palace home was far from completed and his successors, lacking their ancestor's architectural enthusiasms, never really made a full fist of it, though two wings were subsequently attached to the rotunda with the East Wing becoming the family home in the 1820s, and the other now turned into a luxury hotel (see below).

On public display in the **house** are paintings by a number of leading artists, most notably Velázquez, Titian, Gainsborough and Reynolds, as well as a fine collection of Georgian silver and Regency furniture. There's also the iconic *Death of Wolfe* by Benjamin West (1738–1820). The British general James Wolfe inflicted a crushing defeat on the French outside Québec City in 1759, but was killed during the battle. West's painting transformed this grubby colonial conflict into a romantic extravagance, with the dying general in a Christ-like pose, a pale figure held tenderly by his subordinates. West presented the first version of his painting to the Royal Academy of Arts in 1771 and it proved so popular that he spent much of the next decade painting copies. After the house, most visitors proceed to ramble round the **park**, pausing at the so-called Fairy Lake and popping into the walled garden.

ACCOMMODATION

★**Ickworth Hotel** Horringer, IP29 5QE ☎01284 735 350, ⓦickworthhotel.co.uk. This superb hotel occupies an extraordinary location – the East Wing of Ickworth House (see above), its imposing stonework and high-ceilinged corridors added to the house's original rotunda in the early nineteenth century. The facilities are outstanding – there's a basement spa and a pool – and, although the rooms vary, the finest are stunning, with the commodious "Grand Tour" room big enough to accommodate a magnificent antique bed, two fine old sofas, a splendid chandelier and a capacious built-in wardrobe. Add to this a large bathroom and views out across the surrounding parkland and it's hard to imagine somewhere much better. Breakfast (included) is taken in the conservatory, as are lunches, and the hotel restaurant is a fine affair as well – try, for instance, the Horringer pheasant with sautéed potatoes, spinach and roasted pumpkin purée. Mains average around £22. Advance reservations – even if you're a hotel resident – are advised. Lunch daily noon–2pm; afternoon tea daily 3–5pm; dinner daily 7–9.30pm. **£120**

THE HERVEYS OF ICKWORTH

The Sixth Marquess of Bristol, **Victor Frederick Cochrane Hervey** (1915–85) gave **Ickworth House** and its grounds to the National Trust in the 1950s in lieu of death duties with the proviso that the Herveys could continue to live in the East Wing. The Herveys had a long-standing reputation for eccentricity, but the Sixth Marquess trumped his predecessors by masterminding the activities of a gang of jewel thieves – he was sent down for three years in 1939 – before amassing a fortune in various business activities. Neither does he appear to have been a good father and his son, **Frederick William John Augustus Hervey** (1954–99), the Seventh Marquess of Bristol, had a particularly troubled life, whittling away a vast fortune in a frenzy of cocaine, heroin and rent boys. At Ickworth, the antics of the seventh marquess antagonized his landlord, the National Trust, who just about bit his hand off when he offered to sell his remaining rights to them in 1998. The Herveys no longer have any connection with Ickworth, though the hotel (see p.313) displays photos of this unloveable brood.

West Stow Country Park and Anglo-Saxon Village

Icklingham Rd, West Stow, IP28 6HG • Daily 10am–5pm • £5, children (5–16yrs) £3 • ☎ 01284 728718, ⓦ weststow.org

This unusual attraction, located among wooded heathland seven miles northwest of Bury St Edmunds via the A1101, comprises around a dozen re-created **Anglo-Saxon houses** on the site of what was originally a late Iron Age village, whose layout was fully excavated in the 1960s. The attached **visitor centre** examines the nature of Anglo-Saxon society and explores the various controversies surrounding the houses: it's agreed they were thatched, but the key debate is whether the Anglo-Saxons lived in pits or on wooden floors. The village is popular with school parties and there's a programme of special events and displays, while the adjacent **Country Park** provides pleasant wooded walks and has a lake with bird hides.

Pakenham Water Mill

Mill Rd, Pakenham, IP31 2NB • Early April to late Sept Thurs 10am–4.30pm, Sat & Sun 1.30–5pm • Milling on the first Thurs morning of each month 10–11.30am, plus July & Aug Sun 2–3.30pm • £4.50 • ☎ 01359 230275, ⓦ pakenhamwatermill.org.uk

On the edge of the village of **PAKENHAM**, about six miles northeast of Bury St Edmunds via the A143, stands **Pakenham Mill**, the last working water mill in Suffolk. Visitors can wander around the old workings, examine the antique bread oven and brewing vat, and finish off with a cuppa and a cake at the tearoom.

Wyken Vineyards

Wyken Rd, Stanton, IP31 2DW • **Gardens** April–Sept Mon–Fri & Sun 2–6pm • £4 • **Restaurant** Mon–Thurs & Sun noon–2pm, Fri & Sat noon–2pm & 7–10pm • ☎ 01359 250287 • **Store** Daily 10am–6pm, plus Fri & Sat 7–10pm • ☎ 01359 250262, ⓦ wykenvineyards.co.uk

Deep in the countryside, nine miles northeast of Bury St Edmunds, **Wyken Vineyards** is an exercise in diversification, with something for just about everyone: woodland walks; a flock of Shetland sheep and a small herd of Red Poll cattle on the farm; a well-regarded vineyard; a restaurant in the old barn that specializes in meat, game and vegetables from the estate; formal gardens surrounding the Elizabethan manor house; an excellent farmers' market (Sat 9am–1pm); and a very good arts, crafts and gifts country store.

Newmarket

NEWMARKET, just fifteen miles from Bury St Edmunds, is dedicated to the **racehorse** – or more specifically the flat (fence-less) horse racing season, which runs from April to early November. There are farriers, betting shops and bloodstock agents, two racecourses, stud farms and stables, saddlers and jockey-barracks, plus vets galore and nigh on three thousand horses. As you approach the town, its equine credentials are announced with a wide sweep of carefully maintained **heathland**, and it's here that the country's leading racehorses are put through their paces – and have been since horserace-loving King Charles II put the place on the map, moving his court to Newmarket once or twice a year. Nowadays, the Dubai Royal Family is the dominant economic force, but they don't control the training grounds – that's down to the **Jockey Club**, whose 150 members gather in discreet premises in the centre of town. Otherwise, Newmarket's centre is really rather undistinguished, but make no mistake, there's big money here: a top **thoroughbred** can go for £2 million or more and every aspect of the animal's life is carefully (and expensively) monitored, from the food they eat and the mares the stallions mate with (or "cover") through to each horse's exercise regime. This ultra-scientific approach is part of an attempt to cut the odds, reduce the uncertainties, but in the end it's all a gamble – and that's the thrill. The casual visitor is kept very much on the outside of the racing, but there are ways to gain an insight: the obvious ploy is to drive out along the **Heath Road** to watch the horses training on **The Gallops**, the wide heath just to the east of the town centre latticed with white posts and rails; horses have right of way till 1pm, when the heath reverts to common land. You can also go to the races (see box, p.316), take a guided tour (see box, p.317), pop into the **Horseracing Museum** and, although access is limited, visit the **National Stud** and the **Jockey Club**.

National Horseracing Museum

8

99 High St, CB8 8JH • Mon–Sat 10am–5pm, Sun 10am–4pm • £6.50 • ☎ 01638 667333, ⓦ nhrm.co.uk

The **National Horseracing Museum** starts at the beginning, with an intriguing section on the "Origins of Racing 1600–1900", which includes paintings and prints, a

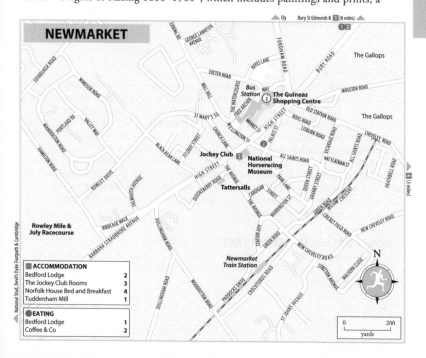

stuffed horse's head or two and examples of early jockey gear. There's also a fascinating display on the evolution of the **thoroughbred**: remarkably enough, all are descendants of just three, early eighteenth-century "**Foundation Sires**" (Darley Arabian, Godolphin Arabian and Byerley Turk), Arabian stallions noted for their speed and agility, which were bred with English mares, renowned for their strength and courage. Other sections of the museum include a Jockeys' Hall of Fame, a selection of racehorse paintings and the skeleton of one of the most successful sires of all time, **Hyperion**, who galloped off into the stable in the sky in 1960; there's a statue of him outside the Jockey Club next door. Finally, the museum has a small hands-on section aimed at kids, who can dress up in racing silks and weigh themselves before mounting a (vigorous) horse simulator. Plans are afoot to develop and expand the museum, funds permitting.

The Jockey Club

101 High St, CB8 8JL · Teas & tours by advance reservation only: Sun afternoon once monthly or once every two months · £28 · ☎ 01638 663101, ⓦ jockeyclubrooms.co.uk

Founded in 1750, the **Jockey Club** has precious little to do with jockeys, but a lot to do with those wealthy enough to own Newmarket's racehorses. For most of its history, the club controlled the sport, but these regulatory functions were surrendered a few years ago and passed to the newly founded **British Horseracing Authority** in 2007. Since then, the Jockey Club has been free to concentrate on its commercial interests and the operation of its extensive estate – in particular the club owns Newmarket's large horse-training grounds. A little tentatively, the club has also opened its doors to outsiders for weddings, special events and **teas and tours**. High Tea is taken in the Coffee Room, a handsome Georgian salon with leather benches, discreet little alcoves, lots of horsey paintings and heavy drape curtains. The tour includes a scoot through a series of rooms, including the portrait gallery, card room and boardroom – all spiced up with tales of horses and their riders.

National Stud

Newmarket, CB8 0XE (off the A1304) · ☎ 01638 663464, ⓦ nationalstud.co.uk · Tours Daily mid-Feb to Sept; 90min; advance bookings required with Discover Newmarket · £11 · ☎ 08447 489200, ⓦ discovernewmarket.co.uk · Two miles southwest of Newmarket, next to the July Racecourse; at the Racehorse Statue roundabout take the same exit as for the July Racecourse and follow the signs

Owned and operated by the Jockey Club, the **National Stud** was established in 1916 to ensure that the British cavalry had decent horses to ride – just as the poor animals were being slaughtered in their hundreds during World War I. **Tours**, which are by bus and on foot, include visits to the foaling unit, the nursery paddocks and the stallion house, plus a peek inside the covering (mating) shed; the breeding season runs from February to June. The economics of the Stud dwarf the prize money offered to the winners of the races: a top-ranking stallion can cover 120 mares per year at a rate of £65,000 per session.

HORSE RACING IN NEWMARKET

Newmarket has two racecourses, Rowley Mile and July Racecourse. They share the same box office and website (☎ 01638 675500, ⓦ newmarket.thejockeyclub.co.uk). There are five classic flat races every year:

1000 Guineas Late April/early May, Newmarket
2000 Guineas Late April/early May, Newmarket

The Oaks Early June, Epsom Downs Racecourse
The Derby First Saturday in June, Epsom Downs Racecourse
St Leger September, Doncaster Racecourse

Devil's Dyke

The finest surviving Anglo-Saxon earthwork in East Anglia, the **Devil's Dyke** cuts a dead-straight line across the chalky downs to the west of Newmarket, running northwest the eight miles from Ditton Green to Reach. A **footpath** runs along the top of the dyke, providing wide views over the surrounding countryside, and making a pleasant day-long excursion. You can join the path at its midway point just outside Newmarket: turn right off the main road at the Racehorse Statue roundabout and keep going to the end of the road (200m or so) and you'll spot the Devil's Dyke sign.

ARRIVAL AND INFORMATION   NEWMARKET

By train The station is south of the town centre, a 10min walk from the High Street. Services run hourly to Bury St Edmunds (20min), Cambridge (25min) and Ipswich (1hr).
By bus Most buses pull into the station in The Guineas, abutting Fred Archer Way and to the north of the High St.

Services include Cambridge (Mon–Sat hourly, Sun every 2–3hr; 40min) and Ipswich (every 2hr; 1hr 40min).
Tourist office Part of the District Council offices in The Guineas shopping centre (Mon–Fri 9am–5pm & Sat 10am–4pm; ☏ 01638 719749, ⓦ westsuffolk.gov.uk).

ACCOMMODATION

IN TOWN
Bedford Lodge 11 Bury Rd, CB8 7BX ☏ 01638 663175, ⓦ bedfordlodgehotel.co.uk. The best hotel in town, the *Bedford Lodge* occupies a former stables in substantial grounds a 10min walk east of the centre. The 55 spacious guest rooms and suites are decorated in an attractive modern style with lots of pastel shades. There's a spa and a fitness suite, too, plus a good restaurant (see below). **£140**
The Jockey Club Rooms 101 High St, CB8 8JL ☏ 01638 663101, ⓦ jockeyclubrooms.co.uk. Members of the Jockey Club have been staying in chichi accommodation at the back of the main building for many decades, but these eighteen bedrooms are now available to the public. Each is decorated in an easy-going, genteel country-house style, with extravagant bathrooms, and the setting is as tranquil as tranquil can be. Advance reservations are recommended; note that some periods are reserved for club members. **£160**

OUT OF TOWN
Norfolk House Bed and Breakfast 141 High St, Cheveley, CB8 9DG ☏ 01638 730424, ⓦ norfolkhouse .biz. Smart B&B with two well-appointed guest rooms, one en suite, in an appealing Georgian country home. Price includes tea and cake on arrival and use of the outdoor swimming pool in summer. In the village of Cheveley, about three miles southeast of Newmarket via the B1063. **£85**
Tuddenham Mill High St, Tuddenham, IP28 6SQ ☏ 01638 713552, ⓦ tuddenhammill.co.uk. This deluxe hotel is sited in a sympathetically renovated old water mill about eight miles northeast of Newmarket in the village of Tuddenham. No luxury has been skimped on in the kitting out of the fifteen smart guest rooms, which come complete with walk-in showers, whopping baths, Italian contemporary furniture and, de rigueur for this sort of boutique hotel, fine Egyptian-cotton bed linen. **£120**

EATING

Bedford Lodge 11 Bury Rd, CB8 7BX ☏ 01638 663175, ⓦ bedfordlodgehotel.co.uk. Excellent hotel (see above) restaurant, serving modern British dishes like braised shin of beef with a red-wine glaze and horseradish creamed potato. Mains around £22. Mon–Fri noon–2pm & 7–9.30pm, Sat

7–9.30pm, Sun 12.30–2.30pm & 7–9pm.
Coffee & Co 12–14 Palace St, CB8 8EP ☏ 01638 611000, ⓦ coffeeandco.info. This bright, pleasant little café serves scrumptious light meals, snacks and sandwiches. Very friendly too. Mon–Sat 8am–5.30pm, Sun 10am–2.30pm.

GUIDED TOURS OF NEWMARKET

One sure-fire way of getting a handle on Newmarket's **horse racing culture** is to take a guided tour with **Discover Newmarket** (☏ 0844 7489200, ⓦ discovernewmarket.co.uk). Dates and itineraries vary considerably, depending on what's happening and what's open, but their most popular offering is the **Country Mile Tour** (7hr; £80 per person). The tour, which is by minibus, usually starts at the National Stud (see opposite) and includes time watching the horses on The Gallops and visits to a stable and horse-training yard. Sometimes it also includes a visit to **Tattersalls** (ⓦ tattersalls.com), whose world-famous horse auctions take place about sixteen days a year in their large premises in the town centre. On the tour, you'll also have a chance to see the various sorts of training track – the most sophisticated are of sand fibre doused in hot Vaseline. Advance reservations required.

BLACK-TAILED GODWIT

Contexts

History

On the map, Norfolk and Suffolk look something like a sack on the back of the rest of England, pushing out into the North Sea. This hints at the region's isolation, but doesn't tell the whole story as the forests of Essex to the south and the sticky marshes of the Fens to the west pretty much cut the two counties off until the seventeenth century – and it was another hundred years before the journey overland from London to Norwich looked more tempting than the sea cruise. It was the incoming Angles who gave the counties their names (the North Folk and the South Folk) and they threw in the name of the region too (East Anglia), though nowadays no one can agree on what exactly constitutes East Anglia: some add one or other of Lincolnshire, Cambridgeshire and Essex, too.

The Stone Ages

Norfolk and Suffolk have been inhabited for over half a million years and although the earliest archeological evidence is necessarily scant, an assortment of Old Stone Age (Paleolithic) bones and flint tools has been found in coastal deposits near **Happisburgh** in northeast Norfolk. The comings and goings of these migrant peoples were dictated by the fluctuations of several ice ages. The last spell of intense cold began about 17,000 years ago, and it was the final thawing of this last **Ice Age** around 5000 BC that caused the British Isles to separate from the European mainland. Perhaps surprisingly, the sea barrier did nothing to stop further migrations of nomadic hunters into the region, the main magnet being the game that inhabited its forests. These Middle Stone Age (Mesolithic) people needed tools and weapons, and the easy-to-work surface flint of Norfolk and Suffolk was ideal. One of the richest Mesolithic sites in East Anglia is Kelling Heath (see p.134), near Weybourne, where a scattering of around one hundred Mesolithic flint artefacts have been discovered.

In about 3500 BC, a new wave of colonists reached England from the continent, probably via Ireland, bringing with them a **New Stone Age** (Neolithic) culture based on farming and the rearing of livestock. These were the first people to make some impact on the environment, clearing forests, enclosing fields and constructing defensive ditches around their villages. They were also the first to mine flint from the subterranean seams of chalk, the prime example being Grimes Graves near Thetford (see p.212), where these early miners sank shafts through no less than 10ft of sand and clay before quarrying a 20ft band of chalk, a remarkable effort given the crudeness of their tools. In most of England, the most profuse relics of this Neolithic culture are their graves, usually stone-chambered, turf-covered mounds (called **long barrows**), but here in agricultural Norfolk and Suffolk almost all were lost to the plough ages ago, a rare exception being the two barrows at Broome Heath, near Bungay in Suffolk.

6000 BC	3000 BC	2500 BC	2050 BC
End of the last Ice Age; the sea separates Britain from the continent.	Neolithic flint mining begins in Grimes Graves, near Thetford.	Beginning of the Bronze Age.	Construction of Seahenge in Norfolk – no one is quite sure why.

The Bronze Age

The transition from the Neolithic to the **Bronze Age** began around 2500 BC with the importation from northern Europe of artefacts attributed to the **Beaker Culture** – named from the distinctive cups found at many burial sites. In East Anglia as elsewhere, the spread of the Beaker Culture along established trade routes helped stimulate the development of a comparatively well-organized social structure with an established aristocracy. Many of Britain's stone and timber circles were completed at this time (including Stonehenge in Wiltshire) while many others belong entirely to the Bronze Age, including Norfolk's remarkable **Seahenge**, which was discovered on the coast at Holme-next-the-Sea in 1998 – and transferred to a King's Lynn museum a few years later (see p.173). Dated to around 2050 BC, the Seahenge was almost certainly some kind of ceremonial site, perhaps with astronomical significance, though some have argued that this was where the dead were brought to speed the process of decay.

The Iron Age

Covering the period from about 700 BC to the Roman conquest beginning in 43 AD, the British **Iron Age** saw the consolidation of a relatively sophisticated farming economy with a social hierarchy dominated by a druidic priesthood. These early Britons gradually developed better methods of metal working, forging not just weapons but also coins and ornamental works, thus creating the first recognizable indigenous art – as famously demonstrated by the wonderfully crafted, gold neck ring – or Great Torc – found at Snettisham and now displayed in the British Museum. The tribes' principal contribution to the landscape was a network of **hillforts** and other defensive works stretching over the entire country, and there are the remains of such fortifications at a dozen or so places in Norfolk and Suffolk, including Clare, Narborough, South Creake, Holkham and Thetford. These earthworks suggest endemic tribal warfare, a situation further complicated by the appearance of bands of Celts, who arrived in numbers from central Europe in around 600 BC. In Norfolk and Suffolk, the origins of the dominant tribe, the **Iceni**, are open to debate: some have argued they were a Germanic people, others that they were invading Celts from France and Belgium, yet others insist they were descendants of the prehistoric inhabitants of the region – or a combination of all three. Whatever their origins, the Iceni – the "People of the Horse" – traded widely: they were familiar with Mediterranean artefacts, and the long-distance Icknield Way, running south from their tribal heartland to the Chiltern Hills and Berkshire, was named after them.

Roman conquest and resistance

The Roman invasion of Britain began hesitantly, with small cross-Channel incursions led by **Julius Caesar** in 55 and 54 BC. Almost a century later, in **August 43 AD**, the Romans warmed to the task, landing a substantial force in Kent, from where they fanned out, soon establishing a base along the estuary of the Thames. Joined by a menagerie of elephants and camels, the Romans soon reached Camulodunum (Colchester) and within four years were dug in on the frontier of south Wales. Inter-tribal rivalries among the Britons dampened resistance, but the Romans did come a military cropper when they tangled with the Iceni under their queen **Boudicca** – or Boadicea – in 60 AD (see box opposite).

55 BC	43 AD	60 AD	630
Chickens reach Norfolk – and cross the road with Julius Caesar.	The Romans invade Britain and overrun East Anglia.	Boudicca and her Iceni ravage Essex.	Mass baptisms after Sigebert, the Anglo-Saxon king of East Anglia, opts for Christianity.

BOUDICCA

Among the many tribes of Iron Age Britain, the **Iceni** were one of the more powerful. By the first century BC, they had settled most of Norfolk and Suffolk, with their tribal heartland located just outside what is now Bury St Edmunds in and around Ixworth, Icklingham and West Stow (see p.314). In 43 AD, **Prasutagus**, the chief of the Iceni, allied himself to the Romans during their conquest of Britain. Initially, this suited the Iceni very well, but just five years later, when the Iceni were no longer useful, the Romans attempted to disarm them and, although the tribe rebelled, they were soon brought to heel. Rubbing salt into the wound, the Romans confiscated the property of Prasutagus upon his death and when his wife, **Boudicca** – aka Boadicea – protested, they flogged her and raped her daughters. Enraged, Boudicca determined to take her revenge, quickly rallying the Iceni and their allies before setting off on a rampage across southern Britain in 60 AD.

As the ultimate symbol of Roman oppression, the Temple of Claudius in Colchester was the initial focus of hatred, but, once Colchester had been razed, Boudicca turned her sights elsewhere. She laid waste to London and St Albans, massacring over seventy thousand citizens and inflicting crushing defeats on the Roman units stationed there. She was far from squeamish, ripping traitors' arms out of their sockets and torturing every Roman and Roman collaborator in sight. The Roman governor Suetonius Paulinus eventually defeated her in a pitched battle, which cost the Romans just four hundred lives and the Britons untold thousands. Boudicca knew what to expect from the Romans, so she opted for suicide, thereby ensuring her later reputation as a patriotic Englishwoman, who died fighting for liberty and freedom – claims that Boudicca would have found incomprehensible.

The Romans ruled England for over three centuries. For the first time, the country began to emerge as a clearly identifiable entity with a defined political structure and, in general terms at least, peace brought prosperity. Commerce flourished, cities prospered and Latin became the language of the Romano-British ruling elite, though local traditions were allowed to coexist alongside imported customs. The benefits of the Roman occupation were, however, largely lost on the Iceni, whose lands were traduced when their rebellion was crushed. It took decades for the region to recover and East Anglia long remained peripheral to the Roman interest, though the legions did keep a beady eye on the Iceni, running two military roads into their heartland from the garrison town of Camulodunum: one followed the route of today's **Peddars Way** (see p.210); the other, the Pye Road, went to **Venta Icenorum**, an administrative centre whose scant remains lie just outside Norwich in the village of Caistor St Edmund.

The Anglo-Saxon onslaught

By the middle of the third century AD, the **Roman Empire** was in trouble with frequent collapses of central authority, its military commanders ever more inclined to act independently. And there was the problem of the **Germanic Saxons**, who had begun to raid England's eastern shore. In response, the Romans built a series of coastal defences, known as the **Saxon Shore**, stretching along the coast from Norfolk to the Isle of Wight and including forts at Brancaster and Burgh Castle. These strongholds, holding mixed garrisons of soldiers, sailors and cavalry, frustrated the Saxons for sixty years or more, but by the end of the fourth century England had become irrevocably detached from what remained of the Roman Empire and, by then, the **Saxons** – and the **Angles**, also

840	869	1066	1072
Danish Vikings invade East Anglia; fear and panic spread.	Edmund, the last Saxon king of East Anglia, comes to a sticky end.	King Harold, the last Saxon king of England, comes to an even stickier end.	Rebellion in Ely: Hereward the Wake resists the Normans, but is defeated.

from northern Germany – had begun settling England themselves. By the end of the sixth century, the Angles and the Saxons had all but eliminated Romano-British culture and England was divided into the **kingdoms** of Northumbria, Mercia, East Anglia, Kent and Wessex. So complete was the Anglo-Saxon domination of England, through conquest and intermarriage, that some ninety percent of English place names today have an Anglo-Saxon derivation.

Anglo-Saxon East Anglia

Little is known for sure about the Anglo-Saxon kingdom of **East Anglia**, but it seems to have been created in about 520 AD by the Germanic Angles, who had dispossessed or absorbed the Iceni. One of its early kings was an obscure figure by the name of **Wuffa**, who established a dynasty – the Wuffingas – in the late sixth century. His grandson, **Raedwald**, who died in about 624, appears to have extended his authority well beyond the region and is generally regarded as being the chieftain commemorated by the principal ship burial at **Sutton Hoo** (see p.246). The treasures of Sutton Hoo proclaim the wealth and power of the warrior aristocracy who ruled East Anglia, hanging around their communal halls, drinking mead and listening to the lyre. Life for their subjects was, predictably enough, much harsher with most of them eking out a precarious living in small farming communities like the re-created Anglo-Saxon village in **West Stow** (see p.314). It was a barter economy – there was no money – and effectively an illiterate one too, until, that is, the Church introduced the elite to Latin. Raedwald flirted with Christianity, but it was **Sigebert**, his stepson, who turned East Anglia **Christian**, welcoming the services of Felix, a priest-evangelist, whom he installed as bishop in Dunwich.

For decades, the marshy fenlands of Lincolnshire and Cambridgeshire had protected East Anglia from the rival kingdom of Mercia to the west, but the most powerful of the Mercian kings, **Offa**, overcame this natural barrier and conquered the region in about 794.

The Danish onslaught

After the death of Offa in 796, Wessex gained the upper hand among the Anglo-Saxon kingdoms, and by 825 the kings of Wessex had conquered or taken allegiance from all the other English kingdoms, including East Anglia. Their triumph was, however, short-lived. Carried here by their longboats, the **Vikings** – in this case mostly Danes – had started to raid the east coast towards the end of the eighth century; these raids soon turned into a migration. By 870, the Danes had conquered Northumbria, Mercia and East Anglia, where, in 869, they murdered King Edmund at Hoxne (see p.310). Thereafter, the Danes set their sights on Wessex, whose new king was the exceptionally talented **Alfred the Great**. Despite the odds, Alfred successfully resisted the Danes and eventually a truce was signed, fixing the border between Wessex and Danish territory: Danish land, the **Danelaw**, lay to the north of a line drawn between London and Chester – and included East Anglia. Alfred died in 899 and his successor, **Edward the Elder**, capitalized on his efforts, establishing his supremacy over the Danelaw to become the de facto overlord of all England. The relative calm continued until the Vikings returned in force to milk the king of Wessex for all the money they could, though the ransom paid – the **Danegeld** – brought only temporary relief and, in 1016, the Danes took control of the whole of England.

1085	1096	1190	1256
The Normans compile the Domesday Book, which details who owns what, does what and lives where.	Work begins on Norwich Cathedral – stonemasons hit the good times.	King Richard complains that in England it is "cold and always raining," and joins the Third Crusade.	The calendar is getting out of sync, so a decree installs a leap year – one leap day every four years.

Danish rule and Norman conquest

The first Danish king of England was **Canute**, a shrewd and gifted ruler, who took a gamble – or paid off some military indebtedness – when he appointed Thorkell the Tall to be the Jarl of East Anglia in 1017. It didn't work. Thorkell's relationship with Canute broke down irretrievably when the jarl stayed loyal to his wife even after she was found guilty of poisoning Thorkell's son by his first marriage with the help of a witch – heady stuff even by Viking standards. Neither did Canute's carefully constructed Anglo-Scandinavian empire last much beyond the king's death, soon brought to ruin by his two disreputable sons. Thereafter, the Saxons regained the initiative, putting **Edward the Confessor** on the English throne in 1042. On Edward's death, **Harold**, the Earl of Wessex, became king, but it was a disputed succession, the end result being the invasion of William, Duke of Normandy, who famously routed the Saxons – and killed Harold – at the **Battle of Hastings** in 1066.

Norman East Anglia

William I imposed a Norman aristocracy on his new subjects, rewarding his leading retainers with vast estates – within a decade ten of William's relatives owned thirty per cent of English land. In Norfolk, the Bigod and Warenne families led the territorial charge, and the Bigods were large landowners in Suffolk too. Other beneficiaries included Richard Fitzgilbert, who ended up with 95 lordships in Suffolk, where he made Clare his base, and Robert Malet, who accrued 221 Suffolk holdings with his headquarters in Eye. What was left of the Anglo-Saxon aristocracy must have viewed all this with a mix of horror and trepidation, but William crushed any acts of resistance – like Hereward the Wake's rebellion in Ely (see p.183) – with great brutality. William and his Norman successors also overawed their new subjects with a series of strongholds – the **castles** at Norwich, Eye, Castle Rising and Castle Acre are prime examples – and encouraged the establishment of **monasteries** like those at North Creake, Binham and Little Walsingham.

There were, however, exceptions to the usual pattern of dispossession and castellation, principally in Bury St Edmunds, where the Normans did not erect a castle and also permitted Abbot Baldwin, who had been a physician to Edward the Confessor, to stay in post. Perhaps the single most effective controlling measure, however, was the compilation of the **Domesday Book** between 1085 and 1086, which recorded who owned what and where. The Domesday Book paints a rosy picture of Norwich, one of the country's largest and most important towns with no less than 1320 burgesses, indicating a population of about 10,000 inhabitants.

Medieval tribulations

William I died in 1087, but his kingdom was soon wracked by **civil war** as rival sets of feudal barons slugged it out for control of the English throne. This bitter conflict lasted for several centuries during which, in 1214, a large group of disgruntled barons gathered in the abbey church of Bury St Edmunds to swear to bring King John to heel. The following year they famously forced John to accept the **Magna Carta**, a charter guaranteeing their rights and privileges, but, charter or not, the struggle between central and local power rumbled on for decades.

1349	1381	1549	1605
The Black Death reaches Norfolk and Suffolk; Hunstanton gets a dose first.	Peasants' Revolt convulses East Anglia.	More discontented peasants: Kett and his rebels occupy Norwich.	Gunpowder Plot: the Catholic Guy Fawkes plans to blow up the Houses of Parliament, but fails.

The whole balance of medieval society was, however, much more profoundly affected by the **Black Death**, which reached Norwich in 1349. It's impossible to know what percentage of the Norfolk and Suffolk population died from the Black Death, especially as its ravages varied from parish to parish, but it's likely that most towns and villages lost between twenty and fifty percent of their inhabitants. Further visitations of the plague followed shortly afterwards and the scarcity of labour that followed gave the peasantry more economic clout than they had ever had before. Predictably, the landowners attempted to restrict the concomitant rise in wages, thereby provoking the widespread rioting that culminated in the **Peasants' Revolt of 1381**, though the immediate spark was lit by the imposition of a swingeing poll tax. In Norfolk, the peasantry seized Norwich and proceeded to take bloody revenge on their oppressors. Their leader, a dyer by the name of Geoffrey Litster, even installed himself in the castle, making four gentlemen knights wait upon him while he banqueted. Unluckily for Litster, his feasting did not last long: in London, the Peasants' Revolt was crushed after the murder of its leader, Wat Tyler, and, with the forces of reaction rallying, Bishop Henry Despenser marched on Norwich and crushed the revolt forthwith; the **Despenser Reredos** in Norwich Cathedral (see p.42) celebrates his success.

The fifteenth to early seventeenth centuries

Throughout most of the fifteenth century, the kings of England were preoccupied with the Anglo-French **Hundred Years' War** (effectively till 1454) and the **Wars of the Roses**, a protracted civil war between two rival sets of barons – the Yorkists and the Lancastrians – which only ended with the death of Richard III at Bosworth Field in 1485. One result was the dislocation and transformation of the wool trade with Flanders (see box opposite); another was Richard III's replacement by **Henry VII**, the first of the **Tudors**, which was when England began to assume the status of a major European power. After Henry VII came **Henry VIII**, who is best remembered for his separation of the English Church from Rome and his establishment of an independent Protestant church – the **Church of England**. Famously, Henry's motives were all to do with his quest to divorce Catherine of Aragon for her failure to provide him with a son, rather than any doctrinal issues – Henry was never a Protestant himself – but his break with Rome in the **Reformation** shattered the traditional alliance of church and state that had dominated medieval England: pope and bishops, kings and dukes were supposedly the representatives of God on earth, and Henry's schism stood the country on its intellectual head. The whole of England was convulsed by religious debate, nowhere more so than in Norfolk and Suffolk where the seeds of **Protestantism** had already fallen on fertile ground among both the region's merchants, whose burgeoning wealth and independence had never been easy to accommodate within a rigid caste society, and their employees, the skilled cloth workers and their apprentices, who had a tradition of opposing arbitrary authority.

Enclosure and rebellion

In the late 1530s, one of the consequences of Henry's break with Rome was the **Dissolution of the Monasteries**, which gave both king and nobles the chance to get their hands on valuable monastic property. This was a windfall for the large landowners, many of whom had already started expanding their estates by summarily fencing in

1642	1645	1660	1734
The English Civil War begins; most of Norfolk and Suffolk supports Parliament against the king.	Cromwell creates the formidable New Model Army; East Anglians are its backbone.	The Restoration: Charles II takes the throne – and digs up the body of Oliver Cromwell to prove his point.	Work starts on Holkham Hall.

THE WOOL TOWNS OF NORFOLK AND SUFFOLK

Since the thirteenth century, the **wool trade**, which involved the export of raw wool from England to the weavers of Flanders, had become a mainstay of the English economy. In **East Anglia** as elsewhere, the main beneficiaries were the owners of the flocks, often the monasteries, and the wool merchants, few in number but extraordinarily rich. During the fifteenth century, however, protectionist tariffs, war and taxation combined to boost domestic cloth-making and the towns of **southern Suffolk** – Lavenham, Hadleigh and Kersey for instance – flourished. Helped by refugee Flemish weavers, Suffolk's cloth workers learnt how to produce top-quality, short-fibre woollens (rather than the traditional, long-fibre worsteds) in a complex cottage industry that involved at least six separate procedures: washing, sorting, scouring and soaking in oil; carding; spinning; weaving; fulling and bleaching; dyeing and finishing. It was a dynamic industry too, with each village developing its own speciality – Lavenham's was blue broadcloth – but one in which the workforce was soon in thrall to the wool and cloth merchants, a perennial source of bitterness and discontent. In the event, the success of the Suffolk cloth industry was short-lived as its products could not compete with the lighter, stronger "new draperies" developed elsewhere in England and, although the industry survived for another hundred years or so, its salad days were over by 1550. In **Norwich**, the textile industry lasted longer, partly as a result of a further influx of Flemish weaver refugees, who fled here from the Spanish Netherlands to avoid the tender mercies of the Inquisition in the 1560s.

common land to graze their flocks of sheep, acts of **enforced enclosure** which threatened the very livelihood of their poorer neighbours. Out of fear and anger, a great concourse of country folk gathered outside Norwich in 1549 under the general leadership of **Robert Kett**. Here they engaged in a sort of prototype sit-down strike, the "rebels" organizing themselves into a rudimentary mini-state, holding Protestant religious services and buying supplies before ultimately occupying Norwich itself. They were convinced that the obvious justice of their cause would persuade the government to punish the land grabbers, but they were wrong: instead, the government dispatched an army of mercenaries, who butchered the rebels; Kett was hung over the walls of Norwich castle, his death purposefully prolonged as an example to all.

The crushing of Kett's rebellion gave the green light for further acts of enclosure and East Anglia seethed with discontent, especially at the treatment of one of the region's most popular Protestant preachers and pamphleteers, **William Prynne** (1600–69). In punishment for his assorted diatribes against church and state, Prynne had already had his ears cropped, but that did not deter him at all and in 1636 his *Newes from Ipswich* had him up in court again: at something of a loss as to how to punish him, the judge ordered the remaining stumps of his ears be chopped off – and the crowds cheered and threw flowers in front of Prynne as he approached the place of punishment.

The English Civil War

Elizabeth I steered a skilful course between the religious factions that might have stretched her authority, but her successors – **James I and Charles I** – were much less prudent, clinging to an absolutist vision of the monarchy – the divine right of kings – that was totally out of step with the Protestant leanings of the majority of their subjects. It was a recipe for disaster, and sure enough disaster came with the outbreak of the **English Civil**

1754	1846	1862	1902
Charles Wesley tours Norfolk; Methodism takes root.	Opening of Ipswich train station. General delirium.	Royal family buys Sandringham; locals delighted (mostly).	First football game between Ipswich and Norwich – beginning of the "Old Farm derby".

War between Parliament and king in 1642. The Royalist forces ("Cavaliers") were initially successful, but afterwards key regiments of the Parliamentarian army ("Roundheads") were completely overhauled by **Oliver Cromwell** (1599–1658). The kernel of the **New Model Army** that Cromwell created came from the small freeholders and skilled craftsmen of Norfolk and Suffolk – butchers, weavers, dyers, shoemakers and men like Philip Skippon, a minor gentleman from West Lexham in Norfolk, who became a major general. Well drilled and well trained, the New Model cut its teeth at the Battle of Naseby and thereafter simply brushed the Royalists aside, the end result – after endless royal shenanigans – being the **king's execution** in January 1649.

For the next eleven years, England was a **Commonwealth** – at first a true republic, then, after 1653, a **Protectorate** with Cromwell as the Lord Protector and commander in chief. The turmoil of the Civil War and the pre-eminence of the army unleashed a furious legal, theological and political debate in every corner of the country, but especially in Norfolk and Suffolk. This milieu spawned a host of proto-communist sects, the most notable of whom were the **Levellers**, who demanded wholesale constitutional reform, as well as a battery of **Nonconformist** religious groups, including the **Quakers**, who established a dissenting tradition that long remained a feature of Norfolk and, to a lesser extent, Suffolk life. There was a less palatable side to all this religious fervour too, most notably the New Model's savage treatment of Irish Catholics and, in East Anglia, the multiple denunciations of witchcraft which fed the "trials" of the so-called **Witchfinder General**, Suffolk's own Matthew Hopkins (c.1620–1647), who managed to kill around three hundred "witches" in just a couple of years.

Cromwell died in 1658 and two years later the monarchy was restored in the shape of **Charles II**, the exiled son of the previous king: the dissenting Protestants of Norfolk and Suffolk knew what was coming next – the return of the old regime, and lots more enforced enclosures.

The eighteenth century

With the decline of the cloth trade (see p.325) Norfolk and Suffolk had become much more reliant on **agriculture**, and by the 1750s East Anglia was providing London with much of its wheat and meat. A buoyant agricultural sector encouraged the region's larger landowners to enclose yet more tracts of common land and, between 1792 and 1815, no fewer than one million acres were lost to East Anglia's landless labourers, tenants and lease holders, who were no longer allowed to graze their animals, collect firewood or do pretty much anything else on land they had used (but not legally owned) for centuries. It was, as E.P. Thompson declared in his seminal *The Making of the English Working Class*, "a plain enough case of class robbery".

With their newly enlarged estates, the big landowners of Georgian East Anglia could get down to some serious money-making, and in this they were helped by two of their number who pioneered ways of improving the fertility of the land. First up was Raynham's second **Viscount Townshend** (1674–1738) – aka "Turnip Townshend"– who spent the last years of his life experimenting with all things agricultural, one of his most important innovations being a four-year rotation of crops – wheat, turnips, barley and clover – which helped stop soil exhaustion and increased yields. The second great pioneering figure was Holkham's **Coke of Norfolk** (1754–1842), who, among much else,

1915	1920s	1942	1946	1950
German Zeppelins bomb Norfolk: little damage; light casualties; great fear.	Mass unemployment; work schemes create a string of urban parks in Norwich and Ipswich.	German air force bombs Norwich in the so-called Baedeker raids.	Bernard Matthews leaves school; turkeys frightened.	Soap rationing ends in Britain – a general clean-up follows.

imported new machinery, experimented with pig breeding and improved the quality of the sandy soils of his estate with marl (a crumbly mixture of clays, calcium and magnesium carbonates). Inevitably, not all the region's landowners were so "agricultural", most notably **Robert Walpole** (1676–1745), generally regarded as England's **first prime minister**, who built himself a real show-off pile, Houghton Hall, and stuffed it with paintings and assorted treasures – not much interest in turnips there, then.

The nineteenth century

Powerful aristocrats like Coke, Townshend and Walpole gave eighteenth-century East Anglia a lot of clout, but the situation was transformed by the **Industrial Revolution**, which gathered pace after the defeat of Napoleon at the Battle of Waterloo in 1815. In the space of a few decades, England turned from an agricultural to a manufacturing economy and the cities of the Midlands and the North mushroomed, while East Anglia was effectively marooned, becoming little more than a rural backwater. There were, of course, exceptions – Cromer became a fashionable resort, Ipswich built a huge new dock, and much of the region was linked to the railway network in the 1840s and 1850s – but these developments went against the general tide.

Even worse, the prolonged agricultural **depression** that hit England in the mid-1870s stretched the finances of large and small landowners alike, its effects deepened by the availability – and importation – of cheap grain from North America. Neither did the introduction of **death duties** in 1894 do the big estates any favours, and as a result many landowners sold up and several hundred country houses were simply demolished. The situation of the agricultural labourers as a whole was even worse, though there was something of a fightback with the establishment of the **National Agricultural Labourers' Union** in 1872. At its high point, the union had over 86,000 members, over one-tenth of the farm workforce in England, and in 1885, their leader, a farm labourer by the name of **Joseph Arch**, became the MP for Northwest Norfolk, which was to remain a union stronghold for several decades.

The twentieth century

As was the case in most of Europe, the outbreak of **World War I** was greeted by cheering crowds in both Norfolk and Suffolk, but the reality was grim: both counties lost thousands of men in the war, the effects compounded by many joining up as groups of "pals" – the "Sandringham Company", which recruited from the King's estate at Sandringham, was, for example, badly mauled at Gallipoli. More unusually, a squadron of German ships bombarded Lowestoft and Great Yarmouth to limited effect in 1916 and there were periodic Zeppelin bombing raids on the likes of Norwich, Harwich and Ipswich.

There were more hard times in the **depression** of the 1930s – though Norfolk and Suffolk were not as badly affected as the country's more industrialized regions – and precious little cheering in the early days of **World War II**, especially as many believed that the Germans would invade England via Norfolk or Suffolk. Indeed, there were frantic efforts to protect the coastline: hundreds of mines were laid offshore; the shoreline was festooned with barbed wire and anti-tank traps; dozens of concrete pillboxes were constructed just inland; and Shingle Street (see p.248) was forcibly

1953	1959	1970s	1990
Freak weather conditions bring flooding to the Norfolk coast; many die in what amounts to a major disaster.	BBC *Look East* begins; regional news boosted?	Great Yarmouth booms on the back of North Sea oil.	In Norfolk, Mrs Thatcher praises "the common sense of the housewife with her food"; turkeys still frightened (see 1946).

THE STRANGE CAREER OF FRED COPEMAN

Rural Norfolk and Suffolk may be true-blue Tory today, but Fred Copeman (1907–1983) bucked the trend. Born in Wangford, near Southwold, Copeman joined the Royal Navy at the tender age of 12. Harsh naval training did not, however, break his spirit; when the government cut sailors' pay in 1931, he organized the Invergordon Mutiny of the Atlantic Fleet. For his mutinous pains, Copeman was ejected from the Navy after which he became a trade union organizer and Communist Party member. In 1936 he left England to join the International Brigades fighting Franco in Spain. Described by one of his comrades as a "great bull of a man… completely without physical fear", Copeman was badly wounded and shipped back to England, where his urgent radicalism gradually faded away: he ended his days as a Labour Party councillor in south London.

evacuated. In the event, the Germans never arrived, but the **American air force** did, occupying around 700 hastily constructed air-strips from where they could fly off to bomb the continent. In 1943, the airmen were joined by thousands of American soldiers in the lead-up to D-Day and the effect of this amicable invasion on the East Anglian population was quite striking – in particular the Americans went down well with many local women, who found them a breath of fresh air.

The 1970s and 1980s

In many ways the **1970s and the 1980s** have proved to be the decisive decades for Norfolk and Suffolk: the ports of the east coast, particularly Felixstowe, boomed as trade moved from England's west coast to the east; small electronics companies moved into East Anglia by the dozen; commuters could speed their way to the capital with the electrification of the London–Norwich rail line in 1987; Norwich's University of East Anglia began to establish an academic name for itself; and, partly as a result of EU subsidies, big farmers made big profits with fewer men – the agricultural workforce was reduced to a fraction of what it had once been. The aristocracy got in on the act too when they realized they no longer had to bulldoze their country houses as uneconomic, but could turn them into tourist attractions instead – and the Queen duly obliged by opening Sandringham up to the general public in 1977.

Norfolk and Suffolk today

Amid all the good news in the 1970s and 1980s, there were two major problems: **property** prices spiked with the incoming tide of commuters and second-home owners, so local families had to move away. Many villages were left strangely deserted, looking normal enough but with no actual community – "pastiche suburbia", in the words of one commentator. This remains a problem today, though a scattering of charitable housing trusts does provide affordable homes across the region. The other issue was **agriculture**. By the mid-1990s hundreds of hedgerows had been uprooted, acres of marshland drained and scores of ditches and ponds filled; pesticides and nitrates had affected water quality, and fields had been consolidated as never before, creating the so-called "prairie farming" that scars some of the region. Here the news is better, as concerted efforts by conservationists are slowly turning back the agricultural clock; the most obvious sign to visitors is the many restaurants serving local, seasonal produce. Now that is indeed good news.

1994	1996	2007	2010	2015
Channel Tunnel opens to traffic – continent no longer isolated.	Delia Smith and husband become majority shareholders in Norwich City Football Club.	Smoking banned in enclosed public places in England and Wales.	Bernard Matthews dies.	General Election: Norwich South (Labour) and Norfolk North (Lib Dem) marooned in a sea of Tory blue.

Wildlife

With barely a ridge in sight, never mind a mountain Norfolk and Suffolk
are low-lying, but this does not mean they are uniform – far from it. The
two counties hold a mix of habitats, from farmland and forest through to
salt marshes, mudflats, sand dunes, sandy beaches, pebble beaches and
the occasional sea cliff – think Cromer and Hunstanton. These varied
habitats support a varied wildlife, though it's for its birds that the region
wins most praise.

Mammals

As in most of rural England, **mammals** such as foxes, hedgehogs, badgers, stoats and
weasels are relatively common. The region's rivers support a wide range of mammals
too, including otters and water voles, though these are threatened by an alien species,
the mink. Similarly, grey squirrels, originally from North America, have pretty much
wiped out the native **red squirrel**, though Pensthorpe Nature Reserve (see p.145) near
Fakenham is doing its best to protect and conserve some of the reds. There is a
significant **bat** population in East Anglia, with the pipistrelle and brown long-eared the
most common, and a 200-strong breeding colony of **Daubenton's bat** in the Broads.
The region also has more than half the UK population of the very rare **barbastelle bat**.

Common seals

The Wash and its neighbouring coastline has the largest population of **common seals** in
Europe. They are distinguished from the more populous **grey seal** by the V-shaped
slant to their nostrils. Lumpen and ungainly on land, their grey or brown dappled fur
clearly visible, these large mammals look sleek and streamlined once in the water. They
can remain underwater for up to ten minutes at a time, are able to dive to a depth of
160ft, and can swim 30 miles just to feed. They frequently stay out at sea for several
days, only heading for land to rest, give birth, suckle their young and moult. The males
play no part in rearing pups, opting instead to fight with other males to guarantee their
opportunity to mate again. Females give birth to a single pup in the summer, their rich
milk allowing the pup to double in weight in three to four weeks. Females live for
around thirty years, males usually peg out ten years earlier.

Harbour porpoises

At around 6ft long, **harbour porpoises** are one of the smallest ocean mammals.
Grey-backed, but paler underneath, they are round-headed and they make regular
appearances along the Norfolk coast, particularly between January and April. Much
smaller than their dolphin relatives, they are hard to spot, especially as they are also shy
and rarely break the surface for long, and your best chance of a good sighting is in
shallow waters.

Reptiles

The pride of East Anglia's reptilian crew is the endangered **natterjack toad**, which is
found in the coastal dunes and salt marshes of Norfolk, especially Holme Dunes
National Nature Reserve. With yellow- or red-coloured warts covering its brown or
green skin, it's most easily distinguished by the yellow stripe down its back. It's not a
great swimmer and walks rather than hops. The male's rasping mating call can be heard

THE TOP SIX BIRDWATCHING SITES

NWT Cley Marshes (see p.137). The best known of the NWT's reserves and one of the oldest reserves in the country, where the saline lagoons, grazing marsh and reedbeds attract wintering and migrating waterbirds. Spring and autumn are best to see these visitors arriving and departing but there's good birding all year round.

NWT Hickling Broad Nature Reserve (see p.88). Overlooking the Broads' largest area of open water, the reedbeds, water meadows and woodland of this excellent reserve provide a rich habitat for bittern, bearded tit, water rail, marsh- and hen-harriers and cranes. Boat trips – which take you to hides only accessible by boat – are available from April to September.

RSPB Minsmere (see p.266). Up to thirty percent of the UK's breeding population of bittern are to be found at Minsmere, where they are most easily spotted in winter. The reserve is also of particular importance for its populations of marsh harrier, pied avocet, bearded tit and reed bunting.

RSPB Snettisham (see p.163). In the winter, the inter-tidal mudbanks and salt marshes of the Wash receive the UK's largest influx of visiting waterbirds, over 300,000 waders and wildfowl – waders arriving ahead of the wildfowl (ducks and geese). The RSPB reserve at Snettisham provides a perfect place to spot them in number and, as the tide rises and their feeding grounds recede, you can expect amazing flight displays.

RSPB Strumpshaw Fen (see p.115). To catch a glimpse of a kingfisher or bearded tit or hear the song of sedge and reed warblers, head for this RSPB reserve, part of its Fen Restoration Project, which removes scrub to encourage bitterns and other fenland wildlife. Best in spring and autumn.

RSPB Titchwell Marsh (see p.159). Spring is perhaps the best time to visit Titchwell with migrating waders arriving by the hundred in April and May, and marsh harriers performing their dancing displays, but there's good birding all year given the range of habitats.

for miles between April and June, in the evenings and after rain. The region's coastal heaths also hold a small population of **adders**, a mildly venomous snake with a brown skin and a lozenge pattern down its back. They slither off if they sense people coming, but can sometimes be spotted basking on warm rocks in sunny weather.

Birds

No argument, Norfolk and Suffolk provide the best birding in the UK. The region's long and varied coastline, its inland waterways, estuary, fen, heathland, grazing marshes, woodland, fields and hedgerows all combine to offer an outstanding variety of habitats for a wonderful range of birds, both resident and migratory. There are three main agencies concerned with the preservation of these habitats, the **Norfolk Wildlife Trust** (NWT; ⓦnorfolkwildlifetrust.org.uk), which has around thirty reserves; the **Suffolk Wildlife Trust** (SWT; ⓦsuffolkwildlifetrust.org), with over fifty reserves; and the **Royal Society for the Protection of Birds** (RSPB; ⓦrspb.org.uk) with sixteen reserves across both counties. In addition, the **National Trust** (ⓦnationaltrust.org.uk) protects and conserves certain key locations – for example, Blakeney Point – as does **Natural England** (ⓦnaturalengland.org.uk), which has, for instance, overall responsibility for Scolt Island. Finally, the **Broads** have been designated a (sort of) National Park (ⓦbroads-authority.gov.uk) with all the wildlife protections that that involves.

GLOSSARY OF SELECTED BIRDS

ALL-YEAR RESIDENTS

Avocet A distinctively patterned, black-and-white wader, long-legged with a long upturned bill. Likes shallow, slightly saline water and mud. Found among the coastal lagoons of the east coast during the summer. Emblem of the RSPB.

Barn owl Instantly recognizable large white owl, which is generally seen hunting across open country. Can appear in car headlights as a ghostly apparition. Best seen at dusk but sometimes also seen during the day floating across farmland. Very common across rural Norfolk and Suffolk.

Bearded tit Tawny-brown tit with a grey head, black moustache and bright yellow eye. A beautiful bird found entirely in reedbeds and localized to the east and south coasts of England. While commonly known as a tit, it is in fact more closely related to the parrotbill family. To add further confusion, it is also sometimes referred to as a bearded reedling. Patience and calm weather are needed to spot this bird as it can be hard to locate in the reeds, but it is a sociable and noisy creature that is easily identified by a loud pinging call.

Bittern A secretive and rare member of the heron family with a stripey, mottled-brown plumage. The bittern relies on the shelter and deep water of the reeds to hunt for fish. Hard to spot, it's often most easily sighted in winter, when it leaves the reeds to find areas of water that have not frozen over. The bittern is one of the most threatened species in the UK. Listen for the booming calls in spring as they enter the breeding season. Restricted to a habitat of wet reedbeds.

Black-tailed godwit Large, handsome wader characterized by exceptionally long legs. Usually stands tall and upright. The summer plumage is very bold and colourful with a coppery-red head and breast; the winter plumage is grey and dull. From autumn to late winter it can be found in flocks in small, sheltered, muddy estuaries.

Common crane Very large, long-legged and long-necked bird with a 6ft wingspan. Has a grey body with thick black legs. Found in reedbeds, lakes and marshy areas. Large groups will gather in spring for graceful dancing courtship displays. Most readily seen in the Norfolk Broads, where there is a small resident population.

Common crossbill Member of the finch family, looks quite chunky and parrot-like with a distinctive hooked bill, dark wings with bright pink/red rich rump. It uses its bill to prise seeds, insects, buds and berries from cones and twigs. Found in spruce, larch and pine trees. Needs easy access to pools so it can drink frequently.

Dunlin Common small wader with a dull grey-brown head and back with long, tapered, very slightly curved black bill and short black legs. When in a large flock, it's often seen dashing and sweeping out at sea and back to shore again in spectacular manoeuvres.

Goldeneye Very shy but strikingly beautiful black-and-white duck. It has black markings on a dazzling white body and a black head with a large distinctive white spot between a yellow eye and a short black beak. Widespread in winter on lakes and estuaries.

Knot Larger and stockier than the dunlin, the knot is a sociable wader with winter plumage of a pale grey back and shortish bill. Summer plumage is a reddish-brown coppery head, back and underparts. Often found in huge numbers mingling with dunlins to form dense packs when roosting at high tide and dramatically swarming over mudflats to feed.

Lapwing Comical-looking, pigeon-sized wader with a black cap and wispy crest. Plumage is dark green and purple and it has a white chest. The wings are broad and rounded and distinctly flappy in flight. Also known as the peewit due to its distinctive call. Found predominantly around farmland and in open countryside.

Little egret Stunning small white heron with long black legs. Generally solitary bird of marshy, flooded grassy areas. Spends much of its time standing still or wading in shallow water hunting for prey.

Oystercatcher Medium-sized wader with striking black-and-white body with a vivid orange bill. Often gathers in large and noisy flocks. Found on sandy, muddy and rocky beaches.

Redshank A medium-sized, very abundant, grey-looking wader. It has long red legs and a long straight bill. Tends to congregate away from other waders and can be distinctly noisy. Probes and picks at mud searching for insects, worms and molluscs. Found on estuaries, salt marshes and freshwater pools.

Ringed plover Small wader with a brown back, white chest, black-and-white ring around neck and orange bill with a black tip. Fairly common and generally found in coastal areas, particularly shingle and gravel beaches.

Ruff Medium-sized wader appearing in mid-autumn on wetland areas. Has a very plain brown/grey winter plumage, but in the spring the male transforms and has a stunning broad feathery ruff of varying colours. Can appear quite sedate compared with other waders. Males often display in groups to females with mock battles.

Snow bunting Beautiful little bunting with a snowy plumage. Bright white chest and grey/brown back. Most commonly seen in the winter on coastal sites on seashore shingle.

Stonechat Has a black head, rust-red chest and white patch on the side of the neck. Likes open places with gorse, heather and bushes around coastal areas and dunes. Will often be found perching on top of bushes and has a very distinct call which sounds like two stones being bashed together.

Teal The smallest of the ducks. The male has stunning plumage with a bright green patch on hind wings and a black-yellow triangle under the tail, while the female is pretty drab-looking with no distinct features. The teal is a surface-feeding duck and can be regularly found among the reeds or well-vegetated shore.

Turnstone Similar in size and shape to a dunlin but with a short, tapered bill and beautiful black, white and chestnut-coloured upperparts and a vivid white underside with bright orange legs. Uses bill to turn over stones and pebbles.

Woodlark A small pretty lark, which has a long white stripe over the eye to the back of the neck. Found in open woodland areas and sandy heaths.

MIGRATORY BIRDS

Brent goose More duck-sized than goose, with a black head and black chest with a brown underside and a white patch on the neck. Has a distinctive but pleasant growling call. Often behaves more like a duck by upending on the water to feed. Found on salt marshes and estuaries from late autumn through to early spring. Winter resident.

Golden oriole A striking bird with vivid yellow and black plumage and a bright pink-red bill. Can be secretive and will often hide in dense foliage preferring oak, poplar and chestnut trees. Only seen in the UK from April to Sept.

Little tern Smaller and whiter than the common tern with a sharp yellow bill, white forehead, black cap and pale grey body. A small, quick, agile coastal bird often roosting in noisy colonies – breeding on sand and shingle beaches. Seen in the UK April to Oct.

Marsh harrier Distinguishable from other harriers by its large size. Holds wings in an obvious V while gliding over reedbeds and marshes performing breathtaking courtship displays in spring. A small population is resident all year round, but most are summer visitors.

Nightingale A plain brown rather dull-looking bird with a truly remarkable song. Slightly larger than a robin. A very secretive bird, which sings from deep within bushes. Summer visitor.

Pink-footed goose Pinkish-grey body, small bill with pink band, and pink feet and legs. Breeds in Scandinavia but large numbers spend the winter here in East Anglia, where it feeds in fields, farmland and river estuaries. Winter resident.

Pintail Elegant, dabbling duck with a long black tail, yellow-brown body with a brown head and distinctive white stripe on the neck and breast. Can be found on both salt and fresh water but generally quite rare. Found in the UK from Sept to April.

Sand martin The smallest of the swallow and swift family with a stockier body, all brown upperparts with white underparts. Lacking the longer tail feathers of the swallow and swift, it appears weaker in flight. It bores holes into earth cliffs, sandy riverbanks or soft sandstone to breed in large colonies from April till July. Summer visitor.

Scarlet rosefinch A brown finch with cherry-red head, chest and rump with a brown back. Sporadic breeding in deciduous woodland often near wetland areas. May to Oct.

Spoonbill Unmistakeable large, heron-like white wader with large spatula-shaped black bill, which turns black with age. Wades through water, sweeping its bill side to side hunting for prey. Found on marshes and lakes. Seen in the UK April to Sept.

Spotted flycatcher Plumage is very plain and grey with a streaked forehead. A sharp-eyed and alert little bird that inhabits edges of clearings, where it will sit on a perch and fly out to catch insects mid-air. Summer visitor.

Stone curlew Very distinctive-looking bird with long yellow legs, dark streaky body – which is perfect for camouflage – and round yellow eyes which are well adapted for nocturnal foraging for insects and worms. A bird of the open countryside it visits the UK between April and Sept.

Wryneck Member of the woodpecker family. At a distance may appear fairly brown and dull, but closer inspection will reveal a complex and intricate set of colours and markings. Often appears camouflaged against the bark of the tree. Seen April to Oct.

Books

Dozens of writers of all descriptions have lived or worked in Norfolk and Suffolk – the list below just skims the surface. For specialist, regional publications, Halsgrove (⊚halsgrove.com) are excellent – we've mentioned one of their Norfolk and Suffolk titles below (Burnham Society History Group), but they publish dozens of books about East Anglia and most are competitively priced. Both counties also have websites cataloguing which writers did what, where and when – check out ⊚literarynorfolk.co.uk and ⊚literarysuffolk.paperviewer.co.uk.

TRAVEL AND GENERAL

William Cobbett *Rural Rides.* Adventurer, journalist, soldier, traveller and radical, Cobbett (1763–1835) bemoans the death of rural England and rails against the treatment of the poor as he rides across the shires of England, dropping by Norfolk and Suffolk to see how the locals are getting on.

Roald Dahl *The Mildenhall Treasure.* In 1942, a ploughman by the name of Gordon Butcher unearthed a valuable hoard of Roman silverware, "The Mildenhall Treasure". By all accounts, he seems to have been conned out of his just rewards by the man he worked for and Dahl tells the tale – mostly fact, but some conjecture.

Daniel Defoe *Tour Through the Whole Island of Great Britain.* When he wasn't thinking about desert islands, Daniel Defoe (1659–1731) had other things to do, including this gambol round much of England – including parts of East Anglia – observing the current state of play, both spiritual and economic, in what turned out to be the last years before the Industrial Revolution hit its stride.

David Gentleman *In The Country.* Immaculately illustrated, coffee-table extravaganza from David Gentleman, the well-known watercolourist, lithographer and wood engraver. Sticks to sights and scenes within a half-hour drive of his Suffolk home.

Henry Rider Haggard *A Farmer's Year: Being His Commonplace Book for 1898.* Haggard (1856–1925) may once have been famous for his swashbuckling tales of imperial derring-do, but he was also a Norfolk squire (who preferred writing novels to toiling the land) and these are his assorted reminiscences.

Arthur Mee *Norfolk: The Classic Guide.* Recent reprint of an old guidebook to Norfolk, part of the popular "King's England" series, much of which is as relevant today as it was when originally published in 1940 – which says a lot. Much of the book is an alphabetical list of towns and villages, which serves as both a useful reference and enjoyable period piece.

★**Mike Page & Pauline Young** *Norfolk from the Air; Suffolk from the Air; The Norfolk Coast from the Air; The Suffolk Coast from the Air; A Broads' Eye View.* You will come across this fabulous series in gift and book shops all over Norfolk and Suffolk – and they're almost irresistible if you have any interest in the area at all. Page has been taking to the air to photograph his home region for many years now and – together with Young's text – the books make for an arresting representation of both counties.

J.B. Priestley *English Journey.* The Bradford-born playwright, broadcaster and author's record of his extensive travels around England in the 1930s, including time in East Anglia, may say nothing about contemporary England, but in many ways its quirkiness, and eye for English eccentricity, formed the blueprint for the later Brysons and Therouxs. The East Anglian is, said Priestley, "a solid man. Lots of beef and beer, tempered with the east wind, have gone into the making of him". Enough said.

Peter Sager *East Anglia: Norfolk, Suffolk and Essex.* Sager doesn't half know his East Anglian onions and it shows in this deeply reflective, studied travel guide/travelogue, which draws on many sources. At risk of sounding churlish, however, he does seem a little too pleased with himself when he is speaking to milords and miladies. A Pallas guide last published in 2003.

W.G. Sebald *Rings of Saturn.* Intriguing, ruminative book that is a heady mix of novel, travel and memoir, focusing ostensibly on the author's walking tour of Suffolk – and including several plum historical accounts of those who have lived there, including Joseph Conrad. A UEA academic and highly regarded writer, Sebald was born in Bavaria in 1944 and died in a car crash near Norwich in 2001.

Roger Wardale *Arthur Ransome on the Broads.* Attractively illustrated book that documents Ransome's time on the Broads and the development of his Norfolk stories (see p.335).

Henry Williamson *The Story of a Norfolk Farm.* Published in 1927, *Tarka the Otter* made its author, Henry Williamson

(1895–1977), a household name, which made his liking for Hitler all the more conspicuous to his new neighbours when he bought a farm at Stiffkey in 1936. Williamson only stayed in Norfolk for two years, but he did have time to record his experiences there in what amounts to a rural lament.

HISTORY, SOCIETY AND POLITICS

★**Ronald Blythe** Akenfield: Portrait of an English Village. First published in 1969, this much acclaimed book, a surprising bestseller, is a thoroughly researched investigation into the comings and goings, habits and economics of a Suffolk village on the cusp of change. There's no village of "Akenfield" per se, but the odds are it was based on the author's researches in the hamlets of Akenham, near Ipswich, and Charsfield, near Wickham Market. Peter Hall amplified the book's success by making the film Akenfield five years later. Also worth reading is Blythe's Time By the Sea, describing the author's life in Aldeburgh in the 1950s.

Burnham Society History Group The Book of the Burnhams: The Story of the Seven Burnhams by the Sea. Long before metropolitan tourists started arriving by the Porsche-load, the Burnhams had a long and unusual history – and this book gives the low-down. Lavishly illustrated with more than three hundred photographs. A title in the Halsgrove Community History Series.

Helen Castor Blood & Roses: The Paston Family & the Wars of the Roses. Norman Davis's book (see below) may have published the Paston letters, but Castor gets stuck into their interpretation.

Norman Davis The Paston Letters. Before the family died out in the early eighteenth century, the Pastons were major Norfolk landowners and, unusually, a great treasure-trove of their late medieval letters have survived – and this book prints a selection from 1430 to 1485, when England was wracked by the Wars of the Roses.

Nigel Heard Wool: East Anglia's Golden Fleece. The only readily available book on this subject, though it was published in the 1970s. Thoroughly researched.

David Hoare Standing Up to Hitler: The Story of Norfolk's Home Guard and Secret Army, 1940–44. Enjoyable account of Norfolk's Home Guard plus the so-called "secret army", which was trained to delay and sabotage the German army if, as was feared, it landed on the east coast.

Frank Meeres The Story of Norwich. Filling a historical gap, this well-researched and detailed (256-page) book gives the low-down on Norwich's history from earliest times until the 1990s.

Charlotte Paton The King of the Norfolk Poachers: His Life and Times. East Anglia's Charlotte Paton became intrigued by the life of Fred Rolfe (see below) and her investigations – as revealed in this book – show the man in all his complexity.

Arthur Patterson Wild Fowlers and Poachers. Born in the Yarmouth Rows, the youngest of nine children, Patterson (1857–1935) was passionate about wildlife and spent much of his spare time teaching himself about the plants and animals of Breydon Water. At the age of 71, he wrote this memoir of his lifetime on Breydon – celebrating the punt-gunners, fishermen, wildfowlers, eelers, smelters and poachers that he had known.

Fred Rolfe I Walked by Night: Being the Philosophy of the King of the Norfolk Poachers, Written by Himself. When Fred Rolfe, an elderly mole-catcher, had his memories/memoirs published in the 1930s, they proved extremely popular – lost rural days perhaps, but intriguing all the same. He was greatly helped in his task by the daughter of Rider Haggard (see p.333), Lilias.

Diana Souhami Edith Cavell: Nurse, Martyr, Heroine. The execution of Norfolk's Edith Cavell in World War I did much to embitter Anglo-German relations as well as making Cavell a national hero. Her life, times and death have been trawled over several times, but this detailed book is the pick of the crop.

★**Craig Taylor** Return to Akenfield: Portrait of an English Village in the 21st Century. Well written and well researched, Taylor interviews all and sundry to get the flavour of the village today – powerful stuff and certainly not reassuring. Last edition published in 2007.

★**E.P. Thompson** The Making of the English Working Class. A seminal text – essential reading for anyone who wants to understand the fabric of English society – tracing the birth of the working class between 1780 and 1832, a key period in the history of Norfolk and Suffolk. Outstanding description of the agricultural enclosures.

ART AND ARCHITECTURE

Anthony Bailey John Constable: A Kingdom of his Own. An in-depth look at Constable's life, times and art; no stone is left unturned in what is arguably the best book on its subject.

Julia Blackburn Threads: The Delicate Life of John Craske. Much lauded book whose starting point is the life of the artist John Craske (1881–1943), who produced his eerie paintings and embroideries after some sort of nervous breakdown. Craske was from a fishing family in Sheringham, but Blackburn does not stop there: her quest is wider, as she explores the intricacies of Norfolk and ponders on life and death.

Malcolm Cormack The Paintings of Thomas Gainsborough. Amongst a platoon of books written about Gainsborough, this is perhaps the most authoritative. Especially strong on the influences that moulded Gainsborough's approach to his art. Published in the early 1990s.

Nicholas Groves *The Medieval Churches of the City of Norwich*. Every ecclesiastical nook and cranny is explored in this extensively researched book. Groves clearly loves his churches – and it's an enthusiasm he communicates well.

★**Simon Jenkins** *England's Thousand Best Churches*; *England's Thousand Best Houses*. Two lucid, immaculately researched volumes describing the pick of England's churches and houses, divided by county and with a star rating. Jenkins does, however, seem to struggle to notch up the 1000 houses – why else would he have included Suffolk's Anglo-Saxon Village (see p.314)?

Matthew Rice *Building Norfolk*. Three hundred watercolour illustrations illuminate most of the county's key buildings with separate sections on just about everything you can think of – inns, barns, country houses, farmhouses etc.

FICTION

George Borrow *Lavengro*. Born near East Dereham, George Borrow (1803–81) spent much of his youth in Norwich before starting his extensive travels as a representative of the Bible Society, distant wanderings that were greatly assisted by his remarkable skills as a linguist – though he did return to settle near Lowestoft. Unusually for the day, Borrow felt a great affinity for Gypsies as reflected in both his most famous work, *Romany Rye*, and the semiautobiographical *Lavengro*, with its gentle evocation of Norwich.

Tim Clare *The Honours*. Clare's debut novel may be set in rural Norfolk in the 1930s, but that's pretty much where the realism ends in this fantasy of suspicion and paranoia with the teenage protagonist – Delphine Venner – determined to root out every local secret, however gruesome.

George Crabbe *The Borough; The Village*. Born in Aldeburgh, the poet George Crabbe (1754–1832) had a particularly hard and gruelling life. As a consequence, his poetry packs a gritty punch, whether it's describing the swamps, mudflats and shingle banks of his home town, the furious roll of the sea or the harsh conditions endured by his fellow townsfolk. His poetry inspired Benjamin Britten – *Peter Grimes* is drawn from *The Borough*.

Elly Griffiths *The House at Sea's End*. Griffiths has a real liking for Norfolk and this crime novel makes good use of its coastal Norfolk setting, where human skeletons turn up as a sea cliff is worn away... and hey presto, here comes forensic archeologist Ruth Galloway to clear things up. If you like this one, try the same author's *The Crossing Places*, where the dastardly deed calling for Galloway's attention has been committed on a remote Norfolk beach; *The Outcast Dead*, with more skeletons and more mystery, this time in Norwich; and *A Room Full of Bones*, which finds us asking who has killed the curator of a local museum? Be assured, Ruth Galloway will root the guilty out.

L.P. Hartley *The Go-Between*. Famous book, famous film, all to do with class and sexual desire in Edwardian Norfolk – rural Norfolk at that. Inspired by Hartley's stay at Bradenham Hall, near Thetford, in 1909.

★**P.D. James** One of the UK's most popular writers, P. D. James had a long association with both Norfolk and Suffolk and several of her crime novels are set here – for example *Unnatural Causes* (Minismere and Dunwich); *Death in Holy Orders* (Covehithe); and *Devices and Desires* (the Norfolk coast).

Jim Kelly *Death Wore White*. King's Lynn may seem a fairly safe place to go, but not in this detective novel, which starts with two bodies and lots of suspects. Appealing descriptions of the north Norfolk coast are a bonus. Other Kelly detective novels with an East Anglian setting include *At Death's Window* and *Death on Demand*.

★**Jon McGregor** *This isn't the Sort of Thing that Happens to Someone like You*. Set in the fenland, these unsettling tales tell of unruly actions and disturbing events – a sugar beet crashes through a car windscreen, a barn bursts into flame. Tasty stuff.

Arthur Ransome *Coot Club*. Ransome (1884–1967) spent several years living in south Suffolk on and around the River Stour, but Breydon Water serves as the setting for the dramatic climax to this particular story: the Hullabaloos are shipwrecked here, leaving Mrs Barrable and the children safe, albeit run aground in the fog. Break open the ginger beer – and press on with Ransome's *The Big Six*: same cast, same (Broads) location.

Ruth Rendell (aka Barbara Vine). A long-time Suffolk resident, Rendell, who died in 2015, featured the county in many of her top-selling crime novels, including *Make Death Love Me*, which begins with a robbery at a Suffolk bank; *The Brimstone Wedding* (Bury St Edmunds); *A Fatal Inversion* (Polstead and Nayland); and *Gallowglass* (Sudbury). In the early 1990s, she also compiled *Ruth Rendell's Suffolk*, in which a handsome set of photographs illustrated her favourite places.

★**Graham Swift** *Waterland*. Written in 1983, *Waterland* is essentially a family saga set in East Anglia's fenlands – excellent on the subtle appeal of this wide-skied, unerringly eerie landscape. The book went down a storm when it was published and a decade later it was turned into a film, *Waterland*, starring Jeremy Irons.

Small print and index

ABOUT THE AUTHORS

Martin Dunford is one of the founders and the former publisher of Rough Guides and has worked in travel publishing for over thirty years. He is the author of more than ten guidebooks and also works as a freelance writer and as a publishing and digital consultant to the travel industry. He writes regularly about Norfolk and Suffolk for various publications, such as UK travel site coolplaces.co.uk, and shares his time between Horning, Norfolk, and Blackheath, London, with his wife and two daughters.

Phil Lee Like many a Midlander, Phil has been holidaying in Norfolk since he was knee-high (in the bathers his mother knitted for him) and he was delighted to be asked to help prepare the new edition of this book. Phil has been writing for Rough Guides for well over twenty years. His other books in the series include Norway, Belgium & Luxembourg, Amsterdam, England, Mallorca and the Netherlands. He lives in Nottingham, where he was born and raised.

A ROUGH GUIDE TO ROUGH GUIDES

Published in 1982, the first Rough Guide – to Greece – was a student scheme that became a publishing phenomenon. Mark Ellingham, a recent graduate in English from Bristol University, had been travelling in Greece the previous summer and couldn't find the right guidebook. With a small group of friends he wrote his own guide, combining a highly contemporary, journalistic style with a thoroughly practical approach to travellers' needs.

The immediate success of the book spawned a series that rapidly covered dozens of destinations. And, in addition to impecunious backpackers, Rough Guides soon acquired a much broader readership that relished the guides' wit and inquisitiveness as much as their enthusiastic, critical approach and value-for-money ethos.

These days, Rough Guides include recommendations from budget to luxury and cover more than 120 destinations around the globe, as well as producing an ever-growing range of ebooks.

Visit **roughguides.com** to find all our latest books, read articles, get inspired and share travel tips with the Rough Guides community.

Rough Guide credits

Editor: Rebecca Hallett
Layout: Anita Singh
Cartography: Ed Wright
Picture editor: Phoebe Lowndes
Photographer: Diana Jarvis
Proofreader: Diane Margolis
Managing editor: Mani Ramaswamy
Assistant editor: Payal Sharotri

Production: Jimmy Lao
Cover photo research: Nicole Newman
Editorial assistant: Freya Godfrey
Senior pre-press designer: Dan May
Programme manager: Gareth Lowe
Publisher: Keith Drew
Publishing director: Georgina Dee

Publishing information

This second edition published May 2016 by
Rough Guides Ltd,
80 Strand, London WC2R 0RL
11, Community Centre, Panchsheel Park,
New Delhi 110017, India
Distributed by Penguin Random House
Penguin Books Ltd, 80 Strand, London WC2R 0RL
Penguin Group (USA), 345 Hudson Street, NY 10014, USA
Penguin Group (Australia), 250 Camberwell Road,
Camberwell, Victoria 3124, Australia
Penguin Group (NZ), 67 Apollo Drive, Mairangi Bay,
Auckland 1310, New Zealand
Penguin Group (South Africa), Block D, Rosebank Office
Park, 181 Jan Smuts Avenue, Parktown North, Gauteng,
South Africa 2193
Rough Guides is represented in Canada by DK Canada, 320
Front Street West, Suite 1400,Toronto, Ontario M5V 3B6
Printed in China
© Martin Dunford and Phil Lee, 2016
Maps © Rough Guides
Contains Ordnance Survey data © Crown copyright and
database rights 2016

All rights reserved. No part of this publication may be
reproduced, stored in or introduced into a retrieval system,
or transmitted in any form, or by any means (electronic,
mechanical, photocopying, recording or otherwise) without
the prior written permission of the copyright owner.
344pp includes index
A catalogue record for this book is available from the
British Library
ISBN: 978-0-24123-859-2
The publishers and authors have done their best to
ensure the accuracy and currency of all the information
in **The Rough Guide to Norfolk & Suffolk**, however,
they can accept no responsibility for any loss, injury, or
inconvenience sustained by any traveller as a result of
information or advice contained in the guide.
1 3 5 7 9 8 6 4 2

Help us update

We've gone to a lot of effort to ensure that the second
edition of **The Rough Guide to Norfolk & Suffolk** is
accurate and up-to-date. However, things change – places
get "discovered", opening hours are notoriously fickle,
restaurants and rooms raise prices or lower standards. If
you feel we've got it wrong or left something out, we'd like
to know, and if you can remember the address, the price,
the hours, the phone number, so much the better.

Please send your comments with the subject line
"**Rough Guide Norfolk & Suffolk Update**" to mail
@uk.roughguides.com. We'll credit all contributions and
send a copy of the next edition (or any other Rough Guide
if you prefer) for the very best emails.
Find more travel information, connect with fellow
travellers and plan your trip on Ⓦroughguides.com.

Acknowledgements

Martin Dunford Martin would like to thank Rebecca
Hallett for her help throughout this project, Mario and
Sally Tinge, Bruce Hanson at the Broads Authority, Amanda
Bond of Visit Suffolk, Tanya Martin, Jeannette Goodrich,
Roland Blunk, Ben Davenport, Sarah Kershaw, Richard
Whitaker, Zoe Bell, Anne Whelpton and many others from
across both counties. Also, as always, to my co-author and
good friend Phil Lee, and of course my regular playmates
Caroline, Daisy and Lucy, who are always looking forward
to our next trip to Norfolk.

Phil Lee Phil would like to thank his editor, Rebecca
Hallett, for her hard work and attention to detail during
the preparation of this new edition of The Rough Guide to
Norfolk and Suffolk. Special thanks also to Martyn and Chris
Livermore for bags of local information; Paul Dickson for
his help with Norwich; Squeak of Flying Kiwi Inns; Melanie
Cook of Visit Norwich; and Amanda Bond of Visit Suffolk.
And big thanks also to my fellow author, Martin, who is
always a pleasure to work with.

Readers' updates

Thanks to all the readers who have taken the time to write in with comments and suggestions (and apologies if we've
inadvertently omitted or misspelt anyone's name):

Roger and Lesley Barnett; Edward Braisher; Zoe Andrea
Bramhall; Bremer; Jacky Bright; Patti Collins; Stephen Cook;
Annabella Forbes; Emma Forbes; Ben Goodhall; Robert
Harding; Sue Harris; Nick Hart; Caroline and John Horder;
Ed Hutchings; Harry Kretchmer; Kirsty Laifa; Lewis Lawson;

Lucy Mellor; Laura Norton; Martin Peters; Alyson Roxburgh;
Adrian Smith; Clive and Rosemary South; David Stubbs;
David Walsh; Jennifer Wood; Jenny Wood; Tim Woods;
Grace Wylie.

Photo credits

All photos © Rough Guides except the following:
(Key: t-top; c-centre; b-bottom; l-left; r-right)

Index

Maps are marked in grey

Map symbols

The symbols below are used on maps throughout the book

✈	Airport	灯	Lighthouse	🍶	Distillery	▬▬▬	Motorway
★	Bus/taxi stop	⛳	Golf course	🍺	Brewery	═══	Dual carriageway
⚓	Ferry stop	🌳	Country park	⊛	Watermill	‒‒‒	Road
🚢	Boat	⊙	Statue	🍎	Orchard/cider farm	═○═	Railway (& stop)
ℹ	Tourist infomation	🏛	Abbey/monastery	Marsh		═○═	Private/light railway (& stop)
✉	Post office	∴	Archeological site/ruins	Park		- - -	Footpath
♦	Museum	🏰	Castle	Cemetery		— -	Ferry route
♦	Place of interest	🐘	Zoo/wildlife park	Beach		▬▬	Wall
P	Parking	❀	Amusement park	Building			
⊠	Gate	⚙	Racing circuit	Church			
🏛	Stately home/historic house	⊤	Public gardens	Stadium			

Listings key

- Accommodation
- Eating
- Drinking and nightlife
- Shopping